The Irish Cup

SPONSORED BY

N. IRELAND'S PREMIERE COMPETITION
SPONSORED BY N. IRELAND'S FAVOURITE ALE.

THE NORTHERN IRELAND football
Y E A R B O O K

The Northern Ireland Football Yearbook 1996/97

© Marshall Gillespie

ISBN 0 90752044 8

Published by: Tudor Journals Limited, 97 Botanic Avenue, Belfast BT7 1JN, Northern Ireland.
Telephone: (01232) 320088; Fax No: (01232) 323163.

Printed by The Universities Press Ltd.

Editor: Marshall Gillespie, 92 Belvoir Close, Fareham, Hants PO16 OPR.
Telephone: (01329) 314417

Front Cover: Portadown v Ballyclare.
Photograph reproduced by kind permission of Century Newspapers Ltd.

ACKNOWLEDGEMENTS

Thank you once again to the many people, listed below, who have contributed their valuable time and support in helping me compile the information for this year's book, it is, as always, much appreciated.

Billy Graham, Jim Palmer, Liam Heffron, George Brown, Darren Fullerton, Martin Harris, Shaun O'Neill, Roy Kitson, Terry Ferry, George Wright, Michael Gallagher, Paul Treanor, John Duffy, Grant Cameron, Hunter McClelland, John Smedley, Dawson Simpson, Colin Hopkins, George Ruddell, Roy France, Sam Robinson, Kevin Hughes, Michael Rudd, Jimmy Davis, Paddy Hunter, Trevor Clydesdale, Brian Courtney, Brian Weir, Ray Sanderson, Damian Wilson, Norman Wallace, Alan Woolley, Fred Magee, Liam Kelly, Noel McClure, Raymond Loughrey, Ernest Downey, Dennis Clarke, Ulrich Matheja, David Alcorn, Barry Hugman, Mike Hammond, Dave Howard, Shane McIlvenny, Allen Gillespie, Marguerita Gillespie. Photographs provided by Michael Reeves, David Hunter, Roy Cathcart, Mark Bain and Thomas Sewell. Members of the A.F.S; staff at Central Library, Belfast, Enniskillen Library and Colindale Library, London; The U.T.V. Sports team of Linda Brien, Stephen Watson, Adrian Logan and Desmond Fahey for their continued support; Bryan Hamilton; Jim Magilton for kindly agreeing to do the Foreword; Bill Campbell, Lesley Bell, Darren Downing, Jacquie Ferguson and, Paula McVeigh at Tudor Journals Ltd.

My Mother, Mavis and Father, Jim, who still, after all these years, consistently send me over an enormous amount of local papers every week, which makes my job so much easier. My wife Paula who, even after seven editions of the book, continues to support and encourage me when deadlines loom and the book is far from finished. To Kate, my daughter, who at four years of age is already being groomed to take over editorial control when I retire!

Sources:
News Letter, Belfast Telegraph, The Sunday Life, The Sunday World, Tyrone Constitution, Impartial Reporter, Tyrone Times, Newtownards Chronicle, Co.Down Spectator, Ballymena Times and Guardian, Carrick Times, Newry Reporter, Irish League Club Programmes, World Soccer, Rothmans Football Yearbooks, European Football Yearbooks, Ultimate Football Guide 1996, Footballers Factfile.

THE NORTHERN IRELAND football
Y E A R B O O K

1 9 9 6 / 9 7

IN ASSOCIATION WITH

S E V E N T H   E D I T I O N

EDITED BY
MARSHALL GILLESPIE

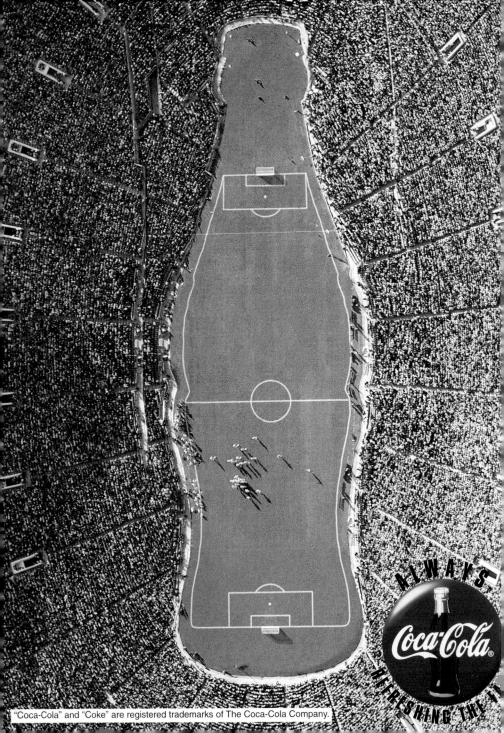

CONTENTS

THE NORTHERN IRELAND **football** YEARBOOK

INTRODUCTION

This is the seventh edition of the Northern Ireland Football Yearbook, which is now widely acknowledged by football writers, administrators and fans throughout the Province as the essential guide to have on Irish League football.

Once again the publishers, Tudor Journals Ltd, have done a wonderful job in maintaining the high standards they have set in previous years and my thanks goes to Bill Campbell and his team for their continued support and professionalism.

As always I am indebted to UTV and Mike McCann in particular for sponsoring the Yearbook for a fourth consecutive year, their coverage of Irish League football is second to none and hopefully the publication will help make life a little bit easier for Linda Brien and Co. in the coming season.

Whether the first season of Promotion and Relegation was a success is debatable. The Premier League clubs seemed to be content with new format. However for First Division clubs it was a season of unmitigated struggle with a number of teams admitting to be so much in debt that they were in danger of folding. Fundamental changes, in my view, are needed in the structure of the two Divisions, with hopefully a two tier system with ten clubs in each Division being the answer. Whatever the outcome of the Irish Football League meeting is it may already be too late for some teams in the Irish League.

On the International front, Bryan Hamilton made steady progress with a young and still relatively inexperienced team. N.Ireland only just missed out in qualifying for EURO 96 and finished off their group with a truly magnificent performance against Austria at Windsor Park. A creditable draw with Germany in May provided the team with further evidence of their progress and was a real confidence booster for the forthcoming World Cup Qualifiers. Realistically N.Ireland chances of making it to France are slim with only one team sure to qualify from the group, but I'm forever the optimist and as Jimmy Greaves says.........

Marshall Gillespie
December 1996

GUIDE TO THE YEARBOOK

IRISH LEAGUE CLUB SECTION

This year each of the sixteen clubs have been allocated seven pages. Information for each club includes:
* Details of Club Personnel
* Review of the Season
* Team Photograph for 1995/96
* Manager Profile
* Results and Line-Ups for all Smirnoff Premier League or First Division matches 1995/96
* Transfers during 1995/96
* List of Honours
* Player Profiles
* Complete Appearances and Goalscorers for 1995/96

EXPLANATORY NOTES

Within the line-ups pages in the Club Section an asterisk (*) a cross (†) and a circle (o) indicates which players were replaced by substitutes.

In the Appearances and Goalscorers pages, appearances as substitute are shown in brackets thus 3+(2) indicates that the player concerned made three full appearances and two as substitute.

Penalty goals are indicated in brackets, prefixed with the letter 'p'; thus 5(2p) shows that five goals were scored of which two were penalties.

Abbreviations used within the Appearances and Goalscorers page and elsewhere in the book are as follows:

UC - Ulster Cup
GC - Sun Life Gold Cup
ILC - Wilkinson Sword Irish League Cup
CC - Coca-Cola Cup
BIC - Bass Irish Cup
CAS - Calor County Antrim Shield
PL - Premier League
FD - First Division
INC - Irish News Cup
MUC - McEwans Mid-Ulster Cup
NWC - North West Senior Challenge Cup
CS - McEwans Charity Shield
CWC - European Cup Winners-Cup
UEF - UEFA Cup
BRC - Bob Radcliffe Cup
IC - McEwans Intermediate Cup
SKC - Smirnoff 'B' Division Knockout Cup
SS - Calor Steel & Sons Cup
NWIC - North West Intermediate Cup

All information within the Club Section is correct up until the end of 1995/96.

PLAYERS DIRECTORY

As ever I have tried to improve the Players Directory to include as many details as possible on the 500 or so players who appeared in the Irish League during 1995/96.
I have endeavoured this year to include transfer information up until the end of August 1996 so as to keep the Directory as up to date as possible for the 1996/97 season.
Below is an example of what information is contained for most players.

BARKER, Ritchie (F) (LINFIELD)
Born: 30.05.1975 Sheffield
Ht: 6.1 *Wt:* 13.05
Status: Professional
Career: Sheffield Wednesday (Jul.'93) 0 - 0; Doncaster Rovers (Sep.'95) 5+1 - 0; Ards (Jan.'96 loan) 7 - 3; Linfield (Aug.'96):
Int.Hon: England U.18; U.15:

Unfortunately there are players throughout the directory whose details were not available to me, so if any player wants their details included in full in next years edition please get in touch.

NB: I have only included League appearances and goals for each player and not that of the many Cup Competitions played throughout the season. League details are collated from my own records so if they differ from other sources please get in contact with me.

INTERNATIONAL PLAYERS DIRECTORY

This is a new feature within this years edition. The format used is along the same lines as the Irish League Players directory, except I have included transfer fees for all players.
I have only included players who are regular members of the current International squad and those who play regular first team football with English or Scottish League clubs. At the end of the Directory I have included a selection of younger players attached to English and Scottish clubs and who are probably on the verge of a first team breakthrough during the forthcoming season.

'B' DIVISION CLUB SECTION

As space within the Yearbook is always tight the decision was made to cut the pages allocated to 'B' Division clubs from three to two. Therefore included in this Section for each club is the following:

* Details of Club Personnel
* Team Photographs for 1995/96 (where available)
* Playing Staff for 1995/96
* List of Honours
* Transfers during 1995/96
* Results and Goalscorers for all League and Cup matches for 1995/96
* List of Goalscorers

Unfortunately goalscorers in certain matches for Ballymoney United, Brantwood, Cookstown United and Tobermore United have not been located and also not every club had a team photograph taken. Anyone wishing to help with supplying either information or photographs for any 'B' Division Club please contact me direct.

NB: Again all information is correct up until the end of 1995/96.

The remainder of the book should be self explanatory. If anyone notices any errors or omissions within the Yearbook, I would appreciate the feedback to where corrections should be made and these will be corrected in the next edition.

Surely an Irish Football League programme has never been looked forward to with such a mixture of emotions than the season of 1995/96.

The Irish league decision to introduce a two-tier structure divided opinion across the Province, but while almost certainly it will be revised to some degree next year there can be no doubt that after the thrills and excitements of last season P and R is here to stay. In the Premier League every game was a big game, every point vital, and every week seemed to bring a new twist.

Eight sides had been designated into an elite section, and if we thought Crusaders' triumph in the Championship in 1995 had been spectacular, what was to unfold in the dramatic final weeks of the first-ever Premier campaign was enthralling, as nerve-tingling and compelling a climax to a year of exciting football as we have ever witnessed - and it was followed, we know, by tens of thousands of fans on UTV, the football channel.

Crusaders, Glenavon and Linfield were in early non-domestic action, UEFA Cup competition demanding that Roy Walker, Nigel Best and Trevor Anderson had their troops ready for European combat in early August. Crusaders and Linfield made brave but early exits, but Mourneview Park ambitions for 1995/96 were boosted by an excellent win over Icelandic opposition and then a glamour fixture with German giants Werder Bremen.

The visitors showed their technical precision in the first leg in Lurgan, and in Bremen the style was added in superb fashion as 'super Mario' Basler and the magnificent Bode set up a 5-0 win. But Glenavon had been no 'cannon fodder' in either match, and Dermot O'Neill, Lee Doherty, Mark Glendinning, Stevie McBride and Glenn Ferguson never looked out of place on such a stage.

But soon it was back to the urgent business back home, and there was as much action in the committee rooms and in the courts as there was on the pitch as the IFL Cup competitions got underway. Glenavon and Portadown were at the centre of several controversies.

Marc Kenny found himself unwittingly at the eye of a long-running storm over his eligibility. The Dubliner - having managed to arrive at Mourneview via Coleraine without ever kicking a ball for the Bannsiders! — was then told a ban picked up at Clandeboye Park had not been properly fulfilled, and a semantic and legal argument ensued which brought little credit, but a lot of headlines, to Northern Ireland soccer. That delayed the Gold Cup competition, while over at Shamrock Park another eligibility row was brewing. The gifted teenager Gareth Fulton was, said the Irish League, not properly registered, so the Ulster Cup was thrown into chaos, with - at one stage - no fewer than six teams claiming a semi-final berth! That too was eventually 'sorted', but the UTV cameras seemed to have taken up permanent residence outside Irish League and IFA headquarters so enduring were these problems.

The Ports had already featured in the pre-season anticipation, Garry Haylock's sensational transfer of allegiance from Linfield causing a rift between the clubs which was only partially healed when, after months of argument, Portadown paid a nominal fee for the most feared striker in the League. Haylock had insisted he was a free agent in the summer of 1995, and Linfield felt it had been cheated of its most valuable asset.

Eventually the football got underway, and Cup competitions suggested that the Mid-Ulster 'Big Two' and, perhaps, a highly motivated Crusaders were the sides to watch in the new Premier League, in which every goal was recorded by UTV's unprecedented coverage. But Tommy Cassidy was gradually reshaping Glentoran, Trevor Anderson was rebuilding at Windsor Park, and Roy Coyle, Marty Quinn and Paul Malone probably would have accepted that survival in the treacherous Premier League waters was the priority at Ards, Cliftonville and Bangor respectively.

In the First Division the incentive was clear - promotion back into the 'major league', and pre-season favourites were Ballymena, where Alan Fraser had expensively revamped United. Distillery, Coleraine and, just possibly, Omagh Town, where Roy McCreadie had already conjured miracles despite poor support and a necessity to draw on players from the North and West of the Province.

It was the financial imperatives at St.Julian's Road which were to pervade the First Division campaign and to leave an enduring legacy, particularly at Omagh, Newry and at East Antrim's triumvirate of Larne, Carrick Rangers and Ballyclare Comrades, where Alan Campbell was back in management.

In the early weeks the leadership of both sections changed as often as the weather, but by December a certain pattern was emerging. As predicted Portadown never dropped 'off the pace' and Glenavon had the firepower, and now the defensive organisation, to be real Championship contenders.

But Crusaders' defiant defence of a title won with such spirit was really eye-catching. The side was often convincing, and even on an 'off day' the ability to grind out a result made them a team to fear. Linfield's up-and-down form continued to frustrate the Windsor faithful and the management, and Glentoran surely were non-runners given the surgery Cassidy was involved with at the Oval.

Christmas and the New Year provided a feast of frantic, exciting fare for the big Premier League crowds the League had hoped for, and as 1996 dawned Portadown, Glenavon and Crusaders were involved in an enthralling battle for supremacy. Crusaders, with Stephen Baxter, Sid Burrows, Kevin McKeown and Glenn Dunlop reprising their heroics of the previous season, had the edge in consistency. Glenavon could be thrilling but inconsistent, and though Ronnie McFall had Gary Peebles, Haylock and particularly Peter Kennedy in devastating form the team could still manage to summon surprise failure out of expected triumph.

Who would have imagined that genuine title contenders could concede seven goals to fierce 'derby rivals Glenavon and still stay in contention?

Linfield revived briefly in January without ever really threatening the cartel developing at the top. Liam Coyle had arrived at the Oval, scoring spectacularly on his debut, only to go 'absent without leave' immediately, providing the season with another off-field 'cameo' to keep our viewers entertained and mystified.

A late-night summit meeting with manager Cassidy, a public proclamation on UTV Live of his allegiance to the 'Cock 'n Hens', and Coyle, surely the classiest 'act' in the country, was back in the Oval fold. Slowly but surely the Glens were developing into a major force, but the Championship was never a realistic target in 1996.

A titanic struggle in the Premier League, but by February its first 'P and R' recruit was already decided. Kenny Shiels had survived an attempted boardroom 'coup' in the autumn, been sacked and reinstated in the time it takes to draw breath, and his players responded with a seventeen-match run which relegated the rest of the First Division to also-rans. It was a spectacularly decisive First Division title victory, Sammy Shiels and Tony 'Stormin' Gorman leading actors as the opposition crumbled, with Pat McAllister's arrival from Cliftonville perhaps the key to Coleraine's barnstorming success.

The focus was now almost entirely on the Premier League. Into April, and the Easter holiday programme couldn't separate Crusaders and Portadown, these two now clearly the principals. Odd points were dropped, but neither could really seize the advantage. The Ports and the Crues looked set for a last-day-of-the-season showdown at Seaview, the victors there destined to be the first premier League champions.

But then Roy Walker's team slipped up at Solitude, where Marty Quinn had consolidated the Reds' future in the top flight and, to the delight of many neutrals, brought the club its first trophy in a decade with a splendidly attractive Coca-Cola Cup triumph.

On that same penultimate afternoon Glenavon went to Shamrock Park and looked set to undermine their greatest rivals, only for the almost forgotten Ian Ferguson to conjure up three points which brought the title, suddenly and surprisingly, to Portadown. Ronnie McFall, veteran of so many campaigns and the wiliest manager of them all, had invested heavily and reaped a lucrative dividend!

A season which had provided some marvelously exciting soccer for the crowds and, through *UTV Live* and *Saturday Sport,* enjoyed the highest-ever profile for the game, had gone virtually 'to the wire'.

In our annual review of the local soccer year in 'The League', the moments which shaped a footballing season were remembered in front of an audience which included the players, managers and administrators who had taken centre stage. The big occasions were revisited, and Glen Dunlop heard Tommy Docherty acclaim his exceptional strike as 'Goal of the Season'.

The winners were there in Studio One, and losers of a sort too. Paul Malone had decided he couldn't harness the resources he needed to stave off relegation for Bangor, and he gave way to Andy Dougan and George Dunlop, while Billy Hamilton's cheery reign at Distillery ended amicably, the former international striker allowing Paul Kirk to show his mettle at New Grosvenor this season.

Assistant manager Lindsay McKeown was a casualty of Linfield's barren season, but how long before this colourful and vibrant stalwart returns to brighten our afternoons - and screens! - with that unmistakable trademark hairstyle!

Peter Watson reluctantly left Newry, unable to get the cash or the players to realise his ambitions for the club. Colin Crawford and Alan Campbell saw enough at Carrick Rangers and Ballyclare to hint at better times ahead.

And now, with even greater anticipation, we all look forward to 1996/97 and a whole new series of surprises and dramas, triumphs and minor disasters. So, keep right up-to-date with the news, the views and the action right from the 'kick-off' have Marshall Gillespie's superb Northern Ireland Football Yearbook by your side as the soccer stories of 1996/97 unfold in *UTV Live* and on *Saturday Sport.* On UTV of course, the football channel.

UTV Foreword

UTV Sports Team (*left to right*) Nigel Carr, Mark Robson, Bruce McKendry, Linda Brien, Des Fahy, Stephen Watson, Adrian Logan. *(Photograph Courtesy of UTV)*

UTV Sport is delighted yet again to have joined forces with Marshall Gillespie in his annual tour de force, The Northern Ireland Football Yearbook.

This is the seventh edition of what has become the definitive guide to Irish League soccer, and Marshall's tireless harnessing of all there is that's worth knowing about the game here never fails to impress the reader. We at UTV Sport like so many of you at home, find that the Yearbook is not just essential reading but a thoroughly entertaining companion throughout what is a packed programme of domestic League and Cup competition.

UTV's commitment to local soccer was expanded even further last season, with our UEFA Cup travels with Glenavon, and with even more cameras being employed each week to provide comprehensive coverage of the first inaugural season of Premier League and First Division football. On UTV Live at Six the game received unprecedented attention, and every weekend the afternoon action was brought first to your screens by the Saturday Sport team.

In the Yearbook Marshall brings all the highlights of the 1995/96 season vividly back to life, his narrative complemented by a statistical record which will solve those good-natured arguments amongst fans and add to everyone's fund of knowledge about a sport which has never enjoyed such a high profile.

We know that our extended highlights coverage of the end-of-season Premier League race was widely appreciated by supporters of football in Northern Ireland, and UTV Sport is determined to maintain and even advance its initiatives in promoting 'the beautiful game'.

Of course we will continue to bring you the stories of the day on UTV Live, and profile the players, the managers and the issues which, together, make soccer in the Province so vibrant. Ronnie McFall's Portadown knows it will face even more determined challenges in 1996/97, with Nigel Best sworn to wrestling the championship away from Glenavon's Mid-Ulster rivals.

Marshall Gillespie gives you all the background to the key figures and the clubs which make Northern Ireland football 'tick'. The Yearbook is no mere statistical reference point, it is an authoritative guide to the domestic game without which no self-respecting UTV Sport viewer would feel complete!

The UTV Sport team will keep you ahead of the news and the action each day and on Saturdays, and the Northern Ireland Football Yearbook is a splendid addition to your sporting library which in its attention to detail and clear affection for the game reflects and endorses the commitment to the game of UTV, the football channel.

Linda Brien — Sports Editor, UTV

THE NORTHERN IRELAND
football
Y E A R B O O K

When approached by Marshall to write a Foreword for his excellent yearbook, I have to be honest and admit I did not know of the books existence. However, having studied the publication in detail I was amazed by the amount of detail Marshall had gone into on not only the local soccer scene but the International front as well.

The Yearbook in my opinion is on a par with any of the numerous publications which cover the game in England and Marshall should be proud of the contribution he is making in promoting Irish League soccer in not just Northern Ireland but throughout the UK as well.

Having played briefly with Distillery in the Irish League myself it was interesting to browse through the Players Directory and come across players I have known and how they have progressed over the years.

With so many of the present day International team having started their careers in the Irish League I am sure this book will be of immense interest to them.

Congratulations to Marshall for yet another superb publication and I for one will be taking it with me on my International trips abroad to wile away the hours.

Jim Magilton
Southampton and Northern Ireland

FINAL LEAGUE TABLES FOR 1995/96

SMIRNOFF PREMIER LEAGUE 1995/96

		Home					Away					Total					
	P	W	D	L	F	A	W	D	L	F	A	W	D	L	F	A	Pts	GD
1 Portadown	28	10	3	1	38	21	6	5	3	32	19	16	8	4	61	40	56	+21
2 Crusaders	28	9	2	3	26	15	6	5	3	19	17	15	7	6	45	32	52	+13
3 Glentoran	28	6	5	3	26	20	7	2	5	30	18	13	7	8	56	38	46	+18
4 Glenavon	28	5	3	6	26	18	8	2	4	21	14	13	5	10	47	32	44	+15
5 Linfield	28	5	4	5	11	14	6	4	4	23	21	11	8	9	34	35	41	-1
6 Cliftonville	28	4	6	4	11	18	2	5	7	16	30	6	11	11	27	48	29	-21
7 Ards	28	3	4	7	17	21	3	3	8	12	22	6	7	15	29	43	25	-14
8 Bangor	28	2	2	10	12	28	1	3	10	11	26	3	5	20	23	54	14	-31

SMIRNOFF FIRST DIVISION 1995/96

		Home					Away					Total					
	P	W	D	L	F	A	W	D	L	F	A	W	D	L	F	A	Pts	GD
1 Coleraine	28	12	1	1	49	13	9	3	2	33	15	21	4	3	82	28	67	+54
2 Ballymena Utd.	28	6	5	3	21	13	7	5	2	17	12	13	10	5	38	25	49	+13
3 Omagh Town	28	6	5	3	25	18	6	2	6	25	25	12	7	9	50	43	43	+7
4 Distillery	28	5	3	6	16	17	5	4	5	19	17	10	7	11	35	34	37	+1
5 Ballyclare Com.	28	4	2	8	15	28	6	1	7	14	20	10	3	15	29	48	33	-19
6 Carrick Rangers	28	6	3	5	16	18	3	0	11	16	38	9	3	16	32	56	30	-24
7 Larne	28	4	3	7	16	17	3	4	7	15	19	7	7	14	31	36	28	-5
8 Newry Town	28	6	1	7	22	24	1	4	9	9	34	7	5	16	31	58	26	-27

TOP GOALSCORERS IN PREMIER LEAGUE 1995/96

	Name:	Club:	Goals:
1	Garry Haylock	Portadown	20 (2 pens)
2	Stephen Baxter	Crusaders	11
3	Peter Kennedy	Portadown	10
4	Glenn Ferguson	Glenavon	9 (1 pen)
5	Glen Little	Glentoran	9
6	Stephen McBride	Glenavon	9 (1 pen)
7	Glenn Hunter	Crusaders	8
8	Raymond McCoy	Glenavon	8
9	Justin McBride	Glentoran	8

TOP GOALSCORERS IN FIRST DIVISION 1995/96

	Name:	Club:	Goals:
1	Sammy Shiels	Coleraine	25
2	Anthony Gorman	Coleraine	16
3	Michael McHugh	Omagh Town	14 (1 pen)
4	Thomas Cleland	Distillery	11 (1 pen)
5	Crawford McCrae	Larne	11
6	Jim Barr	Newry Town	10
7	Barry Forshaw	Ballyclare Comrades	8
8	Mark McWalter	Ballymena United	8 (1 pen)

IRISH LEAGUE CHAMPIONS 1890/91 - 1995/96

Season:	Champions:	Season:	Champions:
1890/91	Linfield	1947/48	Belfast Celtic
1891/92	Linfield	1948/49	Linfield
1892/93	Linfield	1949/50	Linfield
1893/94	Glentoran	1950/51	Glentoran
1894/95	Linfield	1951/52	Glenavon
1895/96	Distillery	1952/53	Glentoran
1896/97	Glentoran	1953/54	Linfield
1897/98	Linfield	1954/55	Linfield
1898/99	Distillery	1955/56	Linfield
1899/00	Belfast Celtic	1956/57	Glenavon
1900/01	Distillery	1957/58	Ards
1901/02	Linfield	1958/59	Linfield
1902/03	Distillery	1959/60	Glenavon
1903/04	Linfield	1960/61	Linfield
1904/05	Glentoran	1961/62	Linfield
1905/06	Cliftonville & Distillery (Joint Holders)	1962/63	Distillery
1906/07	Linfield	1963/64	Glentoran
1907/08	Linfield	1964/65	Derry City
1908/09	Linfield	1965/66	Linfield
1909/10	Cliftonville	1966/67	Glentoran
1910/11	Linfield	1967/68	Glentoran
1911/12	Glentoran	1968/69	Linfield
1912/13	Glentoran	1969/70	Glentoran
1913/14	Linfield	1970/71	Linfield
1914/15	Belfast Celtic	1971/72	Glentoran
1915/16	No Competition	1972/73	Crusaders
1918/19	No Competition	1973/74	Coleraine
1919/20	Belfast Celtic	1974/75	Linfield
1920/21	Glentoran	1975/76	Crusaders
1921/22	Linfield	1976/77	Glentoran
1922/23	Linfield	1977/78	Linfield
1923/24	Queen's Island	1978/79	Linfield
1924/25	Glentoran	1979/80	Linfield
1925/26	Belfast Celtic	1980/81	Glentoran
1926/27	Belfast Celtic	1981/82	Linfield
1927/28	Belfast Celtic	1982/83	Linfield
1928/29	Belfast Celtic	1983/84	Linfield
1929/30	Linfield	1984/85	Linfield
1930/31	Glentoran	1985/86	Linfield
1931/32	Linfield	1986/87	Linfield
1932/33	Belfast Celtic	1987/88	Glentoran
1933/34	Linfield	1988/89	Linfield
1934/35	Linfield	1989/90	Portadown
1935/36	Belfast Celtic	1990/91	Portadown
1936/37	Belfast Celtic	1991/92	Glentoran
1937/38	Belfast Celtic	1992/93	Linfield
1938/39	Belfast Celtic	1993/94	Linfield
1939/40	Belfast Celtic	1994/95	Crusaders
1940/41	No Competition	Premier League 1995/96	Portadown
1946/47	No Competition	First Division 1995/96	Coleraine

IRISH LEAGUE CHAMPIONS:
Linfield– 42; Glentoran — 19; Belfast Celtic — 14; Distillery — 6; Glenavon — 3; Crusaders — 3; Portadown – 3; Cliftonville — 2; Ards, Coleraine, Derry City, Queen's Island —1.

Ground: Castlereagh Park, Newtownards. (10,000) Founded: 1902.
Tel: 01247 813370

Ards 1995/96

Back Row L-R: Gary Walker, Paul Dunnion, Dwaine Shanley, Paul McBride, Paul Kee, William Murphy,
Barney Bowers, Gary O'Sullivan.
Front Row L-R: Ritchie Barker, Martin McCann, Michael Boyle, Paul Mooney, Paul Cullen, Michael Kelly.
(Photograph courtesy of Jim Palmer, Newtownards Chronicle)

President:
Mr.H.H.Cavan
Chairman:
Mr.H.Owens
Hon.Secretary:
Mr.K.Lowry
Hon.Treasurer:
Mr.T.Hillen
Manager:
Roy Coyle
Asst.Manager:
Jimmy Brown
Reserve Team Manager:
George Bowden
Team Attendant:
John Wilton
Physiotherapist:
Billy Barker
Club Colours:
Red & Blue shirts,
White shorts, Red socks

Summary of 1995/96 Season

Coming to the end of season 1994/95 there was more than a little optimism at Castlereagh Park. For the second season in succession manager Roy Coyle had guided Ards to a trophy - the League Cup, and even better than that a place in the new Premier League had been 'grabbed'.

'Grabbed' in style in fact because seasons of sixth place and then fourth place put out hopes that Ards could not only hold their own in the Premier League but also even emerge as "dark horses" in the race for the inaugural Championship.

Things though began to go 'downhill' in the summer even before the 95/96 season had begun. 'Player of the Year' Kevin Brady, decided that a club near his Dublin home would suit him better so he left for Bohemians.

He had been the lynchpin of the defence and he was soon followed by ace striker Darren Erskine - and if there was some joy that Ards had been awarded £35,000 by a League Tribunal for his move to Linfield, thought of spending that money soon disappeared.

Coyle might have hoped for a large chunk to re-build his side after arguably losing his top two players but financial problems with Ards meant the money went else-where and the manager ended up spending the pricely sum of £5,000 all season!!

So what happened on the field afterwards can hardly have been too surprising - a vintage season it was not, forgettable in fact in very many ways but at least and perhaps amazingly Coyle managed to organise and motivate his low-cost outfit to keep them in the Premier League at Bangor's expense.

Dublin Junior player Dwaine Shanley strengthened the squad early on, Michael Boyle arrived from Larne in a swop for David Straney and in September Glentoran veteran Barney Bowers arrived for that £5,000 fee.

Results weren't too good though. The League Cup was surrendered at home to First Division Coleraine in the second round. Ards were non-qualifiers in both the Ulster Cup and Gold Cup, and before Christmas there was a second round Co.Antrim Shield exit to Crusaders - also at Castlereagh Park.

The Premier League had begun with on-loan Scot Pat Flannery threatening to have a great season but Ards had to wait until their eighth game for a win (3-0 at home to Cliftonville).

Portadown though saw off the Ards challenge in the Bass Irish Cup quarter-final winning 2-1 at Ards and the Coca-Cola Cup semi-final defeat, 3-1 to Cliftonville at the Oval, was a big disappointment.

It was a very 'nervy' end to a poorish season and obvious to all that something had to be done. Thankfully Roy Coyle was signed up for a new contract which keeps him at Castlereagh Park for three more seasons so that reason alone must raise Ards' hopes again for the 96/97 season.

Jim Palmer

MANAGER PROFILE — ROY COYLE

Date of Birth: 31/01/1946 Belfast.
Date of Appointment: October 1993.

PREVIOUS CLUBS
As Player: Ballymena United; Glentoran; Sheffield Wednesday; Grimsby Town; Linfield.
As Manager: Linfield; Ards; Derry City:

HONOURS
As Player
5 caps for Northern Ireland.
Glentoran – **Irish League Championship**:1969/70 and 1971/72.
City Cup: 1969/70. **Co.Antrim Shield**: 1970/71.
Linfield – **Irish League Championship**; 1977/78; 1978/79; 1979/80. **Irish Cup**; 1977/78. **Ulster Cup**; 1977/78 and 1978/79. **Co. Antrim Shield**; 1976/77.

As Manager
Linfield – **Irish League Championship**; 1977/78; 1978/79; 1979/80; 1981/82; 1982/83; 1983/84; 1984/85; 1985/86; 1986/87; 1988/89. **Irish Cup**: 1977/78; 1979/80; 1981/82. **Gold Cup**: 1979/80; 1981/82; 1983/84; 1984/85; 1987/88; 1988/89; 1989/90. **Ulster Cup:** 1977/78; 1978/79; 1979/80; 1984/85. **Co.Antrim Shield**: 1976/77; 1980/81; 1981/82; 1982/83; 1983/84. **Irish League Cup:** 1986/87.
Derry City – **League Cup**: 1991/92.
Ards – **Co.Antrim Shield**: 1993/94.
     Irish League Cup: 1994/95

SMIRNOFF PREMIER LEAGUE RECORD 1995/96

No.	Date:	Ven:	Opponents:	Result:	H.T:	Pos:	Goalscorers:
1	Sep 30	A	Cliftonville	0-0 D	0-0	-	-
2	Oct 7	H	Glenavon	1-1 D	1-0	4	Flannery (30)
3	Oct 14	A	Portadown	1-3 L	1-1	6	Shanley (18)
4	Oct 21	H	Crusaders	0-0 D	0-0	6	-
5	Oct 28	A	Glentoran	2-3 L	1-3	7	Boyle (10,66)
6	Nov 4	A	Bangor	1-2 L	1-0	8	Maloney (28)
7	Nov 11	H	Linfield	2-3 L	0-2	8	Boyle (83), Flannery (pen 89)
8	Nov 18	H	Cliftonville	3-0 W	1-0	7	(P) Cullen (5,58), McLaughlin (77)
9	Nov 25	A	Glenavon	0-3 L	0-3	7	-
10	Dec 2	H	Portadown	1-1 D	1-0	7	Mooney (pen 25)
11	Dec 9	A	Crusaders	2-1 W	0-1	6	McGreevy (57), (P) Cullen (77)
12	Dec 16	H	Glentoran	1-4 L	0-2	7	McCann (72)
13	Jan 1	A	Linfield	0-0 D	0-0	-	-
14	Jan 6	A	Cliftonville	0-1 L	0-1	7	-
15	Jan 13	H	Glenavon	1-2 L	0-0	7	Boyle (53)
16	Jan 27	A	Portadown	3-1 W	0-0	7	Boyle (56), Barker (77,90)
17	Jan 30	H	Bangor	3-0 W	1-0	-	McLaughlin (17), Bowers (50), Morrison (82)
18	Feb 3	H	Crusaders	0-1 L	0-1	7	-
19	Feb 10	A	Glentoran	1-3 L	0-1	7	Barker (66)
20	Feb 17	A	Bangor	1-0 W	0-0	6	(P) Cullen (55)
21	Mar 2	H	Linfield	1-2 L	0-1	6	Morrison (50)
22	Mar 16	H	Cliftonville	2-2 D	0-1	6	McLaughlin (72), McCann (81)
23	Mar 23	A	Glenavon	1-3 L	1-1	6	McCann (33)
24	Mar 30	H	Portadown	0-2 L	0-0	6	-
25	Apr 6	A	Crusaders	0-2 L	0-2	7	-
26	Apr 8	H	Glentoran	0-2 L	0-0	-	-
27	Apr 20	H	Bangor	2-1 W	0-1	7	Mooney (pen 52), (P) Cullen (69)
28	Apr 27	A	Linfield	0-0 D	0-0	7	-

Final League Position: 7th

PREMIER LEAGUE LINE-UPS 1995/96

MATCH No	P.Kee 23	P.McBride 18+(3)	R.Morrison 25+(1)	M.Kelly 15	P.Mooney 25	B.Bowers 23+(1)	C.Cullen 14+(2)	D.Shanley 20+(4)	P.Flannery 11+(1)	M.Boyle 22+(2)	P.Cullen 25+(1)	A.Hawkins 2	M.Simpson 1+(2)	W.Murphy 10+(5)	G.O'Sullivan 9+(11)	J.Willis 6+(1)	D.Smyth 1	K.Maloney 4	P.McLaughlin 16	B.Campbell 1	D.McGreevy 7+(2)	M.McCann 18+(1)	G.Walker 0+(4)	R.Barker 7	P.Dunnion 0+(2)	C.Getty 1+(1)	A.Beattie 0+(3)	S.Bibbo 4	P.Gray 0+(2)	Referee
1	1	2	3	4	5	6	7	8	9	10	11																			H.Barr
2	1	2†	8	4	5	6°		3*	9	7	10	11	12*	14†	15°															N.Cowie
3	1		11	4	5	6		7	9	2	12*	10*	8†	3	14†															M.Ross
4	1	2	11	4	5	3*	10	8	9	12*	6					7														G.Douglas
5	1	2	11	4	5	6	10	8*	9	3			12*			7														D.Magill
6		12*	11†	4*	5	6	8		9	10	7			14†			1	2	3											T.Deegan
7	1		11	4		6	2*	14†	9	10	8				12*	7†		5	3											F.McDonald
8	1			4		6			9	10	8				12*	7†		5*	3	2	11	14†								L.Irvine
9	1		8	4	5	6	9		12*	10				14†				2*	3		7†	11								M.Ross
10	1	12*		4	5	6		14†	9	2	10				11†				3*		7	8								E.Millar
11	1	14†	8	4	5	6		12*	9†	11			2						3*		7	10								F.McDonald
12	1*	2	8†		5	6		3	9		11			4	12*						7	10	14†							H.Barr
13	1	2	8		5			4		11*	9			6					3		7†	10	12*							G.Keatley
14	1	2	8	4	5	3	14†			12*	11°			6*							7†	10		9	15°					J.Ferry
15	1	2	12*	4	5	6		7*		11	8								3			10		9						F.McDonald
16	1	2	8	4	5	6		12*		11*	7								3			10		9						A.Snoddy
17	1	2	8†		5	6*		4		7	11			15°	12*				3		14†	10		9°						R.Lutton
18	1	2	8		5	6*		4		7	11			14†	12*				3			10†		9						L.Irvine
19	1	2	8†	4*	5		12*	10		11	7°			6					3		14†			9		15°				E.Millar
20	1	2	8		5		4	10		11	7			6					3					9						N.Cowie
21	1	2	8†				4*	5		11	7			6	12*				3			10		9	14†					R.Luton
22	1	2	8		5	9*		4†		11	7			6	12*				3			10			14†					G.Keatley
23	1	2	8		5	14†	9*	4			7			6†	11				3			10					12*			D.Magill
24	1		8		5	4	9	2			7			6*	11				3			10	12*							A.Snoddy
25			8		5	4	9	3		10	7			6	11*						2						12*	1		M.Ross
26			8		5	6	9	4		11†	7			14†	2*				3			10						1	12*	G.Keatley
27		2	8		5	3†	9	4		11	7			6	12*						10*	14†						1		A.Snoddy
28		2	8		5	3	9	4		11*	7			6	14†							10						1	12†*	N.Cowie

TRANSFERS C/S '95 TO APRIL '96

Players Signed:

Michael Kelly (Ballyclare Comrades Jun.'95), Darren Hall (Glentoran Jul.'95), Gary O'Sullivan (Shamrock Rovers Jul.'95), Michael Boyle (Larne Aug.'95), Ritchie Breza (American Soccer Federation Aug.'95), Steve Elliott (American Soccer Federation Aug.'95), Patrick Flannery (Greenock Morton (Sco loan) Aug.'95), Larry O'Shea (Shelbourne (Shelbourne Aug.'95), Mark Simpson (Greenock Morton (Sco loan) Aug.'95), Barney Bowers (Glentoran Sep.'95), Andy Hawkins (Dunfermline (Sco loan) Oct.'95), Paul McLaughlin (Derry City Nov.'95), Kyle Maloney (Coleraine (loan) Nov.'95), Dean Smyth (Ballymena United (loan) Nov.'95), Ritchie Barker (Sheffield Wednesday (Eng loan) Jan.'96), John Hill (Australia Jan.'96), David Johnstone (Dromara Village Jan.'96), Jim Murray (Distillery Jan.'96), Paul Gray (Bangor Mar.'96), Salvatore Bibbo (Sheffield United (Eng loan) Apr.'96)

Players Transferred:

Dean May (Ballymena United c/s'95), Kevin Brady (Bohemians Jun.'95), Darren Erskine (Linfield Jul.'95), David Straney (Larne Aug.'95), Ritchie Breza (Distillery Sep.'95), Andy Hawkins (Dunfermline (Sco loan rtn) Oct.'95), Mark Simpson (Greenock Morton (Sco loan rtn) Oct.'95), Dean Smyth (Ballymena United (loan rtn) Nov.'95), John Clapham (Abbey Villa Dec.'95), Ian Bustard (Larne Jan.'96), Patrick Flannery (Greenock Morton (Sco loan rtn) Jan.'96), Kyle Maloney (Coleraine (loan rtn) Jan.'96), Ritchie Barker (Sheffield Wednesday (Eng loan rtn) Feb.'96), Salvatore Bibbo (Sheffield United (Eng loan rtn) Apr.'96).

HONOURS

Irish League, Champions/Premier League	(1)	1957/58/7th 1995/96
Irish Cup, Winners:	(4)	1926/27, 1951/52, 1968/69, 1973/74.
Gold Cup, Winners:	(2)	1953/54, 1973/74.
Ulster Cup, Winners:	(1)	1973/74.
Irish League Cup, Winners:	(1)	1994/95.
Co.Antrim Shield, Winners:	(3)	1956/57, 1971/72, 1993/94.
Blaxnit Cup, Winners:	(1)	1974/75.
Irish League 'B' Division, Champions:	(1)	1957/58.
IFA Intermediate Cup, Winners:	(1)	1970/71.
George Wilson Cup, Winners:	(2)	1957/58, 1982/83.

Most Capped Player: Andy Bothwell 5 caps (N.Ireland)

PLAYER PROFILE – PAUL CULLEN

Ards top scorer for the 95/96 season was Dubliner Paul Cullen with 15 goals which included a four goal blast against 'B' Division side Cookstown United in the Bass Irish Cup in January.

That maybe gives some indication of Ards' lack of scoring form during a season in which they had lost top marksman Darren Erskine to Linfield. Erskine and Cullen had in fact been joint scorers for Ards the previous season - both notching 19 apiece. Paul is now 27 years of age, he hails from Dublins' seaside resort Bray and it was with hometown 'Bray Wanderers' that he began his career as a teenager before going on to University.

That was University College Dublin and as 'U.C.D.' played in the Senior League so did Paul who also turned out for the Irish Universities and in the World Student games. His career mirrored that of Ards teammate Gary O'Sullivan as both moved onto Shamrock Rovers and after three seasons both came to Ards 'on-loan'. Cullen was first to sign permanantly for Roy Coyle and that was hardly surprising as he and Erskine had struck up a very profitable partnership up front.

Unfortunately when that was broken with Erskines transfer, so Cullen's form began to fade as no regular front man stayed long enough to assist the Southerner whose best position is supporting a bigger man up front rather than being an 'out and out striker himself.

During the summer Ards re-signed Harry McCourt from Derry City and hopefully Cullen will be able to strike up a similar rapport with McCourt like he had with Erskine.

Interestingly Ards had three Southern travellers last season in Cullen, O'Sullivan and Dwaine Shanley and a more high-powered 'Mastermind' trio you couldn't imagine! Cullen is an Accountant, O'Sullivan a Consulting Engineer and Shanley a Lecturer!

Jim Palmer.

ARDS APPEARANCES FOR 1995/96

Name:	UC	GC	ILC	CC	BIC	CAS	PL	Total
1 Paul Mooney	4	3	2	3	3	1+(1)	25	41+(1)
2 Paul Kee	4	3	2	4	3	2	23	41
3 Michael Boyle	4	2	2	4	2+(1)	2	22+(2)	38+(3)
4 Paul Cullen	4	3	1	2	3	1	25+(1)	39+(1)
5 Paul McBride	4	3	2	4	3	1+(1)	18+(3)	35+(4)
6 Dwaine Shanley	4	2	2	3	3	1	20+(4)	35+(4)
7 Raymond Morrison	1+(1)	1+(1)	-	2	2	1	25+(1)	32+(3)
8 Gary O'Sullivan	4	3	2	-(1)	1+(1)	1	9+(11)	20+(13)
9 Barney Bowers	-	-	-	2	1	2	23+(1)	28+(1)
10 Michael Kelly	4	3	2	2	1	1	15	28
11 William Murphy	2	3	-	4	3	-(1)	10+(5)	22+(6)
12 Martin McCann	-	-	-	3	2+(1)	2	18+(1)	25+(2)
13 Paul McLaughlin	-	-	-	3	2	1	16	22
14 Patrick Flannery	4	3	-	-	-	2	11+(1)	20+(1)
15 Chris Cullen	-	1+(2)	-	1	1	-	14+(2)	17+(4)
16 Declan McGreevy	-	-(1)	-	-(1)	-	2	7+(2)	9+(4)
17 Ritchie Barker	-	-	-	3	2	-	7	12
18 John Wills	2	-	1	-	-	-	6+(1)	9+(1)
19 Paul Dunnion	-	1+(1)	1	1+(2)	-(1)	-(1)	-(2)	3+(7)
20 Mark Simpson	3+(1)	2	-	-	-	-	1+(2)	6+(3)
21 Gary Walker	-	-	2	2	-	-	-(4)	4+(4)
22 Kyle Maloney	-	-	-	-	-	1	4	5
23 Salvatore Bibbo	-	-	-	-	-	-	4	4
24 Con Getty	-	-	-	1	1	-	1+(1)	3+(1)
25 Andy Beattie	-	-	-	-(1)	-	-	-(3)	-(4)
26 Larry O'Shea	-(2)	-	1	-	-	-	-	1+(2)
27 Brian Campbell	-	-	-	-	-	1	1	2
28 Darren Hall	-	-	2	-	-	-	-	2
29 Andy Hawkins	-	-	-	-	-	-	2	2
30 Paul Gray	-	-	-	-	-	-	-(2)	-(2)
31 Stuart Kelly	-	-	-(2)	-	-	-	-	-(2)
32 Michael McGaw	-	-	-(2)	-	-	-	-	-(2)
33 Jim Murray	-	-	-	-(1)	-(1)	-	-	-(2)
34 Dean Smyth	-	-	-	-	-	-	1	1
35 Ritchie Breza	-(1)	-	-	-	-	-	-	-(1)
36 David Johnstone	-	-	-	-(1)	-	-	-	-(1)

ARDS GOALSCORERS FOR 1995/96

Name:	UC	GC	ILC	CC	CAS	BIC	PL	Total
1 Paul Cullen	3	3	-	-	-	4	5	15
2 Michael Boyle	1	1	1	3	-	2	5	13
3 Patrick Flannery	3	2	-	-	1	-	2(1p)	8(1p)
4 Ritchie Barker	-	-	-	1	-	3	3	7
5 Martin McCann	-	-	-	1	1	1	3	6
6 Raymond Morrison	1	-	-	-	-	2	2	5
7 Paul McLaughlin	-	-	-	-	1	-	3	4
8 Barney Bowers	-	-	-	2	-	-	1	3
9 Paul Mooney	-	1p	-	-	-	-	2p	3p
10 Paul Dunnion	-	-	1	-	-	-	-	1
11 Paul McBride	-	-	1	-	-	-	-	1
12 Declan McGreevy	-	-	-	-	-	-	1	1
13 Kyle Maloney	-	-	-	-	-	-	1	1
14 William Murphy	-	-	-	1	-	-	-	1
15 Dwaine Shanley	-	-	-	-	-	-	1	1
16 Own Goals	-	1	-	-	-	-	-	1
Total	8	8	3	8	3	12	29	69

**Ground: Dixon Park, Harrier Way, Ballyclare (4,500) Founded: 1919.
Tel: 019603 52319**

NO PHOTOGRAPH AVAILABLE FOR **1995/96**

President:
Mr.V.Lea
Chairman:
Mr.G.Herron
Secretary:
Mr.D.Horner
Treasurer:
Mr.D.Higgins
Manager:
Alan Campbell
Club Colours:
Red shirts, Red shorts,
Red socks

Summary of 1995/96 Season

Ballyclare Comrades began the season with yet another new manager, their fifth in as many seasons. And it did not take Alan Campbell, the former Glenavon and Ballymena United boss, long to realise the task facing him. The perennial close season exodus from Dixon Park saw the previous seasons top two goalscorers at the club, Peter Moran and Patrick O'Connell, depart along with Michael Kelly, Philip Lecky and David Armstrong. Their replacements were made up of players who came from 'B' Division or Amateur League clubs, so it was no surprise that they made a disastrous start. A defeat against Banbridge Town in the opening round of the League Cup was followed by three Ulster Cup maulings by Distillery, Glenavon and Cliftonville, in which the Comrades conceded a staggering 19 goals! The new boss patched the defence up in time for the Gold Cup campaign against Portadown, Ards and Omagh Town but a lack of punch up front meant that Comrades were still pointless after seven games.

Ballyclare eventually got off the mark with a draw in their opening League match at home to Newry Town and their first victory a fortnight later over eventual runaway Champions Coleraine, led to a pitchside protest by the Bannsiders' fans demanding Kenny Shiels' resignation, but a barren spell then followed before a few good results either side of Christmas lifted them off the bottom of the table.

THE NORTHERN IRELAND
football
Y E A R   B O O K

Despite another slump in their fortunes during February, a second win against Coleraine and a 1-0 victory over Distillery on the last day meant that Ballyclare finished the season in fifth place, ahead of East Antrim rivals Carrick Rangers and Larne.

In the Bass Irish Cup, Comrades survived a fifth round scare before eventually squeezing past Tobermore United on a 3-2 scoreline but not unexpectedly went out at the next hurdle to reigning League Champions Crusaders.

As with most First Division clubs money at Dixon Park is very tight, so while the likes of Trevor Anderson and Ronnie McFall contemplate their next 'big signing' Alan Campbell will once again have to be content with scouring the the Junior Leagues for the types of players who he hopes will turn Ballyclare into a promotion winning side in 1996/97.

Liam Heffron.

MANAGER PROFILE - ALAN CAMPBELL

Date of Birth: 11/09/1944 Belfast
Date of Appointment: June 1995

PREVIOUS CLUBS:
As Player: Coleraine; Grimsby Town; Glenavon:

As Manager: Glenavon (Player/Manager); Ballymena United; Distillery; Ballymena United; Sotiras (Cyprus): Ypsonnas (Cyprus); Grove United:

HONOURS:
As Player: Coleraine - **Irish Cup,** 1964/65

As Manager: Ballymena United - **Irish Cup,** 1980/81
                                  Ulster Cup, 1980/81
                                  Co.Antrim Shield, 1979/80

THE NORTHERN IRELAND
football
Y E A R B O O K

TRANSFERS C/S'95 TO APRIL '96

Players Signed:

Nicky Blair (Carniny Rangers c/s'95), Alan Campbell (Cookstown United Jul.'95), James Irwin (Cookstown United Jul.'95), Tony Kearns (Donegal Celtic Jul.'95), Marcus Walker (Grove United Jul.'95), Liam McCann (Cookstown United Aug.'95), Neill Mitchell (Larne Tech. Old Boys Aug.'95), Nigel Clarke (Randalstown Sky Blues Sep.'95), Chris Gallagher (Ballymena League Sep.'95), Allen Huxley (Bangor (loan) Sep.'95), Keith Kelly (Dromara Village Sep.'95), Harry Laughlin (R.I.R. Sep.'95), Barry Forshaw (U.U.J. Oct.'95), Kenny Higgins (Ballynure Oct.'95), Gavin McCrystal (Cliftonville Oct.'95), Kenny Neilly (Broadway Celtic Oct.'95), Jonathan Field (Carrick Rangers Nov.'95), David Keery (Ballymena United Nov.'95), Robert Young (Carniny Rangers Nov.'95), Anton Boyle (Donegal Celtic Dec.'95), Raymond Bell (Islandmagee Jan.'96), Ray Davidson F.C.Enkalon Jan.'96), Stewart Galbraith (Islandmagee Jan.'96), Darren Munn (Islandmagee Jan.'96), Mervyn Pattison (Moyola Park Jan.'96), Michael Beckinsale (Larne Feb.'96), Graham Mellon (Moyola Park Feb.'96), David Rainey (Knockbreda Paris Apr.'96).

Players Transferred:

Michael Beckinsale (Larne c/s'95), Raymond Bell (Islandmagee c/s'95), Stewart Galbraith (Islandmagee c/s'95), Peter Moran (Omagh Town c/s'95), Darren Munn (Islandmagee c/s'95), Patrick O'Connell (Bangor May'95), Michael Kelly (Ards Jun.'95), Philip Leckey (Coleraine Jul.'95), Jason Murtagh (Bangor Jul.'95), David Armstrong (Larne Aug.'95), Bill Cardwell (Larne Aug.'95), John Johnston (Bangor Oct.'95), Keith Kelly (Released Oct.'95), Harry Loughins (Released Oct.'95), Gary McCormick (Dundela Nov.'95), Frank Wilson (Carrick Rangers Nov.'95), Sean McGreevy (Omagh Town Feb.'96), Gavin McCrystal (Chimney Corner Mar.'96).

HONOURS

Irish League / First Division		11th 1991/92 / 5th 1995/96
Irish League 'B'Division, Champions:	(6)	1960/61, 1962/63, 1973/74, 1977/78, 1979/80, 1988/89
IFA Intermediate Cup, Winners:	(9)	1925/26, 1949/50, 1950/51, 1953/54, 1959/60, 1960/61, 1962/63, 1963/64, 1989/90
Steel & Sons Cup, Winners:	(6)	1943/44, 1960/61, 1974/75, 1981/82, 1984/85, 1986/87
George Wilson Cup, Winners:	(4)	1956/57, 1961/62, 1963/64, 1993/94
'B'Division Knockout Cup, Winners:	(2)	1983/84, 1988/89.

SMIRNOFF FIRST DIVISION RECORD 1995/96

No.	Date:	Ven:	Opponents:	Result:	H.T.	Pos:	Goalscorers:
1	Sep 30	H	Newry Town	1-1 D	1-1	-	O'Connor (14)
2	Oct 7	A	Larne	0-2 L	0-0	7	-
3	Oct 14	H	Coleraine	1-0 W	1-0	6	Irwin (38)
4	Oct 21	A	Carrick Rangers	0-3 L	0-1	6	-
5	Oct 28	H	Ballymena United	1-3 L	1-0	6	O'Connor (15)
6	Nov 4	A	Omagh Town	3-1 W	1-1	5	Bell (20), Campbell (61,74)
7	Nov 11	H	Distillery	0-2 L	0-2	6	-
8	Nov 18	A	Newry Town	0-2 L	0-1	7	-
9	Nov 25	H	Larne	2-3 L	1-1	8	Higgins (34), Campbell (56)
10	Dec 2	A	Coleraine	0-2 L	0-0	8	-
11	Dec 9	H	Carrick Rangers	2-1 W	2-0	8	Forshaw (37), Campbell (41)
12	Dec 16	A	Ballymena United	0-0 D	0-0	7	-
13	Jan 1	A	Distillery	2-1 W	1-0	-	Forshaw (15), Young (63)
14	Jan 6	H	Newry Town	3-2 W	1-1	7	Forshaw (36,55), Higgins (65)
15	Jan 13	A	Larne	1-0 W	1-0	5	Young (8)
16	Jan 27	H	Coleraine	0-2 L	0-2	5	-
17	Feb 3	A	Carrick Rangers	3-0 W	1-0	3	O'Connor (27), Forshaw (79), Young (86)
18	Feb 6	H	Omagh Town	1-2 L	0-1	-	Higgins (55)
19	Feb 10	H	Ballymena United	0-1 L	0-0	4	-
20	Feb 17	A	Omagh Town	0-3 L	0-1	6	-
21	Mar 2	H	Distillery	0-3 L	0-1	6	-
22	Mar 16	A	Newry Town	0-3 L	0-3	7	-
23	Mar 23	H	Larne	1-1 D	1-1	6	Forshaw (29)
24	Mar 30	A	Coleraine	3-1 W	1-0	6	Forshaw (44,60), Young (67)
25	Apr 6	H	Carrick Rangers	3-2 W	1-1	5	(S) Galbraith (43), Orchin (80,82)
26	Apr 8	A	Ballymena United	1-2 L	0-0	-	Young (75)
27	Apr 20	H	Omagh Town	0-5 L	0-1	5	-
28	Apr 27	A	Distillery	1-0 W	0-0	5	(L) Galbraith (79)

Final League Position: 5th

FIRST DIVISION LINE UPS 1995/96

MATCH No	S.McGreevy 10	B.Allsopp 26	A.Kearns 26	P.Hall 8	A.Morrison 25	P.O'Connor 14	F.McCusker 10+(11)	H.Loughins 2	A.Campbell 17+(1)	K.Kelly 2	J.Irwin 7+(1)	F.Wilson 1+(1)	L.Galbraith 19+(4)	A.Finnegan 5+(1)	B.Forshaw 20+(1)	K.Neilly 2+(6)	M.Walker 20+(3)	C.Bell 17	P.Orchin 4+(2)	A.Blair 0+(1)	N.Blair 12+(3)	D.Keery 1+(1)	K.Higgins 8+(2)	D.McCusker 18	R.Young 15+(1)	N.Clarke 1+(1)	S.Galbraith 9+(1)	A.Boyle 1+(5)	G.Mellon 8	Referee
1	1	2	3	4	5	6	7	8*	9	10	11	12*																		M.Adair
2	1	2	3	4	5	11	–	8†	9*	10	7	6	12*	14†																F.Hiles
3	1	2	3	4	5*	7	–	–	8	–	11	–	–	6	9	10	12*													P.Thompson
4	1	2	3	4	5†	7	–	–	8	–	11	–	12*	6	9	10*	14†													F.Hiles
5	1	7	3	4	5	10	–	–	8	–	–	12*	6	9*	–	2	11													T.Deegan
6	1	7	3	4	5	10	8	–	9	–	–	–	6	–	–	2	11													H.Barr
7	1	7	3	4	5	8	–	–	9	–	–	–	–	6	–	12*	2	11	10*											B.Kane
8	1	7	3	4	5	–	8	–	9	–	10	–	6	–	12*	–	2	11	–	14†15°										M.Ross
9	1	7	3	–	5	–	–	–	10*	–	6	–	–	–	–	12*	4	11	–	–	2	8	9							H.O'Neill
10	–	7	3	–	5	–	12*	–	10	–	6	–	–	–	–	–	4	11	–	–	2	14†	9†	1	8*					D.Taylor
11	–	7	3	–	5	–	6	–	10†	–	14†	–	12*	–	8	–	4	11	–	–	2	–	9*	1	–					F.Hiles
12	–	7	3	–	–	–	6	–	11	–	–	–	8	–	–	4	5	–	–	2	–	9	1	–	10					L.Irvine
13	–	7	3	–	5	–	–	–	4	–	–	–	6	8	10	12*	–	–	–	2	–	9*	1	11	–					T.Deegan
14	–	7	3	–	5	–	6†	–	4	–	–	–	8	–	10	–	14†	11	–	–	2	–	9*	1	–	12*				A.Snoddy
15	1	8	3	–	5	7	–	–	12*	–	–	–	6	–	9	–	4	11†	–	–	2	–	14†	–	10*	–				D.Taylor
16	–	–	3	–	5	6	7	–	9†	–	–	–	8*	–	10	12*	4	11	–	–	2	–	–	–	1	14†	–			R.Penney
17	–	7	3	–	5	8	–	–	–	–	–	–	6	–	10	–	4	9	–	–	2	–	–	1	11	–				M.Ross
18	–	7	3	–	–	5	–	–	–	–	–	–	6	–	10	12*	4	9	–	–	2	–	8*	1	11	–				E.Millar
19	–	7	3	–	–	5	–	–	9	–	–	–	6†	–	10*	12*	4	8	–	–	2	–	–	1	11	–	14†			G.Keatley
20	–	7	3*	–	5	8	–	10	–	–	–	–	6	–	9	–	–	–	–	2	–	14†	1	11	–	4†	12*			J.Peden
21	–	–	–	–	5	7	9*	–	–	–	–	–	8	–	10	–	4	–	–	–	12*	–	–	1	11	–	6	2	3	D.Taylor
22	–	7	3	–	5	–	10	–	–	–	–	–	6	–	9	–	4	–	–	–	–	–	–	1	11	–	8	12*	2	F.McDonald
23	–	7	–	–	5	–	–	–	–	–	–	6*	–	9	–	4	3	14†	–	–	–	–	10†	1	11	–	8	12*	2	E.Millar
24	–	7	3	–	5	–	–	–	–	–	–	–	6	–	10	–	4	9	12*	–	–	–	–	1	11*	–	8	–	2	D.Malcolm
25	–	7	3	–	5	–	–	–	–	–	–	–	6	–	9	–	4	–	10	–	–	–	–	1	11	–	8	–	2	P.Thompson
26	–	7	3	–	5*	–	–	–	–	–	–	–	8	–	9	–	4	10	–	–	–	–	–	1	11	–	6	12*	2	T.Deegan
27	–	7	3*	–	5	–	–	–	–	–	–	–	6	–	9	–	4	–	10	–	14†	–	–	1	11	–	8	12*	2†	M.Hutton
28	–	7	3	–	5	–	4	–	–	–	–	–	6	–	9	–	–	10	–	–	–	–	–	1	11	–	8	–	2	D.Chambers

PLAYER PROFILE - PATRICK O'CONNOR

Patrick O'Connor was one of only two professional players at Dixon Park last season (the other was Damien McCusker). But the big midfielder is adamant the Comrades is no amateur set-up.

"Far from it," he says. "There isn't a lot of cash about, but Alan Campbell is a fantastic manager. Too good for this level of football."

Campbell's been around a few corners on the soccer scene, and he's used his experience to put together a Ballyclare side for virtually nothing.

O'Connor is one of the men he plucked from the obscurity of Junior soccer with U.U.J. and although the Comrades may not be the most fashionable of clubs, Pat's happy to be there.

"When I left Larne I thought I'd blown my chance of senior soccer so it's nice to be given a second chance at 26," he says.

In only his first season back in the Irish League, O'Connor, a P.E. Teacher at Hazelwood Integrated College in Belfast, learned quickly to adapt to the higher level. He was one of the stars as Ballyclare Comrades ruffled more than a few feathers in a see-saw campaign.

Don't forget, they were the only team to beat runaway champions Coleraine twice and they also scored their customary success against Premier League top dogs Portadown. Second at one stage in the First Division, they eventually had to settle for fifth.

O'Connor reflects, "That wasn't bad under the circumstances. With our limited resources, we were pleased to finish ahead of our local rivals Carrick Rangers and Larne."

Pat is picked to play in midfield, but says he feels equally at home in defence. He's a bit of a sporting all-rounder really. The Anderstown man is a former Irish table tennis International and he also had four years playing County football for Antrim.

Peter Taggart.

BALLYCLARE COMRADES APPEARANCES FOR 1995/96

Name:	UC	GC	ILC	CC	BIC	CAS	FD	Total
1 Tony Kearns	-	3	1	2	2	1	26	35
2 Allan Morrison	2	3	-	2	2	1	25	35
3 Brendan Allsopp	-	3	-	1	2	1	26	33
4 Marcus Walker	2	-(1)	-	1	2	1	20+(3)	26+(4)
5 Lee Galbraith	1+(1)	-(1)	-	2	1	-(1)	19+(4)	23+(7)
6 Alan Campbell	3	3	1	1	1	1	17+(1)	27+(1)
7 Colin Bell	2	2	-(1)	2	2	1	17	26+(1)
8 Barry Forshaw	-	-	-	2	1	-	20+(1)	23+(1)
9 Damien McCusker	-	-	-	2	2	-	18	22
10 Patrick O'Connor	-	3	1	1	2	-	14	21
11 Robert Young	-	-	-	2	2	1	15+(1)	20+(1)
12 Fergal McCusker	3	2	1	2	-(1)	-(1)	10+(1)	18+(3)
13 Nicky Blair	-	-	-	2	1+(1)	1	12+(3)	16+(4)
14 Sean McGreevy	2	3	1	-	-	1	10	17
15 James Irwin	3	3	1	-	-	1	7+(1)	15+(1)
16 Kenny Higgins	-	-	-	-(1)	1	1	8+(2)	10+(3)
17 Paul Hall	1	3	-	-	-	-	8	12
18 Stewart Galbraith	-	-	-	-	1	-	9+(1)	10+(1)
19 Tony Finnegan	1	1+(1)	-	-	-	-	5+(1)	7+(2)
20 Graham Mellon	-	-	-	-	-	-	8	8
21 Frank Wilson	3	2	1	-	-	-	1+(1)	7+(1)
22 Paul Orchin	1	-(1)	-	-	-	-	4+(2)	5+(3)
23 Kenny Neilly	-	-	-	-	-	-	2+(6)	2+(6)
24 Anton Boyle	-	-	-	-	-(1)	-	1+(5)	1+(6)
25 Keith Kelly	-	2	-	-	-	-	2	4
26 Glenn Larmour	2+(1)	-	1	-	-	-	-	3+(1)
27 Neill McGivern	2	-	1	-	-	-	-	3
28 Brett McCrum	-(2)	-	1	-	-	-	-	1+(2)
29 Harry Loughins	-	-	-	-	-	-	2	2
30 Liam McCann	2	-	-	-	-	-	-	2
31 Nigel Clarke	-	-	-	-	-	-	1+(1)	1+(1)
32 Jason Greer	1+(1)	-	-	-	-	-	-	1+(1)
33 David Keery	-	-	-	-	-	-	1+(1)	1+(1)
34 John Johnston	-	-	1	-	-	-	-	1
35 Brian McNulty	1	-	-	-	-	-	-	1
36 Neill Mitchell	1	-	-	-	-	-	-	1
37 Anthony Blair	-	-	-	-	-	-	-(1)	-(1)
38 Alan McIlwaine	-(1)	-	-	-	-	-	-	-(1)

BALLYCLARE COMRADES GOALSCORERS FOR 1995/96

Name:	UC	GC	ILC	CC	BIC	CAS	FD	Total
1 Barry Forshaw	-	-	-	2	2	-	8	12
2 Kenny Higgins	-	-	-	-	-	2	3	5
3 Robert Young	-	-	-	-	-	-	5	5
4 Alan Campbell	-	-	-	-	-	-	4	4
5 Patrick O'Connor	-	-	-	-	-	-	3	3
6 Stewart Galbraith	-	-	-	-	1	-	1	2
7 Paul Orchin	-	-	-	-	-	-	2	2
8 Colin Bell	-	-	-	-	-	-	1	1
9 Lee Galbraith	-	-	-	-	-	-	1	1
10 James Irwin	-	-	-	-	-	-	1	1
11 Fergal McCusker	1	-	-	-	-	-	-	1
Total:	1	0	0	2	3	2	29	37

Ground: The Showgrounds, Warden Street, Ballymena. (8,000) Founded: 1928.
Tel: 01266 652049

Ballymena United 1995/96

Back Row L-R: Jason Allen, Fintan McConville, Robbie Beck, Tom McCourt, Mark Carlisle, Ally Mauchlen
Front Row: L-R: Nigel Boyd, Des Loughery, Peter Murray, John McConnell, James Steele
(Photograph courtesy of Shaun O'Neill, Ballymena Guardian)

President:
Mr.W.A.Anderson
Chairman:
Mr.E.McLaughlin
Secretary:
Mr.D.Stirling
Treasurer:
Mr.J.Gray
Manager:
Alan Fraser
Asst.Manager:
Eric Bowyer
Club Colours:
Sky Blue shirts,
White shorts,
Sky Blue socks

Summary of the Season 1995/96

It's far from a 'funny old game'. United fans assured themselves that promotion in two years would be acceptable. But when it didn't come in the first season of the League's new two-tier system, you could hear Sky Blue groans stampeding their way along Warden Street.

It seems so ironic now. How we guffawed way back in May 1995 when Paul Muir's right boot cleared United's goaline to condemn Coleraine to First Division football. How deeply depressing then that the Ballycastle Road men should twist the bayonet by turning last season's title into a one-horse race. But there the pessimism ends for another 12 months....

Showgrounds boss, Alan Fraser, is safe in the United hot-seat, an indication of the high esteem in which he is increasingly held in Ballymena. His much-publicised big-money buys at the start of last season have turned United into a hard team to beat. More Arsenal than Ajax, granted, but it's working.

Robbie Beck, Jason Allen (everyone's player-of-the-season), club captain John McConnell, Stephen Stewart and Nigel Boyd have added a steely backbone to United in the past number of months. Ally Mauchlen and Mark McWalter (top goalscorer with 13 goals), who were set for pastures new during the summer, missed most of the campaign through injury, while highly-rated striker Tom McCourt lost his starting place for reasons best known to himself.

The statistics speak for themselves. Ballymena conceded a mere 25 League goals thanks largely to messrs. Beck, Allen and McConnell. It was the best defensive record in the two divisions. But you only have to look at the other end of the scale (38 goals scored in 28 League games) to recognise the team's frailties. How many times did Alan Fraser complain about his side's impotence in front of goal last season? Quite a few, I'd wager.

THE NORTHERN IRELAND
football
Y E A R B O O K

This year United will hope to wrestle Bangor, Distillery and possibly Omagh out of the way to secure Premier League football in the 1997/98 campaign. But boss Fraser is confident this year's Sky Blues will be a "threat and a force to be reckoned with". Speaking at the end of last season the former Glenavon supremo said " I am pleased with the players. Throughout the season they gave me 100 per cent and I couldn't fault them in any way."

On the plus side, the Showgrounds outfit can only improve on last year's failings and the club's Steel & Sons Cup win by the Reserves squad also augurs well for the season ahead.

Now we can merely hope and pray that the sound of a rippling net returns to Warden Street. It would make Mr. Alan Fraser (and countless others) very happy indeed.......

Darren Fullerton.

MANAGER PROFILE — ALAN FRASER

Date of Birth: 25/10/52; Lurgan.
Date of Appointment: March 1995.

PREVIOUS CLUBS:
As Player: Linfield; Glenavon; Carrick Rangers:
As Manager: Carrick (Coach); Ballymena United (Coach); Glenavon (Reserve Team Manager); Linfield (First Team Coach): Glenavon.

HONOURS:
As Player: Irish League Representative 1 cap;
Linfield – **Irish League Championship**; 1974/75; 1977/78; 1978/79; **Irish Cup**; 1977/78 and 1979/80; **Gold Cup**; 1979/80; **Ulster Cup**; 1974/75; 1977/78; 1978/79; 1979/80; **City Cup**; 1973/74; **Co.Antrim Shield**; 1972/73

As Manager:
Glenavon – **Irish Cup**; 1991/92

31

SMIRNOFF FIRST DIVISION RECORD 1995/96

No:	Date:	Ven:	Opponents:	Result:	H.T:	Pos:	Goalscorers:
1	Sep 30	H	Carrick Rangers	3-1 W	3-0	-	Loughery (11,21), Burn (34)
2	Oct 7	A	Newry Town	2-1 W	1-1	1	McCourt (31), McWalter (pen 60)
3	Oct 14	A	Omagh Town	0-0 D	0-0	1	-
4	Oct 21	H	Distillery	0-1 L	0-1	3	-
5	Oct 28	A	Ballyclare Comrades	3-1 W	0-1	3	McWalter (70), Murray (86), Curry (89)
6	Nov 4	H	Larne	0-0 D	0-0	3	-
7	Nov 11	A	Coleraine	1-1 D	0-0	3	Murray (61)
8	Nov 18	A	Carrick Rangers	1-1 D	0-0	3	Burn (60)
9	Nov 25	H	Newry Town	0-0 D	0-0	3	-
10	Dec 2	H	Omagh Town	2-0 W	2-0	3	Murray (22), McWalter (83)
11	Dec 9	A	Distillery	1-0 W	0-0	2	Murray (60)
12	Dec 16	H	Ballyclare Comrades	0-0 D	0-0	2	-
13	Jan 1	H	Coleraine	1-2 L	1-1	-	McWalter (27)
14	Jan 6	H	Carrick Rangers	1-2 L	0-1	2	Murray (75)
15	Jan 13	A	Newry Town	0-1 L	0-1	3	-
16	Jan 31	A	Larne	0-0 D	0-0	-	-
17	Feb 3	H	Distillery	1-1 D	1-1	2	Steele (31)
18	Feb 10	A	Ballyclare Comrades	1-0 W	0-0	2	McConnell (74)
19	Feb 16	H	Larne	2-2 D	1-1	-	Loughery (27,59)
20	Feb 27	A	Omagh Town	2-2 D	0-2	-	McConnell (48), McWalter (82)
21	Mar 2	A	Coleraine	0-4 L	0-3	4	-
22	Mar 16	A	Carrick Rangers	2-0 W	1-0	3	Moors (31,60)
23	Mar 23	H	Newry Town	3-0 W	1-0	3	Steele (9,66), (C) Moore (69)
24	Mar 30	H	Omagh Town	2-0 W	0-0	2	(C) Moore (63), McWalter (88)
25	Apr 6	A	Distillery	3-1 W	1-0	2	(C) Moore (30), Murray (60), Burn (69)
26	Apr 8	H	Ballyclare Comrades	2-1 W	0-0	-	McWalter (47), Allen (pen 64)
27	Apr 20	A	Larne	1-0 W	0-0	2	Carlisle (73)
28	Apr 27	H	Coleraine	4-3 W	0-1	2	Loughery (59), Burn (66), Allen (86), McWalter (90)

Final League Position: 2nd

FIRST DIVISION LINE-UPS 1995/96

MATCH No	D.Smyth 7	A.Mauchlen 13+(2)	S.Stewart 18+(1)	J.Allen 27	J.McConnell 23	P.Burn 21+(2)	D.Loughery 16+(5)	M.McWalter 19+(1)	T.McCourt 10	P.Muir 21+(2)	N.Boyd 17+(4)	B.Patton 3+(6)	P.Murray 21	S.Lynch 0+(2)	L.Curry 6+(6)	R.Beck 21+(1)	D.Moore 9+(4)	F.McConville 19	J.Gilmore 4+(4)	J.Steele 6+(5)	M.Carlisle 16	C.Moore 7+(2)	K.Wylie 0+(1)	C.Moors 3	J.Booth 1	M.Kerr 0+(1)	Referee
1	1	2	3	4	5	6	7	8*	9	10	11	12*															D.Magill
2	1	2	3	4	5	14†	7	8*	9	10	6†	12*	11														G.Dobbin
3	1	2	–	4	5	6	7*	8	9	10	3	12*	11														T.Gillanders
4	1	2	–	4	5	6	7	9†	–	10*	3	8	11	12*	14†												D.Chambers
5	–	2*	12*	4	5	6	7	8	–	10	3	9†	11	–	14†	1											T.Deegan
6	–	–	3	4	5	6	7	8†	9	10*	2	–	11	–	14†	1	12*										R.Lutton
7	–	–	3	4	5	6	7	8	–	10	–	–	11	–	–	1	2	9									A.Snoddy
8	–	14†	3	4	5	6	7	8	–	10	–	–	11	–	12*	1	2	9									G.Dobbin
9	–	–	3	4	5	6	12*	8	–	10†	11*	14†	–	–	7	1	2	9									D.Malcolm
10	–	–	3	4	–	10	–	8	–	5	6*	–	11	–	7†	1	2	9	12*	14†							T.Deegan
11	–	–	3	4	2	10	–	8	–	5	6	–	11	–	7	1	–	9	–	–							R.Lutton
12	–	–	3	4	2	10	–	8	–	5	6*	12*	11	–	7	1	–	9	–	–							L.Irvine
13	–	–	3	4	5	9	12*	8†	–	10	6	14†	11	–	7*	1	–	–	–	–	2						D.Taylor
14	–	14†	–	4	5	6†	12*	–	9	10	3	8	11	–	7*	1	–	–	–	–	2						R.Lutton
15	–	8*	–	4	5	–	10	–	9°	3	11	–	6†	–	12*	1	14†	7	–	15°	2						E.Millar
16	–	8	–	4	5	–	10	–	9	–	3	–	11	–	–	1	–	7	–	12*	2	6*					J.Peden
17	–	8	–	4	5	–	10	–	9	–	3*	–	6†	15°	–	1°	14†	7	–	11	2	–	12*				R.Lutton
18	1	8†	3	4	5	–	10	–	9	14†	12*	–	–	–	–	6	7*	–	11	2	–	–					G.Keatley
19	1	8*	3	4	5	–	10	14†	9	12*	6	–	–	–	–	7	–	11†	2	–	–						L.Irvine
20	1°	–	3	4†	5	14†	10	11	–	7	6	–	–	–	–	15°	8	–	–	–	2	12*	–	9*			F.Hiles
21	–	4	3†	–	5	6*	10	11	–	8	14†	–	–	–	–	1	7	–	–	2	12*	–	9				M.Ross
22	–	8	–	4	–	6	–	–	–	5	–	3	–	–	–	1	7*	12*	10	2	–	–	9	11			D.Taylor
23	–	–	–	4	5	6	–	–	–	3	–	–	11†	–	14†	1	12*	7	8	9	2	10*	–	–			N.Cowie
24	–	–	–	4	–	6	12*	–	–	3*	–	11	–	–	–	1	5	7	8	9	2	10	–	–			J.Ferry
25	–	–	3	4	–	6	–	11	–	–	12*	–	9*	–	–	1°	5	7	8	14†	2	10†	–	–	–	15°	F.Hiles
26	–	–	3	4	–	6	–	11	–	–	12*	–	9*	–	–	1	5	7	8	–	2	10	–	–	–	–	T.Deegan
27	–	6*	3	4	5	8	12*	11	–	–	–	–	9	–	–	1	–	7	14†	–	2	10†	–	–	–	–	J.Peden
28	–	–	3	4	5	8	10	11	–	6†	–	–	–	–	–	1	–	7	14†	12*	2	9*	–	–	–	–	D.Taylor

TRANSFERS C/S'95 TO APRIL '96

Players Signed:

Dean May (Ards c/s'95), Jason Allen (Linfield Jun.'95), John McConnell (Linfield Jun.'95), Mark McWalter (Coleraine Jul.'95), David Moore (Dundela Jul.'95), Stephen Stewart (Crusaders Jul.'95), Nigel Boyd (Linfield Aug.'95), Thomas McCourt (Larne Aug.'95), Ally Mauchlen (Glenavon Aug.'95), Robert Beck (Glenavon Oct.'95), Peter Murray (Portadown Oct.'95), Dean Smyth (Ards (loan rtn) Nov.'95), Chris Moors (West Ham United (Eng loan) Feb.'95), Damian Grant (Crusaders (loan rtn) Apr,'96), Dean Smyth (Cliftonville (loan rtn) Apr.'96).

Players Transferred:

Jonathan Speak (Finn Harps Jun.'95), Stephen Doey (Dundela Jul.'95), Jim McCloskey (Bangor Jul.'95), Trevor McMullan (Crusaders Jul.'95), Stephen Whelan (Newry Town Jul.'95), Danny Crainie (Ross County (Sco) Aug.'95), Damian Grant (Crusaders (loan) Oct.'95), Tony Hall (Waterford Nov.'95), David Keery (Ballyclare Comrades Nov.'95), Dean Smyth (Ards (loan) Nov.'95), Dean May (R.U.C. Feb.'96), Stephen Lynch (Coleraine Mar.'96), Chris Moors (West Ham United (Eng loan rtn) Mar.'96), Dean Smyth (Cliftonville (loan) Apr.'96).

HONOURS

Irish League Championship/First Division		Best Position; Runners-up (2) 1938/39; 1979/80/2nd 1995/96
Irish Cup Winners:	(6)	1928/29; 1939/40; 1957/58; 1980/81; 1983/84; 1988/89
Gold Cup Winners:	(1)	1974/75
Ulster Cup Winners:	(2)	1960/61; 1980/81
City Cup Winners:	(1)	1971/72
Co. Antrim Sheild Winners:	(4)	1947/48; 1950/51; 1975/76; 1979/80
Steel & Sons Cup Winners:	(1)	1995/96*
Louis Moore Cup Winners:	(1)	1952/53*
George Wilson	(2)	1989/90*;1990/91*
Festival of Britain Cup	(1)	1952

Trophies won by Ballymena United Reserves.

Most capped player: J. McNinch (3caps N. Ireland)

PLAYER PROFILE - JASON ALLEN

It's a wonder Trevor Anderson hasn't received thank you notes by the bundle at Windsor Park. Visit Jason Allen and his wife Julie at their Dundonald home and you'll be surrounded by silverware. Compliments of grateful Ballymena United supporters.

Jason (25) has worked his way into the hearts of those hardy souls who watched United's promotion campaign falter in the Braid breeze last season. But despite the disappointment of Ballymena failing to gain Premier League football, the former Northern Ireland schoolboy and Oldham Athletic reserve player couldn't be happier with his new club.

"The Ballymena fans have been fantastic," he said, "It is a great honour to pick up all last season's Player of the Year awards from the supporters' clubs and hopefully I will be able to continue in the same vein next year."

Jason, who decided to turn his back on Linfield following a much-publicised Irish Cup Final dispute in 1995, admits he once considered throwing away his boots for good. But, thankfully, things are a lot different now.

"There were some summers when I wasn't looking forward to the season ahead, but this year I can't wait," he said, "I'm really bubbling and hopefully this year will go well for the club. The fans deserve success."

Jason believes manager Alan Fraser has assembled a squad capable of winning this season's First Division title.

"I expect the club to gain promotion this year." He said, "The boss has a settled team playing decent football at the moment so I think we're more than capable of going up. Bangor will prove our toughest opposition but I am feeling very positive about this year's campaign. Last year we did very well against Premier teams like Glentoran and Crusaders so I don't think we're too far away from a team that can challenge for major honours," he added.

Reflecting on last season, Jason admits that a lack of firepower and misfortune played a role in United's disjointed year.

"We were a bit unlucky at times and the goals didn't seem to go in at the right time," he said, "Before I came to Ballymena I'm not even sure if I'd played in a 0-0 game before!"

Jason who scored two goals last season (against Ballyclare Comrades and Coleraine), places a lot of credit on the shoulders of fellow central-defender John McConnell.

"You would definitely want John in the trenches with you," he laughed, "I know I gained a lot of recognition from the supporters, but John's style of play helps me immensely."

To Sky Blue fans, Jason Allen and John McConnell have performed wonders for a United team that has started to believe in itself again.

And to think they're both former Linfield men. Get me that address for Windsor Park......

Darren Fullerton.

BALLYMENA UNITED APPEARANCES FOR 1995/96

Name:	UC	GC	ILC	CC	BIC	CAS	FD	Total
1 Jason Allen	3	3	2	2	4	3	27	44
2 John McConnell	3	3	2	2	4	2	23	39
3 Nigel Boyd	3	4	2	1	4	3	17+(4)	34+(4)
4 Paul Muir	1+(1)	4	-	1	3+(1)	1+(2)	21+(2)	31+(6)
5 Des Loughery	3	2+(2)	-	2	4	-(1)	16+(5)	27+(8)
6 Fintan McConville	3	1+(1)	2	2	4	3	19	34
7 Stephen Stewart	3	3	2	1	1	3	18+(1)	31+(1)
8 Phil Burn	1	2	2	-	1	3	21+(2)	30+(2)
9 Robert Beck	-	1	-	1	3	3	21+(1)	29+(1)
10 Mark Carlisle	2+(1)	3	-	2	4	-	16	27+(1)
11 Peter Murray	-	-	-	1	3	2	21	27
12 Mark McWalter	1	-	1	-	2	3	19+(1)	26+(1)
13 Ally Mauchlen	2	2	2	-	2	1	13+(2)	22+(2)
14 David Moore	-	2	-(1)	2	-(3)	3	9+(4)	16+(8)
15 Thomas McCourt	2	3	2	2	-	-	10	19
16 Colin Moore	2+(1)	1+(1)	1+(1)	-	2	-(1)	7+(2)	13+(6)
17 Lindsay Curry	-	1	-	-	-(1)	3	6+(6)	10+(7)
18 Dean Smyth	-	3	2	1	1	-	7	14
19 Jason Gilmore	1	-	1+(1)	-	-(1)	-(1)	4+(4)	6+(7)
20 Barry Patton	-	3	-	-	-	-(1)	3+(6)	6+(7)
21 James Steele	-	-	-	1	-	-	6+(5)	7+(5)
22 Stephen Lynch	-(2)	-	1+(1)	-	-	-	-(2)	1+(5)
23 Chris Moors	-	-	-	-	2	-	3	5
24 John Heron	-	3	-	-	-	-	-	3
25 Dean May	3	-	-	-	-	-	-	3
26 Alan Craig	-	-	-	1+(1)	-	-	-	1+(1)
27 Jeff Booth	-	-	-	-	-	-	1	1
28 Mark Beattie	-	-	-	-(1)	-	-	-	-(1)
29 Matthew Kerr	-	-	-	-	-	-	-(1)	-(1)
30 Keith Wylie	-	-	-	-	-	-	-(1)	-(1)

BALLYMENA UNITED GOALSCORERS FOR 1995/96

Name:	UC	GC	ILC	CC	BIC	CAS	FD	Total
1 Mark McWalter	-	-	1	-	-	4	8(1p)	13 (1p)
2 Des Loughery	1	-	-	-	3	-	5	9
3 Peter Murray	-	-	-	-	-	-	6	6
4 Phil Burn	-	1	-	-	-	-	4	5
5 Colin Moore	-	-	-	-	2	-	3	5
6 Lindsay Curry	-	-	-	-	-	2	1	3
7 Chris Moors	-	-	-	-	1	-	2	3
8 James Steele	-	-	-	-	-	-	3	3
9 Jason Allen	-	-	-	-	-	-	2(1p)	2(1p)
10 John McConnell	-	-	-	-	-	-	2	2
11 Thomas McCourt	-	-	-	1	-	-	1	2
12 Mark Carlisle	-	-	-	-	-	-	1	1
13 Fintan McConville	-	-	-	-	1	-	-	1
14 Barry Patton	-	1	-	-	-	-	-	1
15 Own Goals	-	-	-	-	-	1	-	1
Total:	1	2	1	1	7	7	38	57

Ground: Clandeboye Park, Clandeboye Road, Bangor (5,000) Founded: 1918. Tel: 01247 457712

Bangor 1995/96
(Photograph courtesy of Roy Kitson, Co. Down Spectator)

President:	Mr.J.Apperson
Chairman:	Mr.H.Ashe
Hon.Secretary:	Mr.F.Anderson
Hon.Treasurer:	Mr.W.Palmer
Press Liaison:	Roy Kitson
Manager:	Andy Dougan
Asst.Manager:	George Dunlop
Reserve Team Manager:	Stephen McKee
Youth Team Manager:	Jim McCloskey
Physiotherapist:	Bill Massey
Club Colours:	Gold shirts, Royal Blue shorts, Gold socks

Summary of 1995/96 Season.

Despite the fact that Bangor ended the season with a trophy victory - the Mid-Ulster Cup, there can be no doubt that this was a disastrous year for the 'Seasiders' which saw the club relegated from the Premier League into the First Division. The main objective when the season started had been to secure the place fortuitously won in the Premier League, but everyone realised that the odds were against survival. The loss of players such as Tim Dalton, Ricky McEvoy, Marc Kenny and Mark Glendinning under controversial circumstances meant that new manager Paul Malone had to be something of a miracle worker to rebuild a team in a few short weeks.

New players were brought to the club at the start of the season, striker P.J. O'Connell from Ballyclare Comrades, midfielder Michael Cash from Larne and Michael McKeown from Glenavon and others in the course of the first weeks of the season, however it was soon evident that the team did not possess the quality required.

The season opened with a League Cup victory over Dungannon Swifts, but the writing was already on the wall when Cliftonville hammered Bangor 6-1 in the second round. Bangor did succeed in reaching the quarter-final stage of the Gold Cup, but the misfortune which dogged the club last term was evident when the quarter-final tie against Crusaders at Seaview had to be abandoned due to torrential rain with Bangor leading 2-1 after 55 minutes on October 24. When the game was replayed a month later, Bangor lost 2-1.

Just three days before that, however, manager Paul Malone had resigned following a 6-1 League defeat at home to Glentoran. At that stage Bangor were bottom of the table with only four points from their first nine League games. Team affairs were handed to the Reserve management team of Andy Dougan and George Dunlop. It was felt that the 'drop' might possibly be avoided by bringing over full-time players from England on short-term contracts.

Although this proved an expensive venture Bangor used nine such players during the course of the season, such as Martin Williams and Derek Simpson from Reading, Mike Davis from Bristol Rovers, Matt Green and Will Davies from Derby County and Darren Holmes from Sheffield Wednesday. Certainly performances improved, but the team never managed to get off the foot of the table and in the end Bangor finished in bottom position in the Premier League with 14 points. One indication of Bangor's plights was that 51 players were used during the season.

The only ray of sunshine was the Mid-Ulster Cup success at the end of the season. Following home wins over Coagh United, by 3-0 and Newry Town 2-1 Bangor won the trophy, which they had entered for the first time, when they defeated Dungannon Swifts 3-1 at Shamrock Park.

Curiously Bangor had begun and ended the season with victories over Dungannon, but there had been precious little else to cheer and now the management team must aim to achieve a quick return to the Premier League.

Roy Kitson.

MANAGER PROFILE — ANDY DOUGAN

Date of Birth: 02.01.1956
Date of Appointment: December, 1995

Previous Clubs:
As Player: Glentoran; Bangor; Ballyclare Comrades:
As Manager/Coach: Bangor (Reserve Team Manager)

Honours:
As Player:
Glentoran: **Irish League Championship:** 1976/77
Gold Cup: 1976/77 and 1977/78
Ulster Cup: 1976/77
City Cup: 1974/75
Co.Antrim Shield: 1977/78
Ballyclare Comrades: **Steel & Sons Cup:** 1981/82

As Manager:
None

TRANSFERS C/S'95 TO MAY '96

Players Signed:

Paul McCartan (Cliftonville c/s'95), Patrick O'Connell (Ballyclare Comrades May '95), David Haggan (Northern Telecom Jun.'95), Keith Percy (Glenavon Jun.'95), John Campbell (Carrick Rangers Jul.'95), Michael Cash (Larne Jul.'95), Rod Collins (Bohemians Jul.'95), Jim McCloskey (Ballymena United Jul.'95), Michael McKeown (Glenavon Jul.'95), Jason Murtagh (Ballyclare Comrades Jul.'95), Brian Irwin (Dundalk Aug.'95), Gary McKinstry (Dungannon Swifts Sep.'95), Paul Miskelly (Carrick Rangers Sep.'95), Lee Thorpe (Blackpool (Eng loan) Sep.'95), John Byrne (St.Patricks Ath. (loan) Oct.'95), Marc Falconer (Clyde (Sco loan) Oct.'95), Allen Huxley (Ballyclare Comrades (loan rtn) Oct.'95), John Johnston (Ballyclare Comrades Oct.'95), Hillyard Mendes (Chelsea (Eng loan) Oct.'95), Michael Davis (Bristol Rovers (Eng loan) Nov.'95), Jackie Coulter (Carrick Rangers Dec.'95), Derek Simpson (Reading (Eng loan) Dec.'95), Martin Williams (Reading (Eng loan) Dec.'95), Dominic Barclay (Bristol City (Eng loan) Jan.'96), Niall Currie (Distillery Jan.'96), Will Davies (Derby County (Eng loan) Feb.'96), Matthew Green (Derby County (Eng loan) Feb.'96), Darren Holmes (Sheffield Wednesday (Eng loan) Mar.'96), Brain Kennedy (Distillery Mar.'96), Richard McEvoy (Glentoran Mar.'96), John Johnston (Loughgall (loan rtn) May.'96).

Players Transferred:

Timothy Dalton (Portadown c/s'95), Richard McEvoy (Glentoran c/s'95), Alan Murphy (Glenavon c/s'95), Rod Collins (Bohemians (loan) Jun.'95), Niall Currie (Glenavon Jun.'95), Rod Collins (Glentoran Jul.'95), Mark Glendinning (Glenavon Jul.'95), Marc Kenny (Coleraine Jul.'95), Richard Snodgrass (Crusaders Aug.'95), Peter Batey (Glentoran Sep.'95), Tony Clarke (Dungannon Swifts Sep.'95), Allen Huxley (Ballyclare Comrades (loan) Sep.'95), Jonathon Magee (Portadown Sep.'95), Michael Surgeon (Coleraine Sep.'95), Lee Thorpe (Blackpool (Eng loan rtn) Oct.'95), Marc Falconer (Clyde (Sco loan rtn) Nov.'95), Hillyard Mendes (Chelsea (Eng loan rtn) Nov.'95), John Byrne (St.Patricks Ath. Dec.'95), David McCallan (Coleraine Dec.'95), Gary McKinstry (Dungannon Swifts Dec.'95), Dominic Barclay (Bristol City (Eng loan rtn) Jan.'96), Michael Davis (Bristol Rovers (Eng loan rtn) Jan.'96), Ray McGuinness (Finn Harps Jan.'96), Nigel Melly (Omagh Town Jan.'96), Jason Murtagh (Loughgall Jan.'96), Derek Simpson (Reading (Eng loan rtn) Jan.'96), Martin Williams (Reading (Eng loan rtn) Jan.'96), John Johnston (Loughgall (loan) Feb.'96), Allen Huxley (Dundela Mar.'96), Will Davies (Derby County (Eng loan rtn) Apr.'96), Matthew Green (Derby County (Eng loan rtn) Apr.'96), Darren Holmes (Sheffield Wednesday (Eng loan rtn) Apr.'96), John Johnston (Loughgall May '96).

HONOURS

Irish League Championship / Premier League,		Best Position: Runners Up 1990/91 / 8th 1995/96
Irish Cup, Winners:	(1)	1992/93
Ulster Cup, Winners:	(2)	1991/92, 1994/95
City Cup, Winners:	(2)	1970/71, 1975/76
Irish League Cup, Winners:	(1)	1992/93
Co.Antrim Shield, Winners:	(3)	1969/70, 1974/75, 1988/89
'B' Division Section 2, Champions:	(2)	1993/94*,1994/95*.
Steel & Sons Cup, Winners:	(4)	1923/24, 1940/41*, 1944/45*, 1994/95*.
Intermediate League, Champions:	(3)	1940/41*, 1942/43*, 1943/44*.
IFA Intermediate Cup, Winners:	(3)	1941/42*, 1943/44*, 1944/45*.
Louis Moore Cup, Winners:	(1)	1973/74*.
George Wilson Cup, Winners:	(2)	1992/93*1994/95*.
IFA Youth Cup, Winners:	(1)	1989/90.
McElroy Cup, Winners:	(1)	1946/47*.

Won by Bangor Reserves

SMIRNOFF PREMIER LEAGUE RECORD 1995/96

No.	Date:	Ven:	Opponents:	Result:	H.T.	Pos:	Goalscorers:
1	Sep 30	H	Portadown	0-3 L	0-1	-	-
2	Oct 7	A	Glentoran	1-1 D	0-0	6	Thorpe (68)
3	Oct 14	H	Linfield	1-2 L	0-1	8	Percy (49)
4	Oct 21	A	Glenavon	0-1 L	0-1	8	-
5	Oct 28	H	Crusaders	1-2 L	0-1	8	Byrne (pen 83)
6	Nov 4	H	Ards	2-1 W	0-1	6	Morrow (55), Irwin (pen 72)
7	Nov 11	A	Cliftonville	1-2 L	0-1	7	Irwin (65)
8	Nov 18	A	Portadown	2-4 L	1-3	8	Bailie (13), Irwin (75)
9	Nov 25	H	Glentoran	1-6 L	0-1	8	(M) Davis (69)
10	Dec 2	A	Linfield	0-0 D	0-0	8	-
11	Dec 9	H	Glenavon	0-1 L	0-0	8	-
12	Dec 16	A	Crusaders	0-2 L	0-1	8	-
13	Jan 1	H	Cliftonville	3-2 W	2-1	-	Coulter (pen 25), (M) Davis (40), Williams (89)
14	Jan 6	H	Portadown	0-0 D	0-0	8	-
15	Jan 13	A	Glentoran	0-3 L	0-1	8	-
16	Jan 27	H	Linfield	0-2 L	0-0	8	-
17	Jan 30	A	Ards	0-3 L	0-1	-	-
18	Feb 3	A	Glenavon	1-0 W	0-0	8	(W) Davies (87)
19	Feb 10	H	Crusaders	0-2 L	0-0	8	-
20	Feb 17	H	Ards	0-1 L	0-0	8	-
21	Mar 2	A	Cliftonville	1-1 D	0-0	8	Green (pen 58)
22	Mar 16	A	Portadown	3-4 L	2-3	8	(W) Davies (28,83), McCombe (41)
23	Mar 23	H	Glentoran	1-1 D	1-0	8	Holmes (45)
24	Mar 30	A	Linfield	1-2 L	0-1	8	McEvoy (68)
25	Apr 6	H	Glenavon	1-2 L	0-1	8	O'Connell (61)
26	Apr 9	A	Crusaders	0-1 L	0-0	-	-
27	Apr 20	A	Ards	1-2 L	1-0	8	Spiers (35)
28	Apr 27	H	Cliftonville	2-3 L	1-3	8	McCombe (18), O'Connell (60)

Final League Position: 8th

Match No	P.Miskelly 11	J.Bailie 20+(1)	S.Hill 1	E.Spiers 25	M.McKeown 23	A.McCombe 15	K.Percy 14	M.Cash 13+(1)	G.McKinstry 3+(1)	L.Thorpe 3	K.Morrow 7+(20)	B.Irwin 8+(8)	R.Hill 13+(3)	J.Byrne 8+(1)	D.Eddis 3+(2)	J.Murtagh 5+(2)	R.McGuinness 7+(2)	A.Huxley 6	J.Mendes 4	J.McNamara 5+(2)	J.Johnston 1	M.Falconer 1	P.O'Connell 13+(9)	G.Ferguson 3	S.McPherson 2	G.Wilkinson 0+(5)	M.Davis 5	R.Dornan 16	J.Coulter 10+(1)	Referee
1	1	2	3†	4	5	6	7	8	9°	10°	11	12°	14†			15°														F.Hiles
2	1	2		4	5		7	6	9†	10°	11		3	8	12°	14†														A.Snoddy
3	1	2		4	5		7		12°	10°	11°	15	6°	8†	14†	9	3													N.Cowie
4		2		4	5		7	6	9†		12°		11			10	3	1	8°	14†										D.Taylor
5				4	5		7	6			12°	14†		15°		10	3	1	9	11°	2°	8†								E.Millar
6		14†		4	5		7	3†		12°	8		2			10	6	1	11			9°								T.Deegan
7		6		4	5		7				10	8		2				1	9†	14†			12°	3	11°					J.Ferry
8		11		4	5	2	7	6°		10†	8		9			12°		1					14†	3						R.Lutton
9	1	2		4	5		7†	3			11°	8		6		10°	14†						12°		15°	9				D.Taylor
10	1			4	5		2				12°	8°	11	7°			3						10†		14†	15°	9	6		F.Hiles
11	1			4			7†				9°	15°	11	6°			3						10		14†	12°	8	5	2	A.Snoddy
12	1			4			7	6			12°	15°	11			3°							10†		9°		8	5	2	M.Ross
13	1			4	5		11°	6			12°									14†							9	3	2	F.McDonald
14	1			4	5		11°	6			12°	9†								14†								3	2	T.Deegan
15	1			4	5			6			12°	14†										11°						3	2	J.Ferry
16		8		4		5		6			10°	7					1		11				12°			14†		3	2†	F.McDonald
17		8		4		5		6†			14†	9	7		11					15°			12°					3	2°	R.Lutton
18		6			4	5					12°		11		7								10°					3	2	H.Barr
19		6			4		14†		12°		11		7°										10					3†	2	F.Hiles
20		7			4	5					14†		6										10	11				3°	2†	N.Cowie
21		2		4	6	5					12°		11										10					3		T.Deegan
22		2		4	6	5					12°												10°							N.Cowie
23		2		4	6	5					12°												10°					3		F.Hiles
24		2		4	6	5					12°												10°							D.Taylor
25		2		4	6	5					12°		14†										10°							F.McDonald
26	1	2		4°	6	5					12°												10					3		N.Cowie
27		2°		4	6	5°			12°	14†	15°												10					3		A.Snoddy
28		2°		4		5					12°	15°	6										10					3†	14†	L.Irvine

Also Played:

D.Nelson Ma.12 No.14† Ma.13 No.7 Ma.14 No.7 Ma.15 No.7 Ma.20 No.12* = 3+(2)
D.Simpson Ma.13 No.8† Ma.14 No.8 Ma.15 No.8 = 3
M.Williams Ma.13 No.10 Ma.14 No.10 Ma.15 No.10 = 3
D.Barclay Ma.15 No.9† Ma.16 No.9° = 2
C.Bell Ma.16 No.15° Ma.17 No.10° = 1+(1)
N.Currie Ma.17 No.1 Ma.18 No.1 Ma.19 No.1 Ma.20 No.1 Ma.21 No.1 Ma.22 No.1 Ma.23 No.1Ma.24 No.1 Ma.25 No.1 Ma.27 No.1† = 10
M.Green Ma.18 No.8 Ma.19 No.8 Ma.20 No.8 Ma.21 No.8* Ma.22 No.8 Ma.23 No.8 Ma.24 No.8 Ma.25 No.8 Ma.26 No.8 Ma.27 No.8 Ma.28 No.8 = 11
W.Davies Ma.18 No.9 Ma.19 No.9 Ma.20 No.9 Ma.21 No.9 Ma.22 No.9 Ma.23 No.9 Ma.24 No.9 Ma.25 No.9 Ma.26 No.9Ma.27 No.9 Ma.28 No.9 = 11
D.Holmes Ma.21 No.7 Ma.22 No.7 Ma.23 No.7 Ma.24 No.7 Ma.25 No.7† Ma.26 No.7 Ma,27 No.7 Ma.28 No.7° = 8
B.Kennedy Ma.22 No.3 Ma.24 No.3 Ma.25 No.3 = 3
R.McEvoy Ma.22 No.11 Ma.23 No.11 Ma.24 No.11 Ma.25 No.11 Ma.26 No.11 Ma.27 No.11 Ma.28 No.11 = 7
A.Fox Ma.28 No.1 = 1

PLAYER PROFILE - RAYMOND HILL

Raymond Hill has been a 'permanent fixture' at Clandeboye Park for the past eight seasons, indeed Raymond's quiet and unassuming manner conceals a skilful and determined player who has played his full part in the successes won by Bangor in recent seasons. He began his career as a fullback, but is now employed in either a defensive role or in midfield.

Born on December 5, 1961, Raymond began his career with Armagh Boys Club and then joined Portadown, where he played for the third team at 14 years of age. Indeed he made his debut for the first team at the tender age of 15 against Ballymena United. Raymond also won many schoolboy international caps. Indeed he was named as Portadown's '13th man' for the Irish Cup Final against Cliftonville in 1979.

The following season Raymond was a member of the Portadown Irish Youth Cup winning team and he also played in all the games for the N.Ireland Youth team which qualified for the Final tournament in East Germany.

Raymond stayed with Portadown until the summer of 1984 when he joined Ards. By coincidence his first game for Ards was a 4-1 Gold Cup victory against Bangor. The goalscorer for the Seasiders was Raymond with an own goal!

Raymond played 185 senior games and scored 11 goals for Ards until Bangor manager John Flanagan signed him in September 1988. Since then he has played under Nigel Best, Roddy Collins, Paul Malone and Andy Dougan. He says: "I suppose the highlights were the Irish Cup Finals against Ards when we eventually won at the third attempt, and then my first European matches against the gifted players of Czech side Sigma Olomouc." Incidentally he is one of only two players to play in all Bangor's European matches. The other was central defender Stephen Brown. Outside of football Raymond is a teacher at Dromore High School he is married to Deborah and they have two daughters, Ruth (10) and Lindsey (8). In his spare time he enjoys playing cricket and golf though hopes to continue playing football for as long as possible!

Bangor's recent Mid-Ulster win signified yet another personal milestone for Raymond. It provided the midfielder with a winner's medal of course but it also marked his 750th senior appearance in Irish League football.

Raymond has now played 206 League matches for Bangor, just two short of Stephen Brown's record. With no sign of Raymond or Bangor wishing to end their association it looks as if Hill will shortly be able to claim that record too.

Roy Kitson

BANGOR APPEARANCES FOR 1995/96

Name:	UC	GC	ILC	CC	BIC	CAS	MUC	PL	Total
1 Eddie Spiers	2	4	-	2	1	1	3	25	38
2 Keith Morrow	-	1+1	-	-(2)	-(1)	-	1+(2)	7+(20)	9+(26)
3 John Bailie	-(1)	4	-(1)	1	1	1	3	20+(1)	30+(3)
4 Patrick O'Connell	3	-(1)	2	1	-	1	2	13+(9)	22+(10)
5 Michael McKeown	-	3	-	1	-	-	3	23	30
6 Alistair McCombe	3	4	2	1	-(1)	1	2	15	28+(1)
7 Brian Irwin	3	1+(2)	2	1+(1)	1	1	-(1)	8+(8)	17+(12)
8 Raymond Hill	3	2+(2)	2	-	-	-	2(1)	13+(3)	22+(6)
9 Keith Percy	3	4	-	1	1	1	-	14	24
10 Reg Dornan	3	1	-	-	1	-	2	14	24
11 Michael Cash	-	1+(1)	-	2	1	1	-	16	23
12 Paul Miskelly	-	4	-	1	1	1	-	13+(1)	18+(2)
13 Raymond McGuinness	-	1	2	1+(1)	1	-(1)	1	7+(2)	12+(4)
14 Jackie Coulter	-	-	-	2	1	-	1	10+(1)	14+(1)
15 Will Davies	-	-	-	-	-	-	2	11	13
16 Matthew Green	-	-	-	-	-	-	2	11	13
17 Jason Murtagh	3	1	1	-	-	1	-	11	13
18 Jeffrey McNamara	-	1	1+(1)	2	-	-	-	5+(2)	11+(2)
19 John Byrne	-	1	-	-	-	-	-	5+(2)	9+(3)
20 Niall Currie	-	-	-	-	-	1	-	8+(1)	10+(1)
21 Darren Holmes	-	-	-	-	-	-	-	10	10
22 Allen Huxley	-	-	-(1)	1	1	1	2	8	10
23 Richard McEvoy	-	-	-	-	-	-	2	6	9+(1)
24 David Eddis	-(1)	-(2)	-	-	-	-	2	7	9
25 Gary Wilkinson	1	-(1)	-	-(1)	-	-	1	3+(2)	4+(5)
26 Dean Nelson	-	-	-	1	-(1)	-	-(1)	-(5)	1+(8)
27 Pete Batey	3	2	2	-	-	-	1	3+(2)	5+(3)
28 John Campbell	2	2	2	-	-	-	-	-	7
29 Michael Davis	-	1	-	-	-	-	-	-	6
30 Gary McKinstry	-	2	-	-	-	-	-	5	6
31 David Haggan	3	-	2	-	-	-	-	3+(1)	5+(1)
32 Stephen Hill	-	3	-	1	-	-	-	-	5
33 Derek Simpson	-	-	-	1	-	-	-	1	5
34 Martin Williams	-	-	-	1	1	-	-	3	5
35 Gary Ferguson	-	-	-	1	1	-	-	3	5
36 Brian Kennedy	-	-	-	-	-	1	1	3	4
37 Hillyard Mendes	-	-	-	-	-	-	-	4	4
38 Lee Thorpe	-	1	-	-	-	-	-	3	4
39 Stuart McPherson	-(1)	-	-	-(1)	-	-	-	3	4
40 Dan Tierney	-(2)	-	2	-	-	-	-	2	2+(2)
41 Dominic Barclay	-	-	-	1	-	-	-	-	2+(2)
42 Colin Bell	-	-	-	-	-	-	-	2	3
43 Tony Clarke	-	-	2	-	-	-	-(1)	1+(1)	1+(2)
44 Steven Eachus	-	-	-	-	-	-	2	-	2
45 Paul McCartan	-(1)	-	-	-	-	-(1)	-	-	-(2)
46 Michael Surgeon	-	-	-(2)	-	-	-	-	-	-(2)
47 Marc Falconer	-	-	-	-	-	-	-	-	1
48 Andy Fox	-	-	-	-	-	-	-	1	1
49 John Johnston	-	-	-	-	-	-	-	1	1
50 Jonathan Swift	1	-	-	-	-	-	-	-	1
51 Andrew Massey	-	-	-	-	-	-	-(1)	-	-(1)

BANGOR GOALSCORERS FOR 1995/96

Name:	UC	GC	ILC	CC	BIC	CAS	MUC	PL	Total
1 Brian Irwin	-	1	1	2(1p)	-	1	-	3(1p)	8 (2p)
2 Will Davies	-	-	-	-	-	2	3	5
3 Patrick O'Connell	-	-	-	-	1	1	2	4
4 Keith Morrow	-	1	-	-	-	1	2	4
5 Eddie Spiers	1	-	-	-	1	1	3
6 Michael Cash	-	1	-	-	1	1	3
7 Michael Davis	-	-	-	1	-	2
8 Raymond Hill	1	-	-	-	1	-	2
9 Alister McCombe	-	-	-	-	2	2
10 John Bailie	-	-	-	-	2	2
11 Pete Batey	1	-	-	-	1	1
12 John Byrne	-	-	-	-	1	1
13 John Campbell	-	-	-	1p	1p
14 Jackie Coulter	-	-	-	1p	1p
15 David Eddis	-	-	-	1	1
16 Matthew Green	-	-	-	1p	1p
17 Darren Holmes	-	-	-	1	1
18 Richard McEvoy	-	-	-	1	1
19 Michael McKeown	-	-	-	1	1
20 Gary McKinstry	-	1	-	1	1
21 Jason Murtagh	-	1	-	1	1
22 Keith Percy	-	-	-	1	1
23 Lee Thorpe	-	-	-	1	1
24 Dan Tierney	-	1	-	1
25 Martin Williams	-	-	-	1	1
Total:	3	5	3	2	0	3	8	23	47

Ground: Taylors Avenue, Carrickfergus (5,000) Founded: 1919.
Tel: 019603 51009

NO PHOTOGRAPH AVAILABLE FOR **1995/96**

President:
Mr.R.Davidson
Chairman:
Mr.D.Kelly
Secretary:
Mr.G.Wright
Treasurer:
Mr.J.O'Neill
Manager:
Colin Crawford
Asst.Manager:
John Muldoon
Commercial Manager:
Jim McGrory
Club Colours:
Tan shirts,
Black shorts,
Tan socks

Summary of 1995/96 Season:

Carrick Rangers completed the season battling to avoid the humiliation of being the first team to finish bottom of the heap in the newly created First Division. A bizarre encounter in which opponents Newry Town were reduced to ten men after one of the players left the field following a dispute with the manager ended in Carrick's favour. The game was then caught up in allegations over a betting coup. Such a finale complemented the club's controversial build up to the 1995/96 campaign.

Top striker Sammy Shiels, still under contract to Taylor's Avenue, was spotted turning out in a pre-season game for Coleraine, which led to a £2,000 fine for the latter. Talented goalkeeper Paul Miskelly was also on his way from Carrick. On the field, things began promisingly with consecutive victories in August over junior opponents Cookstown United and Banbridge Town in the League Cup. There then followed an eight goal Ulster Cup thriller against Omagh with the honours shared.

Alas, the first meeting with a Premier side, the then champions Crusaders, led to a four-goal thrashing and an exit from the tournament. Things went from bad to worse with a 6-2 defeat by Omagh Town in the League Cup.

Another four goal thumping, this time by Cliftonville marked the beginning and the end of interest in the Gold Cup, but a win over Larne and a courageous draw with Glentoran should have provided a boost before things got underway in earnest.

Rangers made a disastrous debut in the First Division losing 3-1 at Ballymena and there were two more defeats before they picked up their points against neighbours Ballyclare in the second of nine East Antrim derbies for Colin Crawford's team!

The writing was on the wall when Coleraine visited Taylor's Avenue in November and triumphed 3-0, leaving little doubt as to where the one promotion place was going.

By now Crawford had recruited the services of former favourite Winston Armstrong, one of few additions to the squad as the harsh reality of life in the cash strapped lower division dawned.

THE NORTHERN IRELAND
football
Y E A R B O O K

A distraction from the weekly grind of the League was a County Antrim Shield clash with Cliftonville and the home side were not among those complaining about the fairness of a penalty kick shoot out as they triumphed. The joy was short-lived as Portadown put Carrick out in the next round.

Mid-Ulster provided little encouragement in the Coca-Cola Cup either, the big freeze over Christmas meant the home tie with Glenavon was the only one to go ahead on schedule but the visitors' 3-0 success rendered the second leg academic.

The new year saw Carrick put together a run which took them to second place with giant stopper Tom McLeister and flying winger Philip Macauley providing the main inspiration. The month of January did have its hiccup in the form of a tricky Irish Cup match away to the R.U.C, with the visitors having to come from behind to win 3-2. Armstrong scored the winner in the next round against Newry to set up thoughts of a repeat of the previous season's run all the way to the final. Then came the draw and back to reality, a quarter-final trip to Glenavon ended in defeat.

By now Carrick had plummeted back to the lower end of the table and it was a case of commencing a rebuilding programme. It was farewell to veteran forward Geoff Ferris and hello to youngsters such as David Lowry and Stephen Smyth. during the close season experienced defender John Muldoon stepped up as assistant to Crawford and they have indicated they will be putting their trust in youth in what could be a make or break year for the club.

Terence Ferry.

MANAGER PROFILE - COLIN CRAWFORD

Date of Birth: 18/02/1960 Doagh

Date of Appointment: January 1995 (Caretaker P/Manager December 1994)

PREVIOUS CLUBS:

As Player: Bangor; Sunderland; Linfield; Carrick Rangers; Glenavon; Ballyclare Comrades:

As Manager: Ballyclare Comrades (Player/Manager)

HONOURS:

As Player: N.Ireland U.18 Youth International (2 caps); Irish League Representative (2 caps)

Linfield: **Irish League Championship:** 1981/82; 1982/83; 1983/84; 1984/85; 1985/86; 1986/87.

Gold Cup: 1981/82 and 1984/85.

Ulster Cup: 1984/85.

Co.Antrim Shield: 1982/83.

Irish League Cup: 1986/87.

Glenavon: **Irish Cup:** 1991/92.

As Manager: None.

SMIRNOFF FIRST DIVISION RECORD 1995/96

No:	Date:	Ven:	Opponents:	Result:	H.T:	Pos:	Goalscorers:
1	Sep 30	A	Ballymena United	1-3 L	0-3	-	Ferris (47)
2	Oct 7	H	Omagh Town	2-3 L	1-0	8	Armstrong (4), Sinclair (67)
3	Oct 14	A	Distillery	1-3 L	0-0	8	Coulter (pen 90)
4	Oct 21	H	Ballyclare Comrades	3-0 W	1-0	8	Kirk (22), McLeister (61), Ferris (66)
5	Oct 28	A	Larne	1-0 W	0-0	5	Sinclair (64)
6	Nov 4	H	Coleraine	0-3 L	0-2	6	-
7	Nov 11	A	Newry Town	3-2 W	2-0	5	Armstrong (22,37), Ferris (82)
8	Nov 18	H	Ballymena United	1-1 D	0-0	4	Macauley (71)
9	Nov 25	A	Omagh Town	0-1 L	0-0	6	-
10	Dec 2	H	Distillery	0-0 D	0-0	6	-
11	Dec 9	A	Ballyclare Comrades	1-2 L	0-2	6	Sinclair (82)
12	Dec 16	H	Larne	1-0 W	1-0	5	Armstrong (1)
13	Dec 26	A	Coleraine	0-6 L	0-4	-	-
14	Jan 1	H	Newry Town	3-1 W	1-0	-	Donaghey (5), Sinclair (75), Doherty (pen 79)
15	Jan 6	A	Ballymena United	2-1 W	1-0	4	McDermott (8), Sinclair (86)
16	Jan 13	H	Omagh Town	2-0 W	1-0	2	Sinclair (38), Donaghey (75)
17	Feb 3	H	Ballyclare Comrades	0-3 L	0-1	4	-
18	Feb 10	A	Larne	1-3 L	0-1	5	McDermott (66)
19	Feb 14	A	Distillery	1-2 L	1-2	-	Donaghey (43)
20	Feb 17	H	Coleraine	2-5 L	1-2	7	(F) Wilson (22), McGarvey (77)
21	Mar 2	A	Newry Town	0-1 L	0-0	7	-
22	Mar 16	H	Ballymena United	0-2 L	0-1	6	-
23	Mar 23	A	Omagh Town	2-6 L	2-2	8	Sinclair (17), (F) Wilson (43)
24	Mar 30	H	Distillery	0-0 D	0-0	8	-
25	Apr 6	A	Ballyclare Comrades	2-3 L	1-1	8	Macauley (1), (F) Wilson (90)
26	Apr 9	H	Larne	1-0 W	0-0	-	Doherty (76)
27	Apr 20	A	Coleraine	1-5 L	1-1	7	Doherty (pen 13)
28	Apr 27	H	Newry Town	1-0 W	1-0	6	Doherty (39)

Final League Position: 6th

FIRST DIVISION LINE-UPS 1995/96

Match No	R.Hillen 3	K.McDermott 21+(2)	C.Crawford 8+(4)	J.Kirk 9+(3)	T.McLeister 24	J.Coulter 9	H.Sinclair 24+(1)	B.Donaghey 22+(4)	D.Doherty 11+(9)	G.Ferris 18+(2)	W.Wilson 18+(5)	D.Gordon 0+(2)	J.Kerr 0+(1)	W.Armstrong 17+(4)	A.Gilmore 19	J.Muldoon 20+(1)	J.Dillon 25	J.McGarvey 18+(3)	P.Macauley 23+(2)	F.Wilson 11+(5)	J.McRoberts 0+(1)	C.McManus 0+(1)	K.Miller 0+(3)	D.Lowry 7	S.Smyth 1	Referee
1	1	2	3	4	5	6	7†	8	9*	10	11	12*14†														D.Magill
2	1	4	3	2*	5	6	7	8	12*10	11	-	-		9												L.Irvine
3	1	4	-	11	5	2	7	8*	12*10	6	14†			9†	3°	15°										E.Millar
4	-	8°	3†	9	5	6	7	15°	12*10	14†	-	-	-	-	4	1	2	11*								F.Hiles
5	-	8	3	9*	5	6	7	12*-	10	-	-	-	-	-	4	1	2	11								D.Taylor
6	-	8	3†	9	5	6	7°	12*-	10	14†	-	-	15°	-	4*	1	2	11								G.Douglas
7	-	8	3	-	5	6	12*7	-	10	-	-	-	-	9	-	4*	1	2	11							T.Deegan
8	-	4	3	-	5	6	-	8	10	7	-	-		9			1	2	11							G.Dobbin
9	-	4	3†	-	5*	6°	-	8	10	-	14†			9			1	2	11	7	12*	15°				F.McDonald
10	-	4	-	-	5	-	7	8	12*10	-	-			9*	3		1	2	11	6						J.Peden
11	-	8	12*-	-	-	5	4	-	10	7				9	3		1	2	11	6*						F.Hiles
12	-	8	-	-	5	-	7	9	-	12*6				10*	3	4	1	2	11							G.Keatley
13	-	-	15°	-	5	-	7*	6	14†10	8				9°	3	4	1	2	11†	12*						L.Irvine
14	-	8	-	-	5	-	7	6	14†10	-				9†	3	4	1	2	11*	12*						E.Millar
15	-	8*	-	-	5	-	7	6	14†10	15°				9†	3	4	1	2	11°	12*						R.Lutton
16	-	8	-	-	5	-	7	6	12*10	-				9*	3	4	1	2	11							B.Kane
17	-	8°	14†	12*	5	-	7	6	9*	10	15°				4		1	2	11	3†						M.Ross
18	-	8	-	-	5	-	7†	6	9*	-	10				3	4	1	2	11	14†	-	12*				D.Malcolm
19	-	8	-	-	5	-	7	6	9	-	10			11*	3	4	1		12*	2						E.Millar
20	-	8	-	-	5	-	7	6	9	15°	11*			10°	3	4	1	12*	14†	2†						H.Barr
21	-	8*	-	-	-	-	6	9	10†7	-	-			14†	3	4	1		11	2		12*	5			J.Ferry
22	-	8	14†	12*	-	-	5	6	9°	10	2			15°	3	4†	1		11*	7						D.Taylor
23	-	-	-	14†	-	-	9	6†	15°	10	8				3	4	1	2	11°	7*			12*	5		A.Snoddy
24	-	-	-	-	6	-	9	8	-	-	10				3	4	1	2	11	7					5	T.Deegan
25	-	-	-	-	6	-	9	8	-	-	10			12*		4	1	2	11	7				5	3	P.Thompson
26	-	-	2	6	-	7	-	8	-	10				9	3	4	1		11					5		D.Malcolm
27	-	12*-	2	6	-	7†	14†	8	-	10*				9	3°	4	1	15°	11					5		F.Hiles
28	-	15°	-	2	6	-	7	-	8	-	10°			9	3†	4	1	12*	11	14†				5		R.Lutton

TRANSFERS C/S'95 TIL APRIL '96

Players Signed:

Jonathan Field (Chimney Corner c/s'95), Tom McLeister (Tobermore United Aug.'95), John McGarvey (Ballymoney United Sep.'95), Winston Armstrong (Distillery Oct.'95), Frank Wilson (Ballyclare Comrades Nov.'95), Dean May (R.U.C. Mar.'96).

Players Transferred:

John Campbell (Bangor Jul.'95), Sammy Shiels (Tobermore United Aug.'95), Darren Crawford (R.U.C. Sep.'95), Paul Miskelly (Bangor Sep.'95), Jonathan Field (Ballyclare Comrades Nov.'95), Michael Press (Chimney Corner Nov.'95), Jackie Coulter (Bangor Dec.'95), Dean Gordon (Barn United Dec.'95), Colin Woods (Harland & Wolff Welders Feb.'96).

HONOURS

Irish League / First Division		Best Position: 8th 1988/89 / 6th 1995/96
Irish Cup, Winners	(1)	1975/76
Co.Antrim Shield, Winners	(1)	1992/93
Irish League 'B' Division, Champions	(6)	1961/62, 1972/73, 1974/75, 1976/77, 1978/79, 1982/83
Steel & Sons Cup, Winners	(2)	1961/62, 1967/68
IFA Intermediate Cup, Winners	(2)	1975/76, 1976/77
Louis Moore Cup, Winners	(2)	1963/64, 1969/70
Amateur League, Champions	(2)	1948/49, 1951/52
Most capped player: None		

PLAYERS PROFILE - JOHN MULDOON

John Muldoon has no difficulty in explaining why he is full of enthusiasm for his 18th season in the Irish League. He simply "loves playing football". Further incentives are the chance to pass 500 outings in senior soccer and the need to lead by example as the new assistant manager of Carrick Rangers.

His decision to accept greater responsibility may seem strange given his unhappy experience at Ballyclare Comrades where he shared the manager's role with Colin Crawford, the current number one at Carrick. The pair broke with the Dixon Park club in less than harmonious circumstances in 1994.

"The events at Ballyclare, where I was joint manager, soured me and I nearly paced the game up. I knew I was not going to a big club but several had asked me to go into the 'B' Division and do some coaching."

"Then Kenny Shiels, who was manager of Carrick at the time, asked me to come along to Taylor's Avenue, and I have been there since. It is a friendly club and they are a nice bunch of lads."

However, early on he found himself caught up in further turmoil. Shiels left to become manager at Coleraine, followed by several key players, which led to uncertainty. Crawford, who had also made the short move from Comrades, moved into the hot seat, but the team's league form nose dived during the transitional period.

"When Kenny and a number of important players left the club it was a bit of a shock. there was a bit of turmoil but we managed to keep our best performances for the Irish Cup and made it all the way to the Final. That was a great bonus."

Although on the losing side that day to Linfield, Muldoon has tasted success in his long career including Northern Ireland under-18 and Irish League representative honours.

He was also part of an Irish Cup winning squad at Bangor and remembers successful campaigns in the League cup and Ulster Cup too. His senior debut was for Cliftonville back in 1979 and during 12 years service with the Belfast outfit he served with distinction at left-back and enjoyed a County Antrim Shield triumph.

The affable taxi driver was hampered last season due to injury, forcing him to take the radical step of playing no football during the break. "I had a back injury and it was hurting a hamstring. This summer I took a complete rest and it seems alright.

Fitness will feature high on the agenda as Carrick, like many provincial clubs battling in the harsh financial climate created by the controversial two-tier system, make an even more determined push to gain access to the Premier elite. "Colin and I have the same ideas on how we play football and how we go about training. He is the boss and I can be the link between the players. we will be concentrating on fitness and getting a squad of young players balanced with experienced heads."

Terence Ferry.

CARRICK RANGERS APPEARANCES 1995/96

Name:	UC	GC	ILC	CC	BIC	CAS	FD	Total
1 Philip Macauley	3	3	3	1+(1)	3	2	23+(2)	38+(3)
2 Brian Donaghey	1+(2)	3	1+(1)	2	3	2	22+(4)	34+(7)
3 Hugh Sinclair	3	3	3	2	2	1	24+(1)	38+(1)
4 Kel McDermott	3	2	3	1+(1)	2+(1)	2	21+(2)	34+(4)
5 Warren Wilson	3	3	3	2	1+(2)	1	18+(5)	31+(7)
6 Geoff Ferris	3	3	3	2	1+(2)	2	18+(2)	32+(4)
7 Tom McLeister	1	3	-	2	3	1	24	34
8 John Dillon	-	-	-	2	3	2	25	32
9 John Muldoon	2+(1)	1	3	1	2	1	20+(1)	30+(2)
10 Dean Doherty	2	-(1)	3	1+(1)	1+(1)	1+(1)	11+(9)	19+(13)
11 Anthony Gilmore	2	2	1	2	3	1	19	30
12 John McGarvey	-	-	2	2	3	2	18+(3)	27+(3)
13 Winston Armstrong	-	-	-	1+(1)	3	1	17+(4)	22+(5)
14 Colin Crawford	2+(1)	2+(1)	2+(1)	-	1	1	8+(4)	16+(7)
15 Frank Wilson	-	-	-	1+(1)	2+(1)	1+(1)	11+(5)	15+(8)
16 James Kirk	-(3)	2+(1)	-(2)	-	-	-	9+(3)	11+(9)
17 Jackie Coulter	3	3	3	-	-	1	9	19
18 Reg Hillen	3	3	3	-	-	-	3	12
19 David Lowry	-	-	-	-	-	-	7	7
20 Michael Press	2	-	-(1)	-	-	-	-	2+(1)
21 Dean Gordon	-	-	-	-	-	-(1)	-(2)	-(3)
22 Keith Millar	-	-	-	-	-	-	-(3)	-(3)
23 John Jamison	-	-(1)	-	-(1)	-	-	-	-(2)
24 Jackie Kerr	-	-	-	-	-	-(1)	-(1)	-(2)
25 Stephen Smyth	-	-	-	-	-	-	1	1
26 Conor McManus	-	-	-	-	-	-	-(1)	-(1)
27 Joe McRoberts	-	-	-	-	-	-	-(1)	-(1)

CARRICK RANGERS GOALSCORERS 1995/96

Name:	UC	GC	ILC	CC	BIC	CAS	FD	Total
1 Geoff Ferris	-	-	-	1	1	2	3	7
2 Hugh Sinclair	-	-	-	-	-	-	7	7
3 Winston Armstrong	-	-	-	-	2	-	4	6
4 Dean Doherty	-	-	2	-	-	-	4(2p)	6(2p)
5 Jackie Coulter	3p	-	1	-	-	-	1p	5(2p)
6 Philip Macauley	-	1	1	-	1	-	2	5
7 Frank Wilson	-	-	-	-	1	-	3	4
8 Colin Crawford	2	-	1p	-	-	-	-	3(1p)
9 Brian Donaghey	-	-	-	-	-	-	3	3
10 James Kirk	-	1	1	-	-	-	1	3
11 Kel McDermott	-	-	-	-	-	-	2	2
12 John McGarvey	-	-	-	-	-	-	1	1
13 Tom McLeister	-	-	-	-	-	-	1	1
14 Warren Wilson	-	1	-	-	-	-	-	1
Total:	5	3	6	1	5	2	32	54

Ground: Solitude, Cliftonville Street, Belfast BT14 (17,000) Founded: 1879
Tel: 01232 754628

Cliftonville 1995/96

Back Row L-R: Paul Madden (Groundsman), Harry Press (Team Attendant), Ciaran Feehan, Tommy McDonald,
Michael Donnelly, Ian Hill, Paul Stokes, F.Jardine (Physio), John Campbell (Club Doctor).
Middle Row L-R: Brendan Lynch (Physio), Pat Cavanagh, James McFadden, Paul Rice, Marty Quinn (Manager),
Jim Boyce (Chairman), Rory O'Boyle (Asst.Manager), Damian Davey, Ron Manley, Kieran Loughran.
Front Row L-R: Jonathan Cross, Seamus Heath, Gary Sliney, Tim McCann, Martin Tabb, Gerry Flynn, Joe Kerr,
Mark O'Neill, C.Pettigrew (mascot) Trophy: Coca-Cola Cup.
(Photograph courtesy of John Duffy)

President:	**Summary of 1995/96 Season**
Mr.B.Andrews	
Chairman:	
Mr.J.Boyce	
Secretary:	
Mr.J.Duffy	
Hon.Treasurer:	
Mr.J.Greer	
Manager:	
Marty Quinn	
Asst.Manager:	
Rory O'Boyle	
Physiotherapist:	
Brendan Lynch	
Club Colours:	
Red shirts, White shorts,	
Red socks	

President: Mr.B.Andrews
Chairman: Mr.J.Boyce
Secretary: Mr.J.Duffy
Hon.Treasurer: Mr.J.Greer
Manager: Marty Quinn
Asst.Manager: Rory O'Boyle
Physiotherapist: Brendan Lynch
Club Colours: Red shirts, White shorts, Red socks

Summary of 1995/96 Season

Cliftonville's objective for last season was primarily that of maintaining the club's Premier League status in the new two tier set-up. Beforehand the Reds were considered to be a possibility for the drop to the First Division. as it turned out the side spent much of the season vying with Ards to stay clear of Bangor who eventually became the first Irish League club to suffer relegation. Overall the League performances were disappointing, but Portadown apart, the Reds looked quite capable of holding their own against the fancied outfits. The inability to put together a string of consistently good results, and more so a first team squad of sufficient depth and quality consigned Cliftonville to the lower half of the table throughout the League campaign.

The bonus for the Reds came in the shape of qualification for the Inter-Toto cup, courtesy of their sixth place finish in the League, and of course no Reds fan could possibly forget the long awaited trophy success, as the side swept aside Glentoran's challenge in the Coca-Cola Cup Final. Great joy and delight all round followed the 3-1 victory at Windsor Park over the East Belfast club.

Like the local saying about bus services, 'For a long time there are none, and then two or three appear in quick succession' Reds fans very much hope the same now applies in the quest for silverware.

THE NORTHERN IRELAND
football
Y E A R B O O K

The 1996/97 season may not prove to be as worrysome for struggling Premier League sides given that further changes in the set-up, namely an increase to ten clubs, looks to be on the cards next season. Nevertheless Reds manager Marty Quinn will obviously be hoping to improve on the side's showing in the inaugural Premier league season. Several promising young players have come through the ranks to boost the strength of the first team squad. The addition last season of Dubliner Paul Stokes at long last saw the arrival of a much sought after consistent striker.

As usual optimism abounds at Solitude for the new season. The Coca-Cola Cup success hopefully will prove to be the breakthrough the Reds have long been seeking.

Michael Gallagher.

MANAGER PROFILE — MARTY QUINN

Date of Appointment: November 1994
(Initially Caretaker/Manager from October 1994)

PREVIOUS CLUBS:
As Player: Star of the Sea; Cliftonville; Distillery:
As Manager: Distillery;
Cliftonville (Reserve Team Manager);
Cliftonville (Asst.Manager)

HONOURS:
As Player:
Cliftonville - Irish Cup: 1978/79;
Gold Cup 1980/81;
Co.Antrim Shield 1978/79:
Distillery - Co.Antrim Shield 1985/86:

As Manager:
Cliftonville - Coca-Cola Cup 1995/96

TRANSFERS C/S'95 TO APRIL'96

Players Signed:

Ciaran Feehan (Glenavon c/s'95), Seamus Heath (Derry City Aug.'95), Gavin McCrystal (Larne Aug.'95), Paul Ramsey (St.Johnstone (Sco) Aug.'95), Rod Collins (Coleraine Oct.'95), Mark Grugel (Everton (Eng) loan) Oct.'95), Ian McParland (Eastern Athletic (HK) Nov.'95), pat Cavanagh (Distillery Dec.'95), Paul Stokes (Newry Town Dec.'95), Martin Hayes (Dover Jan.'96), Jonathan Cross (Wrexham (Wal loan) Feb.'96), Dean Smyth (Ballymena United (loan) Apr.'96

Players Transferred:

Gary Clifford (Chimney Corner c/s'95), Paul McCartan (Bangor c/s'95), Paul Ramsey (Torquay United (Eng) Aug.'95), Patrick McAllister (Coleraine Sep.'95), Gavin McCrystal (Ballyclare Comrades Oct.'95), Rod Collins (Released Nov.'95), Mark Grugel (Everton (Eng loan rtn) Nov.'95), Ian McParland (Released Jan.'96), Martin Hayes (Released Feb.'96), Jonathan Cross (Wrexham (Wal loan rtn) Apr.'96), Dean Smyth (Ballymena United (loan rtn) Apr.'96).

HONOURS

Irish League, Champions/Premier League:	(2)	1905/06 (shared with Distillery), 1909/10/6th 1995/96
Irish Cup, Winners:	(8)	1882/83, 1887/88, 1896/97, 1899/00, 1900/01, 1906/07, 1908/09, 1978/79
Gold Cup, Winners:	(3)	1923/24, 1933/34, 1980/81
Coca-Cola Cup, Winners:	(1)	1995/96
Co.Antrim Shield, Winners:	(5)	1892/93, 1894/95, 1898/99, 1926/27, 1979/80
Pioneer Cup, Winners:	(9)	1953/54, 1954/55, 1956/57, 1957/58, 1958/59, 1967/68, 1981/82, 1983/84, 1987/88
'B' Division, Champions:	(2)	1953/54*, 1980/81*
Steel & Sons Cup, Winners:	(6)	1900/01*, 1902/03*, 1907/08*, 1908/09*, 1914/15*, 1922/23*
IFA Intermediate, Winners:	(3)	1886/87*, 1900/01*, 1902/03*
Irish Youth League, Champions:	(1)	1992/93

Trophies won by Cliftonville Olympic

Most capped player: J.Clugston 14 caps N.Ireland

SMIRNOFF PREMIER LEAGUE RECORD 1995/96

No:	Date:	Ven:	Opponents:	Result:	H.T:	Pos:	Goalscorers:
1	Sep 30	H	Ards	0-0 D	0-0	-	-
2	Oct 7	A	Portadown	1-6 L	1-4	8	Sliney (9)
3	Oct 14	H	Glentoran	0-0 D	0-0	7	-
4	Oct 21	A	Linfield	0-0 D	0-0	7	-
5	Oct 28	H	Glenavon	2-2 D	1-1	6	Collins (37), Feehan (59)
6	Nov 4	A	Crusaders	0-1 L	0-0	7	-
7	Nov 11	H	Bangor	2-1 W	1-0	6	Strang (1,54)
8	Nov 18	A	Ards	0-3 L	0-1	6	-
9	Nov 25	H	Portadown	0-3 L	0-2	6	-
10	Dec 2	A	Glentoran	1-1 D	0-1	6	Donnelly (75)
11	Dec 9	H	Linfield*	1-1 D	1-0	7	Strang (11)
12	Dec 16	A	Glenavon	2-1 W	0-0	6	McParland (80), O'Neill (86)
13	Dec 26	H	Crusaders	1-4 L	1-2	-	Tabb (32)
14	Jan 1	A	Bangor	2-3 L	1-2	-	Donnelly (8), Stokes (67)
15	Jan 6	H	Ards	1-0 W	1-0	6	Donnelly (25)
16	Jan 13	A	Portadown	1-4 L	0-0	6	Flynn (72)
17	Jan 27	H	Glentoran	1-0 W	1-0	6	Stokes (35)
18	Feb 3	A	Linfield	1-3 L	1-1	6	Rice (pen 19)
19	Feb 10	H	Glenavon	0-1 L	0-0	6	-
20	Feb 17	A	Crusaders	1-1 D	0-1	7	Cavanagh (87)
21	Mar 2	H	Bangor	1-1 D	0-0	7	Kerr (81)
22	Mar 16	A	Ards	2-2 D	1-0	7	Donnelly (16), McCann (60)
23	Mar 23	H	Portadown	0-4 L	0-3	7	-
24	Mar 30	A	Glentoran	1-2 L	0-1	7	Stokes (46)
25	Apr 6	H	Linfield*	0-0 D	0-0	6	-
26	Apr 9	A	Glenavon	1-1 D	0-1	-	Stokes (53)
27	Apr 20	H	Crusaders	2-1 W	1-0	6	Stokes (14,49)
28	Apr 27	A	Bangor	3-2 W	3-1	6	Donnelly (pen 23), Feehan (28), Stokes (40)

Matches played at Windsor Park for security reasons.

Final League Position: 6th

PREMIER LEAGUE LINE-UPS 1995/96

MATCH No	P.Rice 24	I.Hill 25	G.Flynn 27	M.Tabb 22+(1)	J.Kerr 24	S.Strang 11+(3)	T.McCann 25+(2)	G.Sliney 21	C.Feenan 9+(11)	T.McDonald 21+(1)	M.O'Neill 17+(7)	R.Manley 7+(8)	R.Collins 6	M.Donnelly 25	M.Grugel 2	I.McParland 3+(3)	J.McFadden 1	S.Heath 6+(6)	P.Stokes 14	P.Cavanagh 2+(4)	M.Hayes 3	J.Cross 8	D.Smyth 4	K.Loughran 0+(2)	D.Davey 1	J.Quinn 0+(1)	D.McGlinchy 0+(1)	Referee
1	1	2	3	4	5	6*	7	8	9	10	11	12*																H.Barr
2	1	2	3	4	5	6	7	8	9	10	11	–																F.McDoanld
3	1	2	3	4	5	14†	7°	8	15°	10	6†	12*	9*	11														D.Magill
4	1	2	3	–	5	–	7	8	12*	10	6	14†	4†	11		9*												R.Lutton
5	1	2	3	–	5	6†	12*	8	7	10	14†	–	9	11		4*												G.Keatley
6	1	2	3	–	5	6	7	8	9*	10	12*	–	4	11	–													M.Ross
7	1	2	3	12*	5	6	7	8	14†	10	–	4†	9*	11	–													J.Ferry
8	1	2	3	–	5	6	7	8*	–	10	12*	14†	9†	11	–	4												L.Irvine
9	1	2	3	–	5	6*	12*	8†	15°	10	14†	7°	–	11	–	9	4											H.Barr
10	1	2	3	4	5	6	7	–	–	10	8	9	–	11	–													F.McDonald
11	1	2	3	4	5	6*	7	–	–	10	8	9	–	11	–	12*	–											G.Keatley
12	1	2†	3	4	5	–	7	8	15°	10	6	9°	–	11*	–	14†	–	12*										E.Millar
13	1	2	3†	4	5	–	7	8	15°	10	6*	9°	–	11	–	14†	–	12*										R.Lutton
14	1	2	–	4	5	–	7	8†	14†	10	6	12*	–	11*	–	3	–	15°	9									F.McDonald
15	1	2	3	4	5	–	7	8	–	–	6	–	11	–	–	–	12*	9	10*									J.Ferry
16	1	2	3	4	5	15°	7	8	14†	–	6	–	11†	–	–	–	12*	9°	10									F.Hiles
17	1	2	3	4	5	6	7	–	–	–	9	–	11	–	–	–	–	10	–	8								D.Magill
18	1	2	3	4	–	6°	7†	–	–	5	14†	15°	–	11	–	–	–	9	10*	12*	8							N.Cowie
19	1	–	3	4	5	–	7	–	6	2	9	10*	–	11	–	–	–	14†	–	12*	8†							D.Taylor
20	1	2	3	4	5	15°	7	–	9°	6†	8	14†	–	–	–	–	11*	10	12*	–								F.McDonald
21	1	2	3	4	5	–	7	–	14†	6†	–	–	–	11	–	–	–	8	10*	12*	–	9						T.Deegan
22	1	2	3	4	5	–	7	8	–	–	–	–	11	–	–	–	6	10	–	–	9							G.Keatley
23	1	2	3	4†	5	–	7	8*	12*	14†	15°	–	11	–	–	–	6	10	–	–	9*							R.Lutton
24	1	2	3	4	5	–	7	8	–	–	12*	–	11	–	–	–	6	10	–	–	9*							M.Ross
25	–	2	3	4	5	–	7	8	12*	–	6	–	11	–	–	–	–	10	–	–	9*	1						A.Snoddy
26	–	–	3	4	–	–	7	8	5	2	6	–	11	–	–	–	–	10	–	–	9*	1	12*					J.Ferry
27	–	–	3	4	–	–	7	8	5	2	6	12*	11	–	–	–	–	10*	–	–	9	1	–					F.McDonald
28	–	2°	3	4	–	–	–	8	7	6†	–	–	11	–	–	–	–	10	–	–	9*	1	15°	5	12*	14†		L.Irvine

PLAYER PROFILE - TIM McCANN

Tim McCann has firmly established himself as one of the best right sided attacking players in Irish League football.

His ability to get down the right flank at considerable pace has led to many Cliftonville goals. His reputation was enhanced by his fine performance in last season's Coca-Cola Floodlit Cup Final when his opportunism saw him grab the Reds equaliser against Glentoran. Typical McCann wing play then saw him combine well with Paul Stokes for the latter to spectacularly score the third and decisive goal in the 3-1 victory. A television audience was able to witness a typical piece of McCann magic, something which Reds fans had become used to since his debut in 1990.

Tim's fine display in the Cliftonville jersey have naturally attracted the attention of the cross channel clubs. Last season Blackpool had him over on a trial period, and although no transfer has yet materialised, the Bloomfield club are keeping tabs on him.

Sheffield United are another club to have shown interest in the speedy winger. Despite pushing 25, local lad Tim has not given up hopes of breaking into the full-time professional ranks on the other side of the Irish Sea.

Last season Tim underlined his commitment to the Reds by renewing his contract at a time when it was feared by the fans that attractive offers from other local clubs could lure him away from Solitude. A product of the local Newington Youth Club and Cliftonville's own youth and reserve sides, Tim is now very much a key performer in Reds line-ups. Somehow or other the Reds attacking flair is lacking whenever he is absent. Just how long Cliftonville can continue to hold on to him remains to be seen. Despite his own ambitions in the game Cliftonville fans will be quite happy for him to keep adding to his 200 plus appearances for the club.

Michael Gallagher.

CLIFTONVILLE APPEARANCES FOR **1995/96**

Name:	UC	GC	ILC	CC	BIC	CAS	PL	Total
1 Gerry Flynn	3	5	3	5	2	1	27	46
2 Tim McCann	3	4	3	5	2	1	25+(2)	43+(2)
3 Ian Hill	3	5	3	4+(1)	2	1	25	43+(1)
4 Paul Rice	3	5	3	5	2	1	24	43
5 Joe Kerr	3	4	3	5	2	1	24	42
6 Martin Tabb	3	5	3	5	2	1	22+(1)	41+(1)
7 Michael Donnelly	2	2	3	5	1	1	25	39
8 Gary Sliney	1+(1)	4	3	4+(1)	1	-(1)	21	34+(3)
9 Tommy McDonald	3	4	3	1	1	1	21+(2)	34+(2)
10 Ciaran Feehan	3	3+(1)	3	1+(2)	1+(1)	-(1)	9+(11)	20+(16)
11 Mark O'Neill	-	2+(3)	-(1)	3+(1)	1	-	17+(7)	23+(12)
12 Shaun Strang	2	5	2	1	2	-(1)	11+(3)	23+(4)
13 Ron Manley	1+(1)	3+(1)	-(1)	-(1)	-(1)	1	7+(8)	12+(13)
14 Paul Stokes	-	-	-	5	2	-	14	21
15 Seamus Heath	1+(1)	1+(2)	-	2+(1)	1	-	6+(6)	11+(10)
16 Jonathan Cross	-	-	-	2	-	-	8	10
17 Pat Cavanagh	-	1	-	1	-	-	2+(4)	4+(4)
18 Ian McParland	-	-	-	-	-	1	3+(3)	4+(3)
19 Rod Collins	-	-	-	-	-	-	6	6
20 Martin Hayes	-	1	-	1	-	-	3	5
21 Dean Smyth	-	-	-	-	-	-	4	4
22 James McFadden	-	-	-	-(1)	-(1)	1	1	2+(2)
23 Pat McAllister	1	1+(1)	-	-	-	-	-	2+(1)
24 Kieran Loughran	-	-	-(1)	-	-	-	-(2)	-(3)
25 Mark Grugel	-	-	-	-	-	-	2	2
26 Damien Davey	-	-	-(1)	-	-	-	1	1+(1)
27 Joe Quinn	1	-	-	-	-	-	-(1)	1+(1)
28 Gavin McCrystal	-(2)	-	-	-	-	-	-	-(2)
29 Paul Ramsey	-	-	1	-	-	-	-	1
30 Sean Craig	-	-(1)	-	-	-	-	-	-(1)
31 Sam Erskine	-(1)	-	-	-	-	-	-	-(1)
32 David McGlinchey	-	-	-	-	-	-	-(1)	-(1)

CLIFTONVILLE GOALSCORERS FOR **1995/96**

Name:	UC	GC	ILC	CC	BIC	CAS	PL	Total
1 Paul Stokes	-	-	-	5	-	-	7	12
2 Ciaran Feehan	1p	1	5	2	-	-	2	11 (1p)
3 Michael Donnelly	-	-	3	-	1	1	5	10
4 Tim McCann	1	2	1	1	1	-	1	7
5 Shaun Strang	-	2	2	-	-	-	3	7
6 Gary Sliney	1	1	-	1	-	1	1	5
7 Gerry Flynn	1	1	-	-	-	-	1	3
8 Ron Manley	3	-	-	-	-	-	-	3
9 Jonathan Cross	-	-	-	2	-	-	-	2
10 Paul Rice	-	-	-	-	1p	-	1p	2p
11 Martin Tabb	-	-	-	-	1	-	1	2
12 Pat Cavanagh	-	-	-	-	-	-	1	1
13 Rod Collins	-	-	-	-	-	-	1	1
14 Joe Kerr	-	-	-	-	-	-	1	1
15 Ian McParland	-	-	-	-	-	-	1	1
16 Mark O'Neill	-	-	-	-	-	-	1	1
Total:	7	7	11	11	4	2	27	69

Ground: The Showgrounds, Ballycastle Road, Coleraine (8,000) Founded: 1927
TEL: 01265 53655/43724

Coleraine 1995/96
Back Row: L-R: Eamon Doherty, John McIvor, David O'Hare, Michael Surgeon, Paul Gaston, Stephen Young .
Front Row: L-R: Oliver McAuley, Sammy Shiels, Patrick McAllister, 'Dixie Shiels' (mascot), Anthony Gorman, Greg O'Dowd.
(Photograph courtesy of Grant Cameron, Coleraine Chronicle)

President: Dr.J.Love	**Summary of 1995/96 Season**

President:
Dr.J.Love
Chairman:
Mr.W.Harte
Secretary:
Mr.F.Monahan
Treasurer:
Mr.G.Doherty
Manager:
Kenny Shiels
Asst.Manager:
Billy McKeag
Reserve Team Manager:
Raymond Starrett
Colours:
Blue and White vertical
striped shirts,
Blue shorts, White socks

Summary of 1995/96 Season

Who could have dreamed up the script for Coleraine's season? There was still hurt and dejection over relegation to the First Division. The bad feeling lingered on into the new season so much so that - ominously - after only 13 games, manager Kenny Shiels was dramatically sacked by some Directors three matches into the First Division Championship. Within 48 hours Shiels was reinstated for one game and then given the backing of the full board.

The side never looked back after that major hiccough. They ran away with the First Division title, so far in front in the new year that it was obvious nobody could catch them. In the end the Bannsiders won the crown with a massive 18 points, losing only three times in 28 games.

Early season form had been good too with the side reaching the quarter-finals of the Wilkinson Sword Irish League Cup, topping Section B of the Ulster Cup a head of Premiership sides Portadown and Bangor, but losing to Linfield in the last eight.

The Bass Irish Cup saw a dismal exit in the fifth round at Newry Town, but the whole future of senior soccer in the North West was rekindled dramatically by the inaugural Irish News Cup which paired Coleraine and Derry City for the first time in more than a decade. Coleraine defeated City over two legs and Omagh Town in the Final. The competition may be expanded from four teams in years to come.

THE NORTHERN IRELAND
football
Y E A R B O O K

Other plus points were the addition of a new covered enclosure at the Sperrin End of the Showgrounds, the appointment of a female marketing consultant, Ballycastle woman Deidre McNeill, a Promotions Manager, and a fundraising committee as the club prepares to meet the challenge of a new era.

Anthony Gorman's transfer to Windsor Park was a big blow to Coleraine during the close season, however the 'Bosman ruling' allowed Coleraine to take advantage of out of contact trio Brendan Aspinall, Andy Ramage and Robbie Brunton who all joined the Showgrounds outfit from Sligo Rovers. It is very unlikely the coming season will be as profitable as the previous one, with Kenny Shiels main priority to consolidate Coleraine's position within the Premier League.

Grant Cameron.

MANAGER PROFILE — KENNY SHEILS

Date of Birth: 27/04/1956 Magherafelt.

Date of Appointment: December 1994

PREVIOUS CLUBS
As Player: Bridgend United; Tobermore United; Coleraine; Distillery; Tobermore United; Larne; Ballymena United; Tobermore United; Harland & W.W, Carrick Rangers.
As Manager: Tobermore United (Player/Manager), Carrick Rangers.

Honours
As Player: Tobermore U; North West Senior Challenge Cup; 1989/90.North West Intermediate Cup; 1988/89 and 1989/90.
Coleraine North West Senior Challenge Cup 1994/95

As Manager: Tobermore U; As above.
Carrick R; Co.Antrim Shield; 1992/93.
Coleraine, First Division Champions 1995/96
Irish News Cup 1995/96.

SMIRNOFF FIRST DIVISION RECORD 1995/96

No:	Date:	Ven:	Opponents:	Result:	H.T:	Pos:	Goalscorers:
1	Sep 30	A	Omagh Town	2-2 D	1-1	-	Gorman (pen 42),Gaston (71)
2	Oct 7	H	Distillery	2-1 W	0-0	3	Surgeon (72), Doherty (75)
3	Oct 14	A	Ballyclare Comrades	0-1 L	0-1	4	-
4	Oct 21	H	Larne	1-0 W	1-0	4	O'Dowd (38)
5	Oct 28	H	Newry Town	8-0 W	1-0	2	Shiels (12,73,86), O'Dowd (52), Surgeon (57,71), Gorman (pen 62), Gaston (80)
6	Nov 4	A	Carrick Rangers	3-0 W	2-0	2	Gorman (42), McIvor (44), Shiels (83)
7	Nov 11	H	Ballymena United	1-1 D	0-0	2	Shiels (60)
8	Nov 18	H	Omagh Town	5-2 W	2-2	2	McAllister (5,63), Gorman (39,pen 51), O'Dowd (76)
9	Nov 25	A	Distillery	1-1 D	1-0	2	O'Dowd (14)
10	Dec 2	H	Ballyclare Comrades	2-0 W	0-0	1	McIvor (72), Gorman (89)
11	Dec 9	A	Larne	2-0 W	1-0	1	Gorman (27), McIvor (70)
12	Dec 16	A	Newry Town	4-1 W	2-0	1	Surgeon (11), Gorman (15,78), Shiels (90)
13	Dec 26	H	Carrick Rangers	6-0 W	4-0	-	Shiels (10,14,68), Gorman (25,38), Doherty (53)
14	Jan 1	A	Ballymena United	2-1 W	1-1	-	Muir (og 34), Shiels (88)
15	Jan 6	A	Omagh Town	4-0 W	2-0	1	Shiels (19,35,72), Doherty (75)
16	Jan 13	H	Distillery	4-2 W	3-2	1	Gaston (2), Gorman (12), Shiels (28), McIvor (59)
17	Jan 27	A	Ballyclare Comrades	2-0 W	2-0	1	Gaston (36), (N) Blair (og 38)
18	Feb 3	H	Larne	3-2 W	3-0	1	Gaston (23), McAllister (40), McCallan (43)
19	Feb 10	H	Newry Town	5-0 W	4-0	1	O'Dowd (15,63), Gorman (30), Shiels (39,44)
20	Feb 17	A	Carrick Rangers	5-2 W	2-1	1	McCallan (2,27,90), Shiels (60,63)
21	Mar 2	H	Ballymena United	4-0 W	3-0	1	Shiels (16,35,46), McCallan (26)
22	Mar 16	H	Omagh Town	2-1 W	1-1	1	Shiels (19), Gorman (83)
23	Mar 23	A	Distillery	1-1 D	1-1	1	McCallan (39)
24	Mar 30	H	Ballyclare Comrades	1-3 L	0-1	1	McIvor (80)
25	Apr 6	A	Larne	2-1 W	0-1	1	McAllister (57), Gorman (pen 85)
26	Apr 8	A	Newry Town	2-1 W	0-0	-	Shiels (57), O'Dowd (78)
27	Apr 20	H	Carrick Rangers	5-1 W	1-1	1	Shiels (26,47), McIvor (49,77), Surgeon (90)
28	Apr 27	A	Ballymena United	3-4 L	1-0	1	McAllister (34,84), Gorman (75)

Final League Position: 1st

FIRST DIVISION LINE-UPS 1995/96

MATCH No	D.O'Hare 25	O.McAuley 19+(1)	T.Huston 16+(3)	J.Hagan 2	G.Philson 4+(2)	A.Gorman 27	P.McAllister 26+(1)	E.Doherty 26+(1)	M.Surgeon 19+(9)	G.Beckett 2+(4)	P.Gaston 28	K.Maloney 0+(5)	D.Patton 3+(9)	J.McIvor 24+(2)	S.Young 25	S.Shiels 26+(1)	F.O'Donnell 0+(1)	G.O'Dowd	S.Clanachan 2+(2)	D.McCallan 9+(2)	E.Canning 1	S.Lynch 0+(4)	M.Patterson 2	Referee
1	1	2	3	4†	5	6	7	8	9°	10	11	12*	14†	15*										G.Douglas
2	1	-	3	-	5	6	7	2	9	10*	11	-	8	-	4	12*								D.Taylor
3	1	-	3	-	5	6	10*	2	9	-	11	12*	8†	-	4	7	14†							P.Thompson
4	1	-	3	-	-	6	10	2	9	-	5	-	-	11	4	7	-	8						F.McDonald
5	1	-	3	-	15°	6†	10	2	9	-	5°	12*	14†	11*	4	7	-	8						R.Lutton
6	1	-	3	-	-	6	10	2	9	-	5	-	-	11	4	7	-	8						G.Douglas
7	1	-	3	-	-	6	10	2	9†	14†	5	-	12*	11*	4	7	-	8						A.Snoddy
8	1	12*	3*	-	4	6	10	2	9	-	5	-	-	11	-	7	-	8						T.Gillanders
9	1	-	-	3	-	6	10	2	9	12*	5	-	-	11	4	7*	-	8						N.Cowie
10	1	3	-	-	-	6	10	2	9*	12*	5	-	-	11	4	7	-	8						D.Taylor
11	1	3	-	-	12*	6	10	2*	9	-	5	-	-	11	4	7	-	8						N.Cowie
12	1	3	15°	-	-	6	10	2	9*	12*	5	-	14†	11†	4	7	-	8°						T.Deegan
13	1	3	-	-	-	6	10	2†	9	-	5	-	12*	11	4	7	-	8*	14†					L.Irvine
14	1	3	14†	-	-	6	10	2	9*	-	5	-	12*	11	4	7	-	8†	-					D.Taylor
15	1	3	12*	-	-	6	10	2	9	-	5	-	-	11*	4	7	-	8	-					N.Cowie
16	1	3	-	-	-	6	10	2	9*	-	5	-	-	11	4	7	-	8	-	12*				H.Barr
17	1	3	-	-	-	6	10	2	8	-	5	-	-	11	4	7	-	-	-	9				R.Penney
18	1	2	3	-	-	6	10	-	8*	-	5	-	14†	11†	4	7	-	12*	-	9				P.Thompson
19	1	2	3	-	-	6	10	14†	15°	-	5†	-	12*	11*	4	7	-	8	-	9°				A.Snoddy
20	1	2*	3	-	-	-	10	6	14†	-	5	12*	-	11	4	7	-	8†	-	9				H.Barr
21	1	2	3	-	-	6	-	10	12*	-	5	-	14†	11†	4	7	-	8*	-	9				M.Ross
22	1	2	3*	-	-	6	12*	10	14†	-	5	-	-	11	4	7	-	8	-	9†				G.McCay
23	-	3	-	-	-	6	10*	2	12*	-	5	-	-	11†	4	7	-	8	-	9	1	14†		F.McDonald
24	-	3	-	-	-	6	10	2	8	-	5	-	11†	12*	4*	7	-	-	-	9	-	14†	1	D.Malcolm
25	1	3	-	-	-	6	10	2	14†	-	5	-	-	11*	-	7	-	8	4	9†	-	12*		R.Lutton
26	-	-	3*	-	-	6	10	2	12*	-	5	15°	-	11†	9	7	-	8°	4	-	-	14†	1	E.Millar
27	1	2	3	-	-	6	10*	9	14†	-	5°	-	-	11	4	7	-	8†	15°	12*	-	-	-	F.Hiles
28	1	2	3*	-	-	6	10	5	12*	-	9	-	-	11	4	7	-	8	-	-	-	-	-	D.Taylor

TRANSFERS c/s'95 TO APRIL '96

Players Signed:

James Hagan (Crusaders c/s'95), Kyle Maloney (Derry City Jun.'95), Francis O'Donnell (Park Jun.'95), Marc Kenny (Bangor Jul.'95), Philip Leckey (Ballyclare Comrades Jul.'95), Charlie Oatway (Cardiff City (Wal loan) Aug.'95), Rod Collins (Glentoran Sep.'95), Patrick McAllister (Cliftonville Sep.'95), Sammy Shiels (Tobermore United Sep.'95), Michael Surgeon (Bangor Sep.'95), Stephen McCombe (Cookstown United Oct.'95), Greg O'Dowd (Shamrock Rovers (loan) Oct.'95), Greg O'Dowd (Shamrock Rovers Nov.'95), David McCallan (Bangor Dec.'95), Chris Larkin (Larne (loan rtn) Jan.'96), Kyle Maloney (Ards (loan rtn) Jan.'96), Gary Matthewson (Oxford United Stars Feb.'96), Stephen Lynch (Ballymena United Mar.'96), Mark Patterson (Islandmagee Mar.'96).

Players Transferred:

Thomas McCallion (Derry City c/s'95), Gary Smyth (Donegal Celtic c/s'95), Alan Ewing (Linfield Jun.'95), Stuart McLean (Linfield Jun.'95), Marc Kenny (Glenavon Jul.'95), Mark McWalter (Ballymena United Jul.'95), Philip Leckey (Larne Aug.'95), Harry Love (R.U.C. Aug.'95), Stephen McCombe (Cookstown United Aug.'95), Stephen McDowell (Larne Sep.'95), Charlie Oatway (Cardiff City (Wal loan rtn) Sep.'95), Brian Robson (Distillery Sep.'95), Richard Wade (Ballymoney United Sep.'95), Rod Collins (Cliftonville Oct.'95), Billy McCurdy (Ballymoney United Oct.'95), Chris Larkin (Larne (loan) Nov.'95), Kyle Maloney (Ards (loan) Nov.'95), Gary Beckett (Derry City Dec.'95), Francis O'Donnell (Omagh Town Dec.'95), Graeme Philson (West Ham United (Eng) Dec.'95), Stephen Campbell (Livingstone (Sco) Jan.'96).

HONOURS

Irish League/First Division Champions:		1973/74 / 1995/96
Irish Cup, Winners:	(4)	1964/65, 1971/72, 1974/75, 1976/77
Gold Cup, Winners:	(4)	1931/32, 1957/58, 1968/69, 1975/76
Ulster Cup, Winners:	(7)	1965/66, 1968/69, 1969/70, 1972/73, 1975/76, 1985/86, 1986/87
City Cup, Winners:	(2)	1953/54, 1968/69
Irish News Cup, Winners	(1)	1995/96
Irish League Cup, Winners:	(1)	1987/88
Blaxnit Cup, Winners:	(2)	1968/69, 1969/70
George Wilson Cup, Winners:	(2)	1954/55*, 1985/86*
IFA Intermediate Cup, Winners:	(2)	1964/65*, 1968/69*
Louis Moore Cup, Winners:	(2)	1953/54*, 1974/75*
Irish Junior Cup, Winners:	(1)	1927/28
IFA Youth Cup, Winners:	(6)	1967/68, 1969/70, 1973/74, 1974/75, 1992/93, 1993/94

* Trophies won by Coleraine Reserves

Most capped players: Felix Healy (4); Des Dickson (4) both N.Ireland

PLAYER PROFILE - SAMMY SHIELS

Sammy Shiels arrived at Coleraine in a blaze of publicity but for all the wrong reasons!

The striker, who had been with his brother Kenny at Carrick Rangers, left Taylor's Avenue following an horrific time when he was close to death after a collision with Newry Town keeper Brendan Keeley.

But an appearance for Kenny's Coleraine in a pre-season friendly at Tobermore United caused Carrick to protest at their player turning out without permission and Coleraine were fined £2,000. However, after signing briefly for Tobermore, his former club, Sammy teamed up with big brother Kenny again at The Showgrounds and his comeback story began to read like something out of a 'Roy of the Rovers' episode.

The 29 year old, who has always scored goals, quickly began to settle into the groove and the goals were not long in coming. He hit 28 goals in 36 appearances to clinch the club's top goalscorer award from Tony Gorman who netted 25.

It was just reward for a player who demonstrated a courage which few will ever comprehend. "He came through the most difficult time. We thought the worst at one time but he was a fighter and pulled through," says Kenny. "Although he scored goals it took him a few weeks to settle down at Coleraine. He just kept getting better and better."

His team-mates will tell you that while his goalscoring is a feature, it is his unselfish style which they most appreciate. Shiels possesses tremendous vision and can see and seize opportunities to create openings.

Sammy. a quiet man, lives in Maghera. He started his senior career at Ballymena United and went on to Tobermore. He then signed for Ards
in August 1990 and he was among the goals at Castlereagh Park until being transferred to Dungannon Swifts. Next stop was at Carrick Rangers where he won a Co.Antrim Shield medal.

Coleraine looks like being his final senior port of call. Sammy has become a popular player with the fans who see him as the first comparable replacement to legendary goalscorer Dessie Dickson.

Grant Cameron.

COLERAINE APPEARANCES FOR 1995/96

Name:	UC	GC	ILC	CC	BIC	NWC	INC	FD	Total
1 Paul Gaston	4	3	3	3	1	2	4	28	48
2 Anthony Gorman	4	3	3	3	1	2	4	27	47
3 Eamon Doherty	4	2	3	2+(1)	1	2	2+(1)	26+(1)	42+(3)
4 David O'Hare	4	3	3	3	1	-	4	25	43
5 Oliver McAuley	4	3	3	3	1	2	4	19+(1)	39+(1)
6 John McIvor	-(1)	1+(2)	-	3	1	2	4	24+(2)	35+(5)
7 Michael Surgeon	1	-	-	3	1	1+(1)	3+(1)	19+(9)	28+(11)
8 Sammy Shiels	-	-	-	3	1	2	4	26+(1)	36+(1)
9 Stephen Young	1	-	-	3	1	2	4	25	36
10 Patrick McAllister	-	-	-	3	1	1	4	26+(1)	35+(1)
11 Thomas Huston	4	2	3	1	-	1	2	16+(3)	19+(3)
12 Greg O'Dowd	-	-	-	1+(1)	1	-	3	22+(1)	27+(2)
13 David Patton	3+(1)	2	3	-(1)	-	-(1)	-(3)	3+(9)	11+(15)
14 David McCallan	-	-	-	2	-(1)	2	2	9+(2)	15+(3)
15 Kyle Maloney	4	2+(1)	3	-	-	1+(1)	-(1)	-(5)	10+(8)
16 Graeme Philson	4	3	3	-	-	-	-	4+(2)	14+(2)
17 Gary Beckett	4	1	3	-	-	-	-	2+(4)	10+(4)
18 Francis O'Donnell	1+(2)	1+(1)	1+(2)	-	-	-	-	-(1)	3+(6)
19 Charlie Oatway	2	3	2	-	-	-	-	-	7
20 Stuart Clanachan	-	-	-	-	-	-(1)	-	2+(2)	2+(3)
21 Stephen Lynch	-	-	-	-	-	-(1)	-	-(4)	-(5)
22 Mark Patterson	-	-	-	-	-	2	-	2	4
23 James Hagan	-	-	-	-	-	-	-(1)	2	2+(1)
24 Rod Collins	-	2	-	-	-	-	-	-	2
25 Brian Robson	-(1)	1	-	-	-	-	-	-	1+(1)
26 Eamon Canning	-	-	-	-	-	-	-	1	1
27 Sean Harkin	-	1	-	-	-	-	-	-	1
28 Chris Larkin	-	-(1)	-	-	-	-	-	-	-(1)
29 Richard Wade	-	-	-(1)	-	-	-	-	-	-(1)

COLERAINE GOALSCORERS FOR 1995/96

Name:	UC	GC	ILC	CC	BIC	NWC	INC	FD	Total
1 Sammy Shiels	-	-	-	-	-	1	2	25	28
2 Anthony Gorman	3	1	1	2	-	-	2	16(4p)	25
3 David McCallan	-	-	-	1	-	1	5	6	13
4 John McIvor	-	-	-	1	1	1	-	7	10
5 Greg O'Dowd	-	-	-	-	-	-	2	7	9
6 Patrick McAllister	-	-	-	-	-	-	1	6	7
7 Paul Gaston	-	-	-	-	-	-	-	5	5
8 Michael Surgeon	-	-	-	-	-	-	-	5	5
9 Eamon Doherty	-	-	1	-	-	-	-	3	4
10 Gary Beckett	1	-	1	-	-	-	-	-	2
11 Rod Collins	-	1	-	-	-	-	-	-	1
12 Thomas Huston	-	-	-	-	-	-	1	-	1
13 Kyle Maloney	-	-	1	-	-	-	-	-	1
14 Francis O'Donnell	1	-	-	-	-	-	-	-	1
15 David Patton	-	-	1	-	-	-	-	-	1
16 Stephen Young	-	-	-	-	-	-	1	-	1
17 Own Goals	-	-	-	-	-	-	1	2	3
Total:	5	2	5	4	1	3	15	82	117

Ground: Seaview, Shore Road, Belfast BT15 3PL (9,000) Founded: 1908
Tel: 01232 370777

Crusaders 1995/96

Back Row L-R: Aaron Callaghan, Kirk Hunter, Michael Deegan, Kevin McKeown, Glenn Dunlop,
Donal O'Brien, Steven Livingstone, Frank Darby, Martin Murray.
Front Row L-R: Gary McCartney, Glenn Hunter, Derek Carroll, Sid Burrows, Stephen Baxter,
Liam Dunne, Trevor McMullan, Robert Lawlor.
(Photograph by Michael Reeves)

Chairman:
Mr.J.Semple
Treasurer:
Mr.R.White
Secretary:
Mr.H.Davison
Manager:
Roy Walker
Asst.Manager:
Roy McDonald
Reserve Team Manager:
Jim O'Rourke
Club Colours:
Red/Black shirts,
Black shorts,
Red socks

Summary of the Season 1995/96

Successive defeats in competitive games No.57 and No.58 ultimately meant that Crusaders were unable to claim either of the big two prizes on offer last season and Seaview was consumed by gloom for a few days as a consequence.

It would be wrong though to let that last couple of weeks take away from what was another tremendous season for the boys in red-and-black.

Roy Walker's side won the Gold Cup for only the second time in their history, were losing finalists in the League Cup and County Antrim Shield and also reached the semi-final stages of the Ulster Cup and the Irish Cup.

Arguably though, Walker's greatest achievement of the nine months was once more keeping the Crues in the race for the Championship until the penultimate Saturday of the League programme. Runners-up spot may have been poor consolation at the time but it earned entry into European competition for the third time in four seasons and sustained a record of consistency unknown at Seaview for 25 years.

The Crusaders manager also bought wisely once again. Quality rather than quantity was again the name of the Walker game. The two new arrivals were sturdy defender Trevor McMullan (29) and midfielder Donal O'Brien (27). Both very experienced players.

McMullan arrived after a second spell with Ballymena United but is best remembered as a long-serving Larne defender with a number of Inter-League appearances behind him. O'Brien, whose career seemed to be a mix of spells in Australia interspersed with those at Derry City, came to Seaview after a season with Glentoran where he had become something of a cult figure until the emergence of Glen Little squeezed him out. Both gave sterling service in their first season at

THE NORTHERN IRELAND
football
Y E A R B O O K

Seaview and their ability to play in a variety of different roles proved invaluable. There were 48 goals from the front pair of Stephen Baxter and Glenn Hunter. Baxter, with 30 goals, struck a rich vein of form, actually scoring five times in an early Gold Cup meeting against his previous club Distillery. Hunter's strike against Silkeborg in the UEFA Cup was the first goal scored by Crusaders in European competition for 27 years!

The Crues remain as mean as ever at the back. Goalkeeper Kevin McKeown kept 22 clean sheets in 58 appearances and continued to pull off the type of save that can make the difference between winning and losing and the Scot was called up to the 'B' International squad by Craig Brown in October.

There were some formidable defenders in front of McKeown. Glenn Dunlop (himself a N.Ireland 'B' International) and Aaron Callaghan, backed up by Derek Carroll and Robert Lawlor all made life difficult for opposing attacks. The Reserve team also had an encouraging season, finishing third in the 'B' Division with only three defeats in their 28 games with a much younger side than often in the past.

In another, and not well publicised innovation, the club formed it's own Under-18 and Under-16 sides to perform competitively throughout the season. One only has to look at the success of club captain Sid Burrows, a product of former nursery club Carnmoney Colts, to see what benefits can ensue from nurturing local youngsters.

The very best news for Crues fans came in the summer when Roy Walker confirmed that he would continue at the helm in 1996/97. The young Crues boss had been inconsolable at the season's end. His disappointment was understandable but there is still an awful lot that he and his happy Seaview band can achieve. His decision to remain was the right one.

John Smedley.

MANAGER PROFILE — ROY WALKER

Date of Birth: 20/07/1958 Belfast.
Date of Appointment: September 1989.

PREVIOUS CLUBS:
As Player: Luton Town; Ards; Glenavon; Portadown; Crusaders.
As Manager: None.

HONOURS:
As Player: None.

As Manager: Irish League Championships; 1994/95
Irish League Championship; 1994/95.
Ulster Cup; 1993/94. **Co.Antrim Shield**; 1991/92.
Gold Cup; 1995/96.

TRANSFERS C/S '95 TO APRIL '96

Players Signed:

Trevor McMullan (Ballymena United Jul.'95), Donal O'Brien (Glentoran Aug.'95), Richard Snodgrass (Bangor Aug.'95), Damian Grant Ballymena United (loan) Oct.'95), Paul English (Linfield Dec.'95), Colin Ramirez (Gibraltar Dec.'95), Peter Eccles (Home Farm (loan rtn) Feb.'96), Martin Lawlor (Drogheda United Feb.'96), Damien Redden (Nottingham Forest Feb.'96), Frank Darby (Athlone Town Mar.'96).

Players Transferred:

Robert Craig (Loughgall c/s'95), James Hagan (Coleraine c/s'95), Gary Murray (Larne Jun.'95), Stephen Stewart (Ballymena United Jul.'95), David Henry (Nottingham Forest Sep.'95), James Gardiner (Loughgall Oct.'95), Peter Eccles (Home Farm (loan) Dec.'95), Colin Ramirez (Distillery Mar.'96), Damian Grant (Ballymena United (loan rtn) Apr.'96).

HONOURS:

Irish League, Champions/Premier League:	(3)	1972/73, 1975/76, 1994/95 / 2nd 1995/96
Irish Cup, Winners:	(2)	1966/67, 1967/68
Gold Cup, Winners:	(2)	1985/86, 1995/96
Ulster Cup, Winners:	(3)	1953/54, 1963/64, 1993/94
Co.Antrim Shield, Winners:	(5)	1959/60, 1964/65, 1968/69, 1973/74, 1991/92
Carlsberg Cup, Winners:	(1)	1973/74
Pollard Cup, Winners:	(1)	1903/04
Empire Cup, Winners:	(1)	1905/06
Irish Alliance League, Champions:	(3)	1915/16, 1916/17, 1917/18
Lyttle Trophy, Winners:	(3)	1915/16, 1917/18, 1924/25
Braithwaite Cup, Winners:	(1)	1919/20
Irish Intermediate League, Champions:	(7)	1922/23, 1925/26, 1926/27, 1928/29, 1930/31, 1932/33, 1948/49
IFA Intermediate Cup, Winners:	(3)	1926/27, 1937/38, 1938/39
McIlroy Cup, Winners:	(3)	1929/30, 1931/32, 1947/48
Steel & Sons Cup, Winners:	(8)	1922/23, 1926/27, 1928/29, 1930/31, 1933/34, 1936/37, 1947/48, 1953/54*
George Wilson Cup, Winners:	(1)	1952/53*
Louis Moore Cup, Winners:	(1)	1972/73*

*Won by Crusaders Reserves

Most capped player: Albert Campbell 2 N.Ireland

SMIRNOFF PREMIER LEAGUE RECORD 1995/96

No:	Date:	Ven:	Opponents:	Result:	H.T:	Pos:	Goalscorers:
1	Sep 30	H	Glentoran	2-1 W	1-0	-	Dunlop (27), Baxter (70)
2	Oct 7	A	Linfield	2-1 W	0-1	2	Callaghan (48), Murray (61)
3	Oct 14	H	Glenavon	1-2 L	1-1	3	(G) Hunter (17)
4	Oct 21	A	Ards	0-0 D	0-0	3	-
5	Oct 28	A	Bangor	2-1 W	1-0	2	McMullan (41), Burrows (73)
6	Nov 4	H	Cliftonville	1-0 W	0-0	2	(K) Hunter (90)
7	Nov 11	A	Portadown	1-1 D	0-1	2	(G) Hunter (90)
8	Nov 18	A	Glentoran	1-3 L	1-0	3	Baxter (53)
9	Nov 25	H	Linfield	3-0 W	2-0	3	(K) Hunter (17,20), Baxter (86)
10	Dec 2	A	Glenavon	0-4 L	0-1	3	-
11	Dec 9	H	Ards	1-2 L	1-0	3	(K) Hunter (44)
12	Dec 16	H	Bangor	2-0 W	1-0	3	Morgan (6), Dunlop (90)
13	Dec 26	A	Cliftonville	4-1 W	2-1	-	Baxter (4), Burrows (37,81), (G) Hunter (59)
14	Jan 1	H	Portadown	3-1 W	1-1	-	(G) Hunter (37,80), Baxter (63)
15	Jan 6	H	Glentoran	1-3 L	1-0	2	Murray (25)
16	Jan 13	A	Linfield	1-0 W	0-0	2	Murray (70)
17	Jan 27	H	Glenavon	1-0 W	0-0	1	Dunne (68)
18	Feb 3	A	Ards	1-0 W	1-0	1	Baxter (18)
19	Feb 10	A	Bangor	2-0 W	0-0	1	Callaghan (46), Baxter (70)
20	Feb 17	H	Cliftonville	1-1 D	1-0	1	O'Brien (32)
21	Mar 2	A	Portadown	1-1 D	1-0	1	Murray (10)
22	Mar 16	A	Glentoran	2-2 D	2-1	1	Baxter (12,40)
23	Mar 23	H	Linfield	4-2 W	0-0	1	Dunne (52), Burrows (65), Baxter (85,88)
24	Mar 30	A	Glenavon	1-1 D	1-1	2	(G) Hunter (36)
25	Apr 6	H	Ards	2-0 W	2-0	2	O'Brien (24), (G) Hunter (30)
26	Apr 9	H	Bangor	1-0 W	0-0	-	Darby (77)
27	Apr 20	A	Cliftonville	1-2 L	0-1	2	Tabb (og 47)
28	Apr 27	H	Portadown	3-3 D	1-3	2	(G) Hunter (8), McMullan (50), Livingstone (59)

Final League Position: 2nd

PREMIER LEAGUE LINE-UPS 1995/96

MATCH No	K.McKeown 28	T.McMullan 24+(1)	G.McCartney 7+(5)	G.Dunlop 24	A.Callaghan 14	K.Hunter 6+(10)	M.Murray 20+(3)	L.Dunne 24	S.Baxter 26	G.Hunter 19+(5)	S.Burrows 24+(1)	D.O'Brien 20+(2)	R.Lawlor 24	S.Livingstone 8+(3)	M.Deegan 13+(3)	D.Carroll 23	S.Mellon 1+(1)	P.Dwyer 0+(1)	C.Morgan 1+(4)	M.Lawlor 0+(1)	F.Darby 2	Referee
1	1	2	3	4	5	6*	7	8	9	10	11	12*										J.Ferry
2	1	2	3	4	5	–	6	8	9	10*	11	12*	7									G.Keatley
3	1	2*	3	4	5	–	6†	8	9	10	11	–	7	12*	14†							A.Snoddy
4	1	2	12*	4*	–	–	–	8	9	10	11	6	5	7	–	3						G.Douglas
5	1	2	–	4	5	–	6	–	9	12*	11*	10	8	7	–	3						E.Millar
6	1	2	3*	4	–	15°	6	–	9	10†	11	–	5°	–	8	7	12*	14†				M.Ross
7	1	2	3	4	–	–	6	–	9	12*	11	–	5	7*	8	10	–	–				D.Magill
8	1	2	3	4	–	14†	6	8	9	12*	11	–	–	7	10*	5†	–	–				G.Keatley
9	1	2	–	4	–	6†	12*	8	9	–	11	7	5	–	–	10	3*	–	14†			L.Irvine
10	1	2	3	–	4	6	12*	8°	9	–	11	10*	5	–	14†	7†	–	–	15°			H.Barr
11	1	–	–	4	2	6*	10	–	9	–	11	8	5	7	–	3	–	–	12*			F.McDonald
12	1	12*	–	4	3	–	6	8	–	14†	11	–	5	7*	10	2	–	–	9†			M.Ross
13	1	2	–	–	12*	6	8	9	10	11	7	5*	–	4	3	–	–	–				R.Lutton
14	1	2	–	–	12*	6	8	9*	10	11	4	5	–	7	–	–	–					J.Ferry
15	1	2	–	–	14†	6	8	9†	10	–	4	5	11	7	3*	–	–	12*				H.Barr
16	1	2	12*	4	–	14†	6	8	9†	10	11*	5	–	–	7	3	–	–	–			M.Ross
17	1	2	–	4	11	–	6	8	9	10	–	7	5	–	–	3						M.Ross
18	1	2	–	4	11	–	6	8	9	10*	–	7	5	–	12*	3						L.Irvine
19	1	2	–	4	11	14†	6	8	9†	10*	12*	7	5	–	–	3						F.Hiles
20	1	2°	–	4	10	14†	6†	8	9	12*	11*	7	5	–	–	3	–	–	15°			F.McDonald
21	1	2	–	4	7	–	6	8	9	10	11	–	5	–	–	3						D.Magill
22	1	–	12*	4	7	10*	–	8	9	–	11	6	5	–	2	3	–	–	–			A.Snoddy
23	1	–	–	4	3	6*	–	8	9	10	11	7	–	12*	2	–	–	–	–			G.Keatley
24	1	2	–	4	–	–	–	8	9	10	11	7	5	–	6	3	–	–	–			L.Irvine
25	1	2	12*	4	–	–	–	8	9	10	11	7	5*	–	6	3	–	–	–			M.Ross
26	1	2	–	4	–	–	6*	8	9	10	11	7	–	12*	–	3	–	–	–		5	N.Cowie
27	1	2	–	4	–	14†	12*	8	9	10	11	7	5	–	–	3*	–	–	–		6†	F.McDonald
28	1	2	12*	4	–	14†	6†	8	–	10	11	7	5	9	–	3*	–	–	–			D.Magill

PLAYER PROFILE - STEPHEN BAXTER

When Stephen Baxter joined the Crues after an average type of season with Distillery, there were some eyebrows raised among the Shore Road club's supporters. That was less than two years ago but here we are, just two season's on, and those same fans would find it hard to believe if the name Baxter was missing from the starting line up.

The tall, long-legged striker has been playing Irish League football for ten years. The bulk of that time was spent with Linfield but, like some of his new Seaview colleagues, Baxter has gone on to prove that life after Windsor Park can be much more fun.

His first season with Crusaders was a good one but the second, last season, was even better for 'Stanley' (his dressing room nickname). Big Baxter swiftly proved that he was no one-season wonder, improving on his 22-goal tally of 1994/95 with 30 goals in 1995/96.

The 30 year old is not just a goalscorer. He makes a fine target man, leads the line well and his very presence can cause panic in the opposing defence. There is no doubt that Stephen is a far better player now than when he was in the season before he joined Crusaders. Whether that is because he is surrounded by better players, is benefiting from increased confidence or is now putting all he has learnt before into the Crusaders cause is questionable.

"I think that the key to any success I can claim at Seaview is the fact that you are so rapidly accepted by your dressing-room colleagues here," explained Stephen. "Roy Walker is so adept at taking players like myself who have spent long spells with other clubs and then convincing us that we are still as good, if not better, than we were before."

"The other thing that is so important to strikers like myself is the confidence you gain when you are surrounded by good players. It's those same players who help to carve out chances for myself and that's something I thrive on," added Baxter.

Like several of his Seaview predecessors, part-time professional Baxter brings a full-time professional approach to the game he loves to play.

What so often surprises his opponents is the skill of 'Stanley' when the ball is on the floor. They expect him to make life difficult when the ball is in the air as he makes most of his 6' 2". Stephen doesn't disappoint them! But it's his control and shooting power that opponents sometimes underestimate, as they find to their cost!

Crusaders fans will not be making the same mistake. They have seen the big man bang in 52 goals in two seasons and look good for more next term. They also know that Baxter's continued presence inevitably will lead to goalscoring opportunities for others.

John Smedley.

CRUSADERS APPEARANCES FOR 1995/96

Name:	UC	GC	ILC	CC	BIC	CAS	UEF	PL	Total
1 Kevin McKeown	4	6	5	3	5	4	2	28	57
2 Trevor McMullan	5	4+(2)	5	3	5	3+(1)	2	24+(1)	51+(4)
3 Stephen Baxter	5	3+(1)	5	1	5	3	2	26	50+(1)
4 Liam Dunne	5	5+(1)	4+(1)	1	5	2	2	24	48+(2)
5 Glenn Hunter	5	3+(1)	5	3	5	2+(1)	1	19+(5)	43+(7)
6 Donal O'Brien	5	5	5	3	4+(1)	4	-	20+(2)	46+(3)
7 Glen Dunlop	3	3	3	3	5	4	2	24	47
8 Sid Burrows	3	6	3	1	4	3	2	24+(1)	46+(1)
9 Martin Murray	2	3+(1)	5	-	4	2+(2)	-	20+(3)	36+(6)
10 Derek Carroll	3	2+(4)	2	-	3	4	-	23	37+(4)
11 Robert Lawlor	2	3	-	-	4	3	-	24	36
12 Aaron Callaghan	4	4	5	1	1+(1)	3	2	14	34+(1)
13 Gary McCartney	3	5	3	3	1	-(2)	2	7+(5)	24+(7)
14 Steven Livingstone	3+(1)	2	2	2	-(2)	1+(2)	2	8+(3)	20+(8)
15 Kirk Hunter	1+(1)	3	-(1)	1	1+(2)	-	2	6+(10)	14+(14)
16 Michael Deegan	-(1)	2	-	1	2+(1)	2	-	13+(3)	20+(5)
17 Chris Morgan	-	2	-(2)	2+(1)	-(1)	2	-(2)	1+(4)	7+(10)
18 Paul Dwyer	-(1)	-(1)	2	3	-	-(1)	-(1)	-(1)	5+(5)
19 Stuart Mellon	1+(1)	-	-	-(3)	-(1)	1	-	1+(1)	3+(6)
20 Peter Eccles	-(1)	4	-	-	-	1	-	-	5+(1)
21 Frank Darby	-	-	-	-	1	-	-	2	3
22 James Gardiner	-(1)	-	-(1)	-	-	-	1	-	1+(2)
23 Colin Ramirez	-	-	-	2	-	-	-	-	2
24 Damian Grant	1	-(1)	-	-	-	-	-	-	1+(1)
25 Martin Lawlor	-	1	-	-	-	-	-	-(1)	1+(1)
26 Roy Walker	-	-	1	-	-	-	-	-	1
27 Philip Cowan	-	-	-	-(1)	-	-	-	-	-(1)
28 Paul English	-	-	-	-(1)	-	-	-	-	-(1)

Crusaders Goalscorers for 1995/96

Name:	UC	GC	ILC	CC	BIC	CAS	UEF	PL	Total
1 Stephen Baxter	5(1p)	7(1p)	2(1p)	-	5(1p)	-	-	11	30 (4p)
2 Glenn Hunter	4	-	1	1	3	-	1	8	18
3 Sid Burrows	-	-	3	1	-	-	-	4	8
4 Kirk Hunter	-	2	-	-	-	-	-	4	6
5 Donal O'Brien	-	1	1	-	-	2	-	2	6
6 Aaron Callaghan	1	1	-	-	-	-	-	2	4
7 Steven Livingstone	1	1	-	-	-	1	-	1	4
8 Martin Murray	-	-	-	-	-	-	-	4	4
9 Glen Dunlop	-	1	-	-	-	-	-	2	3
10 Liam Dunne	-	-	-	-	1	-	-	2	3
11 Trevor McMullan	-	-	-	-	-	-	-	2	2
12 Frank Darby	-	-	-	-	-	-	-	1	1
13 Michael Deegan	-	-	-	-	-	1	-	-	1
14 Gary McCartney	-	-	-	-	1	-	-	-	1
15 Stuart Mellon	-	-	-	1	-	-	-	-	1
16 Chris Morgan	-	-	-	-	-	-	-	1	1
17 Own Goals	-	-	1	-	-	-	-	1	2
Total:	**11**	**13**	**8**	**3**	**10**	**4**	**1**	**45**	**95**

Ground: New Grosvenor Stadium, Lambeg, Lisburn (14,000) Founded: 1879
Tel: 01232 301148/620178/629148

Distillery 1995/96
Back Row L-R: Brian Robson, Darren Brush, Roy Allen, David Collins, Aidan McAleenan, Thomas Cleland, Ian Curliss, Stephen Small, Andrew McDonald.
Front Row L-R: William Totten, John Drake, Brian Kennedy, Philip Dykes, Philip Mitchell.
(Photograph by David Hunter)

President:
Mr.N.Dalzell
Chairman:
Mr.M.McKnight
Secretary:
Mr.C.Oakes
Treasurer:
Mr.D.Milliken
Manager:
Paul Kirk
Asst.Manager:
Frankie Parks
Youth Team Manager:
Raymond Alexander
Club Colours:
White shirts,
Dark Blue shorts,
White socks

Summary of 1995/96 Season
For Distillery the writing was on the wall for the 1995/96 as early as the first game of the season. In that match a 1-0 home League Cup defeat at the hands of 'B' Division side Harland & Wolff Welders provided a dark backdrop to what was to be a season of great gloom for everyone at New Grosvenor. And yet it had some bright spots along the way. A semi-final place in the Ulster Cup was only denied by a penalty shoot out defeat at the hands of Crusaders, a debut final appearance in the Mid-Ulster Cup was thwarted by a crazy refereeing decision which saw fit to award Dungannon Swifts a match winning hotly disputed penalty with only one minute left to play, and a fine run of form at the start of the League campaign which sadly fizzled out into nothing. Indeed with a quarter of the League matches having been played out, the 'Whites' were four points clear at the top of the First Division and well on course for instant promotion, and then disaster struck. Three points from the next nine games left the side in mid-table and effectively killed off all Distillery hopes of a speedy return to the elite of Irish League football.

Change was needed at New Grosvenor but few believed it would take place so rapidly and dramatically as it did. On 14th February, manager Billy Hamilton, after having earlier announced his intentions to resign at the end of the season, was replaced by former Glentoran Colts supremo Paul Kirk. Kirk immediately went about the task of rebuilding the team from scratch replacing experience with youthful determination. Indeed within six months of his appointment as manager only three players who had featured as regulars under Billy Hamilton were still playing an active role at the club. Kirk has adopted the team to suit his style of play, placed the emphasis on youth, and has also done his best to cut costs, a vital exercise if the club is to survive life in the First Division. Indeed, as with the rest of the teams playing in the new First Division, survival is the order of the day with the very existence of clubs such as Distillery in the melting pot.

And so we enter a new season with the very real shadow of the executioner hanging over those clubs which fail to make it into next seasons 10 team Premier League. Failure for the 'Whites' could mean the end of the road and surely that, after all the struggles the club has endured over the last 20 years, would be the ultimate blow to the Distillery faithful. Here's hoping it's not the case. *Colin Hopkins.*

MANAGER PROFILE — PAUL KIRK

Date of Appointment: February 1996

PREVIOUS CLUBS:
As Player: Linfield; Glentoran; Ballymena United; Crusaders; Ards; Waterford United; Portadown; Ballyclare Comrades:
As Manager/Coach: Glentoran (Youth Team Coach):

HONOURS:
As Player:
Northern Ireland U-18 International
Crusaders: **Irish League Championship**: 1975/76
Waterford: FAI Cup: 1979/80
Ballyclare Comrades: 'B'Division Knockout Cup: 1983/84

As Manager: None

SMIRNOFF FIRST DIVISION RECORD 1995/96

No:	Date:	Ven:	Opponents:	Result:		H.T:	Pos:	Goalscorers:
1	Sep 30	H	Larne	1-0	W	1-0	-	Cleland (42)
2	Oct 7	A	Coleraine	1-2	L	0-0	5	Cleland (52)
3	Oct 14	H	Carrick Rangers	3-1	W	0-0	2	Dykes (48), Cleland (61,76)
4	Oct 21	A	Ballymena United	1-0	W	1-0	1	Cleland (45)
5	Oct 28	H	Omagh Town	3-2	W	1-1	1	Mitchell (pen 30), Robson (59), Cleland (89)
6	Nov 4	H	Newry Town	2-1	W	0-1	1	Allen (47), Moore (83)
7	Nov 11	A	Ballyclare Comrades	2-0	W	2-0	1	Cleland (13), Robson (26)
8	Nov 18	A	Larne	0-2	L	0-0	1	-
9	Nov 25	H	Coleraine	1-1	D	0-1	1	McAleenan (57)
10	Dec 2	A	Carrick Rangers	0-0	D	0-0	2	-
11	Dec 9	H	Ballymena United	0-1	L	0-0	3	-
12	Dec 16	A	Omagh Town	1-3	L	0-0	3	Small (73)
13	Jan 1	H	Ballyclare Comrades	1-2	L	0-1	-	Brady (78)
14	Jan 6	H	Larne	0-1	L	0-0	3	-
15	Jan 13	A	Coleraine	2-4	L	2-3	4	Hall (22), Hillis (26)
16	Feb 3	A	Ballymena United	1-1	D	1-1	5	Cleland (pen 34)
17	Feb 6	A	Newry Town	5-2	W	3-2	-	Cleland (1), Hillis (15), Mitchell (44,76), Allen (48)
18	Feb 10	H	Omagh Town	0-1	L	0-1	3	-
19	Feb 14	H	Carrick Rangers	2-1	W	2-1	-	Small (18), Cleland (30)
20	Feb 17	H	Newry Town	1-1	D	1-0	2	Totten (7)
21	Mar 2	A	Ballyclare Comrades	3-0	W	1-0	3	Robson (33,55), Walker (og 90)
22	Mar 16	A	Larne	1-3	L	0-1	4	Hall (82)
23	Mar 23	H	Coleraine	1-1	D	1-1	4	Brush (1)
24	Mar 30	A	Carrick Rangers	0-0	D	0-0	4	-
25	Apr 6	H	Ballymena United	1-3	L	0-1	4	Cleland (90)
26	Apr 8	A	Omagh Town	0-0	D	0-0	-	-
27	Apr 20	A	Newry Town	2-0	W	2-0	4	Moore (4), Mitchell (45)
28	Apr 27	H	Ballyclare Comrades	0-1	L	0-0	4	-

Final League Position: 4th

FIRST DIVISION LINE-UPS 1995/96

Match No	D.Collins 18	J.Drake 24	I.Curliss 12	R.Allen 28	D.Brush 27	B.Kennedy 15+(2)	W.Totten 19+(3)	A.McAleenan 11+(2)	P.Dykes 5+(3)	P.Mitchell 21+(1)	T.Cleland 24	B.Robson 16+(8)	R.Moore 12+(10)	S.Small 16+(5)	R.Brezza 0+(1)	N.Currie 8	J.Magee 0+(2)	A.Hall 17	G.Hillis 12+(3)	J.Murray 0+(3)	T.Brady 4	S.Rogan 3+(1)	D.Toal 7+(3)	C.Ramirez 3	D.Spence 3+(3)	M.Magill 1+(3)	A.McDonald 2	J.McAtee 0+(1)	Referee
1	1	2	3	4	5	6	7	8	9	10	11																		D.Malcolm
2	1	2	3	4	5	6	7†	8°	9*	10	11	12*	14†	15°															D.Taylor
3	1	2	3°	4	5	6*	7	12*	9†	10	11	–	15°	8	14†														E.Millar
4	1	2	3	4	5	–	7†	8	9*	10	11	12*	14†	6	–														D.Chambers
5	1	2	3	4	5	6	7*	8	14†	10	11	9†	12*	–	–														G.McKay
6	–	2	3	4	5	6	7†	8°	–	10*	11	9	14†	12*	–	1	15°												R.Penney
7	–	2	3	4	5	6	–	–	10	11	9	7	8	–		1													B.Kane
8	–	2	3†	4	5	6*	–	–	11	10	–	9	7	12*	–	1	14†	8											G.Douglas
9	–	2	3	4	5	6	–	7	12*	10	11	8*	–	–	–	1	–	–	9										N.Cowie
10	–	2	3	4	5	6	–	7	–	10	11	8*	–	–	–	1	–	–	9	12*									J.Peden
11	–	2	3°	4	5	6	14†	7†	12*	10	11	8*	–	15°	–	1	–	–	9	–									R.Lutton
12	–	2	–	4	5	–	7*	6	–	10	11	12*	–	8	–	1	–	3	9†	14†									D.Taylor
13	1	2	3*	4	6	12*	7	–	–	10†	–	9°	15°	11	–	–	–	–	8	14†	5								T.Deegan
14	1	2	–	4	9	6	7	–	–	–	–	12*	11*	10	–	–	–	3	8	–	5								M.Ross
15	–	–	–	4	6	3	7	–	–	10	–	11*	12*	2	–	1	–	–	8	9	–	5							H.Barr
16	1	–	–	4	5	3	7	–	–	–	11*	–	12*	6	–	–	–	–	8	9	–	–	2	10					R.Lutton
17	1	–	–	4	5	3	7	–	–	10	11	12*	–	6	–	–	–	–	8	9*	–	–	2	–					A.Snoddy
18	1	2	–	4	5	3†	7	–	–	10	11	15°	12*	6	–	–	–	–	8*	9°	–	–	–	14†					T.Deegan
19	1	2	–	4	5	–	7	12*	–	11	14†	10	6*	–	–	–	–	3	9†	–	–	–	8	–					E.Millar
20	1	2	–	4	5	–	7*	–	8	11	12*	10	–	–	–	–	–	3	9	–	–	–	6						R.Lutton
21	1	2	–	4	5°	15°	12*	8*	–	10†	11	9	6	7	–	–	–	3	–	–	–	–	14†						D.Taylor
22	1	2	–	4	–	–	12*	–	10	11*	9°	7	6	–	–	–	–	3	–	–	5	–	14†	8†	15°				P.Thompson
23	1	2	–	4	5	–	7	–	–	11	10*	9†	8	–	–	–	–	3	12*	–	–	–	–	6	14†				F.McDonald
24	1	2†	–	4	5	–	7*	–	–	11	10	9	8	–	–	–	–	3	15°	–	14†	6°	–	–	12*				T.Deegan
25	1	2	–	4	5	–	7	–	–	11	8†	9	10*	–	–	–	–	3	12*	–	–	6	–	14†	–				F.Hiles
26	1	2	–	4	5	–	–	–	–	10	11	8	7	–	–	–	–	3	–	–	6*	–	9	12*					J.Peden
27	–	2	–	4	5	–	–	–	–	10	11†	8	7	–	–	–	–	3	–	–	6*	–	9	14†			1	12*	H.O'Neill
28	–	–	–	4	5	–	7	10†	–	14†	11	–	15°	12*	–	–	–	3	–	–	–	2	–	6*	9°	8	1	–	D.Chambers

TRANSFERS C/S'95 TO APRIL '96

Players Signed:

Ian Curliss (Portadown Aug.'95), Andrew McDonald (Linfield Aug.'95), Ritchie Breza (Ards Sep.'95), Mark Magill (Linfield Sep.'95), Brian Robson (Coleraine Sep.'95), Mark Herbert (Ballynahinch United Oct.'95), Jonathon Magee (Portadown Oct.'95), Robert Moore (Glentoran Oct.'95), Niall Currie (Glenavon Nov.'95), Gary Hillis (Larne Nov.'95), Jerome McAtee (Glentoran Mar.'96), Colin Ramirez (Crusaders Mar.'96), David Spence (Glentoran Mar.'96).

Players Transferred:

Simon Houston (Glentoran c/s'95), Winston Armstrong (Carrick Rangers Oct.'95), Ritchie Breza (Galway United Oct.'95), John Kennedy (Glentoran Oct.'95), Pat Cavanagh (Cliftonville Dec.'95), Jonathon Magee (Dungannon Swifts Dec.'95), Niall Currie (Bangor Jan.'96), Jim Murray (Ards Jan.'96), Noel Richardson (Armagh City Jan.'96), Brian Kennedy (Bangor Mar.'96).

HONOURS

Irish League, Champions/First Division:	(6)	1895/96, 1898/99, 1900/01, 1902/03, 1905/06 (shared with Cliftonville); 1962/63 / 4th 1995/96
Irish Cup, Winners:	(12)	1883/84, 1884/85, 1885/86, 1888/89, 1893/94, 1895/96, 1902/03, 1904/05, 1909/10, 1924/25, 1955/56, 1970/71
Gold Cup, Winners:	(5)	1913/14, 1919/20, 1924/25, 1929/30, 1993/94
Ulster Cup, Winners:	(1)	1957/58
City Cup, Winners:	(5)	1904/05, 1912/13, 1933/34, 1959/60, 1962/63
Co.Antrim Shield, Winners:	(14)	1888/89, 1892/93, 1895/96, 1896/97, 1899/00, 1902/03, 1904/05, 1914/15, 1918/19, 1919/20, 1945/46, 1953/54, 1963/64, 1985/86.
Intermediate Cup, Winners:	(2)	1903/04*, 1947/48*.
Irish Junior Cup, Winners:	(1)	1887/88*
George Wilson Cup, Winners:	(4)	1956/57*, 1981/82*, 1987/88*, 1992/93*
Louis Moore Cup, Winners:	(1)	1951/52*

Trophies won by Distilley II

Most capped player: Ollie Stanfield 30 caps Ireland

PLAYER PROFILE - ALAN HALL

Since new manager Paul Kirk took over the reins in charge of Distillery in February 1996, to say some players have moved on would be a complete understatement. Indeed only three players who featured in the side before Kirk's appointment still feature in the sides present plans, one such player being Whites stalwart Alan Hall.

Alan Hall joined Distillery from Wigan Athletic as an 18 year old in December 1988 and prior to the start of this season, which incidentally is his benefit year at the club, had notched up no less than 253 appearances for the Whites. Modest as usual however Alan refuses to highlight his great loyalty to the club by declaring "When Billy Hamilton was in charge there were at least four or five players who stayed on throughout his whole time in charge and it just so happens that I'm one of them".

There have being several highlights for Alan in his Distillery career to date with one of them being rather surprisingly the 1994 Budweiser Cup Final defeat against Portadown - a match which saw Distillery lead 2-0 with only 11 minutes remaining before eventually losing 4-2. "That was my only cup final appearance to date" says Alan "and that, plus our great run in the 1992 League season are by far my best memories at Distillery." Asked about his thoughts on the new manager, Alan came across very enthusiastic; "Paul (Kirk) has came in with a lot of new ideas and a lot of new faces and there certainly seems to be a new wave of energy and desire at the club and he seems really determined to make sure that things get off the ground at Distillery." Alan did however voice his concern at the two tier system now in operation in Northern Irish football commenting that "My fear is that every season the gap between Premier and First Divisions will simply get larger and larger and that it will become much harder for the smaller sides to compete. The gap in resources, skills and so forth is certainly becoming more and more obvious as time marches on. That said hopefully we can make promotion this time around although being realistic, we're still a very young side and it really is a case of whether or not we can gel quickly enough to succeed this time around. There's no doubt we now we have a lot of skilful players at Distillery so we can just hope we can all work well as a team as this is the only way to succeed. Of the other teams in the League I would think Bangor would be the team to beat in that they have had a season in the Premier and should be more experienced than most of the First Division sides. Omagh Town as well could be a surprise packet in the title chase."

Alan knows the season ahead will be a difficult one but it is one which he intends to commit his usual 110% to ensure the success of Distillery Football Club.

Colin Hopkins.

DISTILLERY APPEARANCES FOR **1995/96**

Name:	UC	GC	ILC	CC	BIC	CAS	MUC	FD	Total
1 Roy Allen	4	3	1	2	2	1	2	28	43
2 Darren Brush	4	3	1	1	1	1	2	27	40
3 John Drake	4	2	1	2	2	1	2	24	38
4 William Totten	3	3	-(1)	2	1+(1)	-(1)	1+(1)	19+(3)	29+(7)
5 Philip Mitchell	4	3	1	2	1	1	-	21+(1)	33+(1)
6 Thomas Cleland	1+(1)	2+(1)	1	-	1	1	2	24	32+(2)
7 Stephen Small	3+(1)	2	1	2	2	-	2	16+(5)	28+(6)
8 Brian Robson	-	-	-	1+(1)	-(2)	1	2	16+(8)	20+(11)
9 David Collins	4	3	1	1	1	-	2	18	30
10 Robert Moore	-	-	-	1+(1)	2	1	2	12+(10)	18+(11)
11 Brian Kennedy	3	3	1	2	1	-	-	15+(2)	25+(2)
12 Aidan McAleenan	4	2	1	1	1+(1)	1	-(1)	11+(2)	21+(4)
13 Alan Hall	-	-	-	1	2	1	2	17	23
14 Gary Hillis	-	-	-	1	2	-	-	12+(3)	15+(3)
15 Philip Dykes	4	3	1	-	-	-(1)	-	5+(3)	13+(4)
16 Ian Curliss	1	2+(1)	-	-	-	-	-	12	15+(1)
17 Damien Toal	-	-	-	-(1)	1+(1)	-	2	7+(3)	10+(5)
18 Niall Currie	-	-	-	1+(1)	1	1	-	8	11+(1)
19 Tom Brady	-	1	-	2	1	-	-	4	8
20 Jim Murray	1+(2)	-(1)	1	-	-	-	-	-(3)	2+(6)
21 David Spence	-	-	-	-	-	-	1	3+(3)	4+(3)
22 Winston Armstrong	3	1+(1)	-(1)	-	-	-	-	-	4+(2)
23 Mark Magill	-	-	-	-	-(1)	-	-(1)	1+(3)	1+(5)
24 Stephen Rogan	-	-	-	-(1)	-	-	-	3+(1)	3+(2)
25 Colin Ramirez	-	-	-	-	-	-	-	3	3
26 Jonathon Magee	-	-	-	-	-	1	-	-(2)	1+(2)
27 Andrew McDonald	-	-	-	-	-	-	-	2	2
28 Kevin McCavanagh	1	-	-	-	-	-	-	-	1
29 Ritchie Breza	-	-	-	-	-	-	-	-(1)	-(1)
30 Pat Cavanagh	-(1)	-	-	-	-	-	-	-	-(1)
31 Jerome McAtee	-	-	-	-	-	-	-	-(1)	-(1)

DISTILLERY GOALSCORERS FOR **1995/96**

Name:	UC	GC	ILC	CC	BIC	CAS	MUC	FD	Total
1 Thomas Cleland	-	-	-	-	-	-	-	11(1p)	11(1p)
2 Philip Mitchell	3	1	-	-	-	-	-	4(1p)	8(1p)
3 Brian Robson	-	-	-	-	-	-	2	4	6
4 Philip Dykes	1	2	-	-	-	-	-	1	4
5 Roy Allen	-	-	-	-	-	-	1	2	3
6 Winston Armstrong	2	1	-	-	-	-	-	-	3
7 Darren Brush	-	1	-	-	-	1	-	1	3
8 Alan Hall	-	-	-	-	1	-	-	2	3
9 Robert Moore	-	-	-	-	1	-	-	2	3
10 William Totten	-	-	-	-	2	-	-	1	3
11 Tom Brady	-	1	-	-	-	-	-	1	2
12 Gary Hillis	-	-	-	-	-	-	-	2	2
13 Aidan McAleenan	1	-	-	-	-	-	-	1	2
14 Stephen Small	-	-	-	-	-	-	-	2	2
15 Jim Murray	1	-	-	-	-	-	-	-	1
16 Own Goals	-	-	-	-	-	-	-	1	1
Total:	**8**	**6**	**0**	**0**	**4**	**1**	**3**	**35**	**57**

Ground: Mourneview Park, Lurgan. (15,000); Founded: 1889.
TEL: 01762 322472

Glenavon 1995/96

Chairman:
Mr.A.Teer
Hon.Secretary:
Mr.T.R.Kerr
Treasurer:
Mr.J.Carpenter
Manager:
Nigel Best
Asst.Manager:
Colin McCurdy
Reserve Team Manager:
David Chisholm
Physio:
Billy Nellins
Club Colours:
Royal Blue shirts,
White shorts,
Royal Blue socks

Summary of 1995/96 Season

Glenavon marked the commencement of the 1995/96 season by qualifying through a round in Europe for the first time in the club's history. The Lurgan Blues scored a brilliant 1-0 away UEFA Cup preliminary round victory over Icelandic side FC Hafnarfjordur to set up a glamour First Round tie with Werder Bremen. Although beaten 0-7 on aggregate by the Bundesliga giants, the Mourneview club had the considerable consolation of substantial revenues from the marketing of the television rights to the First Leg tie at Mourneview Park.

Domestically the Lurgan club made a typically assured start to the season. Six straight wins without a goal conceded took Nigel Best's men through to the semi-final stage of the Wilkinson Sword League Cup and quarter-finals of the Ulster Cup. Glenavon also reached the last eight of the Gold Cup. However, the Lurgan Blues were destined not to contest the final of any of the three competitions. In both the League Cup and Ulster Cup semi-finals the Mourneview side were beaten by neighbours Portadown whilst a long-running dispute with the IFA regarding the eligibility of midfielder Marc Kenny led to the club's eventual withdrawal from the Gold Cup.

Glenavon's European success and encouraging early season form in domestic competition had much to do with the signings made during the summer by manager Best. Experienced goalkeeper Dermot O'Neill arrived from Derry City, N.Ireland 'B' International full back Mark Glendinning came from Bangor and defender Gary Smyth was signed from Glentoran. In addition the Lurgan club bought Dublin-based midfielder Marc Kenny from Coleraine. Later in the season Glenavon added Derry City's Edinburgh-born defender Stuart Gauld and former Celtic and Portadown midfielder Tony Shepherd to the first team squad. The Co.Antrim Shield has always been a competition in which Glenavon have prospered and that record of success continued in 1995/96. Darren Freeman, a

loan signing from Gillingham, marked his debut for the North Armagh club with two goals in a 4-1 victory over Portadown in the semi-finals and Stephen McBride scored twice in a comprehensive 3-0 final win over Crusaders at the end of January. It was Glenavon's first trophy success since winning the Irish Cup in 1992.

January and February saw Glenavon achieve two of it's biggest home wins in post-war football, 1st Liverpool R.R. were beaten 12-0 in the fifth round of the Irish Cup and Portadown were crushed 7-0 in a Premier League fixture. In addition long-serving defender Paul Byrne overtook Wilbur Cush's post war record of 562 club appearances.

An impressive sequence of away victories had lifted Glenavon into a comfortable second place in the Premier League table by mid-December. However, successive home defeats by Cliftonville, Glentoran and Bangor followed by draws against Crusaders and Cliftonville ended the Lurgan club's title charge by mid-April.

Glenavon qualified for the last four of the Bass Irish Cup following comprehensive wins over Cliftonville and Carrick Rangers. A brilliant second-half equaliser from Stevie McBride proved the highlight of a drawn semi-final tie with Portadown at the Oval; four days later the Lurgan Blues, aided by a double strike from on-loan West Ham striker Danny Shipp, crushed their Mid-Ulster rivals 4-1 to set up a final meeting with Glentoran. Without goalkeeper Dermot O'Neill and midfielder Lee Doherty, both suspended, Glenavon lost 0-1 to the East Belfast men in a disappointing final at Windsor Park.
George Ruddell.

MANAGER PROFILE — NIGEL BEST

Date of Birth: 30.04.1950 Belfast.

Date of Appointment: December 1994.

PREVIOUS CLUBS
As Player: N.U.U.
As Manager: N.U.U. Carrick Rangers(coach); Bangor (coach); Bangor (Asst.Manager) Bangor

HONOURS
As Player: Capped by N.Ireland Universities

As Manager:
Bangor: Irish Cup 1992/93,
Irish League Cup; 1992/93.
Ulster Cup 1994/95.
Glenavon: Co.Antrim Shield 1995/96

TRANSFERS C/S'95 TO MAY '96

Players Signed:

Alan Murphy (Bangor May '95), Dermot O'Neill (Derry City May '95), Niall Currie (Bangor Jun.'95), Darren Murphy (Loughgall Jul.'95), Gary Smyth (Glentoran Jul.'95), Marc Kenny (Coleraine Aug.'95), Donal Gray (Partick Thistle (Sco) Sep.'95), Shane Mulholland (Portadown Oct .'95), Paul Straney (Telford United (Eng) loan) Oct.'95), Stuart Gauld (Derry City Nov.'95), Alex Russell (Rochdale (Eng loan) Nov.'95), Anthony Scappaticci (Newry Town (loan rtn) Nov.'95), Darren Freeman (Gillingham (Eng) Dec.'95), Tony Shepherd (Stranraer (Sco) Feb.'96), Danny Shipp (West Ham United (Eng loan) Feb.'96), Anthony Scappaticci (Newry Town (loan rtn) Mar.'96).

Players Transferred:

Ciaran Feehan (Cliftonville c/s'95), Dean McCullough (Loughgall c/s'95), Chris McKerr (Dungannon Swifts c/s'95), Keith Percy (Bangor Jun.'95), Peter Kennedy (Portadown Jul.'95), Michael McKeown (Bangor Jul.'95), Ally Mauchlen (Ballymena United Aug.'95), Paul Straney (Telford United (Eng loan) Aug.'95), Anthony Scappaticci (Newry Town (loan) Sep.'95), Robert Beck (Ballymena United Oct.'95), Liam Smyth (Larne Oct.'95), Niall Currie (Distillery Nov.'95), Alex Russell (Rochdale (Eng loan rtn) Nov.'95), Darren Freeman (Gillingham (Eng loan rtn) Jan.'96), Nigel Quigley (Retired Jan.'96), Anthony Scappaticci (Newry Town (loan rtn) Jan.'96), Danny Shipp (West Ham United (loan rtn) May '96).

HONOURS

Irish League, Champions / Premier League:	(3)	1951/52, 1956/57, 1959/60 / 4th 1995/96
Irish Cup, Winners:	(4)	1956/57, 1958/59, 1960/61, 1991/92
Gold Cup, Winners:	(3)	1954/55, 1956/57, 1990/91
Ulster Cup, Winners:	(3)	1954/55, 1958/59, 1962/63
City Cup, Winners:	(5)	1920/21, 1954/55, 1955/56, 1960/61, 1965/66
Irish League Cup, Winners:	(1)	1989/90
Budweiser Cup, Winners:	(1)	1988/89
North-South Cup, Winners:	(1)	1962/63
Co.Antrim Shield, Winners:	(2)	1990/91, 1995/96
Mid-Ulster Cup, Winners:	(20)	1897/98, 1901/02, 1904/05, 1905/06; 1906/07; 1907/08; 1908/09; 1909/10; 1910/ 11; 1924/25; 1925/26, 1930/31; 1931/32; 1932/33; 1937/38; 1947/48*; 1957/58*; 1965/66*; 1971/72*; 1976/77*; 1983/84; 1984/85; 1985/86; 1988/89; 1989/90; 1990/91
Mid-Ulster Shield, Winners:	(3)	1909/10*, 1910/11*, 1917/18*
IFA Intermediate Cup, Winners:	(2)	1907/08*, 1910/11*
Irish Junior Cup, Winners:	(1)	1897/98
George Wilson Cup, Winners:	(1)	1963/64*
Bob Radcliffe Cup, Winners:	(1)	1990/91 *
KY Youth League, Champions:	(1)	1991/92

Trophies won by Glenavon Reserves.
Most capped player: Wilbur Cush 8 caps (26) N.Ireland

SMIRNOFF PREMIER LEAGUE RECORD 1995/96

No:	Date:		Ven:	Opponents:	Result:		H.T:	Pos:	Goalscorers:
1	Sep	30	H	Linfield	0-3	L	0-2	-	-
2	Oct	7	A	Ards	1-1	D	0-1	7	McBride (72)
3	Oct	14	A	Crusaders	2-1	W	1-1	4	McCoy (42), Ferguson (66)
4	Oct	21	H	Bangor	1-0	W	1-0	4	McCoy (40)
5	Oct	28	A	Cliftonville	2-2	D	1-1	3	McBride (3,66)
6	Nov	4	H	Portadown	0-1	L	0-0	4	-
7	Nov	11	A	Glentoran	2-0	W	2-0	3	McCoy (5), McBride (8)
8	Nov	18	A	Linfield	3-0	W	1-0	2	McCoy (10), McBride (85), Ferguson (89 pen)
9	Nov	25	H	Ards	3-0	W	3-0	2	McBride (pen 19), Ferguson (25), McCoy (33)
10	Dec	2	H	Crusaders	4-0	W	1-0	2	Glendinning (25), (J) Smyth (57,82), Johnston (89)
11	Dec	9	A	Bangor	1-0	W	0-0	2	McBride (79)
12	Dec	16	H	Cliftonville	1-2	L	0-0	2	McCoy (57)
13	Jan	1	H	Glentoran	2-3	L	1-0	-	(D) Murphy (45), McCoy (72)
14	Jan	6	H	Linfield	2-2	D	0-2	4	Glendinning (66), Freeman (90)
15	Jan	13	A	Ards	2-1	W	0-0	4	Ferguson (84), Johnston (86)
16	Jan	27	A	Crusaders	0-1	L	0-0	4	-
17	Feb	3	H	Bangor	0-1	L	0-0	4	-
18	Feb	10	A	Cliftonville	1-0	W	0-0	4	Johnston (62)
19	Feb	13	A	Portadown	1-2	L	1-1	-	Ferguson (3)
20	Feb	17	H	Portadown	7-0	W	3-0	3	Johnston (4), Shipp (15,54), McBride (23,53), (D) Murphy (67), McCoy (87)
21	Mar	2	A	Glentoran	2-1	W	1-1	3	Ferguson (34,72)
22	Mar	16	A	Linfield	1-2	L	1-2	3	Shipp (41)
23	Mar	23	H	Ards	3-1	W	1-1	3	Johnston (21), Shipp (60,73)
24	Mar	30	H	Crusaders	1-1	D	1-1	3	Shipp (32)
25	Apr	6	A	Bangor	2-1	W	1-0	3	Johnston (4), (D) Murphy (81)
26	Apr	9	H	Cliftonville	1-1	D	1-0	-	Johnston (41)
27	Apr	20	A	Portadown	1-2	L	1-1	3	Ferguson (8)
28	Apr	27	H	Glentoran	1-3	L	0-2	4	Ferguson (90)

Final League Position: 4th

PREMIER LEAGUE LINE-UPS 1995/96

MATCH No	D.O'Neill 25	P.Byrne 16+(3)	M.Glendinning 25	L.Doherty 23	S.Brown 7+(1)	G.Smyth 24	S.Collins 5+(9)	S.Johnston 18+(6)	G.Ferguson 23+(1)	S.McBride 28	M.Kenny 5+(1)	R.McCoy 14+(7)	D.Murphy 18+(8)	N.Birney 1	A.Murphy 4+(1)	J.Smyth 20	S.Burns 2+(1)	A.Russell 4	S.Gauld 16	J.McCartan 2	S.Mulholland 1+(4)	D.Freeman 2	A.Shepherd 11	P.Straney 2	D.Shipp 9	D.Gray 2	D.Grant 1	Referee
1	1	2†	3	4	5	6	7*	8	9	10	11	12*	14†															A.Snoddy
2	1	–	3	4	–	6	12*	8	–	10	7	14†	9	2*	5†	11												N.Cowie
3	1	–	3	4	–	6	–	–	9	10	–	8	2	–	5	11	7											A.Snoddy
4	1	12*	3	4	–	6	–	7*	9	10	–	8	2	–	5	11	–											D.Taylor
5	1	12*	3	4	5	6	–	–	9	10	–	8	2	–	–	11	7*											G.Keatley
6	1	14†	3	4	5†	6	–	12*	9	10	11	8	7*	–	–	–	–	2										N.Cowie
7	1	5	3	4	–	6	–	12*	9	10*	–	8	7	–	–	11	–	2										L.Irvine
8	1	5	3	–	–	6	12*	7	9	10	–	8	4†	–	–	11	14†	2*										A.Snoddy
9	1	5	3	4	–	6†	12*	14†	9	10	–	8*	7	–	–	11	–	2										M.Ross
10	1	2	3	4	–	6	7*	12*	9	10	–	–	8	–	–	11	–	–	5									H.Barr
11	1	2	3	4	–	6	12*	14†	–	10	–	8*	7°	–	–	11	–	–	5	9†	15°							A.Snoddy
12	1	2	3	4†	15°	6	12*	14†	–	10	–	8*	7	–	–	–	–	–	5°	9	–							E.Millar
13	1	2	3	4	–	6	7	–	–	10	–	12*	8*	–	–	11	–	–	5	–	–	9						M.Ross
14	1	2	3	4	6*	–	–	7	9	10	–	8	12*	–	–	–	–	–	5	–	–	–	11					L.Irvine
15	1	2	3	4	6	–	14†	7	9	10	12*	8†	5*	–	–	11	–	–	–	–	–	–	–					F.McDonald
16	1	2	3	4*	5	6	–	7	9	10	–	8	12*	–	–	–	–	11	–	–	–							M.Ross
17	1	2	3	–	–	6	14†	7	9	10	11†	8*	12*	–	–	–	–	–	5	–	–	–	4					H.Barr
18	–	2	3	–	–	6	11	7	9	10	–	–	4	–	–	–	–	–	5	–	–	–	–	–	8	–	1	D.Taylor
19	1	2*	3	–	–	6	11	7	9	10	–	12*	4	–	–	–	–	–	5	–	–	–	–	–	8	–		H.Barr
20	1	–	3	4†	–	6	–	7*	9	10	–	12*	14†	–	2	–	–	–	5	–	–	8	11					A.Snoddy
21	1	–	3	4	–	6	–	7	9	10	–	–	–	–	2	–	–	–	5	–	–	8	11					L.Irvine
22	1	–	3	4	–	6	12*	7†	9	10*	–	–	14†	–	2	–	–	–	5	–	–	8	11					J.Ferry
23	1	5	3	4†	–	6	–	7*	9	10	–	–	12*	–	2	–	–	–	–	14†	–	8	11					D.Magill
24	1	–	–	4	–	6	–	7*	9	10	–	–	3	–	2	–	–	–	5	–	12*	8	11					L.Irvine
25	1	–	–	4	–	6	–	7*	9	10	–	–	3	–	2	–	–	–	5	–	12*	8	11					F.McDonald
26	1	–	3	4	–	–	–	7	9	10	–	12*	–	6	2	–	–	–	5	–	–	8	11*					J.Ferry
27	–	–	3	4	–	6	–	7	9	10*	–	12*	14†	–	–	–	–	–	5	–	–	8	1	11	2†			G.Keatley
28	–	6	–	–	5	–	14†	–	15°	10†	8*	9	3°	–	12*	4	–	–	–	7	–	–	11	2	1			M.Ross

PLAYER PROFILE - LEE DOHERTY

At Mourneview Park Lee Doherty swept all before him last term. The 33 year-old midfielder was voted 'Player of the Season' by Glenavon supporters and supporters' clubs alike. It all added up to a thunderous affirmation of the renaissance in his playing career over the past 12 months. "Yes, I was obviously delighted to be chosen for so many awards," he says. "It wasn't something which I had expected – although I felt personally that things had gone well for me – but it was a terrific boost nonetheless."

Collecting personal honours was a fairly common experience for Lee during 14 success-filled seasons at Windsor Park. News of Lee's intention to leave Linfield had broken in May 1994 shortly after the Blues had clinched their 42nd Championship title and 34th Irish Cup win, pipping Glenavon and Portadown for the League and beating Bangor in the Cup Final. "During my final season I was in and out of the side,' he recalls. "When I got a chance in the team I thought that I did quite well, but as time went on those opportunities became fewer and fewer in number." But there was more to the parting of the ways between Linfield and Lee Doherty than Trevor Anderson's selection policy. "To be honest my dispute with the club was over the length of contract which I was offered at the end of the 1993-94 season. They wanted me to sign a one-year deal and I was adamant that I wanted at least two years." Glenavon, of course, were prepared to satisfy Lee's contractual requirements during the summer of 1994. However, two years later, there was to be no immediate meeting of minds between Lee and the club. "Back in May, when the chairman and I talked about a new deal, I asked for a contract which would have taken me through until the end of the 1997-98 season. Having performed so well during the previous 10 months and feeling as fit as I did I felt confident that I could play for at least two more years at the top level and that's still my view now, but the board of directors were only prepared to talk to me in terms of a 12 month deal. There's no hiding the fact that I was disappointed by the club's approach, but I agreed to put pen to paper nonetheless. I have enjoyed myself so much here that I felt I owed something to the club and the supporters."

Lee, who missed both Glenavon's Co.Antrim Shield win in January and Irish Cup final appearance in May, is optimistic about the Lurgan club's prospects for the 1996/97 campaign. "I feel very excited about our chances of landing silverware this season," he enthuses. "Since Nigel Best came to the club he has been steadily building up a squad. Twelve months ago we brought in the likes of Gary Smyth, Mark Glendinning and Dermot O'Neill, then during the season just past we signed Stuart Gauld and Tony Shepherd. These are all quality players who have been successful at other clubs and know what it taked to win major trophies. Like every other team in the League I still feel we can strengthen further, but if we can avoid injuries and suspensions I would be very hopeful that we'll be in there battling for the major honours again this season."

George Ruddell

GLENAVON APPEARANCES FOR 1995/96

Name:	UC	GC	ILC	CC	BIC	CAS	UEF	PL	Total
1 Stephen McBride	5	3	4	3	6	4	4	28	57
2 Mark Glendinning	5	3	3	3	6	4	4	25	53
3 Dermot O'Neill	5	3	4	3	5	4	4	25	53
4 Gary Smyth	5	3	3	2	6	4	4	24	51
5 Glenn Ferguson	5	3	2	2	6	3	4	23+(1)	48+(1)
6 Sammy Johnston	5	2	4	1	6	3	4	18+(6)	43+(6)
7 Raymond McCoy	3+(2)	-(3)	4	-(2)	2+(3)	2+(1)	2+(2)	14+(7)	27+(20)
8 Lee Doherty	4	3	4	2	5	1	3	23	45
9 John Smyth	4	3	4	1+(1)	5	3	3	20	43+(1)
10 Darren Murphy	2	1	1+(2)	1+(1)	1+(4)	4	1	18+(8)	29+(15)
11 Paul Byrne	3	1+(1)	4	3	1	4	3+(1)	16+(3)	35+(5)
12 Sean Collins	1+(3)	3	1+(3)	1	-(2)	3+(1)	1+(2)	5+(9)	15+(20)
13 Stuart Gauld	-	-	-	3	5	2	-	16	26
14 Stephen Brown	3	1	3	2+(1)	1	-(1)	4	7+(1)	21+(3)
15 Tony Shepherd	-	-	-	1	5	-	-	11	17
16 Alan Murphy	2+(1)	3	2	-	-	-	1+(1)	4+(1)	12+(3)
17 Danny Shipp	-	-	-	-	4	-(1)	-	9	13+(1)
18 Marc Kenny	2	1	-	1	1	1	1	5+(1)	12+(1)
19 Shane Mulholland	-	-	-	1	-	1+(2)	-	1+(4)	3+(6)
20 Darren Freeman	-	-	-	2	-	1	-	2	5
21 Nigel Birney	1+(1)	-	-(1)	-	-	-	1	1	3+(2)
22 Sean Burns	-	-	-	-	-	-(2)	-	2+(1)	2+(3)
23 James McCartan	-	-(1)	-	-	-	-(2)	-	2	2+(3)
24 Alex Russell	-	-	-	-	-	-	-	4	4
25 Paul Straney	-	-	-	-	1	-(1)	-	2	3+(1)
26 Donal Gray	-	-	-	1	-	-	-	2	3
27 Damian Grant	-	-	-	-	-	-	-	1	1
28 Phil McDonagh	-	-	1	-	-	-	-	-	1
29 Craig McAllister	-	-	-	-	-(1)	-	-	-	-(1)

GLENAVON GOALSCORERS FOR 1995/96

Name:	UC	GC	ILC	CC	BIC	CAS	UEF	PL	Total
1 Glenn Ferguson	7	2	-	1	9	2	-	9(1p)	30(1p)
2 Stephen McBride	5(1p)	1	3	1	5	3	-	9(1p)	27(1p)
3 Sammy Johnston	-	-	3	-	1	1	1	7	13
4 Raymond McCoy	-	-	-	1	3	1	-	8	13
5 Danny Shipp	-	-	-	-	2	-	-	6	8
6 Mark Glendinning	-	1	-	2	-	-	-	2	5
7 Darren Murphy	-	1	-	-	1	-	-	3	5
8 Sean Collins	-	-	1	-	-	3	-	-	4
9 Darren Freeman	-	-	-	1	-	2	-	-	4
10 Lee Doherty	-	2	-	-	1	-	-	-	3
11 Marc Kenny	-	-	-	-	1	1	-	-	2
12 Gary Smyth	1	-	1	-	-	-	-	-	2
13 John Smyth	-	-	-	-	-	-	-	2	2
14 Paul Byrne	-	-	-	1	-	-	-	-	1
15 James McCartan	-	-	-	-	-	1	-	-	1
16 Phil McDonagh	-	-	1	-	-	-	-	-	1
Total:	13	7	9	7	23	14	1	47	121

Ground: The Oval, Mersey Street, Belfast BT4 1FG (30,000) Founded: 1882
Tel: 01232 457670

Glentoran 1995/96
(Photograph by Thomas Sewell)

President:	**Summary of 1995/96 Season**
Mr.J.Nelson	In the year when 'Football Came Home' the Bass Irish Cup came home to
Chairman:	East Belfast after a absence of six years. On a sunny May afternoon Lon-
Mr.D.Chick	doner Glen Little was Glentoran's hero with a super strike from 20 yards
Treasurer:	for the only goal of the game against Glenavon.
Mr.E.Brownlee	It had been a strange season for manager Tommy Cassidy and the team.
Secretary:	Despite the signings of Darren Finlay, Pete Batey, Dugald McCarrison
Mr.J.Warren	(loan), John Kennedy and a short-lived "now you see him, now you don't"
Manager:	from Liam Coyle, Cassidy constantly insisted that we were always a cou-
Tommy Cassidy	ple of players short of the finished article. The Glens were good enough to
Asst. Manager:	finish third in the inaugural Premier League without ever really threaten-
Billy Sinclair	ing to reach the top.
Reserve Team Manager:	In the secondary knock-out competitions the best performance was in reach-
Alan Paterson	ing the Coca-Cola Cup Final only to lose 1-3 to Cliftonville.
Physio:	One hoodoo was laid to rest in early November when Linfield were ham-
Mr.J.Miller	mered 4-0 in the League at Windsor Park to end a run of 12 games without
Club Colours:	a win against them. The Blues took some revenge during a farcical Boxing
Green/Black/Red shirts,	Day encounter played on a snow covered pitch for the most part with a
Black shorts,	white ball! This event even warranted a guest appearance clip on BBC2's
Green socks.	Fantasy Football League.
	One pleasing note was the emergence of two stars of the future. At right
	back Colin Nixon replaced the stalwart George Neill while towards the
	end of the season forward Andy Kirk had a run in the first team.

Off the field the club programme, The Gazette, scooped all the awards and the new home and away shirts have been manufactured by Le Coq Sportif. Also an Internet site has been launched on the World Wide Web.

So at the start of 1996/97 the Glens stand at the cross-roads. The potential is there to build on the Irish Cup success and an attractive trip to Prague, but pre-season results suggested that Cassidy is still a way short of his ultimate goal. Only time will tell.

Roy France.

MANAGER PROFILE — TOMMY CASSIDY

Date of Birth: 18/11/1950 Belfast.
Date of Appointment: June 1994.

PREVIOUS CLUBS:
As Player:
Ards Boys; Glentoran; Newcastle United; Burnley; Apoel Nicosia.

HONOURS:
As Player:
N.Ireland International 24 caps and 1 goal
Glentoran – **City Cup;** 1969/70;
Newcastle United – **Anglo-Italian Cup** 1972/73
Texaco Cup 1973/74
Burnley – **3rd Division Championship;** 1981/82;
Apoel – **Cyprus Knockout Cup;** 1984

AS MANAGER:
Cyprus League Championship; 1986.
Glentoran – **Gold Cup** 1994/95, **Irish Cup** 1995/96

SMIRNOFF PREMIER LEAGUE RECORD 1995/96

No:	Date:	Ven:	Opponents:	Result:	H.T.	Pos:	Goalscorers:
1	Sep 30	A	Crusaders	1-2 L	0-1	-	Little (90)
2	Oct 7	H	Bangor	1-1 D	0-0	5	(J) Devine (90)
3	Oct 14	A	Cliftonville	0-0 D	0-0	5	-
4	Oct 21	H	Portadown	1-1 D	0-1	5	Batey (83)
5	Oct 28	H	Ards	3-2 W	3-1	5	(T) Smith (21), Nixon (33), Cunnington (37)
6	Nov 4	A	Linfield	4-0 W	1-0	3	Cunnington (32), McBride (81), McCarrison (84), Little (90)
7	Nov 11	H	Glenavon	0-2 L	0-2	5	-
8	Nov 18	H	Crusaders	3-1 W	0-1	4	McBride (48,84), (T) Smith (75)
9	Nov 25	A	Bangor	6-1 W	1-0	4	Batey (32), Kennedy (70), Cunnington (75), Cook (80,84), McBride (89)
10	Dec 2	H	Cliftonville	1-1 D	1-0	4	Coyle (16)
11	Dec 9	A	Portadown	1-3 L	0-1	4	Batey (6)
12	Dec 16	A	Ards	4-1 W	2-0	4	Finlay (32), Batey (38), (T) Smith (49), McBride (55)
13	Dec 26	H	Linfield	0-3 L	0-1	-	-
14	Jan 1	A	Glenavon	3-2 W	0-1	-	(M) Smyth (74), Little (80,87)
15	Jan 6	A	Crusaders	3-1 W	0-1	3	Cook (74), Mathieson (81), Little (90)
16	Jan 13	H	Bangor	3-0 W	1-0	3	Cook (2), Batey (75), Little (80)
17	Jan 27	A	Cliftonville	0-1 L	0-1	3	-
18	Feb 3	H	Portadown	3-3 D	1-2	3	Nixon (39), Little (56), (T) Smith (75)
19	Feb 10	H	Ards	3-1 W	1-0	3	Coyle (12), Finlay (68), (T) Smith (88)
20	Feb 17	A	Linfield	0-2 L	0-1	4	-
21	Mar 2	H	Glenavon	1-2 L	1-1	5	Coyle (15)
22	Mar 16	H	Crusaders	2-2 D	1-2	5	McBride (18), (J) Devine (pen 51)
23	Mar 23	A	Bangor	1-1 D	0-1	5	Parker (73)
24	Mar 30	H	Cliftonville	2-1 W	1-0	5	Coyle (29), McBride (62)
25	Apr 6	A	Portadown	2-3 L	1-1	5	Little (37), McBride (67)
26	Apr 8	A	Ards	2-0 W	0-0	-	(T) Smith (61,74)
27	Apr 20	H	Linfield	3-0 W	3-0	4	Little (24), (M) Smyth (27), Batey (35)
28	Apr 27	A	Glenavon	3-1 W	2-0	3	Cook (23,36), Kirk (81)

Final League Position: 3rd

PREMIER LEAGUE LINE-UPS 1995/96

Match No	D.Devine 4	G.Neill 4	M.Smyth 24	C.McCaffrey 2	J.Devine 24	D.Parker 16+(4)	J.Quigley 15+(3)	G.Little 22	T.Smith 11+(5)	D.Cook 12+(9)	P.Batey 23	R.McEvoy 1+(2)	D.Finley 8+(6)	A.Mathieson 10+(5)	N.Armstrong 22	J.Kennedy 20+(3)	R.McDowell 0+(1)	C.Nixon 24	D.McCarrison 7+(4)	E.Cunnington 13	D.Kelly 1+(5)	J.McBride 23+(1)	L.Coyle 9+(3)	C.Walker 11+(1)	J.Houston 0+(1)	B.Hutchinson 2	P.Leeman 0+(1)	A.Kirk 0+(1)	S.Elliott 0+(1)	Referee
1	1	2	3	4	5	6*	7	8	9°	10	11	12*	14†	15†°																J.Ferry
2	-	2	3	6†	5	4*	7	8	-	9	11	12*	10	-	1	14†	15°													A.Snoddy
3	-	-	3	-	5	6	7	-	9	12*	-	-	10†	-	1	4	-	2	8*	11	14†									D.Magill
4	-	-	3	-	5	6*	7†	-	-	12*	10	-	-	-	1	4	-	2	9	11	14†	8								H.Barr
5	-	-	3	-	5	-	12*	6	9	-	10	-	-	-	1	4	-	2	7†	11	14†	8*								D.Magill
6	-	-	3	-	5	6	-	8	-	-	10	-	-	-	1	4	-	2	7	11	-	9								J.Fery
7	-	-	3	-	5	6†	12*	8	-	-	10*	-	-	-	1	4	-	2	7	11	14†	9								L.Irvine
8	1	-	3	-	5	6*	12*	8	9	-	10	-	-	-		4	-	2	-	11	-	7								G.Keatley
9	-	-	3	-	5	12*	6	8*	-	14†	10	-	-	-	1	4	-	2	9†	11	-	7								D.Taylor
10	-	-	3	-	5	6	8†	-	-	12*	-	-	14†	-	1	4	-	2	10*	11	-	7	9							F.McDonald
11	-	-	3	-	5	12*	7°	-	9	-	10	-	-	6*	1	4	-	2	14†	11	15°	8†	-							L.Irvine
12	-	-	-	-	5	12*	6	8*	9†	14†	10	-	3	-	1	4	-	2	15°	11	-	7°	-							H.Barr
13	-	2*	-	-	-	6†	8	9	-	10	-	3	14†	-	1	4	-	5	-	11	-	7	-	12*						A.Snoddy
14	-	3°	-	-	-	8	9*	12*	10	-	15°	6	-	-	1	4	-	2	14†	11†	-	7	-	5						M.Ross
15	-	-	3	-	5	-	-	8	12*	9	10	-	-	14†	1	4	-	2	-	11†	-	7	-	6*						H.Barr
16	-	-	3	-	5	-	-	8	14†	9†	10	-	7	15°	1	4	-	2°	12*	-	-	11*	-	6						J.Ferry
17	-	-	3	-	5	6*	-	8	14†	9†	10	-	-	7	1	-	-	2	-	-	11	12*	4							D.Magill
18	-	-	3	-	5	6	-	8	14†	9*	-	-	10†	7	1	-	-	2	-	-	11	12*	4							G.Keatley
19	-	-	3	-	5	-	-	8	9	-	-	-	6*	7	1	14†	-	2	-	-	11	10†	4	12*						E.Millar
20	-	-	3	-	5	-	-	8	14†	12*	10	-	-	7	1	4	-	2	-	-	11	9*	6†	-						D.Magill
21	1	-	3	-	5	12*	6	8	-	9	10	-	-	-		4	-	2	-	-	11*	7	-	-						L.Irvine
22	-	-	3	-	5	-	7	8	-	9*	10	-	-	-	1	4	-	2	-	-	11	12*	6	-						A.Snoddy
23	-	-	3	-	5	6	-	8	-	9	10	-	-	2	1	4	-	-	-	-	11	7	-	-						F.Hiles
24	-	-	3†	-	6	5	8	-	12*	10	-	14†	7	-		4	-	2	-	-	11	9*	-	-	1					M.Ross
25	-	-	3	-	5	6°	7*	8	-	12*	10	-	15°	14†	-	4	-	2†	-	-	11	9	-	-	1					J.Ferry
26	-	-	-	-	5	6	7	-	11	9	10	-	3*	4	1	12*	-	-	-	14†	8†	2	-	-						G.Keatley
27	-	-	3*	-	5	6	-	8	-	9	10	-	12*	-	1	-	-	2	-	-	11	7	4	-	-					D.Magill
28	1	2	-	-	-	6*	10†	7°	9	-	-	3	11	-	-	-	5	-	-	8	-	-	4	-	-		12*	14†	15°	M.Ross

TRANSFERS C/S'95 TO APRIL '96

Players Signed:

Darren Finlay (Doncaster Rovers (Eng) c/s'95), Simon Houston (Distillery c/s'95), Glen Little (Crystal Palace c/s'95), Richard McEvoy (Bangor c/s'95), Rod Collins (Bangor Jul.'95), Derek McGill (Hamilton Academical (Sco) Aug.'95), Pete Batey (Bangor Sep.'95), John Kennedy (Distillery Oct.'95), Dugald McCarrison (Hamilton Academical (Sco) Oct.'95 loan), Liam Coyle (Derry City Dec.'95), Brian Hutchinson (Moyola Park Jan.'96).

Players Transferred:

Darren Hall (Ards Jul.'95), Gary Smyth (Glenavon Jul.'95), Donal O'Brien (Crusaders Aug.'95), Barney Bowers (Ards Sep.'95), Rod Collins (Coleraine Sep.'95), Derek McGill (Released Sep.'95), Robert Moore (Distillery Oct.'95), Dugald McCarrison (Hamilton Academical (Sco) Jan.'96 loan rtn); Roddy McDowell (Omagh Town Feb.'95), Jerome McAtee (Distillery Mar.'96), Richard McEvoy (Bangor Mar.'96); David Spence (Distillery Mar.'96).

HONOURS

Irish League, Champions/Premier League:	(19)	1893/94, 1896/97, 1904/05, 1911/12, 1912/13, 1920/21, 1924/25, 1930/31, 1950/51, 1952/53, 1963/64, 1966/67 1967/68, 1969/70, 1971/72, 1976/77, 1980/81, 1987/88, 1991/92 / 3rd 1995/96.
Irish Cup,Winners:	(16)	1913/14, 1916/17, 1920/21, 1931/32, 1932/33, 1934/35, 1950/51, 1965/66, 1972/73, 1982/83, 1984/85, 1985/86, 1986/87, 1987/88, 1989/90, 1995/96.
Gold Cup, Winners:	(11)	1941/42, 1950/51, 1959/60, 1961/62, 1965/66, 1976/77, 1977/78, 1982/83, 1986/87, 1991/92, 1994/95
Ulster Cup, Winners:	(8)	1950/51, 1952/53, 1966/67, 1976/77, 1981/82, 1982/83, 1983/84, 1988/89.
City Cup, Winners:	(16)	1895/96, 1896/97, 1898/99, 1910/11, 1911/12, 1913/14, 1914/15, 1931/32, 1950/51, 1952/53, 1956/57, 1964/65, 1966/67, 1969/70, 1972/73, 1974/75.
Co.Antrim Shield, Winners:	(20)	1900/02, 1908/09*, 1910/11, 1915/16, 1917/18, 1924/25, 1930/31, 1939/40, 1940/41, 1943/44, 1949/50, 1950/51 1951/52, 1956/57, 1967/68, 1970/71, 1977/78, 1984/85, 1986/87.
Irish League Cup, Winners:	(2)	1988/89, 1990/91
Budweiser Cup, Winners:	(2)	1987/88, 1989/90.
Blaxnit Cup, Winners:	(1)	1972/73
Irish League 'B' Division, Champions:	(6)	1958/59*, 1985/86*, 1986/87*, 1989/90*, 1992/93*, 1995/96*.
Steel & Sons Cup, Winners:	(11)	1904/05*, 1908/09*, 1910/11*, 1914/15*, 1918/19* 1932/33*, 1937/38*, 1957/58*, 1965/66*, 1966/67*, 1989/90*
IFA Intermediate Cup, Winners:	(9)	1893/94*, 1897/98*, 1908/09*, 1912/13*, 1915/16*, 1917/18*, 1930/31*, 1940/41*, 1961/62*
George Wilson Cup, Winners:	(4)	1965/66*, 1966/67*, 1979/80*, 1986/87*,
Louis Moore Cup, Winners:	(2)	1962/63*, 1965/66*
Irish Youth League, Champions	(1)	1995/96.
Irish Youth Cup, Winners:	(9)	1956/57, 1958/59, 1971/72, 1978/79, 1980/81, 1981/82, 1983/84, 1990/91, 1994/95.

Trophies won by Glentoran II
Most Capped player. W. Emerson 6 caps Ireland.

PLAYER PROFILE - ANDY MATHIESON

Glentoran's current beneficiary is Andy Mathieson, now into his twelfth season with the club, since signing way back as an 18 year old in November 1985. He went onto make his debut on Tuesday 6th may 1986 in a 1-1 draw with Cliftonville at The Oval and up to the start of the current season he had amassed 236 appearances (62 as substitute).

Just as important though to Andy is the 200 or so appearances made for Glentoran Seconds, including captaining them to the Steel & Sons Cup success of 1989. Andy netted in that match, a convincing 4-1 victory over East Belfast.

Down the years Andy has represented the Glens in nearly every position but, despite the Mr. Versatile tag, he has managed to score 40 goals for the first team. His most memorable strike came against Linfield at Windsor Park in a Boxing Day 1-1 draw in 1990. Andy recalls, "There were no TV cameras present but there was a hurricane blowing along with sleety rain and snow. I hit a free-kick from about 40 yards out and it went into the top corner. Did I mean it? Of course! After a few drinks it got further .....60 yards, 80 yards, bye-ball line!"

On a more serious note though Andy does now regret agreeing to play in so many different positions. He honestly admits, "It has affected my game. I wish I'd have stayed up front when I was scoring a few goals but at the end of the day I will try and give a 100% no matter what number I'm wearing."

Most people will know Andy had a spell at Old Trafford as a youth, rubbing shoulders with the famous before a brief sortie with Crewe Alexandra. There he played alongside another ex-Man. Utd. youth, David Platt. Andy has no regrets at all about not making it in England, "I represented my country at Under-18 level and had a great chance, but I simply was not good enough for League football. I came back home and still enjoyed myself doing something I love, playing football.

Who can argue with that? In fact during his time at the Oval the Glens have won every local trophy (18 in total) including the double in 1988. Mathieson's most prolific season was the Championship year of 1991/92 when he played in of the Glens 50 games, netting 18 times.

After the benefit season is over Andy has no definite plans for the future. He explains, "My contract is up in October 1997 so I'll see what happens then. Somehow I can't see myself playing for another club against a team I love so I'll probably retire."

If indeed that is the case then the Oval will have lost another trusty servant. All the best Andy.

Roy France.

GLENTORAN APPEARANCES FOR 1995/96

Name:	UC	GC	ILC	CC	BIC	CAS	PL	Total
1 John Devine	4	4	2	5	7	2	24	48
2 Michael Smyth	4	4	2	5	6	2	24	47
3 Justin McBride	1	1	2	5	7	2	23+(1)	41+(1)
4 Glen Little	4	3	2	3	5	1	22	40
5 Colin Nixon	-	1	-	4	6	2	24	37
6 James Quigley	2+(2)	3+(1)	2	3+(1)	2+(2)	1	15+(3)	28+(9)
7 Derek Cook	4	3	-	3	4	-(1)	12+(9)	26+(10)
8 Pete Batey	-	-	-	3	7	2	23	35
9 Darren Parker	1	1+(1)	-	3+(2)	4+(1)	1+(1)	16+(4)	26+(9)
10 Neil Armstrong	-	1	-	4	5	2	22	34
11 Trevor Smith	3	4	2	2	3+(2)	1	11+(5)	26+(7)
12 John Kennedy	-	1	-	2	4	2	20+(3)	29+(3)
13 Darren Finlay	3+(1)	3	1+(1)	1+(1)	2+(1)	-(1)	8+(6)	18+(11)
14 Chris Walker	2	3	-(1)	4	5+(1)	-	11+(1)	25+(3)
15 Andy Mathieson	3	3	-(1)	3	3	-	10+(5)	22+(6)
16 Liam Coyle	-	-	-	2+(2)	4	1	9+(3)	16+(5)
17 Eddie Cunnington	-	1	-	-	1	2	13	17
18 Declan Devine	4	3	2	1	2	-	4	16
19 Dugald McCarrison	-	-(1)	-	1	-	1	7+(4)	9+(5)
20 George Neill	3	3	2	1	-	-	4	13
21 Richard McEvoy	3+(1)	2+(1)	2	-	-	-	1+(2)	8+(4)
22 Damien Kelly	-	-(2)	-	-	-	-(1)	1+(5)	1+(8)
23 Conor McCaffrey	3	-	2	-	-	-	2	7
24 Roddy McDowell	-(1)	-(3)	-	-	-	-	-(1)	-(5)
25 Jonathan Houston	-	-	-	-(2)	-	-	-(1)	-(3)
26 Brian Hutchinson	-	-	-	-	-	-	2	2
27 Barney Bowers	-(1)	-	-(1)	-	-	-	-	-(2)
28 Stuart Elliott	-	-	-	-(1)	-	-	-(1)	-(2)
29 Colin Telford	-	-	-	-	-(1)	-(1)	-	-(2)
30 Derek McGill	-	-	1	-	-	-	-	1
31 Andrew Kirk	-	-	-	-	-	-	-(1)	-(1)
32 Paul Leeman	-	-	-	-	-	-	-(1)	-(1)
33 Robert Moore	-(1)	-	-	-	-	-	-	-(1)

GLENTORAN GOALSCORERS FOR 1995/96

Name:	UC	GC	ILC	CC	BIC	CAS	PL	Total
1 Justin McBride	-	2	1	5	2	1	8	19
2 Glen Little	3	-	-	1	4	-	9	17
3 Derek Cook	3	2	-	1	3	-	6	15
4 Pete Batey	-	-	-	2	1	3	6	12
5 Trevor Smith	1	1	-	2	1	-	7	12
6 Liam Coyle	-	-	-	1	1	-	4	6
7 Michael Smyth	-	-	-	1	1	-	2	4
8 Eddie Cunnington	-	-	-	-	-	-	3	3
9 Darren Finlay	-	-	-	-	1	-	2	3
10 John Devine	-	-	-	-	-	-	2(1p)	2(1p)
11 Dugald McCarrison	-	-	-	-	-	1	1	2
12 Colin Nixon	-	-	-	-	-	-	2	2
13 John Kennedy	-	-	-	-	-	-	1	1
14 Andrew Kirk	-	-	-	-	-	-	1	1
15 Andy Mathieson	-	-	-	-	-	-	1	1
16 James Quigley	-	-	1	-	-	-	-	1
17 Darren Parker	-	-	-	-	-	-	1	1
18 Own Goals	-	-	1	-	1	-	-	2
Total	7	5	3	13	15	5	56	104

Ground: Inver Park, Larne. (6,000); Founded: 1900.
Tel: 01574 74292

NO PHOTOGRAPH AVAILABLE FOR 1995/96

Chairman:
Mr.J.Black
Secretary:
Mr.R.Orr
Treasurer:
Mr.J.Roberts
Manager:
Shay Hamill
Club Colours:
Red shirts,
White shorts,
Red socks

Summary of 1995/96 Season

The failure to score goals was the real reason Larne's results failed so miserably to reflect the quality of their performances last season. However Larne manager Shay Hamill is confident his young squad will get much more reward for their endeavour in the forthcoming season.

In backing up his argument, Hamill crucially cites their matches in the new First Division against the Coleraine side that completely over-ran the opposition and had the title wrapped up months before the end of the campaign.

"Those four games are perfect for illustrating my point. We lost them all by a single goal, and we had four or five chances that went begging in every one of those games," said the Ballymena man, a St.Comgall's PE teacher in Larne.

"Indeed, their manager Kenny Shiels said we were by far the best side they played in the League."

It's a sad fact, indeed, that the Inver Park team only lost by a 1-0 scoreline on no fewer than twelve occasions and in the vast majority of those matches they were the better side and just couldn't get the ball in the net.

The main problem was that they were too dependent on Crawford McCrae to supply the finish. "He is a good player but nobody can carry the responsibility of needing to score in every game" reasoned Hamill.

"It was a good season in many ways but still goes down as an absolute disaster in terms of the record books. We didn't make any worthwhile progress in any of the cup competitions and finished second bottom of the First Division. That makes horrible reading."

THE NORTHERN IRELAND
football
Y E A R B O O K

"The most positive factor was the loyalty of the players. Okay, a couple, Stephen Collier and Robert Robinson, chose to follow David Jeffrey to Windsor Park during the summer. But lads like Larry McMahon, Mark Looney, Eamon McLaughlin and Dubois Elder have all pledged their wholehearted support and I believe we will make significant progress together, and success will be the due reward for their devotion to the club." he assured.

The departure of Jeffrey was singularly disappointing. He was recruited to be influential on and off the field but, after just a year, he felt he could give no more to the East Antrim club, and within weeks was snapped up by his old club Linfield.
Kevin Hughes.

MANAGER PROFILE — SHAY HAMILL

Date of Appointment: February 1995.

Previous Clubs:
As Player: Larne
As Manager: Larne (Reserve Team Manager);
Chimney Corner(Asst. Manager); Ballymena United
(Asst. Manager)

Honours:
As Player; None
As Manager: Chimney Corner - 'B' Championship
1984/85

TRANSFERS C/S'95 TO APRIL '96

Players Signed:

Michael Beckinsale (Ballyclare Comrades c/s'95), Gary Murray (Crusaders Jun.'95), David Armstrong (Ballyclare Comrades Aug.'95), Bill Cardwell (Ballyclare Comrades Aug.'95), Philip Leckey (Coleraine Aug.'95), Mark Looney (Queens University Aug.'95), David Straney (Ards Aug.'95), Stephen McDowell (Coleraine Sep,'95), Colin Stevenson (America Sep.'95), Andy May (Millwall Oct.'95), Liam Smyth (Glenavon Oct.'95), Chris Larkin (Coleraine (loan) Nov.'95), Ian Bustard (Ards Jan.'96), Dermot Doherty (Moyola Park Feb.'96), John McGuigan (Northern Telecom Feb.'96).

Players Transferred:

Colin Bell (Moyola Park c/s'95), Michael Cash (Bangor Jul.'95), Stephen Morrison (Alloa Jul.'95), Michael Boyle (Ards Aug.'95), Harry Kernoghan (Chimney Corner Aug.'95), Thomas McCourt (Ballymena United Aug.'95), Gavin McCrystal (Cliftonville Aug.'96), Gary Hillis (Distillery Nov.'95), Damien McNamee (Dungannon Swifts Nov.'95), Chris Larkin (Coleraine (loan rtn) Jan.'96), Michael Beckinsale (Ballyclare Comrades Feb.'96), Andy May (Released Feb.'96), Gary Murray (Loughgall Apr.'96).

HONOURS

Irish League / First Division		Best Position: 3rd 1925/26 / 7th1995/96
Ulster Cup, Winners:	(2)	1951/52, 1987/88
Irish League 'B' Division Champions:	(11)	1954/55, 1956/57, 1963/64, 1964/65, 1965/66, 1966/67, 1968/69, 1969/70, 1970/71, 1971/72, 1981/82*
Steel & Sons Cup, Winners:	(11)	1909/10, 1941/42, 1942/43, 1956/57, 1958/59, 1959/60, 1964/65, 1968/69, 1969/70, 1970/71, 1971/72
George Wilson Cup, Winners:	(5)	1958/59, 1959/60, 1968/69, 1970/71, 1978/79*
Louis Moore Cup, Winners:	(3)	1956/57 (shared with Banbridge Town), 1958/59, 1979/80,
IFA Intermediate Cup, Winners:	(3)	1942/43, 1958/59, 1969/70
Irish Youth Cup, Winners:	(1)	1977/78
Irish Junior Cup, Winners:	(1)	1900/01

Trophies won by Larne Olympic.

SMIRNOFF FIRST DIVISION RECORD 1995/96

No:	Date:	Ven:	Opponents:	Result:		H.T.	Pos:	Goalscorers:
1	Sep 30	A	Distillery	0-1	L	0-1	-	-
2	Oct 7	H	Ballyclare Comrades	2-0	W	0-0	4	McDowell (64), Armstrong (74)
3	Oct 14	H	Newry Town	1-2	L	0-1	7	McCrae (48)
4	Oct 21	A	Coleraine	0-1	L	0-1	7	-
5	Oct 28	H	Carrick Rangers	0-1	L	0-0	8	-
6	Nov 4	A	Ballymena United	0-0	D	0-0	7	-
7	Nov 11	H	Omagh Town	2-2	D	0-1	7	McMahon (53,90)
8	Nov 18	H	Distillery	2-0	W	0-0	6	McMahon (54), McCrae (78)
9	Nov 25	A	Ballyclare Comrades	3-2	W	1-1	5	Armstrong (4,87), McGreevy (og 83)
10	Dec 2	A	Newry Town	2-3	L	2-2	5	McCrae (9,45)
11	Dec 9	H	Coleraine	0-2	L	0-1	5	-
12	Dec 16	A	Carrick Rangers	0-1	L	0-1	6	-
13	Jan 1	A	Omagh Town	3-1	W	1-1	-	McCrae (27,84), Armstrong (89)
14	Jan 6	A	Distillery	1-0	W	0-0	6	May (68)
15	Jan 13	H	Ballyclare Comrades	0-1	L	0-1	7	-
16	Jan 27	H	Newry Town	1-1	D	0-1	6	McCrae (77)
17	Jan 31	H	Ballymena United	0-0	D	0-0	-	-
18	Feb 3	A	Coleraine	2-3	L	0-3	6	McMahon (49), Armstrong (53)
19	Feb 10	H	Carrick Rangers	3-1	W	1-0	7	Jeffrey (23), Bustard (74), McKnight (79)
20	Feb 16	A	Ballymena United	2-2	D	1-1	-	McMahon (2), Collier (83)
21	Mar 2	H	Omagh Town	1-3	L	0-1	5	Johnston (og 76)
22	Mar 16	H	Distillery	3-1	W	1-0	5	McCrae (16,47,64)
23	Mar 23	A	Ballyclare Comrades	1-1	D	1-1	5	Bustard (37)
24	Mar 30	A	Newry Town	0-2	L	0-0	5	-
25	Apr 6	H	Coleraine	1-2	L	1-0	6	McCrae (45)
26	Apr 9	A	Carrick Rangers	0-1	L	0-0	-	-
27	Apr 20	H	Ballymena United	0-1	L	0-0	6	-
28	Apr 27	A	Omagh Town	1-1	D	0-1	7	Armstrong (69)

Final League Position: 7th

FIRST DIVISION LINE-UPS 1995/96

MATCH No.	R.Robinson 28	N.Murray 20	D.Magill 5+(4)	J.McKinstry 21	D.Jeffrey 14	G.Hillis 5	M.Looney 18	P.Leckey 11+(2)	C.McCrae 25	D.Armstrong 22+(4)	S.McDowell 21+(3)	K.Doherty 0+(2)	E.McLoughlin 9+(3)	L.McMahon 24+(2)	H.McConkey 14	S.Collier 19+(2)	D.McNamee 1	D.Elder 5+(4)	D.Straney 3+(3)	C.McKnight 6+(9)	A.May 10	D.Smyth 2	J.Johnston 3+(3)	E.Adams 1	C.Larkin 1	L.Smyth 3+(1)	S.Findlay 0+(5)	I.Bustard 10	B.McLoughlin 1+(4)	D.Doherty 5	Referee
1	1	2	3	4	5	6	7	8	9†	10	11*	12*	14†																		D.Malcolm
2	1	2	–	4	5	9	7	–	10	12*	3	–	11*	6	8																F.Hiles
3	1	2	–	4	5	11	8	–	10	9	–	12*	6*	7†	3	14†															G.Keatley
4	1	2	–	4	–	10†	7	11*	8	9	–	–	–	6	3	–	5	12*	14†												F.McDonald
5	1	2	–	4	–	8*	6	–	10	9	11	–	–	7	5	3	–	–	–	12*											D.Taylor
6	1	–	2	4	5	–	8	–	7	9*	11	–	–	12*	3	–	–	–	14†	10†	6										R.Lutton
7	1	2	12*	4*	5	–	7	–	8	–	11	–	–	9	3	–	–	–	14†	10†	6										E.Millar
8	1	–	2	–	5	–	7	14†	11	9	4	–	–	10	3	–	–	–	–	12*	8	6									G.Douglas
9	1	2	–	–	5	–	7	6	11	10	8	–	–	9	4	3	–	–	–	–	–	–	12*								H.O'Neill
10	1	2	–	–	5	–	7	6	10	9	11	–	–	4	3	12*	–	–	–	8*	–	–									D.Chambers
11	1	2	12*	–	–	7	5	–	10	9°	11	–	15°	8	4	3	–	–	–	–	6*	14†									N.Cowie
12	1	2	4	–	–	–	–	8	9	11	–	–	14†	7	–	3	–	–	–	12*	–	–	–	–	–	6	5	10			G.Keatley
13	1	2	–	4	–	–	–	7	10	9	8	–	–	5	–	3	–	11	–	6											G.McKay
14	1	2	–	4	–	–	–	–	9	10	8	–	–	5	7	3	–	11	–	6											M.Ross
15	1	2†	–	4	5	–	–	–	8	9	11	–	–	12*	7	3	–	10*	–	6	–	14†									D.Taylor
16	1	2	–	4	–	–	–	8	10	12*	–	–	5	–	6	3	–	–	11*	9	–	–	–	–	–	–	–	7			J.Peden
17	1	–	6	4	5	–	–	7	9	12*	11	–	10	2	3*	–	–	–	–	8											J.Peden
18	1	2	–	4	5	–	–	7†	9	12*	11	–	–	6	–	3	–	14†	10*	8											P.Thompson
19	1	2*	–	4	5	–	–	12*	10°	9	11	–	–	8	–	3	–	–	15°	–	–	–	–	–	–	14†	–	6	–	7	D.Malcolm
20	1	2*	–	4	–	–	–	11	10†	–	14†	–	–	6	–	3	–	–	9	–	–	5	–	8	–	7	–	12*	–		L.Irvine
21	1	2	–	4	–	–	6	11*	9	12*	–	–	10	–	–	3	–	–	–	14†	–	5	–	8†	–	7					F.Hiles
22	1	2*	12*	4	5	–	7	–	9	10	11†	–	–	6	–	3	–	–	15°	–	–	–	–	–	–	–	–	8	14†		P.Thompson
23	1	2†	14†	4	5	–	7	–	9	10	11*	–	–	6	–	3	–	–	15°	–	–	–	–	–	–	–	–	8	12*		E.Millar
24	1	–	–	–	–	–	7	–	9	10	8	–	11	6	–	3	–	4	–	15°	–	–	–	–	–	14†	5	2	–		J.Peden
25	1	–	–	–	–	–	7	–	9†	10	6	–	11*	8	–	3	–	4	–	14†	–	–	–	–	–	12*	5	–	–	2	R.Lutton
26	1	–	–	4	–	–	7	–	–	9	10	–	11	8	–	3	–	2	–	12*	–	–	–	–	–	14†	5	–	–	6*	D.Malcolm
27	1	–	–	4	–	–	7	–	9†	–	–	11*	10	–	–	3	–	5	–	12*	–	–	–	–	–	14†	8	–	–	6	J.Peden
28	1	–	–	4	–	–	6	–	–	10†	12*	–	11	8	–	3	–	5	–	9	–	–	–	–	–	15°	7°	14†	2*	–	E.Millar

ALSO PLAYED: J.McGuigan Ma.24 No.12 Ma.25 No.2 = 1+(1)*

PLAYER PROFILE – CRAWFORD MCCRAE

Crawford McCrae has a unique distinction in local football, he has scored nine goals in a single match!

That was four years ago when he was playing for Crusaders Reserves who were 10-1 winners that day in a 'B' Division match against Carrick Rangers at Taylor's Avenue, his hometown team.

During his time at Seaview Crawford went on to win a Gold Cup and Ulster Cup winners medal with Crusaders but an enforced absence through injury was his downfall and he couldn't command a regular first team place when he returned.

That was something he didn't want. He had suffered more than enough of the hard life with his previous club, Linfield, and he was itching for first team football on a weekly basis. The lad had given his heart and soul for the blue jersey of Linfield, spending five years at Windsor Park and, when he had his apprenticeship served, discovered that he rarely got beyond the substitutes bench.

Having joined the Belfast club as a schoolboy, he won a host of honours at underage level including two cup and three league medals with the Colts, and also a 'B' Division Championship medal with the Swifts.

The glory of playing for Linfield was great and he enjoyed his years there, but the opportunity he craved to make it into the first team week in week out never materialised.

When Roy Walker brought him to the Shore Road club his dream seemed to have come true. But, after that spell on the sidelines and his failure to command a regular slot, he became disillusioned once more.

Then came the chance to join Larne and he jumped at it. Injury once more threatened his progress but, after regaining full fitness he was an instant hit this time, and he finished last season as top scorer with 14 goals.

"I'm enjoying it tremendously. The club has obvious financial problems but the players showed their feelings for the management and supporters by voluntarily taking a cut in wages last year to play their part in our survival." he revealed.

"Not many groups of players would have done that, but that is an indication of how much we enjoy playing for Larne. Everybody at the club works hard, none more so than manager Shay Hamill. He has a great rapport with us. I'm enjoying my football more than ever before and I just hope I can keep on scoring plenty of goals for the club." said the 25 year-old Storeman.
Kevin Hughes.

LARNE APPEARANCES FOR 1995/96

Name:	UC	GC	ILC	CC	BIC	CAS	FD	Total
1 Robert Robinson	3	3	2	2	2	2	28	42
2 David Armstrong	3	3	2	1+(1)	1	2	22+(4)	34+(5)
3 Larry McMahon	1	2	-(1)	2	2	2	24+(2)	33+(3)
4 John McKinstry	3	3	2	2	2	-	21	33
5 Stephen Collier	3	3	2	1	2	1	19+(2)	31+(2)
6 Crawford McCrae	-	1	-	1	1	2	25	30
7 Noel Murray	2	2	2	1	2	1	20	30
8 Stephen McDowell	-	-	-	1	1+(1)	2	21+(2)	25+(4)
9 Mark Looney	3	3	2	-	-	2	18	28
10 Harry McConkey	3	2+(1)	1	2	1	2	14	25+(1)
11 Philip Leckey	1+(2)	2+(1)	-	2	2	1+(1)	11+(2)	19+(6)
12 David Jeffrey	2	3	2	1	-	2	14	24
13 Eamon McLaughlin	3	2	2	1	-	1	9+(3)	18+(3)
14 Colin McKnight	-	-	-	1	1	-(1)	6+(9)	8+(10)
15 Darryn Magill	-(2)	-(2)	-	-(1)	-(1)	1	5+(4)	6+(10)
16 Andy May	-	-	-	1	2	-	10	13
17 David Straney	2	1+(1)	1+(1)	1	-	-	3+(3)	8+(5)
18 Gary Hillis	1+(2)	1+(2)	1	-	-	-	5	8+(4)
19 Ian Bustard	-	-	-	-	1	-	10	11
20 Jackie Johnston	-	-	-	1+(1)	1	-(2)	3+(3)	5+(6)
21 Dubois Elder	-	-	-	-(1)	-	-	5+(4)	5+(5)
22 Liam Smyth	-	-	-	1	1	1+(1)	3+(1)	6+(2)
23 Gary Murray	3	2	2	-	-	-	-	7
24 Dermot Doherty	-	-	-	-	-	-	5	5
25 Bryan McLoughlin	-	-	-	-	-	-	1+(4)	1+(4)
26 Stuart Findlay	-	-	-	-	-	-	-(5)	-(5)
27 David Smyth	-	-	-	-	-	-(1)	2	2+(1)
28 Damien McNamee	-	-	1	-	-	-	1	2
29 John McGuigan	-	-	-	-	-	-	1+(1)	1+(1)
30 Kieran Doherty	-	-	-	-	-	-	-(2)	-(2)
31 Eddie Adams	-	-	-	-	-	-	1	1
32 Chris Larkin	-	-	-	-	-	-	1	1

LARNE GOALSCORERS FOR 1995/96

Name:	UC	GC	ILC	CC	BIC	CAS	FD	Total
1 Crawford McCrae	-	-	-	-	1	2	11	14
2 David Armstrong	-	1	-	-	1	1	6	9
3 Larry McMahon	-	-	-	-	-	-	5	5
4 Ian Bustard	-	-	-	-	-	-	2	2
5 Stephen Collier	-	-	-	-	1	-	1	2
6 Gary Murray	-	-	2	-	-	-	-	2
7 David Jeffrey	-	-	-	-	-	-	1	1
8 Mark Looney	-	-	1	-	-	-	-	1
9 Stephen McDowell	-	-	-	-	-	-	1	1
10 Colin McKnight	-	-	-	-	-	-	1	1
11 Andy May	-	-	-	-	-	-	1	1
12 Own Goals	-	-	-	-	-	-	2	2
Total:	**0**	**1**	**3**	**0**	**3**	**3**	**31**	**41**

Ground: Windsor Park, Belfast (28,500)   Founded: 1886.
Tel: 01232 323703

NO PHOTOGRAPH AVAILABLE FOR 1995/96

President:
Mr.W.Weir
Chairman:
Mr.W.McCoubrey
Hon.Treasurer:
Mr.D.Crawford
Secretary:
Mr.D.Brooks
Manager:
Trevor Anderson
Asst.Manager:
David Jeffrey
Physiotherapist:
Terry Hayes
Club Colours:
Royal Blue shirts,
White shorts,
Red socks

Summary of 1995/96 Season

Goals or to be precise, the lack of goals, dominated the 1995/96 season for Linfield. Beginning with the controversial departure of Garry Haylock, top scorer for the previous two seasons, the main talking point among fans at the start of the new Premier League set-up was could he be replaced. Nine long barren months later after enduring a full month without a single goal the same fans were reflecting on this fact, the combined tally of Linfield's top four goalscorers didn't match Haylocks total for Portadown!

Paul Millar's 13 goals was the lowest post war total for Linfield's leading goalscorer and even more depressing on this front was the poor contribution of 7 goals from Darren Erskine recruited to fill the void after Haylock's departure. After the high of Liverpool's visit to Windsor Park in early August Linfield got down to business with an unsuccessful tiring trip to the Ukraine in the European Cup-Winners' Cup. The Wilkinson Sword League Cup provided Linfield with an early victory over cross town rivals Glentoran but the interest in this competition ended at Shamrock Park with the first of three penalty kick deciders the club were to contest. In the Ulster Cup a meeting with Crusaders in the semi-final produced one of the highlights of the season with a traditional spirited performance from a young Linfield side forced by injury to use reserve goalkeeper Andrew Caldwell in an outfield role. The Blues once again overcame Glentoran in the quarter-final of the Gold Cup despite being reduced to ten men when Dessie Gorman was sent-off. However Linfield were to lose both the Ulster and Gold Cup Finals to Portadown and Crusaders respectively.

THE NORTHERN IRELAND
football
Y E A R B O O K

In the inaugural Premier League the Belfast Blues didn't offer a serious challenge after a very indifferent first half of the season. The inability to put together a consistent run meant the end to the club's season following their exit from the Irish Cup at Seaview in early March. The clashes with Crusaders in particular had a significant impact on the Blues progress in 1995/96 as in nine meetings with the Shore Road club Linfield managed to win only one!

Injuries to key players including newcomers Stuart McLean and Alan Byrne made team selection difficult for manager Trevor Anderson at crucial stages of the season but this wasn't offered as an excuse as other clubs suffered similar losses. The return of David Jeffrey as assistant manager in April was seen by many supporters as the first step to restoring passion and commitment within the club and the promised close season signings must prove themselves worthy of the task ahead. Too often during last season performances didn't match the stature of the players brought into the side, many recruited by Linfield on the strength of their reputation with other clubs. Although several young players were groomed during periods of injury and suspension with some success, the quality in depth would appear to be low judging by the number of fringe players transfer listed in May.

Michael Rudd

MANAGER PROFILE — TREVOR ANDERSON

Date of Birth: 03/03/1951 Belfast
Date of Appointment: October 1992

Previous Clubs:
As Player: Portadown; Manchester United; Swindon Town; Peterborough United; Linfield:
As Manager: Linfield (Youth Team Coach)

Honours:
As Player: N.Ireland International 22 caps 4 goals;
Irish League Representative 3 caps 1 goal
Linfield – **Irish League Championship**; 1979/80; 1981/82; 1982/83; 1983/84; 1984/85; 1985/86:
Irish Cup; 1979/80 and 1981/82:
Gold Cup; 1979/80; 1981/82; 1983/84; 1984/85:
Ulster Cup; 1979/80 and 1984/85:
Co.Antrim Shield; 1980/81; 1981/82; 1982/83; 1983/84:
Tyler All Ireland Cup; 1980/81

As Manager:
Linfield – **Irish League Championship**; 1992/93 and 1993/94;
Irish Cup; 1993/94 & 1994/95 **Budweiser Cup;** 1993/94;
Irish League Cup; 1993/94.
Co. Antrim Shield; 1994/95

SMIRNOFF PREMIER LEAGUE RECORD 1995/96

No:	Date:	Ven:	Opponents:	Result:	H.T:	Pos:	Goalscorers:
1	Sep 30	A	Glenavon	3-0 W	2-0	-	Brown (og 32), Fenlon (42), Erskine (74)
2	Oct 7	H	Crusaders	1-2 L	1-0	3	Fenlon (45)
3	Oct 14	A	Bangor	2-1 W	1-0	2	Ray.Campbell (44,65)
4	Oct 21	H	Cliftonville	0-0 D	0-0	2	-
5	Oct 28	A	Portadown	2-3 L	1-1	4	Erskine (35), Byrne (73)
6	Nov 4	H	Glentoran	0-4 L	0-1	5	-
7	Nov 11	A	Ards	3-2 W	2-0	4	Fenlon (pen 29,37), Ray.Campbell (56)
8	Nov 18	H	Glenavon	0-3 L	0-1	5	-
9	Nov 25	A	Crusaders	0-3 L	0-2	5	-
10	Dec 2	H	Bangor	0-0 D	0-0	5	-
11	Dec 9	A	Cliftonville*	1-1 D	0-1	5	Gorman (88)
12	Dec 16	H	Portadown	1-0 W	1-0	5	Erskine (23)
13	Dec 26	A	Glentoran	3-0 W	1-0	-	Ewing (22,57), McCoosh (68)
14	Jan 1	H	Ards	0-0 D	0-0	-	-
15	Jan 6	A	Glenavon	2-2 D	2-0	5	Johnston (9), Erskine (28)
16	Jan 13	H	Crusaders	0-1 L	0-0	5	-
17	Jan 27	A	Bangor	2-0 W	0-0	5	Millar (80,82)
18	Feb 3	H	Cliftonville	3-1 W	1-1	5	Ray.Campbell (32), Erskine (78), Millar (83)
19	Feb 10	A	Portadown	1-1 D	0-0	5	Fenlon (70)
20	Feb 17	H	Glentoran	2-0 W	1-0	5	Millar (36,70)
21	Mar 2	A	Ards	2-1 W	1-0	4	Johnston (23), Millar (67)
22	Mar 16	H	Glenavon	2-1 W	2-1	4	Beatty (7), Millar (38)
23	Mar 23	A	Crusaders	2-4 L	0-0	4	Ray.Campbell (47), Ewing (75)
24	Mar 30	H	Bangor	2-1 W	1-0	4	Ray.Campbell (45), Fenlon (83)
25	Apr 6	A	Cliftonville*	0-0 D	0-0	4	-
26	Apr 9	H	Portadown	0-1 L	0-1	-	-
27	Apr 20	A	Glentoran	0-3 L	0-3	5	-
28	Apr 27	H	Ards	0-0 D	0-0	5	-

Both matches played at Windsor Park for security reasons.
Final League Position: 5th

PREMIER LEAGUE LINE-UPS 1995/96

Match No	W.Lamont 15	A.Dorman 22	J.Easton 10+(1)	A.Ewing 14+(6)	S.McLean 3	S.Beatty 17+(3)	Ray.Campbell 21+(1)	D.Gorman 13+(2)	D.Erskine 15+(9)	P.Fenlon 22	N.Bailie 28	P.Millar 15+(2)	J.Hill 3	T.McIlroy 1+(5)	J.Hosick 4+(3)	D.Crawford 13	J.Spiers 24	P.McGee 7+(3)	A.Caldwell 0+(1)	P.Crothers 7	A.Byrne 4+(1)	J.Marks 1+(3)	M.Norbury 1	I.McCoosh 19	R.Johnston 12	P.Knell 5+(3)	R.McLaughlin 1+(1)	Rob.Campbell 5	P.McShane 5+(1)	M.Gamble 1	Referee
1	1	2	3	4	5	6	7	8*	9	10	11	12*																			A.Snoddy
2	1		3		5	6	7	8	9	10	11			4*	2†	12*	14†														G.Keatley
3		2		4	5*	6	7		9		11			10	8	1	3	12*													N.Cowie
4	1	2		4		6	7		9	10	11			12*	8*		5	3†	14†												R.Lutton
5	1		3			6	7	8*	9	10	11			12*			5			2	4										L.Irvine
6	1			3		6	7	8†	9*	10	11			14†	4		5			2		12*									J.Ferry
7	1	2				6	7		9	10	11	8					5				4	3									F.McDonald
8	1	2	3	4*		6	7			10	11	8					5							12*	9						A.Snoddy
9	1	2	3*	4†			7		9	10	11	6			14†		5							12*		8					L.Irvine
10		2				6	7		9†	10	11			14†		1	5				4*			3	8	12*					F.Hiles
11		2		14†		6	7†	8	12*	10	11			4*		1								3	9		5				G.Keatley
12		2		4					9		11					1	5			3				6	8	10		7			N.Cowie
13		2		4					9		11					1	5			3				6	8	10		7			A.Snoddy
14		2		4*		12*		14†	9†		11					1	5			3				6	8	10		7			G.Keatley
15		2		4		12*			9		11					1	5			3				6	8	10*		7			L.Irvine
16		2		4		12*		14†	9†		11					1	5			3				6	8	10*		7			M.Ross
17	1	2	3*			6	14†	7†		10	11	9					5							4	8	12*					F.McDonald
18	1	2	3	12*		6	7		14†	10*	11	9					5							4	8†						N.Cowie
19	1	2	3	5†		6	7		12*	10	11	9					5							4	8*	14†					J.Ferry
20	1	2		4			7	8*	12*	10	11	9					5							3					6		D.Magill
21	1	2	3			6*	7			10	11	9		12*			5	4						8							R.Lutton
22	1	2	3*			6	7	8†	14†	10	11	9					5	12*						4							J.Ferry
23	1	2		12*		6	7	8		10	11	9					5	3*						4							G.Keatley
24				4			7	8	14†	10	11	9†				1	5	12*						6					3	2*	D.Taylor
25		2°	12*		3		7	8†	14†	10*	11	9				1	5	6						4					15°		A.Snoddy
26							7	8*	12*	10†	11	9	2			1	5	6						4				14†	3		H.Barr
27			12*				7	8°	5°	10*	11	9	2†			1	5	6			14†			4					3		D.Magill
28		2	15°	14†				9	10†	11		12*				1	5	6		7°				4	8*				3		N.Cowie

TRANSFERS MAY'95 TO APRIL '96

Players Signed:
Alan Ewing (Coleraine Jun.'95), Stuart McLean (Coleraine Jun.'95), Darren Erskine (Ards Jul.'95), Paul Millar (Cardiff City Aug.'95), Alan Byrne (Shelbourne Oct.'95), Jamie Marks (Leeds United (Eng loan) Oct.'95), Mike Norbury (Doncaster Rovers (Eng loan) Nov.'95), Paul McGee (Bohemians (loan rtn) Jan.'96).

Players Transferred:
Jason Allen (Ballymena United Jun.'95), Garry Haylock (Portadown Jun.'95), John McConnell (Ballymena United Jun.'95), Gary Peebles (Portadown Jul.'95), Nigel Boyd (Ballymena United Aug.'95), Andy McDonald (Distillery Aug.'95), Mark Magill (Distillery Sep.'95), Paul McGee (Bohemians (loan) Oct.'96), Jamie Marks (Leeds United (Eng loan rtn) Nov.'96), Mike Norbury (Doncaster Rovers (Eng loan rtn) Nov.'96), Paul English (Crusaders Dec.'95), Jim Rankin (Ballyclare Comrades Mar.'96).

HONOURS:

Irish League, Champions/ Premier League:	(42)	1890/91, 1891/92, 1892/93, 1894/95, 1897/98, 1901/02, 1903/04, 1906/07, 1907/08, 1908/09, 1910/11, 1913/14, 1921/22, 1922/23, 1929/30, 1931/32, 1933/34, 1934/35, 1948/49, 1953/54, 1954/55, 1955/56, 1958/59, 1959/60, 1960/61, 1961/62, 1965/66, 1968/69, 1970/71, 1974/75, 1977/78, 1978/79, 1979/80, 1981/82, 1982/83, 1983/84, 1984/85, 1985/86, 1986/87, 1988/89, 1992/93, 1993/94 / 5th 1995/96.
Irish Cup, Winners:	(35)	1890/91, 1891/92, 1892/93, 1894/95, 1897/98, 1898/99, 1901/02, 1903/04, 1911/12, 1912/13, 1914/15, 1915/16, 1918/19, 1921/22, 1922/23, 1929/30, 1930/31, 1933/34, 1935/36, 1938/39, 1941/42, 1944/45, 1945/46, 1947/48, 1949/50, 1952/53, 1959/60, 1961/62, 1962/63, 1969/70, 1977/78, 1979/80, 1981/82, 1993/94, 1994/95.
Gold Cup, Winners:	(30)	1920/21, 1921/22, 1923/24, 1926/27, 1927/28, 1928/29, 1930/31, 1935/36, 1936/37, 1942/43, 1948/49, 1949/50, 1950/51, 1955/56, 1957/58, 1959/60, 1961/62, 1963/64, 1965/66, 1967/68, 1968/69, 1970/71, 1972/73, 1979/80, 1981/82, 1983/84, 1984/85, 1987/88, 1988/89, 1989/90.
Ulster Cup, Winners:	(15)	1948/49, 1955/56, 1956/57, 1959/60, 1961/62, 1964/65, 1967/68, 1970/71, 1971/72, 1974/75, 1977/78, 1978/79, 1979/80, 1984/85, 1992/93.
Co.Antrim Shield, Winners:	(36)	1888/89, 1903/04, 1905/06, 1906/07, 1907/08, 1912/13, 1913/14, 1916/17, 1921/22, 1922/23, 1927/28, 1928/29, 1929/30, 1931/32, 1932/33, 1933/34, 1934/35, 1937/38, 1941/42, 1948/49, 1952/53, 1954/55, 1957/58, 1958/59, 1960/61, 1961/62, 1962/63, 1965/66, 1966/67, 1972/73, 1976/77, 1980/81, 1981/82, 1982/83, 1983/84, 1994/95.
City Cup, Winners:	(22)	1894/95, 1897/98, 1899/00, 1900/01, 1901/02, 1903/04, 1907/08, 1909/10, 1919/20, 1921/22, 1926/27, 1928/29, 1935/36, 1937/38, 1949/50, 1951/52, 1957/58, 1958/59, 1961/62, 1963/64, 1967/68, 1973/74.
Irish League Cup, Winners:	(3)	1986/97, 1991/92, 1993/94.
Budweiser Cup, Winners:	(1)	1993/94.
Tyler Cup, Winners:	(1)	1980/81.
Blaxnit Cup, Winners:	(1)	1970/71.
North South Cup, Winners:	(1)	1961/62.
Top Four Trophy, Winners:	(2)	1966/67, 1967/68.
Irish League 'B' Div. Champions:	(13)	1951/52*, 1952/53*, 1975/76*, 1977/78*, 1978/79*, 1979/80*, 1982/83*, 1983/84*, 1984/85*, 1987/88*, 1988/89*, 1990/91*, 1991/92*.
Steel & Sons Cup, Winners:	(8)	1895/96*, 1898/99*, 1915/16*, 1939/40*, 1946/47*, 1948/49*, 1972/73*, 1983/84*.
IFA Intermediate Cup, Winners:	(11)	1896/97*, 1898/99*, 1900/01*, 1921/22*, 1924/25*, 1928/29*, 1945/46*, 1948/49*, 1955/56*, 1956/57*, 1971/72*.
George Wilson Cup, Winners:	(8)	1953/54*, 1961/62*, 1965/66*, 1977/78*, 1980/81*, 1983/84*, 1984/85*, 1988/89*.
Louis Moore Cup, Winners:	(3)	1970/71*, 1971/72*, 1977/78*.
Irish Junior Cup, Winners:	(3)	1891/92*, 1895/96*, 1906/07*.
IFA Youth Cup, Winners	(9)	1957/58, 1959/60, 1960/61, 1961/62, 1966/67, 1968/69, 1976/77, 1987/88, 1988/89.

Indicates trophies won by Linfield Swifts.
Most capped player; Robert G. Milne 27 caps for Ireland.

PLAYER PROFILE - IAN McCOOSH

Linfields' tough tackling all rounder Ian McCoosh has been at Windsor Park nine years although it is only within the past four seasons that he has made his presence felt. He joined Linfield in August 1987, a few months before his sixteenth birthday from Lisburn Youths, the former team of clubmate John Easton.

Ian's progress in Linfield Rangers side was hampered by two separate leg breaks over an eighteen month period, but this sickening experience was only a temporary setback for the brave Lisburn lad.

The first representative appearance of his career was made before his initial leg break when capped at Under-16 Youth level against Greece at Coleraine in September 1987. Further honours were gained at the end of 1988/89 season when again selected for the Northern Ireland Youth side this time at Under-17 level when he played against Scotland in Glasgow and the Republic of Ireland at Mourneview Park.

Whilst starring in the Rangers side Ian, in a defensive role, won two IFA Youth Cup medals and helped his team-mates Crawford McCrae, Noel Bailie, Darrin Wallace and David McCallan, all future first teamers, to many trophy successes in Dunmurry and District League.

The experience gained playing in the Liege Under-20 Tournament in July 1988 prepared Ian when promoted later that year to the Swifts side where he initially occupied a defensive position, but gradually with his eye for goalscoring opportunities moved to an attacking midfield role.

Two successive 'B' Division Championship medals were followed by a winners medal in the 1991 Liege Tournament and a further representative honour in a Junior International against North wales Coast F.A. when he scored one of Northern Ireland's goals.

Season 1991/92 saw him established as midfield anchorman in a Swifts side regularly complimented with first team players assisting his development at Windsor Park. Ian's goalscoring tally increased dramatically during this season with a couple of hat-tricks bringing him into double figures for the first time. Every medal except the Steel & Sons Cup was won during his spell in a very talented Swifts side.

The breakthrough to senior football came during Eric Bowyer's rein as Linfield manager and Ian's full debut was made against Coleraine on 5th September 1992 having already made six appearances as sub.. Within 16 weeks a first senior winners medal (the Ulster Cup) and his first senior goal, against Carrick Rangers, were confidently achieved.

In the past four seasons Ian has made 128 first team appearances with 15 goals to his credit and although not always an automatic choice he has nevertheless continued to give 110% commitment when selected. 'Basher', as he is known to fans and colleagues alike, attracted the attention of Glenavon a few seasons back but is firmly committed to Linfield his only senior club.

Linfield fans sincerely hope that Ian's thunderbolt goal against Portadown in last season's Ulster Cup Final will be repeated more often in the future as the powerhouse, who works as motor mechanic, continues to provide the drive in the Blues engine room.

Michael Rudd.

LINFIELD APPEARANCES FOR 1995/96

Name:	UC	GC	ILC	CC	BIC	CAS	CWC	PL	Total
1 Noel Bailie	6	6	3	3	3	1	2	28	52
2 Pat Fenlon	5+(1)	6	1+(1)	2	3	1	1	22	41+(2)
3 Darren Erskine	4+(2)	3+(1)	3	1	1+(1)	1	2	15+(9)	30+(13)
4 Alan Dornan	4	6	2	3	3	1	1	22	42
5 Raymond Campbell	4	6	3	1	2	1	2	21+(1)	40+(1)
6 Stephen Beatty	3+(2)	5	3	2	1	1	2	17+(3)	34+(5)
7 Jeff Spiers	1	3	-	3	3	1	2	24	37
8 Paul Millar	4+(1)	4+(1)	3	2+(1)	3	-	-	15+(2)	31+(5)
9 Wesley Lamont	4	6	3	2	2	1	2	15	35
10 Alan Ewing	3+(1)	1+(1)	-	1+(2)	2+(1)	-	2	14+(6)	23+(1)
11 Ian McCoosh	1+(1)	3	2	3	2	1	-(1)	19	31+(2)
12 John Easton	4	5	3	2	1	1	2	10+(1)	28+(1)
13 Dessie Gorman	4+(1)	3	2	1	1+(1)	-	1	13+(2)	25+(4)
14 Paul McGee	2+(2)	1+(1)	1+(2)	-	1+(1)	-	1	7+(3)	13+(9)
15 Richard Johnston	1	3	-	2	2	-	-	12	20
16 Darren Crawford	2	-	-	1	1	-	-	13	17
17 Philip Knell	1	1+(2)	-	1+(1)	-(1)	-(1)	-	5+(3)	8+(8)
18 Stuart McLean	5	3	3	-	-	-	1	3	15
19 Peter Crothers	1	-	1	1	-	-	1	7	11
20 Robert Campbell	1	-(1)	-	2+(1)	-	-	-	5	8+(2)
21 Pat McShane	1+(1)	-	-	-	1	-	-	5+(1)	7+(2)
22 Tommy McIlroy	2	-	-	-	1	-	-	1+(5)	4+(5)
23 Jackie Hosick	1	-	-	-	-	-	-	4+(3)	5+(3)
24 Jonathan Hill	2	-	-	-	-	-	-	3	5
25 Alan Byrne	-	-	-	-	-	-	-	4+(1)	4+(1)
26 Jamie Marks	-	-	-	-	-	-(1)	-	1+(3)	1+(4)
27 Ryan McLaughlin	-	1	-	-	-	-	-(1)	1+(1)	2+(2)
28 Andrew Caldwell	-(1)	-	-(1)	-	-(1)	-	-	-(1)	-(4)
29 Mike Norbury	-	-	-	-	-	1	-	1	2
30 Maurice Gamble	-	-	-	-	-	-	-	1	1

LINFIELD GOALSCORERS FOR 1995/96

Name:	UC	GC	ILC	CC	BIC	CAS	CWC	PL	Total
1 Pat Fenlon	3(1p)	2(1p)	-	-	1p	-	1	6(1p)	13(4p)
2 Paul Millar	-	1	1	2	2	-	-	7	13
3 Raymond Campbell	-	-	1	-	-	-	-	6	7
4 Darren Erskine	-	-	2	-	-	-	-	5	7
5 Dessie Gorman	-	3	-	1	2	-	-	1	7
6 Ian McCoosh	1	-	2	2	-	-	-	1	6
7 Alan Ewing	1	1	-	-	-	-	-	3	5
8 Richard Johnston	-	-	-	-	3	-	-	2	5
9 Stuart McLean	2	-	1	-	-	-	-	-	3
10 Stephen Beatty	1	-	-	-	-	-	-	1	2
11 Paul McGee	2	-	-	-	-	-	-	-	2
12 Alan Byrne	-	-	-	-	-	-	-	1	1
13 Alan Dornan	-	1	-	-	-	-	-	-	1
14 Jackie Hosick	1	-	-	-	-	-	-	-	1
15 Philip Knell	-	-	-	1	-	-	-	-	1
16 Ryan McLaughlin	-	1	-	-	-	-	-	-	1
17 Jeff Spiers	-	-	-	-	1	-	-	-	1
18 Own Goals	-	-	-	-	-	-	-	1	1
Total:	11	9	7	6	9	0	1	34	77

NEWRY TOWN

Ground: The Showgrounds, Newry (15,000) Founded: 1923
TEL: 01693 64551

Newry Town 1995/96
Back Row L-R: Peter Magee, Alan Berry, Brendan Keeley, Ciaran O'Kane, Tommy Mooney.
Front Row L-R: Tom Clarke, Ryan Watson, Kieran McParland, Ollie Ralph, Matthew Shields, John Feehan.
(Photograph courtesy of Jimmy Davis, Newry Reporter)

President: Mr.J.Grant **Chairman:** Mr.W.McVicker **Treasurer:** Mr.T.Preston **Secretary:** Mr.E.Cole **Manager:** Matt Bradley **Asst.Manager:** Ollie Ralph **Physio:** Declan McLaughlin **Club Colours:** Blue/White striped shirts, White shorts, Blue socks	**Summary of 1995/96 Season** Newry Town Football Club's Management Committee, Players and supporters must have been very much relieved to see the end of the 1995/96 season. Throughout the whole period enthusiasm was at a very low ebb and this was reflected in all departments throughout the club. True, the club started the season off on a bright note, but a series of defeats didn't help it's cause and from there on it was a struggling outfit. True, unlike other First Division clubs, Newry Town were fortunate to be at home to several top Premier League teams in various cup competitions, but, unfortunately, the main bulk of supporters of these clubs didn't think it was worth their while coming to Newry as the results were a forgone conclusion and as a consequence gate receipts suffered. Home support, too, dwindled away and only the really dedicated fans turned up to support the club at home games, but they got very little to cheer about. Then, just when it seemed as if Newry Town were about to turn the corner with a good cup run in prospect, their manager, Peter Watson, resigned, and this certainly didn't help matters. The resignation signalled the return of Matt Bradley as the club's manager. Matt, it will be recalled, steered the club to great heights in the late eighties, when he took over the position the club was in a more-or-less similar position after the resignation of Jim Hume.

On this occasion, however, try as he did, Matt Bradley was unable to steer Newry Town away from the 'wooden spoon' position in the League table and for the second time since the club returned to the senior scene in 1983 Newry Town had the embarrassment of having to reapply for senior status. They were duly reinstated at the expense of the up and coming Donegal Celtic, the Intermediate League side.

After the last ball had been kicked to end the disastrous season, the 'few men' still at the helm of the sinking club vowed to battle on and stated that never again would Newry Town be placed in such an embarrassing position.

At the Annual General Meeting there was a feeling of renewed determination prevailing and this could well result in a new lease of life oozing through all ranks of the club in the years to come.

Manager Matt Bradley has a mammoth task on his hands to make Newry Town a force in the First Division this coming season, but he has been in this position with the club before so there is a glimmer of hope for Newry Town's long suffering supporters.

Jimmy Davis.

MANAGER PROFILE — MATT BRADLEY

Date of Appointment: February 1996

PREVIOUS CLUBS:
As Player: Bangor; Drogheda United; Finn Harps; Newry Town:

As Manager: Newry Town (player/manager)

HONOURS:
As Player:
Drogheda United: **League Cup**; 1983/84
Newry Town: **Mid-Ulster Cup**; 1986/87

As Manager:
Newry Town: **Co.Antrim Shield**; 1986/87;
          Mid-Ulster Cup; 1986/87, 1989/90

TRANSFERS C/S'95 TO APRIL '96

Players Signed:

Stephen McQuaid (Camlough Rovers c/s'95), Fred Scappaticci (Banbridge Town c/s'95), Stephen Whelan (Ballymena United Jul.'95), Jim Barr (Park View Aug.'95), Tom Clarke (Neilstown Rangers (ROI) Aug.'95), Anthony Scappaticci (Glenavon (loan) Sep.'95), Anthony Scappaticci (Glenavon (loan) Jan.'96), Matthew Shields (Park View Mar.'96), Larry Griffen (Banbridge Town Mar.'96).

Players Transferred:

John Tumilty (Armagh City c/s'95), Des Edgar (Loughgall Jul.'95), Tom Gray (Banbridge Town Jul.'95), Raymond Byrne (Portadown Aug.'95), Larry Griffen (Banbridge Town Aug.'95), Anthony Scappaticci (Glenavon (loan rtn) Nov.'95), Paul Stokes (Cliftonville Dec.'95), Mark Gracey (Banbridge Town Feb.'96), Anthony Scappaticci (Glenavon (loan rtn) Mar.'96), Steven Thompson (Banbridge Town Mar.'96).

HONOURS:

Irish League/First Division:		Best Position: 3rd 1927/28 / 8th 1995/96.
Co.Antrim Shield, Winners:	(1)	1987/88
Mid-Ulster Cup, Winners:	(11)	1936/37, 1956/57, 1963/64, 1966/67, 1968/69, 1974/75, 1977/78, 1978/79, 1984/85, 1986/87, 1989/90
Irish League 'B'Division, Champions:	(2)	1959/60, 1980/81
IFA Intermediate Cup, Winners:	(3)	1957/58, 1966/67, 1980/81

Most capped player: None

SMIRNOFF FIRST DIVISION RECORD 1995/96

No:	Date:	Ven:	Opponents:	Result:	H.T:	Pos:	Goalscorers:
1	Sep 30	A	Ballyclare Comrades	1-1 D	1-1	-	Barr (11)
2	Oct 7	H	Ballymena United	1-2 L	1-1	6	Ralph (37)
3	Oct 14	A	Larne	2-1 W	1-0	5	(N) Watson (32), Ralph (88)
4	Oct 21	H	Omagh Town	1-2 L	0-1	5	(R) Watson (67)
5	Oct 28	A	Coleraine	0-8 L	0-1	7	-
6	Nov 4	A	Distillery	1-2 L	1-0	8	(S) Feehan (8)
7	Nov 11	H	Carrick Rangers	2-3 L	0-2	8	Clarke (pen 55), Barr (62)
8	Nov 18	H	Ballyclare Comrades	2-0 W	1-0	8	(S) Feehan (19), Barr (77)
9	Nov 25	A	Ballymena United	0-0 D	0-0	7	-
10	Dec 2	H	Larne	3-2 W	2-2	7	(S) Feehan (5), Barr (39,90)
11	Dec 9	A	Omagh Town	0-1 L	0-0	7	-
12	Dec 16	H	Coleraine	1-4 L	0-2	8	Mooney (58)
13	Jan 1	A	Carrick Rangers	1-3 L	0-1	-	Magee (65)
14	Jan 6	A	Ballyclare Comrades	2-3 L	1-1	8	Clarke (31), (C) O'Kane (59)
15	Jan 13	H	Ballymena United	1-0 W	1-0	8	Clarke (24)
16	Jan 27	A	Larne	1-1 D	1-0	8	Clarke (44)
17	Feb 3	H	Omagh Town	2-2 D	2-1	8	Barr (10,20)
18	Feb 6	H	Distillery	2-5 L	2-3	-	Clarke (pen 10, pen 29)
19	Feb 10	A	Coleraine	0-5 L	0-4	8	-
20	Feb 17	A	Distillery	1-1 D	0-1	8	Mooney (59)
21	Mar 2	H	Carrick Rangers	1-0 W	0-0	8	(C) O'Kane (83)
22	Mar 16	H	Ballyclare Comrades	3-0 W	3-0	8	Barr (25,40), Ralph (39)
23	Mar 23	A	Ballymena United	0-3 L	0-1	7	-
24	Mar 30	H	Larne	2-0 W	0-0	7	Barr (55), Clarke (pen 68)
25	Apr 6	A	Omagh Town	0-4 L	0-3	7	-
26	Apr 8	H	Coleraine	1-2 L	0-0	-	(J) Shields (82)
27	Apr 20	H	Distillery	0-2 L	0-2	8	-
28	Apr 27	A	Carrick Rangers	0-1 L	0-1	8	-

Final League Position: 8th

FIRST DIVISION LINE-UPS 1995/96

MATCH No	M.Campbell 11	K.McParland 15+(3)	A.Berry 7	C.O'Kane 22+(1)	F.Scappaticci 22	O.Ralph 23	S.Whelan 11+(3)	M.Gracey 6+(1)	B.O'Kane 21+(3)	J.Barr 22+(3)	T.Clarke 22+(2)	P.Stokes 3+(2)	R.Watson 23+(1)	T.Mooney 19+(3)	S.Feehan 11+(5)	N.Watson 10+(5)	S.Thompson 1+(1)	C.O'Hare 1	B.Keeley 16	N.Courtney 11+(4)	C.Lennon 2+(1)	M.McMahon 0+(3)	P.Magee 14+(1)	A.Scappaticci 7	N.Rees 0+(1)	L.Griffen 3	J.Shields 2+(3)	J.Feehan 2+(1)	S.Courtney 0+(2)	M.Shields 2	Referee
1	1	2†	3	4	5	6	7°	8	9	10	11*	12*	14†	15°																	M.Adair
2	1	–	3	4	5	6•	14†	10†	2	9	11	–	8	7	12*																G.Dobbin
3	1	14†	3	4	5	6	15°	–	2	9*	11†	12*	8	7	–	10°															G.Keatley
4	1	–	3°	4	5	6†	14†	–	2	12*	11	9	8	7	–	10*	15°														J.Peden
5	–	–		4	5	6	10*	11	2	12*	–	9	8	7	–	–	3	1													R.Lutton
6	–	–		4	5	6	7	3	12*	–	–	9	8	–	10*	2	–	–	1	11											R.Penney
7	–	–		4	5°	6	7	3	12*	14†	11	–	8	–	9	2	–	–	1	10	15°										T.Deegan
8	–	–	2	–	6	7	5	12*	10	11	–	8	14†	9	–	–	–		1	4	3										M.Ross
9	–	12*	–	2	5	6	–	14†	3	10	11*	–	8†	–	9	7	–	–	1	4	–										D.Malcolm
10	–	12*	–	2*	5	6	–	–	3	10	11	–	–	8†	9	7	–	–	1	4	–	14†									D.Chambers
11	–	2	–	–	5	6	–	–	3	10	11	–	8	12*	9†	7*	–	–	1	4	–	14†									H.Barr
12	–	2	–	–	5	6	–	–	3	10	11	–	8	7	9	–	–	–	1	4	–	14†	12*								T.Deegan
13	1	4	–	2	5	6†	–	–	3	10	–	8°	9	15°	14†	–	–			12*	11*	–		7							E.Millar
14	1	–	–	2	5	6	–	–	3	10	11	–	–	9	12*	8*	–	–		4	–	–		7							A.Snoddy
15	1	8	–	2	5	6	–	–	4	10	11	–	9	–	–	–	–							7		3					E.Millar
16	1	8	–	–	5	6	–	–	3	10	11	2	–	–	9*	–	–			12*				7	4						J.Peden
17	1	8	–	12*	5	6*	–	–	4	10	11	2	9	–	–	–	–							7		3					F.Hiles
18	1	8	–	–	5*	–	–	–	4	10	11	2°	9	6	14†	–	15°							7		3	12*				A.Snoddy
19	1	8	–	2	5	–	–	4	10°	11*	–	6	9	15°	14†	–	12*	–						7		3†	–				A.Snoddy
20	–	–	11	5	6*	10	–	4	–	7	–	2	8	9	12*	–	–		1	–	–	3	–								R.Lutton
21	–	–	7	5	6	9	–	4*	10	12*	–	2	11	–	–	–			1	–	–	8	3								J.Ferry
22	–	9	–	7	5	6	–	–	3	10	11	–	2	–	–	–			1	–	–	8	–	4							F.McDonald
23	–	8	–	6	5	–	7	–	10	11†	–	2	–	12*	–				1	3	–	9*	–	4	14†						N.Cowie
24	–	9	–	5	–	6	7	–	3	10	12*	–	2	8	–	–			1	–	–	11	–	4*	–						J.Peden
25	–	2	–	5	–	6†	–	3	10	11*	–	4	8	12*	–				1	–	9	–	–	14†							D.Taylor
26	–	2	4	3	–	–	7†	–	8	11	–	–	6	9*	–	–			1	5	–	–	14†	12*	–	10					E.Millar
27	–	2	3	5	–	6	–	–	11	–	4	8	–	–	–				1	–	–	9	–	–	10	12*	7				H.O'Neill
28	–	–	5	–	–	–	–	–	11	–	3	2	10	9*	–				1	7	–	8	–	–	6	4	12*	–			R.Lutton

PLAYER PROFILE - JIM BARR

A through and through Newry man who was deemed a few years ago as not being good enough to play senior football for his home town club, was in February 1996 presented with the Bass Irish Cup 'Personality of the Round' following Newry Town's shock 2-1 defeat of Coleraine.

When 27 year-old Jim Barr, who resides in Newry, joined Newry Town from National League of Ireland club Finn Harps in September 1992, he was unable to command a permanent place on the team and his senior football career seemed over when he decided to join local Carnbane League club Park View.

However Jim decided to give Irish League football one last crack when he again 'came home' at the beginning of last season.

At first he wasn't very impressive as it looked as if he once again was going to lose his chance to establish a reputation for himself in the Irish League, but his perseverance to keep going and his determination to improve his game eventually won him a permanent place in the Newry team.

Jim Barr started his Irish League career with Newry Town back in the late eighties, but after just one substitute appearance against Ards in 1987 Jim felt it was better to kick start his career elsewhere and joined League of Ireland side Monaghan United in October 1989.

After two successful seasons with Monaghan, where he not only won a regular place in the team but also ended up top scorer in his second season at Gortakeegan, Jim signed for First Division club Finn Harps in the summer of 1991. He lasted only one season with the Co.Donegal side, before deciding to return home.

The introduction of Promotion and Relegation in the Irish League has so far had a disastrous effect on the smaller clubs like Newry Town. Whereas the likes of Portadown and Linfield can splash out £30/40 thousand on a proven goalscorer, Newry Town have to rely on the home grown talents of players such as Jim Barr. If in the forthcoming season Jim can match or better his 15 goal tally of the last campaign then who knows what lies in store for the local boy made good!

Jimmy Davis

NEWRY TOWN APPEARANCES 1995/96

Name:	UC	GC	ILC	CC	BIC	CAS	MUC	FD	Total
1 Jim Barr	-(2)	1+(2)	2	2	2	1	2	22+(3)	32+(7)
2 Ollie Ralph	3	3	2	1	2	1	2	23	37
3 Tom Clarke	3	3	1	1	2	1	2	22+(2)	35+(2)
4 Barry O'Kane	3	1	2	2	2	-(1)	1	21+(3)	32+(4)
5 Ciaran O'Kane	-	3	2	2	2	1	2	22+(1)	34+(1)
6 Tom Mooney	2	2+(1)	-	2	2	-(1)	2	19+(3)	29+(5)
7 Kieran McParland	3	3	2	2	1	-	2	15+(3)	28+(3)
8 Fred Scappaticci	1	1	-	2	2	1	-	22	29
9 Brendan Keeley	3	3	2	-	1	1	2	16	28
10 Ryan Watson	-	1	-	1	1	1	-	23+(1)	27+(1)
11 Stephen Whelan	3	2	2	-(1)	-(1)	1	1	11+(3)	20+(5)
12 Neil Watson	1+(1)	-(1)	2	1	-	-(1)	1	10+(5)	15+(8)
13 Stephen Feehan	-	1+(1)	-	1	-(1)	1	-(1)	11+(5)	14+(8)
14 Niall Courtney	-(1)	-	-(2)	-(1)	-	1	1	11+(4)	13+(8)
15 Peter Magee	-	-	-	1	2	-	2	14+(1)	19+(1)
16 Mark Campbell	-	-(1)	-(1)	2	1	-	-	11	14+(2)
17 Mark Gracey	2	3	2	-	-	1	-	6+(1)	14+(1)
18 Paul Stokes	3	2+(1)	2	-	-	-	-	3+(2)	10+(3)
19 Anthony Scappaticci	-	1	-	2	2	-	-	7	12
20 Alan Berry	-	1	-	-	-	-	1	7	9
21 Stephen McQuaid	3	1	1+(1)	-	-	-	-	-	5+(1)
22 Steven Thompson	3	1	-	-	-	-	-	1+(1)	5+(1)
23 Matthew Shields	-	-	-	-	-	-	1+(1)	2	3+(1)
24 John Shields	-	-	-	-	-	-	-	1+(3)	1+(3)
25 Larry Griffen	-	-	-	-	-	-	-	3	3
26 John Feehan	-	-	-	-	-	-	-	2+(1)	2+(1)
27 Cathal Lennon	-	-	-	-	-	-	-	2+(1)	2+(1)
28 Maurice McMahon	-	-	-	-	-	-	-	-(3)	-(3)
29 Shane Courtney	-	-	-	-	-	-	-	-(2)	-(2)
30 Nigel Rees	-	-	-	-(1)	-	-	-	-(1)	-(2)
31 Colin O'Hare	-	-	-	-	-	-	-	1	1
32 David McGrath	-	-	-(1)	-	-	-	-	-	-(1)
33 David White	-(1)	-	-	-	-	-	-	-	-(1)

NEWRY TOWN GOALSCORERS FOR 1995/96

Name:	UC	GC	ILC	CC	BIC	CAS	MUC	FD	Total
1 Jim Barr	-	1	-	1	2	-	2	10	16
2 Tom Clarke	-	1p	1	-	-	-	1	7 (4p)	10 (5p)
3 Ollie Ralph	-	1	-	-	-	-	-	3	4
4 Stephen Feehan	-	-	-	-	-	-	-	3	3
5 Tom Mooney	-	-	-	1	-	-	-	2	3
6 Ciaran O'Kane	-	-	-	-	-	1	-	2	3
7 Peter Magee	-	-	-	-	-	-	1	1	2
8 Neil Watson	-	-	1	-	-	-	-	1	2
9 Stephen McQuaid	1	-	-	-	-	-	-	-	1
10 John Shields	-	-	-	-	-	-	-	1	1
11 Ryan Watson	-	-	-	-	-	-	-	1	1
12 Stephen Whelan	-	-	1	-	-	-	-	-	1
Total:	**1**	**3**	**3**	**2**	**2**	**1**	**4**	**31**	**47**

Ground: St.Julian's Road, Omagh (8,000)   Founded: 1964
Tel: 01662 242927 Fax:01662 242927

NO PHOTOGRAPH AVAILABLE FOR 1995/96

Chairman:
Mr.N.Hunter
Treasurer:
Mr.G.McCullough
Secretary:
Mr.P.Hunter
Manager:
Roy McCreadie
Asst.Manager:
Sean Davis
Physio:
Paddy Hunter
Team Attendant:
Kevin Lunny
Club Colours:
White shirts, Black shorts,
White/Red socks

Summary of 1995/96 Season

Town's 1995/96 season started with a heart stopping League Cup victory at Loughgall in August, 3-1 down with nine minutes left they scrambled back to draw level and won the match in extra time with a wonder goal from full back Stephen Johnston. This victory put Town on their way to an eventual semi-final outing against Crusaders who were to prove too tough a nut to crack in this and the Gold Cup semi-final in December.

The introduction of former Republic of Ireland U.21 International Michael McHugh added an extra bite up front and the young Ramelton man was to top the scoring charts with 25 goals, a club record. McHugh however only hit form late in the season, too late for an impression to be made on Coleraine's runaway lead at the top of the table.

In the League it was a case of so near yet so far, on 28th October a victory at Distillery would have put Town top, a point would have put them level on top, sadly a late goal for the Whites denied Omagh the points and left them in third position. From then on the season went on a roller coaster ride, a run of bad form in November and mixed fortunes over Christmas sealed Town's fate in the new First Division and another difficult season in the basement of the Irish League.

The inaugural Irish News Cup kicked off in December with Omagh eventually meeting Coleraine in the Final, a 12-2 aggregate defeat was avenged in the North West Cup Final with Town hammering the Bannsiders 5-1 in the April decider.

THE NORTHERN IRELAND
football
Y E A R B O O K

Dungannon were ousted in the Irish Cup fifth round but were defeated 3-1 in the next round by Champions elect Portadown who avenged their Gold Cup defeat by Omagh at St.Julians Road.

On the awards front Michael McHugh's four goals at Ballyclare in April earned him a 'Crystal Ball' and Joe McBreartys third clean sheet in a month earned him the monthly goalkeeper award.

The forthcoming season is virtually make or break for not only Omagh Town but for all First Division teams. Basically the only way to survive is to win promotion, no doubt that's what Roy McCreadie plans to do. What Town wouldn't give for another 25 McHugh goals this season!

Paddy Hunter

Manager Profile — Roy McCreadie

Date of Birth: 23/03/1960 Nottingham.
Date of Appointment: June 1994.

Previous Clubs:
As Player: Coleraine; Portadown; Omagh Town.
As Manager: Omagh Town (Player/Manager).

Honours:
As Player: Irish League Representative; 3 caps;
Coleraine – **Ulster Cup**; 1985/86;
Portadown – **Irish League Championship**;
1989/90 and 1990/91;
Ulster Cup; 1990/91;
Omagh T – **Budweiser Cup**; 1991/92.

As Manager:
Budweiser Cup; 1991/92;
North West Senior Challange Cup; 1995/96

SMIRNOFF FIRST DIVISION RECORD 1995/96

No:	Date:	Ven:	Opponents:	Result:	H.T:	Pos:	Goalscorers:
1	Sep 30	H	Coleraine	2-2 D	1-1	-	Crilly (36), Donnelly (78)
2	Oct 7	A	Carrick Rangers	3-2 W	0-1	2	Crilly (66), (M) O'Donnell (68), Mooney (80)
3	Oct 14	H	Ballymena United	0-0 D	0-0	3	-
4	Oct 21	A	Newry Town	2-1 W	1-0	2	Crilly (39), Mooney (87)
5	Oct 28	A	Distillery	2-3 L	1-1	4	Mooney (22), Crilly (75)
6	Nov 4	H	Ballyclare Comrades	1-3 L	1-1	4	McHugh (13)
7	Nov 11	A	Larne	2-2 D	1-0	4	Gallagher (26), (R) McCreadie (74)
8	Nov 18	A	Coleraine	2-5 L	2-2	5	Mooney (16), McAllister (og 21)
9	Nov 25	H	Carrick Rangers	1-0 W	0-0	4	Crilly (55)
10	Dec 2	A	Ballymena United	0-2 L	0-2	4	-
11	Dec 9	H	Newry Town	1-0 W	0-0	4	McIntyre (72)
12	Dec 16	H	Distillery	3-1 W	0-0	4	McHugh (60), McIntyre (75), Johnston (78)
13	Jan 1	H	Larne	1-3 L	1-1	-	Donnelly (22)
14	Jan 6	H	Coleraine	0-4 L	0-2	5	-
15	Jan 13	A	Carrick Rangers	0-2 L	0-1	6	-
16	Feb 3	A	Newry Town	2-2 D	1-2	7	Mooney (1), Crilly (90)
17	Feb 6	A	Ballyclare Comrades	2-1 W	1-0	-	McDowell (20,57)
18	Feb 10	A	Distillery	1-0 W	1-0	6	McHugh (40)
19	Feb 17	H	Ballyclare Comrades	3-0 W	1-0	3	McHugh (49), (B) McCreadie (53), Kavanagh (59)
20	Feb 27	H	Ballymena United	2-2 D	2-0	-	McDowell (24), Mooney (31)
21	Mar 2	A	Larne	3-1 W	1-0	2	McHugh (11,88), Kavanagh (49)
22	Mar 16	A	Coleraine	1-2 L	1-1	2	Kavanagh (44)
23	Mar 23	H	Carrick Rangers	6-2 W	2-2	2	Gallagher (7,84), McHugh (35,90), Crilly (51), Mooney (73)
24	Mar 30	A	Ballymena United	0-2 L	0-0	3	-
25	Apr 6	H	Newry Town	4-0 W	3-0	3	Melly (4), (B) McCreadie (16), McHugh (19,72)
26	Apr 8	H	Distillery	0-0 D	0-0	-	-
27	Apr 20	A	Ballyclare Comrades	5-0 W	1-0	3	Donnelly (21), McHugh (53,54,pen 69,76)
28	Apr 27	H	Larne	1-1 D	1-0	3	Donnelly (13)

Final League Position: 3rd

FIRST DIVISION LINE-UPS 1995/96

MATCH No	A.Blake 11	S.Johnston 26	M.Magill 22+(1)	M.Donnelly 20	D.McCaul 6+(1)	E.Kavanagh 22+(1)	M.Mooney 24	J.Quigg 14	E.McIntyre 10+(4)	J.Crilly 24	M.McHugh 23+(2)	B.McCreadie 4+(15)	D.O'Neill 2+(13)	M.O'Donnell 5+(2)	J.McBrearty 13	P.Moran 0+(1)	K.Moore 9+(3)	M.Gallagher 21+(1)	A.Gray 11	J.McElroy 10+(8)	S.Doherty 6+(1)	M.McDevitt 1+(1)	F.O'Donnell 1+(1)	S.McGreevy 3	N.Melly 13	R.McDowell 7+(2)	R.McCreadie 1	C.McCullagh 0+(1)	R.Sheridan 0+(1)	Referee
1	1	2°	3	4	5	6	7	8	9*	10	11†	12*	14†	15°																G.Douglas
2	–	2	3	4	5	–	7	8	–	10	11	12*	6†	9*	1		14†													L.Irvine
3	1	2	3	5	–	6	7	8	–	10	11†	–	12*	9*	–	–	4	14†												T.Gillanders
4	1	2	3	5	–	6	7	–	11†	10	–	14†	12*	9*	–	–	4	8												J.Peden
5	1	2	3†	5	–	6	7	8	12*	10	11*	14†	–	9	–	–	4	–												G.McKay
6	1	2	3	5	–	6	7	8	14†	10	11	12*	–	9	–	–	4	–												H.Barr
7	1	2	3†	–	5	–	7	8	9*	10	11	12*	14†	–	–	–	–	6	4											E.Millar
8	1	2	3	–	7	–	6	8*	9†	10	11	14†	–	15°	–	–	–	5°	4	12*										T.Gillanders
9	1	2*	3	5	–	–	7	8	9†	10	–	14†	–	–	–	–	–	11	6	12*	4									F.McDonald
10	1°	–	3	5	–	–	–	8	7	10	11	9*	14†	–	–	–	–	2	6†	12*	4	15°								T.Deegan
11	1	2	3	5	14†	6	10	8	12*	–	11*	15°	–	–	–	–	9†	–	7*	4										H.Barr
12	–	2	3	5	4†	15°	7	8	9*	10	11	–	12*	–	1	–	–	–	6°	14†	–	–								D.Taylor
13	1	2	3	5	4†	11	10†	8	9*	–	–	–	12*	15°	–	–	–	6	–	7	–	–	14†							G.McKay
14	–	2	3	5	–	6	10	8	9	–	11	–	7	–	–	–	–	–	–	4	1	–								N.Cowie
15	–	2	3†	5°	–	6	10	8	9	–	11	14†	15°	–	1	–	–	7*	–	12*	4	–	–							B.Kane
16	–	2	3	–	–	6	9	–	–	10	11*	12*	–	–	–	–	7	–	8	4	–	–	–	–	1	5				F.Hiles
17	–	2	3	–	–	6†	7°	–	–	10	12*	9*	14†	–	–	15°	8	–	4	–	–	–	–	–	1	5	11			E.Millar
18	–	2°	3	9	–	6	7	–	–	10	12*	–	15°	–	14†	–	8	–	4	–	–	–	–	–	1*	5	11†			T.Deegan
19	–	–	–	–	–	6	–	–	–	10	11	9*	12*	–	1	–	14†	8	3	2°	15°	–	–	–	5	7	4†			J.Peden
20	–	2	–	–	–	6	7*	–	–	10	11	12*	–	–	1	–	4	8	3	–	–	–	–	–	5	9	–			F.Hiles
21	–	2	–	5	–	6	7	–	–	10	11	–	–	–	1	–	–	8	3	–	–	–	–	–	4	9	–			F.Hiles
22	–	2	–	5	–	6	9	–	–	10	11	–	–	–	1	–	7	8*	3	12*	–	–	–	–	4	–	–			G.McKay
23	–	2	14†	4°	–	6	9	–	–	10	11	–	12*	–	1	–	7	8*	3†	15°	–	–	–	–	5	–	–			A.Snoddy
24	–	2	–	–	–	6*	7	–	–	10	11	–	–	–	1	–	4	8	3	12*	–	–	–	–	5	9	–			J.Ferry
25	–	2*	3	–	–	6	7°	–	–	10	11	9†	12*	–	1	–	8	–	4	–	–	–	–	–	5	–	–	14†	15°	D.Taylor
26	–	2	3	7*	–	6	–	–	14†	10	11	12*	–	–	1	–	8	–	5	–	–	–	–	–	4	9†	–	–	–	J.Peden
27	–	7	3	9	–	6	–	–	–	10	11	–	–	–	1	–	–	2	8	–	5	–	–	–	4	12*	–	–	–	M.Hutton
28	–	2	3	9†	–	6	7*	–	–	10	11	12*	–	–	1	–	8	–	5	–	–	–	–	–	4	14†	–	–	–	E.Millar

TRANSFERS C/S'95 TO APRIL '96

Players Signed:

Peter Moran (Ballyclare Comrades c/s'95), Andrew Crawford (Glenavon Aug.'95), Leo Devine (Bristol City Aug.'95), Colm McCullagh (Glenavon Aug.'95), Michael McHugh (Scarborough Aug.'95), Ross Murray (Glenavon Aug.'95), Paul Quinn (Glenavon Aug.'95), Ryan Sheridan (Glenavon Aug.'95), Martin Gallagher (Finn Harps Sep.'95), Mark McDevitt (Derry City Nov.'95), Francis O'Donnell (Coleraine Dec.'95), Nigel Melly (Bangor Jan.'96), Roddy McDowell (Glentoran Feb.'96), Sean McGreevy (Ballyclare Comrades Feb.'96).

Players Transferred:

Thomas Mohan (Derry City c/s'95), Peter Moran (Limavady United (Oct.'95), Kevin O'Neill (Released Oct.'95), Dermot Hillen (Ballinamallard United Jan.'96), Dermot McCaul (Dungannon Swifts Jan.'96), John Quigg (Finn Harps Jan.'96).

HONOURS:

Irish League / First Division		Best Position: 8th 1991/92 / 3rd 1995/96
Budweiser Cup, Winners:	(1)	1991/92
North West Senior Challenge Cup, Winners:	(3)	1990/91, 1992/93, 1995/96
Smirnoff 'B' Div. Knockout Cup, Winners:	(1)	1989/90
Fermanagh & Western League, Champions	(2)	1966/67, 1974/75*
Kennedy Cup, Winners:	(4)	1979/80, 1980/81, 1986/87, 1989/90
Mulhern Cup, Winners:	(4)	1965/66, 1966/67, 1969/70, 1974/75
North West League, Champions:	(1)	1971/72
Tom McDaid Cup, Winners:	(4)	1981/82, 1982/83, 1983/84, 1986/87
Alan Brunt Cup, Winners:	(3)	1986/87, 1990/91, 1992/93, 1994/95
Laird Cup, Winners:	(2)	1989, 1990, 1991, 1992

Most capped player: None

* Trophies won by Omagh Town Reserves.

PLAYER PROFILE - MARK DONNELLY

Mark Donnelly played his first game in an Omagh Town shirt when he was 14 albeit in the youth team but still the young Donnelly, who had only recently come to Omagh from Portrush, was already creating a buzz whenever he appeared.

Coming from a footballing family it was always expected that youngest in the household Mark would also make his 'mark' in the footballing world. 'ODGIE' as he is known, played with Town reserves before Danny Rouse brought him into the first team along with the likes of Davy Malcomson, Brendan Johns, Paul McAnea and brothers Trevor and Liam Donnelly.

Mark was by now making a name for himself whether it was defending or attacking. He went for a trial to Dundee before going to Dungannon Swifts, Ards and Monaghan United before returning to the fold at Omagh when the club entered Senior Soccer in 1990.

In 1994 Donnelly collected the supporters 'Player of the Year' and in 1995 he won a 'Guinness Player of the Month' award. However the illustrious club 'Player of the Year' award has eluded him mainly due to injuries and suspensions.

A hard hitting centre-half who has indeed been an accomplished striker in his day, Mark Donnelly is one of the most popular players at Omagh Town and indeed in the Irish League. Well known as a fiery soul Mark has mellowed with age (he's now 29) but will always give 100% and knock in the odd goal.

Mark, married to Donna has a daughter and lives in Omagh as does his footballing brothers Liam and Trevor. Liam now plays in the Fermanagh and Western League with Shelbourne while Trevor is with Fivemiletown.

Paddy Hunter.

OMAGH TOWN APPEARANCES FOR 1995/96

Name:	UC	GC	ILC	CC	BIC	NWC	INC	FD	Total
1 Stephen Johnston	3	3+(1)	4	2	2	2	2	26	44+(1)
2 Michael McHugh	2	4+(1)	2	2	2	2	4	23+(2)	41+(3)
3 Eamon Kavanagh	3	4	4	2	2	1	3	22+(1)	41+(1)
4 John Crilly	2	5	3	1	2	2	2	24	41
5 Martin Mooney	2+(1)	5	2	1+(1)	1	1	3	24	39+(2)
6 Mark Donnelly	3	5	4	2	2	1	2	20	39
7 Michael Magill	3	5	2	1	1	1	3	22+(1)	38+(1)
8 Martin Gallagher	-	2	-	1	2	2	3	21+(1)	31+(1)
9 Barry McCreadie	-(3)	2	-(4)	-	1	-	1+(1)	4+(15)	8+(23)
10 John Quigg	3	4	4	2	1	-	2	14	30
11 Emmett McIntyre	2	3+(2)	4	2	-(1)	-	1+(1)	10+(4)	22+(8)
12 Donal O'Neill	1	2+(2)	-(2)	1	1	-(2)	2+(2)	2+(13)	9+(21)
13 Tony Blake	3	5	4	-	2	-	-(1)	11	25+(1)
14 John McElroy	-	-	-	1	-(1)	2	4	10+(8)	17+(9)
15 Dermot McCaul	2	3	3	1	1	-	2	6+(1)	18+(1)
16 Tony Gray	-	1	2	-	-	2	1+(2)	11	17+(2)
17 Kevin Moore	1	-	2	-	-	2	1	9+(3)	15+(3)
18 Joe McBrearty	-	-	-	1	-	-	2	13	16
19 Nigel Melly	-	-	-	-	1	1	1	13	16
20 Stephen Doherty	-	2	-	1+(1)	-(1)	-	2	6+(1)	11+(3)
21 Roddy McDowell	-	-	-	-	1	-(1)	-	7+(2)	8+(3)
22 Mark O'Donnell	-	-(3)	-	-	-	-	-	5+(2)	5+(5)
23 Mark McDevitt	-	-	-	1	-	2	2	1+(1)	6+(1)
24 Peter Moran	2	-	2+(2)	-	-	-	-	-(1)	4+(3)
25 Declan Sheridan	1+(1)	-	2	-	-	-	-	-	3+(1)
26 Colm McCullagh	-	-	-	-	-	-(2)	-(1)	-(1)	-(4)
27 Sean McGreevy	-	-	-	-	-	-	-	3	3
28 Dermot Hillen	-(1)	-	-(1)	-	-	-	-(1)	-	-(3)
29 Ryan Sheridan	-	-	-	-	-	-(1)	-	-(1)	-(2)
30 Leo Devine	-	-	-	-	-	1	-	-	1
31 Roy McCreadie	-	-	-	-	-	-	-	1	1
32 Kevin O'Neill	-	-	-	-	-	-	1	-	1
33 Francis O'Donnell	-	-	-	-	-	-	-	-(1)	-(1)
34 Darren Walker	-	-	-	-	-	-(1)	-	-	-(1)

OMAGH TOWN GOALSCORERS FOR 1995/96

Name:	UC	GC	ILC	CC	BIC	NWC	INC	FD	Total
1 Michael McHugh	-	2	1	1	-	3	4	14 (1p)	25 (1p)
2 John Crilly	1	-	-	-	-	3	-	7	11
3 Eamon Kavanagh	1p	1p	2 (1p)	-	-	1	2	3	10 (3p)
4 Martin Mooney	-	1	2	-	-	-	-	7	10
5 Mark Donnelly	-	2	1	-	1	1	-	4	9
6 Barry McCreadie	1	2	1	-	1	-	-	3	8
7 Stephen Johnston	1	-	1	-	-	2	-	1	5
8 Emmett McIntyre	-	-	2	-	1	-	-	2	5
9 Martin Gallagher	-	-	-	-	-	1	-	3	4
10 Roddy McDowell	-	-	-	-	-	-	-	3	3
11 Peter Moran	-	-	3	-	-	-	-	-	3
12 John Quigg	1	-	1	-	1	-	-	-	3
13 John McElroy	-	-	-	-	1	-	-	-	1
14 Michael Magill	-	-	-	-	-	1	-	-	1
15 Nigel Melly	-	-	-	-	-	-	1	-	1
16 Mark O'Donnell	-	-	-	-	-	-	1	-	1
17 Donal O'Neill	-	-	-	-	-	1	-	-	1
18 Declan Sheridan	1	-	-	-	-	-	-	-	1
19 Ryan Sheridan	-	-	-	-	-	1	-	-	1
20 Own Goals	-	-	-	-	-	-	-	1	1
Total:	6	8	14	1	5	12	8	50	104

Ground: Shamrock Park, Brownstown Road, Portadown (15,000) Founded: 1924
Tel: 01762 332726

Portadown 1995/96
(Photograph by Michael Reeves)

Chairman:
Mr.M.Hunniford

Secretary:
Mr.L.Singleton

Treasurer:
Mr.T.Vaughan

Manager:
Ronnie McFall

Coach:
Bob Nesbitt

Reserve Team Coach:
Barry McCullough

Physiotherapist:
Derek McKinlay

Team Attendant:
George Richardson

Club Colours:
Red shirts, Red shorts,

Summary of 1995/96 Season

Portadown climaxed a glorious and in some ways an astonishing season by winning the inaugural Premier League Championship and finishing with three trophies - just one less than their greatest ever season in 1990/91.

Manager Ronnie McFall had every reason to feel proud as he reflected on the success of a Portadown season which was blighted for long spells by legislative hassle. At one time the Ports were booted out of the Ulster Cup after defeating Crusaders in the final because the authorities held that Gareth Fulton, their talented young full back was not eligible. Portadown were eventually reinstated and allowed to keep the trophy and Fulton was cleared, but not before there had been threats of the matter finishing up in the Courts.

Then there was the furore over the signing of ex-Linfield man Garry Haylock, with Portadown appearing at one time to have signed the Yorkshireman without having to pay a fee. Once again the threats of litigation swirled around and in the end Portadown and Linfield reached on a fee.

In the Premier League campaign Portadown looked well on the way to fulfilling expectations when after only eleven games they had eight wins and three draws under their belt. The first doubts began to appear when they lost their first game to Linfield in December and when on New Year's day closest challengers Crusaders won a titanic battle 3-1 at a tension filled Seaview to really throw the title race open. Portadown managed to stop the losing run with a nervous scoreless draw against Bangor at Clandeboye Park and then thrashed the impressive Cliftonville 4-1. However, Ards really upset the applecart in a snowstorm at Shamrock Park in January when they deservedly won 3-1. It was a test of character for Portadown and they responded with fighting draws against Glentoran and Linfield, but a sensational 7-0 defeat at the hands of Glenavon at Mourneview Park in February was a milestone. Portadown had been minus half a team through injury in that game, but the result still merited a council of war and at a no-holds barred session Ronnie McFall called on his players to prove they had what it takes to win titles.

From then on it was roses all the way, and Portadown recovered their poise with a 1-1 draw against Crusaders in a game McFall's men couldn't afford to lose - defeat would have allowed the Belfast side to open a gap at the top of the table.

After the crunch game with Crusaders, Portadown won five on the trot before their penultimate game at home to great rivals Glenavon and it was an afternoon which was to decide the destination of the Premier League. Portadown had to battle like tigers to win 2-1 and it was roars of jubilation when word came through on hundreds of transistors that Cliftonville had beaten Crusaders, the one team who could have pipped the Ports. It also spoiled what would have been a deciding game at Seaview in the last match and transformed this into a day of Portadown victory celebrations.

Having achieved so much in the face of adversity it was hardly surprising that McFall was promising that given better luck with injuries his team will be in there bidding strongly to retain their title next campaign.

Brian Courtney.

MANAGER PROFILE — RONNIE MCFALL

Date of Appointment: December 1986.

PREVIOUS CLUBS:
As Player: Dundee United; Portadown; Ards; Glentoran.
As Manager: Glentoran.

HONOURS:
As Player: N.Ireland Youth International; Irish League Representative (1 cap); Portadown – **Gold Cup**; 1971/72; **Texaco Cup**; 1973/74; **Carlsberg Cup**; 1972/73; Glentoran –
Irish League Championship; 1976/77;
Gold Cup; 1976/77 and 1977/78;
Ulster Cup; 1976/77.

As Manager:
Glentoran – **Irish League Championship**;
1980/81; **Irish Cup** – 1982/83;
Gold Cup – 1982/83;
Ulster Cup – 1981/82, 1982/83,1983/84;
Portadown – **Irish League Championship** –
1989/90, 1990/91, 1995/96; **Irish Cup** – 1990/91;
Gold Cup – 1992/93; **Ulster Cup** – 1990/91, 1995/96;
Budweiser Cup – 1990/91, 1992/93 and 1994/95;
Mid-Ulster Cup – 1992/93, 1993/94 and 1994/95;
Irish League Cup – 1995/96.

TRANSFERS C/S'95 TO APRIL '96

Players Signed:

Timothy Dalton (Bangor c/s'95), Garry Haylock (Linfield Jun.'95), Peter Kennedy (Glenavon Jul.'95), Gary Peebles (Linfield Jul.'95), Raymond Byrne (Newry Town Aug.'95), Jonathon Magee (Bangor Sep.'95), Paul Carlyle (Derry City Dec.'95), Scott Leitch (Hearts (Sco loan) Jan.'96), Ian Ferguson (St.Johnstone (Sco loan) Feb.'96), Derek Rae (Motherwell (Sco loan) Feb.'96), Jamie Woodsford (Luton Town (Eng loan) Feb.'96), Kevin Bain (Dundee (Sco loan) Mar.'96).

Players Transferred:

Sandy Fraser (Derry City Jul.'95), Ian Curliss (Distillery Aug.'95), Lindsay Hamilton (East Fife (Sco) Aug.'95), Andy Kennedy (St.Mirren (Sco) Aug.'95), Tony Shepherd (Ayr United (Sco) Aug.'95), Gareth Johnston (Queens University Oct.'95), Jonathon Magee (Distillery Oct.'95), Peter Murray (Ballymena United Oct.'95), Wesley Boyle (Leeds United (Eng) Feb.'96), Scott Leitch (Hearts (Sco loan rtn) Feb.'96), Derek Rae (Motherwell (Sco loan rtn) Feb.'96), Ian Ferguson (St.Johnstone (Sco loan rtn) Mar.'96), Kevin Bain (Dundee (Sco loan rtn) Apr.'96), Jamie Woodsford (Luton Town (Eng loan rtn) Apr.'96).

HONOURS:

Irish League/Premier League Champions:	(3)	1989/90, 1990/91 / 1995/96
Irish Cup, Winners:	(1)	1990/91
Gold Cup, Winners:	(6)	1933/34, 1937/38, 1952/53, 1971/72, 1978/79, 1992/93
Ulster Cup, Winners:	(2)	1990/91, 1995/96
Wilkinson Sword Irish League Cup	(1)	1995/96
City Cup, Winners:	(1)	1938/39
Budweiser Cup, Winners	(3)	1990/91, 1992/93, 1994/95
Texaco Cup, Winners:	(1)	1973/74
Carlsberg Cup, Winners:	(1)	1972/73
Mid Ulster Cup, Winners:	(18)	1898/99, 1899/00, 1902/03, 1905/06, 1907/08, 1909/ 10, 1931/32, 1933/34, 1960/61*, 1962/63*, 1964/65*, 1969/70*, 1980/81, 1981/82, 1982/83, 1992/93, 1993/94,1994/95
Mid Ulster Shield, Winners:	(2)	1927/28*, 1928/29*
IFA Youth Cup, Winners:	(1)	11979/80

Trophies won by Portadown Reserves

Most capped player: Wilbur Cush (3) N.Ireland

SMIRNOFF PREMIER LEAGUE RECORD FOR 1995/96

No.	Date:	Ven:	Opponents:	Result:	H.T.	Pos:	Goalscorers:
1	Sep 30	A	Bangor	3-0 W	1-0	-	Major (27), Kennedy (46), Haylock (70)
2	Oct 7	H	Cliftonville	6-1 W	4-1	1	Candlish (3,11,39), Haylock (20,56), Kennedy (62)
3	Oct 14	H	Ards	3-1 W	1-1	1	Russell (20), Haylock (pen 64), Candlish (66)
4	Oct 21	A	Glentoran	1-1 D	1-0	1	Kennedy (31)
5	Oct 28	H	Linfield	3-2 W	1-1	1	Kennedy (11,57), Peebles (53)
6	Nov 4	A	Glenavon	1-0 W	0-0	1	Haylock (50)
7	Nov 11	H	Crusaders	1-1 D	1-0	1	Haylock (8)
8	Nov 18	H	Bangor	4-2 W	3-1	1	(I.J) Ferguson (28), McKeown (og 38), Haylock (44,87)
9	Nov 25	A	Cliftonville	3-0 W	2-0	1	Candlish (26), Strain (38,57)
10	Dec 2	A	Ards	1-1 D	0-1	1	Haylock (68)
11	Dec 9	H	Glentoran	3-1 W	1-0	1	(I.J) Ferguson (40), Boyle (75), Haylock (84)
12	Dec 16	A	Linfield	0-1 L	0-1	1	-
13	Jan 1	A	Crusaders	1-3 L	1-1	-	Carlyle (27)
14	Jan 6	A	Bangor	0-0 D	0-0	1	-
15	Jan 13	H	Cliftonville	4-1 W	0-0	1	Haylock (53,62,82), Casey (88)
16	Jan 27	H	Ards	1-3 L	0-0	2	Evans (89)
17	Feb 3	A	Glentoran	3-3 D	2-1	2	Haylock (17), Kennedy (45), Casey (50)
18	Feb 10	H	Linfield	1-1 D	0-0	2	Casey (50)
19	Feb 13	H	Glenavon	2-1 W	1-1	-	(I) Ferguson (38), Strain (74)
20	Feb 17	A	Glenavon	0-7 L	0-3	2	-
21	Mar 2	H	Crusaders	1-1 D	0-1	2	Woodsford (85)
22	Mar 16	H	Bangor	4-3 W	3-2	2	Woodsford (36,45), Kennedy (44,89)
23	Mar 23	A	Cliftonville	4-0 W	3-0	2	Major (25), Woodsford (29,35,55)
24	Mar 30	A	Ards	2-0 W	0-0	1	Kennedy (59), Haylock (78)
25	Apr 6	H	Glentoran	3-2 W	1-1	1	Haylock (17), Davidson (55), Kennedy (70)
26	Apr 9	A	Linfield	1-0 W	1-0	-	Haylock (26)
27	Apr 20	H	Glenavon	2-1 W	1-1	1	(I.J) Ferguson (27), Haylock (pen 67)
28	Apr 27	A	Crusaders	3-3 D	3-1	1	Casey (3), Haylock (11,25)

Final League Position: 1st

PREMIER LEAGUE LINE-UPS 1995/96

MATCH No	T.Dalton 22	G.Fulton 13+(1)	G.Davidson 22	R.Casey 26	B.Strain 24	P.Major 20	G.Peebles 22+(1)	M.Russell 7+(2)	G.Haylock 25	J.Magee 1+(1)	P.Kennedy 23	P.Murray 0+(1)	N.Candlish 19+(6)	C.McKeever 1	R.Gallagher 0+(2)	R.Byrne 17	I.J.Ferguson 12+(3)	M.Keenan 6+(1)	A.Stewart 16+(2)	W.Boyle 1+(1)	P.Carlyle 8+(4)	P.Evans 3+(4)	S.Leitch 3	I.Ferguson 3	D.Rae 2	J.Woodsford 6	K.Bain 6	Referee
1	1	2	3*	4	5	6	7	8	9	10†	11	12*	14†															F.Hiles
2	1	–	3	4	5	6	10	8	9	12*	11	–	7*	2†	14†													F.McDonald
3	1	–	3	4	5	2	10	8	9	–	11	–	7*	–	–	6	12*											M.Ross
4	1	–	3	4	5	2	10	8	9	–	11	–	7*	–	–	6	12*											H.Barr
5	–	2	3	4	5	–	8	12*	9	–	11	–	7*	–	–	6	10	1										L.Irvine
6	–	–	3	4	5	2	7	8	9	–	11	–	12*	–	–	6	10*	1										N.Cowie
7	–	2*	3	4	5	–	7	8	9	–	11	–	–	–	–	6	10	1	12*									D.Magill
8	1	2	3	4	5	–	–	8*	9	–	11	–	12*	–	–	6	10	–	7									R.Lutton
9	1	–	3	4	5	2	8	–	9	–	11	–	7	–	–	6	10	–	–									H.Barr
10	1	2	3	4	–	–	8	–	9	–	11	–	7	–	–	6	10	–	5									E.Millar
11	1	2	3	4	5	–	8	–	9	–	11	–	7*	–	–	6	10	–	–	12*								L.Irvine
12	1	2	3	4	5	–	8	–	9	–	11	–	12*	–	–	6	10	–	–	7*								N.Cowie
13	1	2*	3	4	5	–	–	–	9	–	11	–	8	–	–	6	10	–	12*	–	7							J.Ferry
14	1	–	3	4	5	2	–	–	9	–	11	–	10*	–	8	12*	–	6	–	7								T.Deegan
15	1	–	–	4	5	2	8	–	9	–	11	–	–	–	–	6	10	–	3	–	–	7						F.Hiles
16	1	2	3	4	5	–	8	–	9	–	11	–	12*	–	–	–	–	6†	–	7*	14†	10						A.Snoddy
17	1	2*	–	4	5	3	8	–	9	–	11	–	10	–	–	–	–	6	–	12*	–	7						G.Keatley
18	–	2	–	4	5	3	8	–	–	–	11	–	10	–	–	–	1	6	–	–	–	7	9					J.Ferry
19	–	–	–	–	5	2	8	–	–	–	10	–	–	3	–	1	6	–	7	11	–	9	4					H.Barr
20	–	14†	–	–	5	2	8	–	–	–	10	–	12*	3†	–	1	6	–	7	11	–	9	4*					A.Snoddy
21	1	–	–	4	5	2	8	–	9	–	11	–	10*	–	–	3	–	6	–	12*	–	–	–	7				D.Magill
22	1	–	3	4	5	2	–	–	9	–	11	–	12*	–	–	–	–	6	–	7	–	–	–	–	10		8*	N.Cowie
23	1	–	3	4	5*	2	–	–	9	–	11	–	10	–	–	–	–	6	–	12*	–	–	–	7			8	R.Lutton
24	1	–	3	4	5	2	12*	–	9	–	11	–	7*	–	–	–	–	6	–	–	–	–	–	10			8	A.Snoddy
25	1	–	3	4	5*	2	10	–	9	–	11	–	–	–	–	–	–	6	–	12*	14†	–	–	7†			8	J.Ferry
26	1	5	3	4	–	2	10	–	9	–	11	–	–	–	–	–	–	6	–	–	–	–	–	7			8	H.Barr
27	1	–	3	4	–	2	8	–	9	–	–	10	–	–	11*	–	6	–	7	12*	–	–	–	5				G.Keatley
28	1°	5	3	4*	–	2†	8	14†	9	–	–	10	–	–	6	11	15°	–	7	12*	–	–	–	–				D.Magill

PLAYER PROFILE - PETER KENNEDY

Peter Kennedy had no real challenger when it came to selecting Portadown's 'Player of the Year', in spite of the fact that there were others who contributed in no small measure to the team's highly successful season. Garry Haylock for one, and his 41 goals, were crucial in the push for the League Championship and the generally outstanding season. There were others like battling midfielder Robert Casey, reliable full back Philip Major, and tigerish Gregg Davidson, one of the finest competitors in the Irish League.

But Kennedy - 'PK' to his host of admirers - was simply the best and few observers would quarrel with that assessment. He was voted Guinness 'Player of the Year' by the Northern Ireland Football Writers, and also collected the prestigious Castlereagh Glentoran Supporters Club award - only the third Portadown player to do so since it was inaugurated.

Signed from deadly rivals Glenavon at the end of the previous season, Kennedy was in storming and relentless form for the season, only missing out in the closing weeks when an injury sidelined him for the final League games against Glenavon and Crusaders - and cruelly for him and Portadown - the Bass Irish Cup replay against the Lurgan Club.

But Kennedy had done enough to deserve the accolades and in the 49 matches he played he scored 18 goals, most of them in the memorable category.

Playing left side of midfield his creative and hard-running qualities were allied to lethal finishing, an explosive and exciting cocktail, and it was an asset which Portadown exploited to the full.

Kennedy also collected almost all the Portadown supporters club awards, and in spite of missing out in the final two games which clinched the championship the season finished on a high. His injury collected in the Bass Irish Cup semi-final had appeared at first to be crochet ligament damage, a worrying prospect for player and club. Fortunately the eventual diagnosis confirmed it was cartilage trouble and Kennedy quickly had the operation with the firm prospect of being in action in time for the start of the season.

"He is a super player and we are fortunate to have him" said manager Ronnie McFall, delighted that Kennedy signed a one-year extension to his contract just before the end of the season. How long Portadown can hold him is a valid question as cross-channel clubs were showing more than a passing interest in his form towards the end of the season.

Biggest surprise was that 'PK' wasn't selected for the Northern Ireland 'B' squad but if he continues to produce form on this scale in the new season, it will surely only be a matter of time before he forces himself into the reckoning.
Brian Courtney.

PORTADOWN APPEARANCES FOR 1995/96

Name:	UC	GC	ILC	CC	BIC	CAS	MUC	PL	Total
1 Garry Haylock	6	4	5	4	5	2	-	25	51
2 Robert Casey	5	3	3	4	5	3	-	26	49
3 Peter Kennedy	6	3	5	4	5	3	-	23	49
4 Brian Strain	5	4	5	3	1	2	-	24	44
5 Gary Peebles	5	4	3	3	4	1	-	22+(1)	42+(1)
6 Timothy Dalton	4	2+(2)	2	4	5	2	-	22	41+(2)
7 Philip Major	5	4	5	3	4	1	-	20	42
8 Neil Candlish	1+(2)	1+(1)	-	2+(2)	2+(1)	2+(1)	1	19+(6)	28+(13)
9 Gregg Davidson	2+(1)	4	-(3)	1	3	3	-	22	35+(4)
10 Raymond Byrne	3+(1)	3	2	3	2	3	1	17	34+(1)
11 Gareth Fulton	3+(1)	1+(1)	2	1+(3)	5	2+(1)	1	13+(1)	28+(7)
12 Alfie Stewart	1	-	-	3	4	3	-	16+(2)	27+(2)
13 Iain J. Ferguson	2	1	2	1	1	3	-	12+(3)	22+(3)
14 Martin Russell	5	3	5	-	-	-	1	7+(2)	21+(2)
15 Paul Carlyle	-(1)	-	-	4	3+(1)	-	1	8+(4)	16+(6)
16 Michael Keenan	2+(1)	2	3	-(1)	-	1	1	6+(1)	15+(3)
17 Paul Evans	2	-(1)	-	-(1)	1+(1)	-	1	3+(4)	7+(7)
18 Peter Murray	4	2	5	-	-	-	-	-(1)	11+(1)
19 Wesley Boyle	-(2)	1+(1)	3	-	-	1	-	1+(1)	6+(4)
20 Jamie Woodsford	-	-	-	1	2	-	-	6	9
21 Kevin Bain	-	-	-	-	2	-	-	6	8
22 Conor McKeever	2	-	1	-	-(1)	-	1	1	5+(1)
23 Jonathon Magee	1	2	-(1)	-	-	-	-	1+(1)	4+(2)
24 Rory Gallagher	-	-	-	1	1	-(1)	1	-(2)	3+(3)
25 Scott Leitch	1	-	-	1	-	-	-	3	5
26 Ian Ferguson	-	-	-	1	-	-	-	3	4
27 Michael Coll	-	-	2	-	-	1	-	-	3
28 Barry Meehan	1	-	2	-	-	-	-	-	3
29 Derek Rae	-	-	-	-(1)	-	-	-	2	2+(1)
30 Jonathan Turkington	-	-	-	-	-	-(1)	1	-	1+(1)
31 Richard Clarke	-	-	-	-	-	-	1	-	1
32 Mark Herbert	-(1)	-	-	-	-	-	-	-	-(1)
33 Glenn McCullough	-	-	-	-	-	-(1)	-	-	-(1)
34 Mark Savage	-	-	-	-	-	-(1)	-	-	-(1)

PORTADOWN GOALSCORERS FOR 1995/96

Name:	UC	GC	ILC	CC	BIC	CAS	MUC	PL	Total
1 Garry Haylock	7	4	2	4	3	1	-	20(2p)	41(2p)
2 Peter Kennedy	-	-	1	1	4(1p)	2	-	10	18(1p)
3 Robert Casey	1	2	1	-	2	-	-	4	10
4 Gary Peebles	3	3	1	2	-	-	-	1	10
5 Neil Candlish	1	-	-	-	1	-	1	5	8
6 Iain J. Ferguson	1	-	2	-	-	1	-	3	7
7 Jamie Woodsford	-	-	-	-	-	-	-	6	6
8 Brian Strain	-	1	1	-	-	-	-	3	5
9 Philip Major	-	-	-	1	1	-	-	2	4
10 Wesley Boyle	-	-	-	-	-	1	-	1	2
11 Paul Evans	-	1	-	-	-	-	-	1	2
12 Ian Ferguson	-	-	-	1	-	-	-	1	2
13 Raymond Byrne	-	-	-	-	-	1	-	-	1
14 Paul Carlyle	-	-	-	-	-	-	-	1	1
15 Gregg Davidson	-	-	-	-	-	-	-	1	1
16 Scott Leitch	-	-	-	1	-	-	-	-	1
17 Peter Murray	-	-	1	-	-	-	-	-	1
18 Martin Russell	-	-	-	-	-	-	-	1	1
19 Own Goals	1	-	1	-	-	-	-	1	3
Total	14	11	10	10	11	6	1	61	124

RECORDS SECTION

CURRENT TOP LEAGUE GOALSCORERS

The following is a list of players who have scored 50 or more goals in the Irish League Championship (including the new Premier League and First Division) up until the end of the 1995/96 season and who made at least one League appearance last season.

Name:	Clubs:	Goals:
1 Ollie Ralph	Newry Town (130)	130
2 Stephen McBride	Linfield (5); Glenavon (123)	128
3 Raymond McCoy	Coleraine (77); Glenavon (33)	110
4 Stephen Baxter	Ards (21); Linfield (51); Distillery (6); Crusaders (21)	99
5 Glenn Ferguson	Ards (14); Glenavon (81)	95
6 Glenn Hunter	Distillery (1); Crusaders (30); Linfield (17); Crusaders (40)	88
7 Darren Erskine	Ards (70); Linfield (5)	75
8 Ron Manley	Glentoran (60); Cliftonville (14)	74
9 Raymond Morrison	Glentoran (66); Ards (4)	70
10 Sammy Shiels	Ards (11); Carrick Rangers (34); Coleraine (25)	70
11 Barry McCreadie	Coleraine (23); Bangor (25); Omagh Town (2); Ballymena Utd(4); Omagh Town (13)	67
12 Thomas Cleland	Distillery (9); Glentoran (2); Distillery (50)	61
13 Thomas McCourt	Carrick Rangers (15); Larne (44); Ballymena United (1)	60
14 Garry Haylock	Linfield (36); Portadown (20)	56
15 Kirk Hunter	Crusaders (50)	50

ALL TIME RECORDS IN IRISH LEAGUE CHAMPIONSHIP 1890/91 – 1995/96

HIGHEST WIN:

Home:	Linfield	14	Oldpark	0	15th November 1890
	Glentoran	15	Oldpark	1	15th September 1891

POST WAR:

	Linfield	11	Bangor	1	
	Glenavon	10	Bangor	0	24th December 1966

Away:	Bangor	0	Distillery	11	12th November 1966

HIGHEST AGGREGATE SCORE:

(16)	Glentoran	15	Oldpark	1	5th September 1891

Post War:

(15)	Glenavon	9	Coleraine	6	24th December 1955

HIGHEST SCORING DRAW:

	Larne	6	Distillery	6	
	Glentoran	6	Bangor	6	

MOST GOALS SCORED IN A SEASON: 116 in 26 matches by Belfast Celtic in 1928/29.

POST WAR: 85 in 22 matches by Linfield in 1967/68.

FEWEST GOALS SCORED IN A SEASON: 3 in 10 matches by Cliftonville in 1921/22.

Post War: 12 in 26 matches by Carrick Rangers in 1985/86.

MOST GOALS CONCEDED IN A SEASON: 130 in 26 matches by Queen's Island in 1928/29.

Post War: 100 in 22 matches by Cliftonville in 1964/65.

FEWEST GOALS CONCEDED IN A SEASON: 4 in 10 matches by Linfield in 1915/16.

Post War: 13 in 22 matches by Linfield in 1982/83.

MOST POINTS IN A SEASON: 2pts a win: 48 in 26 matches by Belfast Celtic in 1928/29. 3pts a win: 77 in 30 matches by Portadown in 1990/91 and Glentoran in 1991/92.

MOST WINS IN A SEASON: 24 in 30 matches by Glentoran in 1991/92.

FEWEST WINS IN A SEASON: 0 in 22 matches by Cliftonville in 1961/62. This unenviable record was also achieved by Milford in 1890/91; St.Columb's Court in 1901/02; and Bohemians in 1904/05 who all played 14 matches their respective season. In a 10 match Championship season the following teams also failed to secure a victory North Staffordshire 1898/99, Derry Celtic 1900/01, Glenavon 1915/16 and Belfast United 1916/17.

MOST HOME WINS IN A SEASON: 13 in 13 matches by Derry Celtic in 1936/37 and 1937/38.

Post War: 11 in 11 matches by Glenavon in 1956/57; Glentoran in 1976/77 and Linfield in 1979/80.

MOST AWAY WINS IN A SEASON: 12 in 15 matches by Portadown in 1990/91.

LONGEST UNDEFEATED RUN: 49 games by Belfast Celtic: The sequence started in the home match v Portadown on 10/09/1927 when they drew 1-1 and ended in a home match v Bangor on 20/08/1929 when they were beaten 2-1. Their record during this time was – P: 49 W: 40 D: 9 L: 0 F: 224 A: 60.

LONGEST UNDEFEATED SEQUENCE FROM START OF SEASON: 26 games by Belfast Celtic in 1928/29 which was the complete league season.

Post War: Glentoran also went through the entire 22 match programme in 1980/81 undefeated.

LONGEST UNDEFEATED SEQUENCE AT HOME: 47 by Derry City. The run commenced with a 3-1 win against Distillery on 03/11/1934 and lasted until they lost 5-2 to Ballymena United on 20/08/1938.

Post War: 39 by Linfield. The sequence started with a 0-0 draw against Crusaders on 13/12/1952 and was ended by Ballymena United when they were beaten 2-1 on 25/02/1956.

LONGEST WINNING RUN: 22 games by Linfield. It started with a 5-0 home win against Glentoran on 12/01/1980 and lasted until the following season when they were beaten 2-1 by Glentoran at The Oval on 10/01/1981.

LONGEST LOSING RUN: 21 Games by Cliftonville. When Cliftonville lost 4-1 at home to Linfield on 02/12/1967 it took them nearly a year to end the sequence when they beat Glenavon 5-3 at Mourneview Park on 09/11/1968.

LEAGUE CHAMPIONSHIPS:

3 in a row: This Feat has been achieved by Linfield on four occasions:

1890/91 - 1892/93; 1906/07 -1908/09; 1953/54 - 1955/56; 1977/78 -1979/80

4 in a row: Belfast Celtic won four consecutive titles between 1925/26 and 1928/29

6 in a row: Held jointly between Belfast Celtic and Linfield;

Celtic won their six titles in 1935/36; 1936/37; 1937/38; 1938/39; 1939/40 and then had to wait til after the war to win the 1947/48 Championship. Linfield achieved the feat more recently between 1981/82 and 1986/87.

MOST LEAGUE GOALS IN A SEASON: This record is held by Fred Roberts of Glentoran who scored 55 goals during 1930/31 season.

BASS IRISH CUP REVIEW 1995/96

Glentoran players celebrate their success over Glenavon after a six year gap.
(Photograph by Michael Reeves.)

With the proliferation of minor competitions, local football fans could be forgiven for asking who won what last season. It's very easy to lose interest if your team isn't involved. But there's one knock-out trophy which continues to capture the imagination of Ulster soccer year after year. The cup - the Bass Irish Cup of course.

And it's a piece of silverware which has a particularly special place in the hearts of Glentoran supporters. The Glens just couldn't stop winning it in the eighties, including five out of six from 1982 - 1988. They kicked off the nineties with a success in the competition as well, beating Portadown 3-0 in the Final at Windsor Park.

But they went into last season's cup on the back of six years of failure. And they made an inauspicious start in their bid to regain the trophy, going a goal down early on against 'B' Division no hopers Limavady United at the Oval in January.

The sixth round stage was a relatively comfortable 2-0 victory against Distillery at the Oval, goals there for Darren Finlay and Derek Cook, the Scottish striker who had netted twice against Limavady.

The quarter-finals saw two remarkable games against Ballymena. In the first, a scoreless draw at the Oval, Glens goalkeeper Declan Devine sustained back and facial injuries and was replaced by midfielder Pete Batey. Devine missed the replay, but made it back for the Final. Fit again Neil Armstrong returned for the quarter-final rematch at Ballymena Showgrounds, but couldn't prevent the home side racing into a 2-0 lead after 20 minutes.

It looked as if the cup dream had ended for Tommy Cassidy's team, but an inspired comeback sparked by a goal from ex-Ballymena defender Michael Smyth and completed with a Glen Little hat-trick, saw the Glens to a hard earned 4-2 victory against the First Division side.

The semi-final against Crusaders went to a second match as well. The Glens were saved by a goal from substitute Trevor Smith to give them a replay. Justin McBride scored a cracking goal in the rematch at Windsor and the Glens eventually went through 2-1 winners after a breathtaking last minute strike from Liam Coyle. Without doubt his most telling contribution during a short stay at the Oval and one Glenmen will remember him for in years to come.

The Final against Glenavon saw another deserved victory for the East Belfast side. They were on top for most of the match, but it took a late, long range wonder goal from Glen Little to secure a 1-0 win, the Cup and a place in Europe. For a change, Little didn't pick up the 'man-of-the-match' award, that went to full-back Darren Finlay who had an outstanding game against Stevie McBride in what proved to be his last match for the Lurgan club.

Peter Taggart.

BASS IRISH CUP 1995/96

FIRST ROUND

23rd September, 1995

Armoy United	2	East Belfast	6	Ballynahinch United	3	Rathfriland Rangers	0
Bangor Amateurs	2	Shorts Brothers	3	Bridgend United	1	First Shankill N.I.S.C.	3
Downshire Young Men	2	Cookstown Royals	0	Dromara Village	0	Annagh United	0
Drummond United	0	Dromore Amateurs	1	First Bangor O.B.	2	Abbey Villa	2
First Liverpool R.R.	4	Ballymacash Rangers	1	Harland & Wolff Welders	5	Civil Service	2
Islandmagee	3	AFC Craigavon	1	Killymoon Rangers	1	Wellington Recreation	3
Magherfelt Sky Blues	0	Portstewart	1	Malachians	4	Comber Recreation	0
Queens University	2	Hanover	2	Roe Valley	2	Killyleagh Youth Club	0
Seapatrick	2	Barn United	2	Sirocco Works	v	Richhill	
Tandragee Rovers	4	Donard Hospital	2	*(Richhill withdrew)*			

FIRST ROUND REPLAYS

27th September, 1995

Annagh United	2	Dromara Village	0	Barn United	3	Seapatrick	4
Hanover	3	Queens University	1				

28th September, 1995

Abbey Villa	0	First Bangor O.B.	1

First Round Byes: Ards Rangers; Bessbrook United; Cullybackey; Dungiven Celtic; Glebe Rangers; Larne Tech Old Boys; Laurelvale; Northern Telecom; Orangefield Old Boys; Portglenone; Saintfield United; Southend United; U.U.C:

SECOND ROUND

14th October, 1995

Annagh United	3	Portglenone	2	Ards Rangers	1	Glebe Rangers	1
Ballynahinch United	0	First Liverpool R.R.	4	Cullybackey	5	Sirocco Works	4
East Belfast	1	Northern Telecom	1	Harland & Wolff Welders	5	Hanover	2
Islandmagee	2	Dungiven Celtic	2	Larne Tech Old Boys	2	First Shankill N.I.S.C.	0
Malachians	2	Bessbrook United	2	Orangefield Old Boys	4	Saintfield United	2
Portstewart	3	Southend United	0	Seapatrick	3	First Bangor O.B.	2
Shorts Brothers	2	Dromre Amateurs	2	Tandragee Rovers	4	Roe Valley	1
U.U.C.	2	Laurelvale	4	Wellington Recreation	8	Downshire Young Men	1

SECOND ROUND REPLAYS

17th October, 1995

Dungiven Celtic	3	Islandmagee	0

18th October, 1995

Bessbrook United	3	Malachians	3 (aet Malachians won 3-2 on pens)
Dromore Amateurs	1	Shorts Brothers	3

19th October, 1995

Downshire Young Men	2	Wellington Recreation	0	Glebe Rangers	5	Ards Rangers	6
Northern Telecom	1	East Belfast	2				

THIRD ROUND

29th November, 1995

Annagh United	1	Harland & Wolff Welders	3	Cullybackey	2	Ards Rangers	3
Dungiven Celtic	3	Seapatrick	0	First Liverpool R.R.	2	Orangefield Old Boys	1
Laurelvale	1	East Belfast	2	Malachians	2	Downshire Young Men	1
Portstewart	2	Tandragee Rovers	1	Shorts Brothers	0	Larne Tech Old Boys	0

THIRD ROUND REPLAYS

29th November, 1995

Larne Tech. Old Boys	3	Shorts Brothers	2

Clubs exempt til Fourth Round: Armagh City; Ballinamallard United; Ballymoney United; Banbridge Town; Brantwood; British Telecom; Chimney Corner; Coagh United; Cookstown United; Crewe United; Crumlin United; Donegal Celtic; Drumaness Mills; Dundela; Dungannon Swifts; Dunmurry Recreation; F.C.Enkalon; Kilmore Recreation; Limavady United; Loughgall; Moyola Park; Park; R.U.C; Tobermore United:

BASS IRISH CUP 1995/96
FOURTH ROUND

9th December, 1995

Ballinamallard United	1	Crumlin United	1	Ballymoney United	1	Larne Tech. Old Boys	3
Banbridge Town	3	Loughgall	3	British Telecom	0	Dungiven Celtic	2
Crewe United	2	Cookstown United	4	Drumaness Mills	2	East Belfast	3
Dundela	1	Harland & Wolff Welders	1	Dungannon Swifts	2	Moyola Park	0
Dunmurry Recreation	0	Armagh City	1	First Liverpool R.R.	1	Portstewart	1
Kilmore Recreation	3	Coagh United	2	Limavady United	1	Ards Rangers	1
Malachians	4	F.C.Enkalon	3	Park	2	Chimney Corner	2
R.U.C.	v	Donegal Celtic (Donegal Celtic withdrew)					
Tobermore United	1	Brantwood	0				

Fourth Round Replays

12th December, 1995

Crumlin United	4	Ballinamallard United	0

13th December, 1995

Dundela	3	Harland & Wolff Welders	0	Limavady United	2	Ards Rangers	1
Loughgall	1	Banbridge Town	4	Portstewart	0	First Liverpool R.R.	1

14th December, 1995

Chimney Corner	2	Park	0

FIFTH ROUND

20th January, 1995

Ards (6) 10   Cookstown United (0) 0
Boyle (11,14), Barker (15,17,52),
McCann (24), (P) Cullen (30,59,69,79)

Ards: Kee, McBride, Murphy, (M) Kelly, Mooney, (P) Cullen, Shanley, Bowers, Barker, McCann, Boyle. *Subs:* O'Sullivan replaced Bowers; Dunnion replaced McCann; *Sub not used:* Walker:
Cookstown Utd: Talbot, Donnelly, Hudson, Monaghan, Taggart, Shannon, (J) McGuickin, (S) Hunter, Montgomery, McElhatton, Kelly. *Subs:* Devine replaced Kelly; Corr replaced Hudson; McAllister replaced McElhatton:
Referee: M.Ross (Londonderry)

Armagh City (0) 2   Dundela (0) 1
McAleavey (70), Casey (75)   Whiteside (51)

Armagh C: Pollock, Cochrane, Richardson, Haire, Murphy, McAleavey, Fay, Neill, Casey, Tumilty, Willis. *Subs not used:* Lavery; Montgomery; McGeown:
Dundela: Miskelly, Fyfe, McKee, McCormick, Lennox, Whiteside, Caskey, Doey, Hanvey, Coulter, Snodden. *Subs:* Fettis replaced Doey McCarroll replaced Caskey Parker replaced Whiteside. *Referee:* F.Hiles (Newtownards)
Booked: Murphy (Armagh City): *Sent Off:* Alan Murphy (Armagh City):

Bangor (0) 0   Portadown (3) 4
                  Kennedy (3,45), Haylock (11),
                  Casey (76)

Bangor: Huxley, Coulter, McGuinness, Spiers, Dornan, Cash, Bailie, Simpson, Williams, Irwin, Percy. *Subs:* Nelson replaced Simpson; McCombe replaced Nelson; Morrow replaced Dornan:
Portadown: Dalton, Fulton, Davidson, Casey, Gallagher, Stewart, Carlyle, Peebles, Haylock, (I.J) Ferguson, Kennedy. *Sub:* Candlish replaced Carlyle; *Subs not used:* Evans; Keenan (gk):
Referee: J.Peden (Richhill)
Booked: Irwin (Bangor); (I.J) Ferguson (Portadown):

Chimney Corner (0) 0   Ballymena United (1) 1
                         Loughery (22)

C.Corner: Hartley, Press, Tully, Clifford, Stitt, Mallon, Tumilty, Trainor, Kernoghan, McGurnaghan, Patterson. *Subs:* McCloskey replaced ? Clements replaced Tully; McAlea replaced Kernoghan:
Ballymena Utd: Beck, Carlisle, Boyd, Allen, McConnell, Murray, McConville, Mauchlen, (C) Moore, Loughery, McWalter. *Subs:* (D) Moore replaced Mauchlen; Curry replaced McWalter; Muir replaced Boyd:
Referee: D.Taylor (Tandragee)
Booked: Mallon (Chimney Corner): *Sent Off:* Paul Tumilty (Chimney Corner):

Crumlin United (0) 0 Linfield (3) 8
Johnston (8,48,70), Gorman (30,65), Millar (41,86), Spiers (46)

Crumlin Utd: McFarland, McAuley, Flaherty, (B) Tennyson, McGrath, Duffy, Byrne, Curry, Donnelly, Magilton, Lenaghan. *Subs:* Scannell replaced ? Brady replaced ? (E) Tennyson replaced ?
Linfield: Crawford, Dornan, McCoosh, Ewing, Spiers, Beatty, Millar, Gorman, Johnston, Fenlon, Bailie. *Subs:* Knell replaced Gorman; Erskine replaced Johnston; Caldwell (gk) replaced Crawford:
Referee: E.Millar (Bangor)

Crusaders (3) 4 Dungiven Celtic (0) 0
(G) Hunter (3,8), McCartney (5), Baxter (51)

Crusaders: McKeown, McMullan, Carroll, Dunlop, (R) Lawlor, (K) Hunter, O'Brien, Dunne, Baxter, (G) Hunter, McCartney. *Subs:* Mellon replaced (K) Hunter; Morgan replaced McCartney Livingstone replaced O'Brien:
Dungiven C: (W) Harkin, (S) McLaughlin, (M) McCloskey, Haslett, McGonigle, Gaile, McKeever, Kelly, (L) McCloskey, Quigg, (J) McLaughlin. *Subs:* (S) Harkin replaced ? McVey replaced ? O'Reilly replaced ?
Referee: F.McDonald (Newry)

Distillery (3) 4 Larne Tech. Old Boys (1) 2
Hall (30), Totten (31,51), (K) McAllister (43), Holden (68)
Moore (33)

Distillery: Currie, Drake, Kennedy, Allen, Brady, Small, Totten, Hall, Hillis, Mitchell, Moore. *Subs:* Robson replaced Hillis; Toal replaced Allen; McAleenan replaced Mitchell:
Larne Tech: Sluman, (F) McAllister, Cowie, Hamilton, Holden, Cahoon, Brown, Brownlow, Robinson, (K) McAllister, Brunker. *Subs:* McCourt replaced (F) McAllister; Thompson replaced Robinson; Ferguson replaced Brunker:
Referee: N.Cowie (Bangor)

Dungannon Swifts (0) 2 Omagh Town (1) 4
McNamee (61), O'Hagen (65) *Quigg (25), (B) McCreadie (55), McElroy (86), McIntyre (90)*

Dungannon Sw: Vance, Gregg, McCrory, Coll, Clarke, Jer.Robinson, Jennings, McNamee, O'Hagen, Magee, Smyth. *Subs:* Shaw replaced Clarke; Montgomery replaced Jer.Robinson; *Sub not used:* D.Robinson:
Omagh T: Blake, Johnston, (D) O'Neill, McCaul, Donnelly, Kavanagh, Gallagher, Quigg, (B) McCreadie, Crilly, McHugh. *Subs:* McIntyre replaced (B) McCreadie; McElroy replaced McCaul; Doherty replaced Gallagher:
Referee: D.Magill (Belfast)
Booked: Smyth, O'Hagen, Coll (Dungannon Swifts); Johnston (Omagh Town)

East Belfast (2) 4 Malachians (0) 1
Kavanagh (og4), Grattan (12,82), King (77)
(G) Dougherty (90)

E.Belfast: McKenzie, Blackstock, Pavis, Martin, (G) Murray, (C) Dougherty, Irvine, Grattan, McDowell, Adair, (G) Dougherty. *Subs:* Shannon replaced Martin *Subs not used:* (B) Murray; Wright:
Malachians: Hickey, McAlea, McNally, Adams, Kavanagh, Lynn, Adair, Magee, Duffy, Girvan, Lewsley. Subs: King replaced Adams; Brien replaced ? Hood replaced ?
Referee: H.Barr (Bangor)

Glenavon (6) 12 First Liverpool R.R. (0) 0
McBride (6,31,53,74), McCoy (15,66), Ferguson (34,41,68,85), Johnston (40), Kenny (76)

Glenavon: O'Neill, Byrne, Glendinning, Doherty, Brown, (G) Smyth, Johnston, McCoy, Ferguson, McBride, Kenny. *Subs:* Collins replaced Johnston; McAllister replaced (G) Smyth; (D) Murphy replaced Doherty:
First Liverpool: Hendron, Spiers, Evans, McCabe, Graham, Jones, Piggott, McAleese, Walker, McCleary, White. *Subs:* Tweedie replaced Walker; Patterson replaced McAleese; Kelly replaced Walker:
Referee: T.Deegan (Ballynahinch)

Glentoran (1) 4 Limavady United (1) 1
Batey (43), Cook (47,89), Moran (26)
McBride (48)

Glentoran: Armstrong, Nixon, (M) Smyth, Walker, (J) Devine, Mathieson, Cunnington, Little, Cook, Batey, McBride. *Subs:* (T) Smith replaced Batey Quigley replaced Cunnington; *Subs not used:* Finlay.
Limavady Utd: Crown, Nutt, McCreadie, Davies, King, McCallum, (M) Mullan, Law, Neill, Moran, Painter. *Subs:* Harrison replaced Law, White replaced Neill, Morrow replaced Painter. *Referee:* D.Malcolm (Bangor)

Kilmore Recreation (0) 0 Cliftonville (1) 3
Tabb (42), McCann (67), Donnelly (82)

Kilmore Rec: Travers, Mullan, Swail, Trainor, Owens, Oakes, Gelston, Kennedy, McCarthy, Smith, McPhillips. *Subs:* Healey ? Madine ? Curran ?
Cliftonville: Rice, Hill, Flynn, Tabb, Kerr, Strang, McCann,

BASS IRISH CUP 1995/96

Sliney, O'Neill, Stokes, Donnelly. Subs: Feehan replaced Strang; McFadden replaced Stokes; *Sub not used:* Heath
Referee: J.Ferry (Londonderry)

Larne   (1)   3   Banbridge Town   (0)   0
Collier (41), Armstrong (63),
McCrae (73)

Larne: Robinson, McConkey, Collier, McKinstry, (N) Murray, May, Leckey, McCrae, McMahon, Armstrong, (S) McDowell. *Subs:* Johnston ? Jeffrey ? (2) Smyth
Banbridge T: Napier, Mullan, Scappaticci, Griffen, Gray, McStravick, Johnston, White, Clarke, Brannigan, Douglas. *Subs:* Maguire replaced White; (K) Buchanan replaced Mullan; Andrews replaced Brannigan:
Referee: P.Thompson (Bangor)

Newry Town   (1)   2   Coleraine   (1)   1
Barr (22,66)   McIvor (1)

Newry T: Campbell, (C) O'Kane, (A) Scappaticci, (B) O'Kane, (F) Scappaticci, Ralph, Magee, McParland, Mooney, Barr, Clarke. *Sub:* (S) Feehan replaced Ralph; *Subs not used:* (N) Watson; (N) Courtney:
Coleraine: O'Hare, Doherty, McAuley, Young, Gaston, Gorman, Shiels, O'Dowd, Surgeon, McAllister, McIvor. *Sub:* McCallan replaced Surgeon; *Subs not used:* Hagan; Canning (gk):
Referee: R.Lutton (Lurgan)

R.U.C.   (1)   2   Carrick Rangers   (0)   3
Young ( ), Millen (60)   Armstrong (55), Macauley (61), (F)
Wilson (85)

R.U.C: Matthews, Ferguson, (D) Crawford, Spratt, (J) Crawford, Mercer, Millen, McFadden, Macartney, Young, Leckey. *Subs:* Hunter replaced Macartney. *Subs not used:* Love, McClean:
Carrick R: Dillon, McGarvey, Gilmore, Muldoon, McLeister, Donaghey, Sinclair, McDermott, Armstrong, Ferris, Macauley. *Subs:* (F) Wilson replaced Muldoon; (W) Wilson replaced Donaghey; *Sub not used:* Doherty:
Referee: L.Irvine (Limavady)

Tobermore United   (1)   2   Ballyclare Comrades (1)   3
Crooks (42,47)   Forshaw (6,53),
*   (S) Galbraith (87)*

Tobermore Utd: Stewart, Todd, (A) Moore, Nelson, Young, Leacock, Patterson, Crooks, Taylor, McKay, Reid. *Subs:* O'Doherty replaced ? Kelly ? Wray ?
Ballyclare C: (D) McCusker, (N) Blair, Kearns, Walker, Morrison, (S) Galbraith, Allsopp, O'Connor, Young, Forshaw, Bell. *Sub:* (F) McCusker replaced (N) Blair; *Subs not used:* Higgins; Irwin:
Referee: G.Keatley (Bangor)

Ards (0) 1   Larne   (0)
Morrison (83)

Ards: Kee, McBride, McLaughlin, (C) Cullen, Mooney, Murphy, (P) Cullen, Morrison, Barker, Shanley, Boyle. *Subs:* Murray replaced Boyle; McCann replaced Shanley; *Sub not used:* O'Sullivan:
Larne: Robinson, (N) Murray, Collier, McKinstry, Johnston, (L) Smyth, Bustard, Leckey, McMahon, May, McKnight. *Subs:* Magill replaced Bustard; (S) McDowell replaced May (B); *Sub not used:* ( ) McLoughlin:
Referee: H.Barr (Bangor)

Ballyclare Comrades   (0)   0   Crusaders (0)   1
*   Dunne (84)*

Ballyclare Com: (D) McCusker, Allsopp, Kearns, Walker, Morrison, Bell, O'Connor, (L) Galbraith, Higgins, Campbell, Young. *Subs:* (N) Blair replaced Higgins; Boyle replaced Campbell; *Sub not used:* Forshaw:
Crusaders: McKeown, McMullan, Carroll, Dunlop, (R) Lawlor, Murray, O'Brien, Dunne, Baxter, (G) Hunter, Burrows. *Sub:* Callaghan replaced Carroll; *Subs not used:* Deegan; (K) Hunter:
Referee: L.Irvine (Limavady)

Ballymena United   (2)   4   Armagh City   (0)   0
(C) Moore (2,65), Loughery (11,60)

Ballymena Utd: Smyth, Carlisle, Stewart, Allen, McConnell, Boyd, McConville, Muir, (C) Moore, Loughery, McWalter. *Sub:* (D) Moore replaced Allen; *Subs not used:* Murray; Beck (gk):
Armagh C: Pollock, Cochrane, Richardson, Haire, Murphy, McAleavey, Fay, Neill, Casey, Tumilty, Willis. *Sub:* McGeown replaced Willis; *Subs not used:* Lavery; Williamson:
Referee: A.Snoddy (Carryduff)
Sent Off: Oliver McGeown (Armagh City):

Carrick Rangers   (1)   1   Newry Town   (0)   0
Armstrong (7)

Carrick R: Dillon, McGarvey, Gilmore, Muldoon, McLeister, Donaghey, Sinclair, (F) Wilson, Armstrong, Doherty, Macauley. *Subs:* Ferris replaced Armstrong; (W) Wilson replaced Doherty; McDermott replaced McGarvey:
Newry T: Keeley, (B) O'Kane, (C) O'Kane, (A) Scappaticci, (F) Scappaticci, Ralph, (R) Watson, Magee, Barr, Clarke, Mooney. *Sub:* Whelan replaced Clarke; *Subs not used:* (N) Watson; (N) Courtney:
Referee: N.Cowie (Bangor)
Booked: McLeister (Carrick Rangers): *Sent Off:* Thomas McLeister (Carrick Rangers):

BASS IRISH CUP 1995/96

Glenavon (2) 3   **Cliftonville (1) 1**
McCoy (26), Ferguson (34),   *Rice (pen 29)*
(D) Murphy (85)

Glenavon: O'Neill, (J) Smyth, Glendinning, Doherty, Gauld,
(G) Smyth, Johnston, Shepherd, Ferguson, McBride, McCoy.
Subs: Collins replaced Johnston; (D) Murphy replaced McCoy;
Sub not used: Byrne:
Cliftonville: Rice, Hill, Flynn, Tabb, Kerr, McDonald, McCann,
Strang, Feehan, Stokes, Heath. *Sub:* Manley replaced Strang;
Subs not used: Loughran; Cavanagh:
Referee: G.Keatley (Bangor)
Booked: Kerr, McDonald, Stokes (Cliftonville):

Glentoran (1) 2   **Distillery (0) 0**
Cook (9), Finlay (77)

Glentoran: Armstrong, Nixon, (M) Smyth, Kennedy, (J) Devine,
Finlay, (T) Smith, Mathieson, Cook, Batey, McBride. *Subs:*
Telford replaced Cook; Quigley replaced Mathieson; *Sub not
used:* Parker:
Distillery: Collins, Drake, Hall, Allen, Brush, McAleenan,
Small, Moore, Hillis, Toal, Cleland. *Subs:* Magill replaced
McAleenan; Totten replaced Hillis; Robson replaced Moore:
Referee: J.Ferry (Londonderry)
Booked: (J) Devine (Glentoran); Allen (Distillery):

Linfield (1) 1   **East Belfast (0) 0**
Fenlon (pen 33)

Linfield: Lamont, Dornan, McCoosh, Ewing, Spiers, McShane,
Ray.Campbell, Erskine, Millar, Fenlon, Bailie. *Sub:* McGee re-
placed McCoosh; *Subs not used:* Easton; McIlroy:
E.Belfast: Millen, Pavis, (B) Murray, Irwin, (G) Murray, Craig,
Irvine, Grattan, Dougherty, McDowell, Shannon. *Subs:* McCaw
replaced Grattan; Wright replaced Dougherty; Lee replaced
McDowell:
Referee: M.Ross (Carrickfergus)
Booked: Spiers (Linfield); McDowell, Lee (East Belfast):

Portadown (1) 3   **Omagh Town (0) 1**
Casey (27), Haylock (82,90)   *Donnelly (59)*

Portadown: Dalton, Major, Fulton, Casey, Strain, Byrne,
Carlyle, Peebles, Haylock, Candlish, Kennedy. *Subs not used:*
McKeever; Evans; Keenan (gk):
Omagh T: Blake, Johnston, Magill, Donnelly, Melly, Kavanagh,
Mooney, Gallagher, McDowell, Crilly, McHugh. *Subs not used:*
McElroy; Moore; (D) O'Neill:
Referee: E.Millar (Bangor)
Booked: Kennedy, Byrne (Portadown); Donnelly (Omagh
Town); *Sent Off:* Mark Donnelly (Omagh Town):

QUARTER-FINALS
9th March, 1996

Crusaders (0) 2   **Linfield (0) 0**
Baxter (pen 52,84)

Crusaders: McKeown, McMullan, Carroll, Dunlop, (R) Lawlor,
Murray, Callaghan, Dunne, Baxter, (G) Hunter, Burrows. *Subs:*
Deegan replaced Baxter; (K) Hunter replaced (G) Hunter;
O'Brien replaced (K) Hunter:
Linfield: Lamont, Dornan, Easton, McIlroy, Spiers, McGee,
Ray.Campbell, Johnston, Millar, Fenlon, Bailie. *Subs:* Ewing
replaced McIlroy; Gorman replaced Johnston; *Sub not used:*
Erskine:
Referee: H.Barr (Bangor)
Booked: (K) Hunter, Murray, Callaghan (Crusaders); McGee,
Spiers (Linfield):

Glenavon (2) 3   **Carrick Rangers (0) 1**
Ferguson (24,37,62)   *Ferris (69)*

Glenavon: O'Neill, (J) Smyth, Glendinning, Doherty, Gauld,
(G) Smyth, Johnston, Shepherd, Ferguson, McBride, Shipp.
Subs not used: Collins; Byrne; (D) Murphy:
Carrick R: Dillon, McGarvey, Gilmore, (W) Wilson, McLeister,
Donaghey, Crawford, McDermott, Armstrong, (F) Wilson,
Macauley. *Subs:* Ferris replaced Armstrong; Doherty replaced
Crawford; *Sub not used:* Lowry:
Referee: M.Ross (Carrickfergus)

Glentoran 0   **Ballymena United 0**

Glentoran: (D) Devine, Nixon, (M) Smyth, Kennedy, (J)
Devine, Parker, Quigley, Coyle, Cook, Batey, McBride. *Sub:*
Walker replaced (D) Devine; *Subs not used:* Mathieson; Telford:
Ballymena Utd: Beck, Carlisle, Muir, Allen, McConnell,
Murray, McConville, Mauchlen, Moors, Loughery, Boyd. *Subs
not used:* (D) Moore; (C) Moore; Smyth (gk):
Referee: L.Irvine (Limavady)
Booked: Walker (Glentoran); Mauchlen and McConnell
(Ballymena United):

Portadown (0) 2   **Ards (0) 1**
Kennedy (47), Candlish (51)   *Morrison (55)*

Portadown: Dalton, Major, Fulton, Casey, Byrne, Stewart,
Evans, Carlyle, Haylock, Candlish, Kennedy. Sub: McKeever
replaced Evans; *Subs not used:* Turkington; Keenan (gk):
Ards: Kee, McBride, McLaughlin, Shanley, Mooney, Murphy,
(P) Cullen, Morrison, Getty, McCann, O'Sullivan. *Sub:* Boyle
replaced O'Sullivan; *Subs not used:* Johnston; Walker:
Referee: J.Ferry (Londonderry)

135

QUARTER-FINALS REPLAY
13th March, 1996

Ballymena United (2) 2   **Glentoran** (2) 4
Moors (24), McConville (26)   *(M) Smyth (39), Little (44,49,88)*

Ballymena Utd: Beck, Carlisle, Muir, Allen, McConnell, Murray, McConville, Burn, Moors, Loughery, Boyd. Subs: (D) Moore replaced Loughery; Gilmore replaced McConnell; *Sub not used:* Smyth (gk):
Glentoran: Armstrong, Nixon, (M) Smyth, Kennedy, (J) Devine, Walker, Quigley, Little, Cook, Batey, McBride. *Subs:* Parker replaced Quigley; *Subs not used:* Coyle: Mathieson:
Referee: L.Irvine (Limavady)

SEMI-FINALS
12th April, 1996

Venue: Windsor Park, Belfast
Glentoran (1) 2   **Crusaders** (2) 2
McKeown (og 32),   *Baxter (17),*
(T) Smith (78)   *(G) Hunter (41)*

Glentoran: Armstrong, Walker, (M) Smyth, Kennedy, (J) Devine, Parker, Mathieson, Little, Coyle, Batey. *Subs:* Finlay replaced Kennedy; (T) Smith replaced Parker; *Sub not used:* Cook:
Crusaders: McKeown, McMullan, Deegan, Dunlop, Darby, Murray, O'Brien, Dunne, Baxter, (G) Hunter, Burrows. *Subs not used:* Livingstone; (K) Hunter; Mellon:
Referee: H.Barr (Bangor)
Booked: (M) Smyth (Glentoran); McMullan (Crusaders):

13th April, 1996

Venue: The Oval, Belfast
Glenavon (0) 1   **Portadown** (1) 1
McBride (48)   *Kennedy (22)*

Glenavon: O'Neill, (J) Smyth, Glendinning, Doherty, Gauld, (G) Smyth, Johnston, Shepherd, Ferguson, McBride, Shipp. *Subs:* McCoy replaced Shipp; (D) Murphy replaced Johnston; *Sub not used:* Straney (gk):
Portadown: Dalton, Major, Davidson, Casey, Fulton, Stewart, Woodsford, Bain, Haylock, Peebles, Kennedy. *Subs not used:* Carlyle; Evans; Keenan (gk):
Referee: L.Irvine (Limavady)
Booked: O'Neill (Glenavon):

SEMI-FINAL REPLAYS
16th April, 1996

Venue: Windsor Park, Belfast
Glentoran (1) 2   **Crusaders** (1) 1
McBride (23), Coyle (89)   *Baxter (40)*

Glentoran: Armstrong, Nixon, (M) Smyth, Walker, (J) Devine, Parker, (T) Smith, Little, Coyle, Batey, McBride. *Subs not used:* Cook; Finlay:
Crusaders: McKeown, McMullan, Deegan, Dunlop, (R) Lawlor, Murray, O'Brien, Dunne, Baxter, (G) Hunter, Burrows. *Subs:* Livingstone replaced Dunne; (K) Hunter replaced Murray; *Subs not used:* Darby:
Referee: H.Barr (Bangor) replaced by N.Cowie (Carryduff) after 51 mins.
Booked: (J) Devine, Little (Glentoran); McMullan, (R) Lawlor, O'Brien (Crusaders):

17th April, 1996

Venue: The Oval, Belfast
Glenavon (2) 4   **Portadown** (1) 1
Shipp (26,59), Ferguson (34),   *Major (19)*
Doherty (56)

Glenavon: O'Neill, (J) Smyth, Glendinning, Doherty, Gauld, (G) Smyth, Johnston, Shepherd, Ferguson, McBride, Shipp. *Subs:* McCoy replaced Ferguson; (D) Murphy replaced McBride; *Sub not used:* Straney (gk):
Portadown: Dalton, Major, Davidson, Casey, Fulton, Stewart, Woodsford, Bain, Haylock, Peebles, Kennedy. *Subs:* Carlyle replaced Woodsford; Evans replaced Kennedy; *Sub not used:* Keenan (gk). *Referee:* L.Irvine (Limavady)

FINAL
4th May, 1996

Venue: Windsor Park, Belfast   Att: 10,000
Glentoran (0) 1   **Glenavon** (0) 0
Little (75)

Glentoran: (D) Devine, Nixon, Finlay, Walker, (J) Devine, Parker, (T) Smith, Little, Coyle, Batey, McBride. *Subs not used:* Cook; Mathieson; Armstrong (gk):
Glenavon: Straney, (J) Smyth, Glendinning, (D) Murphy, Gauld, (G) Smyth, Johnston, Shepherd, Ferguson, McBride, Shipp. *Sub:* McCoy replaced McBride (77 mins); *Subs not used:* Brown; Byrne:
Referee: A.Snoddy (Carryduff)
Booked: Gauld (Glenavon): Walker (Glentoran):

Irish Cup Finals 1880/81-1995/96

Season	Winner		Runner-up	
1880/81	Moyola Park	1	Cliftonville	0
1881/82	Queens Island	1	Cliftonville	0
1882/83	Cliftonville	5	Ulster	0
1883/84	Distillery	5	Wellington Park	0
1884/85	Distillery	2	Limavady	0
1885/86	Distillery	1	Limavady	0
1886/87	Ulster	3	Cliftonville	1
1887/88	Cliftonville	2	Distillery	1
1888/89	Distillery	5	Belfast YMCA	4
1889/90	Gordon Highlanders	3	Cliftonville	0
	(after 2-2 draw)			
1890/91	Linfield	4	Ulster	2
1891/92	Linfield	7	Black Watch	0
1892/93	Linfield	5	Cliftonville	1
1893/94	Distillery	3	Linfield	2
	(after 2-2 draw)			
1894/95	Linfield	10	Bohemians	1
1895/96	Distillery	3	Glentoran	1
1896/97	Cliftonville	3	Sherwood Forsesters	1
1897/98	Linfield	2	St.Columbs Hall	0
1898/99	Linfield	1	Glentoran	0
1899/00	Cliftonville	2	Bohemians	1
1900/01	Cliftonville	1	Freebooters	0
1901/02	Linfield	5	Distillery	1
1902/03	Distillery	3	Bohemians	1
1903/04	Linfield	5	Derry Celtic	0
1904/05	Distillery	3	Shelbourne	0
1905/06	Shelbourne	2	Belfast Celtic	0
1906/07	Cliftonville	1	Shelbourne	0
	(after 0-0 draw)			
1907/08	Bohemians	3	Shelbourne	1
	(after 1-1 draw)			
1908/09	Cliftonville	2	Bohemians	1
	(after 0-0 draw)			
1909/10	Distillery	1	Cliftonville	0
1910/11	Shelbourne	2	Bohemians	1
	(after 0-0 draw)			
1911/12	Linfield awarded cup. Final not played.			
1912/13	Linfield	2	Glentoran	0
1913/14	Glentoran	3	Linfield	1
1914/15	Linfield	1	Belfast Celtic	0
1915/16	Linfield	1	Glentoran	0
	(after 1-1 draw)			
1916/17	Glentoran	2	Belfast Celtic	0
1917/18	Belfast Celtic	2	Linfield	0
	(after two 0-0 draws)			
1918/19	Linfield	2	Glentoran	1
	(after 1-1 and 0-0 draws)			
1919/20	Shelbourne awarded cup. Final not played.			
1920/21	Glentoran	2	Glenavon	0
1921/22	Linfield	2	Glenavon	1
1922/23	Linfield	2	Glentoran	0
1923/24	Queens Island	1	Willowfield	0
1924/25	Distillery	2	Glentoran	1
1925/26	Belfast Celtic	3	Linfield	2
1926/27	Ards	3	Cliftonville	2
1927/28	Willowfield	1	Larne	0
	(after 1-1 draw)			
1928/29	Ballymena	2	Belfast Celtic	1
1929/30	Linfield	4	Ballymena	3
1930/31	Linfield	3	Ballymena	0
1931/32	Glentoran	2	Linfield	1
1932/33	Glentoran	3	Distillery	1
	(after two 1-1 draws)			
1933/34	Linfield	5	Cliftonville	0
1934/35	Glentoran	1	Larne	0
	(after two 0-0 draws)			
1935/36	Linfield	2	Derry City a.e.t.	1
	(after 0-0 draw)			
1936/37	Belfast Celtic	3	Linfield	0
1937/38	Belfast Celtic	2	Bangor	0
	(after 0-0 draw)			
1938/39	Linfield	2	Ballymena United	0
1939/40	Ballymena United	2	Glenavon	0
1940/41	Belfast Celtic	1	Linfield	0
1941/42	Linfield	3	Glentoran	1
1942/43	Belfast Celtic	1	Glentoran	0
1943/44	Belfast Celtic	3	Linfield	1
1944/45	Linfield	4	Glentoran	2
1945/46	Linfield	3	Distillery	0
1946/47	Belfast Celtic	1	Glentoran	0
1947/48	Linfield	3	Coleraine	0
1948/49	Derry City	3	Glentoran	1
1949/50	Linfield	2	Distillery	1
1950/51	Glentoran	3	Ballymena United	1
1951/52	Ards	1	Glentoran	0
1952/53	Linfield	5	Coleraine	0
1953/54	Derry City	1	Glentoran	0
	(after 2-2 and 0-0 draws)			
1954/55	Dundela	3	Glenavon	0
1955/56	Distillery	1	Glentoran	0
	(after 2-2 and 1-1 draws)			
1956/57	Glenavon	2	Derry City	0
1957/58	Ballymena United	2	Linfield	0
1958/59	Glenavon	2	Ballymena United	0
	(after 1-1 draw)			
1959/60	Linfield	5	Ards	1
1960/61	Glenavon	5	Linfield	1
1961/62	Linfield	4	Portadown	0
1962/63	Linfield	2	Distillery	1
1963/64	Derry City	2	Glentoran	0
1964/65	Coleraine	2	Glenavon	1
1965/66	Glentoran	2	Linfield	0
1966/67	Crusaders	3	Glentoran	1
1967/68	Crusaders	2	Linfield	0
1968/69	Ards	4	Distillery a.e.t	2
	(after 0-0 draw)			
1969/70	Linfield	2	Ballymena United	1
1970/71	Distillery	3	Derry City	0
1971/72	Coleraine	2	Portadown	1
1972/73	Glentoran	3	Linfield	2
1973/74	Ards	2	Ballymena United	1
1974/75	Coleraine	1	Linfield	0
	(after 1-1 and 0-0 draws)			
1975/76	Carrick Rangers	2	Linfield	1
1976/77	Coleraine	4	Linfield	1
1977/78	Linfield	3	Ballymena United	1
1978/79	Cliftonville	3	Portadown	2
1979/80	Linfield	2	Crusaders	0
1980/81	Ballymena United	1	Glenavon	0
1981/82	Linfield	2	Coleraine	1
1982/83	Glentoran	2	Linfield	1
	(after 1-1 draw)			
1983/84	Ballymena United	4	Carrick Rangers	1
1984/85	Glentoran	1	Linfield	0
	(after 1-1 draw)			
1985/86	Glentoran	2	Coleraine	1
1986/87	Glentoran	1	Larne	0
1987/88	Glentoran	1	Glenavon	0
1988/89	Ballymena United	1	Larne	0
1989/90	Glentoran	3	Portadown	0
1990/91	Portadown	2	Glenavon	1
1991/92	Glenavon	2	Linfield	1
1992/93	Bangor	1	Ards	0
	(after two 1-1 draws)			
1993/94	Linfield	2	Bangor	0
1994/95	Linfield	3	Carrick Rangers	1
1995/96	Glentoran	1	Glenavon	0

Crusaders players are bouyant after narrowly beating Linfield 1-0 in the final of the Gold Cup to lift the trophy for only the second time in their history.
(Photograph by Michael Reeves).

THE SUN LIFE GOLD CUP 1995/96

9th September, 1995

SECTION A

Crusaders (2) 5   Distillery (2) 2
Baxter (26,pen 27,58, 77,90)   Armstrong (21), Brady (45)

Crusaders: McKeown, McMullan, McCartney, Callaghan, Eccles, (K) Hunter, Murray, O'Brien, Baxter, (G) Hunter, Burrows. *Subs:* Carroll replaced Eccles; Dunne replaced (K) Hunter; *Sub not used:* Hamer (gk):
Distillery: Collins, Drake, Kennedy, Allen, Brush, Brady, Totten, Small, Armstrong, Mitchell, Dykes. *Subs:* Murray replaced Dykes; Cleland replaced Armstrong; Curliss replaced Brady:
Referee: F.Hiles (Newtownards)

Newry Town (0) 1   Linfield (0) 3
Barr (77)   Gorman (54,70),
*   Fenlon (pen 63)*

Newry T: Keeley, McParland, (A) Scappaticci, (C) O'Kane, Gracey, Ralph, McQuaid, Mooney, Whelan, Stokes, Clarke. *Subs:* Barr replaced McQuaid; (S) Feehan replaced (A) Scappaticci; *Sub not used:* Campbell (gk):
Linfield: Lamont, Dornan, Easton, Millar, McLean, Beatty, Ray.Campbell, Gorman, Erskine, Fenlon, Bailie. *Sub:* Ewing replaced Millar; *Subs not used:* McGee; Caldwell (gk)
Referee: N.Cowie (Bangor)
Booked: McQuaid (Newry Town)

SECTION B

Ballymena United (1) 2   Coleraine (0) 0
Patton (13), Burn (83)

Ballymena U: Smyth, Carlisle, Stewart, Allen, McConnell, Boyd, Burn, Patton, McCourt, Muir, Heron. *Sub:* Loughery replaced Patton; *Subs not used:* Steele; Gilmore:
Coleraine: O'Hare, Harkin, McAuley, Gaston, Philson, Gorman, Robson, Doherty, Oatway, Beckett, O'Donnell. *Subs:* McIvor replaced O'Donnell; Maloney replaced Harkin; *Sub not used:* Hagan
Referee: G.Keatley (Bangor)
Booked: Carlisle (Ballymena United); Doherty, Philson, O'Hare, Beckett (Coleraine):

Glenavon (1) 1   Bangor (0) 0
Glendinning (19)

Glenavon: O'Neill, Collins, Glendinning, Doherty, Brown, (G) Smyth, (A) Murphy, Johnston, Ferguson, McBride, (J) Smyth. *Sub:* McCoy replaced (A) Murphy; *Subs not used:* Byrne; Currie (gk):
Bangor: Miskelly, Bailie, (S) Hill, Spiers, McKeown, McComb, Percy, Batey, Campbell, Murtagh, (R) Hill. *Sub:* Eddis replaced Murtagh, Wilkinson replaced McKeown; *Sub not used:* Irwin
Referee: M.Ross (Carrickfergus)
Booked: Murtagh, Wilkinson (Bangor)

SECTION C

Ballyclare Comrades (0) 0   Portadown (0) 1
*   Peebles (56)*

Ballyclare C: McGreevy, Allsopp, Kearns, Hall, Morrison, Wilson, (F) McCusker, Irwin, Campbell, O'Connor, Bell. *Sub:* Walker replaced (F) McCusker; *Subs not used:* (L) Galbraith; Finnegan:
Portadown: Keenan, Major, Murray, Casey, Strain, Byrne, Boyle, Russell, Haylock, Peebles, Davidson. *Subs:* Dalton (gk) replaced Davidson; *Subs not used:* Fulton; McArdle:
Referee: A.Snoddy (Carryduff)
Sent Off: Michael Keenan (Portadown)

Omagh Town (1) 2   Ards (2) 2
McHugh (2,88)   Mooney (pen 26),
*   Johnston (og 45)*

Omagh T: Blake, Johnston, McGill, Donnelly, McCaul, Kavanagh, Mooney, (D) O'Neill, McIntyre, Crilly, McHugh. *Sub:* (M) O'Donnell replaced (D) O'Neill; *Subs not used:* Moran; Moore:
Ards: Kee, McBride, Murphy, (M) Kelly, Mooney, O'Sullivan, Simpson, Shanley, Flannery, (P) Cullen, Dunnion. *Subs:* (C) Cullen replaced Simpson; Morrison replaced Dunnion; *Sub not used:* O'Shea:
Referee: R.Lutton (Lurgan)
Booked: Johnston (Omagh Town); Morrison (Ards):

SECTION D

Cliftonville (1) 4   Carrick Rangers (0) 0
McCann (5), Sliney (51),
Strang (75), Feehan (89)

Cliftonville: Rice, Hill, Flynn, Tabb, Kerr, Strang, McCann, Sliney, Feehan, McDonald, Manley. *Subs:* O'Neill replaced Manley; *Sub not used:* Heath, Davey
Carrick R: Hillen, Sinclair, Gilmore, Muldoon, McLeister, Coulter, (W) Wilson, Donaghey, Crawford, Ferris, Macauley. *Subs:* Kirk replaced (W) Wilson; *Sub not used:* Doherty; Dillon (gk)
Referee: L.Irvine (Limavady)

Larne (0) 0   Glentoran (0) 2
*   Cook (79,84)*

Larne: Robinson, McConkey, Collier, Jeffrey, McMahon, Looney, (G) Murray, Armstrong, Hillis, (E) McLoughlin. Subs: Straney replaced Hillis; Leckey replaced (E) McLoughlin; *Sub not used:* Magill:
Glentoran: (D) Devine, Neill, (M) Smyth, Walker, (J) Devine, Mathieson, McEvoy, Little, (T) Smith, Cook, Finlay. *Subs:* Quigley replaced Finlay; McDowell replaced Little; *Sub not used:* Bowers:
Referee: G.Douglas (Comber)

15th September, 1995

SECTION C

Omagh Town (1) 1 Portadown (0) 1
Donnelly (44) *Haylock (60)*

Omagh T: Blake, Johnston, Magill, Donnelly, McCaul, Kavanagh, Mooney, Quigg, McIntyre, Crilly, McHugh. *Sub:* (M) O'Donnell replaced McIntyre; *Subs not used:* (D) O'Neill; Moore:
Portadown: Dalton, Major, Davidson, Peebles, Strain, Byrne, Murray, Russell, Haylock, Magee, Kennedy. *Subs:* Candlish replaced Magee; Fulton replaced Byrne; *Sub not used:* Whitmarsh (gk):
Referee: H.Barr (Bangor)
Booked: Kavanagh (Omagh Town); Major (Portadown):

16th September, 1995

SECTION A

Distillery (1) 3 Newry Town (0) 0
Brush (20), Dykes (66,68)

Distillery: Collins, Drake, Curliss, Allen, Brush, Kennedy, Totten, McAleenan, Dykes, Mitchell, Cleland. *Subs not used:* Small; Armstrong; Quinn:
Newry T: Keeley, McParland, Thompson, (C) O'Kane, Gracey, Ralph, (S) Feehan, Mooney, Barr, (R) Watson, Clarke. *Subs:* (N) Watson replaced Barr; Stokes replaced McParland; *Sub not used:* Campbell (gk):
Referee: M.Ross (Carrickfergus)

Linfield (1) 1 Crusaders (1) 1
Fenlon (10) *(K) Hunter (15)*

Linfield: Lamont, Dornan, Easton, Millar, McLean, Beatty, Ray.Campbell, Gorman, Erskine, Fenlon, Bailie. *Sub:* McGee replaced Gorman; *Subs not used:* Ewing; Crawford (gk):
Crusaders: McKeown, McMullan, McCartney, Murray, Eccles, (K) Hunter, Livingstone, Dunne, O'Brien, (G) Hunter, Burrows. *Subs:* Carroll replaced Murray; Dwyer replaced Livingstone; *Sub not used:* Morgan:
Referee: D.Magill (Belfast)
Booked: Millar (Linfield); (K) Hunter (Crusaders):

SECTION B

Bangor (1) 1 Ballymena United (0) 0
Campbell (20)

Bangor: Miskelly, Bailie, (S) Hill, Spiers, McKeown, McCombe, Percy, Batey, Campbell, McKinstry, (R) Hill. *Subs:* Morrow replaced Campbell; Eddis replaced Batey; Cash replaced (S) Hill:
Ballymena U: Smyth, Carlisle, Stewart, Allen, McConnell, Boyd, Burn, Patton, McCourt, Muir, Heron. *Subs:* Loughery replaced Carlisle; (C) Moore replaced Stewart; *Sub not used:* May (gk):
Referee: E.Millar (Bangor)

Coleraine (0) 1 Glenavon (2) 3
Gorman (85) *Ferguson (34), Doherty (43),*
(D) Murphy (81)

Coleraine: O'Hare, McAuley, Huston, Gaston, Philson, Gorman, Maloney, Doherty, Collins, Patton, Oatway. *Sub:* McIvor replaced McAuley; *Subs not used:* O'Donnell; Hagan:
Glenavon: O'Neill, (D) Murphy, Glendinning, Doherty, (A) Murphy, (G) Smyth, Collins, Johnston, Ferguson, McBride, (J) Smyth. *Subs:* McCoy replaced Collins; Byrne replaced Johnston; *Sub not used:* Currie (gk):
Referee: T.Deegan (Ballynahinch)
Booked: Collins (Coleraine):

SECTION C

Ards (1) 3 Ballyclare Comrades (0) 0
Flannery (44), (P) Cullen (56),
Boyle (73)

Ards: Kee, McBride, Murphy, (M) Kelly, Mooney, O'Sullivan, Simpson, Shanley, Flannery, (P) Cullen, Boyle. *Sub:* (C) Cullen replaced Simpson; *Subs not used:* Elliott; Dunnion:
Ballyclare C: (S) McGreevy, Allsopp, Kearns, Hall, Morrison, Wilson, Finnegan, Irwin, Campbell, Kelly, O'Connor. *Subs:* (L) Galbraith replaced Wilson; Orchin replaced Campbell:
Referee: F.McDonald (Newry)

SECTION D

Carrick Rangers (1) 2 Larne (0) 0
Macauley (10), (W) Wilson (65)

Carrick R: Hillen, Donaghey, (W) Wilson, McDermott, McLeister, Coulter, Sinclair, Kirk, Crawford, Ferris, Macauley. *Subs not used:* Doherty; Gilmore; Dillon (gk):
Larne: Robinson, (N) Murray, Collier, McKinstry, Jeffrey, McMahon, Looney, Leckey, McConkey, Armstrong, (G) Murray. *Subs:* Magill replaced McKinstry; Hillis replaced McConkey; Straney:
Referee: D.Taylor (Trandragee)

Glentoran (0) 0 Cliftonville (1) 1
Flynn (15)

Glentoran: (D) Devine, Neill, (M) Smyth, Walker, (J) Devine, Mathieson, Quigley, Little, (T) Smith, Cook, Finlay. *Subs:* McEvoy replaced Neill; McDowell replaced (M) Smyth; *Sub not used:* Bowers:
Cliftonville: Rice, Hill, Flynn, Tabb, Kerr, Strang, McCann, Sliney, Feehan, McDonald, Manley. *Subs:* O'Neill replaced Strang; McAllister replaced Manley; *Sub not used:* Heath:
Referee: J.Ferry (Londonderry)
Booked: Cook (Glentoran); Hill, Strang, Feehan, Kerr (Cliftonville): *Sent Off:* Tim McCann (Cliftonville):

21st September, 1995

SECTION B

Ballymena United (0) 0   Glenavon (1)   3
                                    Ferguson (10), McBride (58),
                                    Doherty (87)

Ballymena U: Smyth, (D) Moore, Stewart, Mauchlen, McConnell, Boyd, Loughery, Patton, McCourt, Muir, Heron. *Subs* McConville replaced McConnell; *Subs not used:* (C) Moore; Gilmore:
Glenavon: O'Neill, Byrne, Glendinning, Doherty, (A) Murphy, (G) Smyth, Collins, Kenny, Ferguson, McBride, (J) Smyth. *Subs:* McCoy replaced (J) Smyth; McCartan replaced McBride; *Sub not used:* Currie (gk):
Referee: R.Lutton (Lurgan)
Booked: McConville (Ballymena United):

22nd September, 1995

SECTION B

Bangor   (1)   3   Coleraine (1)   1
McKinstry (31), Morrow (49),   Collins (20)
Cash (68)

Bangor: Miskelly, Bailie, (S) Hill, Spiers, McKeown, McCombe, Percy, Cash, McKinstry, Thorpe, Morrow. *Subs:* (R) Hill replaced Percy; Irwin replaced Thorpe; *Sub not used:* Murtagh
Coleraine: O'Hare, McAuley, Huston, Gaston, Philson, Gorman, Oatway, Maloney, Collins, Patton, McIvor. *Subs:* O'Donnell replaced Maloney; Larkin replaced Patton:
Referee: L.Irvine (Limavady)

SECTION C

Ballyclare Comrades (0) 0   Omagh Town (1) 1
                                    Kavanagh (pen 34)

Ballyclare C: McGreevy, Allsopp, Kearns, Hall, Morrison, Irwin, (F) McCusker, O'Connor, Campbell, Kelly, Bell. *Sub:* Finnegan replaced Bell; *Subs not used:* Walker; (D) McCusker (gk):
Omagh T: Blake, Johnston, Magill, Donnelly, McCaul, Kavanagh, Mooney, Quigg, McIntyre, Crilly, McHugh. *Subs:* (D) O'Neill replaced Kavanagh; (M) O'Donnell replaced McHugh; *Sub not used:* Moran:
Referee: J.Peden (Richhill)
Booked: Kelly (Ballyclare Comrades); Magill and McCaul (Omagh Town):

Portadown   (4)   7   Ards   (1)   3
Peebles (6), Strain (8),   (P) Cullen (43,90),
Haylock (30,38,88), Casey (50),   Flannery (56)
Evans (77)

Portadown: Keenan, Fulton, Davidson, Casey, Strain, Major, Peebles, Russell, Haylock, Magee, Kennedy. *Subs:* Evans replaced Peebles; Dalton (gk) replaced Keenan; *Sub not used:* Gallagher
Ards: Kee, McBride, Murphy, (M) Kelly, Mooney, O'Sullivan, (C) Cullen, Boyle, Flannery, (P) Cullen, Morrison. *Subs:*

Dunnion replaced O'Sullivan; McGreevy replaced Dunnion;
Sub not used: Simpson:
Referee: G.Douglas (Comber)
Booked: Haylock and Casey (Portadown); Murphy (Ards):
Sent Off: William Murphy (Ards):

23rd September, 1995

SECTION A

Distillery   (1)   1   Linfield (1)   1
Mitchell (13)   Ewing (23)

Distillery: Collins, Small, Curliss, Allen, Brush, Kennedy, Totten, McAleenan, Dykes, Mitchell, Cleland. *Sub:* Armstrong replaced Curliss; *Subs not used:* McKavanagh; McEnhill (gk):
Linfield: Lamont, Dornan, Easton, Ewing, McLean, Beatty, Ray.Campbell, McGee, Erskine, Fenlon, Bailie. *Sub:* Millar replaced McGee; *Subs not used:* Hosick; Crawford (gk):
Referee: H.Barr (Bangor)
Booked: Brush (Distillery):

Newry Town   (2)   2   Crusaders (1)   3
Clarke (pen 12), Ralph (19)   (K) Hunter (28), Callaghan
                               (67), Dunlop (77)

Newry T: Keeley, McParland, Berry, (C) O'Kane, (F) Scappaticci, Ralph, Whelan, Gracey, (B) O'Kane, Stokes, Clarke. *Subs:* Barr replaced   ? Mooney replaced   ?
Campbell (gk) replaced Keeley:
Crusaders: McKeown, (R) Lawlor, McCartney, Dunlop, Callaghan, Eccles, (K) Hunter, Dunne, O'Brien, (G) Hunter, Burrows. *Subs:* Baxter replaced (G) Hunter; McMullan replaced Eccles; Carroll replaced McCartney:
Referee: P.Thompson (Bangor)

SECTION D

Carrick Rangers (1) 1   Glentoran (1)   1
Kirk (2)   (T) Smith (18)

Carrick R: Hillen, Gilmore, (W) Wilson, McDermott, McLeister, Coulter, Sinclair, Donaghey, Kirk, Ferris, Macauley. *Subs:* Doherty replaced Macauley; Crawford replaced Gilmore; Jamison (gk) replaced Sinclair:
Glentoran: (D) Devine, Neill, (M) Smyth, Walker, (J) Devine, Mathieson, Quigley, McEvoy, (T) Smith, Cook. *Subs:* Parker replaced (T) Smith; Kelly replaced McEvoy; McDowell replaced Cook:
Referee: T.Deegan (Ballynahinch)

Larne   (1)   1   Cliftonville (0)   0
Armstrong (13)

Larne: Robinson, (N) Murray, Collier, McKinstry, Jeffrey, Leckey, Looney, Straney, McCrae, Armstrong, (E) McLoughlin. *Subs:* Hillis replaced Straney; Magill replaced Collier; McConkey replaced (E) McLoughlin:
Cliftonville: Rice, Hill, Flynn, Tabb, Kerr, Strang, McDonald, Sliney, Feehan, McAllister, Manley. *Subs:* Heath replaced Sliney; Craig replaced Feehan; O'Neill replaced Hill
Referee: F.Hiles (Newtownards)

141

FINAL TABLES

SECTION A

	P	W	D	L	F	A	Pts	GD
1 Crusaders	3	2	1	0	9	5	7	+4
2 Linfield	3	1	2	0	5	3	5	+2
3 Distillery	3	1	1	1	6	6	4	-
4 Newry Town	3	0	0	3	3	9	0	-6

SECTION B

	P	W	D	L	F	A	Pts	GD
1 Glenavon *	3	3	0	0	7	1	9	+6
2 Bangor	3	2	0	1	4	2	6	+2
3 Ballymena United	3	1	0	2	2	4	3	-2
4 Coleraine	3	0	0	3	2	8	0	-6

SECTION C

	P	W	D	L	F	A	Pts	GD
1 Portadown	3	2	1	0	9	4	7	+5
2 Omagh Town	3	1	2	0	4	3	5	+1
3 Ards	3	1	1	1	8	9	4	-1
4 Ballyclare Comrades	3	0	0	3	0	5	0	-5

SECTION D

	P	W	D	L	F	A	Pts	GD
1 Cliftonville	3	2	0	1	5	1	6	+4
2 Glentoran	3	1	1	1	3	2	4	+1
3 Carrick Rangers	3	1	1	1	3	5	4	-2
4 Larne	3	1	0	2	1	4	3	-3

* Glenavon were dismissed from the competition for fielding Marc Kenny during the group matches whilst he was still serving a suspension. Ballymena United, who were the third placed team in Section B replaced Glenavon in the Quarter-Finals.

QUARTER-FINALS

24th October, 1995

Crusaders (1)	1	Bangor (0)	2

O'Brien (29)   *Murtagh (48), O'Connell (53)*

(match abandoned after 56 minutes due to severe weather conditions)

Linfield (0)	0	Glentoran (1)	1

Cunnington (15)

(match abandoned after 60 mins due to severe weather conditions)

28th November, 1995

Crusaders (1)	2	Bangor (0)	1

Baxter (28,49)   *Irwin (54)*

Crusaders: McKeown, Carroll, McCartney, Callaghan, Eccles, Deegan, Morgan, Dunne, Baxter, O'Brien, Burrows. *Subs:* Murray replaced Burrows; McMullan replaced Dunne; *Sub not used:* (G) Hunter:
Bangor: Miskelly, Percy, McGuinness, Spiers, McCombe, Dornan, Byrne, Irwin, Davis, McNamara, Bailie. *Subs:* (R) Hill replaced Bailie; O'Connell replaced McNamara; *Sub not used:* Wilkinson ?
Referee: D.Magill (Belfast)

Linfield (0)	2	Glentoran (2)	2

Gorman (68), McLaughlin (71)   *McBride (19,37)*
(aet Linfield won 4-3 on pens)
Penalty Shoot Out:
Linfield: Beatty, Ray.Campbell, Knell, Fenlon (all scored):
Glentoran: Devine (scored), Quigley (missed), Kennedy, Cunnington (both scored), Parker (missed):

Linfield: Lamont, Dornan, McLaughlin, McCoosh, Spiers, Beatty, Ray.Campbell, Gorman, Johnston, Fenlon, Bailie. *Sub:* Knell replaced McLaughlin; *Subs not used:* Hosick; Crawford (gk):
Glentoran: Armstrong, Nixon, (M) Smyth, Kennedy, (J) Devine, Parker, McBride, Little, (T) Smith, Quigley, Cunnington. *Subs:* McCarrison replaced Little; Kelly replaced (T) Smith; *Sub not used:* Cook:
Referee: A.Snoddy (Carryduff)
Sent Off: Gorman (Linfield)

Omagh Town (1)   4   **Portadown (2)   2 aet**
Donnelly (23), (B) McCreadie (50,111),   *Peebles (14), Casey (44)*
Mooney (121)

Omagh T: Blake, Gallagher, Magill, Doherty, Donnelly, Gray, Mooney, Quigg, (B) McCreadie, Crilly, McHugh. *Subs:* McIntyre replaced McHugh; (D) O'Neill replaced (B) McCreadie; *Sub not used:* McElroy:
Portadown: Dalton, Major, Davidson, Casey, Strain, Byrne, Candlish, Peebles, Haylock, (I.J) Ferguson, Kennedy. *Sub:* Boyle replaced Strain; *Subs not used:* Fulton; Keenan (gk):
Referee: R.Lutton (Lurgan)
Booked: Mooney, Gray, Doherty (Omagh Town)

17th January, 1996
Cliftonville (0)   1   **Ballymena United (0)   0**
McCann (58)

Cliftonville: Rice, Hill, Flynn, Tabb, Kerr, Strang, McCann, Sliney, O'Neill, Cavanagh, Donnelly. *Subs:* Heath replaced Sliney; Feehan replaced Cavanagh; *Sub not used:* McFadden:
Ballymena U: Beck, Carlisle, Boyd, Allen, Muir, McConville, Curry, Mauchlen, (C) Moore, Loughery, (D) Moore. *Subs not used:* Steele; Craig; Smyth (gk):
Referee: N.Cowie (Belfast)

SEMI-FINALS
12th December, 1995
Venue: The Oval, Belfast
Crusaders (1)   1   **Omagh Town (0)   0**
Livingstone (6)

Crusaders: McKeown, McMullan, McCartney, Dunlop, (R) Lawlor, Deegan, Livingstone,Dunne, Morgan, Callaghan, Burrows. *Subs:* (G) Hunter replaced Morgan; Carroll replaced McCartney; Grant (gk) replaced Dunne:
Omagh T: Blake, Gallagher, Magill, Doherty, Donnelly, Kavanagh, Mooney, Quigg, (B) McCreadie, Crilly, (D) O'Neill. *Subs:* McHugh replaced (D) O'Neill; McIntyre replaced (B) McCreadie; Johnston replaced Kavanagh:
Referee: G.Keatley (Bangor)
Booked: Kavanagh (Omagh Town)

31st January, 1996
Venue: Windsor Park, Belfast
Linfield (0)   2   **Cliftonville (0)   1**
Dornan (60), Millar (72)   *Strang (78)*

Linfield: Lamont, Dornan, Easton, McCoosh, Spiers, Beatty, Ray.Campbell, Johnston, Millar, Fenlon, Bailie. *Sub:* Knell replaced Johnston; *Subs not used:* Erskine; Ewing:
Cliftonville: Rice, Hill, Flynn, Tabb, McDonald, Strang, McCann, Hayes, O'Neill, Heath, Donnelly. *Subs:* Manley replaced Hill; *Subs not used:* Davey Sliney:
Referee: L.Irvine (Limavady)
Booked: Dornan and Knell (Linfield); Heath and O'Neill (Cliftonville):

FINAL
13th February, 1996
Venue: The Oval, Belfast   Att: 3,076
Crusaders (1)   1   **Linfield (0)   0**
O'Brien (10)

Crusaders: McKeown, McMullan, (M) Lawlor, Dunlop, (R) Lawlor, Murray, O'Brien, Dunne, Baxter, Carroll, Burrows. *Subs not used:* (K) Hunter:
Linfield: Lamont, Dornan, Easton, McCoosh, Spiers, Knell, Ray.Campbell, Johnston, Millar, Fenlon, Bailie. *Subs:* Rob.Campbell replaced Knell (56 min); Erskine replaced Johnston (70 min); Ewing replaced McCoosh (78 min):
Referee: A.Snoddy (Carryduff)
Booked: McCoosh (Linfield); Dunlop (Crusaders):

GOLD CUP WINNERS 1911/12 TO 1995/96

19/11/12	Belfast Celtic		1954/55	Glenavon
1912/13	–		1955/56	Linfield
1913/14	Distillery		1956/57	Glenavon
1914/15	Shelbourne		1957/58	Linfield
1915/16			1958/59	Coleraine
to	No competition		1959/60	Linfield
1918/19			1960/61	Glentoran
1919/20	Distillery		1961/62	Linfield
1920/21	Linfield		1962/63	Glentoran
1921/22	Linfield		1963/64	Linfield
1922/23	Cliftonville		1964/65	Derry City
1923/24	Linfield		1965/66	Linfield
1924/25	Distillery		1966/67	Glentoran
1925/26	Belfast Celtic		1967/68	Linfield
1926/27	Linfield		1968/69	Linfield
1927/28	Linfield		1969/70	Coleraine
1928/29	Linfield		1970/71	Linfield
1929/30	Distillery		1971/72	Portadown
1930/31	Linfield		1972/73	Linfield
1931/32	Coleraine		1973/74	Ards
1932/33	Cliftonville		1974/75	Ballymena United
1933/34	Portadown		1975/76	Coleraine
1934/35	Belfast Celtic		1976/77	Glentoran
1935/36	Linfield		1977/78	Glentoran
1936/37	Linfield		1978/79	Portadown
1937/38	Portadown		1979/80	Linfield
1938/39	Belfast Celtic		1980/81	Cliftonville
1939/40	Belfast Celtic		1981/82	Linfield
1940/41	Belfast Celtic		1982/83	Glentoran
1941/42	Glentoran		1983/84	Linfield
1942/43	Linfield		1984/85	Linfield
1943/44	Belfast Celtic		1985/86	Crusaders
1944/45	–		1986/87	Glentoran
1945/46	Belfast Celtic		1987/88	Linfield
1946/47	Belfast Celtic		1988/89	Linfield
1947/48	Belfast Celtic		1989/90	Linfield
1948/49	Linfield		1990/91	Glenavon
1949/50	Linfield		1991/92	Glentoran
1950/51	Linfield		1992/93	Portadown
1951/52	Glentoran		1993/94	Distillery
1952/53	Portadown		1994/95	Glentoran
1953/54	Ards		1995/96	Crusaders

SUMMARY OF WINNERS 1911/12 – 1995/96: 30 Linfield; 11 Glentoran, 10 Belfast Celtic; 6 Portadown, 5 Distillery; 4 Coleraine; 3 Cliftonville, Glenavon; 2 Ards, Crusaders, 1 Ballymena United, Derry City, Shelbourne.

Portadown
Irish League Champions

ULSTER CUP 1995/96

19th August, 1995

SECTION A

Carrick Rangers (1) 4   Omagh Town (3) 4
Crawford (29),Coulter   Quigg (22), Kavanagh
(pen 49, pen 79, pen 90)   (pen 27),(D) Sheridan (43),
*   Crilly (60)*

Carrick R: Hillen, Press, Crawford, Muldoon, Sinclair, Coulter, (W) Wilson, McDermott, Doherty, Ferris, Macauley. **Subs:** Kirk replaced Doherty; Donaghey replaced (W) Wilson; **Sub not used:** Dillon (gk):
Omagh T: Blake, Johnston, Magill, Moore, Donnelly, Moran, Kavanagh, Quigg, McIntyre, Crilly, (D) Sheridan. **Subs:** (B) McCreadie replaced McIntyre; Mooney replaced Moran; **Sub not used:** Hillen:
Referee: F.Hiles (Newtownards)
Booked: Quigg, Magill, Moore, McIntyre (Omagh Town):

Crusaders (2) 4   Glentoran (1) 3
Baxter (26), Livingstone (38),   (T) Smith (16), Little
(G) Hunter (46,73)   (59,64)

Crusaders: McKeown, McMullan, McCartney, Carroll, Murray, O'Brien, Livingstone, Dunne, Baxter, (G) Hunter, Burrows. **Sub:** Dwyer replaced McCartney; **Subs not used:** Morgan; Henry (gk):
Glentoran: (D) Devine, Neill, (M) Smyth, Walker, (J) Devine, Mathieson, Quigley, Little, (T) Smith, Cook, McBride. **Subs:** McEvoy replaced (M) Smyth; Finlay replaced McBride; **Sub not used:** Armstrong (gk):
Referee: N.Cowie (Bangor)

SECTION B

Ballyclare Comrades (0) 0   Distillery (4) 6
*   Mitchell (9,28),*
*   Armstrong (36,68),*
*   McAleenan (42), Murray (90)*

Ballyclare C: McGreevy, Larmour, Wilson, Mitchell, McCann, McGivern, Irwin, (F) McCusker, Campbell, Bell. **Subs:** McCrum replaced Greer; (L) Galbraith replaced Bell:
Distillery: Collins, Drake, Kennedy, Allen, Brush, McAleenan, Totten, Small, Armstrong, Mitchell, Dykes. **Sub:** Murray replaced Dykes; **Subs not used:** Bradley; Richardson:
Referee: D.Taylor (Tandragee)

Glenavon (2) 2   Cliftonville (0) 0
(G) Smyth (18), Ferguson (30)

Glenavon: O'Neill, Byrne, Glendinning, Doherty, Brown (G) Smyth, McCoy, Johnston, Ferguson, McBride, Collins. **Subs not used:** (D) Murphy; Birney; Stitt (gk):
Cliftonville: Rice, Hill, Flynn, Tabb, Kerr, Strang, McCann, McDonald, Feehan, Quinn, Donnelly. **Sub:** McCrystal replaced Quinn; **Subs not used:** McNamee; Davey:
Referee: G.Keatley (Bangor)
Booked: Tabb and McDonald (Cliftonville): *Sent Off:* Michael Donnelly (Cliftonville):

SECTION C

Newry Town (1) 1   Bangor (2) 2
McQuaid (32)   Batey (11), (R) Hill (34)

Newry T: Keeley, (B) O'Kane, Thompson, McParland, Gracey, Ralph, McQuaid, (N) Watson, Whelan, Stokes, Clarke. **Subs:** Barr replaced   ; (N) Courtney replaced   ; **Sub not used:** Campbell (gk):
Bangor: Haggan, Campbell, Dornan, Percy, McComb, (R) Hill, Irwin, Batey, O'Connell, Murtagh, Wilkinson. **Subs:** Tierney replaced Wilkinson; McCartan replaced Irwin; **Sub not used:** Eachus (gk):
Referee: D.Magill (Belfast).

Portadown (0) 0   Coleraine (2) 2
*   Gorman (34), Beckett (40)*

Portadown: Dalton, Fulton, McKeever, Major, Strain, Murray, Evans, Russell, Haylock, Meehan, Kennedy. **Subs:** Boyle replaced Evans; Herbert replaced McKeever; Keenan (gk) replaced Dalton:
Coleraine: O'Hare, McAuley, Huston, Gaston, Philson, Gorman, Maloney, Doherty, Patton, Beckett, Oatway. **Subs not used:** Wade; Hagan; O'Donnell:
Referee: R.Lutton (Lurgan)

Section D

Ards (1) 2   Linfield (0) 0
Flannery (26,62)

Ards: Kee, McBride, Wills, (M) Kelly, Mooney, Simpson, Boyle, Shanley, Flannery, (P) Cullen, O'Sullivan. **Sub:** O'Shea replaced Boyle; **Subs not used:** Dunnion; McNamara (gk):
Linfield: Lamont, Dornan, Easton, Ewing, McLean, McGee, Ray.Campbell, Millar, Erskine, Fenlon, Bai-

lie. *Subs:* Gorman replaced Fenlon; Beatty replaced McGee; *Sub not used:* Caldwell (gk):
Referee: T.Deegan (Ballynahinch)

Larne   (0)   0   Ballymena United (1)   1
Loughery (33)

Larne: Robinson, (N) Murray, Collier, McKinstry, Jeffrey, Looney, (G) Murray, McConkey, Straney, Armstrong, (E) McLoughlin. *Subs:* Hillis replaced Straney; Leckey replaced McConkey; *Sub not used:* McCorry (gk):
Ballymena U: May, Mauchlen, Stewart, Allen, McCormick, (C) Moore, McConville, Burn, Loughery, McWalter, Boyd. *Subs:* Lynch replaced (C) Moore; Carlisle replaced Mauchlen; *Sub not used:* Gilmore:
Referee: J.Ferry (Londonderry)
Booked: (N) Murray, McConkey, Jeffrey (Larne); McConnell and Lynch (Ballymena United):

25th August, 1995.

SECTION A

Glentoran   (1)   2   Omagh Town   (0)   1
Cook (44,52)   *Johnston (49)*

Glentoran: (D) Devine, Neill, (M) Smyth, McCaffrey, (J) Devine, Mathieson, McEvoy, Little, (T) Smith, Cook, Finlay. *Subs:* Quigley replaced Neill; McDowell replaced (T) Smyth; *Sub not used:* Collins:
Omagh T: Blake, Johnston, Magill, McCaul, Donnelly, Mooney, Kavanagh, Quigg, McInytre, Crilly, McHugh. *Subs:* (D) Sheridan replaced McHugh; (B) McCreadie replaced Magill; *Sub not used:* Moore:
Referee: P.Thompson (Bangor)
Booked: Cook and McDowell (Glentoran); McCaul, Magill, (B) McCreadie (Omagh Town):

SECTION B

Cliftonville   (0)   0   Distillery   (1)   1
Dykes (22)

Cliftonville: Rice, Hill, Flynn, Tabb, Kerr, Strang, McCann, Sliney, Feehan, McDonald, Heath. *Subs:* Manley replaced Heath; McCrystal replaced Strang; *Sub not used:* Davey:
Distillery: Collins, Drake, Kennedy, Allen, Brush, McAleenan, Totten, Small, Armstrong, Mitchell, Dykes. *Sub:* Murray replaced Totten; *Sub not used:* Toal; McEnhill (gk):
Referee: D.Malcolm (Bangor)

SECTION C

Coleraine   (0)   1   Bangor   (0)   1
Gorman (84)   *Spiers (87)*

Coleraine: O'Hare, McAuley, Huston, Gaston, Philson, Gorman, Maloney, Doherty, Patton, Beckett, Oatway. *Sub:* O'Donnell replaced Oatway; *Subs not used:* Wade; Hagan:
Bangor: Haggan, Percy, Dornan, Spiers, (R) Hill, McCombe, Irwin, Batey, O'Connell, Murtagh, Swift. *Sub:* Tierney replaced Irwin; *Subs not used:* Eddis; Eachus (gk):
Referee: A.Snoddy (Carryduff)

Portadown   (1)   3   Newry Town   (0)   0
Haylock (13), (I.J) Ferguson (67),
Peebles (89)

Portadown: Keenan, Major, Murray, Casey, Strain, Byrne, Peebles, Russell, Haylock, (I.J) Ferguson, Kennedy. *Subs not used:* Meehan; Fulton; Whitmarsh (gk)
Newry T: Keeley, (B) O'Kane, Thompson, McParland, Gracey, Ralph, McQuaid, Mooney, Whelan, Stokes, Clarke. *Sub:* Barr replaced Stokes; *Subs not used:*(N) Watson; Campbell (gk):
Referee: D.Taylor (Tandragee)

26th August, 1995.

SECTION A

Crusaders   (1)   4   Carrick Rangers   (0)   0
Baxter (33, pen 88),
Callaghan (46),
(G) Hunter (51)

Crusaders: McKeown, McMullan, Carroll, Murray, Callaghan, O'Brien, Livingstone, Dunne, Baxter, (G) Hunter, Burrows. *Sub:* Mellon replaced McMullan; *Subs not used:* Gardiner; Hamer (gk):
Carrick R: Hillen, Press, Gilmore, Muldoon, Sinclair, Coulter, (W) Wilson, McDermott, Doherty, Ferris, Macauley. *Subs:* Kirk replaced Ferris; Crawford replaced McDermott; Donaghey replaced Coulter:
Referee: J.Peden (Richhill)
Booked: Livingstone, O'Brien, McDermott (Crusaders)

Glenavon (1)   6   Ballyclare Comrades (0)   0
Ferguson (35,68,82),
McBride (70,76,pen79)

Glenavon: O'Neill, Byrne, Glendinning, Doherty, Brown, (G) Smyth, McCoy, Johnston, Ferguson, McBride, (J) Smyth. *Subs:* Birney replaced Byrne; Collins replaced Doherty; *Sub not used:* Currie (gk):
Ballyclare Com: McNulty, Larmour, Wilson, Morrison, McCann, (L) Galbraith, Orchin, Irwin, Campbell, (F) McCusker, Walker. *Subs:* McCrum replaced (F) McCusker; McIlwaine replaced Orchin; *Sub not used:* McGreevy (gk):
Referee: T.Deegan (Ballynahinch)

SECTION D

Ards 0)   1   Larne (0)   0
(P) Cullen (74)

Ards: Kee, McBride, Wills, (M) Kelly, Mooney, O'Sullivan, Simpson, Shanley, Flannery, (P) Cullen, Boyle. *Sub:* O'Shea replaced Simpson; *Subs not used:* McGreevy; McNamara (gk):
Larne: Robinson, McConkey, Collier, McKinstry, Jeffrey, Looney, Leckey, (G) Murray, Straney, Armstrong, (E) McLoughlin. *Subs:* Hillis replaced Straney; Magill replaced Jeffrey; *Sub not used:* McCorry (gk):
Referee: H.Barr (Bangor)
Booked: McKinstry, (G) Murray, Collier (Larne):

Linfield (3)   3   Ballymena United (0)   0
McGee (17), Fenlon (pen 19),
Ewing (45)

Linfield: Lamont, Dornan, McShane, Ewing, McLean, McGee, Ray.Campbell, Gorman, Millar, Fenlon, Bailie. *Subs:* Erskine replaced Ewing; McCoosh replaced Dornan; *Sub not used:* Caldwell (gk):
Ballymena Utd: May, Carlisle, Stewart, Allen, McConnell, Muir, McConville, Gilmore, Loughery, McCourt, Boyd. *Subs:* Lynch replaced Loughery; (C) Moore replaced Gilmore; *Sub not used:* Smyth (gk):
Referee: M.Ross (Carrickfergus)

2nd September, 1995

SECTION A

Glentoran (0)   2   Carrick Rangers (0)   1
Cook (51), Little (60)   Crawford (83)

Glentoran: (D) Devine, Neill (M) Smyth, McCaffrey, (J) Devine, Mathieson, McEvoy, Little, (T) Smith, Cook, Finlay. *Subs:* Quigley replaced McEvoy; Bowers replaced Neill; *Sub not used:* McDowell:
CarricK R: Hillen Sinclair, Crawford, Gilmore, McLeister, Coulter, (W) Wilson, McDermott, Donaghey, Ferris, Macauley. *Subs:* Kirk replaced (W) Wilson; Muldoon

replaced McDermott; *Sub not used:* Dillon (gk):
Referee: H.Barr (Bangor)
Booked: (M) Smyth (Glentoran):

Omagh Town (0)   1   Crusaders (0)   0
(B) McCreadie (83)

Omagh T: Blake, Johnston, Magill, McCaul, Donnelly,(D) O'Neill, Kavanagh, Quigg, Mooney, Moran, McHugh. *Subs:* (B) McCreadie replaced McHugh; Hillen replaced Moran; *Sub not used:* Doherty:
Crusaders: McKeown, McMullan, Mellon, Dunlop, Callaghan, O'Brien, Livingstone, Dunne, Baxter, (G) Hunter, Carroll. *Subs:* Gardiner replaced Baxter; Eccles replaced Carroll; *Sub not used:* Murray:
Referee: G.Douglas (Comber)

SECTION B

Cliftonville (3)   7   Ballyclare Comrades (1)   1
Feehan (pen 7), Flynn (30), (F) McCusker (8)
McCann (35), Manley (66,
80,85), Sliney (75).

Cliftonville: Rice, Hill, Flynn, Tabb, Kerr, McDonald, McCann, Manley, Feehan, McAllister, Donnelly. *Subs:* Sliney replaced Flynn; Heath replaced Donnelly; Erskine replaced Feehan:
Ballyclare C: McGreevy, Walker, Finnegan, Hall, Morrison, Wilson, Irwin, (F) McCusker, Campbell, Bell, McGivern. *Subs:* Larmour replaced   ; Greer replaced:
Referee: E.Millar (Bangor)

Distillery (0)   0   Glenavon (0)   1
Ferguson (56)

Distillery: Collins, Drake, Brush, McAleenan, McCavanagh, Allen, Murray, Small, Armstrong, Mitchell, Dykes. *Subs:* Cleland replaced Murray; *Subs not used:* Kennedy; McEnhill (gk):
Glenavon: O'Neill, Byrne, Glendinning, Doherty, (A) Murphy, (G) Smyth, McCoy, Johnston, Ferguson, McBride, (J) Smyth. *Sub:* Collins replaced McCoy; *Subs not used:* Birney; Currie (gk):
Referee: D.Magill (Belfast)

SECTION C

Bangor (0)   0   Portadown (4)   4
Spiers (og 15), Haylock
(20,37,44)

Bangor: Haggan, Campbell, Dornan, Spiers, (R) Hill, McCombe, Percy, Batey, O'Connell, Murtagh, Irwin. *Subs:* Bailie replaced McCombe; Eddis replaced\O'Connell; McPherson replaced Irwin:
Portadown: Keenan, Major, Murray, Casey, Strain, Byrne, Peebles, Russell, Haylock, (I.J) Ferguson, Kennedy. *Subs:*

Boyle replaced Casey; Fulton replaced Kennedy; *Sub not used:*Whitmarsh (gk)
Referee: N.Cowie (Carryduff)

Coleraine (1)   2   Newry Town (0)   0
Gorman (16), O'Donnell (71)

Coleraine: O'Hare, McAuley, Huston, Gaston, Philson, Gorman, Maloney, Doherty, Patton, Beckett, O'Donnell. *Subs:* Robson replaced Beckett; McIvor replaced Huston; *Sub not used:* Hagan:
Newry T: Keeley, (B) O'Kane, Thompson, McParland, (F) Scappaticci, Ralph, McQuaid, Mooney, Whelan, Stokes, Clarke. *Subs:* White replaced McQuaid; (N) Watson replaced Whelan; Campbell (gk) replaced Keeley:
Referee: J.Ferry (Londonderry)

SECTION D

Ballymena United (0)   0   Ards (1)   4
Flannery (15), (P)
Cullen (55,65),
Boyle (63)

Ballymena U: May, Carlisle, Stewart, Allen, McConnell, (C) Moore, McConville, Mauchlen, Loughery, McCourt, Boyd. *Sub:* Muir replaced Mauchlen; *Subs not used:* Gilmore; Smyth (gk):
Ards: Kee, McBride, Murphy, (M) Kelly, Mooney, O'Sullivan, Simpson, Shanley, Flannery, (P) Cullen, Boyle. *Subs:* O'Shea replaced O'Sullivan; Morrison replaced Simpson; Breza replaced Boyle:
Referee: L.Irvine (Limavady)

Linfield (1)   2   Larne (0)   0
Fenlon (16), McGee (84)

Linfield: Lamont, Dornan, Easton, Millar, McClean, Beatty, Ray.Campbell, Gorman, Erskine, Fenlon, Bailie. *Subs:* McGee replaced Easton; Ewing replaced Millar; *Sub not used:* Caldwell (gk):
Larne: Robinson, McConkey, Collier, McKinstry, (N) Murray, McMahon, Looney, (G) Murray, Hillis, Armstrong, (E) McLoughlin. *Subs:* Leckey replaced Armstrong; Magill replaced (G) Murray; *Sub not used:* Straney:
Referee: R.Lutton (Lurgan)
Booked: Millar (Linfield); (E) McLoughlin and (N) Murray (Larne):

FINAL TABLES

SECTION A	P	W	D	L	F	A	Pts	GD
1 Crusaders	3	2	0	1	8	4	6	+4
2 Glentoran	3	2	0	1	7	6	6	+1
3 Omagh Town	3	1	1	1	6	6	4	-
4 Carrick Rangers	3	0	1	2	5	10	1	-5

SECTION B	P	W	D	L	F	A	Pts	GD
1 Glenavon	3	3	0	0	9	0	9	+9
2 Distillery	3	2	0	1	7	1	6	+6
3 Cliftonville	3	1	0	2	7	4	3	+3
4 Ballyclare Comrades	3	0	0	3	1	19	0	-18

SECTION C	P	W	D	L	F	A	Pts	GD
1 Coleraine	3	2	1	0	5	1	7	+4
2 Portadown	3	2	0	1	7	2	6	+5
3 Bangor	3	1	1	1	3	6	4	-3
4 Newry Town	3	0	0	3	1	7	0	-6

SECTION D	P	W	D	L	F	A	Pts	GD
1 Ards	3	3	0	0	7	0	9	+7
2 Linfield	3	2	0	1	5	2	6	+3
3 Ballymena United	3	1	0	2	1	7	3	-6
4 Larne	3	0	0	3	0	4	0	-4

NB: Top two teams from each section qualified fo the Quarter-Finals of the competition.

QUARTER-FINALS

3rd October, 1995.

Ards (1)   1   Portadown (0)   2
Morrison (44)   Peebles (67), Casey (69)

Ards: Kee, McBride, Murphy, (M) Kelly, Mooney, O'Sullivan, Boyle, Shanley, Flannery, (P) Cullen, Morrison. *Sub:* Simpson replaced O'Sullivan; *Subs not used:* McGreevy; Dunnion:
Portadown: Dalton, McKeever, Murray, Casey, Strain, Major, Peebles, Russell, Haylock, Magee, Kennedy. *Subs:* Davidson replaced McKeever; Candlish replaced Magee; *Sub not used:* Whitmarsh (gk):
Referee: J.Ferry (Londonderry)

Coleraine (0)   0   Linfield (1)   1
McLean (15)

Coleraine: O'Hare, McAuley, Huston, Young, Philson, Gorman, Maloney, Doherty, Surgeon, Beckett, Gaston. *Subs:* O'Donnell replaced Maloney; Patton replaced McAuley; *Sub not used:*Platt (gk) not used:
Linfield: Lamont, Hill, Easton, McIlroy, McLean, Beatty, Ray.Campbell, Millar, Erskine, Fenlon, Bailie. *Sub:* McGee replaced McIlroy; *Subs not used:* Spiers; Crawford (gk):
Referee: L.Irvine (Limavady)

Crusaders (1)   1   **Distillery (1)   1**

(G) Hunter (8)   *Mitchell (42)*

(aet Crusaders won 6-5 on pens)

Penalty Shoot Out:

Crusaders: McMullan, Dunne, Baxter, McKeown, O'Brien, Callaghan (all scored):

Distillery: Mitchell, Small, Brush, Dykes, Cleland (all scored); McAleenan (missed):

Crusaders: McKeown, McMullan, McCartney, Dunlop, Callaghan, (K) Hunter, (R) Lawlor, Dunne, Baxter, (G) Hunter, O'Brien. *Sub:* Livingstone replaced (K) Hunter; *Subs not used:* Carroll; Snodgrass (gk):

Distillery: Collins, Drake, Curliss, Allen, Brush, Kennedy, Totten, McAleenan, Dykes, Mitchell, Cleland. *Subs:* Small replaced Curliss; Cavanagh replaced Totten; *Sub not used:* McEnhill (gk):

Referee: M.Ross (Carrickfergus)

Glenavon (1)   2   **Glentoran (0)   0**

McBride (29), Ferguson (74)

Glenavon: O'Neill, Birney, Glendinning, Kenny, Brown, (G) Smyth, (D) Murphy, Johnston, Ferguson, McBride, (J) Smyth. *Subs:* McCoy replaced Kenny; (A) Murphy replaced Brown; *Subs not used:* Collins:

Glentoran: (D) Devine, Parker, (M) Smyth, Walker, (J) Devine, McEvoy, Quigley, Little, Cook, McCaffrey, Finlay. *Sub:* Moore replaced McEvoy; *Sub not used:* Spence; McDowell:

Referee: G.Keatley (Bangor)

Booked: Quigley (Glentoran):

SEMI-FINALS

10th October, 1995

Venue: The Oval, Belfast

Crusaders (2)   2   **Linfield (1)   3** aet

Baxter (10,25)   *Beatty (26), Hosick (90),*
McLean (114)

Crusaders: Grant, McMullan, McCartney, Dunlop, Callaghan, O'Brien, (R) Lawlor, Dunne, Baxter, (G) Hunter, Burrows. *Subs:* (K) Hunter replaced Baxter; Deegan replaced McCartney; *Sub not used:* Carroll:

Linfield: Crawford, Hill, Easton, McIlroy, McLean, Beatty, Hosick, Gorman, Erskine, Fenlon, Bailie. *Subs:* Millar replaced Erskine; McShane replaced Hill; Caldwell (gk) replaced Millar:

Referee: H.Barr (Bangor)

Booked: Dunne (Crusaders); McLean (Linfield): *Sent Off:* O'Brien (Crusaders); Fenlon (Linfield):

11th October, 1995

Venue: Mourneview Park, Lurgan

Glenavon (1)   2   **Portadown (0)   3**

McBride (8), Ferguson (57) *Candlish (51), Haylock (64,82)*

Glenavon: O'Neill, (D) Murphy, Glendinning, Doherty, (A) Murphy, (G) Smyth, Kenny, Johnston, Ferguson, McBride, (J) Smyth. *Subs:* Collins replaced Johnston; McCoy replaced Kenny; *Sub not used:* Birney:

Portadown: Dalton, Fulton, Davidson, Casey, Strain, Major, Candlish, Russell, Haylock, Peebles, Kennedy. *Sub:* Byrne replaced Fulton; *Subs not used:* Magee; Keenan (gk):

Referee: D.Magill (Belfast)

Booked: Russell (Portadown):

FINAL

16th January, 1996

Venue: Windsor Park, Belfast.   *Att:* 4,061

Portadown (0)   2   **Linfield (0)   2**

Haylock (72), Peebles (93) *McCoosh (86), Fenlon (100)*
(aet Portadown won 5-3 on pens)

Penalty Shoot Out:

Portadown: Haylock, Kennedy, Casey, Peebles, Candlsih (all scored):

Linfield: Fenlon, Beatty, Erskine (all scored); Bailie (missed):

Portadown: Dalton, Fulton, Davidson, Casey, Stewart, Byrne, Evans, Peebles, Haylock, Leitch, Kennedy. *Subs:* Carlyle replaced Evans (71 min); Candlish replaced Byrne (116 min); *Sub not used:* Keenan (gk)

Linfield: Crawford, Dornan, Crothers, Ewing, Spiers, McCoosh, Rob.Campbell, Gorman, Johnston, Knell, Bailie. *Subs:* Beatty replaced Crothers (63 min); Fenlon replaced Knell (76 min); Erskine replaced Rob.Campbell (80 min): *Referee:* D.Magill (Belfast)

Booked: Davidson, Stewart, Evans (Portadown); Ewing and McCoosh (Linfield):

Ulster Cup Winners 1948/49 – 1995/96

Year	Winner	Score	Runner-up	Score	Notes
1948/49	Linfield	3	Ards	0	
1949/50	Larne	2	Ballymena United	1	
1950/51	Glentoran	2	Linfield	1	
1951/52	Competition not played*				
1952/53	Glentoran	3	Distillery	0	
1953/54	Crusaders	2	Linfield	1	
1954/55	Glenavon	3	Coleraine	1	
1955/56	Linfield	5	Coleraine	1	
1956/57	League Format: Linfield 20pts from 11 games.				
1957/58	Distillery	4	Glentoran	1	
	(after 1-1 draw)				
1958/59	Glenavon	2	Crusaders	0	
1959/60	Linfield	4	Crusaders	1	
	(after 1-1 draw)				
1960/61	Ballymena United	3	Glenavon	1	
1961/62	Linfield	2	Glentoran	0	
1962/63	Glenavon	1	Coleraine	0	
1963/64	Crusaders	1	Glenavon	0	
	(after 2-2 draw)				
1964/65	Linfield	1	Glentoran	0	
1965/66	League Format: Coleraine 17 pts from 11 games.				
1966/67	League Format: Glentoran 21 pts from 11games.				
1967/68	League Format: Linfield 20 pts from 11 games.				
1968/69	League Format: Coleraine 20 pts from 11 games.				
1969/70	League Format: Coleraine 20 pts from 11 games.				
1970/71	League Format: Linfield 18 pts from 11 games.				
1971/72	League Format: Linfield 18 pts from 11 games.				
1972/73	League Format: Coleraine 16 pts from 10 games.				
1973/74	League Format: Ards 19 pts from 11 games.				
1974/75	League Format: Linfield 18 pts from 11 games.				
1975/76	League Format: Coleraine 19 pts from 11 games.				
1976/77	League Format: Glentoran 17 pts from 11 games.				
1977/78	League Format: Linfield 18 pts from 11 games.				
1978/79	League Format: Linfield 17 pts from 11 games.				
1979/80	League Format: Linfield 17 pts from 11 games.				
1980/81	League Format: Ballymena Utd 18 pts from 11games.				
1981/82	League Format: Glentoran 19 pts from 11 games.				
1982/83	League Format: Glentoran 19 pts from 11 games.				
1983/84	Glentoran	5	Coleraine	2 aet.	
1984/85	Linfield	2	Larne	2 aet.	
	(Linfield won 3-2 on pens)				
1985/86	Coleraine	5	Portadown	0 aet	
1986/87	Coleraine	1	Linfield	0	
1987/88	Larne	2	Coleraine	1	
1988/89	Glentoran	5	Larne	1	
1989/90	Glentoran	3	Glenavon	1	
1990/91	Portadown	1	Glenavon	1 aet.	
	(Portadown won 3-2 on pens)				
1991/92	Bangor	3	Crusaders	1	
1992/93	Linfield	2	Ards	0	
1993/94	Crusaders	1	Bangor	0	
1994/95	Bangor	2	Linfield	1	
1995/96	Portadown	2	Linfield	2 aet.	
	(Portadown won 5-3 on pens)				

Summary of Winners 1948/49 - 1995/96:

15 Linfield, 9 Glentoran, 7 Coleraine, 3 Crusaders, Glenavon, 2 Ballymena United, Bangor, Larne, Portadown 1, Ards, Distillery.

* Ulster Cup not played for in 1951/52, instead the Festival of Britain Cup was played for which was won by Ballymena United.

It was becoming a bit of a standing joke in local soccer circles, Cliftonville record in knock-out competitions.

Not only did they have an alarming habit of falling at the semi-final and final hurdles, but their failure in penalty kick shoot-outs was legend. "Some reports said we had lost twenty in a row, but that's a bit of an exaggeration," explains manager Marty Quinn. "But in the past decade I think we only were successful once in penalty shoot-outs."

The main problem for Quinn and Co. of course was their failure to win a trophy. Fifteen barren years at Solitude was hard to stomach for all concerned.

But after flat beer for a decade and a half the Reds finally got the real thing in 1995/96 - the Coca-Cola Cup.

Marty Quinn was a member of the Solitude side that lifted the Gold Cup in the 1980/81 season and he put players in the picture about what was required this time around. "I told them that they couldn't continue to let themselves and the fans down in these competitions. I told them we had the quality to win trophies and that people were saying we just didn't have the determination to do it. They were desperate to prove the critics wrong and they did."

The path to the final started at St.Julian's Road in Omagh where the Reds scored a 1-0 first-leg win, enough to take them through after the Solitude rematch ended 1-1. Two goals from new signing Paul Stokes helped them to a 3-0 success against First Division champions-elect Coleraine in the quarters, and Ards were 3-1 semi-final victims, goals there for Stokes, Gary Sliney, and loan signing from Wrexham Jonathan Cross. A comfortable victory, and the same in the Final. The same score as the semi as well, Glentoran well beaten by the Reds at their second home Windsor Park. Tim McCann, Cross and Stokes were the Cliftonville marksmen in a night to remember.

Manager Quinn has the last word. "Yes it was nice to end up in the winners' enclosure at last. It was a memorable occasion, really well organised by the sponsors and very enjoyable. It gave the players and fans a taste for success and I'm sure it won't be another fifteen years before we win another trophy!"

Peter Taggart.

COCA - COLA CUP 1995/96

FIRST ROUND, FIRST LEG

30th December, 1995

Carrick Rangers (1)   1   Glenavon (1)   3
Ferris (10)   Glendinning (19), Byrne
                                    (77), Freeman (80)

Carrick R: Dillon, McGarvey, Gilmore, Muldoon, McLeister, Donaghey, Sinclair, (W) Wilson, Armstrong, Ferris, Macauley. *Subs:* Doherty replaced Ferris; McDermott replaced Sinclair; (F) Wilson replaced (W) Wilson:

Glenavon: O'Neill, Byrne, Glendinning, Doherty, Gauld, (G) Smyth, Collins, Mulholland, Freeman, McBride, (J) Smyth. *Subs:* Brown replaced Gauld; McCoy replaced Collins; (D) Murphy replaced Mulholland:

Referee: A.Snoddy (Carryduff)

Booked: Armstrong and Sinclair (Carrick Rangers)

9th January, 1996

Ballyclare Comrades (1)   2   Portadown (1)   1
Forshaw (35,75)   Major (44)

Ballyclare Com: (D) McCusker, (N) Blair, Kearns, Walker, Morrison, (F) McCusker, Allsopp, (L) Galbraith, Bell, Forshaw, Young. *Sub:* Higgins replaced Forshaw; *Subs not used:* Clarke; Adams:

Portadown: Dalton, Major, Davidson, Casey, Strain, Byrne, Carlyle, Candlish, Haylock, (I.J) Ferguson, Kennedy. *Subs:* Fulton replaced Carlyle; *Subs not used:* Evans, Keenan (gk)

Referee: T.Gillanders (Belfast)

Booked: (F) McCusker, Young (Ballyclare Comrades); Byrne (Portadown); *Sent Off:* Gregg Davidson and Peter Kennedy (Portadown):

Coleraine (2)   2   Bangor (0)   0
Gorman (15,18)

Coleraine: O'Hare, Doherty, McAuley, Young, Gaston, Gorman, Shiels, O'Dowd, Surgeon, McAllister, McIvor. *Sub:* Patton replaced O'Dowd; *Subs not used:* Maloney; Hagan:

Bangor: Miskelly, Coulter, Simpson, Spiers, McKeown, Cash, Nelson, McNamara, O'Connell, Williams, Percy. *Subs:* Irwin replaced O'Connell; Morrow replaced Percy; McGuinness replaced Nelson:

Referee: J.Peden (Richhill)

Distillery (0)   0   Linfield (1)   4
                    Gorman (5), McCoosh
                    (83,88), Knell (90)

Distillery: Collins, Drake, Kennedy, Allen, Brady, Small, Totten, McAleenan, Brush, Mitchell, Robson. *Subs:* Moore replaced Totten; Rogan replaced Robson; Currie (gk) replaced Collins:

Linfield: Crawford, Dornan, Crothers, Ewing, Spiers, McCoosh, Rob.Campbell, Gorman, Johnston, Knell, Bailie. *Sub:* Millar replaced Gorman; *Subs not used:* Fenlon; Beatty:

Referee: F.Hiles (Newtownards)

Booked: Gorman (Linfield): *Sent Off:* John Drake (Distillery):

Omagh Town (0)   0   Cliftonville (0)   1
                    Feehan (82)

Omagh T: McDevitt, Johnston, Magill, Doherty, Donnelly, Kavanagh, (D) O'Neill, Quigg, McIntyre, Mooney, McHugh. *Subs not used:* Gray; McElroy; (F) O'Donnell:

Cliftonville: Rice, Hill, Flynn, Tabb, Kerr, O'Neill, McCann, Sliney, Stokes, Cavanagh, Donnelly. *Subs:* Feehan replaced Cavanagh; Manley replaced Stokes; Heath replaced O'Neill:

Referee: F.McDonald (Newry)

Booked: Donnelly (Omagh Town); Sliney (Cliftonville):

17th January, 1996

Larne (0)   0   Ards (2)   3
                    Boyle (20,31), Bower (53)

Larne: Robinson, McConkey, Collier, McKinstry, Jeffrey, May, Leckey, Johnston, McCrae, McMahon, Straney. *Subs:* Magill replaced Leckey; Armstrong replaced Straney; *Sub not used:* (L) Smyth:

Ards: Kee, McBride, Murphy, (M) Kelly, Mooney, Bowers, Shanley, Walker, Barker, McCann, Boyle. *Sub:* Dunnion replaced Bowers; *Subs not used:* Armstrong; Johnston:

Referee: E.Millar (Bangor)

Booked: Jeffrey, Johnston, McMahon (Larne); Barker (Ards):

Newry Town (1) 2   **Glentoran (1)** 2
Barr (9), Mooney (73)   *McBride (18), (T) Smith*
                                (75)

Newry T: Campbell, (C) O'Kane, (A) Scappaticci, (B) O'Kane, (F) Scappaticci, Ralph, Magee, McParland, Mooney, Barr, Clarke. *Subs not used:* (N) Courtney; (S) Feehan; (N) Watson:
Glentoran: Armstrong, Neill, (M) Smyth, Walker, (J) Devine, Parker, Mathieson, McCarrison, (T) Smith, Quigley, McBride. *Subs:* Houston replaced (M) Smyth; Finlay replaced Neill; Elliott replaced McCarrison:
Referee: G.Keatley (Bangor)
Booked: Magee, (F) Scappaticci, (C) O'Kane(Newry Town); Quigley (Glentoran):

23rd January, 1996

Ballymena United (0) 0   **Crusaders (0)** 2
Att: 300   *(G) Hunter (68), Mellon*
                                (73)

Ballymena Utd: Beck, Carlisle, Muir, Allen, McConnell, Boyd, McConville, (D) Moore, McCourt, Loughery, Murray. *Subs:* Craig replaced Muir; Beattie replaced McCourt; *Sub not used:* Wylie:
Crusaders: McKeown, McMullan, McCartney, Dunlop, Callaghan, Dwyer, O'Brien, Livingstone, Baxter, (G) Hunter, Ramirez. *Subs:* Mellon replaced Ramirez; English replaced McCartney; Morgan replaced Baxter:
Referee: N.Cowie (Carryduff)

FIRST ROUND, SECOND LEG

9th January, 1996

Glenavon (1) 3   **Carrick Rangers (0)** 0
Ferguson (13), Glendinning (47),
McCoy (56)
(Glenavon won 6-1 on aggregate)

Glenavon: O'Neill, Byrne, Glendinning, Doherty, Gauld, Brown, Gray, Kenny, Ferguson, McBride, Freeman. *Subs:* (J) Smyth replaced Freeman; McCoy replaced Gray; *Sub not used:* (D) Murphy:
Carrick R: Dillon, McGarvey, (F) Wilson, Gilmore, McLeister, Donaghey, Sinclair, McDermott, Doherty, Ferris, (W) Wilson. *Subs:* Armstrong replaced Ferris; Macauley replaced (W) Wilson; Jamison (gk) replaced Dillon:
Referee: E.Millar (Bangor)

23rd January, 1996

Ards (1) 2   **Larne (0)** 0
                                  Att: 200
Barker (38), Bowers (52)
(Ards won 5-0 on aggregate)

Ards: Kee, McBride, McLaughlin, (M) Kelly, Mooney, Bowers, Walker, Murphy, Barker, McCann, Boyle. *Subs:* McGreevy replaced Walker; Johnston replaced Mooney; Dunnion replaced Bowers:
Larne: Robinson, (N) Murray, McConkey, McKinstry, (E) McLaughlin, (L) Smyth, Leckey, McKnight, McMahon, Armstrong, (S) McDowell. *Subs:* Johnston replaced (S) McDowell; Elder replaced Leckey; McCrae
Referee: D.Magill (Belfast)

Bangor (1) 2   **Coleraine (1)** 2
Irwin (16,pen 56)   *McIvor (27),*
Att: 400   *McCallan (77)*
(Coleraine won 4-2 on aggregate)

Bangor: Huxley, Coulter, McGuinness, Spiers, McCombe, Cash, (S) Hill, Bailie, Barclay, Irwin, McNamara. *Subs:* Morrow replaced McGuinness; Wilkinson replaced (S) Hill; McPherson replaced McNamara:
Coleraine: O'Hare, Doherty, McAuley, Young, Gaston, Gorman, Shiels, Surgeon, McCallan, McAllister, McIvor. *Subs not used:* O'Dowd; Patton; Hagan:
Referee: R.Lutton (Lurgan)

Cliftonville (0) 1   **Omagh Town (1)** 1
Stokes (80)   *McHugh (7)*
Att: 200
(Cliftonville won 2-1 on aggregate)

Cliftonville: Rice, Hill, Flynn, Tabb, Kerr, Strang, McCann, Sliney, O'Neill, Stokes, Donnelly. *Subs:* McFadden replaced Strang; Feehan replaced Stokes; *Sub not used:* Heath:
Omagh T: McBrearty, Johnston, McElroy, McCaul, Donnelly, Kavanagh, Gallagher, Quigg, McIntyre, Crilly, McHugh. *Subs:* Mooney replaced McIntyre; Doherty replaced McCaul; *Sub not used:* (D) O'Neill:
Referee: M.Hutton (Londonderry)
Booked: Sliney (Cliftonville); Donnelly (Omagh Town):
Sent Off: Gary Sliney (Cliftonville):

Glentoran (2)   **7**   **Newry Town (0)**   **0**

Att: 800

(T) Smith (4), McBride (21,60,75),
Little (80), Batey (82), (M) Smyth (85)
(Glentoran won 9-2 on aggregate)

Glentoran: Armstrong, Nixon, (M) Smyth, Walker, (J) Devine, Finlay, Mathieson, Little, (T) Smith, Batey, McBride. **Subs:** Parker replaced Nixon; Quigley replaced Mathieson; Coyle replaced Finlay:
Newry T: Campbell, (C) O'Kane, (A) Scappaticci, (B) O'Kane, (F) Scappaticci, (R) Watson, (N) Watson, McParland, Mooney, Barr, (S) Feehan. **Subs:** Whelan replaced (A) Scappaticci; Rees replaced (N) Watson; (N) Courtney replaced Feehan:
Referee: T.Deegan (Ballynahinch)
Booked: Barr and McParland (Newry Town):

Linfield (1)   **1**   **Distillery (0)**   **0**

Att: 505

Millar (33)
(Linfield won 5-0 on aggregate)

Linfield: Lamont, Dornan, Easton, McCoosh, Spiers, Beatty, Rob.Campbell, Johnston, Millar, Fenlon, Bailie. **Subs:** Ewing replaced Spiers; Knell replaced Rob.Campbell; **Sub not used:** Caldwell (gk):
Distillery: Currie, Drake, Kennedy, Allen, Brady, Small, Totten, Hall, Hillis, Mitchell, Moore. **Subs:** Toal replaced Mitchell; Robson replaced Totten; **Sub not used:** McAleenan:
Referee: M.Ross (Carrickfergus)

Portadown (2)   **3**   **Ballyclare Comrades (0) 0**

Att: 800

Leitch (10), Peebles (43),
Haylock (86)
(Portadown won 4-2 on aggregate)

Portadown: Dalton, Fulton, Gallagher, Casey, Strain, Stewart, Carlyle, Peebles, Haylock, Leitch, Kennedy. **Subs:** Evans replaced Haylock; Candlish replaced Peebles; **Sub not used:** Keenan (gk):
Ballyclare Com: (D) McCusker, (N) Blair, Kearns, O'Connor, Morrison, (F) McCusker, (L) Galbraith, Bell, Campbell, Forshaw, Young. **Subs not used:** Neilly; Higgins; Irwin:
Referee: D.Taylor (Tandragee)

6th February, 1996

Crusaders (0)   **0**   **Ballymena United (0)**   **1**

McCourt (74)
(Crusaders won 2-1 on aggregate)

Crusaders: McKeown, McMullan, Dwyer, Dunlop, Ramirez, (K) Hunter, O'Brien, Livingstone, Morgan, (G) Hunter, McCartney. **Subs:** Cowan replaced (K) Hunter; Mellon replaced Ramirez; **Sub not used:** English:
Ballymena Utd: Smyth, Carlisle, Stewart, Allen, McConnell, (D) Moore, McConville, Craig, McCourt, Loughery, Steele. **Subs not used:** Wylie; Sloan; Quinn:
Referee: H.Barr (Bangor)
Booked: (K) Hunter (Crusaders); Craig (Ballymena United):

Quarter-Finals

6th February, 1996

Cliftonville (0)   **3**   **Coleraine (0)**   **0**

Stokes (46,48),
Feehan (55)

Cliftonville: Rice, McDonald, Flynn, Tabb, Kerr, Feehan, McCann, Hayes, O'Neill, Stokes, Donnelly. **Subs:** Sliney replaced Hayes; Hill replaced O'Neill; **Sub not used:** Manley:
Coleraine: O'Hare, McAuley, Huston, Young, Gaston, Gorman, Shiels, Surgeon, McCallan, McAllister, McIvor. **Subs:** Doherty replaced Young; O'Dowd replaced McIvor; **Sub not used:** Hagan:
Referee: M.Ross (Carrickfergus)
Booked: Stokes, Donnelly (Cliftonville); McAllister (Coleraine): *Sent Off:* Paul Stokes (Cliftonville):

McBride (20)   *Murphy (18), Boyle (90)*

Glenavon: O'Neill, Byrne, Glendinning, (D) Murphy, Gauld, (G) Smyth, Brown, Shepherd, Ferguson, McBride, Johnston. **Subs not used:** Kenny; Collins; McCoy:
Ards: Kee, McBride, McLaughlin, (C) Cullen, Mooney, Murphy, (P) Cullen, Morrison, Barker, Shanley, Boyle. **Sub:** Murray replaced (C) Cullen; **Subs not used:** McGreevy; Walker:
Referee: G.Keatley (Bangor)
Booked: (D) Murphy (Glenavon); (C) Cullen, Mooney (Ards); *Sent Off:* Dermot O'Neill (Glenavon):

Glentoran (0)   **2**   **Linfield (0)**   **1**

Coyle (52), McBride (72) Millar (61)

Glentoran: Armstrong, Nixon, (M) Smyth, Walker, (J) Devine, Parker, Mathieson, Little, Cook, Coyle, McBride. *Sub:* Houston replaced Mathieson; *Subs not used:* Finlay; Telford:

Linfield: Lamont, Dornan, Easton, McCoosh, Spiers, Beatty, Ray.Campbell, Erskine, Millar, Fenlon, Bailie. *Subs:* Rob.Campbell replaced Erskine; Ewing replaced Fenlon; *Sub not used:* Knell:

Referee: F.McDonald (Newry)

Booked: Parker, Walker, Little, McBride (Glentoran); Rob.Campbell (Linfield):

20th February, 1996

Crusaders (0)   **1**   **Portadown (4)**   **6**

Burrows (57)   *Haylock (6,34,36), Kennedy (33), (I) Ferguson (50), Peebles (64)*

Crusaders: McKeown, McMullan, McCartney, Dunlop, Deegan, Dwyer, O'Brien, Dunne, Morgan, (G) Hunter, Burrows. *Sub:* Mellon replaced Dunne; *Subs not used:* Redden; English:

Portadown: Dalton, Major, Peebles, Casey, Byrne, Stewart, Carlyle, (I) Ferguson, Haylock, Candlish, Kennedy. *Subs:* Fulton replaced Casey; Rae replaced Stewart; Keenan (gk) replaced Peebles:

Referee: L.Irvine (Limavady)

SEMI-FINALS

5th March, 1996

Venue: The Oval, Belfast

Ards (0)   **1**   **Cliftonville (2)**   **3**

McCann (90)   *Cross (21), Sliney (35), Stokes (56)*

Ards: Kee, McBride, McLaughlin, Shanley, McCann, Murphy, (P) Cullen, Morrison, Getty, Boyle, Dunnion. *Subs:* O'Sullivan replaced Boyle; Beattie replaced Dunnion; *Sub not used:* Bowers:

Cliftonville: Rice, Hill, Flynn, Tabb, Kerr, Heath, McCann, Sliney, Cross, Stokes, Donnelly. ? Sub not used: Loughran; Cavanagh; Feehan

Referee: J.Ferry (Londonderry)

Booked: McBride, McLaughlin (Ards); Stokes, Hill (Cliftonville):

6th March, 1996

Venue: Mourneview Park, Lurgan

Glentoran (0)   **1**   **Portadown (0)**   **0**

Batey (86)

Glentoran: (D) Devine, Nixon, (M) Smyth, Kennedy, (J) Devine, Parker, Quigley, Coyle, Cook, Batey, McBride. *Subs not used:* Mathieson; Telford; Hutchinson (gk):

Portadown: Dalton, Major, Byrne, Casey, Strain, Stewart, Woodsford, Peebles, Haylock, Carlyle, Kennedy. *Subs:* Fulton replaced Strain; Candlish replaced Peebles;

Referee: H.Barr (Bangor)

FINAL

19th March, 1996

Venue: Windsor Park, Belfast. *Att:* 1,672

Cliftonville (1)   **3**   **Glentoran (1)**   **1**

McCann (42), Cross (47),   *Cook (29)*
Stokes (86)

Cliftonville: Rice, Hill, Flynn, Tabb, Kerr, Heath, McCann, Sliney, Cross, Stokes, Donnelly. *Sub:* O'Neill replaced Donnelly (82 min); *Subs not used:* Feehan; McDonald:

Glentoran: Armstrong, Nixon, (M) Smyth, Kennedy, (J) Devine, Walker, Quigley, Little, Cook, Batey, McBride. *Subs:* Coyle replaced Walker (59 min); Parker replaced Quigley (62 min); *Sub not used:* Mathieson:

Referee: N.Cowie (Carryduff)

Booked: Heath (Cliftonville):

Portadown Players in celebratory mood after their 2-1 victory over Crusaders in the final of the Irish League Cup.

(Photograph by Michael Reeves)

FIRST ROUND

12th August, 1995

Ards (1)   2   Queens University (0)   0
Dunnion (25), Boyle (51)

Ards: Kee, Walker, (M) Kelly, McBride, Mooney, O'Sullivan, Dunnion, Shanley, Hall, (P) Cullen, Boyle. *Subs:* McGaw replaced Hall; (S) Kelly replaced Dunnion; *Sub not used:* McNamara (gk):
Queens: O'Neill, Browne, Graham, Harding, Harty, McNeill, Hume, O'Carroll, Evans, McCourt, Clarke. *Subs:* Bell replaced McCourt; Todd replaced McNeill; Morris replaced O'Carroll:
Referee: P.Thompson (Bangor)

Armagh City (0) 2   Crusaders (2)   3
*Mullen (67), Fay (88)   Baxter (28, pen 31), (G)
                          Hunter (55)*

Armagh C: Pollock, McLoughlin, Cochrane, Lavery, Uprichard, Turkington, Fay, Tumilty, Montgomery, Casey, Hynds. *Sub:* Mullen replaced Uprichard; *Subs not used:* Buchanan; Willis:
Crusaders: McKeown, McMullan, McCartney, Carroll, Callaghan, Murray, O'Brien, Walker, Baxter, (G) Hunter, Dwyer. *Subs:* Morgan replaced Baxter; Dunne replaced Callaghan; *Sub not used:* Hamer (gk):
Referee: D.Taylor (Tandregee).

Ballyclare Comrades (0)   0 Banbridge Town (0) 1(aet)
Brannigan (98)

Ballyclare Com: McGreevy, Larmour, Kearns, Johnston, O'Connor, Wilson, McCrum, (F) McCusker, Campbell, Irwin, McGivern. *Sub:* Bell replaced McCrum; *Subs not used:* Titterington; Eve (gk):
Banbridge T: Napier, Wilson, Maguire, Griffen, Gray, Johnston, McQuaid, Clarke, White, McStravick, Mullan. *Subs:* Adams replaced White; Brannigan replaced McQuaid; *Sub not used:* Burns:
Referee: N.Cowie (Belfast)

Carrick Rangers (0)   1   Cookstown United (0)   0
Doherty (67)

Carrick R: Hillen, McGarvey, Crawford, Muldoon, Sinclair, Coulter, (W) Wilson, McDermott, Doherty, Ferris, Macauley. *Sub:* Press replaced (W) Wilson; *Subs not used:* Gordon; Dillon (gk):
Cookstown Utd: McCombe, Eastwood, Donnelly, (E) Mullan, Taggart, Shannon, McGuckin, Devine, Lawn, (D) Mullan, (S) Hunter. *Subs:* McAllister replaced McGuckin; Bradley replaced Shannon; *Sub not used:* (N) Hunter (gk):
Referee: G.Keatley (Bangor)

Cliftonville (2)   5   Limavady United (0)   0
*Donnelly (8), Feehan (18,52,68),
Strang (65)*

Cliftonville: Rice, Hill, Flynn, Tabb, Kerr, Strang, McCann, Sliney, Feehan, McDonald, Donnelly. *Subs:* O'Neill replaced McCann; Manley replaced Feehan; Loughran replaced Sliney:
Limavady Utd: Crown, Nutt, Law, (D) Mullan, King, McCallum, (M) Mullan, Harrison, Neill, McLaughlin, Painter. *Subs:* Byrne replaced (D) Mullan; McCann replaced Painter; *Subs not used:* O'Donovan

Chimney Corner (0)   0 Ballymena United (1) 1
McWalter (43)

C.Corner: Hartley, (F) O'Kane, Owens, (S) O'Kane, Stitt, Mallon, McGurnaghan, Clements, McAllister, Patterson, McCaig. *Subs:* Caulfield; Trainor, McGrinder:
Ballymena Utd: Smyth, Mauchlen, Stewart, Allen, McConnell, Burn, McConville, Lynch, McCourt, McWalter, Boyd. *Subs:* Gilmore replaced Burn; (C) Moore replaced Lynch; *Sub not used:* May (gk):
Referee: D.Magill (Belfast)
Booked: Mallon and McAllister (Chimney Corner):

Coleraine (2)   3   Ballinamallard United (1) 1
Doherty (20), Gorman (28), Ming (34),   Patton (46).

Coleraine: O'Hare, McAuley, Huston, Gaston, Philson, Gorman, Maloney, Doherty, Patton, Beckett, Oatway. *Sub:* O'Donnell replaced Gorman; *Subs not used:* Wade; Hargan:
Ballinamallard Utd: Gallagher, McGettigan, Bogle, McGlinchey, Doherty, Ballard, Benson, Kelly, Bonner, Ming, Keys. *Subs:* McCutcheon replaced Ballard; Carroll replaced McGettigan; *Sub not used:* Bell:
Referee: M. Ross (Carrickfergus)
Sent Off: Seamus Bonner (Ballinamallard United):

Distillery (0)   0   Harland & Wolff Welders (0) 1
Gallagher (pen 61)

Distillery: Collins, Drake, Kennedy, Allen, Brush, McAleenan, Dykes, Small, Murray, Mitchell, Cleland. *Subs:* Totten replaced McAleenan; Richardson replaced Kennedy; Armstrong replaced Murray:
H & W.W: Blackwood, Doey, Kincaid, Cummings, Trevick, McCrea, Lockhart, Gallagher, Black, Wilson, Doyle. *Subs:* Blair replaced Doyle; *Subs not used:* Dunwoody, Johnston (gk)
Referee: A.Snoddy (Carryduff)
Booked: Collins (Distillery)

Dundela (0)   0   Portadown (0)   1
Haylock (73)

Dundela: Robson, Fyfe, McKee, Harrison, Goddard, Lennox, McCarroll, Doey, Hanvey, Coulter, Parker. *Subs:* Stirling replaced Coulter; Whiteside replaced Parker; *Sub not used:* Miskelly (gk):
Portadown: Dalton, McKeever, Coll, Major, Strain, Murray, Meehan, Russell, Haylock, (I.J.) Ferguson, Kennedy. *Sub not used:* Keenan (gk), Fulton, Gallagher:

Referee: M.Hutton (Londonderry)
Booked: Harrison (Dundela); Strain (Portadown)

Dungannon Swifts (0)	**1**	**Bangor (1)**	**2**
O'Hagen (50)		*Irwin (25), Tierney*	
		(65)	

Dungannon Sw: Vance, Gregg, Kennedy, Anderson, Coll, Crowe, Jennings, Jer.Robinson, O'Hagen, McKinstry, Averill. **Subs:** Denver replaced O'Hagen; Jim.Robinson replaced Averill;
Bangor: Haggen, Campbell, Clarke, McCombe, McGuinness, (R) Hill, Irwin, Batey, O'Connell, McNamara, Tierney. **Subs:** Surgeon replaced Irwin; Bailie replaced McNamara; Huxley replaced Haggen.
Referee: J.Peden (Richhill)

Glenavon (3)	**5**	**Moyola Park (0)**	**0**
(G) Smyth (15), McBride (23),			
Johnston (43,88), McDonagh (60)			

Glenavon: O'Neill, Byrne, (D) Murphy, Doherty, Brown, (G) Smyth, McCoy, Johnston, McDonagh, McBride, (J) Smyth. **Subs:** Collins replaced McDonagh; Birney replaced Byrne; **Sub not used:** Currie (gk):
Moyola Park: Hutchinson, Quinn, Braniff, Pyper, Martin, Doherty, Bell, Mellon, (A) Pattison, Scott, (M) Pattison. **Subs:** McMinn replaced (M) Pattison; Mawhinney replaced Bell; **Sub not used:** Young:
Referee: G.Douglas (Comber) replaced by D.McLoughlin (Omagh)

Glentoran (3)	**3**	**Brantwood (0)**	**0**
McGreevy (og 13), McBride (27),			
Quigley (32)			

Glentoran: (D) Devine, Neill, (M) Smyth, McCaffrey, (J) Devine, McEvoy, Quigley, Little, (T) Smith, Finlay, McBride. **Subs:** Bowers replaced (T) Smith; Walker replaced (M) Smyth; **Sub not used:** Armstrong (gk):
Brantwood: Coey, McGreevy, McIlwrath, Simpson, Hanna, Garrett, Ingram, Maxwell, Barr, McDonald, Mellon. **Subs:** McCullough replaced; Taylor replaced   *Referee:* F.Hiles (Belfast)
Booked: Barr (Brantwood)

Larne (1)	**3**	**Ballymoney United (0)**	**0**
(G) Murray (44,85),			
Looney (50)			

Larne: Robinson, (N) Murray, Collier, McKinstry, Jeffrey, Looney, (G) Murray, McNamee, Hillis, **Sub not used:** Armstrong, (E) McLoughlin Subs: McMahon replaced McNamee; Straney replaced Hillis; McConkey
Ballymoney Utd: (M) Nash, Clyde, Kirgan, Wilkinson, Mitchell, Walker, McKenna, Taylor, McFaul, McCaul, McLaughlin. Subs: (G) Nash; Moody; Smyth (gk)
Referee: T.Deegan (Ballynahinch)
Booked: Jeffrey (Larne)

Linfield (3)	**6**	**R.U.C. (0)**	**0**
Ray.Campbell (5), Erskine (43),			
McCoosh (44,63), McLean (50),			

Millar (68)

Linfield: Lamont, Crothers, Easton, McCoosh, McLean, Beatty, Ray. Campbell, Gorman, Erskine, Millar, Bailie. **Subs:** McGee replaced Beatty; Fenlon replaced Erskine; Caldwell (gk) replaced Lamont:
R.U.C.: Matthews, Morrow, Whiteside, Spratt, Crawford, Millen, Ferguson, McFadden, Macartney, Young, Leckey. **Subs:** Hunter replaced Morrow; Senior replaced Leckey; Ferris (gk) replaced Young:
Referee: R.Lutton (Lurgan)

Loughgall (1)	**3**	**Omagh Town (1)**	**4 (aet)**
Henderson (11)		*Moran (37),*	
Craig (59,76)		*McCreadie (90),*	
		Johnston (107)	
		Kavanagh (pen 86), (B)	

Loughgall: Hanley, Halliday, Leeman, Calvin, (D) McCullough, Edgar, Craig, Blake, Barnes, Henderson, Griffen. **Subs:** Greer replaced Henderson; Hamilton replaced Blake; Duke replaced Craig:
Omagh T: Blake, Johnston, McGill, Moore, McCaul, Donnelly, Kavanagh, Quigg, McIntyre, Moran, Sheridan. **Subs:** (B) McCreadie replaced; Hillen, (D) O'Neill:
Referee: J.Ferry (Londonderry)

Newry Town (2)	**2**	**Tobermore United (0)**	**0**
(N) Watson (7), Whelan (19)			

Newry T: Keeley, (B) O'Kane, Gracey, McParland, (C) O'Kane, Ralph, Barr, (N) Watson, Whelan, Stokes, McQuaid. **Subs:** McGrath replaced McQuaid; (N) Courtney replaced Barr; Campbell (gk) replaced Keeley:
Tobermore U: White, Todd, Leacock, Nelson, McFadden, Kelly, Moran, Livingstone, O'Doherty, McKay, Crooks. **Subs not used:** (A) Moore; (B) Moore:
Referee: H.Barr (Bangor)

SECOND ROUND

15th August, 1995

Ards (1)	**1**	**Coleraine (1)**	**2**
McBride (42)		*Beckett (18), Maloney (48)*	

Ards: Kee, McBride, (M) Kelly, O'Shea, Mooney, O'Sullivan, Walker, Shanley, Hall, Boyle, Wills. **Subs:** McGaw replaced O'Shea; (S) Kelly replaced Hall; **Sub not used:** McNamara (gk):
Coleraine: O'Hare, McAuley, Huston, Gaston, Philson, Gorman, Maloney, Doherty, Patton, Beckett, Oatway. **Sub:** O'Donnell replaced Oatway; **Subs not used:** Hagan; Platt:
Referee: D.Taylor (Tandragee)

Ballymena United (0)	**0**	**Portadown (0)**	**4**
		Murray (57), (I.J) Ferguson	
		(67,80), Strain (85)	

Ballymena Utd: Smyth, Mauchlen, Stewart, Allen, McConnell, Burn, McConville, Gilmore, McCourt, (C) Moore, Boyd. **Subs:** Lynch replaced (C) Moore; (D) Moore replaced Gilmore; **Sub not used:** May (gk):

Portadown: Dalton, Fulton, Coll, Major, Strain, Murray, Meehan, Russell, Haylock, (I.J) Ferguson, Kennedy. *Subs not used:* McKeever; Herbert; Keenan (gk):
Referee: M.Ross (Carrickfergus)
Booked: McConnell (Ballymena United):

Carrick Rangers (1)   3 Banbridge Town (0)   0
Coulter (30), Macauley (55),
Kirk (89)

Carrick R: Hillen, McGarvey, Crawford, Muldoon, Sinclair, Coulter, (W) Wilson, McDermott, Doherty, Ferris, Macauley. *Subs:* Kirk replaced Doherty; Donaghey replaced (W) Wilson; *Sub not used:* Press:
Banbridge T: Napier, Wilson, Maguire, Griffen, Gray, Johnston, McQuaid, Brannigan, Clarke, McStravick, Mullan. *Subs:* Adams replaced McQuaid; Scappaticci replaced Maguire; Burns replaced Clarke:
Referee: H.Barr (Bangor)

Cliftonville (2)   6 Bangor (1)   1
Strang (8), Feehan (36,90),   Murtagh (6)
McCann (55),
Donnelly (76,77)

Cliftonville: Rice, Hill, Flynn, Tabb, Kerr, Strang, McCann, Sliney, Feehan, McDonald, Donnelly. *Sub:* Davey replaced Sliney; *Subs not used:* Manley; Loughran:
Bangor: Haggan, Campbell, Clarke, McCombe, McGuinness, (R) Hill, Irwin, Batey, O'Connell, Murtagh, Tierney. *Subs:* McNamara replaced Tierney; Surgeon replaced O'Connell; *Sub not used:* Huxley (gk).
Referee: D.Magill (Belfast)
Booked: Kerr (Cliftonville); McGuinness and Murtagh (Bangor):

Crusaders (1)   1 Harland & Wolff Welders (0) 0
Cummings (og 40)

Crusaders: McKeown, McMullan, McCartney, Carroll, Callaghan, Murray, O'Brien, Dunne, Baxter, (G) Hunter, Dwyer. *Subs:* Morgan replaced Baxter; *Subs not used:* Cobain; Bell:
H.W.W: Blackwood, Doey, Kincaid, Cummings, Trueick, McCrea, Lockhart, Gallagher, Black, Wilson, Doyle. *Subs:* Dunwoody replaced Doyle; Blair replaced Doey, Johnston replaced Blackwood.
Referee: G.Keatley (Bangor)
Booked: Baxter (Crusaders); Cummings and Gallagher (Harland & W.W); *Sent Off:* Aaron Callaghan (Crusaders); Gary Trueick (Harland & W.W)

Larne (0)   0 Glenavon (1)   1
                    Johnston (49)

Larne: Robinson, (N) Murray, Collier, McKinstry, Jeffrey, Looney, (G) Murray, McConkey, Straney, Armstrong, (E) McLoughlin. *Subs not used:* Hillis; (J) McDowell; McCorry (gk):
Glenavon: O'Neill, Byrne, Glendinning, Doherty, Brown, (A) Murphy, McCoy, Johnston, Collins, McBride, (J) Smyth. *Sub:* (D) Murphy replaced Collins; *Subs not used:*

McDonagh; Currie (gk):
Referee: N.Cowie (Carryduff)
Booked: (G) Murray (Larne); Doherty and (A) Murphy (Glenavon):

Omagh Town (2) 3   Newry Town (1) 1
Moran (8,64),   *Clarke (34)*
McIntyre (23)

Omagh T: Blake, Johnston, Magill, Moore, Donnelly, Kavanagh, Moran, Quigg, McIntyre, Crilly, Sheridan. *Subs:* (B) McCreadie replaced ; (D) O'Neill replaced ; Hillen replaced:
Newry T: Keeley, (B) O'Kane, Gracey, McParland, (C) O'Kane, Ralph, Barr, (N) Watson, Whelan, Stokes, Clarke. *Subs:* Courtney replaced (B) O'Kane; McQuaid replaced Ralph; *Sub not used:* Campbell (gk):
Referee: T.Gillanders (Belfast)

16th August, 1995

Glentoran (0)   0   Linfield (1)   1
                              Erskine (3)

Glentoran: (D) Devine, Neill, (M) Smyth, McCaffrey, (J) Devine, McEvoy, Quigley, Little, (T) Smith, McGill, McBride. *Subs:* Finlay replaced McEvoy; Mathieson replaced McGill; *Sub not used:* Armstrong (gk):
Linfield: Lamont, Dornan, Easton, McCoosh, McLean, Beatty, Ray.Campbell, McGee, Erskine, Millar, Bailie. *Subs not used:* Fenlon; McShane; Caldwell (gk):
Referee: J.Ferry (Londonderry)
Booked: McGill and (T) Smith (Glentoran):

QUARTER-FINALS

29th August, 1995

Carrick Rangers (0)   2 Omagh Town (4) 6
Doherty (64),   *Mooney (18),*
Crawford (pen67)   *McIntyre (39),*
                            Donnelly (40),
                            Quigg (45),
                            McHugh (53),
                            Kavanagh (71)

Carrick R: Hillen, Donaghey, Gilmore, Muldoon, Sinclair, Coulter, (W) Wilson, McDermott, Doherty, Ferris, Macauley. *Subs:* Kirk replaced Macauley; Crawford replaced Coulter; *Sub not used:* Bowes:
Omagh T: Blake, Johnston, Gray, Donnelly, McCaul, Mooney,Kavanagh, Quigg, McIntyre, Crilly, McHugh. *Subs:* (B) McCreadie replaced McIntyre; Moran replaced McHugh; (D) O'Neill replaced Quigg:
Referee: N.Cowie (Carryduff)
Booked: (W) Wilson (Carrick Rangers):

Cliftonville   0   Crusaders   0
(aet Crusaders won 3-0 on pens)

Penalty Shoot Out:
Cliftonville: Feehan, Ramsey, Sliney (all missed)
Crusaders: McMullan, Dunne, Baxter (all scored)

WILKINSON SWORD IRISH LEAGUE CUP 1995/96

Cliftonville: Rice, Hill, Flynn, Tabb, Kerr, Ramsey, McCann, Sliney, Feehan, McDonald, Donnelly. *Subs not used:* McCrystal; Heath; Manley:
Crusaders: McKeown, McMullan, Murray, Dunlop, Callaghan, O'Brien, Livingstone, Dunne, Baxter, (G) Hunter, Burrows. *Subs not used:* Gardiner; Mellon; Carroll:
Referee: A.Snoddy (Carryduff)
Booked: Sliney (Cliftonville):

| Coleraine (0) | 0 | Glenavon (0) | 3 |
| | | McBride (67,75), Collins (86) | |

Coleraine: O'Hare, McAuley, Huston, Gaston, Philson, Gorman, Maloney, Doherty, Patton, Beckett, O'Donnell. *Sub:* Wade replaced Maloney; *Subs not used:* Oatway; Hagan:
Glenavon: O'Neill, Byrne, Glendinning, Doherty, Brown, (G) Smyth, McCoy, Johnston, Ferguson, McBride, (J) Smyth. *Sub:* Collins replaced McCoy; *Subs not used:* Birney; Currie (gk):
Referee: H.Barr (Bangor)

| Portadown | 0 | Linfield | 0 |
| *(aet Portadown won 5-4 on pens)* | | | |

Penalty Shoot Out:
Portadown: Casey, Kennedy, Russell, Strain, Peebles (all scored). Haylock (missed):
Linfield: Fenlon, Ray.Campbell, Erskine, McGee (all scored). Millar, Dornan (both missed):

Portadown: Keenan, Major, Murray, Casey, Strain, Byrne, Boyle, Russell, Haylock, Peebles, Kennedy. *Sub:* Davidson replaced Boyle: *Subs not used:* Fulton; Whitmarsh (og);
Linfield: Lamont, Dornan, Easton, Millar, McLean, Beatty, Ray.Campbell, Gorman, Erskine, Fenlon, Bailie. *Sub:* McGee replaced Gorman; *Sub not used:* McCoosh; Caldwell (gk):
Referee: D.Magill (Belfast)
Booked: Strain, Haylock, Peebles (Portadown); Ray.Campbell, Millar, McLean (Linfield):

SEMI-FINALS

5th September, 1995

Venue: The Oval, Belfast

Crusaders (2)	3	Omagh Town (1)	1
O'Brien (3),		Mooney (27)	
Burrows (41,71),			

Crusaders: McKeown, McMullan, Murray, Dunlop. Callaghan, O'Brien, Livingstone, Dunne, Baxter, (G) Hunter, Burrows. *Sub:* Gardiner replaced (G) Hunter; *Subs not used:* Carroll; Mellon:
Omagh T: Blake, Johnston, Gray, Donnelly, McCaul, Mooney, Kavanagh, Quigg, McIntyre, Crilly, McHugh. *Subs:* (B) McCreadie replaced Gray; Moran replaced McIntyre; *Sub not used:* (D) O'Neill:
Referee: N.Cowie (Bangor)
Booked: Livingstone (Crusaders):

6th September, 1995

Venue: Shamrock Park, Portadown

Portadown (1)	3	Glenavon (0)	0
Peebles (10), Kennedy (58),			
(G) Smyth (og 60)			

Portadown: Keenan, Major, Murray, Casey, Strain, Byrne, Boyle, Russell, Haylock, Peebles, Kennedy. *Subs:* Davidson replaced Kennedy; *Subs not used:* Fulton; Dalton (gk)
Glenavon: O'Neill, Byrne, Glendinning, Doherty, (A) Murphy, (G) Smyth, McCoy, Johnston, Ferguson, McBride, (J) Smyth. *Subs:* (D) Murphy replaced Glendinning; Collins replaced McCoy; *Sub not used:* Currie (gk):
Referee: J.Ferry (Londonderry)
Booked: Peebles (Portadown); Doherty and (G) Smyth (Glenavon):

FINAL

19th September, 1995

Venue: Windsor Park, Belfast *Att:* 2,6000

| Portadown (0) | 2 | Crusaders (0) | 1 |
| Haylock (50), Casey (83) | | Burrows (79) | |

Portadown: Keenan, Fulton, Murray, Casey, Strain, Major, Boyle, Russell, Haylock, Peebles, Kennedy. *Subs:* Davidson replaced Boyle (46 mins); Magee replaced Murray (78 mins); *Sub not used:* Dalton (gk):
Crusaders: McKeown, McMullan, McCartney, Dunlop, Callaghan, O'Brien, Murray, Dunne, Baxter, (G) Hunter, Burrows. *Sub:* (K) Hunter replaced O'Brien (58 min); *Subs not used:* Carroll; (R) Lawlor:
Referee: L.Irvine (Limavady)
Booked: Major and Russell (Portadown); Baxter, Dunlop, (K) Hunter (Crusaders):

PREVIOUS IRISH LEAGUE CUP FINALS

1986/87	Linfield	2		Crusaders	1	
1987/88	Coleraine	1		Portadown	0	(aet)
1988/89	Glentoran	2		Linfield	1	
1989/90	Glenavon	3		Newry Town	1	
1990/91	Glentoran	2		Ards	0	
1991/92	Linfield	3		Larne	0	
1992/93	Bangor	3		Coleraine	0	
1993/94	Linfield	2		Coleraine	0	
1994/95	Ards	0		Cliftonville	0	

(Ards won 2-0 on penalties)

Summary of Winners 1986/87 - 1995/96

3 Linfield; 2 Glentoran; 1 Ards; Bangor; Coleraine; Glenavon; Portadown:

CALOR COUNTY ANTRIM SHIELD 1995/96

<table>
<tr><td colspan="2">

FIRST ROUND

21st November, 1995

</td></tr>
</table>

Glenavon (2)	5	Dundela (0)	0

McBride (16), McCoy (18),
Ferguson (60,76), Collins (71)

Bangor (1)	3	Ballymena United (2)	5

Cash (8), Irwin (73),   *Curry (24,72), McWalter(31,89),*
O'Connell (79)   *McGuinness (og 86)*

Bangor: Huxley, Bailie, Ferguson, Spiers, McCombe, Cash, Percy, Irwin, O'Connell, Murtagh, Byrne. *Subs:* McGuinness replaced Murtagh; McCartan replaced Cash; *Subs not used:* McNamara.
Ballymena Utd: Beck, (D) Moore, Stewart, Allen, McConnell, Mauchlen, Curry, McWalter, McConville, Burn, Boyd. *Subs:* Loughery replaced Curry; Muir replaced Boyd;
Referee: F.Hiles (Newtownards)

Carrick Rangers (1) 2		Cliftonville (1)	2

Ferris (15,96)   *Donnelly (16), Sliney (110)*
(aet Carrick Rangers won 4-3 on pens)

Penalty Shoot Out:
Carrick R: Garvey; (F) Wilson, Crawford, Doherty (all scored); Coulter (missed).
Cliftonville: Sliney, Strang, Donnelly (scored),Feehan, Tabb (both missed)

Carrick R: Dillon, McGarvey, Crawford, Muldoon, McLeister, Coulter, Donaghey, McDermott, Doherty, Ferris, Macauley. *Subs:* (F) Wilson replaced Muldoon. *Subs not used:* Sinclair (W) Wilson.
Cliftonville: Rice, Hill, Flynn, Tabb, Kerr, Manley, McCann, McFadden, McParland, McDonald, Donnelly. *Subs:* Feehan replaced McPorland; Strang replaced McCann; Sliney replaced McFadden.
Referee: E.Millar (Bangor)

Crusaders (0)	1	Linfield (0)	0 (aet)

Livingstone (108)

Crusaders: McKeown, McMullan, Mellon, Dunlop, Eccles, O'Brien, Carroll, Dunne, Baxter, Morgan, Burrows. *Subs:* Murray replaced Eccles; (G) Hunter replaced Baxter; Livingstone replaced Morgan:
Linfield: Lamont, Dornan, Easton, McCoosh, Spiers, Beatty, Ray.Campbell, Norbury, Erskine, Fenlon, Bailie. *Subs:* Knell replaced Norbury; Marks replaced McCoosh; *Sub not used:* Crawford (gk):
Referee: D.Magill (Belfast)
Booked: Dunlop, McMullan, O'Brien (Crusaders); Knell, Erskine (Linfield): *Sent Off:* Stephen Beatty (Linfield):

Distillery (1)	1	Ards (2)	3

Brush (19)   *McLaughlin (35), McCann*
    (42), Flannery (50)

Distillery: Currie, Drake, Hall, Allen, Brush, Moore, Magee, McAleenan, Robson, Mitchell, Cleland. *Subs:* Dykes replaced Magee; Totten replaced Moore; *Sub not used:* Small:
Ards: Kee, Campbell, McLaughlin, (M) Kelly, Maloney, Bowers, McGreevy, Morrison, Flannery, Boyle, McCann. *Subs:* Mooney replaced Campbell; McBride replaced McGreevy; Murphy replaced Flannery:
Referee: M.Ross (Carrickfergus)

Glenavon: O'Neill, Collins, Glendinning, (D) Murphy, Byrne, (G) Smyth, Johnston, McCoy, Ferguson, McBride, (J) Smyth. *Subs:* McCartan replaced McCoy; Mulholland replaced (D) Murphy; Burns replaced Johnston:
Dundela: Robson, Fyfe, McKee, Harrison, Lennox, Caskey, Fettis, Doey, Hanvey, Coulter, Parker. *Subs:* Snodden replaced Doey; McCormick replaced Coulter; *Sub not used:* Whiteside:
Referee: T.Deegan (Ballynahinch)
Booked: (J) Smyth (Glenavon): *Sent Off:* Billy Caskey (Dundela)

Larne (1)	3	Ballyclare Comrades (0)	2 (aet)

Armstrong (34),   *Higgins (47,52)*
McCrae (50,109)

Larne: Robinson, Magill, McConkey, (L) Smyth, Jeffrey, (S) McDowell, Looney, McMahon, Armstrong, McCrae, McLoughlin. *Subs:* McKnight replaced; Leckey replaced; Johnston replaced;
Ballyclare Com: McGreevy, (N) Blair, Kearns, Walker, Morrison, Irwin, Allsopp, Young, Higgins, Campbell, Bell. *Subs:* (F) McCusker replaced; (L) Galbraith replaced;
Referee: P.Thompson (Bangor)

Newry Town (0)	1	Glentoran (3)	4

(C) O'Kane (68)   *Batey (15,30,67), McCarrison*
    (25)

Newry T: Keeley, (C) O'Kane, Gracey, Courtney, (F) Scappaticci, Ralph, Whelan, (R) Watson, (S) Feehan, Barr, Clarke. *Subs:* (B) O'Kane replaced; Mooney replaced; (N) Watson replaced;
Glentoran: Armstrong, Nixon, (M) Smyth, Kennedy, (J) Devine, Quigley, McBride, Little, McCarrison, Batey, Cunnington. *Subs:* Parker replaced Kennedy; Telford replaced Batey; Kelly replaced (M) Smyth:
Referee: D.Malcolm (Bangor)

Portadown (0)	1	Dromara Village (0) 0 (aet)

Haylock (100)

Portadown: Dalton, Fulton, Davidson, Casey, Strain, Byrne, Candlish, Stewart, Haylock, (I.J) Ferguson, Kennedy. *Subs not used:* Boyle; Gallagher; Keenan (gk):
Dromara V: Gregge, Graham, Adams, Johnston, Bustard, (I) Bingham, Woods, Beckett, Doran, Hewitt, Kirk. *Subs:* Cosgrave replaced; (K) Bingham replaced; Morrison replaced
Referee: G.Douglas (Hillsborough)

QUARTER-FINALS

6th December, 1995

Ards (0)	0	Crusaders (1)	1

    D.O'Brien (45)

Ards: Kee, McBride, Shanley, McCann, Mooney, Bowers, McGreevy, (P) Cullen, Flannery, Boyle, O'Sullivan. *Sub:* Dunnion replaced Flannery; *Subs not used:* Walker; Armstrong:

CALOR COUNTY ANTRIM SHIELD 1995/96

Crusaders: McKeown, McMullan, Carroll, Dunlop, (R) Lawlor, Callaghan, Livingstone, O'Brien, Morgan, Murray, Burrows. *Subs:* McCartney replaced McMullan; Dwyer replaced Morgan; *Sub not used:* (K) Hunter: *Referee:* F.Hiles (Newtownards)

Carrick Rangers (0)0   Portadown (2)   4

Boyle (22), Kennedy (39,57), (I.J) Ferguson (65)

Carrick R: Dillon, McGarvey, Gilmore, McDermott, Sinclair, (F) Wilson, (W) Wilson, Donaghey, Armstrong, Ferris, Macauley. *Subs:* Gordon replaced Armstrong; Kerr replaced (F) Wilson; Doherty replaced Ferris: *Portadown:* Dalton, Fulton, Davidson, Casey, Stewart, Byrne, Boyle, Peebles, (I) Ferguson, Candlish, Kennedy. *Subs:* Turkington replaced Candlish; Gallagher replaced Boyle; *Sub not used:* Keenan (gk): *Referee:* A.Snoddy (Carryduff)

Glentoran (0)   1   Ballymena United (0) 2
McBride (88)   McWalter (70,82)

Glentoran: Armstrong, Nixon, (M) Smyth, Kennedy, (J) Devine, Parker, McBride, Coyle, (T) Smith, Batey, Cunnington. *Subs:* Cook replaced (T) Smith; Finlay replaced Parker; *Sub not used:* McCarrison: *Ballymena Utd:* Beck, (D) Moore, Stewart, Allen, Muir, Boyd, Curry, McWalter, McConville, Burn, Murray. *Subs:* Gilmore replaced Murray; (C) Moore replaced Curry; *Sub not used:* Patton: *Referee:* H.Barr (Bangor) *Booked:* Batey (Glentoran); McConville (Ballymena United):

Larne (0)   0   Glenavon (0)   2
                          McCartan (79), Collins (80)

Larne: Robinson, (N) Murray, Collier, McConkey, Jeffrey, Leckey, Looney, McCrae, Armstrong, McMahon, (S) McDowell. *Subs:* Johnston replaced (S) McDowell; (L) Smyth replaced Jeffrey; (D) Smyth replaced Leckey: *Glenavon:* O'Neill, Byrne, Glendinning, Doherty, Gauld, (G) Smyth, Collins, (D) Murphy, Ferguson, McBride, (J) Smyth. *Subs:* Mulholland replaced (D) Murphy; McCartan replaced Ferguson; Burns replaced (J) Smyth: *Referee:* N.Cowie (Carryduff). *Booked:* (L) Smyth (Larne)

SEMI-FINAL

19th December, 1995

Venue: The Oval, Belfast
Crusaders (1)   2   Ballymena United (0) 0
O'Brien (21), Deegan (90)

Crusaders: McKeown, Carroll, Callaghan, Dunlop, (R) Lawlor, Murray, O'Brien, Deegan, Baxter, (G) Hunter, Burrows. *Sub:* McMullan replaced (G) Hunter; *Subs not used:* Morgan; Livingstone: *Ballymena Utd:* Beck, (D) Moore, Stewart, Allen, McConnell, Boyd, Curry, McWalter, McConville, Burn, Murray. *Subs:* Muir replaced McConville; Patton replaced (D) Moore; *Sub not used:* Smyth (gk): *Referee:* A.Snoddy (Carryduff)

20th December, 1995

Venue: Shamrock Park, Portadown
Portadown (1)   1   Glenavon 0)   4 aet)
Byrne (13)   Johnston (71), Freeman (101,104), Collins (103)

Portadown: Keenan, Major, Coll, Casey, Strain, Byrne, Davidson, Stewart, Haylock, (I.J) Ferguson, Kennedy. *Subs:* Candlish replaced Davidson; Fulton replaced (I.J) Ferguson; *Sub not used:* Dalton (gk): *Glenavon:* O'Neill, Mulholland, Glendinning, (D) Murphy, Byrne, (G) Smyth, Collins, Johnston, Freeman, McBride, (J) Smyth. *Subs:* Brown replaced (D) Murphy; McCoy replaced Mulholland; Straney (gk) replaced Freeman: *Referee:* G.Keatley (Bangor) *Booked:* Kennedy, Strain, Haylock (Portadown); Glendinning, Freeman (Glenavon): *Sent Off:* Philip Major (Portadown)

FINAL

30th January, 1996

Venue: The Oval, Belfast. *Att:* 1,700
Crusaders (0)   0   Glenavon (2)   3
                          McBride (15,80), Kenny (42)

Crusaders: McKeown, McMullan, Carroll, Dunlop, (R) Lawlor, Deegan, O'Brien, Dunne, Baxter, (G) Hunter, Callaghan. *Subs:* Murray replaced (R) Lawlor (45 min); McCartney replaced Carroll (45 min); Livingstone replaced McMullan (72 min): *Glenavon:* O'Neill, Byrne, Glendinning, (D) Murphy, Gauld, (G) Smyth, Johnston, McCoy, Ferguson, McBride, Kenny. *Sub:* Collins replaced Kenny (81 min); *Subs not used:* (J) Smyth; Brown: *Referee:* D.Magill (Belfast).

CO. ANTRIM SHIELD WINNERS 1888/89 - 1995/96

1888/89	Distillery	1924/25	Glentoran	1960/61	Linfield
1889/90	Shield Withheld	1925/26	Cliftonville	1961/62	Linfield
1890/91	Black Watch	1926/27	Belfast Celtic	1962/63	Linfield
1891/92	Cliftonville	1927/28	Linfield	1963/64	Distillery
1892/93	Distillery	1928/29	Linfield	1964/65	Crusaders
1893/94	Cliftonville	1929/30	Linfield	1965/66	Linfield
1894/95	Belfast Celtic	1930/31	Glentoran	1966/67	Linfield
1895/96	Distillery	1931/32	Linfield	1967/68	Glentoran
1896/97	Distillery	1932/33	Linfield	1968/69	Crusaders
1897/98	Cliftonville	1933/34	Linfield	1969/70	Bangor
1898/99	Linfield	1934/35	Linfield	1970/71	Glentoran
1899/00	Distillery	1935/36	Belfast Celtic	1971/72	Ards
1900/01	Glentoran	1936/37	Belfast Celtic	1972/73	Linfield
1901/02	Glentoran	1937/38	Linfield	1973/74	Crusaders
1902/03	Distillery	1938/39	Belfast Celtic	1974/75	Bangor
1903/04	Linfield	1939/40	Glentoran	1975/76	Ballymena United
1904/05	Distillery	1940/41	Glentoran	1976/77	Linfield
1905/06	Linfield	1941/42	Linfield	1977/78	Glentoran
1906/07	Linfield	1942/43	Belfast Celtic	1978/79	Cliftonville
1907/08	Linfield	1943/44	Glentoran	1979/80	Ballymena United
1908/09	Glentoran II	1945/46	Distillery	1980/81	Linfield
1909/10	Belfast Celtic	1946/47	Final not played	1981/82	Linfield
1910/11	Glentoran		Shield awarded to Linfield	1982/83	Linfield
1911/12	Not Played	1947/48	Ballymena United	1983/84	Linfield
1912/13	Linfield	1948/49	Linfield Swifts	1984/85	Glentoran
1913/14	Linfield	1949/50	Glentoran	1985/86	Distillery
1914/15	Distillery	1950/51	Ballymena United	1986/87	Glentoran
1915/16	Glentoran	1951/52	Glentoran	1987/88	Newry Town
1916/17	Linfield	1952/53	Linfield	1988/89	Bangor
1917/18	Glentoran	1953/54	Distillery	1989/90	Glentoran
1918/19	Distillery	1954/55	Linfield	1990/91	Glenavon
1919/20	Distillery	1955/56	Ards	1991/92	Crusaders
1920/21	Glentoran	1956/57	Glentoran	1992/93	Carrick Rangers
1921/22	Linfield	1957/58	Linfield	1993/94	Ards
1922/23	Linfield	1958/59	Linfield	1994/95	Linfield
1923/24	Queen's Island	1959/60	Crusaders	1995/96	Glenavon

Summary of Winners 1888/89-1995/96
36 Linfield, 20 Glentoran, 14 Distillery, 8 Belfast Celtic, 5 Cliftonville, Crusaders, 4 Ballymena Utd, 3 Ards, Bangor, 2 Glenavon, 1 Black Watch, Carrick Rangers, Glentoran II, Linfield Swifts, Newry Town, Queen's Island.

McEwans Mid-Ulster Cup 1995/96

First Round

27th January, 1996

Annagh United	0	Laurelvale	1
Bessbrook United	2	Cookstown Royals	1 (aet)
Lurgan Celtic Bhoys	?	Hanover	?
Queens Park Swifts	?	Coalisland Celtic	?
Rathfriland Rangers	2	Seapatrick	3
Tandragee Rovers	11	Southend United	2

3rd February, 1996

Coagh United	7	Scarva Rangers	1
Dromore Amateurs	6	Richhill	1
Killymoon Rangers	0	AFC Craigavon	3
Warrenpoint Town	4	Mountnorris	0

Bye: Bourneview Y.M.

Second Round
10th February, 1996

AFC Craigavon	2	Laurelvale	3
Bessbrook United	4	Tandragee Rovers	2
Bourneview Y.M.	7	Coalisland Celtic	0
Coagh United	4	Seapatrick	0
Warrenpoint Town	0	Lurgan Celtic Bhoys	3

Bye: Dromore Amateurs

Third Round
24th February, 1996

Bessbrook United	1	Laurelvale	2
Coagh United	4	Dromore Amateurs	0
Lurgan Celtic Bhoys	8	Bourneview	0

Fourth Round
9th March, 1996

Armagh City	1	Coagh United	3
Banbridge Town	2	Loughgall	4
Cookstown United	2	Laurelvale	3
Dungannon Swifts	3	Lurgan Celtic Bhoys	3
(aet Dunganonn Swifts won 5-3 on pens)			

Quarter-Finals
1st April, 1996

Dungannon Swifts (2) 5 Laurelvale (0) 0
Jer.Robinson (10), McKinstry (45,71),
McNamee (47), O'Hagen (53)

Dungannon Sw: Vance, Gregg, Averill, Montgomery, McCullough, Jer.Robinson, Jennings, McNamee, O'Hagen, Smyth, McKinstry. *Subs:* McCrory replaced Jer.Robinson; (D) Robinson replaced Smyth; Shaw replaced Jennings;
Laurelvale: McGaw, McLoughlin, Simmons, Guy, Adams, Best, Wilkinson, Turkington, Tate, Conn, Porter.
Subs: McKew replaced Wilkinson; Hynds replaced Best; *Sub not used:* Hamilton:
Referee: J.Peden (Richhill)
Booked: Averill (Dungannon Swifts):

2nd April, 1996

Bangor (2) 3 Coagh United (0) 0
Eddis (17), Morrow (24),
Spiers (90)

Bangor: Miskelly, Coulter, Dornan, Spiers, Kennedy, McKeown, Nelson, Bailie (R) Hill, Morrow, Eddis. *Subs:* Massey replaced Nelson; Wilkinson replaced Kennedy; Bell replaced Eddis:
Coagh Utd: Hassan, Brown, Henry, Jordan, (W) Johnston, Robinson, McMenemy, McCalmont, Murdock, Boyd, Pattison.
Subs not used: Nelson; Haire; (I) Johnston:
Referee: F.McDonald (Newry)

Distillery	**(2)**	**2**	**Portadown**	**(1)**	**1**
Robson (16,30)			*Candlish (44)*		

Distillery: Collins, Drake, Hall, Allen, Brush, Toal, Totten, Robson, Moore, Small, Cleland. *Sub:* Magill replaced Totten;
Subs not used: Hillis; Rogan:
Portadown: Keenan, Fulton, Turkington, Gallagher, McKeever, Byrne, Clarke, Russell, Evans, Candlish, Carlyle. *Subs*: Savage replaced Russell; McCullough replaced Turkington;
Referee: D.Taylor (Tandragee)

Newry Town	**(1)**	**3**	**Loughgall**	**(0)**	**1**
Magee (23), Barr (64,70)			*Griffin (69)*		

Newry T: Keeley, McParland, (B) O'Kane, (N) Watson, (C) O'Kane, Ralph, Whelan, Mooney, Clarke, Barr. Magee.
Sub: (M) Shields replaced ?; *Sub not used:* (N) Courtney:
Loughgall: Hanley, Edgar, Calvin, (D) McCullough, Morwood, Johnston, Duke, Hamilton, Gardiner, Henderson, Griffin.
Subs: Huddleston replaced Calvin Blake replaced Gardiner, (G) McCullough replaced Johnston.
Referee: B.Kane (Newry)

Semi-Finals

18th April, 1996

Venue: Clandeboye Park, Bangor

Bangor	**(2)**	**2**	**Newry Town (1)**		**1**
(W) Davies (6), (R) Hill (23)			*Clarke (29)*		

Bangor: Eachus, Bailie, (R) Hill, Spiers, McCombe, McKeown, Holmes, Green, (W) Davies, O'Connell, McEvoy.
Subs: Irwin replaced O'Connell; Morrow replaced (W) Davies; *Sub not used:* Coulter.
Newry T: Keeley, Berry, McParland, Clarke, (C) O'Kane, Ralph, (N) Courtney, (M) Shields, Mooney, Barr, Magee.
Sub: (S) Feehan replaced Barr; *Subs not used:* (J) Feehan; (N) Watson:
Referee: F.McDonald (Newry)
Booked: (N) Courtney (Newry Town); *Sent Off:* Steven Eachus (Bangor); Niall Courtney (Newry Town):

25th April, 1996

Venue: Stangmore Park, Dungannon

Dungannon Swifts	**(1)**	**2**	**Distillery**	**(0)**	**1**
Jer.Robinson (42), Smyth (pen 89)			*Allen (85)*		

Dungannon S: Vance, Gregg, Clarke, Coll, McKerr, Crowe, Shaw, Montgomery, McKinstry, Smyth, Jer. Robinson.
Sub: McNamee replaced McKinstry; *Subs not used:* O'Hagen; Jennings:
Distillery: Collins, Drake, Hall, Allen, Brush, Small, Moore, Robson, Spence, Toal, Cleland.
Subs: Totten replaced Moore; McAleenan replaced Toal; *Sub not used:* Magill:
Referee: D.Taylor (Tandragee)
Booked: Allen, Small, Brush (Distillery); *Sent Off:* Damian Toal (Distillery)

Final

30th April, 1996

Venue: Shamrock Park, Portadown.   Att: 500

Bangor	**(3)**	**3**	**Dungannon Swifts**	**(0)**	**1**
O'Connell (17), (W) Davies (30), Smyth (57)			*McKeown (37)*		

Bangor: Eachus, Bailie, Dornan, Spiers, McCombe, McKeown, Holmes, Green, (W) Davies, O'Connell, McEvoy.
Subs: (R) Hill replaced McCombe (74 min); Morrow replaced O'Connell (78 min); *Sub not used:* Irwin:
Dungannon S: Vance, Gregg, Clarke, Coll, McKerr, McNamee, Jennings, Shaw, McKinstry, Smyth, Jer.Robinson.
Subs: McCaul replaced Coll (45 min); Crowe replaced McKerr; *Sub not used:* Montgomery:
Referee: R.Lutton (Lurgan)
Booked: McCaul and Gregg (Dungannon Swifts)

NB: Only four teams are involved in this competition, Oxford United and Churchill Kilfennan United as they were the finalists in the North West Intermediate Cup for 1995/96 and Coleraine and Omagh Town who are the only two senior teams from the North West playing in the Irish League.

SEMI-FINALS

5th March, 1996

Venue: The Showgrounds, Coleraine

Coleraine	**(1)**	**2**	**Oxford United Stars**	**(0)**	**1**
McCallan (12), McIvor (70)			Francis (57)		

Coleraine: Patterson, McAuley, Huston, Young, Gaston, Gorman, Shiels, Surgeon, McCallan, Doherty, McIvor.
Subs: Maloney replaced McCallan; Patton replaced Surgeon; Clanachan replaced Young:
Oxford Utd. Stars: Matthewson, Boyle, Slevin, Seydak, Hearn, Ross, Cairn, Francis, McCarron, O'Donnell, Devlin.
Subs: Taylor replaced Slevin; Doherty replaced Cairn; *Sub not used:* McCallion:
Referee: M.Hutton (Londonderry)

28th March, 1996

Venue: St.Julians Road, Omagh

Omagh Town	**(3)**	**7**	**Churchill Kilfennan United**	**(0)**	**1**
Johnston (21), McHugh (36,40,)			Doherty ( )		
Kavanagh ( ), (R) Sheridan ( )					
Crilly (90)					

Omagh T: McDevitt, Johnston, Gray, Moore, McElroy, Kavanagh, Devine, Gallagher, Mooney, Crilly, McHugh.
Subs: (D) O'Neill replaced Gray; (R) Sheridan replaced Devine; McCullagh replaced Kavanagh:
CKU: Line up not available.
Referee: G.McKay (Strabane)

FINAL

11th April, 1996
Venue: The Showgrounds, Coleraine. Att:200

Coleraine	**(0)**	**1**	**Omagh Town**	**(3)**	**5**
Shiels (70)			Magill (30), Donnelly (34), Johnston (45), Crilly (63,64)		

Coleraine: Patterson, Doherty, McAuley, Young, Gaston, Gorman, Shiels, Maloney, McCallan, McAllister, McIvor.
Subs: Surgeon replaced McAllister (65 min); Lynch replaced McCallan (68 min); *Sub not used:* Clanachan:
Omagh T: McDevitt, Moore, Magill, Melly, McElroy, Gray, Johnston, Gallagher, Donnelly, Crilly, McHugh.
Subs: McCullagh replaced Gray (82 min); McDowell replaced McHugh (82 min); (D) O'Neill replaced Gallagher (90 min):
Referee: M.Hutton (Londonderry)
Booked: Donnelly and Moore (Omagh Town)

PREVIOUS YEARBOOKS

THE IRISH FOOTBALL YEARBOOK 1990/91

The first yearbook includes complete statistics of every match played in all competitions during the 1989/90 season. Also every Irish Cup Final line-up since 1882. Copies of this book are still available at a reduced price of just £3

(UK post free, Europe & Eire please add £1 for postage)

IRISH FOOTBALL YEARBOOK 1991/92

The second edition consists of 304 pages featuring team photographs for Irish League and 'B' Division clubs. Plus, for the first time match by match results and goalscorers for all 'B' Division Section One clubs. On the international front a concise record is included of every Northern Ireland match since 1947.

Again copies of this book are still available at a reduced price of just £6.50

(UK post free, Europe & Eire please add £1.50 for postage)

IRISH FOOTBALL YEARBOOK 1992/93

The third edition contained all the usual features relating to the 1991/92 season plus for the first time an Irish League Players Directory listing every player to have appeared in the Irish League for the previous season. Complete match line-ups included for all European games played by Northern Ireland teams since 1957.

A limited number of copies of this book are still available at a reduced price of just £6.50.

(UK post free, Europe & Eire please add £1.50 for postage)

THE NORTHERN IRELAND FOOTBALL YEARBOOK 1993/94

All copies of 1993/94 Yearbook are sold out!

THE UTV NORTHERN IRELAND FOOTBALL YEARBOOK 1994/95

The 1994/95 UTV Football Yearbook priced £7.95 is available from Tudor Journals Limited, 97 Botanic Avenue, Belfast. BT7 1JN. (UK post free, Europe & Eire please add £1.50 for postage).

THE UTV NORTHERN IRELAND FOOTBALL YEARBOOK 1995/96

The 1995/96 UTV Football Yearbook priced £7.95 is available from Tudor Journals Limited, 97 Botanic Avenue, Belfast. BT7 1JN. (UK post free, Europe & Eire please add £1.50 for postage).

NB: 1990/91; 1991/92; 1992/93 yearbooks available only direct from the editor.

Please make cheques payable to;- Marshall Gillespie and send to 92 Belvoir Close, Fareham. PO16 0PR.

IRISH NEWS CUP 1995/96

SEMI-FINAL, FIRST LEG

4th December, 1995

| Omagh Town | (2) | 3 | Finn Harps | (1) | 1 |
McHugh (12,51), Gallagher (44) ... *Speak (29)*

Omagh T: McDevitt, Gallagher, Magill, Doherty, McCaul, (D) O'Neill, McElroy, Quigg, Donnelly, Mooney, McHugh.
Subs: McIntyre replaced McCaul; (B) McCreadie replaced McDevitt; Hillen replaced Mooney:
Finn Harps: Nash, McGinley, Minnock, Scanlon, Reid, Melvin, Devenney, McGranaghan, Speak, Dunleavy, Hegarty.
Subs: Burke replaced McGinley, Lafferty replaced Reid; Toland replaced Devenney:
Referee: J.Ferry (Londonderry)

6th December, 1995

| Derry City | (0) | 0 | Coleraine | (1) | 2 |
Shiels (12,47)

Derry C: O'Dowd, Vaudequin, Creane, Hutton, Curran, Carlyle, Feeney, McKeever, McCourt, Fraser, Mohan. *Subs:* Coyle replaced McKeever;
Coleraine: O'Hare, Doherty, McAuley, Young, Gaston, Gorman, Shiels, O'Dowd, Surgeon, McAllister, McIvor. *Sub:* Patton replaced McIvor; *Subs not used:* Beckett; Philson:
Referee: W.Wallace (Donegal)

SEMI-FINALS, SECOND LEG

19th December, 1995

| Finn Harps | (1) | 1 | Omagh Town | (2) | 3 |
Speak (21) ... *Kavanagh (22), McHugh (33), (D) O'Neill (47)*
(Omagh Town won 6-2 on aggregate)

Finn Harps: Nash, McGinley, Minnock, Toland, Reid, Melvin, Dunleavy, Devanney, Speak, Doherty, Lafferty. *Subs:* Gallagher replaced Lafferty; Macauley replaced Doherty; *Sub not used:* McKeever:
Omagh T: McBrearty, Johnston, Magill, Doherty, McCaul, Kavanagh, McElroy, Quigg, McIntyre, Mooney, McHugh.
Subs: (D) O'Neill replaced McIntyre; Gray replaced McCaul; Blake replaced O'Neill:
Referee: S.Devenney (Newtowncunningham)
Booked: Doherty (Finn Harps); O'Neill and Magill (Omagh Town):

21st December, 1995

| Coleraine | (1) | 1 | Derry City | (0) | 0 |
Carlyle (og 37)
(Coleraine won 3-0 on aggregate)

Coleraine: O'Hare, Doherty, McAuley, Young, Gaston, Gorman, Shiels, O'Dowd, Surgeon, McAllister, McIvor. *Subs not used:* Philson; Huston; Beckett:
Derry C: O'Dowd, Vaudequin, Carlyle, Hutton, Curran, Tohill, Doolin, McCourt, Gorman, Heaney, Mohan. *Subs:* McKeever replaced McCourt; Creane replaced Heaney; *Sub not used:* Coyle:
Referee: L.Irvine (Limavady)

Final - First Leg

31st January, 1996

Omagh Town	(0)	1	Coleraine	(4)	4
Kavanagh (57)			*McCallan (8,40,42), Gorman (17)*		

Omagh T: McBrearty, Johnston, Kavanagh, McElroy, Donnelly, Gray, Mooney, Gallagher, (B) McCreadie, Crilly, McHugh. *Sub:* (D) O'Neill replaced (B) McCreadie (79 min); *Subs not used:* Doherty; McCaul:
Coleraine: O'Hare, McAuley, Huston, Young, Gaston, Gorman, Shiels, Surgeon, McCallan, McAllister, McIvor.
Subs: Hagan replaced Gaston (79 miin); Patton replaced McIvor (79 min); Maloney replaced McAllister (79 min):
Referee: W.Wallace (Donegal)
Booked: Kavanagh (Omagh Town); O'Hare (Coleraine):

Final - Second Leg

13th February, 1996

Coleraine	(3)	8	Omagh Town	(0)	1
McAllister (19), Gorman (30),			*McHugh (54)*		
O'Dowd (33,63), Young (58)					
McCallan (73,78), Huston (84)					
(Coleraine won 12-2 on aggregate)					

Coleraine: O'Hare, Huston, McAuley, Young, Gaston, Gorman, Shiels, O'Dowd, McCallan, McAllister, McIvor. *Subs:* Patton replaced McIvor (61 min); Doherty replaced McAuley (61 min); Surgeon replaced Shiels (61 min):
Omagh T: McDevitt, Gallagher, Magill, Moore, Melly, Kavanagh, McElroy, (D) O'Neill, (K) O'Neill, Crilly, McHugh.
Subs: Gray replaced Gallagher (35 min); McCullagh replaced (K) O'Neill (72 min); Walker replaced Kavanagh (79 min):
Referee: L.Irvine (Limavady)
Booked: O'Hare (Coleraine); Gray and Moore (Omagh Town): *Sent Off:* Michael Magill (Omagh Town):

HONOURS AT A GLANCE 1995/96

	Winners:		Runners Up:	
Premier League	Portadown	56pts	Crusaders	52pts
First Division	Coleraine	67pts	Ballymena United	49 pts
Bass Irish Cup	Glentoran	1	Glenavon	0
Sun Life Gold Cup	Crusaders	1	Linfield	0
Ulster Cup	Portadown	2	Linfield	2
	(aet Portadown won 5-3 on pens)			
Wilkinson Sword League Cup	Portadown	2	Crusaders	1
Coca-Cola Cup	Cliftonville	3	Glentoran	1
Calor Co.Antrim Shield	Glenavon	3	Crusaders	0
McEwans Mid-Ulster Cup	Bangor	3	Dungannon Swifts	1
Irish News Cup	Coleraine	12	Omagh Town	2
	(Aggregate score over two legs)			
N.W. Senior Challenge Cup	Omagh Town	5	Coleraine	1

Wilkinson Sword 'B' Division				
Section I	Loughgall	76pts	Dungannon Swifts	68pts
Section II	Glentoran II	64pts	Bangor Reserves	63pts
McEwans Intermediate Cup	Limavady United	4	Harland & Wolff Welders	2
Calor Steel & Sons Cup	Ballymena United Res	2	Dromara Village	1
	(after 1-1 draw)			
Smirnoff Knockout Cup	Limavady United	3	Banbridge Town	2
Bob Radcliffe Cup	Dungannon Swifts	3	Lurgan Celtic Bhoys	1
N.W. Intermediate Cup	Oxford United Stars	2	CKU	1
George Wilson Cup	Coleraine Reserves	3	Bangor Reserves	2
Irish Youth League	Glentoran Colts	86pts	Linfield Rangers	76pts
IFA Coca-Cola Youth Cup	Kilmore Recreation	2	Portadown Boys	0

TOP GOALSCORERS IN ALL COMPETITIONS FOR 1995/96

PREMIER LEAGUE			FIRST DIVISION		
Name	Club	Goals:	Name	Club	Goals:
1 Garry Haylock	Portadown	20 (2 pens)	1 Sammy Shiels	Coleraine	25
2 Stephen Baxter	Crusaders	11	2 Anthony Gorman	Coleraine	16
3 Peter Kennedy	Portadown	10	3 Michael McHugh	Omagh Town	14 (1 pen)
4 Glenn Ferguson	Glenavon	9 (1 pen)	4 Thomas Cleland	Distillery	11 (1 pen)
5 Glen Little	Glentoran	9	5 Crawford McCrae	Larne	11
6 Stephen McBride	Glenavon	9 (1 pen)	6 Jim Barr	Newry Town	10
7 Glenn Hunter	Crusaders	8	7 Barry Forshaw	Ballyclare Comrades	8
8 Raymond McCoy	Glenavon	8	8 Mark McWalter	Ballymena United	8 (1 pen)
9 Justin McBride	Glentoran	8	9 Tom Clarke	Newry Town	7 (4 pens)
10 Sammy Johnston	Glenavon	7	10 John Crilly	Omagh Town	7
11 Paul Millar	Linfield	7	11 John McIvor	Coleraine	7
12 Trevor Smith	Glentoran	7	12 Martin Mooney	Omagh Town	7
13 Paul Stokes	Cliftonville	7	13 Greg O'Dowd	Coleraine	7
			14 Hugh Sinclair	Carrick Rangers	7

AWARDS FOR 1995/96 SEASON

NORTHERN IRELAND P.F.A. AWARDS

Player of the Year 1996
Not Available When Going To Press

PREVIOUS WINNERS:

1975	Ivan Murray	(Coleraine)	1985	Martin McGaughey	(Linfield)
1976	Warren Feeney	(Glentoran)	1986	Pat McCoy	(Crusaders)
1977	Peter Rafferty	(Linfield)	1987	Raymond McCoy	(Coleraine)
1978	Tom Armstrong	(Ards)	1988	Billy Caskey	(Glentoran)
1979	Roy Walsh	(Glentoran)	1989	Gary Macartney	(Glentoran)
1980	Colin McCurdy	(Linfield)	1990	Ollie Ralph	(Newry Town)
1981	Gary Blackledge	(Glentoran)	1991	Stephen McBride	(Glenavon)
1982	Felix Healy	(Coleraine)	1992	Martin Russell	(Portadown)
1983	Jim Campbell	(Ards)	1993	Paul Byrne	(Bangor)
1984	Jim Cleary	(Glentoran)	1994	Glenn Ferguson	(Glenavon)
			1995	Kevin McKeown	(Crusaders)

Most Promising Newcomer 1996
Not Available When Going To Press

PREVIOUS WINNERS:

1975	Billy Caskey	(Glentoran)	1985	Billy Paton	(Portadown)
1976	Sam Galway	(Larne)	1986	Paul Millar	(Glentoran)
1977	Gerry O'Kane	(Cliftonville)	1987	George O'Boyle	(Linfield)
1978	Mal Donaghy	(Larne)	1988	Michael Hughes	(Carrick Rangers)
1979	Brian Quinn	(Larne)	1989	Lindsay Curry	(Ballymena Utd)
1980	Tony McCall	(Ballymena Utd)	1990	Noel Bailie	(Linfield)
1981	Nigel Worthington	(Ballymena Utd)	1991	Glenn Hunter	(Linfield)
1982	Peter Dunlop	(Cliftonville)	1992	Justin McBride	(Glentoran)
1983	Raymond McCoy	(Coleraine)	1993	Paul Byrne	(Bangor)
1984	Lee Doherty	(Linfield)	1994	Peter Kennedy	(Glenavon)
			1995	Stephen Livingstone	(Crusaders)

Roy Stewart/Sean Mullan Merit Trophy 1996
Not Available When Going To Press

PREVIOUS WINNERS:

1976	Billy Neill		1985	Harry Hegan	(Crusaders)
1977	Bertie Peacock		1986	Mervyn Bell	(Dundela)
1978	Joy Williams	(BBC)	1987	Billy Nixon	(Cliftonville)
1979	Cliftonville F.C.		1988	Jimmy McAlinden	
1980	Ivan Little & Billy Kennedy		1989	Jimmy Todd	(Ards)
		(Editors of Linfield Prog.)	1990	Ralph McGuicken	(Bangor)
1981	Roy Marshall	(IFA)	1991	Billy McCready	(Ballymena Utd)
1982	Bob Bishop	(Man Utd N.I. Rep)	1992	Malcolm Brodie	(Belfast Telegraph)
1983	Len Hiller	(Linfield Physio)	1993	Mervyn Brown	
1984	Tony Curley	(Coleraine)	1994	Billy Crawford	(Glentoran Groundsman)
			1995	Tom Douglas	(Secretary PFA)

NORTHERN IRELAND FOOTBALL WRITERS' ASSOCIATION AWARDS
Player of the Year 1996
Peter Kennedy   (Portadown)

PREVIOUS WINNERS:

1970	Des Dickson	(Coleraine)	1974	Ivan Murray	(Coleraine)
1971	Bryan Hamilton	(Linfield)	1975	Ivan Murray	(Coleraine)
1972	Billy Humphries	(Ards)	1976	Warren Feeney	(Glentoran)
1973	John McPolin	(Crusaders)	1977	Billy Caskey	(Glentoran)

1978	Jim Martin	(Linfield)	1987	Damien Byrne	(Ards)
1979	Ray McGuigan	(Glenavon)	1988	Alan Paterson	(Glentoran)
1980	Lindsay McKeown	(Linfield)	1989	Martin Magee	(Portadown)
1981	Gary Blackledge	(Glentoran)	1990	Ollie Ralph	(Newry Town)
1982	Felix Healy	(Coleraine)	1991	Stephen McBride	(Glenavon)
1983	George Dunlop	(Linfield)	1992	Raymond Morrison	(Glentoran)
1984	Billy Murray	(Linfield)	1993	Paul Byrne	(Bangor)
1985	Martin McGaughey	(Linfield)	1994	Noel Bailie	(Linfield)
1986	Trevor Anderson	(Linfield)	1995	Kevin McKeown	(Crusaders)

Ulster Young Footballer of the Year 1996
Glen Little   (Glentoran)

PREVIOUS WINNERS:

1972	Brian Craig	(Glenavon)	1984	Jonathan Speak	(Ballymena Utd)
1973	Laurie Todd	(Crusaders)	1985	Alfie Stewart	(Glentoran)
1974	Niall Sloan	(Portadown)	1986	Paul Millar	(Glentoran)
1975	Ronnie McCullough	(Bangor)	1987	George O'Boyle	(Linfield)
1976	Jim Hagan	(Larne)	1988	Mark Glendenning	(Bangor)
1977	Jim Harvey	(Glenavon)	1989	Lindsay Curry	(Ballymena Utd)
1978	Tom Sloan	(Ballymena Utd)	1990	Noel Bailie	(Linfield)
1979	Jim Smyth	(Portadown)	1991	Gary Hughes	(Newry Town)
1980	Tony McCall	(Ballymena Utd)	1992	Justin McBride	(Glentoran)
1981	Nigel Worthington	(Ballymena Utd)	1993	Paul Byrne	(Bangor)
1982	Peter Dunlop	(Cliftonville)	1994	Declan Devine	(Omagh Town)
1983	Raymond McCoy	(Coleraine)	1995	Graeme Philson	(Coleraine)

International Personality of the Year 1996
Steve Lomas   (Manchester City)

PREVIOUS WINNERS:

1985	Pat Jennings	(Arsenal)	1990	No Award made	
1986	Pat Jennings	(Arsenal)	1991	Gerry Taggart	(Barnsley)
1987	Mal Donaghy	(Luton Town)	1992	No Award made	
1988	Michael O'Neill	(Newcastle Utd)	1993	Tommy Wright	(Newcastle United)
1989	No Award made		1994	Jimmy Quinn	(Reading)
			1995	Iain Dowie	(Crystal Palace)

Castlereagh Glentoran Supporters' Club
Ulster Footballer of the Year 1996
Peter Kennedy   (Portadown)

PREVIOUS WINNERS:

1951	Kevin McGarry	(Cliftonville)	1973	Sammy Lunn	(Portadown)
1952	Eric Trevorrow	(Ballymena Utd)	1974	Arthur Stewart	(Ballymena Utd)
1953	Sammy Hughes	(Glentoran)	1975	Eric Bowyer	(Linfield)
1954	Jimmy Delaney	(Derry City)	1976	Warren Feeney	(Glentoran)
1955	Maurice McVeigh	(Glenavon)	1977	Peter Rafferty	(Linfield)
1956	Dick Keith	(Linfield)	1978	Jim Martin	(Linfield)
1957	Wilbur Cush	(Glenavon)	1979	Roy Walsh	(Linfield)
1958	Jackie Milburn	(Linfield)	1980	Lindsay McKeown	(Linfield)
1959	Clancy McDermott	(Coleraine)	1981	George Dunlop	(Linfield)
1960	Billy Neill	(Glentoran)	1982	Felix Healy	(Coleraine)
1961	Albert Campbell	(Crusaders)	1983	Jim Cleary	(Glentoran)
1962	Tommy Dickson	(Linfield)	1984	Bobby Carlisle	(Cliftonville)
1963	Roy Rea	(Glentoran)	1985	Martin McGaughey	(Linfield)
1964	Trevor Thompson	(Glentoran)	1986	Pat McCoy	(Crusaders)
1965	Doug Wood	(Derry City)	1987	Raymond McCoy	(Coleraine)
1966	Tommy Leishman	(Linfield)	1988	Alan Paterson	(Glentoran)
1967	Walter Bruce	(Glentoran)	1989	Lindsay McKeown	(Linfield)
1968	Sammy Hatton	(Linfield)	1990	Ollie Ralph	(Newry Town)
1969	Billy McAvoy	(Ards)	1991	Stephen McBride	(Glenavon)
1970	Billy Humphries	(Ards)	1992	Raymond Morrison	(Glentoran)
1971	Bryan Hamilton	(Linfield)	1993	Steve Cowan	(Portadown)
1972	Billy Humphries	(Ards)	1994	Noel Bailie	(Linfield)
			1995	Kevin McKeown	(Crusaders)

NORTHERN IRELAND COACHES' ASSOCIATION

Manager of the Year 1996
Ronnie McFall   (Portadown)

PREVIOUS WINNERS:

1977	Alan Campbell	(Glenavon)		1987	Paul Malone	(Larne)
1978	Roy Coyle	(Linfield)		1988	Tommy Jackson	(Glentoran)
1979	Bertie Neill	(Portadown)		1989	John Flanagan	(Bangor)
1980	Roy Coyle	(Linfield)		1990	Ronnie McFall	(Portadown)
1981	Ronnie McFall	(Glentoran)		1991	Ronnie McFall	(Portadown)
1982	Roy Coyle	(Linfield)		1992	Tommy Jackson	(Glentoran)
1983	Roy Coyle	(Linfield)		1993	Nigel Best	(Bangor)
1984	Roy Welsh	(Distillery)		1994	Trevor Anderson	(Linfield)
1985	Roy Coyle	(Linfield)		1995	Roy Walker	(Crusaders)
1986	Roy Coyle	(Linfield)				

'SUNDAY LIFE' GOALSCORING AWARD
Top Goalscorer 1995/96
Garry Haylock   (Portadown)   41 Goals

PREVIOUS WINNERS:

1989/90	Ollie Ralph	(Newry Town)	42 goals
1990/91	Stephen McBride	(Glenavon)	49 goals
1991/92	Stephen McBride	(Glenavon)	38 goals
1992/93	Steve Cowan	(Portadown)	47 goals
1993/94	Garry Haylock	(Linfield)	37 goals
1994/95	Glen Ferguson	(Glenavon)	49 goals

BY JOHN DUFFY HON.SECRETARY
NORTHERN IRELAND FOOTBALL PROGRAMME COLLECTORS CLUB

At the Annual Football Programme Fair held on the last Saturday in May our Club once again made the presentation of the 'Programme of the Year Award' Glentoran were very worthy winners for the first time since the award was inaugurated in 1983/84 season. It was a close run thing with Glenavon only one point adrift and Portadown a further point away. Last season was a difficult season from a programme point of view especially in the First Division as some teams did not issue any programmes while others chose to issue for the bigger matches. Again in 1996/97 season I would expect the same trend to be repeated. In our awards in 1994/95 we were critical of the price Glenavon charged i.e. £1.50 and we are pleased to see that they took that criticism on board as they reduced the price to £1.00.

On the International front we continue to produce one of the best programmes in the British Isles and it does represent very good value for money. Billy Kennedy has been the editor for over 20 years and still manages to produce the goods. Sometimes I feel it carries too many adverts, but I also realise the economics of producing a programme. For some of our smaller matches the print run has been of the order of 2,500 and this does not give much scope for error. The Irish Football Association also deserve credit for having programmes for all their Finals like the Youth Cup and Intermediate Cup. Once again we had the joint issue for the Irish Cup semi-finals which are again a necessary evil otherwise we will not have a programme. The same applies to the Irish Football League who also had programmes for all their semi-finals and finals. The semi-finals were all joint except the Sun Life Gold Cup which had two separate issues. You may remember there was a dispute between Glenavon and the Irish league which delayed one half of the draw.

Again at this time it is good to say thanks to all those junior sides who took the trouble to produce programmes. Here pride of place must go to Loughgall who issued for every home game, the man behind it is Jim McCrea (Jnr.) who does an excellent job as Editor and his is an example that many other clubs could follow. Armagh City fell by the wayside somewhat last season as they only managed a very small number of programmes.

Finally a mention is due to the smaller Associations such as the County Antrim F.A. who had programmes for the Senior Shield semi-finals and the final plus the Steel & Sons final. They even went to the trouble of having a wrap round sheet issued for the replayed final. The original issue was sold with the addition of the extra four pages. Good luck to all those with an interest in programme collecting.

Northern Ireland Programme Collectors Club Awards 1995/96

1st Glentoran (81 pts); Joint 2nd. Glenavon and Portadown (80 pts); 4th Crusaders (78 pts); 5th Linfield (75 pts); 6th Cliftonville (59 pts); 7th Ards (57 pts); 8th Omagh Town (56 pts); 9th Larne (52 pts); 10th Bangor (49 pts); 11th Carrick Rangers (47 pts); 12th Distillery (34 pts); 13th Ballyclare Comrades; Ballymena United; Coleraine; Newry Town (all 0 pts):

MAJOR FRIENDLY MATCHES 1995/96

14th August, 1995

Venue: Windsor Park, Belfast   *Att:* 25,000

Linfield (0)	0	Liverpool (1)
		Rush (39)

Linfield: Lamont, Dornan, Easton, McCoosh, McLean, Beatty, Ray.Campbell, Gorman, Erskine, Millar, Bailie.
Subs: Fenlon replaced McCoosh; McGee replaced Gorman:

Liverpool: James, Jones, Bjornebye, Scales, Wright, Matteo, McManaman, Collymore, Rush, Barnes, Thomas.
Sub: Harkness replaced Scales:
Referee: A.Snoddy (Carryduff)

8th November, 1995

Venue: Stangmore Park, Dungannon   *Att:* 3,000

Dungannon Swifts (1)	1	Manchester United Reserves (2)	4
M.Crowe (7)		*P.Mulryne (14), D.Baker (2,47,64)*	

Dungannon S: S.Vance, J.Gregg, R.Averill, B.Kennedy, D.Coll, M.Crowe, A.Denver, M.Jennings, A.Shaw, S.Smyth, T.McCrory. *Subs:* R.McAree replaced A.Denver; D.Anderson replaced J.Gregg; A.Hammond replaced B.Kennedy; T.Clarke replaced S.Smyth; G.Mackay replaced ?

Man.Utd.Res: K.Pilkington, M.Clegg, J.O'Kane, C.Casper, P.McGibbon, M.Appleton, T.Cooke, S.Davies, D.Baker, G.Tomlinson, P.Mulryne. *Subs:* C.Murdock replaced C.Casper; R.Wallwork replaced M. Clegg:
Referee: F.McDonald (Newry)

5th December, 1995

Venue: Windsor Park, Belfast   *Att:* 22,000

International Select (1)	2	Manchester United (0)	1
P.Masinga (36), Jimmy Quinn (82)		*P.Scholes (53)*	

Int.Select: G.Rousett (Hearts), J.Wright (Norwich City), S.Bjornebye (Liverpool), M.Gooding (Reading), A.Kernaghan (Manchester City), D.Lennon (Raith Rovers), I.Dumitrescu (Tottenham Hotspur), R.Slater (West Ham United), M.Boogers (West Ham United), P.Masinga (Leeds United), K.Black (Nottingham Forest). *Subs:* T.Wood (Walsall) replaced G.Roussett; B.Hamilton (Hearts) replaced D.Lennon; G.Creaney (Manchester City) replaced P.Masinga; A.Rougier (Raith Rovers) replaced K.Black; James Quinn replaced I.Dumitrescu; Jimmy Quinn (Reading) replaced M.Boogers; J.Nicholl (Raith Rovers) replaced M.Gooding:

Man.Utd: K.Pilkington, P.Parker, D.Irwin, G.Neville, L.Sharpe, D.May, E.Cantona, D.Beckham, B.McClair, A.Cole, P.Scholes. *Subs:* P.McGibbon replaced D. Irwin; S.Davies replaced g. Neville; P.Mulryne replaced Sharpe; M.Appleton replaced McClair; T. Cooke replaced D. Beckham::
Referee: J.Ferry (Londonderry)

MICHAEL GODDARD MEMORIAL MATCH

27th May, 1996

Venue: Wilgar Park, Belfast   *Att:* 3,000

Dundela/Glentoran Select (1)	**2**	**Dungannon Swifts/Linfield Select (1)**	**3**
C.Walker (20), D.Finlay (59)		*P.Millar (pen 42), S.Smyth (54), G.McKinstry (88)*	

Dundela/Glentoran: B.Hutchinson, G.Neill, B.Kennedy, C.Walker, M.Lennox, L.Coyle, J.McBride, S.Doey, S.Hanvey, T.Smith, D.Finlay. *Subs:* N.McKee replaced B.Kennedy (46 min); B.Caskey replaced J.McBride (46 min); B.McCarroll replaced S.Doey (46 min); A.Mathieson replaced S.Hanvey (46 min); I.Coulter replaced T.Smith (46 min); S.Whiteside replaced M.Lennox (60 min):

Dungannon Sw/Linfield: D.Crawford, I.McCoosh, P.McShane, N.Bailie, J.Spiers, M.Crowe, P.Knell, Jer.Robinson, P.Millar, S.Smyth, R.Johnston. *Subs:* G.McKinstry replaced P.Millar (46 min); A.Shaw replaced P.Knell (46 min); P.Vance replaced D.Crawford (46 min); C.McKerr replaced J.Spiers (63 min); T.Clarke replaced P.McShane (75 min): *Referee:* N.Cowie (Carryduff)

ADAMS, Eddie (D) (LARNE)
Career: Larne 1 - 0:

ALLEN, Jason (D) (BALLYMENA UNITED)
Born: 05.11.1970 Belfast
Status: Professional;
Career: Oldham Ath. 0 - 0; IF Tannum (Swe); Linfield
(Oct.'90) 48+3 - 1; Ballymena United (Jun.'95) 27 - 2
Int.Hon: N.Ireland U.19; U.18; U.16

Roy Allen

ALLEN, Roy (D) (BANGOR)
Born: 28.11.1966 Belfast
Status: Amateur; Occupation: Skilled Inspector
Career: Fisher Body; Glenavon (Jul.'90) 0 - 0; Harland
& W.W. (Sep.'90); Bangor (Mar.'92) 8 -1; Distillery
(Dec.'92) 88+3 - 8; Bangor (Aug.'96):

Brendan Allsopp

ALLSOPP, Brendan (D) (BALLYCLARE COMRADES)
Ht: 5.7
Occupation: Schoolteacher
Career: Glenavon 0 - 0; Cookstown United (c/s'90); Ards
(c/s'92) 0 - 0; Ballyclare Comrades (c/s '95) 26 - 0:

ARMSTRONG, David (F) (LARNE)
Born: 21.12.1964 Lisburn
Career: Downshire; Cliftonville (Jan.'88) 28+9 - 9;
Crusaders (Mar.'90) 5 - 0; Ballyclare Comrades (Sep.'90)
53+1 - 24; Glenavon (Aug.'92) 3+2 - 1;
Ballyclare Comrades (Aug.'93) 39+9 - 7;
Larne (Aug. '95) 22+4 - 6:

ARMSTRONG, Neil (G) (GLENTORAN)
Born: Belfast
Ht: 6.0 Wt: 11.08
Status: Professional; Occupation: Student
Career: Lisburn Utd. Youth; Glentoran (c/s'92) 37 - 0:

Winston Armstrong

ARMSTRONG, Winston (F) (CARRICK RANGERS)
Born: 16.01.1965 Lisburn
Ht: 6.1 Wt: 13.00
Status: Professional; Occupation: Skilled Labourer
Career: Dromore Amateurs; Dunmurry Y.M.; Bangor
(1987) 2+1 - 0; Distillery (Mar.'88) 6 - 0; Dunmurry
Y.M. (c/s'88); Carrick Rangers (Oct.'89) 18+8 - 5; Ards
(Oct.'90) 18+1 - 6; Glentoran (Oct.'91) 1+3 - 0;
Distillery (Jul.'92) 31+6 - 14; Carrick Rangers
(Oct.'95) 17+4 - 4:

BAILIE, John (M) (BANGOR)
Career: Bangor (1992) 21+1 - 1:
Status: Professional;
Int.Hon: N.Ireland U.18 Schools.

Noel Bailie

BAILIE, Noel (M) (LINFIELD)
Born: 23.02.1971 Lisburn
Ht: 5.9 Wt:12.00
Status; Professional; Occupation: Civil Servant
Career: Hillsborough B.C; Linfield (1986) 188+4 - 6:
Int.Hon: N.Ireland U.21; U.18; U.18 Schools; U.16;
Irish League Rep.

BAIN, Kevin (M) (PORTADOWN)*
Born: 19.09.1972 Kirkcaldy
Ht: 6.0 Wt: 11.09
Status: Professional; Occupation: Professional Footballer
Career: Abbey Star; Dundee (Jun.'89) 63+6 - 2;
Portadown (Mar.'96 loan) 6 - 0:
Int.Hon: Scotland U.18, U.15 Schools.

BARCLAY, Dominic (F) (BANGOR)*
Born: 05.09.1976 Bristol
Ht: 5.10 Wt: 11.07
Status: Professional;
Career: Bristol City (Jul.'95) 2+2; Bangor (Jan.'96 loan) 2 - 0:

BARKER, Ritchie (F) (LINFIELD)
Born: 30.05.1975 Sheffield
Ht: 6.1 Wt: 13.05
Status: Professional;
Career: Sheffield Wednesday (Jul.'93) 0 - 0;
Doncaster Rovers (Sep.'95) 5+1 - 0; Ards (Jan.'96 loan) 7 - 3;
Linfield (Aug.'96):
Int.Hon: England U.18; U.15:

BARR, Jim (F) (NEWRY TOWN)
Born: 14.12.1967 Newry
Ht: 5.9 Wt: 11.11
Status: Professional; Occupation: Assembly Worker
Career: Newry Town 0+1 - 0; Monaghan United (Oct.'89); Finn Harps (c/s'91) 12+6 - 3; Newry Town (Sep.'92) 7+2 - 0; Park View; Newry Town (Aug.'95) 22+3 - 10:

BATEY, Peter (M) (GLENTORAN)
Born: 31.12.1969 Ashington
Occupation: Landscape Gardener
Career: Army & Combined Services (1989);
Farnborough Town (1991); Bangor (c/s'94) 24 - 4;
Glentoran (Sep.'95) 23 - 6:

BAXTER, Stephen (F) (CRUSADERS)
Born: 01.10.1965 Belfast
Ht: 6.2 Wt: 12.10
Status: Professional; Occupation: Sales Rep
Career: Glentoran 0 - 0; Ards (Jul.'85) 41+2 - 21;
Linfield (Jul.'87) 82+32 - 51; Distillery (Aug.'93) 21+4 - 6; Crusaders (Aug.'94) 51 - 21:
Int.Hon: N.Ireland U.18; U.15

BEATTIE, Andy (F) (ARDS)*
Born: Belfast
Ht: 5.5 Wt: 10.07
Occupation: Joiner
Career: Bangor 0 - 0; Harland & W.W. (1988); Dundela (c/s'91); Ards (Jun.'92) 63+12 - 15; Dundela (c/s'96):

BEATTIE, Mark (F) (BALLYMENA UNITED)
Career: Ballymena United 0 - 0:

BEATTY, Stephen (M) (LINFIELD)
Born: 01.09.1969 Carrickfergus
Status: Professional; Occupation: Storeman
Career: Carrick Rangers 2+1 - 0; Chelsea (Jun.'88) 0 - 0; Aarhus (Den) (1990) 8+4 - 0; Linfield (Nov.'90) 131+12 -13:
Int.Hon: N.Ireland U.21; U.18:

BECK, Robert (G) (BALLYMENA UNITED)
Born: 20.01.1964 Lisburn
Ht: 5.11 Wt: 12.06
Status: Professional; Occupation: Fibreglass Laminator
Career: Distillery (1980) 18 - 0; Glenavon (Sep.'83);
Ballymena United (Oct.'95) 21+1 - 0:

BECKETT, Gary (F) (COLERAINE)*
Born: 24.07.1973 Enniskillen
Ht: 5.10 Wt: 11.07
Status: Amateur; Occupation: Factory Worker
Career: Enniskillen Town United; Omagh Town (Jul.'92) 26+1 - 6; Coleraine (Jun.'94) 26+9 - 3; Derry City
(Dec.'95) 12-1:
Int.Hon: Irish League U.21 Rep.

BELL, Colin (M) (BALLYCLARE COMRADES)
Career: Glenavon; Dungannon Swifts (Oct.'89);
Cookstown United (c/s'92); Ballyclare Comrades (c/s'95) 17 - 1:

BELL, Colin (F) (BANGOR)
Career: Bangor 1+1 - 0:

BERRY, Alan (D) (NEWRY TOWN)
Career: Newry Town (c/s'93) 14+1 - 0:

BIBBO, Salvatore (G) (ARDS)*
Born: 24.08.1974 Basingstoke
Ht: 6.2 Wt: 13.05
Status: Professional; Occupation: Professional Footballer
Career: Crawley Town; Sheffield United (Sep.'93) 0 - 0; Chesterfield (Feb.'95 loan) 1 - 0; Ards (Apr.'96 loan) 4 - 0:

BIRNEY, Nigel (D) (GLENAVON)
Born: 29.11.1964 Enniskillen
Ht: 5.11 Wt: 11.07
Status: Professional; Occupation: Bank Official
Career: Enniskillen Rangers; Distillery (1979) 0 - 0;
Enniskillen Rangers; Dungannon Swifts (c/s'89);
Larne (Aug.'90) 100 - 2; Glenavon (Jun.'94) 21+3 - 0:
Int.Hon: Irish League Rep.

BALIR, Anthony (M) (BALLYCLARE COMRADES)
Career: Ballyclare Comrades 0+1 - 0:

BLAIR, Nicky (D) (BALLYCLARE COMRADES)
Career: Carniny Rangers; Ballyclare Comrades (c/s'95) 12+3 - 0:

BLAKE, Tony (G) (OMAGH TOWN)
Born: 09.12.1971 Letterkenny
Ht: 6.2 Wt: 12.05
Status: Professional; Occupation: Student
Career: Letterkenny Rovers; Derry City; Finn Harps (Mar.'92) 3 - 0; Sligo Rovers 0 - 0; Omagh Town (Oct.'94 loan; Dec.'94) 32 - 0:
Int.Hon: Irish League U.21

BOOTH, Jeff (M) (BALLYMENA UNITED)
Career: Glentoran 0 - 0; Ballymena United (c/s'95) 1 - 0:

BOWERS, Barney (M) (ARDS)
Born: 19.08.1959 Belfast
Ht: 5.10 Wt: 10.10
Status: Professional; Occupation: Sales Rep
Career: Cliftonville (1977); Derby County (1978) 0 - 0; Glentoran (1981) 245+6 - 44; Ards (Sep.'95) 23+1 - 1:
Int.Hon: N.Ireland U.18; Irish League Rep

BOYD, Nigel (F) (BALLYMENA UNITED)
Status: Amateur
Career: Linfield (1990) 4+5 - 2;
Ballymena United (Aug.'95) 17+4 - 0:

BOYLE, Anton (M) (BALLYCLARE COMRADES)
Born: 13.10.1971 Belfast
Career: Bangor 0 - 0; Distillery (c/s'89) 0 - 0; Cliftonville 0+1 - 0; Cookstown United (c/s'94); Donegal Celtic (c/s'95); Ballyclare Comrades (Dec.'95) 1+5 - 0:
Int.Hon: N.Ireland U.16; U.15.

BOYLE, Michael (F) (CLIFTONVILLE)
Born: 23.01.1970 Belfast
Status: Amateur
Career: Distillery (Oct.'90) 8+4 - 3; Larne 7 - 1; Ards (Aug.'95) 22+2 - 5; Cliftonville (Aug.'96):

BOYLE, Wesley (M) (PORTADOWN)*
Born: 30.03.1979 Portadown
Ht: 5.11 Wt: 11.00
Career: Portadown 1+1 - 1; Leeds United (Feb.'96) 0 - 0:
Int.Hon: N.Ireland U.18 Schools; U.17; U.15:

Tom Brady

BRADY, Tom (D) (ARDS)
Born: 28.11.1963 Belfast
Status: Professional; Occupation: Builder
Career: Cromac Albion (Jul.'85); Distillery (Jul.'87) 22 - 1;

Cromac Albion (Jul.'88); Chimney Corner (Aug.'89); Donegal Celtic (Jul.'90); Distillery (Jul.'93) 45 - 4; Ards (c/s'96):

BREZA, Ritchie (F) (DISTILLERY)*
Career: American Soccer Federation; Ards (Aug.'95) 0 - 0; Distillery (Sep.'95) 0+1 - 0; Galway United (Oct.'95) 1-10:

BROWN, Stephen (D) (GLENAVON)
Born: 25.12.1962 Belfast
Ht: 6.0 Wt:12.09
Status: Professional; Occupation: Taxi Driver
Career: Cliftonville; Bangor (Aug.'87) 208 - 19; Glenavon (Mar.'95) 13+1 - 2:
Int.Hon: Irish League Rep.

Darren Brush

BRUSH, Darren (D) (LINFIELD)
Born: 19.08.1974 London
Status: Amateur; Occupation: Storeman
Career: Bangor 0 - 0; Leyton Orient (Aug.'92) 0 - 0; Leyton F.C. (Nov.'93) 0 - 0; Distillery (Mar.'95) 27 - 1; Linfield (May.'96):

BURN, Philip (M) (BALLYMENA UNITED)
Born: 14.01.1969 Edinburgh
Ht: 5.10 Wt: 11.00
Status: Professional
Career: Lochgelly Albert; Raith Rovers (Aug.'88) 39+5 - 1; Glenavon (Oct.'92 loan) 3 - 2; Ballymena United (Nov.'92) 87+6 - 11:

BURNS, Sean (M) (GLENAVON)
Born: Belfast
Ht: 5.10 Wt: 11.13
Status: Amateur; Occupation: Joiner
Career: Bangor 7+2 - 0; Glenavon (Mar.'95) 2+2 - 0:

BURROWS, Sid (M) (CRUSADERS)
Born: 27.03.1964 Belfast
Ht: 5.8 Wt: 11.2
Status: Professional; Occupation: Warehouse Assistant
Career: Ballyclare Comrades; Crusaders (Aug.'82); Linfield (Sep.'86) 84+6 - 14; Crusaders (Apr.'91) 135+1 - 28:
Int.Hon: Irish League Rep.

BUSTARD, Ian (M) (BALLYMENA UNITED)
Born: 30.12.1963 Belfast
Status: Professional
Career: *Harland & Wolff Welders; Larne (Sep.'85)*
105+9 - 13; Glenavon (Jan.'91) 8 - 1; Ards (Jun.'91)
69+5 - 7; Larne (Jan.'96) 10 -2; Ballymena United
(c/s'96)

BYRNE, Alan (M) (LINFIELD)
Born: 12.05.1969 Dublin
Ht: 5.11 Wt: 12.05
Status: Professional; Occupation: Electrician
Career: *Lakelands; Bohemians (Jul.'87); Shamrock*
Rovers (c/s'93) 28+2 - 1; Shelbourne (Aug.'94) 11-0;
Linfield (Oct.'95) 4+1 - 1:
Int.Hon: *League of Ireland Rep.*

BYRNE, John (M) (BANGOR)*
Born: 29.08.1962 Dublin
Ht: 5.11 Wt: 12.00
Status: Professional
Career: *Home Farm; Bohemians; Sligo Rovers (Jul.'90)*
84+3 - 5; St.Pats Athletic (c/s'93) 38+4-0; Bangor
(Oct.'95 loan) 8+1 - 1:

BYRNE, Paul (M) (GLENAVON)
Born: 02.04.1964 Belfast
Ht: 5.11 Wt: 12.00
Status: Professional; Occupation: Student
Career: *Bangor 0 - 0; Cliftonville 0 - 0; Drogheda*
(Aug.'81); Glenavon (Sep.'83):

BYRNE, Raymond (D) (PORTADOWN)
Born: 04.07.1972 Newry
Ht: 6.1 Wt: 11.02
Status: Professional
Career: *Barcroft Y.C; Cleary Celtic Y.C; West End*
Athletic; Millburn United; Newry Town (1989) 16+2 - 0;
Nottingham Forest (Feb.'91) 0 - 0; Northampton Town
(Aug.'94) 2 - 0; Shelbourne (Sep.'94) 18+1 - 0; Newry
Town (Nov.'94) 19 - 0; Portadown (Aug.'95) 17 - 0:

CALDWELL, Andrew (G) (DISTILLERY)
Born: 22.11.1975 Belfast
Ht: 5.10 Wt: 11.09
Status: Professional
Career: *Linfield 0 - 0; Rangers (Jul.'92) 0 - 0;*
Glasgow Perthshire (loan); Linfield (Jun.'94) 0+2 - 0;
Distillery (Aug.'96):
Int. Hon: *N.Ireland U.16; U.15:*

CALLAGHAN, Aaron (D) (CRUSADERS)
Born: 08.10.1966 Dublin
Ht: 5.11 Wt: 11.02
Status: Professional
Career: *Stoke City (Oct.'84) 8+5 - 0; Crewe Alexandra*
(Nov.'85 loan) 8 - 0; Oldham Ath. (Oct.'86) 11+5 - 2;
Crewe Alexandra (May.'88) 148+10 - 6; Preston North
End (Aug.'92) 34+2 - 2; Shelbourne (Dec.'93) 13+1 - 1;
Crusaders (Sep.'94 loan; Oct.'94) 39 - 3:
Int.Hon: *Republic of Ireland U.21; U.18:*

CAMPBELL, Alan (F) (BALLYCLARE COMRADES)
Born: 01.10.1965 Belfast
Career: *Distillery; Ballymena United (c/s'84); Coleraine*
(Jun.'85) 16+3 - 13; Distillery (Sep.'87) 16+1 - 2;
Linfield (Jul.'90) 0+2 - 0; Coleraine (Dec.'91 loan) 12 -
2; Ballyclare Comrades (Aug.'92) 11 - 3; Cookstown
United (c/s'94); Ballyclare Comrades (Jul.'95) 17+1 - 4:

CAMPBELL, Brian (D) (ARDS)
Born: 08.02.1968 Dundonald
Status: Professional;
Career: *Ards (1983) 87+11 - 1:*

CAMPBELL, John (D) (BANGOR)
Born: 27.03.1972
Career: *Glenavon 3+5 - 0; Portadown (c/s'91) 12 - 0;*
Armagh City (Nov.'92) 0 - 0; Newry Town (Dec.'92) 14 -
1; Dungannon Swifts (Apr.'94); Carrick Rangers
(Aug.'94) 5 - 0; Bangor (Jul.'95) 0 - 0:

CAMPBELL, Mark (G) (NEWRY TOWN)
Career: *Newry Town (1993) 19+2 - 0:*

CAMPBELL, Raymond (M) (LINFIELD)
Born: 03.101968 Downpatrick
Ht: 5.7 Wt: 10.07
Status: Professional
Career: *Ibrox; Nottingham Forest 0 - 0; Glentoran*
(Jan.'89)102+5 - 10; Linfield (Sep.'93) 64+3 - 9:
Int.Hon: *Irish League Rep.*

CAMPBELL, Robert (F) (LINFIELD)
Born: 05.05.1969 Dundonald
Status: Professional; Occupation: Joiner
Career: *Ards 105+19 - 20; Linfield (Jun.'92) 25+10 - 4:*

CANDLISH, Neil (F) (PORTADOWN)
Born: 02.06.1968 Inverness
Status: Professional; Occupation: Fitness Instructor
Career: *Wishaw Juniors; Motherwell (Aug.'85) 8+3 - 1;*
Kilmarnock (Feb.'88 loan) 3 - 0; Ballymena United
(Nov.'90) 74 - 25; Glentoran (Jun.'93) 23+1 - 5;
Portadown (Sep.'94) 38+9 -12:
Int.Hon: *Irish League Rep.*

CANNING, Eamon (G) (COLERAINE)
Occupation: Student
Career: *Coleraine 1 - 0:*

CARLISLE, Mark (D) (BALLYMENA UNITED)
Born: 21.11.1968 Portadown
Ht: 5.11
Career: *Chimney Corner (1985); Ballymena United*
(Jun.'92) 105+1 - 1:

CARLYLE, Paul (M) (PORTADOWN)
Born: 19.07.1967 Londonderry
Ht: 5.11 Wt: 12.07
Status: Professional
Career: *Coleraine(1985) 0 - 0; Derry City (c/s'86);*
Shamrock Rovers (Jan.'87); Derry City (c/s'87);
Coleraine (Oct.'93) 39 - 10; Derry City (Dec.'94) 28+2 -
5; Portadown (Dec.'95) 8+4 - 1:

CARROLL, Derek (D) (CRUSADERS)
Born: 02.10.1959 Dublin
Ht: 5.6 Wt: 11.0
Status: Professional
Career: Dundalk; Liverpool (May.'78) 0 - 0; Athlone Town; Dundalk; Athlone Town; Bohemians (Jul.'89); Galway United (Aug.'91) 25+1 - 0; Crusaders 95+9 - 1: Int.Hon: Republic of Ireland U.21

CASEY, Robert (M) (PORTADOWN)
Born: 20.11.1972 Newry
Status: Professional; Occupation: Civil Servant
Career: Newry Celtic; Portadown (1991) 99+22 - 28

CASH, Michael (M) (BANGOR)
Born: 11.03.1968 Carrickfergus
Status: Professional
Career: Crusaders (Jul.'85) 179+9 - 27; Larne (Jun.'94)14+1 - 2; Bangor (Jul.'95) 13+1 - 0:

CAVANAGH, Pat (F) (CARRICK RANGERS)
Born: 14.10.1973 Belfast
Ht: 6.2
Status: Amateur; Occupation: Student
Career: Ford F.C. (Aug.'93); U.U.J. (Aug.'94); Distillery (Dec.'94) 3+5 - 4; Cliftonville (Dec.'95) 2+4 - 1; Carrick Rangers (Aug.'96): Int.Hon: Irish League U.21 Rep.

CLANACHAN, Stuart (M) (COLERAINE)
Occupation: Student
Career: Coleraine 2+2 - 0: Int.Hon: N.Ireland U.18 Schools.

CLARKE, Nigel (F) (BALLYCLARE COMRADES)
Career: Randalstown Sky Blues; Ballyclare Comrades (Sep.'95) 1+1 - 0:

CLARKE, Richard (M)
Born: 29.05.1979
Ht: 5.9 Wt: 10.07
Occupation: Student
Career: Portadown 0 - 0: Int.Hon: N.Ireland U.18 Schools; U.15:

CLARKE, Tom (F) (NEWRY TOWN)
Career: Neilstown Rangers (ROI); Newry Town (Aug.'95) 22+2 - 7:

CLARKE, Tony (D) (BANGOR)*
Born: 30.10.1968
Ht: 5.7 Wt: 10.09
Career: Portadown; Annagh United; Armagh City (Mar.'90), Bangor (c/s'95) 0 - 0; Dungannon Swifts (Sep.'95):

CLELAND, Thomas (M) (LINFIELD)
Born: 08.08.1968 Belfast
Status: Professional; Occupation: Technical Services Operator
Career: Distillery (Jun.'84) 69+6 - 9; Glentoran (Dec.'88) 23+11 - 2; Distillery (Mar.'92) 103+9 - 50; Linfield (Aug.'96): Int.Hon: N.Ireland U.16; Irish League Rep.

COLL, Michael (D) (PORTADOWN)
Born: 25.02.1974 Londonderry
Career: Institute; Omagh Town (Aug.'91) 46+2 - 0; Portadown (Dec.'93) 4 - 0: Int.Hon: N.Ireland U.18 Schools.

COLLIER, Stephen (D) (LINFIELD)
Born: Ballyclare
Career: Larne (Mar.'93) 40+7 - 1; Linfield (Jul.'96):

David Collins

COLLINS, David (G) (DISTILLERY)
Born: 16.01.1974 Newtownards
Status: Professional; Occupation: Civil Servant
Career: Hillsborough B.C; Glenavon (Jan.'89) 1 - 0; Peterborough United (Jul.'90) 0 - 0; Distillery (Mar.'92) 93+1 - 0; Newry Town (Dec.'94 loan) 5 - 0: Int.Hon: N.Ireland U.21; U.18; U.16; U.16 Schools.

COLLINS, Rod (F) (CLIFTONVILLE)*
Born; 07.08.1961 Dublin
Status: Professional
Career: Bohemians; Athlone Town; Drogheda United; Dundalk; Mansfield Town (Dec.'85) 11+5 - 1; Newport County (Aug.'87) 5+2 - 1; Swansea City 0 - 0; Shamrock Rovers; Dundalk 3+4 - 0; Sligo Rovers (c/s'91) 3+3 - 0; Crusaders (Nov.'91) 53+8 - 24; Bohemians (Nov.'93 loan) 0 - 0; Bangor (May.'94) 21+3 - 5; Bohemians (Jun.'95 loan); Glentoran (Jul.'95) 0 - 0; Coleraine (Sep.'95) 0 - 0; Cliftonville (Oct.'95) 6 - 1; Home Farm Everton 6+2 - 1:

COLLINS, Sean (M) (GLENAVON)
Born: 01.01.1974 Belfast
Ht: 5.6 Wt: 10.04
Status: Professional; Occupation: Factory Worker
Career: Norwich City (Apr.'89) 0 - 0; Euran Pallo (Fin) (May.'93); Glenavon (Dec.'93) 21+15 - 3: Int.Hon: N.Ireland U.18:

COOK, Derek (F) (GLENTORAN)
Born: 26.04.1968 Irvine
Ht: 6.0 Wt: 12.06
Status: Professional; Occupation: Builder
Career: Kilmarnock (1983) 36+11 - 12; Queen of the South (Dec.'89) 13+1 - 3; Stranraer (Jun.'90) 66+33 - 28; Coleraine (Aug.'92) 64+6 - 27; Glentoran (Feb.'95) 22+9 - 8: Int.Hon: Scotland U.19:

COULTER, Jackie (D) (BANGOR)
Born: 12.09.1968 Belfast
Ht: 5.8 Wt: 12.02
Status: Amateur; Occupation: Postman
*Career: **Linfield** (1983); **Bangor** (Jul.'85); **Carrick**
***Rangers** (Dec.'91) 100+10 - 8; **Bangor** (Dec.'95)*
10+1 - 1:

COURTNEY, Niall (M) (NEWRY TOWN)
Born: 01.12.1975 Newry
*Career: **Glenavon** (Sep.'93) 0 - 0; **Finn Harps** (N.I.);*
***Newry Town** 11+4 - 0:*

COURTNEY, Shane (F) (NEWRY TOWN)
*Career: **Newry Town** 0+2 - 0:*

COWAN, Philip (M) (CRUSADERS)
Born: 02.09.1975 Belfast
Status: Amateur
*Career: **Crusaders** 0 - 0:*

COYLE, Liam (F) (GLENTORAN)*
Born: 21.05.1968 Londonderry
Status: Professional;
*Career: **Derry City**; **Coleraine** (Sep.'90) 0 - 0; **Omagh**
***Town** (Jul.'92) 30 - 16; **Derry City** (Aug.'93 68 - 16);*
***Glentoran** (Dec.'95) 9+3 - 4; **Derry City** (Aug.'96):*
*Int.Honours: **N.Ireland International 1 cap**:*

CRAIG, Alan (D) (BALLYMENA UNITED)
Born: 09.08.1975
*Career: **Ballymena United** 2+2 - 0:*
*Int.Hon: **N.Ireland U.18 Schools; U.16**:*

CRAIG, Sean (F) (CLIFTONVILLE)
*Career: **Cliftonville** 0 - 0:*

CRAWFORD, Colin (D) (CARRICK RANGERS)
Born: 18.02.1960 Doagh
Ht: 5.6   Wt:11.00
Status: Professional; Occupation: Coachbuilder
*Career: **Bangor** (1976); **Sunderland** (Sep.'78) 0 - 0;*
***Linfield** (Oct.'81) 105+8 - 4; **Carrick Rangers** (Sep.'87)*
*95+2 - 14; **Glenavon** (Dec.'91) 35+7 - 1; **Ballyclare**
***Comrades** (Sep.'93) 24+6 - 3; **Carrick Rangers** (Nov.'94)*
22+6 - 3:
*Int.Hon: **N.Ireland U.18; Irish League Rep**.*

CRAWFORD, Darren (G) (LINFIELD)
*Career: **Ballymena United** (1987); **F.C.Penerol**;*
***Ballyclare Comrades**; **Larne** (1990) 20 - 0; **Ballymena**
***United**; **Linfield** (Nov.'94) 13 - 0:*

CRILLY, John (M) (OMAGH TOWN)
Born: 29.04.1966 Londonderry
Ht: 5.11 Wt: 11.05
Status: Professional; Occupation: Solicitor
*Career: **Queens University** (1984); **Carrick Rangers** (c/s'86)*
*0 - 0; **Queens University**; **Culduff** (1989); **Omagh Town** (c/*
*s'90) 43+1 - 3; **Ards** (Mar.'92) 3 - 0; **Omagh Town** (Aug.'92)*
104 - 12:

CROSS, Jonathan (F) (CLIFTONVILLE)*
Born: 02.03.1975 Wallasey
Ht: 5.10 Wt: 11.04
Status: Professional
*Career: **Wrexham** (Nov.'92) 79+20 - 10;*
***Cliftonville** (Feb.'96 loan) 8 - 0:*

CROTHERS, Peter (D) (DISTILLERY)
Born: 07.10.1971 Lisburn
*Career: **Lisburn Athletic**; **Linfield** 16+2 - 0; **Distillery***
(Aug.'96):
*Int.Hon: **N.Ireland U.18 Schools; U.16**:*

CULLEN, Chris (D) (ARDS)
Born: 09.06.1971 Downpatrick
Status: Professional
*Career: **Kilmore Recreation**; **Cliftonville** (c/s'91) 3+3 -*
*0; **Linfield** (Jul.'92) 0 - 0; **Drumaness Mills**; **Ards***
(Aug.'94) 31+4 - 0:

CULLEN, Paul (F) (ARDS)
Born: 05.08.1968 Bray
Occupation: Accountant
*Career: **Bray Wanderers**; **UCD** (Jul.'88); **Shamrock**
***Rovers** (c/s'92) 25+7 - 7; **Ards** (Nov.'94 loan; Jan.'95)*
43+4 - 17:

CUNNINGTON, Eddie (M) (GLENTORAN)
Born: 12.11.1969 Bellshill
Ht: 5.8 Wt: 10.7
Status: Professional; Occupation: Footballer
*Career: **Chelsea** (Jan.'87) 0 - 0; **Dunfermline Athletic***
*(Aug.'89) 74+12 - 0; **Dumbarton** (Mar.'94) 13 - 3;*
***Glentoran** (Aug.'94) 30 - 6:*

CURLISS, Ian (D) (DISTILLERY)
*Career: **Dunmurry Recreation**; **Portadown** 149+1 - 6;*
***Distillery** (Aug.'95) 12 - 0:*
*Int.Hon: **Irish League Rep**.*

CURRIE, Niall (G) (BANGOR)
Born: 12.09.1972 Portadown
Status: Professional; Occupation: Factory Worker
*Career: **Portadown** (1987) 0 - 0; **Tandragee**
***Rovers**(1988); **Loughgall** (Aug.'92); **Bangor** (Jul.'94) 8 -*
*0; **Glenavon** (Jun.'95) 0 - 0; **Distillery** (Nov.'95) 8 - 0;*
***Bangor** (Jan.'96) 10 - 0:*

CURRY, Lindsay (M) (BALLYMENA UNITED)
Born: 23.02.1970 Londonderry
Status: Professional
*Career: **Manchester City** (Jul.'86); **Ballymena United** (c/*
*s'88); **Linfield** (Oct.'90) 54+5 - 15; **Larne** (Aug.'93)*
*14+2 - 7; **Ballymena United** (Jun.'94) 7+7 - 1:*
*Int.Hon: **N.Ireland U.19; U.18***

DALTON, Timothy (G) (PORTADOWN)
Born: 14.10.1965 Waterford
Ht: 6.0 Wt: 12.08
Status: Professional
*Career: **Coventry City** (Sep.'83) 0 - 0; **Notts County***
*(Jul.'84) 1 - 0; **Boston; Bradford City** (Sep.'86) 0 - 0;*
Tranmere Rovers** (Dec.'86 loan) 1 - 0; **Cork City

(Feb.'88); **Derry City** *(c/s'88);* **Airdrie** *0 - 0;* **Gillingham** *0 - 0;* **Ernst Borel** *(1993);* **Coventry City** *(c/s'93) 0 - 0;* **Bangor** *(Sep.'93) 42+1 - 0;* **Portadown** *(c/s'95) 22 - 0:* **Int.Hon:** *Republic of Ireland U.17; U.15; Irish League Rep.*

DARBY, Frank (D) (CRUSADERS)
Born: 22.10.1967 Dublin
Status: Professional
Career: **St.Columbans Boys; Athlone Town** *(c/s'92) 104+1 - 5;* **Crusaders** *(Mar.'96) 2 - 1:*

DAVEY, Damien (F) (CLIFTONVILLE)
Status: Amateur
Career: **Cliftonville** *(1993) 4+2 - 0:*

DAVIDSON, Gregg (D) (PORTADOWN)
Born: 24.12.1965 Belfast
Status: Professional
Career: **Crusaders** *(1985);* **Portadown** *(1986) 167+29 - 17:*

DAVIES, Will (F) (BANGOR)*
Born: 27.09.1975 Derby
Ht: 6.2 Wt: 13.01
Status: Professional;
Career: **Derby County** *(Jul.'94) 1+1 - 0;* **Bangor** *(Feb. '96 loan) 11 - 3:*

DAVIS, Michael (F) (BANGOR)*
Born: 19.10.1974 Bristol
Ht: 6.0 Wt: 12.00
Status: Professional;
Career: **Bristol City** *(1987) 0 - 0;* **Yate Town** *(1990);* **Bristol Rovers** *(Apr.'93) 3+14 - 1;* **Hereford United** *(Aug.'94 loan) 1 - 0;* **Bangor** *(Nov.'95 loan) 5 - 2:*

DEEGAN, Michael (M) (CRUSADERS)
Born: 17.03.1964 Dublin
Status: Professional; Occupation: Mechanic
Career: **Home Farm; Tolka Rovers; Crusaders** *(Dec.'94) 25+7 - 1:*

DEVINE, Declan (G) (GLENTORAN)*
Born: 15.09.1973 Londonderry
Ht: 6.2 Wt: 14.04
Status: Professional; Occupation: Football Coach
Career: **Institute;** *Ipswich Town (Jul.'90) 0 - 0;* **Omagh Town** *(Nov.'92 loan) 4 - 0;* **Omagh Town** *(Jun.'93) 21 - 0;* **Glentoran** *(Jul.'94) 18- 0;* **Derry City** *(Aug.'96):* **Int.Hon:** *N.Ireland U.21; U.18; U.17; U.16; U.15:*

DEVINE, John (D) (GLENTORAN)
Born: 27.01.1969 Carrickfergus
Ht: 6.2 Wt: 13.07
Status: Professional; Occupation: Tradesmans Helper
Career: **Chimney Corner; Islandmagee;** **Glentoran** *(Feb.'86) 180+3 - 17:* **Int.Hon:** *N.Ireland International (1 cap); U.23; U.21:*

DEVINE, Leo (M) (OMAGH TOWN)
Career: **Bristol City; Omagh Town** *(Aug.'95) 0 - 0:*

DILLON, John (G) (CARRICK RANGERS)*
Born: 11.07.1976 Coleraine
Ht: 5.10 Wt: 11.00
Status: Amateur; Occupation: Student
Career: **Coleraine** *0 - 0;* **Portstewart; Limavady United** *(Aug.'94);* **Carrick Rangers** *(Sep.'94) 29+1 - 0;* **Limavady United** *(c/s'96):*

DOHERTY, Dean (F) (CARRICK RANGERS)
Born: 14.10.1974 Belfast
Ht: 5.10 Wt: 10.10
Status: Amateur; Occupation: Painter
Career: **Linfield** *(1990) 0 - 0;* **Bangor** *(Jan.'93) 2+6 - 0;* **Carrick Rangers** *(Jan.'95) 19+11 - 5:*

DOHERTY, Dermot (M) (LARNE)
Born: 21.01.1967 Coleraine
Career: **Coleraine** *2+3 - 1;* **Ballymena United** *(c/s'88);* **Coleraine** *(Nov.'90) 10 - 0;* **Tobermore United** *(Jan.'92);* **Ballymena United** *(Jan.'93) 22+2 - 0;* **Moyola Park** *(Dec.'94);* **Larne** *(Feb.'96) 5 - 0:*

DOHERTY, Eamon (D) (COLERAINE)
Born: 04.10.1974 Londonderry
Occupation: Milkman
Career: **Institute** *(Jun.'89);* **Omagh Town** *(Jun.'91) 57+2 - 0;* **Coleraine** *(Jun.'94) 54+1 - 4:* **Int.Hon:** *N.Ireland U.18 Schools*

DOHERTY, Lee (M) (GLENAVON)
Born: 31.03.1963 Belfast
Ht: 5.11 Wt: 11.07
Status: Professional; Occupation: Architectural Engineer
Career: **Linfield** *(1981) 234+7 - 37;* **Glenavon** *(Jul.'94) 45 - 2: Int.Hon:* **N.Ireland International (2 caps); Irish League Rep.**

DOHERTY, Kieran (M) (LARNE)
Career: **Larne** *0+2 - 0:*

DOHERTY, Stephen (D) (OMAGH TOWN)
Born: 07.07.1971 Londonderry
Occupation: Teacher
Career: **Oxford United Stars; Omagh Town** *(Oct.'91) 11+4 - 0:*

DONAGHEY, Brain (M) (OMAGH TOWN)
Born: 09.08.1971 Londonderry
Ht: 5.10 Wt: 11.00
Status: Professional; Occupation: Travel Consultant
Career: **Norwich City** *(Dec.'86) 0 - 0;* **Derry City** *(Feb.'88);* **Coleraine** *(Jul.'89) 55+19 - 10;* **Carrick Rangers** *(Nov.'94) 46+5 - 6;* **Omagh Town** *(c/s'96):*

DONNELLY, Mark (D) (OMAGH TOWN)
Born: 03.03.1967 Coleraine
Ht: 5.11 Wt: 14.00
Status: Professional; Occupation: Painter
Career: **Omagh Town** *(1983);* **Monaghan United; Ards** *(Jul.'88) 8 - 0;* **Dungannon Swifts** *(Dec.'88);* **Omagh Town** *(c/s'89) 142+2 - 24:*

DONNELLY, Michael (M) (CLIFTONVILLE)
Born: 09.05.1964 Belfast
Occupation: Painter & Decorator
Career: **Shorts; Banbridge Town; Cliftonville** *(1987)*
188+5 - 18:

DORNAN, Alan (D) (CRUSADERS)
Born: 30.08.1962 Belfast
Status: Professional; Occupation: Desk-Top Engineer
Career: **Ards; Linfield** *(Aug '86) 242+1 - 8;* **Crusaders**
(May.'96):
Int.Hon: **Irish League Rep.**

DORNAN, Reg (D) (BANGOR)
Born: 09.12.1958 Belfast
Career: **P.O.S.C; Bangor; Ards; Bangor**
(Aug.'88) 148+16 - 2:

John Drake

DRAKE, John (D) (DISTILLERY)
Born: 01.06.1968 Lisburn
Status: Professional; Occupation: Aeronautical Engineer
Career: **Glenavon** *0 - 0;* **Distillery** *(Jul.'87) 59+8 - 1;*
Cliftonville *(Aug.'90) 16 - 0;* **Distillery** *(Feb.'91) 148 - 1:*

DUNLOP, Glenn (D) (CRUSADERS)
Born: 12.05.1968 Belfast
Ht: 6.1 Wt: 12.07
Status: Professional
Career: **Sirocco Works; Crusaders** *(Aug.'91) 107+4 - 5;*
Int.Hon: **N.Ireland 'B' International (1 cap);**
Irish League Rep:

DUNNE, Liam (M) (CRUSADERS)
Born: 01.09.1971 Dublin
Ht: 5.7 Wt: 10.09
Status: Professional
Career: **Belvedere; Bohemians** *(Jul.'90) 12+12 - 0;*
St.Johnstone *(May.'91) 13+12 - 0;* **Bohemians** *(c/s'93)*
13+1 - 4; **Crusaders** *(Dec.'93) 72 - 9;*
Int.Hon: **Republic of Ireland U.21; U.18; Irish**
League Rep.

DUNNION, Paul (M) (ARDS)
Born: 21.10.1969 Strabane
Ht: 5.9 Wt: 10.12
Status: Professional; Occupation: Housing Executive

Employee
Career: **Strabane; Omagh Town** *(Aug.'89) 73+1 - 5;*
Ards *(Jul.'94) 8+3 - 0:*

DWYER, Paul (F) (CRUSADERS)
Born: 11.09.1975 Belfast
Ht: 5.11 Wt: 11.00
Status: Amateur; Occupation: Student
Career: **Lisburn Youth; Saintfield Boys;**
Middlesbrough; Crusaders *(Sep.'94) 0+2 - 0:*

Philip Dykes

DYKES, Philip (F) (DISTILLERY)
Born: 30.7.1967 Belfast:
Status: Professional; Occupation: Production Officer
Career: **9th Bangor O.B; Dunmurry Recreation;**
Distillery *(Sep.'92) 75+18 - 28:*

EACHUS, Steven (G) (BANGOR)
Born: 15.12.1964 East Anglia
Status: Professional
Career: **Linfield; Ballymena United; Comber**
Recreation; Bangor *(Aug.'88) 141 - 0;* **Carrick**
Rangers *(Aug.'94 loan) 2 - 0:*

EASTON, John (D) (LINFIELD)
Born: 22.12.1968 Belfast
Status: Professional
Career: **Lisburn United; Linfield** *(1987) 106+2 - 1:*

ECCLES, Peter (D) (CRUSADERS)
Born: 24.08.1962 Dublin
Ht: 6.2 Wt: 13.03
Status: Professional
Career: **St.Brendans; Shamrock Rovers** *(1981);*
Kingsway Olympic *(Aus) (c/s'88);* **Dundalk** *(Oct.'88)*
Leicester City *(Nov.'88) 1 - 0;* **Dundalk** *(1989);*
Shamrock Rovers *(Oct.'89);* **Crusaders** *(Jun.'94) 0 - 0;*
Home Farm
(Dec.'95 loan):
Int.Hon: **Republic of Ireland International (1 cap);**
League of Ireland Rep.

EDDIS, David (F) (BANGOR)
Born: 14.01.1965 Bangor
Career: **First Bangor Old Boys; Bangor; Ards**
(Aug.'90) 27+8 - 5; **Harland & Wolff Welders** *(c/s'92);*
Ballyclare Comrades *(Dec.'92) 28+4 - 5;* **First Bangor**
Old Boys
(c/s'94); **Bangor** *(c/s'95) 3+2 - 0:*

ELDER, Dubois (D) (LARNE)
Career: Ballyclare Comrades 4 - 0; Larne 5+4 - 0:

ELLIOTT, Stuart (F) (GLENTORAN)
Career: Glentoran 0+1 - 0:
Int.Hon: N.Ireland U.18 Schools:

ENGLISH, Paul (D) (CRUSADERS)
Born: 16.11.1972 Belfast
Status: Amateur
Career: Linfield (1990) 6 - 0; Crusaders (Dec.'95) 0 - 0:

ERSKINE, Darren (F) (LINFIELD)
Born: 16.05.1966 Donaghadee
Ht: 6.0 Wt: 12.00
Status: Professional; Occupation: Machine Operator
Career: Ards Rangers; Dundela (Mar.'91); Ards (c/s'91)
108+1 - 70; Linfield (Jul.'95) 15+9 - 5:

ERSKINE, Sam (F) (CLIFTONVILLE)
Career: Cliftonville 0 - 0:

EVANS, Paul (F) (PORTADOWN)
Born: 05.09.1974 Banbridge
Status: Amateur; Occupation: Bar Manager
Career: Portadown (1989) 6+9 - 1:
Int.Hon: N.Ireland U.18 Schools:

EWING, Alan (F) (LINFIELD)
Born: 22.12.1968 Johnstone
Ht: 6.1 Wt: 12.08
Status: Professional; Occupation: Plasterer
Career: Beith Juniors; Stranraer (Dec.'88) 53+15 - 7;
Coleraine (Aug.'92) 74+3 - 17; Linfield (Jun.'95)
14+6 - 3:

FALCONER, Marc (F) (BANGOR)*
Born: 04.11.1972 Glasgow
Ht: 5.10 Wt: 11.02
Status: Professional
Career: Campsie Black Watch; Clyde (Jun.'94) 8+11 - 1;
Bangor (Oct.'95 loan) 1 - 0:

FEEHAN, Ciaran (F) (BALLYMENA UNITED)
Born: 06.08.1973 Newry
Ht: 5.11 Wt: 11.07
Status: Amateur; Occupation: Swimming Pool Attendant
Career: Brookvale; Lisburn United Y.C; Tottenham
Hotspur; Bessbrook Wanderers; Portadown (Feb.'91) 0 -
0; Glenavon (Nov.'91) 9+17 - 8; Cliftonville (c/s'95)
9+11 - 2; Ballymena United (Aug.'96):
Int.Hon: N.Ireland U.15:

FEEHAN, John (F) (NEWRY TOWN)
Career: Bessbrook Wanderers; Newry Town 3+1 - 0:

FEEHAN, Stephen (F) (NEWRY TOWN)
Career: Newry Town 15+5 - 5:

FENLON, Pat (M) (LINFIELD)*
Born: 15.03.1969 Dublin
Status: Professional
Career: Chelsea; St.Pats Athletic (c/s'87);
Bohemians (c/s'91) 88 + 29; Linfield (Jan.'94) 62 - 18;
Bohemians (c/s'96):
Int.Hon: Republic of Ireland 'B'; U.21; U.18; U.15;
League of Ireland Rep.

FERGUSON, Gary (D) (BANGOR)
Born: 16.09.1974 Belfast
Ht: 5.11 Wt: 10.11
Status: Professional
Career: Reading (Aug.'91) 0 - 0; Southampton
(Jun.'92) 0 - 0; Bangor (May '94) 12+4 - 4:
Int.Hon: N.Ireland U.18; Irish League U.21 Rep.

FERGUSON, Glenn (F) (GLENAVON)
Born: 10.07.1969 Belfast
Ht: 5.11 Wt: 12.06
Status: Professional; Occupation: Civil Servant
Career: Dungoyne Boys; Fisher Body; Ards (Aug.'87)
50+6 - 14; Glenavon (Aug.'90) 154+2 - 81:
Int.Hon: Irish League Rep.

FERGUSON, Iain J. (F) (PORTADOWN)
Born: 04.08.1962 Newarthill
Ht: 5.9 Wt: 10.0 7
Status: Professional; Occupation: Footballer
Career: Fir Park B.C; Dundee 108+11 - 39; Rangers
(Jun.'84) 25+7 - 6; Dundee (Aug.'87 loan) 2+1 - 2;
Dundee United (Aug.'87) 68+7 - 27; Hearts (Jul.'88)
31+21 - 8; Charlton Ath. (Nov.'89 loan) 1 - 0; Bristol
City (Mar.'90 loan) 8+3 - 2; Motherwell (Dec.'90)
33+17 - 10; Airdrie (Sep.'93) 26+5 - 9; Portadown
(Sep.'94) 33+6 - 14:
Int.Hon: Scotland U.21; U.18:

FERGUSON, Ian (F) (PORTADOWN)*
Born: 05.08.1968 Dunfermline
Ht: 6.1 Wt: 13.12
Status: Professional
Career: Lochgelly Albert; Raith Rovers (Aug.'87)
71+40 - 23; Hearts (Oct.'91) 24+36 - 9; St.Johnstone
(Nov.'93) 25+7 - 4; Portadown (Feb.'96 loan) 3 - 1:

FERRIS, Geoff (F) (CARRICK RANGERS)
Born: 13.03.1962 Limavady
Ht: 5.11 Wt: 12.7
Status: Professional; Occupation: Civil Servant
Career: Limavady United; R.U.C; Glenavon (Aug.'88)
97+16 - 36; Coleraine (Jun.'94) 5+1 - 1; Carrick
Rangers (Nov.'94 loan; Jan.'95) 34+3 - 5:

FINDLAY, Stuart (F) (LARNE)
Career: Larne 0+5 - 0:

FINLAY, Darren (M) (GLENTORAN)
Born: 19.12.1973 Belfast
Ht: 5.4 Wt: 10.00
Status: Professional
Career: Glentoran; Queens Park Rangers (May '92) 0
- 0; Doncaster Rovers ((Jul.'94) 6+2 - 1; Glentoran (c/
s'95) 8+6 - 2:
Int.Hon: N.Ireland 'B'; U.18:

FINNEGAN, Tony (D) (BALLYCLARE COMRADES)
Career: Ballyclare Comrades 5+1 - 0:

FLANNERY, Pat (M) (ARDS)*
Born: 23.07.1976 Glasgow
Ht: 5.11 Wt: 10.12
Status: Professional
Career: Eadie U.18; Greenock Morton (Aug.'94) 2+1 - 0; Ards (Aug.'95 loan) 11+1 - 2:

FLYNN, Gerry (F) (CLIFTONVILLE)
Born: 28.03.1972 Belfast
Status: Professional
Career: Bangor 0 - 0; Hull City (c/s'89) 0 - 0; Ards (Apr.'91) 0 - 0; Ballyclare Comrades (Jun.'91) 35+2 - 5; Cliftonville ((Jan.'93) 57+12 - 8:

FORSHAW, Barry (F) (BALLYCLARE COMRADES)
Born: 07.04.1970 Newry
Career: Killeavey United; Newry Town (1991) 4+2 - 0; U.U.J; Ballyclare Comrades (Oct.'95) 20+1 - 8:

FOX, Andrew (G) (BANGOR)
Occupation: Student Career: Bangor 1 - 0:

FREEMAN, Darren (F) (GLENAVON)*
Born: 22.08.1973 Brighton
Ht: 5.11 Wt: 13.01
Status: Professional
Career: Horsham Town; Gillingham (Jan.'95) 4+7 - 0; Glenavon (Dec.'95) 2 - 1; Fulham (c/s'96):

FULTON, Gareth (D) (PORTADOWN)
Born: 01.03.1978 Belfast
Ht: 5.11 Wt: 10.07
Status: Amateur; Occupation: Student
Career: Portadown (c/s'93) 13+2 - 0:
Int.Hon: N.Ireland U.18; U.18 Schools; U16; U.15:

GALBRAITH, Lee (M) (BALLYCLARE COMRADES)
Status: Amateur
Career: Ballyclare Comrades (1993)19+4 - 1:

Stewart Galbraith

GALBRAITH, Stewart (F) (BALLYCLARE COMRADES)
Career: Ballyclare Comrades 5+2- 1; Islandmagee (c/s'95); Ballyclare Comrades (Jan.'96) 9+1 - 1:

GALLAGHER, Martin (M) (OMAGH TOWN)
Born: Londonderry
Status: Amateur
Career: Cauldaff; Finn Harps (Jun.'92); Omagh Town (Sep.'95) 21+1 - 3:

GALLAGHER, Rory (M) (PORTADOWN)
Born: 22.08.1978 Enniskillen
Ht: 6.1 Wt: 12.00
Occupation: Student
Career: North Fermanagh Boys; Portadown 0+2 - 0:
Int.Hon: N.Ireland U.18 Schools; U.17; U.15:

GAMBLE, Maurice (D) (LINFIELD)
Career: Linfield 1 - 0:

GARDINER, James (F) (CRUSADERS)*
Born: 06.11.1959 Belfast
Status: Professional; Occupation: Bank Official
Career: Portadown; Burnley (May.'78) 0 - 0; Portadown (Nov.'79); Ards (c/s'84) 4+1 - 0; Glenavon (Dec.'84); Crusaders (Aug.'90) 73+7 - 37; Glenavon (Reserve Team Manager, c/s'94); Crusaders (Nov.'94) 4 - 1; Loughgall (Oct.'95):
Int.Hon: N.Ireland U.18

GASTON, Paul (D) (COLERAINE)
Born: 07.12.1972 Ballymoney
Ht: 6.2 Wt: 11.07
Status: Professional; Occupation: Process Operator
Career: Coleraine (Aug.'89) 106+5 - 13; Limavady United (Feb.'93 loan):

GAULD, Stuart (M) (PORTADOWN)
Born: 26.03.1964 Edinburgh
Career: Hearts 21+1 - 0; Derry City (Nov.'95); Glenavon (Nov.'95)16 - 0:

GETTY, Con (F) (ARDS)
Career: Scrabo United; Ards (1995) 1+1 - 0:

GILMORE, Anthony (D) (CARRICK RANGERS)
Born: 05.12.1967 Ballymoney
Ht: 5.8 Wt: 11.00
Status: Professional; Occupation: Labourer
Career: Coleraine (Aug.'83) 0 - 0; Ballymena United (1986) 0 - 0; Coleraine (1986) 94+10 - 0; Omagh Town (Aug.'93 loan) 0 - 0; Ballymoney United (Sep.'93 loan); Carrick Rangers (Feb.'95) 28 - 1:
Int.Hon: N.Ireland U.18:

GILMORE, Jason (M) (BALLYMENA UNITED)
Born: 15.10.1969 Ballymena
Career: Ballymena Utd. (Aug.'91) 41+18 - 5:

GLENDINNING, Mark (D) (GLENAVON)
Born: 02.04.1970 Belfast
Status: Professional; Occupation: Riveter at Shorts
Career: Bangor (1986) 134 - 19; Glenavon (Jul.'95) 25 - 2: Int.Hon: N.Ireland U.21; U.19; U.18; Irish League Rep.

GORDON, Dean (D) (CARRICK RANGERS)*
Born: 27.01.1969 Oxford
Ht: 6.3 Wt: 14.07
Status: Amateur; Occupation: Joiner
Career: Oxford United (1986) 0 - 0; Oxford City (1988);
Linfield (Nov.'91) 0 - 0; Distillery (Mar.'92) 4+1 - 1;
Ballyclare Comrades (Dec.'92) 38+1 - 8; Carrick Rangers
(Aug.'94) 29+2 - 1; Barn United (Dec.'95); Dundela (c/
s'96):

GORMAN, Anthony (M) (LINFIELD)
Born: 05.12.1970 Letterkenny
Ht: 5.10 Wt: 11.07
Status: Professional; Occupation: Sports Supervisor
Career: Letterkenny Rovers; Mansfield Town 0 - 0;
Waterford United (Nov.'88); Galway United; Chesterfield;
Finn Harps (Mar.'89); Sligo Rovers (c/s'91) 19+1 - 3;
Portadown (Aug.'92) 32+6 - 9; Coleraine (Aug.'94) 54 -
25; Linfield (Jul.'96)
Int.Hon: Irish League Rep.

Dessie Gorman

GORMAN, Dessie (F) (LINFIELD)
Born: 13.12.1964 Manchester
Status: Professional
Career: Dundalk (1984); Bourges (Fra); Derry City
(Oct.'90 loan) 21+7 - 7; Shelbourne (c/s'91) 27+14 - 8;
Linfield (Dec.'92) 77+5 - 24:

GRACEY, Mark (F) (NEWRY TOWN)*
Career: Newry Town (c/s'93) 8+3 - 0; Banbridge Town
(Feb.'96):

GRANT, Damian (G) (CRUSADERS)
Born: 06.08.1967 Belfast
Status: Professional
Career: Distillery; Port Vale (Aug.'85) 0 - 0; Ballymena
United (Aug.'87); Crusaders (Oct.'95 loan) 0 - 0; Glenavon
(Apr.'96 loan) 1 - 0; Crusaders (c/s'96):
Int.Hon: N.Ireland U.18:

GRAY, Donal (D) (GLENAVON)
Born: 22.05.1977 Newry
Ht: 5.7 Wt: 12.08
Career: Ballybot; Barcroft; Portadown (Jul.'91) 6+1 - 0;
Partick Thistle (Aug.'94) 0+1 - 0; Glenavon (Sep.'95)
Int.Hon: N.Ireland U.18; U.17; U.16:

GRAY, Paul (F) (ARDS)
Born: 28.01.1970 Portsmouth
Ht: 5.9 Wt: 11.10
Status: Professional
Career: Bangor 16+3 - 3; Luton Town (Jul.'88) 2+5 - 1;
Wigan Ath. (Jun.'91) 2+3 - 0; Bangor (Aug.'93) 9+10 - 1;
Ards (Mar.'96) 0+2 - 0:
Int.Hon: N.Ireland U.21; U.19; U.18; U.16; U.15:

GRAY, Tony (D) (OMAGH TOWN)
Ht: 5.10 Wt: 10.05
Status: Amateur; Occupation: Student
Career: Omagh Town 16+1 - 0:

GREEN, Matt (M) (BANGOR)
Born: 22.10.1975 Northampton
Ht: 5.8 Wt: 11.10
Status: Professional;
Career: Derby County (Jul.'94) 0 - 0; Bangor (Feb.'96
loan) 11 - 1; Bangor (Aug.'96):

GREER, Jason (M) (BALLYCLARE COMRADES)
Career: Cliftonville (1988) 0 - 0; Ballyclare Comrades
0 - 0:

GRIFFEN, Larry (D) (NEWRY TOWN)
Born: 11.05.1969
Occupation: Plasterer

Career: Newry Celtic; Newry Town (c/s'90) 99+5 - 7;
Banbridge Town (Aug.'95); Newry Town (Mar.'96) 3 - 0:

GRUGEL, Mark (M) (CLIFTONVILLE)*
Born: 09.03.1976 Liverpool
Ht: 5.8 Wt: 10.00
Status: Professional
Career: Everton (Nov.'93) 0 - 0; Cliftonville (Oct.'95 loan)
2 - 0:

HAGAN, James (D) (COLERAINE)
Born: 10.08.1956 Monkstown
Status: Professional
Career: Larne (1974); Coventry City (Nov.'77) 12+1 -
0; Torquay Utd. (Sep.'79 loan) 7 - 0; Detroit Express
(Mar.'80 loan) 30 - 0; Seiko Hong Kong (Oct.'80);
Coventry City (Jul.'81) 3 - 0; Birmingham City (May
'82) 124+13 - 0; Real Celta Vigo (Sp) (Aug.'87); Larne
(Aug.'89) 3 - 0; Colchester Utd (Nov.'89) 2 - 0; Larne
(Jan.'90) 5 - 0; IFK Oddevold (Swe) (May '90);
Ballymena Utd. (May '91) 39+2 - 0; Carrick Rangers
(Oct.'93) 10 - 0; Larne (Jan.'94) 16 - 0; Crusaders
(Jan.'95)1+2 - 0; Coleraine (c/s'95) 2 - 0:
Int.Hon: N.Ireland U.18:

HAGGAN, David (G) (BANGOR)
Career: Crusaders 0 - 0; Northern Telecom; Bangor
(Jun.'95) 0 - 0:

HALL, Alan (D) (DISTILLERY)
Born: 02.03.1970 Newtownards
Status: Professional; Occupation: Lifeguard
Career: Bangor 0 - 0; Wigan Ath. (Jul.'86) 0 - 0; Distillery
(Dec.'88) 166+7 - 2:
Int.Hon: N.Ireland U.18; U.15:

HALL, Darren (M) (ARDS)
Born: 13.11.1975 Belfast
Ht: 5.11 Wt: 12.07
Status: Amateur; Occupation: Student
Career: Glentoran (1992) 1+3 - 1; Ards (Jul.'95) 0 - 0:
Int.Hon: N.Ireland U.18; U.18 Schools; U.16; U.15

HALL, Paul (D) (BALLYCLARE COMRADES)*
Career: Harolds Cross Boys; St.James Gate (c/s'90) 60+5
- 0; Dundalk (c/s'94) 0 - 0; Ballyclare Comrades (Sep.'94
loan; Dec.'94) 31 - 2; Finn Harps 3 - 0:

HARKIN, Sean (M) (COLERAINE)
Born: 03.12.1973 Birmingham
Status: Professional
Career: St.Anne's; St.Bernard's; Manchester City
(Dec.'90) 0 - 0; Coleraine (Aug.'94) 1+1:

HAWKINS, Andrew (M) (ARDS)*
Born: 12.10.1975 Cambridge
Ht: 5.9 Wt: 10.04
Status: Professional
Career: Hutchison Vale B.C; Dunfermline Athletic
(Aug.'94) 1+4 - o; Ards (Oct.'95 loan) 2 - 0:

HAYES, Martin (M) (CLIFTONVILLE)*
Born: 21.03.1966 Walthamstow
Ht: 6.0 Wt: 12.04
Status: Professional
Career: Arsenal (Nov.'83) 70+23 - 26; Celtic (Aug.'91)
3+4 - 0; Wimbledon (Feb.'92 loan) 1+1 - 0; Swansea City
(Jan.'93) 44+17 - 8; Southend United (Aug.'95) 1 - 0;
Dover (Sep.'95); Cliftonville (Jan.'96) 3- 0:
Int.Hon: England U.21:

HAYLOCK, Garry (F) (PORTADOWN)
Born: 31.12.1970 Bradford
Ht: 5.11 Wt: 12.00
Status: Professional; Occupation: Footballer
Career: Huddersfield Town (Jul.'89) 10+3 - 4; Shelbourne
(Sep.'90 loan) 11 - 9; Shelbourne (Nov.'91 loan) 22+1 -
13; Shelbourne (Aug.'92) 35+2 - 15; Linfield (Jun.'93)
60 - 36; Portadown (Jun.'95) 25 - 20:
Int.Hon: Irish League Rep.

HEATH, Seamus (M) (CLIFTONVILLE)
Born: 06.12.1961 Belfast
Status: Professional
Career: Cromac Albion; Luton Town (Apr.'79) 0 - 0;
Lincoln City (Aug.'82) 6+1 - 0; Wrexham (Aug.'83) 32 -
1; Tranmere Rovers (Aug.'84) 6+11 - 0; Portadown
(Oct.'86) 4 - 1; B.K.46 (Fin); Glentoran (Oct.'89)10+1 -
0; B.K.46 (Mar.'90); Glentoran (Oct.'90) 27+1 - 0;
Distillery (Jul.'92) 39+4 - 0; Derry City (Aug.'94) 9 - 0;
Cliftonville (Aug.'95) 6+6 - 0:
Int.Hon: N.Ireland U.18:

HERBERT, Andrew (D) (PORTADOWN)
Born: 29.10.1975 Lurgan
Ht: 6.1 Wt: 12.00
Status: Amateur; Occupation: Student
Career: Dungannon Swifts; Glenavon (c/s'91) 1+2 - 0;
Portadown (c/s'95) 0 - 0:
Int.Hon: N.Ireland U.18; U.18 Schools; U.16; U.15:

HERON, John (D) (DISTILLERY)
Born: 19.09.1965 Broughshane
Occupation: Farmer
Career: Chimney Corner; Ballymena United (1986);
Distillery (Aug.'96):

HIGGINS, Kenny (F) (BALLYCLARE COMRADES)
Career: Ballynure; Ballyclare Comrades (Oct.'95) 8+2 -
3:

HILL, Ian (D) (CLIFTONVILLE)
Born: 09.05.1965 Dublin
Ht: 6.0 Wt: 12.03
Status: Professional
Career: Cherry Orchard; Leicester City 0 - 0; Shelbourne
(Sep.'88); Limerick City (Nov.'91 loan) 23 - 0;
St.Pats.Athletic (c/s'92) 59 - 0; Cliftonville (Sep.'94) 52 -
0:

HILL, Jonathan (D) (LINFIELD)
Status: Amateur
Career: Linfield (1993) 6+1 - 0:
Int.Hon: N.Ireland U.16

HILL, Raymond (M) (BANGOR)
Born: 05.12.1961 Armagh
Status: Professional; Occupation: School Teacher
Career: Portadown (1975); Ards (c/s'84); Bangor (Sep.'88)
201+6 -10:
Int.Hon: N.Ireland U.18:

HILL, Stephen (D) (BANGOR)
Career: Leeds United 0 - 0; Bangor (1992) 1 - 0:

HILLEN, Dermot (M) (OMAGH TOWN)*
Born: 30.05.1974 Londonderry
Status: Amateur
Career: Institute; Derry City; Omagh Town (Jul.'92) 12+17
- 0; Park (Nov.'94 loan); Ballinamallard United (Jan.'96):
Int.Hon: N.Ireland U.16; U.15:

HILLEN, Reg (G) (CARRICK RANGERS)
Born: 19.04.1961 Banbridge
Ht: 6.1 Wt: 12.00
Status: Professional; Occupation: Civil Engineer
Career: Portadown (1979); Glentoran (1981) 34 - 0;
Carrick Rangers (c/s'86) 177 - 0:
Int.Hon: N.Ireland U.18:

HILLIS, Gary (F) (DISTILLERY)*
Born: 19.04.1964 Belfast
Status: Professional
Career: Glentoran (1979) 0 - 0; Harland & W.W. (1981);
Crusaders (c/s'84); Glentoran (May '88) 76+24 - 27; Larne
(Jun.'94) 29 - 7; Distillery (Nov.'95) 12+3 - 2; Harland &
Wolff Welders (Jul.'96):

HOLMES, Darren (M) (BANGOR)*
Born: 30.01.1975 Sheffield
Ht: 5.10 Wt: 11.07
Status: Professional
Career: Sheffield Wednesday (Jul.'93); Bangor (Apr.'96
loan) 8 - 1:

HOSICK, Jackie (F) (LINFIELD)
Career: Crusaders 0 - 0; Dunmurry Recreation; Linfield (Aug.'94) 5+6 - 0:

HOUSTON, Jonathan (D) (GLENTORAN)
Status: Professional
Career: Glentoran 0+1 - 0:

HUNTER, Glenn (F) (CRUSADERS)
Born: 23.11.1967 Dromara
Ht: 5.10 Wt: 11.07
Status: Professional
Career: Distillery 13+7 -1; Crusaders (Jul.'89) 47+1 - 30; Linfield (Apr.'91) 28+18 -17; Crusaders (Aug.'93) 72+8 - 40:
Int.Hon: Irish League Rep.

HUNTER, Kirk (M) (CRUSADERS)
Born: 02.10.1963 Belfast
Ht: 6.1 Wt: 13.07
Status: Professional
Career: Crusaders (Sep.'85) 164+26 - 50:
Int.Hon: Irish League Rep.

HUSTON, Thomas (D) (COLERAINE)
Born: 13.06.1963 Randalstown
Ht: 5.8 Wt: 11.07
Status: Professional; Occupation: Haulager
Career: Ballymena United; Larne (Mar.'84); Coleraine (Jan.'95) 21+3 - 0:
Int.Hon: N.Ireland U.18; U.15; Irish League Rep.

HUTCHINSON, Brian (G) (GLENTORAN)
Career: Ballymena United; Larne (c/s'84); Ballymena United; Carrick Rangers; Distillery (c/s'86) 4 - 0; Dungannon Swifts (Sep.'86); Crusaders (Aug.'89) 21 - 0; F.C.Enkalon (c/s'89); Cliftonville (Aug.'90) 14 - 0; Dungannon Swifts (Jul.'91); Moyola Park (c/s '93); Glentoran (Jan.'96) 2 - 0:

HUXLEY, Alan (G) (BANGOR)*
Born: 20.04.1974 Larne
Career: Ballymena United (Sep.'90) 13 - 0; Bangor (Mar.'95) 6 - 0; Ballyclare Comrades (Sep.'95 loan) 0 - 0; Dundela (Mar.'96):
Int.Hon: N.Ireland U.18 Schools:

IRWIN, Brian (F) (BANGOR)
Born: 20.05.1971 Dublin
Career: Barnsley 0 - 0; Home Farm; Kilkenny City (Mar.'91) 3 - 1; Dundalk (c/s'91) 55+16 - 23; Bangor (Aug.'95) 8+8 - 3:

IRWIN, James (M) (BALLYCLARE COMRADES)
Born: 09.02.1965 Fadross
Status: Amateur;
Career: Glenavon (Jul.'83); Barn United (Jul.'85); Portadown (Aug.'87) 3 - 0; Carrick Rangers (Jul.'89) 0+1 - 0; Chimney Corner (Jan.'90); Distillery (Mar.'92) 15+9 - 0; Harland & Wolff Welders (Mar.'94 loan); Dungannon Swifts (c/s'94); Cookstown United (Oct.'94); Ballyclare Comrades (Jul.'95) 7+1 - 1:

JAMISON, John (G) (CARRICK RANGERS)
Career: Carrick Rangers 0 - 0:

JEFFREY, David (D) (LARNE)*
Born: 28.10.1962 Newtownards
Ht: 6.0 Wt: 12.07
Status: Professional; Occupation: Youth Leader
Career: Manchester Utd. (c/s'79) 0 - 0; Linfield (c/s'82) 181+1 - 21; Ards (Jun.'92) 64+1 - 2; Larne (Feb.'95 Player/Coach) 22 - 1; Linfield (Apr.'96 Asst.Manager):
Int.Hon: N.Ireland U.18; U.15; Irish League Rep.

JOHNSTON, Jackie (M) (LARNE)
Career: Cookstown United; Larne (Mar.'95) 6+3 - 0:

JOHNSTON, John (M) (BANGOR)*
Born: 21.03.1972 Newtownards
Status: Professional; Occupation; Taxi-Driver
Career: Ards 0 - 0; Port Vale (1989) 0 - 0; Ards (Mar.'91) 2+3 - 1; Ballyclare Comrades (c/s'92) 69+3 - 4; Bangor (Oct.'95) 1 - 0; Loughgall (Feb.'96 loan); Loughgall (May.'96)
Int.Hon: N.Ireland U.17; U.16; U.15:

JOHNSTON, Richard (F) (LINFIELD)
Born: 15.10.69 Portadown
Status: Professional
Career: Tottenham Hotspur (Aug.'87) 0 - 0; Dunfermline Athletic (Apr.'90) 0 - 0; Linfield (Aug.'90) 56+13 - 16;
Int.Hon: N.Ireland U.18:

Sammy Johnston

JOHNSTON, Sammy (M) (GLENAVON)
Born: 13.04.1967 Glasgow
Ht: 5.10 Wt: 11.07
Status: Professional; Occupation: Electronic Engineer
Career: Bishopbriggs B.C; St.Johnstone (1983) 154+22 - 29; Ayr Utd (Sep.'90) 24 - 9; Partick Thistle (Mar.'91) 38+5 - 4; Ballymena Utd. (Jul.'93) 3+2 - 0; Stranraer (Nov.'93) 2 - 0; Glenavon (Jul.'94) 39+10 - 14:

JOHNSTON, Stephen (D) (OMAGH TOWN)
Born: 11.03.1976 Londonderry
Ht: 5.8 Wt: 10.07
Status: Amateur; Occupation: Student
Career: Derry City; Omagh Town (Aug.'94) 56 - 1:
Int.Hon: N.Ireland U.15:

JOHNSTONE, David (D) (ARDS)
Career: Dromara Village; Ards (Jan.'96) 0 - 0:

KAVANAGH, Eamon (M) (OMAGH TOWN)
Born:14.08.1966 Ballygawley
Ht: 5.10 Wt: 11.02
Status: Professional; Occupation: Engineer
Career: Omagh Town (1982) 45+2 - 9; Glentoran
(Aug.'92) 7+4 - 1; Omagh Town (Feb.'93) 81+2 - 11:

KEARNS, Tony (D) (BALLYCLARE COMRADES)*
Career: Donegal Celtic; Ballyclare Comrades (Jul.'95)
26 - 0; Donegal Celtic (c/s'96):

KEE, Paul (G) (ARDS)
Born: 08.11.1969 Belfast
Ht: 6.3 Wt: 12.05
Status: Professional; Occupation: Coalman
Career: Ards 42 - 0; Oxford Utd (Jun.'88) 56 - 0;
Wimbledon (Apr.'93 loan) 0 - 0; Ards (Dec.'93 loan) 4 -
0; Reading (Mar.'94 loan) 0 - 0; Ards (Jul.'94) 51 - 0:
Int.Hon: N.Ireland International (9 caps); U.23; U.18;
U.16; U.15

KEELEY, Brendan (G) (NEWRY TOWN)
Born: Dublin
Status: Professional; Occupation: Buyer in Plastics
Company
Career: St.Canices; St.Kevins; Newry Town (Aug.'93) 59
- 0:

KEENAN, Michael (G) (PORTADOWN)
Born: 05.04.1956 Newry
Status: Professional; Occupation: Divisional Youth Officer
Career: Newry Town (1965); Oldham Ath. (Sep.'74) 0 -
0; Newry Town (1978); Portadown (1981):
Int.Hon: N.Ireland U.18; Irish League Rep.

KEERY, David (M) (BALLYCLARE COMRADES)
Born: 06.08.1966 Belfast
Career: Glentoran 13+7 - 1; Crusaders (c/s'87) 43 - 1;
Coleraine (Mar.'90) 56 - 4; Ballymena United (1995) 0 -
0; Ballyclare Comrades (Nov.'95) 1+1 - 0:

Damien Kelly

KELLY, Damien (M) (GLENTORAN)
Born: 15.09.1972 Kircubbin
Ht: 5.8 Wt: 11.00
Status: Professional; Occupation: Student
Career: Bangor 2+1 - 0; Glentoran (Aug.'92) 37+18 - 4:

KELLY, Keith (F) (BALLYCLARE COMRADES)*
Career: Rockview Rangers; Glenavon 0+1 - 0; Newry
Town (Jan.'92) 5+5 - 1; Dromara Village; Windmill Stars;
Ballyclare Comrades (Sep.'95) 2 - 0:

KELLY, Michael (D) (ARDS)
Born: 19.06.1970 Londonderry
Status: Professional; Occupation: Work Study Officer
Career: Oxford Utd. Stars; Omagh Town (c/s'91) 0 - 0;
Oxford Utd. Stars (Oct.'91); Derry City 0 - 0; Ballyclare
Comrades (c/s'93) 41+2 - 1; Ards (Jun.'95) 15 - 0:

KELLY, Stuart (D) (ARDS)
Career: Ards (1992) 0 - 0:

KENNEDY, Brian (D) (BANGOR)
Born: 13.07.1970 Lisburn
Status: Amateur; Occupation: Sheet Metal Worker
Career: Lisburn Rangers; Glenavon (Jul.'86) 16+2 - 2;
Lisburn Rangers (Jul.'91); Glenavon (Nov.'91) 28+2 - 2;
Lisburn Rangers (Jul.'93); Crewe Utd. (Nov.'93); Distillery
(Jan.'94) 49+3 - 1; Bangor (Mar.'96) 3 - 0:

John Kennedy

KENNEDY, John (M) (GLENTORAN)
Born: 08.03.1967 Lisburn
Status: Professional; Occupation: Sheet Metal Worker
Career: Hillsborough B.C; Cliftonville (Jul.'82); A.F.C;
(Aug.'85); Cromac Albion (Jul.'87); Distillery (Jan.'89)
139+3 - 3; Glentoran (Oct.'95) 20+3 - 1:

KENNEDY, Peter (M) (PORTADOWN)*
Born: 10.09.1973 Lisburn
Ht: 5.10 Wt: 11.00
Status: Amateur; Occupation: Sheet Metal Worker
Career: Glentoran (1990) 0 - 0; Glenavon (Aug.'90) 36+3
- 7; Portadown (Jul.'95) 23 - 10; Notts County (Aug.'96)
Int.Hon: Irish League U.21 Rep.

KENNY, Marc (M) (GLENAVON)
Born: 17.09.1973 Dublin
Status: Professional
Career: Home Farm; Liverpool (Sep.'90) 0 - 0; Bangor
(Jul.'93) 28+4 - 6; Coleraine (Jul.'95) 0 - 0; Glenavon
(Jul.'95) 5+1 - 0:
Int.Hon: Republic of Ireland U.18; U.16; Irish League
U.21 Rep.

KERR, Jackie (M) (CARRICK RANGERS)*
Status: Amateur
Career: Crusaders (1992) 0 - 0; Carrick Rangers (c/s '95) 0+1 - 0; Loughgall (c/s '96):

KERR, Joe (D) (CLIFTONVILLE)
Born: 23.09.1974 Belfast
Career: Donegal Celtic; Ards (May. '91) 14 - 0; Cliftonville (Jun. '92) 73+1 - 2:

KERR, Matthew (G) (BALLYMENA UNITED)
Career: Ballymena United 0+1 - 0:
Int.Hon: N.Ireland U.15:

KIRK, Andrew (F) (GLENTORAN)
Occupation: Student
Career: Dungoyne Boys; Glentoran (1993) 0+1 - 1:
Int.Hon: N.Ireland U.18 Schools; U.17:

KIRK, James (M) (CARRICK RANGERS)
Born: 01.05.1963 Ballyclare
Ht: 5.8 Wt: 12.00

Status: Amateur; Occupation: Stock Controller
Career: Ballyclare Comrades (1982); Carrick Rangers (c/s '87) 40+9 - 10; Ballyclare Comrades (c/s '89) 61+11 - 8; Carrick Rangers (Dec. '94) 16+4 - 2:

KNELL, Philip (M) (LINFIELD)
Born: 09.10.1968 Belfast
Ht: 5.7 Wt: 10.07
Status: Professional; Occupation: Store Operative
Career: Rangers (1983) 0 - 0; Linfield (c/s '87) 71+25 - 16:
Int.Hon: N.Ireland U.18; U.16:

LAMONT, Wesley (G) (COLERAINE)
Born: 05.04.1964 Belfast
Status: Amateur
Career: F.C.Enkalon; Linfield (Jul. '90) 118 - 0; Coleraine (Aug. '96):
Int.Hon: N.Ireland 'B' International.

LARKIN, Chris (F) (COLERAINE)
Born: 17.10.1977
Status: Amateur
Career: Ballymena Utd. 0 - 0; Coleraine 0+1 - 0; Larne (Nov. '95) 1 - 0:
Int.Hon: N.Ireland U.16; U.15:

LARMOUR, Glenn (D) (BALLYCLARE COMRADES)
Born: 02.08.1964 Belfast
Career: Dunmurry Rec; Crusaders (Dec. '86) 29+6 - 0; Ballyclare Comrades (Dec. '92) 42+3 - 1:

LAUGHLIN, Harry (F) (BALLYCLARE COMRADES)*
Career: Linfield 0 - 0; R.I.R; Ballyclare Comrades (Sep. '95) 2 - 0:

LAWLOR, Martin (M) (CRUSADERS)
Born: 01.03.1958 Dublin
Status: Professional;
Career: Stella Maris; Dundalk (1976); Shamrock Rovers (c/s '91) 21 - 0; Dundalk (c/s '92) 58+3 - 1; Drogheda United (player coach); Crusaders (Feb. '96) 0+1 - 0:
Int.Hon: Republic of Ireland U.21;

LAWLOR, Robert (D) (CRUSADERS)
Born: 14.02.1962 Dublin
Ht: 5.11 Wt: 11.07
Status: Professional
Career: Dundalk; Shamrock Ro. (1987); U.C.D; Sligo Ro; Bohemians; Crusaders (Nov. '91) 93 - 7:
Int.Hon: Republic of Ireland U.18

LECKEY, Philip (M) (LARNE)
Born: 29.10.1969 Belfast
Ht: 5.8 Wt: 10.07
Status: Amateur; Occupation: Civil Servant
Career: Crusaders (1986); Ballyclare Comrades (Aug. '91) 66+9 - 8; Coleraine (Jul. '95) 0 - 0; Larne (Aug. '95) 11+2 - 0:

LEEMAN, Paul (D) (GLENTORAN)
Career: Glentoran 0+1 - 0:

LEITCH, Scott (D) (PORTADOWN)*
Born: 06.10.1969 Motherwell
Ht: 5.9 Wt: 11.08
Status: Professional
Career: Shettleston Juniors; Dunfermline Athletic (Apr. '90) 72+17 - 16; Hearts (Aug. '93) 46+9 - 2; Portadown (Jan. '96 loan) 3 - 0; Swindon Town (Mar. '96 loan) 7 - 0:

LENNON, Cathal (M) (NEWRY TOWN)
Career: Newry Town (1995) 2+1 - 0:

LITTLE, Glen (M) (GLENTORAN)
Born: 15.10.1975 Wimbledon
Ht: 6.3 Wt: 12.07
Status: Professional; Occupation: Footballer
Career: Crystal Palace (Jul. '94) 0 - 0; Derry City (Nov. '94 loan) 3+1 - 0; Glentoran (Dec. '94 loan) 14 - 4; Glentoran (c/s '95) 22 - 9:

LIVINGSTONE, Steven (F) (PORTADOWN)
Born: 07.10.1973 Belfast
Ht: 6.1 Wt: 12.07
Status: Professional
Career: Carrick Rangers 0 - 0; Middlesbrough 0 - 0; Crusaders (Jan. '92) 50+15 - 14; Portadown (Jul. '96):
Int.Hon: N.Ireland U.18; U.16; U.15; Irish League U.21 Rep.

LOONEY, Mark (M) (LARNE)
Career: Queens University; Larne (Aug. '95) 18 - 0:

LOUGHERY, Des (F) (BALLYMENA UNITED)
Born: 22.04.1967 Limavady
Career: Roe Valley; Ballymena United (Nov. '88):

LOUGHRAN, Kieran (D) (CLIFTONVILLE)
Born: 19.09.1964 Belfast
Status: Professional
*Career: **Cliftonville** (1983):*

LOWRY, David (F) (CARRICK RANGERS)
Born: 18.07.1978 Belfast
Ht: 6.2 Wt: 12.07
Occupation: Student
*Career: **Carrick Rangers** (Aug.'93) 7+1 - 0:*

LYNCH, Stephen (M) (COLERAINE)
Born: 25.09.1969 Belfast
Status: Professional
*Career: **Q.P.R.** (Oct.'87) 0 - 0; **Newcastle Utd.** 0 - 0;*
***Portadown** (Mar.'90) 0+1 - 0; **Carrick Rangers** (c/s'91)*
*23+2 - 1; **Crusaders** (May '92) 17+16 - 5; **Ballymena Utd.***
*(Dec.'94) 8+8 - 2; **Coleraine** (Mar.'96) 0+4 - 0:*
*Int.Hon: **N.Ireland U.18; U.16:***

MACAULEY, Philip (M) (CARRICK RANGERS)
Born: 07.10.1972 Belfast
Ht: 5.6 Wt: 10.00
Status: Amateur; Occupation: Leisure Attendant
*Career: **Bournemouth** (1989) 0 - 0; **Linfield** (Aug.'91) 0 -*
*0; **Carrick Rangers** (Aug.'94) 50+5 - 11:*
*Int.Hon: **N.Ireland U.18; U.15***

McALEENAN, Aidan (F) (DISTILLERY)
Born: 29.11.1967 Belfast
Status: Professional
*Career: **Olympia; Distillery** (Aug.'91) 49+6 - 9:*
McALLISTER, Craig (M) (GLENAVON)
*Career: **Bangor; Glenavon** (c/s'92) 0 - 0:*
*Int.Hon: **N.Ireland U.18; U.16:***

McALLISTER, Patrick (M) (COLERAINE)
Born: 03.02.1972 Belfast
Status: Professional
*Career: **Cliftonville** 3+3 - 1; **Dunfermline Ath.** (Jul.'90)*
*2+4 - 0; **Cliftonville** (Aug.'92 loan) 3 - 0; **Cliftonville***
*(Dec.'92) 58+2 - 8; **Coleraine** (Sep.'95) 26+1 - 6:*
*Int.Hon: **Irish League Rep; Irish League U.21 Rep.***

McATEE, Jerome (M) (DISTILLERY)
Born: 16.11.1975 Belfast
Status: Amateur; Occupation: Student
*Career: **Star of the Sea; Glentoran** (Aug.'94) 0 - 0;*
***Distillery** (Mar.'96) 0+1 - 0:*
*Int.Hon: **N.Ireland U.18 Schools:***

McAULEY, Oliver (D) (COLERAINE)
Born: 07.09.1964 Belfast
Ht: 5.7 Wt: 11.00
Status: Professional
*Career: **Cromac Albion; Cliftonville** (1986) 0 - 0;*
Ballyclare Comrades** (Dec.'89) 15+2 - 4; **Chimney Corner
*(c/s'91); **Carrick Rangers** (c/s'92) 68-0; **Coleraine***
(Jan.'95) 29+1-0:

McBREARTY, Joe (G) (OMAGH TOWN)
Born: 11.02.1952 Londonderry
*Career: **Derry City; Omagh Town** (Jul.'91) 34+1 - 0;*
***Westport** (ROI) (Nov.'94 loan):*

McBRIDE, Justin (F) (GLENTORAN)
Born: 16.10.1971 Belfast
Ht: 5.7 Wt: 10.07
Status: Professional; Occupation: Employee in Retail Comp.
*Career: **Carrick Rangers**(1989) 6+3 - 0; **Glentoran***
(Aug.'91) 92+5 - 42:
*Int.Hon: **N.Ireland U.21; U.18***

McBRIDE, Paul (D) (ARDS)
Born: 31.05.1972 Belfast
Ht: 6.1 Wt: 11.07
Occupation: Joiner
*Career: **Crusaders** (Aug.'89) 7+1 - 1; **Harland & W.W.***
*(Jan.'92); **Larne** (c/s'92) 14+2 - 0; **Ards** (Aug.'94) 37+6 -*
0:

Stephen McBride

McBRIDE, Stephen (F) (LINFIELD)
Born: 02.05.1964 Lurgan
Ht: 6.0 Wt: 12.06
Status: Professional; Occupation: Civil Servant
*Career: **Linfield** (1978) 6 - 5; **Motherwell** (Feb.'84) 0+4 -*
*0; **Linfield** (1984) 0 - 0; **Glenavon** (Aug.'85) 249+11 - 123;*
***Linfield** (Jul.'96):*
*Int.Hon: **N.Ireland International (4 caps); U.23; Irish***
League Rep.

McCAFFREY, Conor (D) (ARDS)
Born: 04.11.1969 Belfast
Ht: 5.10 Wt: 12.6
Status: Amateur; Occupation:
*Career: **Drogheda Utd; Glentoran** (Aug.'88) 48+2 - 1; **Ards***
*(Aug.'92) 3 - 0; **Bangor** (Jan.'93) 45+2 - 4; **Glentoran***
*(Jan.'95) 2+2 - 0; **Ards** (May '96):*

McCALLAN, David (F) (COLERAINE)
Born: 26.02.1970 Belfast
Status: Professional
*Career: **Carrick Rangers** (1986) 5+4 - 1; **Linfield** (1987)*
*1 - 0; **Port Vale** (Jun.'89) 0 - 0; **Linfield** (Aug.'89) 6+9 -*
*3; **Mooroolbark** (Aus) (Mar.'90); **Portadown** (Jan.'92)*
*1+1 - 1; **Bangor** (Aug.'92) 49+2 - 34; **Coleraine***
(Dec.'95) 9+2 - 6:
*Int.Hon: **N.Ireland U.18; U.16; U.15:***

McCANN, Liam (M) (BALLYCLARE COMRADES)
Career: Cookstown United; Ballyclare Comrades (Jul.'95)0 - 0:

McCANN, Martin (M) (ARDS)*
Born: Londonderry
Ht: 5.11 Wt: 11.00
Career: Derry City 18+14 - 1; Cliftonville (Nov.'92 loan) 6 - 0; Ards (Aug.'93) 59+12 - 10; Finn Harps (Aug.'96):

McCANN, Tim (M) (CLIFTONVILLE)
Born: 25.09.1971 Belfast
Status: Professional
Career: Newington Y.C; Cliftonville (1990) 110+24 - 16:

McCARRISON, Dugald (M) (GLENTORAN)*
Born: 22.12.1969 Lanark
Ht: 5.8 Wt: 12.00
Status: Professional
Career: Celtic B.C; Celtic (Oct.'87) 0+3 - 0; Ipswich Town (Dec.'90 loan) 0 - 0; Darlington (Oct.'91 loan) 5 - 2; Kilmarnock (Feb.'93) 6+3 - 1; Hamilton Academicals (Aug.'95) 0+3 - 0; Glentoran (Oct.'95 loan) 7+4 - 1:

McCARTAN, James (F) (GLENAVON)
Career: Portadown 0 - 0; Donacloney; Glenavon (c/s'95) 2 - 0:

McCARTAN, Paul (F) (BANGOR)
Born: 02.09.1969 Belfast
Career: Distillery 0 - 0; Newry Town (c/s'88); Distillery (Sep.'90) 25+6 - 3; Newry Town (Jan.'92) 5+6 - 0; Cliftonville (c/s'92) 0+5 - 0; Distillery (Dec.'92) 0 - 0; Newry Town (Oct.'93) 11+5 - 1; Cliftonville (Jan.'95) 0 - 0; Bangor (c/s'95) 0 - 0:

McCARTNEY, Gary (D) (CRUSADERS)
Born: 15.08.1960 Belfast
Ht: 5.11 Wt: 11.00
Status: Professional
Career: Liverpool 0 - 0; Linfield (1980) 69+14 - 5; Bangor (Jun.'89) 74+9 - 2; Crusaders (Dec.'93) 51+7 - 2:
In.Hon: N.Ireland U.18; U.15:

McCARRISON, Dugald (M) (GLENTORAN)*
Born: 22.12.1969 Lanark
Ht: 5.8 Wt: 12.00
Status: Professional
Career: Celtic B.C; Celtic (Oct.'87) 0+3 - 0; Ipswich Town (Dec.'90 loan) 0 - 0; Darlington (Oct.'91 loan) 5 - 2; Kilmarnock (Feb.'93) 6+3 - 1; Hamilton Academicals (Aug.'95) 0+3 - 0; Glentoran (Oct.'95 loan) 7+4 - 1:

McCARTAN, James (F) (GLENAVON)
Career: Portadown 0 - 0; Donacloney; Glenavon (c/s'95) 2 - 0:

McCARTAN, Paul (F) (BANGOR)
Born: 02.09.1969 Belfast
Career: Distillery 0 - 0; Newry Town (c/s'88); Distillery (Sep.'90) 25+6 - 3; Newry Town (Jan.'92) 5+6 - 0; Cliftonville (c/s'92) 0+5 - 0; Distillery (Dec.'92) 0 - 0; Newry Town (Oct.'93) 11+5 - 1; Cliftonville (Jan.'95) 0 - 0; Bangor (c/s'95) 0 - 0:

McCARTNEY, Gary (D) (CRUSADERS)
Born: 15.08.1960 Belfast
Ht: 5.11 Wt: 11.00
Status: Professional
Career: Liverpool 0 - 0; Linfield (1980) 69+14 - 5; Bangor (Jun.'89) 74+9 - 2; Crusaders (Dec.'93) 51+7 - 2:
In.Hon: N.Ireland U.18; U.15:

McCAUL, Dermot (D) (OMAGH TOWN)*
Born: 14.01.1969 Londonderry
Career: Derry City; Omagh Town (Jul.'91) 37+2 - 1; Coleraine (Jun.'93) 3 - 0; Finn Harps (Nov.'93) 3+1 - 0; Omagh Town (Jan.'94 loan) 2 - 0; Omagh Town (c/s'94) 5 - 0; Dungannon Swifts (Jan.'96):

McCAVANAGH, Kevin (D) (DISTILLERY)
Born: 08.11.1969 Belfast
Status: Amateur; Occupation: Royal Mail Driver
Career: British Telecom (1985); Crusaders (Dec.'91) 0 - 0; Distillery (Jan.'93) 1 - 0:

McCOMBE, Alistair (D) (BANGOR)
Born: 20.12.1975 Belfast
Ht: 6.0 Wt: 12.11
Career: Bangor; Dundee Utd (Oct.'92) 0 - 0; Bangor (Jul.'93) 10 - 1:
Int.Hon: N.Ireland U.18; U.18 Schools; U.16:

McCONKEY, Harry (M) (LARNE)
Born: 18.09.1959 Magheraveely
Status: Professional; Occupation: P.E. Teacher
Career: Lisbellaw Utd. (1975); Glenavon (1977); Dungannon Swifts (1980); Chimney Corner (1982); Coleraine (Aug.'86) 2+2 - 0; Carrick Rangers (Nov.'86) 18+1 - 2; Ballyclare Comrades (Jan.'88) 20+5 - 0; Ballymena Utd. (Nov.'91) 8+1 - 1; Carrick Rangers (Nov.'93) 17+1 - 1; Larne (Jun.'94) 24+1 - 0:

McCONNELL, John (D) (BALLYMENA UNITED)
Born: 04.04.1968 Belfast
Status: Professional
Career: S.T.C; Linfield (Dec.'89) 94+3 - 2; Ballymena
United (Jun.'95) 23 - 2:

McCONVILLE, Fintan (M) (BALLYMENA UNITED)
Born: 02.09.1967 Lurgan
Status: Professional
Career: Newry Town; Oxford Utd.(NI); Glenavon (c/s'87)
73+7 - 9; Napier City (NZ) (Feb.'91); Glenavon (Jan.'92)
29+3 - 2; Ballymena Utd (Aug.'93) 61+6 - 2:
Int.Hon: Irish League Rep.

McCOOSH, Ian (LINFIELD)
Born: 06.10.1971 Lisburn
Status: Professional
Career: Linfield (Aug.'87) 52+17 - 3:
Int.Hon: N.Ireland U.17; U.16:

McCORRY, Damien (G) (LARNE)
Born: 13.11.1965 Newry
Career: Newry Town 0 - 0; Monaghan Utd. (Aug.'87);
Larne (Jul.'94) 8+1:

McCOURT, Tom (F) (BALLYMENA UNITED)
Born: Larne
Status: Professional
Career: Creagh Hill Olympic; Carrick Rangers (c/s'89)
42+5 - 15; Larne (Jan.'91) 111+8 - 44; Ballymena United
(Aug.'95) 10 - 1:

McCOY, Raymond (M) (GLENAVON)
Born: 22.03.1964 Carrickmore
Ht: 5.6 Wt: 10.06
Status: Professional; Occupation: Progress Controller
Career: Coleraine (1980) 188+4 - 77; Gisborne City
(Jul.'90); Coleraine (Sep.'90) 0 - 0; Glenavon (Nov.'90)
97+27 - 33:
Int.Hon: N.Ireland International (2 caps); U.21;
Irish League Rep.

McCRAE, Crawford (F) (LARNE)
Born: 19.11.1970 Harlow
Status: Professional
Career: Barn Utd; Linfield (1988) 5+9 - 1; Crusaders
(May.'92) 8+20 - 5; Larne (c/s'94) 34+9 - 13:

McCREADIE, Barry (F) (OMAGH TOWN)
Born: 20.11.1959 Nottingham
Ht: 6.1 Wt: 13.10
Status: Professional; Occupation: Contractor
Career: Coleraine; Derry City; Moyola Park; Coleraine
(c/s'86) 41+3 - 17; Bangor (Nov.'89) 81+8 - 25; Omagh
Town (Sep.'93) 9 - 2; Ballymena Utd (Jan.'94) 8+1 - 4;
Omagh Town (Sep.'94) 27+18 - 13:

McCREADIE, Roy (M) (OMAGH TOWN)
Born: 23.03.1960 Nottingham
Career: Coleraine; Portadown (c/s'87) 53+5 - 3; Omagh
Town (c/s'91) 19+1 - 1;

McCRUM, Brett (M) (BALLYCLARE COMRADES)
Career: Ballymena United (1988); Carrick Rangers
(1990); Ballyclare Comrades 0 - 0:

McCRYSTAL, Gavin (F) (BALLYCLARE COMRADES)*
Born: 27.10.1969 Belfast
Career: Carrick Rangers (1986) 0 - 0; Larne (c/s'91) 49+16
- 7; Cliftonville (Aug.'95) 0 - 0; Ballyclare Comrades
(Oct.'95) 0 - 0; Chimney Corner (Mar.'96):

McCULLAGH, Colm (F) (OMAGH TOWN)
Career: Glenavon 0 - 0; Omagh Town (Aug.'95)

McCULLOUGH, Glenn (D) (PORTADOWN)
Born: 25.01.1979 Portadown
Ht: 6.1 Wt: 11.00
Occupation: Student
Career: Portadown 0 - 0:

Damien McCusker

McCUSKER, Damien (G) (BALLYCLARE COMRADES)
Ht: 6.2
Status: Professional;
Career: Ballyclare Comrades (c/s'95) 18 - 0:

McCUSKER, Fergal (F) (BALLYCLARE COMRADES)
Career: Ballyclare Comrades 10+1 - 0:

McDERMOTT, Kel (M) (CARRICK RANGERS)
Born: 03.11.1962 Belfast
Ht: 5.8 Wt: 10.07
Status: Professional; Occupation: Detached Youth Worker
Career: Manchester Utd. (1979) 0 - 0; Ards (c/s'82); Bury
(1984) 0 - 0; Linfield (Oct.'85) 24+3 - 3; Carrick Rangers
(c/s'89) 32 - 1; Glenavon (Jan.'91) 13+3 - 0; Carrick
Rangers (Mar.'93) 79+4 - 3:
Int.Hon: N.Ireland U.18; U.15:

McDEVITT, Mark (G) (OMAGH TOWN)
Career: Omagh Town 1+1 - 0:

McDONAGH, Phil (F) (DISTILLERY)
Career: Bangor; Glenavon 0 - 0; Distillery (c/s'96):

Andy McDonald

McDONALD, Andy (G) (DISTILLERY)
Born: 30.01.1977 Belfast
Status: Amateur; Occupation: Electrician
Career: *Willowfield; Linfield (Aug.'91) 0- 0; Distillery*
(Aug.'95) 2 - 0:

McDONALD, Thomas (M) (CLIFTONVILLE)
Born: 06.08.1967 Belfast
Ht: 5.8 WT: 11.02
Status: Professional; Occupation: Postman
Career: *Distillery 16 - 1; Larne (Sep.'86) 53+13 - 9;*
Ards (Nov.'90) 75+12 - 8; Cliftonville (Jan.'95) 27+4 -
0:
Int.Hon: **N.Ireland U.15**

McDOWELL, Roddy (F) (OMAGH TOWN)
Born: 25.01.1974 Londonderry
Ht: 5.9 Wt: 11.04
Status: Professional; Occupation: Factory Worker
Career: *Oxford Utd. Stars; Middlesbrough (c/s'90) 0 -*
0; Portadown (Feb.'94 loan) 1 - 0; Glentoran (Aug.'94)
4+4 - 1; Omagh Town (Feb.'96) 7+2 - 3:
Int.Hon: **N.Ireland U.18; U.16; U.15:**

McDOWELL, Stephen (D) (LARNE)
Born: 12.03.1975 Ballymoney
Ht: 5.8 Wt: 10.00
Status: Professional; Occupation: Carpet Fitter
Career: *Manchester City (Jul.'91) 0 - 0; Coleraine*
(Jul.'93) 26+4 - 0; Larne (Sep.'95) 21+3 - 1:

McELROY, John (F) (OMAGH TOWN)
Born: 15.12.1974 Buncrana
Occupation: Student
Career: *Derry City 2 - 0; Omagh Town (Feb.'95)*
10+13 - 0:

McEVOY, Richard (M) (BANGOR)*
Born: 06.08.1970 Gibraltar
Status: Professional
Career: *Luton Town (Aug.'85) 0+1 - 0; Cambridge*
Utd.(Feb.'87 loan) 10+1 - 1; Shamrock Rovers (c/s'88);
Finn Harps (Feb.'91 loan) 4 - 0; Dundalk (c/s'91) 29+3
- 4; Bangor (Oct.'92) 62+8 - 4; Glentoran (c/s'95) 1+2 -
0; Bangor (Mar.'96) 7 - 1; Home Farm (Jul.'96):
Int.Hon: **Republic of Ireland U.18:**

McFADDEN, James (M) (CLIFTONVILLE)
Born: 21.03.1968 Belfast
Status: Professional
Career: *Distillery; Cliftonville (Sep.'86) 15 - 0;*
Crusaders (Jan.'88) 7 - 0; Cliftonville (Feb.'89)
92+20 - 8:
Int.Hon: **Irish League Rep:**

McGARVEY, John (D) (CARRICK RANGERS)
Born: 11.09.1976 Londonderry
Ht: 5.11 Wt: 12.00
Occupation: Nursing Assistant
Career: *Derry City (1991) 4+4 - 0; Ballymoney United*
(Jan.'95); Carrick Rangers (Sep.'95) 18+3 - 1:

McGAW, Michael (F) (ARDS)
Career: *Ards (1995) 0 - 0:*

McGEE, Paul (F) (LINFIELD)
Born: 17.05.1968 Dublin
Ht: 5.6 Wt: 9.10
Status: Professional
Career: *Bohemians; Colchester Utd. (Feb.'89) 3 - 0;*
Wimbledon (Mar.'89) 54+6 - 9; Peterborough Utd.
(Mar.'94) 5+1 - 0; Linfield (Jan.'95) 13+4 - 1;
Bohemians (Oct.'95 loan) 7 - 0:
Int.Hon: **Republic of Ireland U.21**

McDOWELL, Stephen (D) (LARNE)
Born: 12.03.1975 Ballymoney
Ht: 5.8 Wt: 10.00
Status: Professional; Occupation: Carpet Fitter
Career: *Manchester City (Jul.'91) 0 - 0; Coleraine*
(Jul.'93) 26+4 - 0; Larne (Sep.'95) 21+3 - 1:

McELROY, John (F) (OMAGH TOWN)
Born: 15.12.1974 Buncrana
Occupation: Student
Career: *Derry City 2 - 0; Omagh Town (Feb.'95)*
10+13 - 0:

McEVOY, Richard (M) (BANGOR)*
Born: 06.08.1970 Gibraltar
Status: Professional
Career: *Luton Town (Aug.'85) 0+1 - 0; Cambridge*
Utd.(Feb.'87 loan) 10+1 - 1; Shamrock Rovers (c/s'88);
Finn Harps (Feb.'91 loan) 4 - 0; Dundalk (c/s'91) 29+3
- 4; Bangor (Oct.'92) 62+8 - 4; Glentoran (c/s'95) 1+2 -
0; Bangor (Mar.'96) 7 - 1; Home Farm (Jul.'96):
Int.Hon: **Republic of Ireland U.18:**

McFADDEN, James (M) (CLIFTONVILLE)
Born: 21.03.1968 Belfast
Status: Professional
Career: *Distillery; Cliftonville (Sep.'86) 15 - 0;*
Crusaders (Jan.'88) 7 - 0; Cliftonville (Feb.'89)
92+20 - 8:
Int.Hon: **Irish League Rep:**

McGARVEY, John (D) (CARRICK RANGERS)
Born: 11.09.1976 Londonderry
Ht: 5.11 Wt: 12.00
Occupation: Nursing Assistant
Career: Derry City (1991) 4+4 - 0; Ballymoney United
(Jan.'95); Carrick Rangers (Sep.'95) 18+3 - 1:

McGAW, Michael (F) (ARDS)
Career: Ards (1995) 0 - 0:

McGEE, Paul (F) (LINFIELD)
Born: 17.05.1968 Dublin
Ht: 5.6 Wt: 10.0
Status: Professional
Career: Bohemians; Colchester Utd. (Feb.'89) 3 - 0;
Wimbledon (Mar.'89) 54+6 - 9; Peterborough Utd.
(Mar.'94) 5+1 - 0; Linfield (Jan.'95) 13+4 - 1;
Bohemians (Oct.'95 loan) 7 - 0:
Int.Hon: Republic of Ireland U.21

McGREEVY, Declan (D) (BALLYMENA UNITED)
Status: Amateur; Occupation: Civil Service
Career: Cliftonville 0 - 0; Chimney Corner (1994); Ards
(Feb.'95) 9+3 - 1; Ballymena United (c/s'96):

McGREEVY, Sean (G) (OMAGH TOWN)
Born: 04.05.1973 Belfast
Status: Amateur; Occupation: Sports Advisor
Career: Newry Town (1991); Cliftonville (1992) 0 - 0;
Donegal Celtic (1994); Ballyclare Comrades (Feb.'95)
17+1 - 0; Omagh Town (Feb.'96) 3 - 0:

McGILL, Derek (F) (GLENTORAN)*
Born: 14.10.1975 Lanark
Ht: 5.11 Wt: 11.04
Status: Professional
Career: Dunfermline Athletic; Hamilton Academical
(Jun.'93) 17+16 - 4:

McGLINCHEY, David (D) (CLIFTONVILLE)
Career: Cliftonville 0+1 - 0;
Int.Hon: N.Ireland U.18 Schools:

McGRATH, David (M) (OMAGH TOWN)
Career: Newry Town (c/s'92) 0 - 0:

McGUIGAN, John (D) (LARNE)
Career: Northern Telecom; Larne (Mar.'96) 1+1 - 0:

McGUINNESS, Raymond (D) (BANGOR)
Born: 26.04.1965 Londonderry
Status: Professional
Career: Finn Harps (1982); Crusaders; Derry City;
Finn Harps; Omagh Town (cs/'91) 15 - 0; Bangor
(Mar.'92) 17 - 1; Derry City (c/s'94); Bangor (Mar.'95)
14+2 - 0; Finn Harps (Jan.'96 loan) 8 - 0; 11+5 - 0:

McHUGH, Michael (F) (OMAGH TOWN)
Born: 03.04.1971 Donegal
Ht: 5.9 Wt: 11.07
Status: Professional
Career: Bradford City (Dec.'89) 18+13 - 4;
Scarborough (Mar.'94) 1+2 - 0; Omagh Town (Aug.'95)
23+2 - 14:

McILROY, Tommy (F) (DISTILLERY)
Born: Belfast
Status: Professional; Occupation; Baker
Career: Linfield (1992) 11+7 - 4; Distillery (Aug.'96):
Int.Hon: N.Ireland U.21; U.18; U.16; U.15:

McILWAINE, Alan (D) (BALLYCLARE COMRADES)
Career: Crusaders 0 - 0; Ballyclare Comrades (1993)
0 - 0:

McINTYRE, Emmet (F) (OMAGH TOWN)
Born: 06.08.1972 Londonderry
Career: Derry City 0+2 - 0; Omagh Town (Aug.'94)
15+14 - 5:

McIVOR, John (F) (COLERAINE)
Born: 12.07.1973 Londonderry
Ht: 5.8 Wt: 11.05
Status: Professional; Occupation: Roofer
Career: Coleraine (Aug.'89) 133+16 - 11:
Int.Hon: N.Ireland U.16:

McKEEVER, Conor (D) (COLERAINE)
Status: Amateur
Career: Portadown (c/s'92) 5+1 - 0; Coleraine
(Aug.'96):

McKEOWN, Kevin (G) (CRUSADERS)
Born: 12.10.1967 Glasgow
Ht: 6.1 Wt: 13.07
Status: Professional
Career: Wishaw Juniors; Motherwell (Aug.'85) 3 - 0;
Stenhousemuir (Nov.'86 loan) 17 - 0; Stirling Albion
(Mar.'89 loan) 1 - 0; Crusaders (Mar.'89 loan) 6 - 0;
Stenhousemuir (Aug.'89 loan) 11 - 0; Crusaders
(Dec.'90) 168 - 0:
Int.Hon: Scotland U.19; U.18; U.16; U.15; Irish
League Rep.

McKEOWN, Michael (D) (BANGOR)
Born: 03.09.1968 Belfast
Ht: 6.0 Wt: 13.08
Status: Professional; Occupation: Warehouse Supervisor
Career: Hillsborough B.C; Glenavon (Sep.'85) 151+2 -
4; Bangor (Jul.'95) 23 - 0:

McKINSTRY, Gary (F) (BANGOR)*
Born: 07.01.1972
Ht: 5.6 Wt: 11.07
Status: Professional; Occupation: Baker
Career: Portadown; Port Vale (Apr.'90); Distillery
(Jul.'92) 0 - 0; Armagh City (Nov.'92); Dungannon
Swifts (Nov.'94); Bangor (Sep.'95) 3+1 - 0; Dungannon
Swifts (Dec.'95):

McKINSTRY, John (M) (LARNE)
Born: 08.01.1966 Larne
Status: Professional
Career: Larne (1983); Carrick Rangers (Apr.'88) 0 - 0;
Larne (Sep.'88) 136+21 - 7:

McKNIGHT, Colin (F) (LARNE)
Career: Larne (1995) 6+9 - 1:

McLAUGHLIN, Eamon (F) (LARNE)
Career: Ballymena United 0 - 0; Larne (1994) 16+3 - 0:

McLAUGHLIN, Paul (D) (ARDS)
Born: 09.12.1965 Johnstone
Ht: 5.11 Wt: 13.07
Status: Professional
Career: Anniesland United; Queens Park (1983) 151+2 - 4; Celtic (May '89) 2+1 - 0; Partick Thistle (Feb.'91) 73+4 - 0; Derry City (Jul.'93); Ards (Nov.'95) 16 - 3:

McLAUGHLIN, Ryan (D) (LINFIELD)
Born: 14.02.1976
Career: Linfield 2+2 -0:
Int.Hon: N.Ireland U.16:

McLEAN, Stuart (D) (LINFIELD)
Born: 04.11.1972 East Kilbride
Ht: 5.11 Wt: 12.00
Status: Professional
Career: Hamilton Acc. B.C; Hamilton Acc. (Jun.'89) 0+3 - 0; Coleraine (Sep.'92) 82 - 6; Linfield (Jun.'95) 3 - 0:
Int.Hon: Irish League U.21 Rep.

McLEISTER, Tom (D) (CARRICK RANGERS)
Born: 04.09.1970 Ballymena
Ht: 6.2 Wt: 13.00
Occupation: Teacher
Career: Portglenone (1989); Tobermore United (1992); Carrick Rangers (Aug.'95) 24 - 1:

McLOUGHLIN, Bryan (M) (LARNE)
Born: 07.08.1960 Belfast
Status: Professional
Career: Larne; Glenavon (Mar.'88) 45+10 - 9; Ards (Dec.'90) 42+8 - 4; Larne (1994) 8+1 - 0:

McLOUGHLIN, Eamon (F) (LARNE)
Career: Ballymena United 0 - 0; Larne (1994) 7 - 0:

McMANUS, Conor (M) (CARRICK RANGERS)
Career: Carrick Rangers 0+1 - 0:

McMANUS, William (G) (LARNE)
Career: Larne (1994) 2 - 0:

McMAHON, Larry (M) (LARNE)
Ht: 6.2
Career: Ballymena United (1987) 0 - 0; Larne (Aug.'95) 24+2 - 5:

McMAHON, Maurice (F) (NEWRY TOWN)
Career: Newry Town (c/s'94) 0+3 - 0:

McMULLAN, Trevor (M) (CRUSADERS)
Born: 22.11.1965 Ballycastle
Status: Professional; Occupation: Marketing Executive
Career: Ballymena Utd. (Jul.'81); Larne (Jul.'84);

Glenavon (Jul.'92) 20+5 - 4; Coleraine (Oct.'93) 23 - 0; Ballymena Utd. (Jun.'94) 28+1 - 5; Crusaders (Jul.'95) 24+1 - 2:
Int.Hon: Irish League Rep.

McNAMARA, Jeffrey (M) (BANGOR)
Born: 10.11.1970 Bangor
Status: Amateur
Career: Bangor (c/s'91) 8+5 - 0:

McNAMEE, Damien (M) (LARNE)*
Born: 31.10.1967 Coleraine
Status: Professional
Career: Coleraine 0 - 0; Limavady Utd. (Aug.'87); Larne (Aug.'90) 109+6 - 7; Dungannon Swifts (Nov.'95); Chimney Corner (c/s'96):

McNULTY, Brian (G) (BALLYCLARE COMRADES)
Born: 03.04.1960 Belfast
Career: N.U.U; Bangor; Ballyclare Comrades; Coleraine (Aug.'90) 45 - 0; Larne (Oct.'93) 2 - 0; Ballyclare Comrades (Jan.'94) 29 - 0:

McPARLAND, IAN (F) (CLIFTONVILLE)*
Born: 04.10.1961 Edinburgh
Status: Professional
Career: Ormiston Primrose; Notts County (Dec.'80) 190 +31 - 69; Hull City (Mar.'89) 31+16 - 8; Walsall (Mar.'91 loan) 11 - 6; Dunfermline Athletic (Jul.'91) 11+5 - 2; Lincoln City (c/s'92) 3+1 - 0; Northampton (Oct.'92) 11 - 3; Eastern Athletic (HK) (Nov.'95) 3+3 - 1:

McPARLAND, Kieran (M) (NEWRY TOWN)
Status: Amateur
Career: Newry Town (1992) 21+4 - 0:

McPHERSON, Stuart (F) (BANGOR)
Career: Bangor 4+4 - 0:
Int.Hon: Irish League U.21 Rep.

McQUAID, Steve (F) (NEWRY TOWN)
Career: Camlough Rovers (c/s'95) 0 - 0:

McROBERTS, Joe (D) (CARRICK RANGERS)
Born: 11.03.1977 Belfast
Ht: 6.2 Wt: 11.00
Occupation: Store Assistant
Career: Larne (1994); Carrick Rangers (1995) 0+1 - 0:

McSHANE, Pat (D) (LINFIELD)
Career: Portadown 0 - 0; Linfield (1994) 6+2 - 0:
Int.Hon: N.Ireland U.18 Schools:

McWALTER, Mark (F) (BALLYMENA UNITED)*
Born: 20.06.1968 Arbroath
Ht: 5.11 Wt: 10.09
Status: Professional
Career: Arbroath B.C; Arbroath (1984) 61+6 - 20; St.Mirren (Jun.'87) 53+26 - 9; Partick Thistle (Jun.'91) 12+7 - 0; Coleraine (Jul.'93) 32+3 - 17; Ballymena United (Jul.'95) 19+1 - 8; Arbroath (Aug.'96):

MAGEE, Jonathon (F) (DISTILLERY)*
Born: 09.02.1972 Lurgan
Status: Professional; Occupation: Student
Career: Glenavon 0+1 - 0; Dungannon Swifts
(Oct.'89); Linfield (Jan.'90) 12+20 - 5; Bangor
(Jan.'93) 35+4 - 19; Kettering Town (Sep.'95) 0+2 - 0;
Burton Albion (loan); Portadown (Aug.'95) 1+1 - 0;
Distillery (Oct.'95) 1+2 - 0; Dungannon Swifts
(Dec.'95):
Int.Hon: N.Ireland U.21; U.18; U.17; U.16:

MAGEE, Peter (F) (NEWRY TOWN)
Born: 31.10.1967 Newry
Ht: 5.10 Wt: 11.10
Status: Professional
Career: Monaghan United (Aug.'87); Finn Harps (c/
s'91) 25 - 1; Newry Town (Sep.'92) 57+11 - 9:

MAGILL, Darryn (D) (LARNE)
Born: 11.10.1973 Larne
Career: Carrick Rangers; Q.P.R 0 - 0; Ballymena
United (Jun.'92) 19+2 - 2; R.U.C. (c/s'93); Larne (c/
s'94) 24+6 - 0:
Int.Hon: N.Ireland U.18; U.16; U.16 Schools:

MAGILL, Mark (M) (DISTILLERY)
Born: 09.10.1978 Belfast
Status: Amateur; Occupation: Courier
Career: St.Andrews Boys; Linfield (Aug.'94) 0 - 0;
Distillery (Sep.'95) 1+3 - 0:
Int.Honours: N.Ireland U.16:

MAGILL, Michael (D) (OMAGH TOWN)
Ht: 5.11 Wt: 11.07
Status: Amateur; Occupation: Engineer
Career: Coleraine 7+2 - 0; Limavady Utd (Oct.'92);
Omagh Town (Aug.'94) 51+1 - 0:

MAJOR, Philip (D) (PORTADOWN)
Born: 03.02.1968 Belfast
Status: Professional; Occupation: Bank Official
Career: Glentoran (1984) 1+1 - 0; Portadown (c/s'88)
189 - 8:

MALONEY, Kyle (M) (COLERAINE)*
Career: Derry City; Coleraine (Jun.'95) 0+5 - 0; Ards
(Nov.'95 loan) 4 - 1; Institute (c/s'96):

MANLEY, Ron (F) (CLIFTONVILLE)*
Born: 18.08.1961 Belfast
Status: Professional
Career: Glentoran (1977) 143+24 - 59; Morwell
Falcons (c/s'89); Glentoran (Mar.'90) 6+8 - 1;
Cliftonville (Dec.'92) 57+15 - 14; Dundela (c/s'96):
Int.Hon: N.Ireland U.18; U.15

MARKS, Jamie (D) (LINFIELD)*
Born: 18.03.1977 Belfast
Ht: 5.9 Wt: 10.13
Status: Professional
Career: Leeds United; 0 - 0; Linfield (Oct.'95) 1+3 - 0;
Hull City (loan) 4 - 0; Hull City (c/s'96):
Int.Hon: N.Ireland U.18; U.17; U.16; U.15:

MASSEY, Andrew (F) (BANGOR)
Career: Bangor 0 - 0:

MATHIESON, Andy (M) (GLENTORAN)
Born: 09.07.1967 Belfast
Ht: 5.7 Wt: 11.00
Status: Professional; Occupation: Postman
Career: Manchester Utd 0 - 0; Crewe Alex. 0 - 0;
Glentoran (Nov.'85) 104+28 - 19:
Int.Hon: N.Ireland U.18:

MAUCHLEN, Ally (M) (BALLYMENA UNITED)
Born: 29.06.1960 Kilwinning
Ht: 5.8 WT: 11.10
Status: Professional; Occupation: Footballer
Career: Irvine Meadow; Kilmarnock (Aug.'78) 115+8 -
10; Motherwell (Oct.'82) 75+1 - 4; Leicester City
(Aug.'85) 228+11 - 11; Leeds Utd. (Mar.'92 loan) 0 - 0;
Hearts (Jul.'92) 16+2 - 0; Glenavon (Nov.'93 loan) 15 -
0; Glenavon (Jul.'94) 12+1 - 0; Ballymena United
(Aug.'95) 13+2 - 0:

MAY, Andy (M) (LARNE)*
Born: 26.02.1964 Bury
Ht: 5.8 Wt: 11.00
Status: Professional
Career: Manchester City (Mar.'82) 141+9 - 8;
Huddersfield Town (Jul.'87) 112+2 - 5; Bolton
Wanderers (Mar.'88 loan) 9+1 - 2; Bristol City (Aug.'90)
88+2 - 4; Millwall (Jun.'92) 49+5 - 1; Larne (Oct.'95)
10 - 1:
Int.Hon: England U.21:

MAY, Dean (G) (CARRICK RANGERS)
Occupation: Civil Servant
Career: Ards (1994) 2 - 0; Ballymena United (c/s'95) 0 -
0; R.U.C. (Feb.'96); Carrick Rangers (Mar.'96) 0 - 0:

MEEHAN, Barry (F) (PORTADOWN)
Born: 16.05.1973 Newry
Status: Professional
Career: Portadown (1989) 13+9 - 5:

MELLON, Graham (D) (BALLYCLARE COMRADES)
Born: 26.07.1970 Antrim
Career: Ballymena United; Glentoran (Aug.'91) 0 - 0;
Ballymena United (Mar.'92) 3+1 - 1; F.C.Enkalon (c/
s'93); Moyola Park (c/s'95); Ballyclare Comrades
(Feb.'96) 8 - 0:

MELLON, Stuart (D) (CRUSADERS)
Born: 23.05.1974 Bangor
Ht: 5.9 Wt: 10.08
Status: Amateur
Career: Bangor 0 - 0; Crusaders (1994) 1+1 - 0; Central
AFC (NZ loan):

MELLY, Nigel (D) (OMAGH TOWN)
Born: 13.10.1971 Londonderry
Ht: 6.4 Wt:13.03
Status: Professional
*Career: **Derry City** 2+2 - 0; **Celtic** (Jun.'91) 0 - 0;*
***Bangor** (May.'94) 7+1 - 0; **Omagh Town** (Jan.'96)*
13 - 1:

MENDES, Junior (M) (BANGOR)*
Born: 15.09.1976 Balham
Ht: 5.8 Wt: 10.00
Status: Professional
*Career: **Chelsea** 0 - 0; **Bangor** (Oct.'95 loan) 4 - 0:*

MILLAR, Keith (M) (CARRICK RANGERS)
Born: 19.11.1977 Belfast
Ht: 5.8 Wt: 11.00
Occupation: Student
*Career: **Linfield** (1993) 0 - 0; **Carrick Rangers** (1995)*
0+3 - 0:
*Int.Hon: **N.Ireland U.18 Schools; U.16; U.15:***

MILLAR, Paul (F) (LINFIELD)
Born: 16.11.1966 Belfast
Ht: 6.2 Wt: 12.07
Status: Professional
*Career: **Glentoran** 33+7 - 12; **Portadown** (c/s'87) 31+1*
*- 10; **Port Vale** (Dec.'88) 19+21 - 5; **Hereford United***
*(Oct.'90 loan) 5 - 2; **Cardiff City** (Aug.'91) 91+ 29 - 17;*
***Linfield** (Aug.'95) 15+2 - 7:*
*Int.Hon: **N.Ireland 'B'; U.23; U.21:***

MISKELLY, Paul (G) (BANGOR)
Born: 18.06.971 Newtownards
Ht: 5.10 Wt: 13.00
Status: Amateur; Occupation: Storeman
*Career: **Bangor Amateurs** (Sep.'85); **Harland & Wolff***
***Welders** (Aug.'90); **Carrick Rangers** (c/s'93) 38 - 0;*
***Bangor** (Sep.'95) 11 - 0:*

MITCHELL, Neill (D) BALLYCLARE COMRADES)
*Career: **Carrick Rangers** 2+1 - 0; **Larne** (c/s '88) 0 - 0;*
***Larne Tech Old Boys; Ballyclare Comrades** (Aug.'95) 0*
- 0:

MITCHELL, Philip (M) (DISTILLERY)
Born: 03.06.1968 Belfast
Status: Professional; Occupation: Sales Rep.
*Career: **Ards** (Mar.'86) 1+4 - 0; **Dunmurry Rec.***
*(Jan.'88); **Linfield** (Jan.'89) 9+8 - 0; **Ipswich Town***
*(Jul.'90) 0 - 0; **Portadown** (Jun.'91) 11+4 - 1; **Distillery***
(Mar.'92) 101+5 - 26:

Kevin Moore

MOORE, Kevin (D) (OMAGH TOWN)
Ht: 5.11 Wt; 12.02
Occupation: Factory Operative
*Career: **Coleraine** 6 - 1; **Ballymoney Utd.** (Dec.'90);*
***Omagh Town** (Aug.'94) 36+3 - 0:*

MOORE, Robert (F) (DISTILLERY)
Born: 20.07.1972 Antrim
Ht: 5.9 Wt: 10.07
Status: Amateur; Occupation: Joiner
*Career: **Millgreen; Glentoran** (Apr.'93) 0+5 - 0;*
***Distillery** (Oct.'95) 12+10 - 2:*

MOONEY, Martin (M) (OMAGH TOWN)
Ht: 5.6 Wt: 10.00
Occupation: Student
*Career: **Oxford Utd.Stars; Omagh Town** (Aug.'94)*
49+1 - 16:
*Int.Hon: **Irish League U.21 Rep.***

MOONEY, Paul (D) (ARDS)
Born: 10.12.1962 Belfast
Ht: 5.10 Wt: 12.00
Status: Professional; Occupation: Newsagent
*Career: **Linfield** (1979) 153+9 - 8; **Derry City** (May.'91)*
*53+1 - 2;**Ards** (Jul.'93) 64+1 - 3:*
*Int.Hon: **Irish League Rep.***

MOONEY, Thomas (M) (NEWRY TOWN)
Born: 14.12.1973 Newry
Ht: 5.11 Wt: 11.02
Status: Professional
*Career: **Brookvale; Woodside; Celtic Boys; Newry Town***
*0 - 0; **Huddersfield Town** (Jul.'90) 1 - 0; **Glentoran***
*(Aug.'93) 12+5 - 1; **Newry Town** (Oct.'94) 38+4 - 2:*
*Int.Hon: **N.Ireland U.18; U.16; U.16 Schools:***

MOORE, Colin (F) (BALLYMENA UNITED)
Born: 10.10.1974 Ballymena
Occupation: Joiner
*Career: **Cullybackey Blues; Ballymena United** (Aug.'91)*
*2+6 - 0; **Connor; Ballymena United** (c/s'95) 7+2 - 3:*

MOORE, David (D) (BALLYMENA UNITED)
Career: *Dundela*(c/s'93); *Ballymena United* (Jul.'95)
9+4 - 0:

MOORE, Kevin (D) (OMAGH TOWN)
Ht: 5.11 Wt; 12.02
Occupation: Factory Operative
Career: *Coleraine* 6 - 1; *Ballymoney Utd.* (Dec.'90);
Omagh Town (Aug.'94) 36+3 - 0:

MOORE, Robert (F) (DISTILLERY)
Born: 20.07.1972 Antrim
Ht: 5.9 Wt: 10.07
Status: Amateur; Occupation: Joiner
Career: *Millgreen*; *Glentoran* (Apr.'93) 0+5 - 0;
Distillery (Oct.'95) 12+10 - 2:

MOORS, Chris (F) (BALLYMENA UNITED)*
Born: 18.08.1976 Yeovil
Status: Professional
Career: *West Ham United* 0 - 0; *Ballymena United*
(Feb.'96 loan) 3 - 2; *Torquay United* 0+1 - 0:

MORAN, Peter (F) (OMAGH TOWN)*
Status: Amateur; Occupation: Nursing Assistant
Career: *Gransha Hospital*; *Oxford United Stars* (1988);
Limavady United (c/s'90); *Oxford United Stars*
(Oct.'90); *Limavady United* (c/s'91); *Ballyclare
Comrades* (Jun.'94) 24+2 - 6; *Omagh Town* (c/s'95)
0+1 - 0; *Limavady United* (Oct.'95):

MORGAN, Chris (F) (CRUSADERS)
Born: 11.01.1976 Belfast
Ht: 5.11 Wt: 11.00
Status: Amateur; Occupation: Student
Career: *Lisburn Youth*; *Bangor* 0 - 0; *Saintfield Utd.*
(1993); *Crusaders* (c/s'94) 1+8 - 1:
Int.Hon: *N.Ireland U.18 Schools:*

**MORRISON, Allan (D) (BALLYCLARE
COMRADES)**
Born: 22.09.1964 Belfast
Status: Amateur; Occupation: Shipping Manager
Career: *Ballyclare Comrades*; *Bangor*; *Coleraine* (c/
s'88) 40+2 - 2; *Ards* (Sep.'90) 47+6 - 1; *Coleraine*
(May.'93) 10 - 0; *Distillery* (Dec.'93) 0+2 - 0;
Moyola Park (Mar.'94); *Ballyclare Comrades*
(Jun.'94) 48+1 - 0:

MORRISON, Raymond (M) (ARDS)
Born: 06.03.1962 Belfast
Status: Professional
Career: *Glentoran* (Aug.'81) 212+15 - 66; *Ards*
(Sep.'94) 50+3 - 4:
Int.Hon: *Irish League Rep.*

MORROW, Keith (F) (BANGOR)
Career: *Linfield* 0 - 0; *Bangor* (c/s'94) 7+21 - 1:

MUIR, Paul (D) (BALLYMENA UNITED)
Career: *Ballymena Utd.* (1993) 23+3 - 0:

MULDOON, John (D) (CARRICK RANGERS)
Born: 12.01.1962 Belfast
Ht: 6.0 Wt: 12.10
Status: Professional; Occupation: Taxi Driver
Career: *Cliftonville* (1979); *Bangor* (Mar.'91) 51 - 0;
Ballyclare Comrades (c/s'93) 25 - 0; *Carrick Rangers*
(Nov.'94) 36+3 - 3:
Int.Hon: *N.Ireland U.18; Irish League Rep.*

MULHOLLAND, Shane (D) (GLENAVON)
Born: 18.05.1976 Newry
Ht: 6.0 Wt: 12.00
Status: Amateur; Occupation: Student
Career: *Newry Town* (Sep.'90) 0 - 0; *Portadown*
(Sep.'91)

0 - 0; *Glenavon* (Oct.'95) 1+4 - 0:
Int.Hon: *N.Ireland U.18 Schools*

MURPHY, Alan (D) (GLENAVON)
Born: 28.01.1975 Belfast
Ht: 6.1 Wt: 12.07
Status: Amateur; Occupation: Insurance Underwriter
Career: *Bangor* (May.'92) 0 - 0; *Glenavon* (May.'95)
4+1 - 0:
Int.Hon: *N.Ireland U.18 Schools:*

MURPHY, William (D) (ARDS)
Born: 29.01.1974 Belfast
Ht: 6.0 Wt: 12.07
Status: Amateur; Occupation: Laboratory Technician
Career: *Carrick Rangers* (1990) 11+4 - 1; *Ards* (Jul.'92)
44+14 - 2:

MURPHY, Darren (M) (GLENAVON)
Born: 23.01.1975 Portadown
Ht: 5.10 Wt: 10.04
Occupation: Factory Worker
Career: *Portadown* (Jun.'88) 2+2 - 0; *Glenavon*
(Jul.'95) 18+8 - 3:

MURRAY, Gary (M) (LARNE)*
Born: 25.08.1971
Status: Amateur
Career: *Crusaders* (Aug.'92) 0+5 - 1; *Larne* (Jun.'95) 0
- 0; *Loughgall* (Apr.'96):

MURRAY, Jim (F) (ARDS)
Born: 04.08.1970 Belfast
Status: Amateur
Career: *Distillery* (1988) 1+1 - 0; *Crusaders* (Dec.'90) 0
- 0; *Cliftonville* (c/s'92) 0 - 0; *Derry City* (1993) 1+1 - 0;
Distillery (Feb.'94) 1+10 - 0; *Ards* (Jan.'96) 0 - 0:

MURRAY, Martin (M) (CRUSADERS)
Born: 06.10.1958 Dublin
Ht: 5.11 Wt: 12.04
Status: Professional
Career: *Home Farm*; *Everton* (1975) 0 - 0; *Drogheda
Utd.* (Jan.'80); *Dundalk*; *Ashtown Villa*; *St.Pats.
Athletic*; *Crusaders* (Jul.'91) 126+8 - 11:
Int.Hon: *Republic of Ireland U.21; U.18; U.15; League
of Ireland Rep.*

MURRAY, Noel (D) (LARNE)
Born: 29.12.1968 Belfast
Status: Professional
Career: Glentoran 0 - 0; Newry Town (Nov.'89) 30+3 - 0; Derry City (Oct.'92) 24+2 - 0; Cliftonville (Nov.'93) 7+4 - 0; Larne (Feb.'95) 22+3 - 0:

MURRAY, Peter (M) (BALLYMENA UNITED)
Born: 11.11.1963 Belfast
Status: Professional; Occupation: Crane Driver
Career: Glenavon (1979); Cliftonville (1982); Portadown (Dec.'91) 85+10 - 8; Ballymena United (Oct.'95) 21 - 6:
Int.Hon: Irish League Rep.

MURTAGH, Jason (M) (BANGOR)*
Born: 01.05.1970
Ht: 5.11 Wt: 10.08
Occupation: Machine Operative
Career: Coagh United; Newry Town (Mar.'90) 1+2 - 0; Armagh City (Jan.'91); Ballyclare Comrades (Nov.'94) 19+1 - 5; Bangor (Jul.'95) 5+2 - 0; Loughgall (Jan.'96):

NEILL, George (D) (GLENTORAN)
Born: 30.09.1962 Belfast
Ht: 5.9 Wt: 12.10
Status: Professional; Occupation: Teacher
Career: Glentoran (Sep.'78) 259+2 - 1:
Int.Hon: N.Ireland U.18; Irish League Rep.

NEILLY, Kenny (F) (BALLYCLARE COMRADES)
Career: Broadway Celtic; Ballyclare Comrades (Oct.'95) 2+6 - 0:

NELSON, Dean (M) (BANGOR)
Born: 28.03.1973 Belfast
Status: Professional
Career: Ards 0 - 0; Bangor (c/s'89) 33+15 - 4:
Int.Hon: N.Ireland U.16:

NIXON, Colin (D) (GLENTORAN)
Born: 08.09.1978
Ht: 5.11
Status: Amateur; Occupation: Student
Career: St.Andrews Boys Club; Glentoran 24 - 2:
Int. Hon: N.Ireland U.18 Schools; U.16; U.15:

NORBURY, Mike (F) (LINFIELD)*
Born: 22.01.1969 Hemsworth
Ht: 6.1 Wt: 11.10
Status: Professional
Career: Ossett Town (1987); Scarborough (Dec.'89); Ossett Town (1990); Bridlington; Cambridge United (Feb.'92) 11+15 - 3; Preston North End (Dec.'92) 32+10 - 13; Doncaster Rovers (Nov.'94) 19+8 - 5; Linfield (Nov.'95 loan) 1 - 0; Stafford Rangers:

O'BRIEN, Donal (M) (CRUSADERS)
Born: 10.11.1967 Dublin
Ht: 6.1 Wt: 12.07
Status: Professional; Occupation: Football Coach
Career: Croatia (Aus); Derry City (1990) 54+12 - 21; Woolongong Wolves (Aus) (c/s'93); Derry City (Nov.'93) 16+1 - 3; Glentoran (Aug.'94) 17+5 - 4; Crusaders (Aug.'95) 20+2 - 2:

O'CONNELL, Patrick (F) (BANGOR)
Born: 07.10.1973 Dublin
Ht: 5.9 Wt: 11.02
Status: Professional
Career: Home Farm 3 - 1; Leeds Utd. (Jul.'91) 0 - 0; St.Pats.Athletic (Jan.'93) 10+2 - 2; Athlone Town (Jan.'94 loan) 8+1 - 1; Ballyclare Comrades (Oct.'94) 24 - 8; Bangor (May '95) 13+9 - 2:

O'CONNOR, Pat (F) (BALLYCLARE COMRADES)
Occupation: P.E.Teacher
Career: Larne (1993) 2 - 0; U.U.J; Ballyclare Comrades (Jul.'95) 14 - 3:

O'DONNELL, Francis (F) (OMAGH TOWN)
Status: Amateur
Career: Park; Coleraine (Jun.'95)0+1 - 1; Omagh Town (Dec.'95) 0+1 - 0:

O'DONNELL, Mark (F) (OMAGH TOWN)
Born: 09.10.1973 Lisnaskea
Status: Amateur; Occupation: Trainee Accountant
Career: Portadown (1989) 0 - 0; Omagh Town (Jul.'92) 10+1 - 3; Ballinamallard Utd. (c/s'94); Omagh Town (Nov.'94) 19+3 - 6:
Int.Hon: N.Ireland U.16; U.15:

O'DOWD, Greg (F) (COLERAINE)
Born: 16.03.1973 Dublin
Career: Brighton & Hove Albion; Longford Town (c/s'92) 27 - 4; Dundalk (c/s'93) 28 - 2; Shamrock Rovers (1994); Coleraine (Oct.'95 loan; Nov.'95) 22+1 - 7:

O'HARE, Colin (G) (NEWRY TOWN)
Career: Newry Town (c/s'94) 1 - 0:

O'HARE, David (G) (COLERAINE)
Born: 02.03.1972 Newry
Ht: 5.10 Wt: 13.05
Status: Professional; Occupation: Student
Career: Newry Town 0 - 0; U.U.C. (Oct.'90); Coleraine (Oct.'91) 114 - 0:

O'KANE, Barry (F) (NEWRY TOWN)
Status: Amateur
Career: Newry Town (1993) 25+6 - 0:

O'KANE, Ciaran (F) (NEWRY TOWN)
Born: 27.01.1972 Craigavon
Status: Professional
Career: Glenavon 9 - 1; Portadown (c/s'92) 0 - 0; Newry Town (c/s'93) 63+4 - 5:
Int.Hon: N.Ireland U.18 Schools; U.16:

O'NEILL, Dermot (G) (GLENAVON)
Born: 27.11.1960 Dublin
Ht: 5.10 Wt: 12.12
Status: Professional
Career: Dundalk; Bohemians (Jul.'81); Derry City (c/
s'91) 129 - 0; Glenavon (May '95) 25 - 0:

O'NEILL, Donal (D) (OMAGH TOWN)
Born: 23.10.1963 Londonderry
Status: Amateur; Occupation: Factory Operative
Career: Moyola Park; Omagh Town (Jul.'92) 4+8 - 0;
Moyola Park (Aug.'93); Omagh Town (c/s'94) 5+17 - 0:

O'NEILL, Kevin (D) (OMAGH TOWN)*
Born: 04.12.1965 Londonderry
Status: Professional
Career: Limavady United (1983); Derry City (1985);
Finn Harps (1988); Ballymena United (Aug.'89) 4+1 -
0; Roe Valley; Tobermore United (Jan.'91); Omagh
Town (Oct.'91) 26+5 - 3; Moyola Park (Mar.'94);
Omagh Town (c/s'95)
0 - 0: Int.Hon: N.Ireland U.18:

O'NEILL, Mark (M) (CLIFTONVILLE)
Born: 04.10.1972 Dublin
Ht: 5.8 Wt: 10.12
Status: Professional
Career: Leyton Orient (Mar.'91) 0 - 0; St.Pats Athletic
(c/s'93) 25+1 - 1; Ballymena United (Oct.'94 loan) 5- 0;
Cliftonville (Mar.'95 loan) 4+2 - 1; Cliftonville (c/s'95)
17+7 - 1:

O'SHEA, Larry (M) (ARDS)
Career: Shelbourne; Ards (Jul.'95) 0 - 0:

O'SULLIVAN, Gary (M) (ARDS)
Born: 15.02.1969 Dublin
Ht: 5.11 Wt: 11.00
Status: Professional; Occupation: Consulting Engineer
Career: Leicester Celtic; U.C.D; (Jul.'86); Shamrock
Rovers (c/s'92) 15+5 - 0; Cobh Ramblers (Jan.'94 loan)
8+2 - 2; Ards (Oct.'94 loan) 22+2 - 3; Ards (Jul.'95)
9+11 - 0:

OATWAY, Charlie (M) (COLERAINE)*
Born: 28.11.1973 Hammersmith
Ht: 5.7 Wt: 10.10
Status: Professional
Career: Yeading (1990); Cardiff City (Aug.'94) 29+3 -
0; Coleraine (Aug.'95 loan) 0 - 0; Torquay (Dec.'95) 24
- 0:

ORCHIN, Paul (F) (BALLYCLARE COMRADES)
Career: Ballyclare Comrades 4+2 - 2:

PARKER, Darren (D) (GLENTORAN)
Born: 25.08.1974 Ballymena
Ht: 5.9 Wt: 10.03
Status: Amateur; Occupation: Student
Career: Ballymena Utd. (1991) 0 - 0; Glentoran (1992)
48+11 - 2:
Int.Hon: N.Ireland U.18 Schools; U.15:

PATTERSON, Mark (G) (COLERAINE)
Occupation: Student
Career: Watford 0 - 0; Islandmagee; Coleraine (Mar.'96)
0 - 0:

PATTON, Barry (F) (BALLYMENA UNITED)
Born: 22.12.1972 Lifford
Ht: 5.10 Wt: 10.00
Status: Professional
Career: Lifford Celtic; Finn Harps (Sep.'89); Omagh
Town (Nov.'92) 49+1 - 24; Ballymena Utd. (Aug.'94)
29+10 - 11:
Int.Hon: Republic of Ireland U.16:

PATTON, David (F) (LARNE)
Born: 19.03.1976 Coleraine
HT: 6.1 Wt: 12.00
Status: Amateur; Occupation: Student
Career: Killowen Youth; Coleraine (1992) 7+10 - 0;
Larne (c/s'96):

PEEBLES, Gary (M) (PORTADOWN)
Born: 06.02.1967 Johnstone
Ht: 5.11 Wt: 12.09
Status: Professional
Career: Gleniffer Thistle; St.Mirren (1984) 7+1 - 0;
Partick Thistle (Jan.'89) 69+11 - 5; Portadown (Jan.'92
loan) 10+2 - 4; Linfield (May.'93) 48+2 - 14; Portadown
(Jul.'95) 22+1 - 1:

PERCY, Keith (M) (BANGOR)
Born: 07.05.1970 Belfast
Ht: 5.11 Wt: 12.00
Status: Amateur; Occupation: Plumber
Career: New Century; Glenavon 0+1 - 0; Armagh City
(Sep.'89); Glenavon (Jan.'92) 36+9 - 5; Bangor
(Jun.'95) 14 - 1:

PHILSON, Graeme (D) (COLERAINE)*
Born: 24.03.1975 Londonderry
Ht: 6.0 Wt: 11.02
Status: Professional; Occupation: Student
Career: Coleraine (1991)19+13 - 0; Limavady Utd.
(Aug.'94 loan); West Ham United (Dec.'95) 0 - 0:
Int.Hon: N.Ireland U.18 Schools; Irish League U.21
Rep.

PRESS, Michael (CARRICK RANGERS)*
Born: 12.11.1969 Belfast
Ht: 5.9 Wt: 11.00
Status: Amateur; Occupation: Storeman
Career: Cliftonville (1986) 8+4 - 0; Ballyclare Comrades
(c/s'89) 10+4 - 0; Chimney Corner (c/s'91); Cookstown
Utd. (c/s'92); Carrick Rangers (c/s'93) 10+6 - 0;
Chimney Corner (Nov.'95):
Int.Hon: N.Ireland U.16; U.15:

QUIGG, John (OMAGH TOWN)*
Born: 23.07.1965 Londonderry
Status: Professional; Occupation: Family Business
Career: Derry City; Coleraine (Aug.'89) 0 - 0; Finn
Harps (Sep.'89); Derry City (Oct.'92) 2 - 0; Omagh
Town (Aug.'93) 66+1 - 2; Finn Harps (Jan.'96) 7+2 - 0:

QUIGLEY, James (M) (GLENTORAN)
Born: 21.09.1976 Londonderry
Ht: 5.8 Wt: 12.00
Status: Professional; Occupation: Footballer
*Career: **Everton** (May.'94) 0 - 0; **Derry City** (c/s'94) 15+2 - 1; **Glentoran** (Jan.'95) 27+3 - 0:*
*Int.Hon: **N.Ireland U.15; Republic of Ireland U.18; U.16:***

QUINN, Joe (M) (CLIFTONVILLE)
*Career: **Cliftonville** 0+1 - 0:*

RAE, Derek (M) (PORTADOWN)*
Born: 02.08.1974 Glasgow
Ht: 5.10 Wt: 10.10
Status: Professional
*Career: **Rangers Boys Club; Rangers** (Jul.'91) 0 - 0; **Motherwell** (Sep.'94) 0 - 0; **Portadown** (Feb.'96 loan) 2 - 0:*

RALPH, Ollie (F) (NEWRY TOWN)
Born: 08.10.1957 Dundalk
Status: Professional
*Career: **Dundalk; Newry Town** (Aug.'83):*
*Int.Hon: **Irish League Rep.***

RAMIREZ, Colin (M) (DISTILLERY)
Born: 01.02.1971 Gibraltar
Status: Professional; Occupation: Shipping Clerk
*Career: **Recreativo Linense** (Aug.'89); **Glentoran** (Jul.'93) 13+1 - 0; **Recreativo Linense** (Aug.'94); **Crusaders** (Dec.'95) 0 - 0; **Distillery** (Mar.'96) 3 - 0:*

RAMSEY, Paul (M) (CLIFTONVILLE)*
Born: 03.09.1962 Londonderry
Ht: 5.11 Wt: 13.00
Status: Professional
*Career: **Derry Athletic; Leicester City** (Apr.'80) 278+12 - 13; **Cardiff City** (Aug.'91) 69 - 7; **St.Johnstone** (Oct.'93) 31+2 - o; **Cardiff City** (Nov.'94 loan) 11 - 0; **Cliftonville** (Aug.'95) 0 - 0; **Telford United** (Aug.'95); **Torquay United** (Nov.'95) 18 - 0:*
*Int.Hon: **N.Ireland International 14 caps; U.15:***

REES, Nigel (F) (NEWRY TOWN)
Status: Amateur
*Career: **Newry Town** (1992) 0+4 - 0:*

RICE, Paul (G) (CLIFTONVILLE)
Born: 12.08.1970
*Career: **Drumaness Mills; Cliftonville** (1989) 119 - 1:*

RICHARDSON, Noel (D) (DISTILLERY)*
Born: 19.12.1971 Portadown
Status: Amateur; Occupation: Electrician
*Career: **Portadown** (1988) 0 - 0; **Hanover** (1991) 0 - 0; **Distillery** (Dec.'93) 5+2 - 0; **Armagh City** (Jan.'96):*

ROBINSON, Robert (G) (LINFIELD)
Ht: 5.11 Wt: 11.07
Status: Amateur
*Career: **Distillery** 0 - 0; **Larne** (1993) 47+1 - 0; **Linfield** (Aug.'96):*

ROBSON, Brian (F) (BANGOR)
Born: 29.09.1967 Newtownards
Ht: 6.0 Wt: 13.05
Status: Amateur; Occupation: Laundry Worker
*Career: **Portadown** (Aug.'86) 0+2 - 0; **Fisher Body** (1987); **Glenavon** (Aug.'90) 0 - 0; **Harland & W.W.** (Jan.'91); **Carrick Rangers** (Jan.'93) 52+3 - 30; **Coleraine** (Feb.'95) 10 - 1; **Distillery** (Sep.'95)16+8 - 4; **Bangor** (Aug.'96):*

ROGAN, Stephen (D) (DISTILLERY)
Born: 08.01.1974 Downpatrick
Status: Amateur; Occupation: Fitter
*Career: **Ards** (1988) 0 - 0; **Killyleagh Youth Club** (Jul.'92); **Distillery** (Jul.'94) 3+1 - 0:*

RUSSELL, Alex (M) (GLENAVON)*
Born: 17.03.1973 Crosby
Ht: 5.11 Wt: 11.07
Status: Professional
*Career: **Liverpool** (1989) 0 - 0; **Stockport County** (1991); **Morecombe** (1992); **Burscough; Rochdale** (Jul.'94) 22+10 - 1; **Glenavon** (Nov.'95 loan) 4 - 0:*

RUSSELL, Martin (M) (PORTADOWN)
Born: 27.04.1967 Dublin
Ht: 5.9 Wt: 10.05
Status: Professional; Occupation: Footballer
*Career: **Belvedere Y.C; Manchester Utd.** (May.'84) 0 - 0; **Birmingham City** (Oct.'86 loan) 3+2 - 0; **Norwich City** (Jan.'87 loan) 0 - 0; **Leicester City** (Mar.'87) 13+7 - 0; **Scarborough** (Feb.'89) 51 - 9; **Middlesbrough** (Mar.'90) 10+1 - 2; **Portadown** (Aug.'91) 118+3 - 26:*
*Int.Hon: **Republic of Ireland 'B'; U.23; U.21; U.18; Irish League Rep.***

SAVAGE, Mark (M) (PORTADOWN)
Born: 14.04.1977 Lurgan
Ht: 5.11 Wt: 11.07
Occupation: Student
*Career: **Lurgan Town; Glenavon** (Feb.'93) 0 - 0; **Portadown** 0 - 0:*

Tony Scappaticci

SCAPPATICCI, Anthony (D) (NEWRY TOWN)
Born: 07.11.1968 Banbridge
Ht: 5.9 Wt: 11.00
Status: Professional; Occupation: Plasterer

Career: **Banbridge Town; Limerick C; Portadown** *0 - 0;*
Banbridge Town; Glenavon *(Mar. '89)* **128 - 4; Newry
Town** *(Sep. '95 loan)* *0 - 0;* **Newry Town** *(Jan. '96 loan)* *7 -
0;* **Newry Town** *(c/s '96):*
Int.Hon: **Irish League Rep.**

SCAPPATICCI, Fred (D) (NEWRY TOWN)
Career: **Banbridge Town; Ards** *(Apr. '90)* *5 - 0;*
Banbridge Town *(c/s '91);* **Newry Town** *(c/s '95)* *22 - 0:*

SHANLEY, Dwaine (M) (ARDS)
Career: **Sligo Rovers** *8+1 - 1;* **Ards** *(c/s '95)* *20+4 - 1:*

SHEPHERD, Anthony (M) (GLENAVON)
Born: 16.11.1966 Glasgow
Ht: 5.9 Wt: 10.07
Status: Professional
Career: **Celtic B.C; Celtic** *16+12 - 3;* **Bristol City**
(Dec. '88 loan) *2+1 - 0;* **Carlisle Utd.** *(Jul. '89)* *73+2 - 8;*
Motherwell *(Jul. '91)* *3+7 - 0;* **Portadown** *(Jul. '93)* *34 -
4;* **Ayr United** *(Aug. '95)* *10+1 - 0;* **Stranraer** *(Jan. '96)* *2 -
0;* **Glenavon** *(Feb. '96)* *11 - 0:*
Int.Hon: **Scotland U.18; U.15:**

SHERIDAN, Declan (M) (OMAGH TOWN)
Career: **Finn Harps; Omagh Town** *0 - 0:*

SHERIDAN, Ryan (M) (OMAGH TOWN)
Career: **Glenavon** *0 - 0;* **Omagh Town** *(Aug. '95)* *0+1 - 0:*

SHIELDS, John (D) (NEWRY TOWN)
Career: **Newry Town** *(1995)* *1+3 - 1:*

SHIELDS, Matthew (F) (NEWRY TOWN)
Career: **Park View; Newry Town** *(Mar. '96)* *2 - 0:*

SHIELS, Sammy (F) (COLERAINE)
Born: 01.03.1966 Magherafelt
Status: Amateur; Occupation: Factory Worker
Career: **Ballymena Utd** *0 - 0;* **Tobermore Utd** *(c/s '88);*
Ards *(Aug. '90)16+7 - 11;* **Dungannon Swifts** *(Aug. '91);*
Carrick Rangers *(May. '92)* *69+1 - 34;* **Tobermore
United** *(Aug. '95);* **Coleraine** *(Sep. '95)* *26+1 - 25:*

SHIPP, Danny (F) (GLENAVON)*
Born: 25.09.1976 Romford
Ht: 5.11 Wt: 11.13
Status: Professional
Career: **West Ham United** *0 - 0;* **Dagenham** *(loan);*
Glenavon *(Feb. '96 loan)* *9 - 6:*

SIMPSON, Derek (M) (BANGOR)*
Born: 23.12.1978 Lanark
Ht: 5.10 Wt: 10.09
Status: Professional
Career: **Reading** *0 - 0;* **Bangor** *(Dec. '95)* *3 - 0:*

SIMPSON, Mark (M) (ARDS)*
Born: 04.11.1975 Aberdeen
Ht: 6.0 Wt: 12.02
Status: Professional
Career: **Greenock Juniors; Greenock Morton** *(Apr. '95)*
0 - 0; **Ards** *(Aug. '95 loan)* *1+2 - 0:*

SINCLAIR, Hugh, (D) (CARRICK RANGERS)
Born: 20.01.1967 Belfast
Ht: 5.11 Wt: 12.00
Status: Amateur; Occupation: Youth Worker
Career: **Dunmurry Rec; Carrick Rangers** *(Feb. '95)*
28+4 - 7:

SLINEY, Gary (M) (CLIFTONVILLE)*
Born: 02.09.1973 Dublin
Ht: 5.10 Wt: 12.03
Status: Professional
Career: **Home Farm; Manchester City** *(Aug. '90)* *0 - 0;*
Bangor *(Sep. '93)* *0+1 - 0:* **Cliftonville** *(Sep. '93)* *70+2 -
5;* **Home Farm** *(Aug. '96):*
Int.Hon: **Republic of Ireland U.18; U.16; Irish League
U.21 Rep.**

Stephen Small

SMALL, Stephen (M) (CLIFTONVILLE)
Born: 28.05.1969 Belfast
Status: Amateur; Occupation: Youth Worker
Career: **Star of the Sea; Cliftonville** *(Aug. '84)* *1+2 - 0;*
USA (1988); **Distillery** *(Aug. '93)* *43+9 - 4;* **Cliftonville**
(Jun. '96):

SMITH, Trevor (F) (GLENTORAN)
Born: 06.05.1965 Whitburn
Ht: 5.10 Wt: 12.00
Status: Professional; Occupation: Footballer
Career: **Sauchie Juveniles; Dunfermline Ath.** *(Jun. '82)*
75+50 - 14; **Hamilton Acc.** *(Feb. '90 loan)* *3 - 2;*
Kilmarnock *(Feb. '91)* *9+4 - 1;* **Hamilton Acc.** *(Aug. '91)*
47+10 - 21; **Portadown** *(Aug. '93)* *26+1 - 19;* **Glentoran**
(Aug. '94) *41+5 - 22:*
Int.Hon: **Scotland U.15:**

SMYTH, David (M) (LARNE)
Born: 27.11.1963 Ballymena
Career: **Larne** *(Nov. '81);* **Ballymena United** *(Jun. '89)*
39+9 - 0; **Larne** *(1995)* *2 - 0:*
Int.Hon: **N.Ireland U.15:**

SMYTH, Dean (G) (CLIFTONVILLE)
Born: 13.08.1964 Carrickfergus
Status: Professional; Occupation: Lifeguard
Career: **Crusaders; Glentoran** *(Aug. '86)* *63 - 0;*
Ballymena Utd. *(Nov. '93)* *39 - 0;* **Ards** *(Nov. '95 loan)*
1 - 0; **Cliftonville** *(Apr. '96 loan)* *4 - 0;* **Cliftonville**
(May. '96):
Int.Hon: **N.Ireland U.18; U.15; Irish League Rep.**

SMYTH, Gary (D) (GLENAVON)
Born: 20.12.1969 Belfast
Ht: 6.0 Wt: 11.04
Status: Professional; Occupation: Lorry Driver
Career: Holywood; Glentoran (Dec.'88) 83+1 - 5;
Glenavon (Jul.'95) 24 - 0:

SMYTH, John (M) (BALLYMENA UNITED)
Born: 28.04.1970 Dundalk
Ht: 5.10 Wt: 12.06
Status: Professional
Career: Dundalk; Liverpool (May.'87) 0 - 0; Burnley
(Jul.'90) 0 - 0; Wigan Ath. (Sep.'91) 2+6 - 0; Limerick
(Sep.'92) 27 - 4; Glenavon (Jul.'93) 46+4 - 5; Ballymena
United (Aug.'96):
Int.Hon: Republic of Ireland U.18:

SMYTH, Liam (M) (LARNE)
Career: Glenavon; Larne (Oct.'95) 3+1 - 0:

SMYTH, Michael (D) (GLENTORAN)
Born: 19.12.1966 Cullybackey
Ht: 5.9 Wt: 12.07
Status: Professional; Occupation: Senior Purchasing
Officer
Career: Ballymena Utd; Glentoran (Sep.'92) 105 - 4:
Int.Hon: N.Ireland U.18; Irish League Rep.

SMYTH, Stephen (M) (CARRICK RANGERS)
Born: 03.02.1979 Belfast
Ht: 5.11 Wt: 11.07
Occupation: Metal Fabricator
Career: Carrick Rangers 1 - 0:

SPENCE, David (F) (DISTILLERY)
Born: 29.12.1976 London
Status: Amateur; Occupation: Student
Career: Carnmoney Colts; Glentoran (Dec.'93) 0 - 0;
Distillery (Mar.'96) 3+3 - 0:

SPIERS, Eddie (D) (BANGOR)
Born: 28.10.1956 Belfast
Occupation: Civil Servant
Career: Barn Utd; S.T.C; Harland & W.W; Carrick
Rangers (c/s'85) 21+1 - 1; Larne (Jul.'86) 149 - 4;
Bangor (Oct.'93) 66 - 4:

SPIERS, Jeff (D) (LINFIELD)
Born: 02.05.1967 Belfast
Status: Professional
Career: Barn Utd; Crusaders; Barn Utd; Linfield
(Feb.'87) 116+4 - 5:

STEELE, James (F) (BALLYMENA UNITED)
Career: Linfield 0 - 0; Glebe Rangers; Ballymena
United (c/s'95) 6+5 - 3:

STEWART, Alfie (D) (PORTADOWN)
Born: 16.10.1964 Magherafelt
Status: Professional
Occupation: Steel Fixer
Career: Bridgend Utd; Moyola Park (Aug.'80);

Glentoran (Oct.'82) 110+5 - 7; Portadown (Aug.'88)
201+2 - 0:
Int.Hon: N.Ireland U.18; Irish League Rep.

STEWART, Stephen (D) (BALLYMENA UNITED)
Born: 19.08.1963 Belfast
Status: Professional
Career: Linfield 0 - 0; Brantwood; Ballyclare
Comrades; Crusaders (Aug.'86) 177+7 - 11; Ballymena
United (Jul.'95) 18+1 - 0:
Int.Hon: Irish League Rep.

STOKES, Paul (F) (CLIFTONVILLE)
Born: Dublin
Ht: 6.2
Career: Bluebell Utd; Waterford Utd. (Oct.'93) 11+2 -
7; Newry Town (Oct.'94 loan; Nov.'94) 24+3 - 9;
Cliftonville (Dec.'95) 14 - 7:

STRAIN, Brian (D) (PORTADOWN)
Born: 27.08.1964 Newtownards
Status: Professional; Occupation: Chartered Physio-
otherapist
Career: Comber Boys (1974); Comber Rec. (1980); Ards
(1981) 0 - 0; Killyleagh Y.C. (1983); Glentoran (Jul.'85)
8 - 0; Portadown (Jul.'87) 222+2 - 23:
Int.Hon: Irish League Rep.

STRANEY, David (F) (LARNE)*
Born: 07.11.1974 Downpatrick
Ht: 5.8 Wt: 10.07
Occupation: Civil Servant
Career: Middlesbrough 0 - 0; Glenavon 0+1 - 0; Ards
(Jun.'93) 9+18 - 9; Larne (Aug.'95) 3+3 - 0; Kilmore
Recreation (c/s'96):
Int.Hon: N.Ireland U.18 Schools:

STRANEY, Paul (G) (GLENAVON)
Born: 07.10.1975 Downpatrick
Ht: 6.0 Wt: 12.04
Status: Professional
Career: Glenavon 1 - 0; Stoke City (Jun.'93) 0 - 0;
Glenavon (Oct.'94) 15 - 0; Telford United (Aug.'95
loan) 10 - 0:
Int.Hon: N.Ireland U.18; U.16; U.15:

STRANG, Shaun (F) (CLIFTONVILLE)
Born: 31.03.1970 Dunfermline
Ht: 5.7 Wt: 10.04
Status: Professional; Occupation: Dental Technician
Career: Dunfermline Ath. 1 - 0; Raith Rovers (Aug.'90)
6+11 - 3; Cliftonville (Sep.'92 loan) 4 - 1; Cliftonville
(Jun.'93) 61+5- 19:

SURGEON, Michael (M) (COLERAINE)
Born: 04.06.1966 Belfast
Status: Professional
Career: Kelvin O.B; Distillery 0 - 0; Kelvin O.B;
Distillery (1986) 93+12 - 15; Portadown (Dec.'91) 16+7
- 2; Bangor (Jan.'93) 42+24 - 9; Coleraine (Sep.'95)
19+9 - 5:

SWIFT, Jonathan (D) (BANGOR)
Status: Amateur; Occupation: Taxi-Driver
Career: St.Francis; Bangor (Jan.'95) 10 - 1:

TABB, Martin (D) (CLIFTONVILLE)
Born: 04.07.1959 Belfast
Status: Professional
Career: Coleraine (1981); Cliftonville (Jul.'91)
132+1 - 6:

TELFORD, Colin (F) (GLENTORAN)
Born: 14.01.1974 Belfast
Ht: 5.10 Wt: 11.00
Status: Professional; Occupation: Shoptrader
Career: Ballymena Utd . 0 - 0; Carrick Rangers (Oct.'89)
0 - 0; Manchester Utd. (1990) 0 - 0; Raith Rovers
(Sep.'92) 0 - 0; Ballyclare Comrades (Mar.'93 loan) 2 - 1;
Glentoran (Aug.'93) 3+1 - 0; Carrick Rangers (Mar.'95
loan) 0+3 - 0
Int.Hon: N.Ireland U.18; U.17; U.16; U15:

THOMPSON, Steven (D) (NEWRY TOWN)*
Career: Chelsea 0 - 0; Glenavon (Mar.'84) 3+4 - 0;
Portadown (c/s'87) 0 - 0; Banbridge Town (c/s'88);
Newry Town (c/s'94) 19+1 - 0; Banbridge Town
(Mar.'96):

THORPE, Lee (F) (BANGOR)*
Born: 14.12.1975 Wolverhampton
Ht: 6.0 Wt: 11.06
Status: Professional
Career: Blackpool (Jul.'94) 0+3 - 0; Bangor (Sep.'95
loan) 3 - 1:

TIERNEY, Dan (M) (BANGOR)
Career: Bangor (Aug.'95) 0 - 0: Bray Wanderers 2+6 - 0

TOAL, Damien (M) (DISTILLERY)
Born: 11.10.1976 Belfast
Status: Amateur; Occupation: Student
Career: Distillery (Jul.'93) 7+3 - 0:

TOTTEN, William (M) (DISTILLERY)
Born: 09.04.1964 Belfast
Status: Professional
Career: Highfield Y; Linfield (1982) 6+3 - 0; Crusaders
(Jul.'85) 40+2 - 4; Coleraine (Jul.'87) 15+4 - 3;
Glentoran (Aug.'88) 21+13 - 2; Distillery (Mar.'92)
93+10 - 11:

TURKINGTON, Jonathan (F) (PORTADOWN)
Born: Portadown
Ht: 6.1 Wt: 11.00
Career: Portadown 0 - 0:

WADE, Richard (M) (COLERAINE)*
Born: 11.05.1964 Ballymoney
Ht: 5.9 Wt: 10.10
Status: Professional; Occupation: Swimming Pool
Attendant
Career: Ballymena Utd; Coleraine (c/s'82); Linfield
(Dec.'91) 17+2 - 3; Coleraine (Jul.'94) 16+5 - 3;
Ballymoney United (Sep.'95):
Int.Hon: Irish League Rep.

WALKER, Chris (D) (GLENTORAN)
Born: Belfast
Ht: 6.2 Wt: 12.05
Status: Professional
Career: 1st Liverpool; Glentoran (Aug.'94) 27+1 - 1:
Int.Hon: Irish League U.21 Rep.

WALKER, Darren (F) (OMAGH TOWN)
Career: Omagh Town 0 - 0:

WALKER, Gary (M) (DISTILLERY)
Born: Dundonald
Ht: 5.8 Wt: 9.10
Status: Amateur
Career: Ards (1991) 7+13 - 0; Distillery (Aug.'96):

WALKER, Marcus (D) (BALLYCLARE COMRADES)
Career: Grove United; Ballyclare Comrades (Jul.'95)
20+3 - 0:

WALKER, Roy (D) (CRUSADERS)
Born: 20.07.1958 Belfast
Status: Professional
Career: Torrin Boys; Luton Town 0 - 0; Ards (1975);
Glenavon (Jul.'85) 7 - 0; Portadown (Sep.'86) 17 - 0;
Crusaders (Nov.'87) 83+3 - 2:

WATSON, Ryan (M) (NEWRY TOWN)
Born: 03.04.1971 Newry
Status: Amateur; Occupation: Student
Career: Glenavon (Jul.'88) 0+1 - 0; Portadown (Feb.'89)
7+4 - 0; Banbridge Town (Dec.'90); Portadown (Apr.'91)
1 - 0; Distillery (Jul.'92) 24+10 - 1; Newry Town (c/s'95)
23+1 - 1:
Int.Hon: N.Ireland U.18; U.15:

WHELAN, Stephen (M) (NEWRY TOWN)
Born: 29.05.1968 Belfast
Status: Amateur
Career: Distillery 2+1 - 0; Chimney Corner (Sep.'89);
Cookstown United (c/s'90); Portadown (Dec.'90) 0 - 0;
Glenavon (Jan.'92) 1+1 - 0; Newry Town (Dec.'92) 16+1
- 4; Carrick Rangers (Oct.'93) 9+8 - 0; Ballymena Utd.
(c/s'94) 0 - 0; Newry Town (Jul.'95) 11+3 - 0:

WHITE, David (F) (NEWRY TOWN)
Born: 24.04.1976 Newry
Career: Finn Harps; Glenavon (Sep.'92) 0 - 0; Newry
Town (Feb.'95) 6+1 - 1:

WILKINSON, Gary (D) (DISTILLERY)
Born: 30.10.1973
Status: Professional
Career: Ards (c/s'89) 0 - 0; Q.P.R. (c/s'90); Hayes (c/s'92);
Bangor (Jul.'93) 0+6 - 0; Distillery (Aug.'96):
Int.Hon: N.Ireland U.18; U.16; U.15:

WILLIAMS, Martin (M) (BANGOR)*
Born: 12.07.1973 Luton
Ht: 5.9 Wt: 11.02
Status: Professional
Career: Leicester City; Luton Town (Sep.'91) 12+28 - 2;
Colchester United (Mar.'95 loan) 3 - 0; Reading (Aug.'95)
11+3 - 1; Bangor (Dec.'95 loan) 3 - 1:

WILLS, John (D) (ARDS)
Born: 07.11.1971 Tarporley
Ht: 5.8 Wt: 11.00
Status: Professional; Occupation: P.E. Supervisor
Career: Manchester City (Jul.'90) 0 - 0; Maine Road F.C.
(c/s'93); Ards (Aug.'94) 26+1 - 0:

WILSON, Frank (M) (CARRICK RANGERS)
Born: 26.07.1970 Belfast
Status: Amateur; Occupation: Student
Career: U.U.J; Ballyclare Comrades (Nov.'91) 70+11 - 16;
Carrick Rangers (Nov.'95) 11+5 - 3:

WILSON, Warren (M) (CARRICK RANGERS)

Born: 20.11.1976 Belfast
Ht: 5.9 Wt: 10.7
Status: Amateur; Occupation: Painter & Decorator
Career: Carnmoney Colts; Carrick Rangers 33+9- 0:
Int.Hon: N.Ireland U.18:

WOODSFORD, Jamie (F) (PORTADOWN)*
Born: 09.11.1976 Ipswich
Ht: 5.11 Wt: 11.10
Status: Professional
Career: Luton Town (Mar.'95) 2+8 - 0; Portadown
(Feb.'96 loan) 6 - 6:
Int.Hon: England U.18:

WYLIE, Keith (D) (BALLYMENA UNITED)
Born: 20.01.1976 Ballymena
Status: Amateur; Occupation: Student
Career: Ballymena Utd. (1991) 16+4 - 0:
Int.Hon: N.Ireland U.18; U.18 Schools; U.16:

YOUNG, Stephen (M) (COLERAINE)
Born: 02.07.1969 Ballymena
Occupation: Factory Foreman
Career: Galgorm Blues; Ballymoney Utd; Ballymena Utd.
(Mar.'87); Larne (Jun.'94) 10 - 0; Coleraine (Jan.'95) 26 -
0:
Int.Hon: N.Ireland U.15:

Robert Young

YOUNG, Robert (F) (BALLYCLARE COMRADES)
Career: Carniny Rangers; Ballyclare Comrades
(Nov.'95) 15+1 - 5:

NORTH WEST INTERMEDIATE CUP 1995/96

FIRST ROUND

2nd September, 1995

Churchill/Kilfennan United	3	Tamnaherin Celtic	2
Coleraine Reserves	6	Magherfelt Sky Blues	1
Drummond United	3	Garvagh	1
Dungiven Celtic	2	Ballinamallard United	
Limavady United	4	Magilligan	1
Macosquin	1	Draperstown Celtic	2
Park	0	Coleraine Crusaders	1
Roe Valley	3	Ardmore	1
Tobermore United	4	U.U.C.	2

First Round Byes: Bridgend United; Institute; Moyola Park; Omagh Town Reserves; Oxford United Stars; Portstewart; Strabane:

SECOND ROUND

30th September, 1995

Bridgend United	1	Draperstown Celtic	5
Coleraine Reserves	1	Dungiven Celtic	0
Limavady United	2	Moyola Park	3
Oxford United Stars	5	Coleraine Crusaders	0
Portstewart	0	Institute	1
Roe Valley	3	Omagh Town Reserves	0
Strabane	1	Churchill/Kilfennan United	4
Tobermore United	v	Drummond United*	

*Tobermore United walkover into Quarter-Finals.

QUARTER FINALS

28th October, 1995

Churchill/Kilfennan United	3	Roe Valley	2
Coleraine Reserves	2	Draperstown Celtic	1
Institute		Oxford United Stars*	
Tobermore United	2	Moyola Park	1 aet

* Oxford United Stars progressed into Semi-Finals after Institute were dismissed from competition for fielding Cathal Deery who was cup-tied after previously playing for Limavady United in an earlier round.

SEMI FINALS

18th November, 1995

Venue: The Showgrounds, Coleraine

Coleraine Reserves	**0**	**Oxford United Stars**	**2**

Venue: Fortwilliam Park, Tobermore

Tobermore United	**1**	**Churchill/Kilfennan United**	**1**
Taylor		*Doherty*	

(aet C.K.U. won 3-2 on pens)

FINAL

23rd March, 1996

Oxford United Stars	**2**	**Churchill/Kilfennan United**	**1**

CUP-WINNERS' CUP

Preliminary Round, First Leg - 10th August, 1995

Venue: Central Stadium, Donetsk.   Att: 31,000

Shakhtar Donetsk (Ukraine) (3)	**4**	**Linfield (0)**	**1**
Atelkin (10), Matveyev (20),		*Ewing (47)*	
Orbu (31,90)			

Shakhtar: Shutkov, Kochvar, Koval, Pyatenko, Chikhradze, Matveyev, Orbu, Petrov, Spivak, Atelkin, Kriventsov.
Subs: Fedkov replaced Atelkin (15 min); Voskoboinik replaced Fedkov (70 min); Onopko replaced Matveyev (83 min):
Linfield: Lamont, Crothers, Easton, Ewing, McLean, Beatty, Ray.Campbell, McGee, Erskine, Spiers, Bailie. *Subs not used*: Crawford (gk); McCoosh; Dornan; McShane; McLaughlin:
Referee: Mikhail (Slovakia).

Preliminary Round, Second Leg - 24th August, 1995

Venue: Windsor Park, Belfast.   Att: 3,000

Linfield (0)	**0**	**Shakhtar Donetsk (0)**	**1**
(Shakhtar Donetsk won 5-1 on aggregate)		*Voskoboinik (85)*	

Linfield: Lamont, Dornan, Easton, Ewing, Spiers, Beatty, Ray.Campbell, Gorman, Erskine, Fenlon, Bailie.
Subs: McLaughlin replaced Beatty (58 mins); McCoosh replaced Ewing (77 mins); *Sub not used*: Caldwell (gk); Crothers; McShane:
Shakhtar: Nikitin, Kochvar, Koval, Pyatenko, Chikhradze, Matveyev, Orbu, Petrov, Kriventsov, Voskoboinik, Popov. *Subs*: Shutkov replaced Petrov (46 mins); Leonov replaced Kriventsov (78 mins); Fedkov replaced Matveyev (86 mins):
Referee: J.Hirviniemi (Finland)
Sent Off: Nikitin (shakhtar Donetsk)

U.E.F.A. CUP

Preliminary Round, First Leg - 8th August, 1995

Venue: Seaview, Belfast.   Att: 4,000

Crusaders`(0)	**1**	**Silkeborg IF (Denmark) (1)**	**2**
(G) Hunter (67)		*Fernandez (15), Larsen (pen 47)*	

Crusaders: McKeown, McMullan, McCartney, Dunlop, Callaghan, (K) Hunter, Livingstone, Dunne, Baxter, (G) Hunter, Burrows. *Sub*: Morgan replaced (K) Hunter (87 min); *Subs not used*: Gardiner; Dwyer; Walker; Henry (gk):
Silkeborg: Kjaer, Petersen, Larsen, Laursen, Brunn, Kastbjerg, Bordinggaard, Sorensen, Reese, Thygesen, Fernandez. *Sub*: Pedersen replaced Fernandez (60 min), Knudsen replaced Thygesen (70 min):
Referee: H.Van Dijk (Holland)
Booked: Dunne (Crusaders); Fernandez (Silkeborg IF):

Venue: Mourneview Park, Lurgan. Att: 3,500

Glenavon (0)	**0**	**FC Hafnarfjordur (Iceland) (0)**	**0**

Glenavon: O'Neill, Byrne, Glendinning, Doherty, Brown, (G) Smyth, McCoy, Johnston, Ferguson, McBride, (J) Smyth. *Sub*: Collins replaced Johnston (74 mins); *Subs not used*: Burns; (A) Murphy; McDonagh; Currie (gk):
Hafnarfjordur: (S) Arnarson, Ragnarsson, Vidarsson, Sveinsson, Mrazek, (H) Kristjansson, Helgason, Toth, Magnusson, (H) Arnarson, (O) Kristjansson. *Sub*: Stephensen replaced Toth (77 mins); *Subs not used*: Hjartarson; Eriksson; Olafsson; Halldorsson:
Referee: L.M.Frohlich (Germany)
Booked: Hegason; Ragnarsson (FC Hafnarfjordur):

Preliminary Round, Second Leg - 22nd August, 1995

Venue: Silkeborg Stadium, Silkeborg.   Att: 4,339

Silkeborg IF (1)	**4**	**Crusaders (0)**	**0**

Larsen (11), Fernandez (60),
Sommer (69,85)
(Silkeborg won 6-1 on aggregate)

Silkeborg: Kjaer, Knudsen, Larsen, Laursen, Brunn, Duus, Bordinggaard, Sorensen, Reese, Thygesen, Fernandez. **Subs***:* Sommer replaced Reese (61 min); Moldrup replaced Sorensen:
Crusaders: McKeown, McMullan, McCartney, Dunlop, Callaghan, (K) Hunter, Livingstone, Dunne, Baxter, Gardiner, Burrows. **Subs***:* Dwyer replaced (K) Hunter (69 min); Morgan replaced Baxter (83 min); **Subs not used**: Walker; Henry (gk):
Referee: M.Peltola (Finland)
Booked: Dunlop (Crusaders):

Preliminary Round, Second Leg - 23rd August, 1995

Venue: Kaplakriki Stadium, Hafnarfjardar.   Att: 500

FC Hafnarfjardar (0)	**0**	**Glenavon (0)**	**1**
		Johnston (65)	

(Glenavon won 1-0 on aggregate)

Hafnarfjardar: (S) Arnarson, Ragnarsson, Vidarsson, Sveinsson, Mrazek, Toth, Helgason, (H) Kristjansson, Magnusson, (H) Arnarson, (O) Kristjansson. **Subs**: Halldorsson replaced (O) Kristjansson (41 mins); Eriksson replaced Toth (74 mins); **Subs not used**: Olafsson; (L) Arnarson; Hjartarson:
Glenavon: O'Neill, Byrne, Glendinning, Doherty, Brown, (G) Smyth, McCoy, Johnston, Ferguson, McBride, (J) Smyth. **Subs not used**: McDonagh; Birney; Collins; (A) Murphy; Currie (gk):
Referee: W.Young (Scotland)
Booked: (H) Kristjansson; Magnusson (FC Hafnarfjardar); Doherty, Brown (Glenavon):

First Round, First Leg - 13th September, 1995

Venue: Mourneview Park, Lurgan.   Att: 5,500

Glenavon 0)	**0**	**SV Werder Bremen (Germany) (0)**	**2**
		Cardoso (59), Vier (88)	

Glenavon: O'Neill, Birney, Glendinning, Doherty, Brown, (G) Smyth, (A) Murphy, Johnston, Ferguson, McBride, (J) Smyth. **Subs**: Byrne replaced Birney (76 mins); McCoy replaced Brown (79 mins); Collins replaced (J) Smyth (84 min); **Subs not used**: McDonagh; Currie (gk):
Werder Bremen: Rost, (H) Schulz, Baiano, Borowka, Eilts, Bode, Wiedener, Votava, Hobsch, Cardoso, Beschastnykh. **Subs**: Vier replaced Beschastnykh (13 mins); (M) Schulz replaced Cordos (83 mins); Neubarth replaced Hobsch (85 mins); **Subs not used**: Biersdorfer; Gundelach (gk):
Referee: R.Temmink (Holland)
Booked: Doherty (Glenavon):

First Round, Second Leg - 27th September, 1995

Venue: Weserstadion, Bremen.   Att: 13,727

SV Werder Bremen (4)	**5**	**Glenavon (0)**	**0**

Hobsch (26,35,38), Basler (pen 36),
Borowka (65)
(SV Werder Bremen won 7-0 on aggregate)

Werder Bremen: Reck, (H) Schulz, Wolter, Wiedener, Eilts, Borowka, Basler, Votava, Hobsch, Beschastnykh, Bode. **Subs**: Biersdorfer replaced Borowka (66 mins); Albayrak replaced Basler (66 mins) Vier replaced Hobsch (70 min); **Subs not used**: Vier; Neubarth; Rost (gk):
Glenavon: O'Neill, Byrne, Glendinning, Kenny, Brown, (G) Smyth, Collins, Johnston, Ferguson, McBride, (D) Murphy. **Subs**: McCoy replaced Kenny (73 mins); (A) Murphy replaced Brown (78 mins); **Subs not used**: Burns; Birney; Currie (gk):
Referee: A.Hamer (Luxembourg).
Booked: Hobsch (SV Werder Bremen); Kenny (Glenavon):

(Brought to you in association with ARCONADA.............ARMSTRONG ! on location in Corfu!)

Well hey, This'll be a quickie this year then. The simple question is 'Are we in a better position than we were this time last year? ' Now think; this time last year means only one thing. Latvia. Remember them? You may recall the shameful 2-1 hammering we took at their hands. A match, which had we won or drawn it, would have put us in the play-off against Holland. Suffice to say, a year ago we were the worst team in the world, ever, without exception. now were not. We are far from being the best team in the world, well out of the top 30, but I think were better than our FIFA ranking in the low fifties indicates.

This season has seen us play a total of six games. Three were in a tournament I had long since given up hope in, and three were in friendlies. So basically all six were fairly non-competitive matches, or at least did not have the pressure of needing the points.

Versus Liechtenstein - We scored some goals. Four of them in fact, and none of them were rubbish. It was a good training exercise I guess, but it was, due to UEFA's bizarre rules, utterly meaningless. That stout, proud Ulsterman Trevor Wood made his debut. He played for the 'Jersey', knocked some good balls into the 'Channels' and even though he only got twenty minutes, he didn't 'Guern', see? (No need to be Sark-y).

Versus Portugal - we played superbly. Our tactics were spot on, but then, after all it was an away match. Fettis was marvellous, but when we went 1-0 down we looked on for a hiding. However a brilliant free-kick by Hughes screamed into the (albeit off Dowie's backside) for a deserved equaliser.

Versus Austria - Okay, so our pride made a comeback in Portugal, but now we were at home against a side in with a chance of qualification for EURO 96. Naturally we would go to pieces. We'd gone through the entire series unbeaten away - something I don't recall us doing before - but we'd lost it spectacularly at home. We were out - we'd thought we were out even before Latvia - but now we knew that even a point then would have left us with real hope. One more point anywhere would have done. The truth was now horrible. A win tonight, coupled with a defeat in Portugal for the Republic would leave us level on points, but out because of that 4-0 defeat at Windsor by Jack's Boys. That hurt. the team owed us one. So instead, they gave us five and we finished the series in a style totally alien to all followers of Northern Ireland. We let in three and we didn't care, because we'd scored five, rounded off with the kind of goal from O'Neill that I though the European Parliament had barred British teams from even attempting.

We were out, sure, but we'd remembered how to play football. Hamilton duly had his contract renewed and there wasn't a fan in the land who would have argued against it that November night. He'd taken us as close to qualifying as we'd been since 1984 (when we would have made it under EUFA's 1996 ruling).

There was an inkling that we may have a chance in the next series given a favourable draw (you know, favourable draws - those things dished out in their dozens to England, Scotland and the Republic.). Regardless of what the IFA think - we did not get a good draw.

Armenia - unknown; Ukraine - scary; Albania - sound like a soft touch, but then you thought Turkey were a soft touch until recently; Portugal - the one second seeded team we just had to avoid; Germany - well I guess
there had to be one easy team in there somewhere!

Nonetheless, we can do it. We have a few quality players, and reasonable competition for places. We have had three very different friendlies to try out various ideas and players. If were not ready now, well we never will be with the current crop. Fettis has come on well in the past year, Hill and Hunter have shown they work well together, Griffen had a fine debut, the midfield of Hughes, Lomas, Lennon and Gillespie looks strong and well balanced. Dowie is a star who needs a regular partner. Add to those, Tommy Wright, Rowland, Taggart, Fleming, Magilton, O'Neill, O'Boyle, Mulryne, Gray and McMahon and the future starts to look a little less murky.

As I said, the friendlies were different. We were very poor against Norway, who were missing two of their stars in Bohinen and Leonhardsen. The only good thing to come out of this was the inclusion of a 'B' International match, something which we applaud Bryan Hamilton for, and something which must continue and eventually (sooner rather than later) must burn into a competitive Under-21 team.

Against Sweden we fielded what was virtually a 'B' team due to withdrawals because of injuries. McMahon scored an excellent goal and showed some silky touches which made you wonder what he was doing in Spurs reserves for most of the season.

When Germany arrived we put on our standard show, ending up unlucky to only draw due to the euphoria of going ahead lasting slightly too long. This match saw us crowned as moral Champions of Europe (again) as we beat the Germans on penalties, Klinsmann side-footing wide and Moller blasting high over the top. Are you watching Ingerland?
So, on we go, towards France. Till we meet again next year, just one point short of automatic qualification, au revoir, mes petts.

David Alcorn is Editor of ARCONADA...........ARMSTRONG ! the Northern Ireland fanzine.

Neil Lennon - An Appreciation

Neil Lennon should, in my opinion, be one of the first names on the team sheet for our International games. People may argue the case for Dowie, Gillespie, Lomas and these days remarkably even Fettis. Isn't it nice though, to have to even think who our best player might be?

Neil is the kind of player we have been without for what seems like an age - the type who wants the ball, knows how and where to get it, and can do something positive with it when he gets it. We just haven't had that battling, hard tackling, creative and, yes ginger kind of player for far too long. Well except for Steve Lomas, but he's not really ginger, is he?

Neil Lennon started his career in the Irish League with Glenavon, before signing for Manchester City, who also had Gerry Taggart and Gary Fleming on their books at the time and who were about to sign Michael Hughes. After just one appearance for the Maine Road outfit he went to the 'Pride of Cheshire', Crewe Alexandra (of whom I am a fan!). It is impossible to read anything about Crewe without the word's "it is impossible to write anything about Crewe without mentioning the likes of David Platt, Geoff Thomas, Rob Jones and John Pemberton" appearing. It is however a fact that the club has a great reputation for bringing on youngsters and other clubs' 'rejects', and thus, although it was a step down for Neil, it was still a positive move.

He made quite an impact at Gresty Road, and by the time I first saw him in the red and white of the Alex in 1994/95 he had already made his International debut during the tour of '94. It was obvious he was the star player in a typically erratic Crewe side, but he was by no means as regular in the International set-up.

Midway through 1995/96 it was obvious Neil was going to make his big move away from Crewe. I was actually surprised we'd held on to him as long as we did. Eventually it was announced he was off to Coventry to join Ron Atkinsons' batch of recent big money signings. He had agreed terms, but somehow felt it wasn't quite right. On discussing the matter with his parents he decided against the move, feeling that at 24, although he still had a long career ahead, he had to make sure this move was the right one.

So Neil turned down the chance to join a struggling Premiership side and instead joined up with Martin O'Neill at Leicester City, a team hopeful of being a struggling Premiership outfit. I am sure this will turn out to be a good choice as Neil is just the type of player Leicester need to help them prolong their stay in the top League.

David Alcorn is Editor of ARCONADA............ARMSTRONG! The Northern Ireland Fanzine.

European Championship Qualifier (Group Six) - 3rd September, 1995

Venue: Stadio Das Antas, Oporto.   Att: 50,000

| **Portugal (0)** | **1** | **Northern Ireland (0)** | **1** |
| *Domingos (48)* | | *Hughes (67)* | |

Portugal: Baia, Secretario, (J) Costa, Oceano, Couto, Sousa, Figo, Santos, Domingos, (R) Costa, Folha. ***Subs***: Baros replaced (J) Costa (73 mins); Alves replaced (R) Costa (82 mins): ***Subs not used***: Barbosa, Alfredo, Dimas;

N.Ireland: Fettis (Hull City), Morrow (Arsenal), Worthington (Leeds United capt), Hill (Leicester City), Hunter (Wrexham), Lomas (Manchester City), Gillespie (Newcastle United), Magilton (Southampton), Dowie (West Ham United), Lennon (Crewe Alexandra), Hughes (Strasbourg). ***Subs***: Gray (Sunderland) replaced Dowie (76 mins); Rowland (West Ham United) replaced Magilton (79 mins); ***Subs not used***: Wood (Walsall); Wilson (Walsall); McGibbon (Manchester United)
Referee: R.Harrel (France).
Booked: Portugal: Santos: N.Ireland: Dowie; Gillespie:

European Championship Qualifier (Group Six) - 11th October, 1995

Venue: Sportpark, Eschen-Mauren.   Att: 1,100

| **Liechtenstein (0)** | **0** | **Northern Ireland (1)** | **4** |
| | | *O'Neill (36), McMahon (49), Quinn (55), Gray (72)* | |

Liechtenstein: Oehry, Hefti, Frick, Hilti, Hasler, Klaunzer, Telser, Stocker, Schadler, Zech, Oehri.
Subs: Sele replaced Stocker (45 mins); Ospelt replaced Hilti (70 mins); Hanselmann replaced Frick (78 mins):
Subs not used: Kindle; Marxer:

N.Ireland: Fettis (Hull City), Lomas (Manchester City), Worthington (Leeds United capt), Hill (Leicester City), Hunter (Wrexham), Lennon (Crewe Alexandra), McMahon (Tottenham Hotspur), O'Neill (Hibernian), Jimmy Quinn (Reading), Gray (Sunderland), Hughes (Strasbourg). ***Subs***: Wood (Walsall) replaced Fettis (75 mins); McGibbon (Manchester United) replaced McMahon (80 mins); Rowland (West Ham United) replaced Hughes (90 mins):
Subs not used: Wilson (Walsall); Taggart (Bolton Wanderers):
Referee: L.Michel (Slovakia).
Booked: Liechtenstein: none: N.Ireland: none:

European Championship Qualifier (Group Six) - 15th November, 1995

Venue: Windsor Park, Belfast   Att: 8,400

Northern Ireland (2)	**5**	**Austria (0)**	**3**
O'Neill (27,78), Dowie (pen 32),		*Schopp (56), Stumpf (70), Wetl (81)*	
Hunter (53), Gray (64)			

N.Ireland: Fettis (Hull City), Lomas (Manchester City), Worthington (Leeds United capt), Hunter (Wrexham), Hill (Leicester City), Lennon (Crewe Alexandra), Gillespie (Newcastle United), O'Neill (Hibernian), Dowie (West Ham United), Gray (Sunderland), Hughes (Strasbourg). ***Subs***: McDonald (Queens Park Rangers) replaced Gray (78 min); Jimmy Quinn (Reading) replaced Dowie (81 min): ***Subs not used***: Wood (Walsall); Rowland (West Ham United); McGibbon (Manchester United):

Austria: Konsel, Schopp, Kogler, Pfeffer, Feiersinger, Marasek, Pfeifenberger, Kuhbauer, Polster, Herzog, Stoger. ***Subs***: Wetl replaced Herzog (46 min); Stumpf replaced Kuhbauer (46 min): ***Subs not used***: Konrad; Ramusch; Artner:
Referee: L.Sundell (Sweden)

Friendly International - 27th March, 1996

Venue: Windsor Park, Belfast   Att: 5,343

Northern Ireland (0)   **0**   **Norway (1)**   **2**
                                                    Solskjaer (51), Ostenstad (78)

N.Ireland: Fettis (Nottingham Forest), Lomas (Manchester City), Worthington (Leeds United capt), Hill (Leicester City), McDonald (Queens Park Rangers), Lennon (Leicester City), Gillespie (Newcastle United), O'Neill (Hibernian), Dowie (West Ham United), Magilton (Southampton), Hughes (West Ham United). *Subs*: Patterson (Luton Town) replaced Magilton (46 min); Rowland (West Ham United) replaced Worthington (56 min); McMahon (Tottenham Hotspur) replaced O'Neill (61 min): *Subs not used*: Davison (Bolton Wanderers; James Quinn (Blackpool):

Norway: Grodas, Haaland, Johnsen, Berg, Bjornebye, Rudi, Solbakken, Leonhardsen, Fjortoft, Rekdal, Solskjaer. *Subs:* Jakobsen replaced Leonhardsen (24 min); Thorstvedt replaced Grodas (46 min); Ostenstad replaced Fjortoft (74 min); Lundekvam replaced Solbakken (86 min); *Sub not used*: Nilsen:
Referee: J.Ashman (Wales)
Sent Off: Iain Dowie (N.Ireland) (86 mins)

Friendly International - 24th April, 1996

Venue: Windsor Park, Belfast   Att: 5,666

Northern Ireland (0)   **1**   **Sweden (1)**   **2**
McMahon (84)   *Dahlin (22), Ingesson (58)*

N.Ireland: Davison (Bolton Wanderers), Patterson (Luton Town), Worthington (Leeds United capt), Hill (Leicester City), Hunter (Wrexham), Morrow (Arsenal), McCarthy (Port Vale), Lomas (Manchester City), McMahon (Tottenham Hotspur), O'Neill (Hibernian), Rowland (West Ham United). *Subs*: O'Boyle (St.Johnstone) replaced O'Neill (65 min); James Quinn (Blackpool) replaced Worthington (77 min); *Subs not used*: Wood (Walsall); Griffin (St.Johnstone):

Sweden: (B) Andesson, Nilson, (P) Andersson, Bjorklund, Sundgren, Schwarz, Wilbran, Ingesson, Thern, Dahlin, (K) Andersson. *Subs:* Zetterberg replaced Wilbran (45 min); Pettersson replaced (K) Andersson (58 min); Larsson replaced Dahlin (80 min); *Subs not used*:Fedel; Lucic; Mild;
Referee: H.Dallas (Scotland)

Friendly International - 29th May, 1996

Venue: Windsor Park, Belfast   Att: 11,770

Northern Ireland (0)   **1**   **Germany (0)**   **1**
O'Boyle (79)   *Scholl (80)*

N.Ireland: Fettis (Nottingham Forest), Griffin (St.Johnstone), Worthington (Leeds United capt), Hill (Leicester City), Hunter (Wrexham), Lomas (Manchester City), Gillespie (Newcastle United), Magilton (Southampton), Dowie (West Ham United), McMahon (Tottenham Hotspur), Hughes (West Ham United). *Subs*: Rowland (West Ham United) replaced Worthington (46 min); O'Boyle (St.Johnstone) replaced Gillespie (66 min): *Subs not used*: Davison (Bolton Wanderers); Taggart (Bolton Wanderers); Patterson (Luton Town); Mulryne (Manchester United):

Germany: Kahn, Helmer, Kohler, Basler, Eilts, Moller, Scholl, Strunz, Ziege, Bierhoff, Klinsmann (capt). *Subs*: Kuntz replaced Klinsmann (46 min); Bobic replaced Bierhoff (46 min); Bode replaced Ziege (46 min): *Subs not used*: Kopke; Reck; Babbel; Schneider; Hassler:
Referee: W.Young (Scotland)
Booked: Basler, Scholl, Ziege (Germany).
NB: Germany missed two penalties during the match, Klinsmann in the third minute and Moller in the thirty-second minute.

15th August, 1995 - Eschen Att: 2,500

| Liechtenstein (0) | 0 | Portugal (3) | 7 |
| | | *Domingos(25), Paulinho (33), (R) Costa (41,71), Paulo Alves (67,73,90)* | |

16th August, 1995 - Riga   Att: 2,000

| Latvia (1) | 3 | Austria (0) | 2 |
| *Rimkus (13,59), Zeiberlins (88)* | | *Polster (68), Ramusch (78)* | |

6th September, 1995 - Vienna Att: 24,000

| Austria (1) | 3 | Republic of Ireland (0) | 1 |
| *Stoger (3,64,77)* | | *McGrath (74)* | |

6th September, 1995 - Riga   Att: 3,800

| Latvia (0) | 1 | Liechstenstein (0) | 0 |
| *Zeiberlins (83)* | | | |

11th October, 1995 - Vienna Att: 44,000

| Austria (1) | 1 | Portugal (0) | 1 |
| *Stoger (21)* | | *Santos (49)* | |

11th October, 1995 - Dublin   Att: 33,000

| Republic of Ireland (0) | 2 | Latvia (0) | 1 |
| *Aldridge (Pen 61,64)* | | *Rimkus (78)* | |

15th November, 1995 - Lisbon Att: 80,000

| Portugal (0) | 3 | Republic of Ireland (0) | 0 |
| *(R) Costa (59), Helder (78), Cadete (89)* | | | |

Group Six Final Table

	P	W	D	L	F	A	Pts	GD
1 Portugal	10	7	2	1	28	7	23	+21
2 Republic of Ireland	10	5	2	3	17	11	17	+6
3 Northern Ireland	10	5	2	3	21	15	17	+6
4 Austria	10	5	1	4	29	14	16	+15
5 Latvia	10	4	0	6	11	20	12	-9
6 Liechtenstein	10	0	1	9	1	40	1	-39

NORTHERN IRELAND 'B' INTERNATIONAL 1995/96

26th March, 1996

Venue: The Showgrounds, Coleraine. *Att:* 1,600

Northern Ireland (1)	**3**	**Norway Olympic XI (0)**	**0**

Patterson (21), Quinn (60)
Mulryne (87)

N.Ireland: Davison (Bolton Wanderers), Wright (Norwich City), Horlock (Swindon Town), Patterson (Luton Town capt), McGibbon (Manchester United), Lennon (Raith Rovers), McCarthy (Port Vale), Griffin (St.Johnstone), Quinn (Blackpool), O'Boyle (St.Johnstone), Black (Nottingham Forest). *Subs:* Wood (Walsall) replaced Davison (45 min); Robinson (Bournemouth) replaced O'Boyle (45 min); Murdock (Manchester United) replaced Patterson (45 min); Mulryne (Manchester United) replaced Quinn (61 min); Graham (Queens Park Rangers) replaced McCarthy (67 min); *Sub not used:* Casey (Portadown)

Norway: Baardsen, Andersen, Kindevag, Waehler, Tran, Aarsheim, Fjortoft, Hestad, Fermann, Lund, Iversen. *Subs:* Hoiland replaced Andersen (71 min); Helstad replaced Fermann (75 min); Baake replaced Fjortoft (80 min): *Subs not used:* Skjeldestad; Karlsbakk; Pedersen:
Referee: B.Lawlor (Wales)

WORLD CUP QUALIFYING GROUP NINE- FIXTURES

31/08/1996	Armenia	v	Portugal
	Northern Ireland	v	Ukraine
05/10/1996	**Northern Ireland**	v	Armenia
	Ukraine	v	Portugal
09/10/1996	Albania	v	Portugal
	Armenia	v	Germany
09/11/1996	Albania	v	Armenia
	Germany	v	**Northern Ireland**
	Portugal	v	Ukraine
14/12/1996	**Northern Ireland**	v	Albania
	Portugal	v	Germany
29/03/1997	Albania	v	Ukraine
	Northern Ireland	v	Portugal
02/04/1997	Albania	v	Germany
	Ukraine	v	**Northern Ireland**
30/04/1997	Armenia	v	**Northern Ireland**
	Germany	v	Ukraine
07/06/1997	Portugal	v	Albania
	Ukraine	v	Germany
20/08/1997	**Northern Ireland**	v	Germany
	Portugal	v	Armenia
	Ukraine	v	Albania
06/09/1997	Armenia	v	Albania
	Germany	v	Portugal
10/09/1997	Albania	v	**Northern Ireland**
	Germany	v	Armenia
11/10/1997	Armenia	v	Ukraine
	Germany	v	Albania
	Portugal	v	**Northern Ireland**

SCHOOLBOY AND YOUTH INTERNATIONALS 1995/1996

NORTHERN IRELAND UNDER-18 YOUTH INTERNATIONAL1995/96

European Under-18 Championship Preliminary Group 15

2nd October, 1995

Venue: The Oval, Belfast
Northern Ireland (1) 2 Republic of Belarus (0) 0
D.Griffen (42,73)

N.Ireland: D.Wells (Bournemouth), C.McAllister (Glenavon), B.McGlinchey (Manchester City), G.Fulton (Portadown), D.Griffen (St.Johnstone capt), C.Coffey (Arsenal), G.Lyttle (Celtic), J.Douglas (Rangers), D.Larmour (Liverpool), M.Collins (Sheffield United), P.Mulryne (Manchester United). *Sub:* S.Friars (Liverpool) replaced C.McAllister (57 min):

6th October, 1995

Venue: Seaview, Belfast
Northern Ireland (2) 2 Iceland (2) 3
P.Mulryne (28,31)   Sveinsson (23), Gislason (pen 41), Ingimarrsson (73)

N.Ireland: D.Wells (Bournemouth), C.McAllister (Glenavon), B.McGlinchey (Manchester City), G.Fulton (Portadown), D.Griffen (St.Johnstone capt), C.Coffey (Arsenal), G.Lyttle (Celtic), J.Douglas (Rangers), D.Larmour (Liverpool), M.Collins (Sheffield United), P.Mulryne (Manchester United). *Subs:* S.O'Neill (Nottingham Forest) replaced J.Douglas (78 min); S.Friars (Liverpool) replaced M.Collins (87 min); McVeigh (Tottenham Hotspur) replaced C.McAllister (87 min):
Booked: D.Griffen; J.Douglas; M.Collins; G.Lyttle: Sent *Off:* S.Friars:

4th October, 1995

Venue: Clandeboye Park, Bangor
Iceland   0 Republic of Belarus 0

Final Group 15 Table

	P	W	D	L N F	A	Pts	GD
1 Iceland	2	1	1	0 N 3	2	4	+1
2 N.Ireland.	2	1	0	1 N 4	3	3	+1
3 Rep. of Belarus	2	0	1	1 N 0	2	1	-2

NORTHERN IRELAND UNDER-17 INTERNATIONAL 1995/96

Friendly International

15th April, 1996

Venue: Racecourse Ground, Wrexham
Wales (0)   0 Northern Ireland (1)   2
D. Johnston (16), A. Coote (58)

N.Ireland: D.Clyde (Barnsley), L.Burns, C.Deegan, E.McCallion (Coleraine), P.Morgan, R.Gallagher (Portadown), D.Johnston (Blackburn Rovers), A.McShane, D.Fitzgerald (Rangers), A.Kirk (Glentoran), M.McKeever. Subs: W.Boyle (Leeds United) replaced L.Burns; P.Emerson (Leicester City) replaced R.Gallagher; B.Vaugh (Glasgow Celtic) replaced D.Fitzgerald; A.Coote (Norwich City) replaced M.McKeever:

NORTHERN IRELAND UNDER-16 INTERNATIONALs 1995/96

European Under-16 Championship - Mini Tournament

30th October, 1995

Venue: Toulouse
France   3 Northern Ireland   2
R.Graham, D.Healey

N. Ireland: D. Hastings (Lisburn Youth, G. Hunter (East End Hawkes); J. Topley (Glenavon); A. Hughes (Lisburn Youth); P. McKeown (Glasgow Celtic); M. McCleave (Celtic Boys); W. Carlisle (Lisburn Youth); G. Skates (Glentoran); M. Harkin (Wycombe Wanderers), D. Healey (Lisburn Youth); R. Graham (QPR); *Subs:* L. Waterman (Portsmouth) replaced G. Hunter (65 mins); G. Doherty (Derry City) replaced M. Harkin (75 mins); N. Corrigan (Celtic Boys) replaced W. Carlisle (60 mins); *Subs not used:* D. Miskelly (Glentoran); K. Trueman (Lisburn Youth).

1st November, 1995

Venue: Toulouse
Finland (1)   1 Northern Ireland (0)   0
Andersson

N. Ireland: D. Hastings, L. Waterman; J. Topley; A. Hughes; P. McKeown; M. McCleave; N. Corrigan; G. Skates; M. Harkin; D. Healey; R. Graham. *Subs:* K. Trueman replaced M. McCleave (43 mins); W. Carlisle replaced N. Corrigan (60 mins): *Subs not used:* D. Miskelly; G. Hunter; G. Doherty.

NORTHERN IRELAND UNDER-18 SCHOOLS INTERNATIONAL 1995/96

Heinz Centenary Shield - Semi-Final

15th March, 1996

Venue: Dixon Park, Ballyclare.
Northern Ireland (2) 2   Wales (1)
S.Elliott (11), P.Kirk (18)   P.Griffith (34)

N.Ireland: A.Spackman (Castlereagh College), C.Nixon (Regent House), N.Lenehan (Our Lady and St.Patrick's), G.Fulton (St.Malachy's College), S.Clanachan (Coleraine Institute), L.Feeney (Castlereagh College), P.McAtee (St.Malachy's College), K.Millar (East Antrim Institute), A.Kirk (Ashfield), D.McGlinchey (La Salle), S.Elliott (Ashfield). *Subs:* M.Heaney (Orangefield) replaced A.Spackman; S.Barr (Bangor Grammer) replaced D.McGlinchey:

NIE International Challenge

29th March, 1996

Venue: Ballybofey
Republic of Ireland (2) 3 Northern Ireland (2) 2
D.McGlinchey (21)   A.Kirk (2),
D. McGinley (29),   G.Callaghan (32),
B.Meehan (83)

N.Ireland: Line up not available.

NIE International Challenge

13th April, 1996

Venue: Newforge Lane, Belfast
Northern Ireland (0)   1   Scotland (0)   0
S.Clanachan (55)

N.Ireland: A.Spackman, C.Nixon, S.Clanachan, L.Feeney, R.Clarke (North West Institute), J.Anderson (Regent House), K.Millar, D.McGlinchey, S.Elliott, P.McAtee, S.Barr. *Subs:* N.Lenehan replaced S.Elliott (80 min); S.Carson (Grosvenor Grammer) replaced D.McGlinchey (88 min)

Heinz Centenary Shield - Final

25th April, 1996

Venue: Donegal Celtic Park, Belfast
Northern Ireland (0)   1   Switzerland (0)   0
D.McGlinchey (60)

N.Ireland: A.Spackman, C.Nixon, N.Lenehan, G.Fulton, S.Clanachan, L.Feeney, P.McAtee, K.Millar, A.Kirk, D.McGlinchey, S.Elliott. *Subs:* S.Barr replaced N.Lenehan (77 min):

NORTHERN IRELAND UNDER-15 SCHOOLS INTERNATIONAL 1995/96

Adidas Victory Shield

16th February, 1996

Venue: Racecourse Ground, Wrexham
Wales (1)   2   Northern Ireland (1)   1
G.Macklin (og 31),   G.Hamilton (17)
P.Roberts (67)

N.Ireland: G.Shannon (Cookstown High School), P.McCann (Lismore Comp.), G.Macklin (Glengormley High School), R.Culbertson (Ballee High School, Ballymena), S.Holmes (St.Brigid's High School, Londonderry), K.Loughran (St.Louis High School, Ballymena), S.Carson (Ballymoney High School), S.Hawe (Magherafelt High School), R.Martin (Abbey Grammer, Newry), G.Hamilton (Lurgan College), M.McCann (Drumcree High School).
Subs: W.Feeney (Ashfield High School) replaced S.Carson (72 min):

Adidas Victory Shield

23rd February, , 1996

Venue: Riverside Stadium, Middlesbrough *Att:* 7,750
England   0   Northern Ireland   0

N.Ireland: G.Shannon, P.McCann, G.Macklin, S.Holmes, R.Culbertson, K.Loughran, S.Carson, S.Hawe, R.Martin, G.Hamilton, M.McCann. *Subs:* T. McFlynn replaced S. Hawe; D. Logan replaced M. McCann.

SCHOOLBOY AND YOUTH INTERNATIONALS 1995/1996

NIE Challenge International

16th March, 1996

Venue: Crewe Park, ·
Northern Ireland (2)   2 Republic of Ireland (0)   1
S.Hawe (5), R.Culbertson (40) G.Dempster (60)

N.Ireland: P.Prentice (Laurelhill High School), P.McCann, G.Macklin, S.Holmes, R.Culbertson, K.Loughran, S.Carson, S.Hawe, G.Hamilton, M.McCann, W.Feeney. *Subs:* R.Martin replaced W.Feeney (54 min); C.McMullan (Boys Model, Belfast) replaced G.Macklin (79 min):

Adidas Victory Shield

22nd March, 1996

Venue: Windsor Park, Belfast   *Att:* 2,000
Northern Ireland (0)   1   Scotland (0)   0
R.Martin (60)

N.Ireland: G.Shannon, P.McCann, G.Macklin, S.Holmes, R.Culbertson, K.Loughran, S.Hawe, R.Martin, G.Hamilton, M.McCann, D.Logan (St.Malachy's College). *Subs:* S.Carson replaced M.McCann (68 min):

NIE Challenge International

8th May, 1996

Venue: Brandywell, Londonderry
Northern Ireland (0)   0   France (1)   2
P.Le Guen (36),
D.Vandenbossche (60)

N.Ireland: G.Shannon, P.McCann, G.Macklin, K.Loughran, S.Holmes, R.Culbertson, S.Carson, T.McFlynn (St.Patricks, Maghera), R.Martin, G.Hamilton, M.McCann. *Subs:* S.Hawe replaced T.McFlynn; C.McMullan replaced G.Macklin; D.Logan replaced W.Feeney:

International Friendly

13th May, 1996

Venue: Budapest.
Hungary (1)   1   Northern Ireland (0)   0
V.Kerescjes (12)

N.Ireland: G.Shannon, P.McCann, S.Holmes, R.Culbertson, G.Macklin, S.Carson, S.Hawe,

K.Loughran, M.McCann, R.Martin, G.Hamilton. *Subs:* D.Logan replaced S.Carson; W.Feeney replaced G.Hamilton; C.McMullan replaced P.McCann:

International Friendly

16th May, 1996

Venue: Sports Centre Complex, Effretikon.
Switzerland (0)   1   Northern Ireland (0)   0
C.Marguet (75)

N.Ireland:

NORTHERN IRELAND JUNIOR INTERNATIONALS 1995/96

Junior International Quadrangular Tournament (Isle of Man)

SEMI-FINAL

19th April, 1996

Venue: The Bowl, Douglas
Northern Ireland (1)   1   Scotland (0)   0
C.Morgan (45)

N.Ireland: D.Platt (Coleraine), L.Fyfe (Dundela) J.Law (Limavady United), D.Mullan (Limavady United), R.Morwood (Loughgall), Jer.Robinson (Dungannon Swifts), M.Jennings (Dungannon Swifts), M.Snodden (Dundela), C.Morgan (Crusaders), P.Moran (Limavady United), J.Johnston (Banbridge Town). *Subs:* D.Coll (Dungannon Swifts) replaced D.Mullan; J.Steele (Ballymena United) replaced C.Morgan; *Subs not used;* R.Crown (Limavady United); J.Houston (Glentoran); G.Duke (Loughgall):

FINAL

20th April, 1996

Venue: The Bowl, Douglas
Northern Ireland (2)   2   Isle of Man (1)   1
J.Johnston (35), C.Morgan (39) N.Corkill (44)

N.Ireland: D.Platt, L.Fyfe, J.Law, D.Coll, R.Morwood, Jer.Robinson, M.Jennings, M.Snodden, C.Morgan, P.Moran, J.Johnston. *Subs:* J.Houston replaced M.Jennings; J.Steele replaced J.Johnston; *Subs not used:* R.Crown; D.Mullan; G.Duke:

NORTHERN IRELANDS INTERNATIONAL PLAYING RECORD
NORTHERN IRELAND RESULTS AGAINST THE HOME COUNTRIES
KEY:
F = Friendly; **WCQ** = World Cup Qualifier; **WCF** = World Cup Finals; **ECQ** = European Championship Qualifier.

Northern Ireland v England
All matches played in British International Championship unless otherwise stated.

RESULTS

Date:	Venue:	N.I.	Eng.	N.Ireland Goalscorers:
18/02/1882	Bloomfield, Belfast	0	13 L	–
24/02/1883	Aigburth, Liverpool	0	7 L	–
23/02/1884	Ulster Grounds, Belfast	1	8 L	W.McWha
28/02/1885	Whelly Range, Manchester	0	4 L	–
13/03/1886	Ballynafeigh Park, Belfast	1	6 L	J.Williams
05/02/1887	Bramall Lane, Sheffield	0	7 L	–
07/04/1888	Ballynafeigh Park, Belfast	1	5 L	W.Crone
02/03/1889	Anfield, Liverpool	1	6 L	J.M.Wilton
15/03/1890	Ballynafeigh Park, Belfast	1	9 L	J.Reynolds
07/03/1891	Molyneux, Wolverhampton	1	6 L	T.Whiteside
05/03/1892	Solitude, Belfast	0	2 L	–
25/02/1893	Perry Barr, Birmingham	1	6 L	G.Gaffikin
03/03/1894	Solitude, Belfast	2	2 D	O.Stanfield, W.Gibson
09/03/1895	County Cricket Ground, Derby	0	9 L	–
07/03/1896	Solitude, Belfast	0	2 L	–
20/02/1897	Trent Bridge, Nottingham	0	6 L	–
05/03/1898	Solitude, Belfast	2	3 L	James Pyper, J.T.Mercer
18/02/1899	Roker Park, Sunderland	2	13 L	J.McAllen, J.Campbell
17/03/1900	Lansdowne Road, Dublin	0	2 L	–
09/03/1901	The Dell, Southampton	0	3 L	–
22/03/1902	Balmoral Ground, Belfast	0	1 L	–
14/02/1903	Molineux, Wolverhampton	0	4 L	–
12/03/1904	Solitude, Belfast	1	3 L	J.Kirwan
25/02/1905	Ayresome Park, Middlesbrough	1	1 D	R.Williamson (og)
17/02/1906	Solitude, Belfast	0	5 L	–
16/02/1907	Goodison Park, Liverpool	0	1 L	–
15/02/1908	Solitude, Belfast	1	3 L	D.J.Hannon
13/02/1909	Park Avenue, Bradford	0	4 L	–
12/02/1910	Solitude, Belfast	1	1 D	F.W.Thompson
11/02/1911	Baseball Ground, Derby	1	2 L	J.L.Macauley
10/02/1912	Dalymount Park, Dublin	1	6 L	M.Hamill
15/02/1913	Windsor Park, Belfast	2	1 W	W.Gillespie (2)
14/02/1914	Ayresome Park, Middlesbrough	3	0 W	W.Lacey (2), W.Gillespie
25/10/1919	Windsor Park, Belfast	1	1 D	J.Ferris
23/10/1920	Roker Park, Sunderland	0	2 L	–
22/10/1921	Windsor Park, Belfast	1	1 D	W.Gillespie
21/10/1922	The Hawthorns, West Bromwich	0	2 L	–
20/10/1923	Windsor Park, Belfast	2	1 W	W.Gillespie, T.Croft
22/10/1924	Goodison Park, Liverpool	1	3 L	W.Gillespie
24/10/1925	Windsor Park, Belfast	0	0 D	–
20/10/1926	Anfield, Liverpool	3	3 D	W.Gillespie, R.W.Irvine, H.Davey
22/10/1927	Windsor Park, Belfast	2	0 W	H.Jones (og), J.Mahood
22/10/1928	Goodison Park, Liverpool	1	2 L	J.Bambrick

Date:	Venue:	N.I.	Eng.		N.Ireland Goalscorers:
19/10/1929	Windsor Park, Belfast	0	3	L	---
20/10/1930	Bramall Lane, Sheffield	1	5	L	J.Dunne
17/10/1931	Windsor Park, Belfast	2	6	L	J.Dunne, J.Kelly
17/10/1932	Bloomfield Road, Blackpool	0	1	L	–
14/10/1933	Windsor Park, Belfast	0	3	L	–
06/02/1935	Goodison Park, Liverpool	1	2	L	A.E.Stevenson
19/10/1935	Windsor Park, Belfast	1	3	L	G.Brown
18/11/1936	Victoria Ground, Stoke	1	3	L	T.L.Davis
23/10/1937	Windsor Park, Belfast	1	5	L	A.E.Stevenson
16/11/1938	Old Trafford, Manchester	0	7	L	–
28/09/1946	Windsor Park, Belfast	2	7	L	N.Lockhart (2)
05/11/1947	Goodison Park, Liverpool	2	2	D	P.Doherty, D.Walsh
09/10/1948	Windsor Park, Belfast	2	6	L	D.Walsh
16/11/1949	Maine Road, Manchester (WCQ)	2	9	L	S.Smyth, R.A.Brennan
07/10/1950	Windsor Park, Belfast	1	4	L	E.J.McMorran
14/11/1951	Villa Park, Birmingham	0	2	L	–
04/10/1952	Windsor Park, Belfast	2	2	D	C.Tully
11/11/1953	Goodison Park, Liverpool (WCQ)	1	3	L	E.J.McMorran
02/10/1954	Windsor Park, Belfast	0	2	L	–
02/11/1955	Wembley Stadium, London	0	3	L	–
06/10/1956	Windsor Park, Belfast	1	1	D	J.McIlroy
06/11/1957	Wembley Stadium, London	3	2	W	J.McIlroy (pen), S.McCrory, W.Simpson
04/10/1958	Windsor Park, Belfast	3	3	D	W.Cush, R.Peacock, T.Casey
18/11/1959	Wembley Stadium, London	1	2	L	W.Bingham
08/10/1960	Windsor Park, Belfast	2	5	L	W.McAdams (2)
22/11/1961	Wembley Stadium, London	1	1	D	J.McIlroy
20/10/1962	Windsor Park, Belfast	1	3	L	H.Barr
20/11/1963	Wembley Stadium, London	3	8	L	J.Crossan, S.Wislon (2)
03/10/1964	Windsor Park, Belfast	3	4	L	S.Wilson, McLaughlin (2)
10/11/1965	Wembley Stadium, London	1	2	L	W.Irvine
22/10/1966	Windsor Park, Belfast (ECQ)	0	2	L	–
22/11/1967	Wembley Stadium, London (ECQ)	0	2	L	–
03/05/1969	Windsor Park, Belfast	1	3	L	E.McMordie
21/04/1970	Wembley Stadium, London	1	3	L	G.Best
15/05/1971	Windsor Park, Belfast	0	1	L	–
23/05/1972	Wembley Stadium, London	1	0	W	T.Neill
12/05/1973	Goodison Park, Liverpool	1	2	L	D.Clements (pen)
15/05/1974	Wembley Stadium, London	0	1	L	–
17/05/1975	Windsor Park, Belfast	0	0	D	–
11/05/1976	Wembley Stadium, London	0	4	L	–
28/05/1977	Windsor Park, Belfast	1	2	L	C.McGrath
16/05/1978	Wembley Stadium, London	0	1	L	–
07/02/1979	Wembley Stadium, London (ECQ)	0	4	L	–
19/05/1979	Windsor Park, Belfast	0	2	L	–
17/10/1979	Windsor Park, Belfast	1	5	L	V.Moreland (pen)
20/05/1980	Wembley Stadium, London	1	1	D	T.Cochrane
23/02/1982	Wembley Stadium, London	0	4	L	–
28/05/1983	Windsor Park, Belfast	0	0	D	–
04/04/1984	Wembley Stadium, London	0	1	L	–

Date:	Venue:	N.I.	Eng.	N.Ireland Goalscorers:
27/02/1985	Windsor Park, Belfast (WCQ)	0	1 L	–
13/11/1985	Wembley Stadium, London (WCQ)	0	0 D	–
15/10/1986	Wembley Stadium, London (ECQ)	0	3 L	–
01/04/1987	Windsor Park, Belfast (ECQ)	0	2 L	–

Northern Ireland v Scotland

All matches played in British International Championship unless otherwise stated.

RESULTS:

Date:	Venue:	N.I.	Scot.	N.Ireland Goalscorers:
26/01/1884	Ballynafeigh Park, Belfast	0	5 L	–
14/03/1885	Second Hampden, Glasgow	2	8 L	J.T.Gibb (2)
20/03/1886	Ballynafeigh Park, Belfast	2	7 L	J.Condy, S.Johnston
19/02/1887	Second Hampden, Glasgow	1	4 L	F.Browne
24/02/1888	Solitude, Belfast	2	10 L	J.Lemon, W.Dalton
09/03/1889	Ibrox Park, Glasgow	0	7 L	–
29/03/1890	Ballynafeigh Park, Belfast	1	4 L	J.Peden
28/03/1891	Parkhead, Glasgow	1	2 L	O.Stanfield
19/03/1892	Solitude, Belfast	2	3 L	J.Williamson, G.Gaffikin
25/03/1893	Parkhead, Glasgow	1	6 L	G.Gaffikin
31/03/1894	Solitude, Belfast	1	2 L	O.Stanfield
30/03/1895	Parkhead, Glasgow	1	3 L	W.Sherrard
28/03/1896	Solitude, Belfast	3	3 D	J.H.Barron (2), R.Milne (pen)
27/03/1897	Ibrox Park, Glasgow	1	5 L	James Pyper
26/03/1898	Solitude, Belfast	0	3 L	–
25/03/1899	Parkhead, Glasgow	1	9 L	A.L.Goodall
03/03/1900	Solitude, Belfast	0	3 L	–
23/02/1901	Parkhead, Glasgow	0	11 L	–
01/03/1902	Grosvenor Park, Belfast	1	5 L	R.Milne
21/03/1903	Parkhead, Glasgow	2	0 W	M.Connor, J.Kirwan
26/03/1904	Dalymount Park, Dublin	1	1 D	J.Sheridan
18/03/1905	Parkhead, Glasgow	0	4 L	–
17/03/1906	Dalymount Park, Dublin	0	1 L	–
16/03/1907	Parkhead, Glasgow	0	3 L	–
14/03/1908	Dalymount Park, Dublin	0	5 L	–
15/03/1909	Ibrox Park, Glasgow	0	5 L	–
19/03/1910	Windsor Park, Belfast	1	0 W	F.W.Thompson
18/03/1911	Parkhead, Glasgow	0	2 L	–
16/03/1912	Windsor Park, Belfast	1	4 L	J.McKnight (pen)
15/03/1913	Dalymount Park, Dublin	1	2 L	J.McKnight
14/03/1914	Windsor Park, Belfast	1	1 D	S.Young
13/03/1920	Parkhead, Glasgow	0	3 L	–
26/02/1921	Windsor Park, Belfast	0	2 L	–
04/03/1922	Parkhead, Glasgow	1	2 L	W.Gillespie
03/03/1923	Windsor Park, Belfast	0	1 L	–
01/03/1924	Parkhead, Glasgow	0	2 L	–
28/02/1925	Windsor Park, Belfast	0	3 L	–
27/02/1926	Ibrox Park, Glasgow	0	4 L	–
26/02/1927	Windsor Park, Belfast	0	2 L	–
25/02/1928	Firhill Park, Glasgow	1	0 W	J.Chambers

Date:	Venue:	N.I.	Scot.	N.Ireland Goalscorers:
23/02/1929	Windsor Park, Belfast	3	7 L	J.Bambrick (2), R.Rowley
22/02/1930	Parkhead, Glasgow	1	3 L	J.H.McCaw
21/02/1931	Windsor Park, Belfast	0	0 D	–
19/09/1931	Ibrox Park, Glasgow	1	3 L	J.Dunne
12/09/1932	Windsor Park, Belfast	0	4 L	–
16/09/1933	Parkhead, Glasgow	2	1 W	D.Martin (2)
20/10/1934	Windsor Park, Belfast	2	1 W	D.Martin, J.Coulter
13/11/1935	Tynecastle Park, Edinburgh	1	2 L	J.Kelly
31/10/1936	Windsor Park, Belfast	1	3 L	N.Kernaghan
10/11/1937	Pittodrie Stadium, Aberdeen	1	1 D	P.Doherty
08/10/1938	Windsor Park, Belfast	0	2 L	–
27/11/1946	Hampden Park, Glasgow	0	0 D	–
04/10/1947	Windsor Park, Belfast	2	0 W	S.Smyth (2)
17/11/1948	Hampden Park, Glasgow	2	3 L	D.Walsh
01/10/1949	Windsor Park, Belfast (WCQ)	2	8 L	S.Smyth (2)
01/11/1950	Hampden Park, Glasgow	1	6 L	J.K.McGarry
06/10/1951	Windsor Park, Glasgow	0	3 L	–
05/11/1952	Hampden Park, Glasgow	1	1 D	S.D.D'Arcy
03/10/1953	Windsor Park, Belfast (WCQ)	1	3 L	N.Lockhart (pen)
03/11/1954	Hampden Park, Glasgow	2	2 D	W.Bingham, W.McAdams
08/10/1955	Windsor Park, Belfast	2	1 W	J.Blanchflower, W.Bingham
07/11/1956	Hampden Park, Glasgow	0	1 L	–
05/10/1957	Windsor Park, Belfast	1	1 D	W.Bingham
05/11/1958	Hampden Park, Glasgow	2	2 D	E.Caldow (og), J.McIlroy
03/10/1959	Windsor Park, Belfast	0	4 L	–
09/11/1960	Hampden Park, Glasgow	2	5 L	D.Blanchflower (pen), P.McParland
07/10/1961	Windsor Park, Belfast	1	6 L	J.McLaughlin
07/11/1962	Hampden Park, Glasgow	1	5 L	W.Bingham
12/10/1963	Windsor Park, Glasgow	2	1 W	W.Bingham, S.Wilson
25/11/1964	Hampden Park, Glasgow	2	3 L	G.Best, W.Irvine
02/10/1965	Windsor Park, Belfast	3	2 W	D.Dougan, J.Crossan, W.Irvine
16/11/1966	Hampden Park, Glasgow (ECQ)	1	2 L	J.Nicholson
21/10/1967	Windsor Park, Belfast (ECQ)	1	0 W	D.Clements
06/05/1969	Hampden Park, Glasgow	1	1 D	E.McMordie
18/04/1970	Windsor Park, Belfast	0	1 L	–
18/05/1971	Hampden Park, Glasgow	1	0 W	J.Greig (og)
20/05/1972	Hampden Park, Glasgow	0	2 L	–
16/05/1973	Hampden Park, Glasgow	2	1 W	Ma.O'Neill, T.Anderson
11/05/1974	Hampden Park, Glasgow	1	0 W	T.Cassidy
20/05/1975	Hampden Park, Glasgow	0	3 L	–
08/05/1976	Hampden Park, Glasgow	0	3 L	–
01/06/1977	Hampden Park, Glasgow	0	3 L	–
13/05/1978	Hampden Park, Glasgow	1	1 D	Ma.O'Neill
22/05/1979	Hampden Park, Glasgow	0	1 L	–
16/05/1980	Windsor Park, Belfast	1	0 W	W.Hamilton
25/03/1981	Hampden Park, Glasgow (WCQ)	1	1 D	W.Hamilton
19/05/1981	Hampden Park, Glasgow	0	2 L	–
14/10/1981	Windsor Park, Belfast	0	0 D	–
28/04/1982	Windsor Park, Belfast	1	1 D	S.McIlroy

Date:	Venue:	N.I.	Scot.	N.Ireland Goalscorers:
24/05/1983	Hampden Park, Glasgow	0	0 D	–
13/12/1983	Windsor Park, Belfast	2	0 W	N.Whiteside, S.McIlroy
19/02/1992	Hampden Park, Glasgow	0	1 L	–

Northern Ireland v Wales

All matches played in British International Championship unless otherwise stated.

RESULTS:

Date:	Venue:	N.I.	Wales	N.Ireland Goalscorers:
25/02/1882	Acton Park, Wrexham	1	7 L	S.Johnston
17/03/1883	Ballynafeigh Park, Belfast	1	1 D	W.J.Morrow
09/02/1884	Acton Park, Wrexham	0	6 L	–
11/04/1885	Ballynafeigh Park, Belfast	2	8 L	T.B.Molyneux, A.H.Dill
27/02/1886	Acton Park, Wrexham	0	5 L	–
12/03/1887	Ballynafeigh Park, Belfast	4	1 W	O.Stanfield, F.Browne, J.Peden, J.Sherrard
03/03/1888	Acton Park, Wrexham	0	11 L	–
27/04/1889	Ballynafeigh Park, Belfast	1	3 L	J.Lemon
08/02/1890	Shrewsbury	2	5 L	W.Dalton (2)
17/02/1891	Ulsterville, Belfast	7	2 W	W.Dalton, G.Gaffikin, O.Stanfield (4), S. Torrans
27/02/1892	Penrhyn Park, Bangor (Wales)	1	1 D	O.Stanfield
08/04/1893	Ulsterville, Belfast	4	3 W	J.Peden (3), J.M.Wilton
24/02/1894	St.Helens, Swansea	1	4 L	O.Stanfield
16/03/1895	Solitude, Belfast	2	2 D	G.Gaukrodger, W.Sherrard
29/02/1896	Acton Park, Wrexham	1	6 L	E.Turner
06/03/1897	Solitude, Belfast	4	3 W	J.H.Barron, O.Stanfield, John Pyper, J.Peden
19/02/1898	Llandudno Park, Llandudno	1	0 W	J.Peden
04/03/1899	Grosvenor Park, Belfast	1	0 W	J.Meldon
24/02/1900	Llandudno Park, Llandudno	0	2 L	–
23/03/1901	Solitude, Belfast	0	1 L	–
22/02/1902	Cardiff Arms Park, Cardiff	3	0 W	A.Gara (3)
28/03/1903	Solitude, Belfast	2	0 W	A.L.Goodall, J.Sheridan
21/03/1904	Penrhyn Park, Bangor (Wales)	1	0 W	W.McCracken (pen)
08/04/1905	Solitude, Belfast	2	2 D	N.Murphy, C.O'Hagen
02/04/1906	Racecourse Ground, Wrexham	4	4 D	J.Maxwell (2), H.Sloan (2)
23/02/1907	Solitude, Belfast	2	3 L	C.O'Hagen, H.Sloan
11/04/1908	Athletic Ground, Aberdare	1	0 W	H.Sloan
20/03/1909	Grosvenor Park, Belfast	2	3 L	W.Lacey, A.Hunter
11/04/1910	Racecourse Ground, Wrexham	1	4 L	J.Darling (pen)
28/01/1911	Windsor Park, Belfast	1	2 L	W.Halligan
13/04/1912	Ninian Park, Cardiff	3	2 W	J.McCandless (2), B.Brennan
18/01/1913	Grosvenor Park, Belfast	0	1 L	–
19/01/1914	Racecourse Ground, Wrexham	2	1 W	S.Young, W.Gillespie
14/02/1920	The Oval, Belfast	2	2 D	J.McCandless, W.Emerson
09/04/1921	The Vetch Field, Swansea	1	2 L	J.Chambers
01/04/1922	Windsor Park, Belfast	1	1 D	W.Gillespie
14/03/1923	Racecourse Ground, Wrexham	3	0 W	R.W.Irvine (2), W.Gillespie
15/03/1924	Windsor Park, Belfast	0	1 L	–
18/04/1925	Racecourse Ground, Wrexham	0	0 D	–
13/02/1926	Windsor Park, Belfast	3	0 W	W.Gillespie, S.Curran (2)
09/04/1927	Ninian Park, Cardiff	2	2 D	H.Johnston (2)

NORTHERN IRELAND INTERNATIONAL PLAYING RECORD

Date:	Venue:	N.I.	Wales	N.Ireland Goalscorers:
04/02/1928	Windsor Park, Belfast	1	2 L	J.Chambers
02/02/1929	Racecourse Ground, Wrexham	2	2 D	J.Mahood, A.McCluggage
01/02/1930	Celtic Park, Belfast	7	0 W	J.Bambrick (6), A.McCluggage
22/04/1931	Racecourse Ground, Wrexham	2	3 L	J.Dunne, R.Rowley
05/12/1931	Windsor Park, Belfast	4	0 W	J.Kelly (2), W.Millar, J.Bambrick
07/12/1932	Racecourse Ground, Wrexham	1	4 L	S.English
04/11/1933	Windsor Park, Belfast	1	1 D	S.Jones
27/03/1935	Racecourse Ground, Wrexham	1	3 L	J.Bambrick
11/03/1936	Celtic Park, Belfast	3	2 W	T.J.Gibb, A.E.Stevenson, N.Kernaghan
17/03/1937	Racecourse Ground, Wrexham	1	4 L	A.E.Stevenson
16/03/1938	Windsor Park, Belfast	1	0 W	J.Bambrick
15/03/1939	Racecourse Ground, Wrexham	1	3 L	D.Milligan
16/04/1947	WindsorPark, Belfast	2	1 W	A.E.Stevenson, P.Doherty (pen)
10/03/1948	Racecourse Ground, Wrexham	0	2 L	–
09/03/1949	Windsor Park, Belfast	0	2 L	–
08/03/1950	Racecourse Ground, Wrexham (WCQ)	0	0 D	–
07/03/1951	Windsor Park, Belfast	1	2 L	W.Simpson
19/03/1952	Vetch Field, Swansea	0	3 L	–
15/04/1953	Windsor Park, Belfast	2	3 L	E.J.McMorran (2)
31/03/1954	Racecourse Ground, Wrexham (WCQ)	2	1 W	P.McParland (2)
20/04/1955	Windsor Park, Belfast	2	3 L	E.Crossan, J.Walker
11/04/1956	Ninian Park, Cardiff	1	1 D	J.Jones
10/04/1957	Windsor Park, Belfast	0	0 D	-
16/04/1958	Ninian Park, Cardiff	1	1 D	W.Simpson
22/04/1959	Windsor Park, Belfast	4	1 W	P.McParland (2), R.Peacock, J.McIlroy
06/04/1960	Racecourse Ground, Wrexham	2	3 L	W.Bingham, D.Blanchflower (pen)
12/04/1961	Windsor Park, Belfast	1	5 L	D.Dougan
11/04/1962	Ninian Park, Cardiff	0	4 L	–
03/04/1963	Windsor Park, Belfast	1	4 L	M.Harvey
15/04/1964	Vetch Field, Swansea	3	2 W	J.McLaughlin, S.Wilson, M.Harvey
31/03/1965	Windsor Park, Belfast	0	5 L	–
30/03/1966	Ninian Park, Cardiff	4	1 W	W.Irvine, S.Wilson, E.Welsh, M.Harvey
12/04/1967	Windsor Park, Belfast (ECQ)	0	0 D	–
28/02/1968	Racecourse Ground, Wrexham (ECQ)	0	2 L	–
10/05/1969	Windsor Park, Belfast	0	0 D	–
25/04/1970	Vetch Field, Swansea	0	1 L	–
22/05/1971	Windsor Park, Belfast	1	0 W	B.Hamilton
27/05/1972	Racecourse Ground, Wrexham	0	0 D	–
19/05/1973	Goodison Park, Liverpool	1	0 W	B.Hamilton
18/05/1974	Racecourse Ground, Wrexham	0	1 L	–
23/05/1975	Windsor Park, Belfast	1	0 W	T.Finney
14/04/1976	Vetch Field, Swansea	0	1 L	–
03/06/1977	Windsor Park, Belfast	1	1 D	S.Nelson
19/05/1978	Racecourse Ground, Wrexham	0	1 L	–
25/05/1979	Windsor Park, Belfast	1	1 D	D.Spence
23/05/1980	Ninian Park, Cardiff	1	0 W	N.Brotherston
28/05/1982	Racecourse Ground, Wrexham	0	3 L	–
31/05/1983	Windsor Park, Belfast	0	1 L	–
22/05/1984	Vetch Field, Swansea	1	1 D	G.Armstrong

NORTHERN IRELANDS FOREIGN PLAYING RECORD

NORTHERN IRELAND RESULTS AGAINST THE FOREIGN COUNTRIES
KEY:
F = Friendly; **WCQ** = World Cup Qualifier; **WCF** = World Cup Finals; **ECQ** = European Championship Qualifier; **CC** = Canada Cop.
Northern Ireland Score shown first in all cases.

Date:	Venue:	Results:	N.Ireland Goalscorers:
		Albania	
07/05/1965	Windsor Park, Belfast (WCQ)	4 - 1 W	J.Crossan (3,1pen), G.Best
24/11/1965	Kombetar Quemal Stadium, Tirana (WCQ)	1 - 1 D	W.Irvine
15/12/1982	Kombetar Quemal Stadium, Tirana (ECQ)	0 - 0 D	–
27/04/1983	Windsor Park, Belfast (ECQ)	1 - 0 W	I.Stewart
09/09/1992	Windsor Park, Belfast (WCQ)	3 - 0 W	C.Clarke, K.Wilson, J.Magilton
17/02/1993	Kombetar Quemal Stadium, Tirana (WCQ)	2 - 1 W	J.Magilton, A.McDonald
		Algeria	
03/06/1986	3rd March Stadium, Guadalajara (WCF)	1 - 1 D	N.Whiteside
		Argentina	
11/06/1958	Orjans Vall Stadium, Halmstad (WCF)	1 - 3 L	P.McParland
		Austria	
01/07/1982	Vicente Calderon Stadium, Madrid (WCF)	2 - 2 D	W.Hamilton (2)
13/10/1982	Prater Stadium, Vienna (ECQ)	0 - 2 L	–
21/09/1983	Windsor Park, Belfast (ECQ)	3 - 1 W	W.Hamilton, N.Whiteside, Ma.O'Neill
14/11/1990	Prater Stadium, Vienna (ECQ)	0 - 0 D	–
16/10/1991	Windsor Park, Belfast (ECQ)	2 - 1 W	I.Dowie, K.Black
12/10/1994	Prater Staidom, Vienna (ECQ)	2 - 1 W	K.Gillespie, P. Gray
15/11/1995	Windsor Park, Belfast (ECQ)	5 - 3 W	Mi. O'Neill (2), I.Dowie (pen), B.Hunter,P.Gray
		Australia	
11/06/1980	Sydney Cricket Ground, Sydney (F)	2 - 1 W	C.Nicholl, J.O'Neill
15/06/1980	Olympic Park, Melbourne (F)	1 - 1 D	Ma.O'Neill
18/06/1980	Hindmarsh Stadium, Adelaide (F)	2 - 1 W	N.Brotherston, C.McCurdy
		Belgium	
10/11/1976	Stade de Sclessin, Liege (WCQ)	0 - 2 L	–
16/11/1977	Windsor Park, Belfast (WCQ)	3 - 0 W	G.Armstrong (2), C.McGrath
		Brazil	
12/10/1986	Jalisco Stadium, Guadalajara (WCF)	0 - 3 L	–
		Bulgaria	
18/10/1972	Vassil Levski Stadium, Sofia (WCQ)	0 - 3 L	–
26/09/1973	Hillsborough, Sheffield (WCQ)	0 - 0 D	–
29/11/1978	Vassil Levski, Sofia (ECQ)	2 - 0 W	G.Armstrong, W.Caskey
02/05/1979	Windsor Park, Belfast (ECQ)	2 - 0 W	C.Nicholl, G.Armstrong
		Canada	
22/05/1995	Commonwealth Stadium, Edmonton (CC)	0 - 2	–
		Chile	
26/05/1989	Windsor Park, Belfast (F)	0 - 1 L	–
		Colombia	
03/06/1994	Foxboro Stadium, Boston (F)	0 - 2 L	–

Date:	Venue:	Results:	N.Ireland Goalscorers:

Cyprus

03/02/1971	GSP Stadium Nicosia (ECQ)	3 - 0 W	J.Nicholson, D.Dougan, G.Best (pen)
21/04/1971	Windsor Park, Belfast(ECQ)	5 - 0 W	D.Dougan, G.Best (3), J.Nicholson
14/02/1973	GSP Stadium, Nicosia (WCQ)	0 - 1 L	–
08/05/1973	Craven Cottage, London (WCQ)	3 - 0 W	S.Morgan, T.Anderson (2)

Czechoslovakia

08/06/1958	Orjans Vall Stadium, Halmstad (WCF)	1 - 0 W	W.Cush
17/06/1958	Malmo Stadium, Malmo (WCF)	2 - 1 W	P.McParland (2)

Denmark

25/10/1978	Windsor Park, Belfast (ECQ)	2 - 1 W	D.Spence, T.Anderson
06/06/1979	Idraetes Park Stadium, Copenhagen (ECQ)	0 - 4 L	–
26/03/1986	Windsor Park, Belfast (F)	1 - 1 D	A.McDonald
17/10/1990	Windsor Park, Belfast (ECQ)	1 - 1 D	C.Clarke
13/11/1991	Odense Stadium, Odense (ECQ)	1 - 2 L	G.Taggart
18/11/1992	Windsor Park, Belfast (WCQ)	0 - 1 L	–
13/10/1993	Parken Stadium, Copenhagen (WCQ)	0 - 1 L	–

Faroe Islands

01/05/1991	Windsor Park, Belfast (ECQ)1	1 - 1 D	C.Clarke
11/09/1991	Landskrona Idrottsplats, Landskrona	5 - 0 W	K.Wilson, C.Clarke (3,1pen), A.McDonald

Finland

27/05/1984	Pori Stadium, Pori (WCQ)	0 - 1 L	–
14/11/1984	Windsor Park, Belfast (WCQ)	2 - 1 W	J.O'Neill, G.Armstrong

France

12/05/1951	Windsor Park, Belfast (F)	2 - 2 D	R.Ferris (pen), W.Simpson
11/11/1952	Stade de Colombes, Paris (F)	1 - 3 L	C.Tully
19/06/1958	Idrottsparken, Norrkoping (WCF)	0 - 4 L	–
24/03/1982	Parc des Princess, Paris (F)	0 - 4 L	–
04/07/1982	Vicente Calderon Stadium, Madrid (WCF)	1 - 4 L	G.Armstrong
26/02/1986	Parc des Princess, Paris (F)	0 - 0 D	–
27/04/1988	Windsor Park, Belfast (F)	0 - 0 D	–

West Germany/Germany

15/05/1958	Malmo Stadium, Malmo (WCF)	2 - 2 D	P.McParland (2)
26/10/1960	Windsor Park, Belfast (WCQ)	3 - 4 L	W.McAdams (3)
10/05/1961	Olympic Stadium, Berlin (WCQ)	1 - 2 L	J.McIlroy
07/05/1966	Windsor Park, Belfast (F)	0 - 2 L	–
27/04/1977	Muengersdorfer Stadium, Cologne (F)	0 - 5 L	–
17/11/1982	Windsor Park, Belfast (ECQ)	1 - 0 W	I.Stewart
16/11/1983	Volksparkstadion, Hamburg (ECQ)	1 - 0 W	N.Whiteside
02/06/1992	Weserstadion, Bremen (F)	1 - 1 D	M.Hughes
29/05/1996	Windsor Park, Belfast (F)	1 - 1 D	G. O'Boyle

Greece

03/05/1961	Panathanaikos Stadium, Athens (WCQ)	1 - 2 L	J.McIlroy

Date:	Venue:	Results:	N.Ireland Goalscorers:
17/10/1961	Windsor Park, Belfast (WCQ)	2 - 0 W	J.McLaughlin (2)
17/02/1988	Olympic Stadium, Athens (F)	2 - 3 L	C.Clarke (2,1pen)

Honduras

21/06/1982	La Romareda Stadium, Zaragoza (WCF)	1 - 1 D	G.Armstrong

Hungary

19/10/1988	Nep Stadium, Budapest (WCQ)	0 - 1 L	–
06/09/1989	Windsor Park, Belfast (WCQ)	1 - 2 L	N.Whiteside

Iceland

11/06/1977	Lancardalvollur Stadium, Reykavik (WCQ)	0 - 1 L	–
21/09/1977	Windsor Park, Belfast (WCQ)	2 - 0 W	C.McGrath, S.McIlroy

Republic of Ireland

20/09/1978	Lansdowne Road, Dublin (ECQ)	0 - 0 D	–
21/11/1979	Windsor Park, Belfast (ECQ)	1 - 0 W	G.Armstrong
14/09/1988	Windsor Park, Belfast (WCQ)	0 - 0 D	–
11/10/1989	Lansdowne Road, Dublin (WCQ)	0 - 3 L	–
31/03/1993	Lansdowne Road, Dublin (WCQ)	0 - 3 L	–
17/11/1993	Windsor Park, Belfast (WCQ)	1 - 1 D	J.Quinn
16/11/1994	Windsor Park, Belfast (WCQ)	0 - 4 L	–
29/03/1995	Lansdowne Road, Dublin (ECQ)	1 - 1 D	I.Dowie

Israel

10/09/1968	Bloomfield Stadium, Tel Aviv (F)	3 - 2 W	D.Dougan, W.Irvine (2)
03/03/1976	Bloomfield Stadium, Tel Aviv (F)	1 - 1 D	W. Feeney
26/03/1980	Ramat Gan Stadium, Tel Aviv (WCQ)	0 - 0 D	–
18/11/1981	Windsor Park, Belfast (WCQ)	1 - 0 W	G.Armstrong
16/10/1984	Windsor Park, Belfast (F)	3 - 0 W	N.Whiteside, J.Quinn, L.Doherty
18/02/1987	Ramat Gan Stadium, Tel Aviv (F)	1 - 1 D	S.Penney

Italy

25/04/1957	Stadio Olympico, Rome (WCQ)	0 - 1 L	–
04/12/1957	Windsor Park, Belfast (F)	2 - 2 D	W.Cush (2)
15/01/1958	Windsor Park, Belfast (WCQ)	2 - 1 W	J.McIlroy, W.Cush
25/04/1961	Comunale Stadium, Bologna (F)	2 - 3 L	D.Dougan, W.McAdams

Latvia

02/06/1993	National Stadium, Riga (WCQ)	2 - 1 W	J.Magilton, G.Taggart
08/09/1993	Windsor Park, Belfast (WCQ)	2 - 0 W	J.Quinn, P.Gray
26/04/1995	Daugava Stadium, Riga (ECQ)	1 - 0 W	I.Dowie (pen)
07/06/1995	Windsor Park, Belfast (ECQ)	1 - 2 L	I.Dowie

Liechtenstein

20/04/1994	Windsor Park, Belfast (ECQ)	4 - 1 W	J.Quinn (2), S.Lomas, I.Dowie
11/10/1995	Sportpark, Eschen (ECQ)	4 - 0 W	M. O'Neill, G.McMahon, J.Quinn, P.Gray

Lithuania

28/05/1992	Windsor Park, Belfast (WCQ)	2 2 D	K.Wislon, G.Taggart

Date:	Venue:	Results:	N.Ireland Goalscorers:
25/05/1993	Zalgiris Stadium, Vilnius (WCQ)	1 0 W	I.Dowie

Malta

21/05/1988	Windsor Park, Belfast (WCQ)	3 0 W	J.Quinn, S.Penney, C.Clarke
26/04/1989	Ta'Quail Stadium, Valetta (WCQ)	2 - 0 W	C.Clarke, Mi.O'Neill

Mexico

22/06/1966	Windsor Park, Belfast (F)	4 - 1 W	W.Johnston, A.Elder, J.Nicholson, W.Ferguson
11/06/1994	Orange Bowl Stadium, Miami (F)	0 - 3 L	–

Morocco

22/04/1986	Windsor Park, Belfast (F)	2 - 1 W	C.Clarke, J.Quinn

Netherlands

09/05/1962	Feyenoord Stadium, Rotterdam (F)	0 - 4 L	–
17/03/1965	Windsor Park, Belfast (WCQ)	2 - 1 W	J.Crossan, T.Neill
07/04/1965	Feyenoord Stadium, Rotterdam (WCQ)	0 - 0 D	–
13/10/1976	Feyenoord Stadium, Rotterdam (WCQ)	2 - 2 D	C.McGrath, D.Spence
12/10/1977	Windsor Park, Belfast (WCQ)	0 - 1 L	–

Norway

04/09/1974	Ulleval Stadium, Oslo (ECQ)	1 - 2 L	T.Finney
29/10/1975	Windsor Park, Belfast (ECQ)	3 - 0 W	S.Morgan, B.Hamilton, S.McIlroy
27/03/1990	Windsor Park, Belfast (F)	2 - 3 L	J.Quinn, K.Wilson
27/03/1996	Windsor Park, Belfast (F)	0 - 2 L	–

Poland

10/10/1962	Slaski Stadium, Katowice (ECQ)	2 - 0 W	D.Dougan, W.Humphries
28/11/1962	Windsor Park, Belfast (ECQ)	2 - 0 W	J.Crossan, W.Bingham
23/03/1988	Windsor Park, Belfast (F)	1 - 1 D	D.Wilson
06/02/1991	Windsor Park, Belfast (F)	3 - 1 W	G.Taggart (2), J.Magilton

Portugal

16/01/1957	Jose Alvalade Stadium, Lisbon (WCQ)	1 - 1 D	W.Cush
01/05/1957	Windsor Park, Belfast (WCQ)	3 - 0 W	W.Simpson, J.McIlroy(pen), T.Casey
28/03/1973	Highfield Road, Coventry (WCQ)	1 - 1 D	Ma.O'Neill
14/11/1973	Jose Alvalade Stadium, Lisbon (WCQ)	1 - 1 D	L.O'Kane
19/11/1980	Stadium of Light, Lisbon (WCQ)	0 - 1 L	–
29/04/1981	Windsor Park, Belfast (WCQ)	1 - 0 W	G.Armstrong
07/09/1994	Windsor Park, Belfast (ECQ)	1 - 2 L	J.Quinn
03/09/1995	Estadio Das Antas, Oporto (ECQ)	1 - 1 D	M. Hughes

Romania

12/09/1984	Windsor Park, Belfast (WCQ)	3 - 2 W	Iorgulescu (og), N.Whiteside, Ma.O'Neill
16/10/1984	23rd August Stadium, Bucharest (WCQ)	1 - 0 W	J.Quinn
23/03/1994	Windsor Park, Belfast (F)	2 - 0 W	S.Morrow, P.Gray

Spain

15/10/1958	Bernabeu Stadium, Madrid (F)	2 - 6 L	W.Bingham, J.McIlroy
30/05/1963	San Mames Stadium, Bilbao (ECQ)	1 - 1 D	W.Irvine
30/10/1963	Windsor Park, Belfast (ECQ)	0 - 1 L	–

Date:	Venue:	Results:	N.Ireland Goalscorers:
11/11/1970	Sanches Pizjuan Stadium, Seville (ECQ)	0 - 3 L	–
16/02/1972	Boothferry Park, Hull (ECQ)	1 - 1 D	S.Morgan
25/06/1982	Luis Casanova Stadium, Valencia (WCF)	1 - 0 W	G.Armstrong
27/03/1985	Luis Sitjar Stadium, Palma (F)	0 - 0 D	–
07/06/1986	3rd March Stadium, Guadalajara (WCF)	1 - 2 L	C.Clarke
21/12/1988	Ramon Sanchez Stadium, Seville (WCQ)	0 - 4 L	–
08/02/1989	Windsor Park, Belfast (WCQ)	0 - 2 L	–
14/10/1992	Windsor Park, Belfast (WCQ)	0 - 0 D	–
28/04/1993	Ramon Sanchez Stadium, Seville (WCQ)	1 - 3 L	K.Wilson

Sweden

Date:	Venue:	Results:	N.Ireland Goalscorers:
30/10/1974	Fotboll Stadion, Solna (ECQ)	2 - 0 W	C.Nicholl, Ma.O'Neill
03/09/1975	Windsor Park, Belfast (ECQ)	1 - 2 L	A.Hunter
15/10/1980	Windsor Park, Belfast (WCQ)	3 - 0 W	N.Brotherston, S.McIlroy, J.Nicholl
03/06/1981	Rasunda Stadium, Stockholm (WCQ)	0 - 1 L	–
24/04/1996	Windsor Park, Belfast (F)	1 - 2 L	G. McMahon

Switzerland

Date:	Venue:	Results:	N.Ireland Goalscorers:
14/10/1964	Windsor Park, Belfast (WCQ)	1 - 0 W	J.Crossan (pen)
14/11/1964	Stade Olympique, Lausanne (WCQ)	1 - 2 L	G.Best

Turkey

Date:	Venue:	Results:	N.Ireland Goalscorers:
23/10/1968	Windsor Park, Belfast (WCQ)	4 - 1 W	G.Best, E.McMordie, D.Dougan,W.Campbell
11/12/1968	Stade Ali Sam Yen, Istanbul (WCQ)	3 - 0 W	T.Harkin (2), J.Nicholson
30/03/1983	Windsor Park, Belfast (ECQ)	2 - 1 W	Ma.O'Neill, J.McClelland
12/10/1983	19th May Stadium, Ankara (ECQ)	0 - 1 L	–
01/05/1985	Windsor Park, Belfast (WCQ)	2 - 0 W	N.Whiteside (2)
11/09/1985	Ataturk Stadium, Izmir (WCQ)	0 - 0 D	–
12/11/1986	Ataturk Stadium, Izmir (ECQ)	0 - 0 D	–
11/11/1987	Windsor Park, Belfast (ECQ)	1 - 0 W	J.Quinn

Uruguay

Date:	Venue:	Results:	N.Ireland Goalscorers:
29/04/1964	Windsor Park, Belfast (F)	3 - 0 W	J.Crossan (2pens), S.Wilson
18/05/1990	Windsor Park, Belfast (F)	1 - 0 W	K.Wilson

U.S.S.R

Date:	Venue:	Results:	N.Ireland Goalscorers:
10/09/1969	Windsor Park, Belfast (WCQ)	0 - 0 D	–
22/10/1969	Lenin Stadium, Moscow (WCQ)	0 - 2 L	–
22/09/1971	Lenin Stadium, Moscow (ECQ)	0 - 1 L	–
13/10/1971	Windsor Park, Belfast (ECQ)	1 - 1 D	J.Nicholson

Yugoslavia

Date:	Venue:	Results:	N.Ireland Goalscorers:
16/03/1975	Windsor Park, Belfast (ECQ)	1 - 0 W	B.Hamilton
19/11/1975	JNA Stadium, Belgrade (ECQ)	0 - 1 L	–
17/06/1982	La Romareda Stadium, Zaragoza (WCF)	0 - 0 D	–
29/04/1987	Windsor Park, Belfast (ECQ)	1 - 2 L	C.Clarke
14/10/1987	Groavica Stadium, Sarajevo (ECQ)	0 - 3 L	–
12/09/1990	Windsor Park, Belfast (ECQ)	0 - 2 L	–
27/03/1991	Marakana Stadium, Belgrade (ECQ)	1 - 4 L	C.Hill

NORTHERN IRELANDS FULL INTERNATIONAL PLAYING RECORD

1882-1996 – HOME AND AWAY

	Home						Away					
	P	W	D	L	F	A	P	W	D	L	F	A
Albania	3	3	0	0	8	1	3	1	2	0	3	2
Algeria	0	0	0	0	0	0	0	0	0	0	0	0
Argentina	0	0	0	0	0	0	0	0	0	0	0	0
Austria	3	3	0	0	10	5	3	1	1	1	2	3
Australia	0	0	0	0	0	0	3	2	1	0	5	3
Belgium	1	1	0	0	3	0	1	0	0	1	0	2
Brazil	0	0	0	0	0	0	0	0	0	0	0	0
Bulgaria	1	1	0	0	2	0	2	1	0	1	2	3
Canada	0	0	0	0	0	0	1	0	0	1	0	2
Chile	1	0	0	1	0	1	0	0	0	0	0	0
Colombia	0	0	0	0	0	0	0	0	0	0	0	0
Cyprus	1	1	0	0	5	0	2	1	0	1	3	1
Czechoslovakia	0	0	0	0	0	0	0	0	0	0	0	0
Denmark	4	1	2	1	4	4	3	0	0	3	1	7
England	47	3	10	34	44	150	49	3	6	40	36	169
Faroe Islands	1	0	1	0	1	1	1	1	0	0	5	0
Finland	1	1	0	0	2	1	1	0	0	1	0	1
France	2	0	2	0	2	2	3	0	1	2	1	7
Germany/West Germany	4	1	1	2	5	7	4	1	1	2	3	8
Greece	1	1	0	0	2	0	2	0	0	2	3	5
Honduras	0	0	0	0	0	0	0	0	0	0	0	0
Hungary	1	0	0	1	1	2	1	0	0	1	0	1
Iceland	1	1	0	0	2	0	1	0	0	1	0	1
Republic of Ireland	4	1	2	1	3	2	4	0	2	2	1	7
Israel	2	2	0	0	4	0	4	1	3	0	5	4
Italy	2	1	1	0	4	3	2	0	0	2	2	4
Latvia	2	1	0	1	3	2	2	2	0	0	3	1
Liechtenstein	1	1	0	0	4	1	1	1	0	0	4	0
Lithuania	1	0	1	0	2	2	1	1	0	0	1	0
Malta	1	1	0	0	3	0	1	1	0	0	2	0
Mexico	1	1	0	0	4	1	0	0	0	0	0	0
Morocco	1	1	0	0	2	1	0	0	0	0	0	0
Netherlands	2	1	0	1	2	2	3	0	2	1	2	6
Norway	3	1	0	2	5	5	1	0	0	1	1	2
Poland	3	2	1	0	6	2	1	1	0	0	2	0
Portugal	3	2	0	1	5	2	4	0	3	1	3	4
Romania	2	2	0	0	5	2	1	1	0	0	1	0
Scotland	43	9	7	27	42	115	49	6	9	34	39	139
Spain	3	0	1	2	0	3	7	1	2	4	5	17
Sweden	3	1	0	2	5	4	2	1	0	1	2	1
Switzerland	1	1	0	0	1	0	1	0	0	1	1	2
Turkey	4	4	0	0	9	2	4	1	2	1	3	1
Uruguay	2	2	0	0	4	0	0	0	0	0	0	0
U.S.S.R.	2	0	2	0	1	1	2	0	0	2	0	3
Wales	43	15	11	17	75	73	46	11	10	25	51	109
Yugoslavia	3	1	0	2	2	4	3	0	0	3	1	8
Total	**204**	**67**	**42**	**95**	**281**	**404**	**219**	**39**	**45**	**135**	**193**	**523**

1882-1996 – NEUTRAL AND TOTAL

	Neutral						Total					
	P	W	D	L	F	A	P	W	D	L	F	A
Albania	0	0	0	0	0	0	6	4	2	0	11	3
Algeria	1	0	1	0	1	1	1	0	1	0	1	1
Argentina	1	0	0	1	1	3	1	0	0	1	1	3
Austria	1	0	1	0	2	2	7	4	2	1	14	10
Australia	0	0	0	0	0	0	3	2	1	0	5	3
Belgium	0	0	0	0	0	0	2	1	0	1	3	2
Brazil	1	0	0	1	0	3	1	0	0	1	0	3
Bulgaria	1	0	1	0	0	0	4	2	1	1	4	3
Canada	0	0	0	0	0	0	1	0	0	1	0	2
Chile	1	0	0	1	1	2	2	0	0	2	1	3
Colombia	1	0	0	1	0	2	1	0	0	1	0	2
Cyprus	1	1	0	0	3	0	4	3	0	1	11	1
Czechoslovakia	2	2	0	0	3	1	2	2	0	0	3	1
Denmark	0	0	0	0	0	0	7	1	2	4	5	11
England	0	0	0	0	0	0	96	6	16	74	80	319
Faroe Islands	0	0	0	0	0	0	2	1	1	0	6	1
Finland	0	0	0	0	0	0	2	1	0	1	2	2
France	2	0	0	2	1	8	7	0	3	4	4	17
Germany/West Germany	1	0	1	0	2	2	9	2	3	4	10	17
Greece	0	0	0	0	0	0	3	1	0	2	5	5
Honduras	1	0	1	0	1	1	1	0	1	0	1	1
Hungary	0	0	0	0	0	0	2	0	0	2	1	3
Iceland	0	0	0	0	0	0	2	1	0	1	2	1
Republic of Ireland	0	0	0	0	0	0	8	1	4	3	3	12
Israel	0	0	0	0	0	0	6	3	3	0	9	4
Italy	0	0	0	0	0	0	4	1	1	2	6	7
Latvia	0	0	0	0	0	0	4	3	0	1	6	3
Liechtenstein	0	0	0	0	0	0	2	2	0	0	8	1
Lithuania	0	0	0	0	0	0	2	1	1	0	3	2
Malta	0	0	0	0	0	0	2	2	0	0	5	0
Mexico	1	0	0	1	0	3	2	1	0	1	4	4
Morocco	0	0	0	0	0	0	1	1	0	0	2	1
Netherlands	0	0	0	0	0	0	5	1	2	2	4	8
Norway	0	0	0	0	0	0	4	1	0	3	6	7
Poland	0	0	0	0	0	0	4	3	1	0	8	2
Portugal	1	0	1	0	1	1	8	2	4	2	9	7
Romania	0	0	0	0	0	0	3	3	0	0	6	2
Scotland	0	0	0	0	0	0	92	15	16	61	81	254
Spain	2	0	1	1	2	3	12	1	4	7	7	23
Sweden	0	0	0	0	0	0	5	2	0	3	7	5
Switzerland	0	0	0	0	0	0	2	1	0	1	2	2
Turkey	0	0	0	0	0	0	8	5	2	1	12	3
Uruguay	0	0	0	0	0	0	2	2	0	0	4	0
U.S.S.R.	0	0	0	0	0	0	4	0	2	2	1	4
Wales	1	1	0	0	1	0	90	27	21	42	127	182
Yugoslavia	1	0	1	0	0	0	7	1	1	5	3	12
Total	20	4	8	8	19	32	443	110	95	238	493	961

NORTHERN IRELANDS INTERNATIONAL GOALSCORERS 1882-1996

Name:	Goals:	Apps:	Name:	Goals:	Apps:
Clarke C.	13 (2pens)	38	Lockhart N.	3 (1pen)	8
Armstrong G.	12 (1pen)	63	McCandless J.	3	5
Bambrick J.	12	11	McDonald A.	3*	52
Gillespie W.	12	25	McMordie E.	3	21
Quinn.J.	12 (1pen)	46	Martin D.K.	3	10
Stanfield O.	11	30	Morgan S.	3	18
Bingham W.	10	56	Nicholl C.	3	51
Crossan J.	10 (4pens)	24	Spence D.	3	29
McIlroy J.	10 (2pens)	55	Tully C.	3	10
McParland P.	10	34	Blanchflower D.	2 (pens)	56
Best G.	9 (1pen)	37	Browne F.	2	5
Whiteside N.	9	38	Casey T.	2	12
Dougan D.	8	43	Clements D.	2 (1pen)	48
Dowie I.	8 (2 pen)	36	Curran S.	2	3
Irvine W.	8	23	Finney T.	2	14
O'Neill Ma.	8	64	Gibb J.T.	2	10
McAdams W.	7	15	Goodall A.L.	2	10
Peden J.	7	24	Harkin T.	2	5
Wilson S.	7	12	Hughes M.	2*	31
McLaughlin J.	6	12	Johnston H.	2	1
Nicholson J.	6	41	Johnston S.	2	4
Wilson K.	6*	42	Kernaghan N.	2	3
Cush. W.	5	26	Kirwan J.	2	17
Gray P.	5*	17	Lemon J.	2	3
Hamilton W.	5	42	McCluggage A.	2	12
McIlroy S.	5	88	McKnight J.	2 (1pen)	2
Simpson W.	5	12	McMahon G.	2*	7
Smyth S.	5	9	Mahood J.	2	9
Stevenson A.E.	5	17	Maxwell J.	2	7
Taggart G.	5*	35	Milne R.G.	2 (1pen)	27
Walsh D.	5	9	Neill W.J.T	2	59
Anderson T.	4	22	O'Hagan C.	2	11
Dalton W.	4	11	O'Neill J.	2	39
Dunne J.	4	7	Peacock R.	2	31
Gaffikin G.	4	15	Penney S.	2	17
Hamilton B.	4	50	Pyper James	2	7
Kelly J. (Derry C.)	4	11	Rowley R.	2	6
McMorran E.J.	4	15	Sheridan J.	2	6
McGrath C.	4	21	Sherrard W.C.	2	3
Magilton J.	4 (1pen)*	32	Stewart I.	2	31
O' Neill Mi	4*	29	Thompson F.W.	2	12
Sloan H.	4	8	Wilton J.M.	2	7
Barron J.H.	3	7	Young S.	2	9
Brotherston N.	3	27	Barr H.H	1	3
Chambers J.	3	12	Black K.	1*	30
Doherty P.	3 (1pen)	16	Blanchflower J.	1	12
Gara A.	3	3	Brennan B.	1	1
Harvey M.	3	34	Brennan R.A.	1	5
Irvine R.W.	3	15	Brown J.	1	10
Lacey W.	3	23	Campbell J.	1	15

NORTHERN IRELAND INTERNATIONAL GOALSCORERS 1882-1996

Name:	Goals:	Apps:	Name:	Goals:	Apps:
Campbell W.	1	6	Jones J. (Glenavon)	1	3
Caskey W.	1	7	Jones S.	1	2
Cassidy T.	1	24	Lomas S.	1*	12
Cochrane T.	1	26	McAllen J.	1	9
Condy J.	1	3	Macauley J.L.	1	6
Connor M.J.	1	3	McCaw J.H.	1	5
Coulter J.	1	11	McClelland J.	1	53
Croft T.	1	1	McCracken W.	1 (pen)	15
Crone W.	1	12	McCrory S.	1	1
Crossan E.	1	3	McCurdy C.	1	1
D'Arcy S.D.	1	5	McGarry J.K.	1	3
Darling J.	1 (pen)	21	McWha W.	1	7
Davey H.H	1	5	Meldon J.	1	2
Davis T.L.	1	1	Mercer J.T.	1	11
Dill A.H.	1	9	Millar W.	1	2
Doherty L.	1	2	Milligan D.	1	1
Elder A.	1	40	Molyneux T.B.	1	11
Emerson W.	1	11	Moreland V.	1 (pen)	6
English S.	1	2	Morrow S.	1*	19
Feeney W.	1	1	Morrow W.J.	1	3
Ferguson W.	1	2	Murphy N.	1	3
Ferris J.	1	5	Nelson S.	1	51
Ferris R.	1 (pen)	3	Nicholl J.	1	73
Gaukrodger G.	1	1	O'Boyle G.	1*	8
Gibb T.J.	1	1	O'Kane L.	1	20
Gillespie, K	1*	12	Pyper John.	1	9
Halligan W.	1	2	Reynolds J.	1	5
Hamill M.	1	7	Sherrard J.	1	3
Hannon D.J.	1	6	Torrans S.	1	26
Hill C.	1*	14	Turner E.	1	2
Humphries W.	1	14	Walker J.	1	1
Hunter A. (Blackburn R.)	1	53	Welsh E.	1	4
			Whiteside T.	1	1
Hunter A. (Distillery)	1	8	Williams J.	1	2
			Williamson J.	1	3
Hunter B.	1*	6	Wilson D.	1	23
Johnston W.	1	2	Own Goals	5	–

* Denotes Current Internationals.

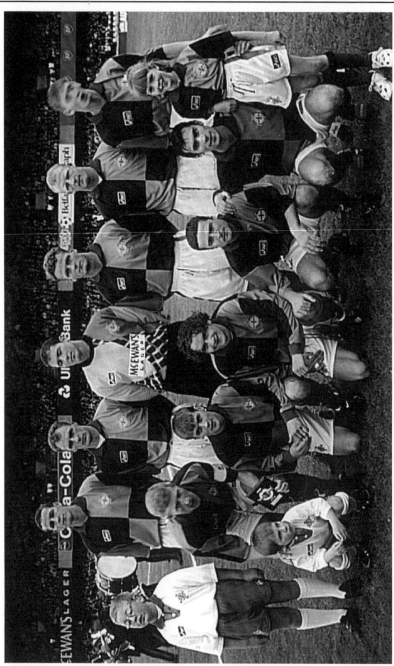

Northern Ireland Team
International friendly between Germany, May 1996

NORTHERN IRELAND INTERNATIONAL APPEARANCES 1882 -1996

Explanatory code for international matches: A represents Austria; Aus, Austrailia; Alb, Alabania; Alg, Algeria; Arg, Argentina; Bel, Belgium; Br, Brazil; Bul, Bulgaria;Can; Canada Ch, Chile; Col, Colombia; Cy, Cyprus; Cz, Czechoslovakia; D, Denmark; E, England; Ei, Eire; F, France; Fa, Faroe Islands; Fi, Finland; G, Germany; Gr, Greece; H, Hungary; Ho, Holland; Hon, Honduras; I, Italy; Ic, Iceland; Is, Israel; Lat, Latvia; Lic, Liechtenstein; Lit, Lithuania; M, Mexico; Ma, Malta; Mo, Morocco; N, Norway; P, Portugal; Pol, Poland; R, Romania; S, Scotland; Se, Sweden; Sp, Spain; Sw, Switzerland; T, Turkey; U, Uruguay; USSR, Russia; W, Wales; WG, West Germany; Y, Yugoslavia;

Aherne, T.	(Belfast C)	1947 v E; 1948 v S; 1949 v W; (with Luton T); 1950 v W (4)
Alexander T.E	(Cliftonville)	1895 v S (1)
Allan, C.	(Cliftonville)	1936 v E (1)
Allen, J.	(Limavady)	1887 v E (1)
Anderson T.	(Manchester U)	1973 v Cy, E, S, W; 1974 v Bul, P;(with Swindon T);1975 v S(sub); 1976 v Is;1977 v Ho Bel, WG, E, S, W, Ic; 1978 v Ic, Ho, Bel; (with Peterborough Utd); S, E, W; 1979 v D(sub) (22)
Anderson W.	(Linfield)	1898 v W, E, S; (with Cliftonville) 1899 v S (4)
Andrews W.	(Glentoran)	1908 v S; (with Grimsby T); 1913 v E, S (3)
Armstrong G.J.	(Tottenham H)	1977 v WG, E, W(sub), Ic(sub); 1978 v Bel, S, E, W; 1979 v Ei, D, Bul, E, Bul, E, S,W, D; 1980 v E, Ei, Is, S, E, W, Aus (3); 1981 v Se (with Watford); P, S, P, S, Se; 1982 v S, Is, E, F, W, Y,Hon, Sp, A, F; 1983 v A, T, Alb, S, E, W; (with Real Mallorca); 1984 v A, WG, E, W, Fi; 1985 v R, Fi, E, Sp; (with WBA), 1986 v T, R(sub), E(sub), F(sub); (with Chesterfield); D(sub), Br(sub) (63)
Baird G.	(Distillery)	1896 v W, E, S (3)
Baird H.C.	(Huddersfield T)	1939 v E (1)
Balfe, J.	(Shelbourne)	1909 v E; 1910 v W (2)
Bambrick J.	(Linfield)	1929 v E, W, S; 1930 v E, W, S; 1932 v W;(with Chelsea); 1935 v W; 1936 v E, S 1938 v S (11)
Banks, S.J.	(Cliftonville)	1937 v W (1)
Barr, H.H.	(Linfield)	1962 v E; (with Coventry C); 1963 v Pol, E (3)
Barron, J.H.	(Cliftonville)	1894 v W, E, S; 1895 v S; 1896 v S; 1897 v E, W (7)
Barry, J.	(Bohemians)	1888 v W, S; 1889 v E; 1900 v S (4)
Baxter, R.A.	(Cliftonville)	1887 v S, W (2)
Bennett, L.V.	(Dublin University)	1889 v W (1)
Best, G.	(Manchester U)	1964 v W, U; 1965 v E, Ho (2), S, Sw (2), Alb; 1966 v S, E, Alb; 1967 v E; 1968 v S; 1969 v E, S, W, T; 1970 v S, E, W, USSR; 1971 v Cy (2), Sp, E, S, W; 1972 v USSR, Sp; 1973 v Bul; 1974 v P; (with Fulham); 1977 v Ho, Bel, WG; 1978 v Ic, Ho (37)
Bingham, W.L.	(Sunderland)	1951 v F; 1952 v E, S, W; 1953 v E, S, F, W; 1954 v E, S, W; 1955 v E, S, W; 1956 v E,S,W; 1957 v E, S, W, P (2), I; 1958 v S, E, W, I (2), Arg, Cz (2), WG, F; (with Luton T); 1959 v E, S, W,Sp;1960 v S, E,W; (with Everton); 1961 v E, S, WG (2), Gr, I; 1962 v E, Gr; 1963 v E, S, Pol (2), Sp;(with Port Vale), 1964 v S, E, Sp (56)
Black, T.	(Glentoran)	1901 v E (1)
Black, K.	(Luton T)	1988 v Fr(sub), Ma(sub); 1989 v Ei, H, Sp (2), Ch(sub); 1990 v H, N, U; 1991 v Y (2), D, A, Pol,Fa;(with Nottingham F);1992 v Fa, A, D, S, Li, G; 1993 v Sp, D(sub), Alb, Ei(sub), Sp; 1994 v D(sub), Ei(sub), R(sub), (30)
Blair, H.	(Portadown)	1931 v S; 1932 v S; (with Swansea) 1934 v S (3)
Blair, J.	(Cliftonville)	1907 v W, E, S; 1908 v E, S (5)
Blair, R.V.	(Oldham Ath)	1975 v Se(sub), S(sub), W; 1976 v Se, Is (5)
Blanchflower, R.D.	(Barnsley)	1950 v S, W; 1951 v E, S; (with Aston Villa); F; 1952 v W; 1953 v E, S, W, F; 1954 v E, S, W; 1955 v E, S, (with Tottenham H); W; 1956 v E, S, W; 1957 v E, S, W, I, P (2); 1958 v E, S, W, I(2),Cz (2), Arg, F, WG; 1959 v E, S, W, Sp; 1960 v E, S, W; 1961 v E, S, W, WG (2); 1962 v E, S, W, Gr, Ho; 1963 v E, S, Pol (2) (56)

Blanchflower, J. (Manchester U)   1954 v W; 1955 v E, S; 1956 v S, W; 1957 v S, E, P; 1958 v S, E, I (2) (12)

Bookman, L.J.O. (Bradford C)   1914 v W; (with Luton T); 1921 v S, W; 1922 v E (4)

Bothwell, A.W. (Ards)   1926 v S, E, W; 1927 v E, W (5)

Bowler, G.C. (Hull C)   1950 v E, S, W (3)

Boyle, P. (Sheffield U)   1901 v E; 1902 v E; 1903 v S, W; 1904 v E (5)

Braithwaite, R.M. (Linfield)   1962 v W; 1963 v P, Sp; (with Middlesbrough); 1964 v W, U; 1965 v E, S, Sw (2), Ho, (10)

Breen, T. (Belfast C)   1935 v E, W; 1937 v E, S, (with Manchester U); W; 1938 v E, S; 1939 v W, S (9)

Brennan, B. (Bohemians)   1912 v W (1)

Brennan, R.A. (Luton T)   1949 v W; (with Birmingham C); 1950 v E, S, W; (with Fulham); 1951 v E (5)

Briggs, W.R. (Manchester U)   1962 v W; (with Swansea T): 1965 v Ho (2)

Brisby, D. (Distillery)   1891 v S (1)

Brolly, T.H. (Millwall)   1937 v W; 1938 v W; 1939 v E, W (4)

Brookes, E.A. (Shelbourne)   1920 v S (1)

Brotherston, N. (Blackburn R)   1980 v S,E, W, Aus (3);1981 v Se, P; 1982 v S, Is, E, F, S, W, Hon(sub), A(sub); 1983 v A(sub), WG, Alb, T, Alb, S(sub), E (sub), W; 1984 v T, 1985 v Is(sub), T (27)

Brown, J. (Glenavon)   1921 v W; (with Tranmere R); 1924 v E, W (3)

Brown,J. (Wolverhampton W) 1935 v E, W; 1936 v E;(with Coventry C); 1937 v E,W; 1938 v S, W; (with Birmingham C), 1939 v E, S, W (10)

Brown, N.M. (Limavady)   1887 v E (1)

Brown, W.G. (Glenavon)   1926 v W (1)

Browne F. (Cliftonville)   1887 v E, S,W; 1888 v E, S (5)

Browne, R.J. (Leeds U)   1936 v E, W; 1938 v E, W; 1939 v E, S (6)

Bruce, W. (Glentoran)   1961 v S; 1967 v W (2)

Buckle, H.R. (Sunderland)   1904 v E; (with Bristol R); 1908 v W (2)

Buckle, J. (Cliftonville)   1882 v E (1)

Burnett, J. (Distillery)   1894 v E, W, S; (with Glentoran); 1895 v E, W (5)

Burnison, J. (Distillery)   1901 v E, W (2)

Burnison,S. (Distillery)   1908 v E; 1910 v E, S; (with Bradford C); 1911 v E, S, W; (with Distillery); 1912 v E; 1913 v W (8)

Burns, J. (Glenavon)   1923 v E (1)

Butler, M.P. (Blackpool)   1939 v W (1)

Campbell, A.C. (Crusaders)   1963 v W; 1965 v Sw (2)

Campbell, D.A. (Nottingham F)   1986 v Mor(sub), Br; 1987 v E, T, (with Notts Co.) E, Y, Y; (with Charlton A); 1988 v Y, T(sub), Gr(sub) Pol(sub) (10)

Campbell, J. (Cliftonville)   1896 v W; 1897 v E, S, W; 1898 v E, S, W; 1899 v E, 1900 v E, S; 1901 v S, W; 1902 v S; 1903 v E; 1904 v S (15)

Campbell, J.P. (Fulham)   1951 v E, S (2)

Campbell, R.M. (Bradford C)   1982 v S, W(sub) (2)

Campbell, W.G. (Dundee)   1968 v S, E; 1969 v T; 1970 v S, W, USSR (6)

Carey, J.J. (Manchester U)   1947 v E, S, W; 1948 v E; 1949 v E, S, W (7)

Carroll, E. (Glenavon)   1925 v S (1)

Casey, T. (Newcastle U)   1955 v W; 1956 v W; 1957 v E, S, W, I, P (2); 1958 v WG, F; (Portsmouth); 1959 v E, Sp (12)

Caskey, W.T. (Derby C)   1979 v Bul, E, Bul, E, D(sub); 1980 v E(sub); (with Tulsa R); 1982 v F(sub) (7)

Cassidy, T. (Newcastle U)   1971 v E(sub); 1972 v USSR(sub); 1974 v Bul(sub), S, E, W; 1975 v N; 1976 v S, E, W; 1977 v WG(sub); 1980 v E, Ei(sub), Is, S, E, W, Aus (3); (with Burnley); 1981 v Se, P; 1982 v Is, Sp(sub) (24)

Caughey, M. (Linfield);   1986 v F(sub), D(sub) (2)

Chambers, R.J. (Distillery)   1921 v W;(with Bury);1928 v E, S, W; 1929 v E, S, W; 1930 v S, W; (with Nottingham For), 1932 v E, S, W (12)

Chatton, H.A. (Partick T)   1925 v E, S; 1926 v E (3)

Christian, J. (Linfield)   1889 v S (1)

Clarke, C.J. (Bournemouth)   1986 v F, D, Mor, Alg(sub), Sp, Br; (with Southampton); 1987 v E, T, Y;

		1988 v Y, T, Gr, Pol, F, Ma; 1989 v Ei, H, Sp (1+1 sub); (with Q.P.R); Ma, Ch; 1990 v H, Ei, N; (with Portsmouth); 1991 v Y(sub), S, A Pol, Y(sub), Fa; 1992 v Fa, D, S, G; 1993 v Alb, Sp, D (38)
Clarke, R.	(Belfast C)	1901 v E, S (2)
Cleary, J.	(Glentoran)	1982 v S, W; 1983 v W(sub); 1984 v T(sub); 1985 v Is (5)
Clements, D.	(Coventry C)	1965 v Ho, W; 1966 v M; 1967 v S, W; 1968 v S, E; 1969 v T (2), S, W; 1970 v USSR, (2), S, E, W; 1971 v Sp, Cy, E, S, W; (with Sheffield W); 1972 v USSR (2), Sp, S, E, W; 1973 v Bul, Cy, P, Cy, E, S,W; (with Everton); 1974 v Bul, P, S, E, W; 1975 v N, Y, E, S, W; 1976 v Se, Y; (with NY Cosmos); E, W (48)
Clugston, J.	(Cliftonville)	1888 v W; 1889 v W, S, E; 1890 v E, S; 1891 v E, W; 1892 v E, S, W; 1893 v E, S, W (14)
Cochrane, D.	(Leeds U)	1939 v E, W; 1947 v E, S, W; 1948 v E, S, W; 1949 v S, W; 1950 v S, E (12)
Cochrane, G.T.	(Coleraine)	1976v N(sub);(with Burnley);1978 v S(sub), E(sub), W(sub);1979 vEi(sub); (with Middlesbrough);D, Bul, E, Bul, E; 1980 v Is, E(sub), W(sub), Aus(1+2 sub); 1981 v Se(sub), P(sub), S, P, S, Se; 1982 v E(sub), F; (with Gillingham); 1984 v S, Fi(sub) (26)
Cochrane, M.	(Distillery)	1898 v S, W, E; 1899 v E; 1900 v E, S, W; (with Leicester Fosse); 1901 v S (8)
Collins, F.	(Celtic)	1922 v S (1)
Condy, J.	(Distillery)	1882 v W; 1886 v E, S (3)
Connell, T.E.	(Coleraine)	1978 v W(sub) (1)
Connor, J.	(Glentoran)	1901 v S,E; (with Belfast C); 1905 v E, S, W; 1907 v E, S; 1908 v E, S; 1909 v W; 1911 v S, E, W (13)
Connor, M.J.	(Brentford)	1903 v S, W; (with Fulham); 1904 v E (3)
Cook, W.	(Celtic)	1933 v E, W, S; (with Everton); 1935 v E; 1936 v S, W; 1937 v E, S, W; 1938 v E, S, W; 1939 v E, S, W (15)
Cooke, S.	(Belfast YMCA)	1889 v E; (with Cliftonville); 1890 v E, S (3)
Coulter, J.	(Belfast C)	1934 v E, S, W; (with Everton); 1935 v E, S, W; 1937 v S, W; (with Grimsby T); 1938 v S, W; (with Chelmsford C); 1939 v S (11)
Cowan, J.	(Newcastle U)	1970 v E(sub) (1)
Cowan, T.S.	(Queen's Island)	1925 v W (1)
Coyle, F.	(Coleraine)	1956 v E, S; 1957 v P; (with Nottingham F); 1958 v Arg (4)
Coyle, L.	(Derry C)	1989 v Ch(sub) (1)
Coyle, R.I.	(Sheffield W)	1973 v P, Cy(sub), W(sub); 1974 v Bul(sub), P(sub) (5)
Craig, A.B.	(Rangers)	1908 v E, S, W; 1909 v S; (with Morton); 1912 v S, W; 1914 v E, S, W (9)
Craig, D.J.	(Newcastle U)	1967 v W; 1968 v W; 1969 v T (2), E, S, W; 1970 v USSR, E, S, W; 1971 v Sp, Cy (2), S(sub); 1972 v USSR, S(sub); 1973 v Cy (2), E, S, W; 1974 v Bul, P; 1975 v N (25)
Crawford, A.	(Distillery)	1889 v E, W; (with Cliftonville); 1891 v E, S, W; 1893 v E, W (7)
Croft, T.	(Queen's Island)	1924 v E (1)
Crone, R.	(Distillery)	1889 v S; 1890 v E, S, W (4)
Crone, W.	(Distillery)	1882 v W;1884 v E,S, W; 1886 v E, S, W; 1887 v E; 1888 v E, W; 1889 v S; 1890 v W (12)
Crooks, W.J.	(Manchester U)	1922 v W (1)
Crossan, E.	(Blackburn R)	1950 v S; 1951 v E; 1955 v W (3)
Crossan, J.A.	(Sparta-Rotterdam)	1960 v E; (with Sunderland); 1963 v Pol, W, Sp; 1964 v S, Sp, E, W, U; 1965 v E, Sw (2), S; (with Manchester C); Ho, W, Ho, Alb; 1966 v S, E, Alb, WG; 1967 v E, S; (with Middlesbrough); 1968 v S (24)
Crothers, C.	(Distillery)	1907 v W (1)
Cumming, L.	(Huddersfield T)	1929 v W, S; (with Oldham A); 1930 v E (3)
Cunningham, W.	(Ulster)	1892 v S, E, W; 1893 v E (4)
Cunningham, W.E.	(St.Mirren)	1951 v W; 1953 v E; 1954 v S; 1955 v S; (with Leicester C); 1956 v S, E, W; 1957 v E, S, P, W, I, P; 1958 v S, I, W, Cz, Arg, WG, Cz, F; 1959 v E, S, W; 1960 v S, E, W; (with Dunfermline A); 1961 v W; 1962 v W, Ho (30)
Curran, S.	(Belfast C)	1926 v S, W; 1928 v S (3)
Curran, J.J.	(Glenavon)	1922 v W; (with Pontypridd); 1923 v E, S; (with Glenavon); 1924 v E (4)

Cush, W.W.	(Glenavon)	1951 v E, S; 1954 v S, E; 1957 v P, W, I, P; (with Leeds U); 1958 v I (2), W, Cz, Arg, WG, Cz, F; 1959 v E, Sp, S, W; 1960 v S, E, W; (with Portadown) 1961 v WG, Gr; 1962 v Gr (26)
Dalton, W.	(YMCA)	1888 v S; (with Linfield); 1890 v W, S; 1891 v W, S; 1892 v W, E, S; 1894 v W, E, S (11)
D'Arcy, S.D.	(Chelsea)	1952 v W; 1953 v E; (with Brentford); S, F, W (5)
Darling, J.	(Linfield)	1897 v E, S; 1900 v S; 1902 v W, S, E; 1903 v E, S, W; 1905 v E, S, W; 1906 v E, S, W; 1908 v W; 1909 v E; 1910 v E, S, W; 1912 v S (21)
Davey, H.H.	(Reading)	1926 v E; 1927 v E, S; 1928 v E; (with Portsmouth); W (5)
Davis, T.L.	(Oldham A)	1937 v E (1)
Davison, J.R.	(Cliftonville)	1882 v E, W; 1883 v E, W; 1884 v S, W, E; 1885 v E (8)
Dennison, R.	(Wolverhampton W)	1988 v F, Ma; 1989 v H, Sp, Ch(sub); 1990 v Ei, U; 1991 v Y, A, Pol, Y, Fa(sub); 1992 v Fa, A, D(sub); 1993 v Sp(sub); 1994 v C(sub) (17)
Devine, A.O.	(Limavady)	1886 v W, E; 1887 v W; 1888 v W (4)
Devine, J.	(Glentoran)	1990 v U(sub) (1)
Dickson, D.	(Coleraine)	1970 v S(sub), W; 1973 v Cy, P (4)
Dickson, T.A.	(Linfield)	1957 v S (1)
Dickson, W.	(Chelsea)	1951 v W, F; 1952 v S, E, W; 1953 v E, S, F, W; (with Arsenal); 1954 v E, W; 1955 v E (12)
Diffin, W.J.	(Belfast C)	1931 v W (1)
Dill, A.H.	(Knock)	1882 v E, W; (with Down Ath); 1883 v W; (with Cliftonville); 1884 v S, W, E; 1885 v E, S, W (9)
Doherty, I.	(Belfast C)	1901 v E (1)
Doherty, J.	(Cliftonville)	1933 v E, W (2)
Doherty, L.	(Linfield)	1985 v Is; 1988 v T(sub) (2)
Doherty, M.	(Derry C)	1938 v S (1)
Doherty, P.D.	(Blackpool);	1935 v E, W; 1936 v E, S; (with Manchester C); 1937 v E, W; 1938 v E, S; 1939 v E, W; (with Derby C);1947 v E; (with Huddersfield T); W; 1948 v E, W; 1949 v S; (with Doncaster R); 1951 v S (16)
Donaghy, M.M.	(Luton T)	1980 v S, E, W; 1981 v Se, P, S(sub); 1982 v S, Is, E, F, S, W, Y, Hon, Sp, F; 1983 v A, WG, Alb, T, Alb, S, E, W; 1984 v A, T, WG, S, E, W, Fi; 1985 v R, Fi, E, Sp, T; 1986 v T, R, E, F, D, Mor, Alg, Sp, Br:1987 v E, T, Is, E, Y; 1988 v Y, T, Gr, Pol, F, Ma; 1989 v Ei, H; (with Manchester U); Sp (2), Ma, Ch, 1990 v Ei, N; 1991 v Y, D, A, Pol, Y, Fa; 1992 v Fa, A, D, S, Li, G; (with Chelsea); 1993 v Alb, Sp, D, Alb, Ei, Sp, Li, La; 1994 v La, D, Ei, R, Lic, C, M (91)
Donnelly, L.	(Distillery)	1913 v W (1)
Doran, J.F.	(Brighton)	1921 v E; 1922 v E, W (3)
Dougan, A.D.	(Portsmouth)	1958 v Cz; (with Blackburn R); 1960 v S; 1961 v E, W, I, Gr; (with Aston Villa); 1963 v Pol,S, Pol;(with Leicester C); 1966 v S, E, Alb, W, WG, M; 1967 v E, S; (with Wolverhampton W); W; 1968 v S, W; 1969 v Is, T(2), E, S, W; 1970 v USSR(2), S, E; 1971 v Sp, Cy(2), E, S, W; 1972 v USSR(2), S, E, W; 1973 v Bul, Cy (43)
Douglas, J.P.	(Belfast C)	1947 v E (1)
Dowd, H.O.	(Glenavon)	1974 v W; (with Sheffield Wed); 1975 v N(sub), Se (3)
Dowie, I.	(Luton T)	1990 v N(sub), U; 1991 v Y, D, A(sub); (with West Ham U); Y, Fa; (with Southampton); 1992 v Fa, A, D(sub), S(sub), Lit; 1993 v Alb (2), Ei, Sp(sub), Lit, Lat; 1994 v Lat, D, Ei(sub), R(sub), Lic, Col, M(sub) (with Crystal Palace) 1995 v A, Ei(2), Lat, Can, Ch, Lat (with West Ham) 1996 v P, A, N, G (36).
Duggan, H.A.	(Leeds U)	1930 v E; 1931 v E, W; 1933 v E; 1934 v E; 1935 v S, W; 1936 v S (8)
Dunlop, G.	(Linfield)	1985 v Is; 1987 v E, Y; 1990 v Ei (4)
Dunne, J.	(Sheffield U)	1928 v W; 1931 v E, W; 1932 v E; 1933 v E, W (7)
Eames, W.L.E.	(Dublin Uni)	1885 v E, S, W (3)
Eglington, T.J.	(Everton)	1947 v S, W; 1948 v S, E, W; 1949 v E (6)
Elder, A.R.	(Burnley)	1960 v W; 1961 v E, WG, S, W, Gr, WG; 1962 v S, Gr, E; 1963 v Pol, E, S, Pol, W, Sp; 1964 v W, U; 1965 v E, Sw (2), S, H, W, H, Alb; 1966 v S, E, 1967 v E, S, W; (Stoke C); 1968 v E, W; 1969 v E(sub),S, W; 1970 v USSR (40)

Elleman, A.R.	(Cliftonville)	1889 v W; 1890 v E (2)
Elwood, J.H.	(Bradford)	1929 v W; 1930 v E (2)
Emerson, W.	(Glentoran)	1920 v E, W, S; 1921 v E; 1922 v E, S; (with Burnley); 1922 v W; 1923 v E, S, W; 1924 v E (11)
English, S.	(Rangers)	1933 v S, W (2)
Enright, J.	(Leeds C)	1912 v S (1)
Falloon, E.	(Aberdeen)	1931 v S; 1933 v S (2)
Farquharson, T.G.	(Cardiff C)	1923 v S, W; 1924 v E, S, W; 1925 v E, S (7)
Farrell, P.	(Distillery)	1901 v S, W (2)
Farrell, P.	(Hibernian)	1938 v W (1)
Farrell, P.D.	(Everton)	1947 v S, W; 1948 v S, E, W; 1949 v E, W (7)
Feeney, J.M.	(Linfield)	1947 v S; (with Swansea T); 1950 v E (2)
Feeney, W.	(Glentoran)	1976 v Is (1)
Ferguson, W.	(Linfield)	1966 v M; 1967 v E (2)
Ferris, J.	(Belfast C)	1920 v E, W; (with Chelsea); 1921 v E, S; (with Belfast C); 1928 v S (5)
Ferris, R.O.	(Birmingham C)	1950 v S; 1951 v F; 1952 v S (3)
Fettis, A.	(Hull C)	1992 v D, Lit; 1993 D; 1994 v M 1995 v P, Ei, Lat, Can, Ch; Lat (10)
Finney, T.	(Sunderland)	1975 v N, E(sub), S, W; 1976 v N, Y, S; (with Cambridge U); 1980 v E, Is, S, E, W; Aus (2) (14)
Fitzpatrick, J.C.	(Bohemians)	1896 v E, S (2)
Flack, H.	(Burnley)	1929 v S (1)
Fleming, J.G.	(Nottingham F)	1987 v E, Is, E, Y; 1988 v T, Gr, Pol; 1989 v Ma, Ch; (with Manchester C); 1990 v H, Ei; (with Barnsley); 1991 v Y; 1992 v Lit(sub), G; 1993 v Alb, Sp, D, Alb, Sp, Lit, Lat; 1994 v Lat, D, Ei, R, Lic, C, M 1995 v P, A, Ei (31)
Forbes, G.	(Limavady)	1888 v W; (with Distillery); 1891 v E, S (3)
Forde, J.T.	(Ards)	1959 v Sp; 1961 v E, WG, S (4)
Foreman, T.A.	(Cliftonville)	1899 v S (1)
Forsyth, J.	(YMCA)	1888 v S, E (2)
Fox, W.T.	(Ulster)	1887 v E, S (2)
Fulton, R.P.	(Belfast C)	1930 v W; 1931 v E, S, W; 1932 v E, W; 1933 v S, E; 1934 v S, E, W; 1935 v S, E, W; 1936 v S, W; 1937 v S, E, W; 1938 v W (20)
Gaffikin, G.	(Linfield)	890 v W, S; 1891 v W, S; 1892 v W, E, S; 1893 v E, S, W; 1894 v W, E, S; 1895 v E, W (15)
Galbraith, W.	(Distillery)	1890 v W (1)
Gallagher, P.	(Celtic)	1920 v E, S; 1922 v S; 1923 v S, W; 1924 v S, W; 1925 v E, S, W; (with Falkirk); 1927 v S (11)
Gallogly, C.	(Huddersfield T)	1951 v E, S (2)
Gara, A.	(Preston N.E)	1902 v W, S, E (3)
Gardiner, A.	(Cliftonville)	1930 v W, S; 1931 v S; 1932 v S, E (5)
Garrett, J.	(Distillery)	1925 v W (1)
Gaston, R.	(Oxford U)	1969 v Is(sub) (1)
Gaukrodger, G.	(Linfield)	1895 v W (1)
Gaussen, A.D.	(Magherafelt)	1884 v S, E; 1888 v W, E; 1889 v E, W (6)
Geary, J.	(Glentoran)	1931 v S; 1932 v S (2)
Gibb, J.T.	(Wellington Park)	1884 v S, W; 1885 v E, S, W; 1886 v S; 1887 v E, S, W; (with Cliftonville) 1889 v S (10)
Gibb, T.J.	(Cliftonville)	1936 v W (1)
Gibson, W.K.	(Cliftonville)	1894 v W, E, S; 1895 v S; 1897 v W; 1898 v W, E, S; 1901 v S, E, W; 1902 v W, S (13)
Gillespie, K.R.	(Manchester U)	1995 v P, A, Ei(with Newcastle U) Ei, Lat, Can,Ch(sub), Lat (sub) 1996 v P,A,N,G (12)
Gillespie, S.	(Hertford)	1886 v W, E, S; 1887 v E, S, W (6)
Gillespie, W.	(Sheffield U)	1913 v E, S,; 1914 v W, E; 1920 v S, W; 1921 v E; 1922 v E, S, W; 1923 v E, S, W; 1924 v E, S, W; 1925 v E, S; 1926 v W, S;1927 v E, W; 1928 v E; 1929 v E; 1931 v E (25)
Gillespie, W.	(West Down)	1889 v W (1)
Goodall, A.L.	(Derby Co)	1899 v W, S; 1900 v W, E; 1901 v E; 1902 v S; 1903 v E, W; (with Glossop),

		1904 v E, W (10)
Goodbody, M.F.	(Dublin University)	1889 v E; 1891 v W (2)
Gordon, H.	(Linfield)	1895 v E, 1896 v E, S (3)
Gordon R.W.	(Linfield)	1891 v S; 1892 v W, E,S; 1893 v E, S, W (7)
Gordon, T.	(Linfield)	1894 v v W; 1895 v E (2)
Gorman, W.C.	(Brentford)	1947 v E, S, W; 1948 v W (4)
Gowdy, J.	(Glentoran)	1920 v E; (with Queen's Island); 1924 v W; (with Falkirk); 1926 v E, S; 1927 v E, S (6)
Gowdy, W.A.	(Hull City)	1932 v S; (with Sheffield Wed); 1933 v S; (with Linfield); 1935 v S, E, W; (with Hibernian); 1936 v W (6)
Graham, W.G.L.	(Doncaster Ro)	1951 v W, F; 1952 v S, E, W; 1953 v S, F; 1954 E, W; 1955 v S, W; 1956 v S, E; 1959 v E (14)
Gray, P.	(Luton Town)	1993 v D(sub), Alb, Ei, Sp; (with Sunderland); 1994 v Lat, D, Ei, R, Lic(sub) 1995 v P, A, Ei, Can, Ch (sub) 1996 v P (sub), Lic, A (17)
Greer, W.	(QPR)	1909 v E, S, W (3)
Gregg, H.	(Doncaster Ro)	1954 v W; 1957 v E, S, P, W, I, P; 1958 v E, I, (with Manchester Utd); 1958 v W, Cz, Arg, WG, F; 1959 v E, W; 1960 v S, E, W; 1961 v E, S; 1962 v S, Gr; 1964 v S, E (25)
Hall, G.	(Distillery)	1897 v E (1)
Halligan, W.	(Derby Co)	1911 v W; (with Wolverhampton W); 1912 v E (2)
Hamill, M.	(Manchester Utd)	1912 v E; 1914 v E, S; (with Belfast Celtic); 1920 v E, S, W; (with Manchester City); 1921 v S (7)
Hamilton, B.	(Linfield)	1969 v T;1971 v Cy (2);E, S, W; (with Ipswich Town); 1972 v USSR (1+1sub), Sp; 1973 v Bul, Cy, P, Cy, E, S, W; 1974 v Bul, S, E, W; 1975 v N, Se, Y, E; 1976 v Se, N, Y, (with Everton); Is, S, E, W;1977 v Ho, Bel, WG, E, S, W, Ic; (with Millwall); 1978 v S, E, W; 1979 v Ei(sub); (with Swindon Town); Bul (2), E, S, W, D; 1980 v Aus (2 sub) (50)
Hamilton, J.	(Knock)	1882 v E, W (2)
Hamilton, R.	(Rangers)	1928 v S; 1929 v E; 1930 v S, E; 1932 v S (5)
Hamilton, W.	(QPR)	1978 v S(sub); (with Burnley); 1980 v S, E, W, Aus (2); 1981 v Se, P, S, P, S, Se; 1982 v S,Is,E, W, Y, Hon, Sp, A, F; 1983 v A, WG, Alb (2), S, E, W; 1984 v A, T, WG, S, E, W, Fi; (with Oxford Utd); 1985 v R, Sp; 1986 v Mor(sub), Alg, Sp(sub), Br(sub) (41)
Hamilton, W.D.	(Dublin Association)	1885 v W (1)
Hamilton, W.J.	(Distillery)	1908 v W (1)
Hamilton, W.J.	(Dublin Association)	1885 v W (1)
Hampton, H.	(Bradford City)	1911 v W, E, S; 1912 v E, W; 1913 v W, E, S; 1914 v E (9)
Hanna, J.D.	(Royal Artillery Portsmouth)	1899 v W (1)
Hanna, J.	(Nottingham For)	1912 v S, W (2)
Hannon, D.J.	(Bohemians)	1908 v E, S; 1911 v E, S; 1912 v W; 1913 v E (6)
Harkin, J.T.	(Southport)	1968 v W; 1969 v T; (with Shrewsbury T); W(sub); 1970 v USSR; 1971 v Sp (5)
Harland, A.I.	(Linfield	1923 v E (1)
Harris, J.	(Cliftonville)	1921 v W (1)
Harris, V.	(Shelbourne)	1906 v E; 1907 v E, W; 1908 v E, S, W; (with Everton); 1909 v E, S, W; 1910 v E, S, W; 1911 v W, E, S; 1912 v E; 1913 v E, S; 1914 v W, S (20)
Harvey, M.	(Sunderland)	1961 v I; 1962 v Ho; 1963 v W, Sp; 1964 v S, Sp, E, W, U; 1965 v E, Sw (2), S, Ho, W, Ho,Alb; 1966 v S, E, Alb, W, WG, M; 1967 v E, S; 1968 v E, W; 1969 v Is, T (2), E; 1970 v USSR; 1971 v Cy, W(sub) (34)
Hastings, J.	(Knock)	1882 v E, W; (with Ulster); 1883 v W; 1884 v S, E; 1886 v E, S (7)
Hatton, S.	(Linfield)	1963 v Pol, S, (2)
Hayes, W.E.	(Huddersfield Town)	1938 v S, E; 1939 v S, E (4)
Healy, P.J.	(Coleraine)	1982 v S, W, Hon(sub); 1984 v A(sub) (4)
Hegan, D.	(WBA)	1970 v USSR; (with Wolverhampton W); 1972 v USSR, S, E; 1973 v Bul, Cy (7)
Henderson, A.W.	(Ulster)	1885 v E, S, W (3)
Hewison, G.	(Moyola Park)	1885 v E, S (2)

Hill, C.F.	(Sheffield Utd)	1990 v N, U; 1991 v Y, Pol; 1992 v A, D (with Leicester City) 1995 v Ei, Lat, 1996 v P, Lic, A, N, Se, G (14)
Hill, M.J.	(Norwich City)	1959 v W: 1960 v W; 1961 v WG; 1962 v S; (with Everton); 1964 v S, Sp, E (7)
Hinton, E.	(Fulham)	1947 v S, W; 1948 v S, E, W; (with Millwall); 1951 v W, F (7)
Hopkins, J.	(Brighton)	1926 v E (1)
Horlock, K.	(Swindon Town)	1995 v La, Can (2)
Houston, J.	(Linfield)	1912 v S, W; 1913 v W; (with Everton); 1913 v E, S; 1914 v S (6)
Houston, W.	(Linfield)	1933 v W (1)
Houston, W.J.	(Moyola Park)	1885 v E, S (2)
Hughes, M.E.	(Manchester City)	1992 v D, S, Lit, G; (with Strasbourg); 1993 v Alb, Sp, D, Ei, Sp, Lit, Lat; 1994 v Lat, D, Ei, R, Lic, C, M 1995 v P, A, Ei(2), Lat, Can, Ch, Lat (26)
Hughes, P.	(Bury)	1987 v E, T, Is (3)
Hughes, W.	(Bolton W)	1951 v W (1)
Humphries, W.	(Ards)	1962 v W; (with Coventry City); 1962 v Ho; 1963 v Pol, E, S, W, Sp; 1964 v S, Sp, E; 1965 v S; (with Swansea T); 1965 v Ho, W (14)
Hunter, A.	(Distillery)	1905 v W; 1906 v E, S, W; (with Belfast Celtic); 1908 v W; 1909 v E, S, W (8)
Hunter, A.	(Blackburn R)	1970 v USSR; 1971 v Cy (2), E, S, W; (with Ipswich Town); 1972 v USSR (2), Sp, S, E, W; 1973 v Bul,Cy, P, Cy, E, S, W; 1974 v Bul, S, E, W; 1975 v N, Se, Y, E, S, W; 1976 v Se, N, Y, Is, S, E, W; 1977 v Ho, Bel, WG, E, S, W, Ic; 1978 v Ic, Ho, Bel; 1979 v Ei, D, S, W, D; 1980 v E, Ei (53)
Hunter, B.	(Wrexham)	1995 v Lat, 1996 v P, Lic, A, Se, G (6)
Hunter, R.J.	(Cliftonville)	1884 v S, W, E (3)
Hunter, V.	(Coleraine)	1962 v E; 1964 v Sp (2)
Irvine, R.J.	(Linfield)	1962 v Ho; 1963 v Pol, E, S, Pol, W, Sp; (with Stoke City); 1965 v W (8)
Irvine, R.W.	(Everton)	1922 v S; 1923 v E, S, W; 1924 v E, S, W; 1925 v E; 1926 v E; 1927 v E, W; 1928 v E, S; (with Portsmouth); 1929 v E; 1930 v S; (with Connah's Quay); 1931 v E; (with Derry City); 1932 v W (15)
Irvine, W.J.	(Burnley)	1963 v W, Sp; 1965 v Sw, S, Ho, W, Ho, Alb; 1966 v S, E, Alb, W, M; 1967 v E, S; 1968 v E, W; (with Preston N.E) 1969 v Is, T, E; (with Brighton H.A.); 1972 v S, E, W (23)
Irving, S.J.	(Dundee)	1923 v S, W; 1924 v E, S, W; 1925 v E, S, W; 1926 v W, S; (with Cardiff City); 1927 v E, S, W; 1928 v E, W, S; (with Chelsea); 1929 v E; 1931 v W (18)
Jackson, T.	(Everton)	1969 v Is, E, S, W; 1970 v USSR (1+1 sub); (with Nottingham For); 1971 v Sp; 1972 v S, E,W;1973 v Cy, E,S,W;1974 v Bul, P, S(sub), E(sub), W(sub); 1975 v N(sub), Se, Y, E, S, W; (with Manchester Utd); 1976 v Se, N, Y; 1977 v Ho, Bel, WG, E, S, W, Ic (35)
Jamison, J.	(Glentoran)	1976 v N (1)
Jennings, P.A.	(Watford)	1964 v W, U; (with Tottenham H), 1965 v E, Sw (2), S, Ho, Alb; 1966 v S, E, Alb, W, WG;1967 v E,S; 1968 v S, E, W; 1969 v Is, T (2), E, S, W; 1970 v USSR (2), S, E; 1971 v Cy (2), E, S, W; 1972 v USSR, Sp, S, E, W; 1973 v Bul, Cy, P, E, S, W; 1974 v P, S, E, W; 1975 v N, Se, Y, E, S, W; 1976 v Se, N, Y, Is, S, E, W; 1977 v Ho, Bel, WG, E, S, W, Ic; (with Arsenal); 1978 v Ic, Ho, Bel; 1979 v Ei, D, Bul, E, Bul, E, S, W, D; 1980 v E, Ei, Is; 1981 v S, P, S, Se; 1982 v S, Is, E, W, Y, Hon, Sp, F; 1983 v Alb, S, E, W; 1984 v A, T, WG, S, W, F; 1985 v R, Fi, E, Sp, T; (with Tottenham H); 1986 v T, R, E, F, D;(with Everton); 1986 v Mor; (with Tottenham H); Alg, Sp, Br (119)
Johnston, H.	(Portadown)	1927 v W (1)
Johnston, R.S.	(Distillery)	1905 v W (1)
Johnston, S.	(Distillery)	1882 v W; 1884 v E; 1886 v E, S (4)
Johnston, S.	(Linfield)	1890 v W; 1893 v S, W; 1894 v E (4)
Johnston, W.	(Oldpark)	1885 v S, W (2)
Johnston, W.C.	(Glenavon)	1962 v W; (with Oldham Ath); 1966 v M(sub) (2)
Jones, J.	(Linfield)	1930 v W, S; 1931 v E, S, W; 1932 v S, E; 1933 v S, E, W; 1934 v S, E, W; 1935 v S, E,W; 1936 v E, S; (with Hibernian); 1936 v W; 1937 v S, E, W;

		(with Glenavon); 1938 v E (23)
Jones, J.	(Glenavon)	1956 v W; 1957 v E, W; (3)
Jones, S.	(Distillery)	1934 v E; (with Blackpool); 1934 v W (2)
Jordan, T.	(Linfield)	1895 v E, W (2)
Kavanagh, P.J.	(Celtic)	1930 v E (1)
Keane, T.R.	(Swansea T)	1949 v S (1)
Kearns, A.	(Distillery)	1900 v W, S, E; 1902 v W, S, E (6)
Kee, P.V.	(Oxford Utd)	1990 v N; 1991 v Y, D, A, Pol, Y, Fa (with Ards) 1995 v A, Ei (9)
Keith, R.M.	(Newcastle Utd)	1958 v E, I, W, Cz, Arg, WG, Cz, F; 1959 v E, Sp, S, W; 1960 v S, E; 1961 v E, WG, S, WG, W, I, Gr; 1962 v W, Ho (23)
Kelly, H.R.	(Fulham)	1950 v E, W; (with Southampton); 1951 v E, S (4)
Kelly, J.	(Glentoran)	1896 v E (1)
Kelly, J.	(Derry City)	1932 v E, W; 1933 v S, E, W; 1934 v W; 1936 v E, S, W; 1937 v S, E (11)
Kelly, P.	(Manchester City)	1921 v E (1)
Kelly, P.M.	(Barnsley)	1950 v S (1)
Kennedy, A.L.	(Arsenal)	1923 v W; 1925 v E (2)
Kernaghan, N.	(Belfast Celtic)	1936 v W; 1937 v S; 1938 v E (3)
Kirkwood, H.	(Cliftonville)	1904 v W (1)
Kirwan, J.	(Tottenham H)	1900 v W; 1902 v W, E; 1903 v E, S, W; 1904 v E, W, S; 1905 v E, S, W; (with Chelsea); 1906 v E, S, W; 1907 v W; (with Clyde); 1909 v S (17)
Lacey, W.	(Everton)	1909 v E, S, W; 1910 v E, S, W; 1911 v W, E, S; 1912 v E; (with Liverpool); 1913 v W; 1914 v W, E, S; 1920 v E, S, W; 1921 v E, S, W; 1922 v E, S; (with New Brighton); 1925 v E (23)
Lawther, R.	(Distillery)	1888 v S, E (2)
Lawther, W.I.	(Sunderland)	1960 v W; 1961 v I; (with Blackburn R); 1962 v S, Ho (4)
Leatham, J.	(Belfast Celtic)	1939 v W (1)
Ledwidge, J.J.	(Shelbourne)	1906 v S, W (2)
Lemon, J.	(Glentoran)	1886 v W; (with Belfast YMCA); 1888 v S; 1889 v W (3)
Lennon, N.	(Crewe Alex)	1994 v M(sub) 1995 v Ch (2)
Leslie, W.	(Belfast YMCA)	1887 v E (1)
Lewis, J.	(Glentoran)	1899 v E, W, S; (with Distillery); 1900 v S (4)
Lockhart, H.	(Rossall School)	1884 v W (1)
Lockhart, N.	(Linfield)	1947 v E; (with Coventry City); 1950 v W; 1951 v W; 1952 v W; (with Aston Villa); 1954 v S, E; 1955 v W; 1956 v W (8)
Lomas, S.M.	(Manchester City)	1994 v R, Lic, Col(sub), M 1995 v P, A, 1996 v P, Lic, A, N, Se, G (12)
Loyal, J.	(Clarence)	1891 v S (1)
Lutton, R.J.	(Wolverhampton W)	1970 v S, E; (with West Ham Utd); 1973 v Cy(sub), S(sub), W(sub); 1974 v P (6)
Lyner, D.	(Glentoran)	1920 v E, W; 1922 v S, W; (with Manchester Utd); 1923 v E; (with Kilmarnock); 1923 v W (6)
Lyttle, J.	(Glentoran)	1898 v W (1)
McAdams, W.J.	(Manchester City)	1954 v W; 1955 v S; 1957 v E; 1958 v S, I; (with Bolton W); 1961 v E, WG, S, WG, W, I, Gr; 1962 v Gr, E; (with Leeds Utd); 1962 v Ho (15)
McAlery, J.M.	(Cliftonville)	1882 v E, W (2)
McAlinden, J.	(Belfast Celtic)	1938 v S; 1939 v S; (with Portsmouth); 1947 v E; (with Southend Utd); 1949 v E (4)
McAllen, J.	(Linfield)	1898 v E; 1899 v E, W, S; 1900 v W, S, E; 1901 v W; 1902 v S (9)
McAlpine, S.	(Cliftonville)	1901 v S (1)
McArthur, A.	(Distillery)	1886 v W (1)
McAuley, J.L.	(Huddersfield T)	1911 v W, E; 1912 v E, S; 1913 v E, S (6)
McAuley, P.	(Belfast Celtic)	1900 v S (1)
McBride, S.D.	(Glenavon)	1991 v D(sub), Pol(sub); 1992 v Fa(sub), D (4)
McCabe, J.J.	(Leeds Utd)	1949 v S, W; 1950 v E; 1951 v W; 1953 v W; 1954 v S (6)
McCabe, W.	(Ulster)	1891 v E (1)
McCambridge, J.	(Ballymena)	1930 v W, S; (with Cardiff City); 1931 v W; 1932 v E (4)
McCandless, J.	(Bradford)	1912 v W; 1913 v W; 1920 v S, W; 1921 v E (5)
McCandless, W.	(Linfield)	1920 v E, W; 1921 v E; (with Rangers); 1921 v W; 1922 v S; 1924 v S, W; 1925 v S; 1929 v W (9)

McCann, P.	(Belfast Celtic)	1910 v E, S, W; 1911 v E; (with Glentoran); 1911 v S; 1912 v E; 1913 v W (7)
McCartney, A.	(Ulster)	1903 v S, W; (with Linfield); 1904 v W, S; (with Everton); 1905 v E, S; (with Belfast Celtic); 1907 v E, W, S; 1908 v E, S, W; (with Glentoran); 1909 v E, S, W (15)
McCashin, J.	(Cliftonville)	1896 v W; 1898 v W, S; 1899 v S (4)
McCavana, W.T.	(Coleraine)	1955 v S; 1956 v S, E (3)
McCaw, D.	(Malone)	1882 v E (1)
McCaw, J.H.	(Linfield)	1927 v W; 1930 v S; 1931 v E, S, W (5)
McClatchey, J.	(Distillery)	1886 v W, E, S (3)
McClatchey, T.	(Distillery)	1895 v S (1)
McCleary, J.W.	(Cliftonville)	1955 v W (1)
McCleery, W.	(Linfield)	1930 v E, W; 1931 v E, S, W; 1932 v S, W; 1933 v E, W (9)
McClelland, J.	(Arsenal)	1961 v WG (2), W, I, Gr; (with Fulham); 1966 v M (6)
McClelland, J.	(Mansfield Town)	1980 v S(sub), Aus (3); 1981 v Se, S; (with Rangers); S, Se(sub); 1982 v S, W, Y, Hon, Sp, A, F; 1983 v A, WG, Alb, T, Alb, S, E, W; 1984 v A, T, WG, S, E, W, Fi; 1985 v R, Is; (with Watford); Fi, E, Sp, T; 1986 v T, F(sub); 1987 v E, T, Is, E, Y; 1988 v T, Gr, F, Ma; 1989 v Ei, H, Sp (2), Ma; (with Leeds Utd); 1990 v N(sub) (53)
McCluggage, A.	(Bradford)	1924 v E; (with Burnley); 1927 v S, W; 1928 v E, W, S; 1929 v E, W, S; 1930 v W; 1931 v E, W (12)
McClure, G.	(Cliftonville)	1907 v W, S; 1908 v W with (Distillery); 1909 v E (4)
McConnell, E.	(Cliftonville)	1904 v W, S: (with Glentoran); 1905 v E; (with Sunderland); 1906 v E; 1907 v E; 1908 v S, W; (with Sheffield Wed); 1909 v S, W; 1910 v E, S, W (12)
McConnell, P.	(Doncaster R)	1928 v W; (with Southport); 1932 v E (2)
McConnell, W.G.	(Bohemians)	1912 v W; 1913 v E, S; 1914 v W, E, S (6)
McConnell, W.H.	(Reading)	1925 v W; 1926 v E, W; 1927 v E, S, W; 1928 v E, W (8)
McCourt, F.J.	(Manchester C)	1952 v E, W; 1953 v E, S, F, W (6)
McCoy, J.	(Distillery)	1896 v W (1)
McCoy, R.	(Coleraine)	1987 v Y(sub) (1)
McCracken, R.	(Crystal Palace)	1921 v E; 1922 v E, S, W (4)
McCracken, W.	(Distillery)	1902 v W, E; 1903 v E; 1904 v E, W, S; (with Newcastle Utd); 1905 v E, S, W; 1907 v E; 1920 v E; 1922 v E, S, W; (with Hull City); 1923 v S (15)
McCreery, D.	(Manchester Utd)	1976 v S(sub), E, W: 1977 v Ho, Bel, WG, E, S,W, Ic; 1978 v Ic, Ho, Bel, S, E, W; 1979 v Ei,D, Bul, E, Bul, W, D; (with QPR); 1980 v E, Ei, S(sub), E(sub), W(sub), Aus (1+1sub); 1981 v Se(sub), P(sub); (with Tulsa R); S, P, Se: 1982 v S, Is, E(sub), F, Y, Ho, Sp, A, F; (with Newcastle Utd); 1983 v A; 1984 v T(sub); 1985 v R, Sp(sub);1986 v T(sub), R, E, F, D, Alg, Sp, Br; 1987 v T, E, Y; 1988 v Y; 1989 v Sp, Ma, Ch; (with Hearts); 1990 v H, Ei, N, U(sub) (67)
McCrory, S.	(Southend Utd)	1958 v E (1)
McCullough, K.	(Belfast Celtic)	1935 v W; 1936 v E; (with Manchester City); 1936 v S; 1937 v S, E (5)
McCullough, W.J.	(Arsenal)	1961 v I; 1963 v Sp; 1964 v S, Sp, E, W, U; 1965 v E, Sw; (with Millwall); 1967 v E (10)
McCurdy, C.	(Linfield)	1980 v Aus(sub) (1)
McDonald, A.	(QPR)	1986 v R, E, F, D, Mor, Alg, Sp, Br; 1987 v E, T, Is, E, Y; 1988 v Y, T, Pol, F, Ma; 1989 v Ei,H, Sp, Ch; 1990 v H, Ei, U; 1991 v Y, D, A, Fa; 1992 v Fa, S, Lit, G; 1993 v Alb, Sp, D, Alb, Ei, Sp, Lit, Lat; 1994 v D, Ei 1995 v P, A, Ei, Lat, Can, Ch, Lat, 1996 v A (sub), N. (52)
McDonald, R.	(Rangers)	1930 v S; 1932 v E (2)
McDonnell, J.	(Bohemians)	1911 v E, S; 1912 v W; 1913 v W (4)
McElhinney, G.	(Bolton W)	1984 v WG, S, E, W, Fi; 1985 v R (6)
McFaul, W.S.	(Linfield)	1967 v E(sub); (with Newcastle Utd); 1970 v W; 1971 v Sp; 1972 v USSR; 1973 v Cy; 1974 v Bul (6)
McGarry, J.K.	(Cliftonville)	1951 v S, W, F (3)
McGaughey, M.	(Linfield)	1985 v Is(sub) (1)
McGibbon, P	(Manchester U)	1995 v Can (sub), Ch, Lat; 1996 v Lic (sub) (4)
McGrath, R.C.	(Tottenham Hots)	1974 v S, E, W; 1975 v N; 1976 v Is(sub); (with Manchester Utd); 1977 v Ho, Bel, WG, E, S, W, Ic; 1978 v Ic, Ho, Bel, S, E, W; 1979 v Bul(sub), E(2 sub) (21)

McGregor, S.	(Glentoran)	1921 v S (1)
McGrillen, J.	(Clyde)	1924 v S; (with Belfast Celtic); 1927 v S (2)
McGuire, E.	(Distillery)	1907 v S (1)
McIlroy, H.	(Cliftonville)	1906 v E (1)
McIlroy, J.	(Burnley)	1952 v S, E, W; 1953 v E, S, W; 1954 v S, E, W; 1955 v E, S, W; 1956 v S, E, W; 1957 v E, S, P, W, I, P; 1958 v S, E, I (2), W, Cz, Arg, WG, Cz, F; 1959 v E, Sp, S, W; 1960 v S, E, W; 1961 v E, WG (2), W, Gr; 1962 v S, Gr, E, Ho; 1963 v Pol, E, S, Pol; (with Stoke City); 1963 v W; 1966 v S, E, Alb (55)
McIlroy, S.B.	(Manchester Utd)	1972 v Sp, S(sub); 1974 v S, E, W; 1975 v N, Se, Y, E, S, W; 1976 v Se, N, Y, S, E,W;1977 v Ho, Bel, E, S, W, Ic; 1978 v Ic, Ho, Bel, S, E, W; 1979 v Ei, D, Bul, E, Bul, E, S, W, D; 1980 v E, Ei, Is, S, E, W; 1981 v Se, P, S, P, S, Se; 1982 v S, Is; (with Stoke City); E, F, S, W, Y, Hon, Sp, Alb, F; 1983 v A, WG, Alb, T, Alb, S, E, W; 1984 v A, T, S, E, W, Fi; 1985 v Fi, E, T; (with Manchester City); 1986 v T, R, E, F, D, Mor, Alg, Sp, Br; 1987 v E(sub) (88)
McIlvenny, P.	(Distillery)	1924 v W (1)
McIlvenny, R.	(Distillery)	1890 v E; (with Ulster) 1891 v E (2)
McKeag, W.	(Glentoran)	1968 v S, W (2)
McKee, F.W.	(Cliftonville)	1906 v S, W; (with Belfast Celtic); 1914 v W, E, S (5)
McKelvey, H.	(Glentoran)	1901 v W (1)
McKenna, J.	(Huddersfield T)	1950 v S, E, W; 1951 v E, S, F; 1952 v E (7)
McKenzie, H.	(Distillery)	1923 v S (1)
McKenzie, R.	(Airdrie)	1967 v W (1)
McKeown, N.	(Linfield)	1892 v W, E, S; 1893 v S, W; 1894 v W, S (7)
McKie, H.	(Cliftonville)	1895 v E, W, S (3)
McKinney, D.	(Hull City)	1921 v S; (with Bradford City); 1924 v S (2)
McKinney, V.J.	(Falkirk)	1966 v WG (1)
McKnight, A.	(Celtic)	1988 v Y, T, Gr, Pol, F, Ma; (with West Ham Utd); 1989 v Ei, H, Sp (2) (10)
McKnight, J.	(Preston NE)	1912 v S; (with Glentoran); 1913 v S (2)
McLaughlin, J.C.	(Shrewsbury T)	1962 v S, Gr, E, W; 1963 v W; (with Swansea T); 1964 v W, U; 1965 v E, Sw (2), W; 1966 v W (12)
McLean, T.	(Limavady)	1885 v S (1)
McMahon G. J.	(Tottenham Hots)	1995 v Can (sub), Ch, Lat; 1996 v Lic, N (sub), Se, G. (7)
McMahon, J.	(Bohemians)	1934 v S (1)
McMaster, G.	(Glentoran)	1897 v E, W, S (3)
McMichael, A.	(Newcastle Utd)	1950 v S, E; 1951 v E, S, F; 1952 v S, E, W; 1953 v E, S, F, W; 1954 v S, E, W; 1955 v E,W;1956 v W; 1957 v E, S, P, W, P, I; 1958 v S, E, I (2), W, Cz, Arg, WG, Cz, F; 1959 v Sp, S, W; 1960 v S, E, W (40)
McMillan, G.	(Distillery)	1903 v E; 1905 v W (2)
McMillan, S.	(Manchester Utd)	1963 v E, S (2)
McMillen, W.S.	(Manchester Utd)	1934 v E; 1935 v S; 1937 v S; (with Chesterfield); 1938 v S, W; 1939 v S, E (7)
McMordie, A.S.	(Middlesbrough)	1969 v Is, T (2), E, S, W; 1970 v USSR, S, E, W; 1971 v Cy (2), E, S, W; 1972 v USSR, Sp, S, E, W; 1973 v Bul (21)
McMorran, E.J.	(Belfast Celtic)	1947 v E; (with Barnsley); 1951 v E, S, W; 1952 v S, E, W; 1953 v E, S, F, (with Doncaster R); 1953 v W; 1954 v E; 1956 v W; 1957 v P, I (15)
McMullan, D.	(Liverpool)	1926 v E, W; 1927 v S (3)
McNally, B.A.	(Shrewsbury T)	1986 v Mor; 1987 v T(sub); 1988 v Y, Gr, Ma(sub) (5)
McNinch, J.	(Ballymena)	1931 v S; 1932 v S, W (3)
McParland, P.J.	(Aston Villa)	1954 v W; 1955 v E, S; 1956 v S, E; 1957 v E, S, P, W; 1958 v S, E, I (2), W, Cz, Arg, WG, Cz, F; 1959 v E, Sp, S, W; 1960 v S, E, W; 1961 v E, WG, S, WG, W, I, Gr; (with Wolverhampton W); 1962 v Ho (34)
McShane, J.	(Cliftonville)	1899 v S; 1900 v W, S, E (4)
McVicker, J.	(Linfield)	1888 v E; (with Glentoran) 1889 v S (2)
McWha, W.B.R.	(Knock)	1882 v E, W; (with Cliftonville); 1883 v E, W; 1884 v E; 1885 v E, W (7)
Mackie, J.	(Arsenal)	1923 v W; (with Portsmouth); 1935 v S, W (3)
Madden, O.	(Norwich City)	1938 v E (1)
Magee, G.	(Wellington Park)	1885 v E, S, W (3)

Magill, E.J.	(Arsenal)	1962 v S, Gr, E; 1963 v Pol, E, S, Pol, W, Sp; 1964 v S, Sp, E, W, U;1965 v E, Sw(2), S, Ho, Alb; 1966 v S; (with Brighton H.A); E, Alb, W, WG, M (26)
Magilton, J.	(Oxford Utd)	1991 v Pol, Y, Fa; 1992 v Fa, A, D, S, Lit, G; 1993 v Alb, D, Alb, Ei, Lit, Lat; 1994 v Lat, D, Ei; (with Southampton); 1994 v R, Lic, Col, M 1995 v P, A, Ei(2) Can, Ch, Lat 1996 v P, N, G (32)
Maginnis, H.	(Linfield)	1900 v W, S, E; 1903 v S, W; 1904 v E, W, S (8)
Mahood, J.	(Belfast Celtic)	1926 v S; 1928 v E, W, S; 1929 v E, W, S; 1930 v W; (with Ballymena); 1934 v S (9)
Manderson, R.	(Rangers)	1920 v W, S; 1925 v E, S; 1926 v S (5)
Mansfield, J.	(Dublin Freebooters)	1901 v E (1)
Martin, C.J.	(Glentoran)	1947 v S; (with Leeds Utd); 1948 v S, E, W; (with Aston Villa); 1949 v E; 1950 v W (6)
Martin, D.	(Bo'ness)	1925 v S (1)
Martin, D.C.	(Cliftonville)	1882 v E, W; 1883 v E (3)
Martin, D.K.	(Belfast Celtic)	1934 v S, E, W; 1935 v S; (with Wolverhampton W); 1935 v E; 1936 v W; (with Nottingham For); 1937 v S; 1938 v E, S; 1939 v S (10)
Mathieson, A.	(Luton Town)	1921 v W; 1922 v E (2)
Maxwell, J.	(Linfield)	1902 v W; 1903 v E, W; (with Glentoran); 1905 v S, W; (with Belfast Celtic); 1906 v W; 1907 v S (7)
Meek, H.L.	(Glentoran)	1925 v W (1)
Mehaffy, J.A.C.	(Queen's Island)	1922 v W (1)
Meldon, J.	(Dublin Freebooters)	1899 v W, S (2)
Mercer, H.V.A.	(Linfield)	1908 v E (1)
Mercer, J.T.	(Distillery)	1898 v W, E, S; 1899 v E; (with Linfield); 1902 v W, E; (with Distillery); 1903 v S,W; (with Derby Co); 1904 v E, W; 1905 v S (11)
Millar, W.	(Barrow)	1932 v W; 1933 v S (2)
Miller, J.	(Middlesbrough)	1929 v W, S; 1930 v E (3)
Milligan, D.	(Chesterfield)	1939 v W (1)
Milne, R.G.	(Linfield)	1894 v W, E, S; 1895 v E, W; 1896 v W, E, S; 1897 v E, S; 1898 v W, E, S z1899 v E, W; 1901 v W; 1902 v W, S, E; 1903 v E, S; 1904 v E, W, S; 1906 v E, S, W (27)
Mitchell, C.	(Glentoran)	1934 v W (1)
Mitchell, E.J.	(Cliftonville)	1933 v S (1)
Mitchell, W.	(Distillery)	1932 v E, W; 1933 v E, W; (with Chelsea); 1934 v S, W; 1935 v S, E; 1936 v E, S; 1937 v S, E, W; 1938 v E, S (15)
Molyneux, T.B.	(Ligoneil)	1883 v E, W; (with Cliftonville); 1884 v S, W, E; 1885 v E, W; 1886 v E, W, S; 1888 v S (11)
Montgomery, F.J.	(Coleraine)	1955 v E (1)
Moore, C.	(Glentoran)	1949 v W (1)
Moore, R.	(Linfield)	1891 v W, E, S (3)
Moore, P.	(Aberdeen)	1933 v E (1)
Moore, R.L.	(Ulster)	1887 v S, W (2)
Moore, W.	(Falkirk)	1923 v S (1)
Moorhead, F.W.	(Dublin University)	1885 v E (1)
Moorhead, G.	(Linfield)	1923 v S; 1928 v S; 1929 v S (3)
Moran, J.	(Leeds City)	1912 v S (1)
Moreland, V.	(Derby Co)	1979 v Bul (2sub), E, S; 1980 v E, Ei (6)
Morgan. F.G.	(Linfield)	1923 v E; (with Nottingham For); 1924 v S; 1927 v E; 1928 v E, W, S; 1929 v E (7)
Morgan, S.	(Port Vale)	1972 v Sp; 1973 v Bul(sub), P, Cy, E, S, W; (with Aston Villa); 1974 v Bul, P, S, E; 1975 v v Se;1976 v se(sub), N, Y; (with Brighton & HA); 1976 v S, W(sub); (with Sparta Rotterdam); 1979 v D (18)
Morrison, R.	(Linfield)	1891 v W, E (2)
Morrison, T.	(Glentoran)	1895 v E, W, S; (with Burnley); 1899 v W; 1900 v W; 1902 v S, E (7)
Morrogh, D.	(Bohemians)	1896 v S (1)
Morrow, S.J.	(Arsenal)	1990 v U(sub); 1991 v A(sub), Pol, Y; 1992 v Fa, S(sub), G(sub); 1993 v Sp(sub), Alb, Ei; 1994 v R, Col, M(sub) 1995 v P, Ei (2) Lat 1996 v P, Se (19).

Morrow, W.J.	(Moyola Park)	1883 v E, W; 1884 v S (3)
Muir, R.	(Oldpark)	1885 v S, W (2)
Mullan G.	(Glentoran)	1983 v Alb(sub), S, E, W (4)
Mulholland, S.	(Belfast Celtic)	1906 v E, S (2)
Mulligan, J.	(Manchester City)	1921 v S (1)
Murphy, J.	(Bradford City)	1910 v E, S, W (3)
Murphy, N.	(QPR)	1905 v E, S, W (3)
Murray, J.M.	(Motherwell)	1910 v E, S; (with Sheffield Wed); 1910 v W (3)
Napier, R.J.	(Bolton W)	1966 v WG (1)

Neill, W.J.T. (Arsenal) 1961 v WG, I, Gr; 1962 v S, Gr, E, W; 1963 v E, Pol, W, Sp; 1964 v S, Sp, E, W, U; 1965 v E, Sw, S, Ho, W, Ho, Alb; 1966 v S, E, Alb, W, WG, M; 1967 v S, W; 1968 v S, E; 1969 v Is, T (2), E, S,W; 1970 v USSR (2), S, E, W; (with Hull City); 1971 v Sp, Cy; 1972 v USSR (2), Sp, S, E, W; 1973 v Bul, Cy, P, Cy, E, S, W (59)

Nelis, P. (Nottingham For) 1923 v E (1)

Nelson, S. (Arsenal) 1970 v E(sub), W; 1971 v Sp, Cy, E, S, W; 1972 v USSR (2), Sp, S, E, W; 1973 v Bul, Cy, P;1974 v S, E; 1975 v Se, Y; 1976 v Se, N, Is, E; 1977 v Bel(sub), WG, W, Ic; 1978 v Ic, Ho, Bel; 1979 v Ei,D,Bul, E, Bul, E, S, W, D; 1980 v E, Ei, Is; 1981 v S, P. S, Se; (with Brighton & HA); 1982 v E, S, Sp(sub) A (51)

Nicholl, C.J. (Aston Villa) 1975 v Se, Y, E, S, W; 1976 v Se, N, Y, S, E, W; 1977 v W; (with Southampton), 1978 v Bel(sub),S, E, W; 1979 v Ei, Bul, E, Bul, E, W; 1980 v Ei, Is, S, E, W, Aus (3); 1981 v Se, P, S, P, S, Se; 1982 v S, Is, E, F, W, Y, Hon, Sp, A, F; 1983 v S(sub), E, W; (with Grimsby T), 1984 v A, T (51)

Nicholl, H. (Belfast Celtic) 1902 v W, E; 1905 v E (3)

Nicholl, J.M. (Manchester Utd) 1976 v Is, W (sub); 1977 v Ho, Bel, E, S, W, Ic; 1978 v Ic, Ho, Bel, S, E, W; 1979 v Ei, D, Bul, E, Bul, E, S, W, D; 1980 v E, Ei, Is, S, E, W, Aus (3); 1981 v Se, P, S, P, S, Se; 1982 v S, Is, E;(with Toronto B); 1982 v F, W, Y, Hon, Sp, A, F; (with Sunderland); 1983 v A, WG, Alb, T, Alb, (with Toronto B); 1983 v S, E, W; 1984 v T; (with Rangers); 1984 v WG, S, E; (with Toronto B); 1984 v Fi; 1985 v R; (with WBA); 1985 v Fi, E, Sp, T; 1986 v T, R, E, F, Alg, Sp, Br (73)

Nicholson, J.J. (Manchester Utd) 1961 v S, W; 1962 v Gr, E, W, Ho; 1963 v Pol, E, S, Pol; (with Huddersfield Town);1965 v Ho, W,Ho, Alb; 1966 v S, E, Alb, W, M; 1967 v S, W; 1968 v S, E, W; 1969 v T (2), E, S, W; 1970 v USSR (2), S, E, W; 1971 v Cy (2), E, S, W; 1972 v USSR (2) (41)

Nixon, R. (Linfield) 1914 v S (1)

Nolan-Whelan, J.V. (Dublin Freebooters) 1901 v E, W; 1902 v W, S (4)

O'Boyle, G. (Dunfermline Ath) 1994 v Col(sub), M (with St. Johnstone) 1995 v P(sub) Lat (sub), Can (sub), Ch (sub) 1996 v Se (sub), G (sub) (8)

O'Brien, M.T. (QPR) 1921 v S; (with Leicester City); 1922 v S, W; 1924 v S, W; (with Hull City); 1925 v E, S, W; 1926 v W; (with Derby Co); 1927 v W (10)

O'Connell, P. (Sheffield Wed) 1912 v E, S; (with Hull City); 1914 v W, E, S (5)

O'Doherty, A. (Coleraine) 1970 v E, W(sub) (2)

O'Driscoll, J.F. (Swansea T) 1949 v E, S, W (3)

O'Hagan, C. (Tottenham Hots) 1905 v S, W; 1906 v E, S, W; (with Aberdeen); 1907 v E, W, S; 1908 v S, W; 1909 v E (11)

O'Hagan, W. (St.Mirren) 1920 v E, W (2)

O'Hehir, J.C. (Bohemians) 1910 v W (1)

O'Kane, W.J. (Nottingham For) 1970 v S(sub), E, W; 1971 v Sp, E, S, W; 1972 v USSR (2); 1973 v P, Cy; 1974 v Bul, P, S, E, W; 1975 v N, Se, E, S (20)

O'Mahoney, M.T. (Bristol R) 1939 v S (1)

O'Neill, C. (Motherwell) 1989 v Ch(sub); 1990 v Ei(sub); 1991 v D (3)

O'Neill, J. (Leicester City) 1980 v Is, S, E, W, Aus (3); 1981 v P, S, P, S, Se; 1982 v S, Is, E, F, S, F(sub); 1983 v A, WG, Alb, T, Alb, S; 1984 v S(sub); 1985 v Is, Fi, E, Sp, T; 1986 v T, R, E, F, D, Mor, Alg, Sp, Br (39)

O'Neill, J.	(Sunderland)	1962 v W (1)
O'Neill, M.A.	(Newcastle Utd)	1988 v Gr, Pol, F, Ma; 1989 v Ei, H, Sp (2sub), Ma(sub), Ch; (with Dundee Utd), 1990 v H(sub), Ei;1991 v Pol; 1992 v Fa(sub), S(sub), G(sub); 1993 v Alb (1+1sub), Ei, Sp, Lit, Lat; (with Hibernian), 1994 v Lic(sub) 1995 v A (sub) Ei 1996 v Lic, A, N, Se (29).
O'Neill, M.H.	(Distillery)	1972 v USSR(sub), with (Nottingham For); 1972 v Sp(sub), W(sub); 1973 v P, Cy, E, S,W;1974 v Bul, P, E(sub), W; 1975 v Se, Y, E, S, 1976 v Y(sub); 1977 v E(sub), S; 1978 v Ic, Ho, S, E, W; 1979 v Ei,D,Bul, E,Bul,D; 1980 v Ei,Is, Aus (3); 1981 v Se, P (with Norwich City); 1981 v P, S, Se, (with Manchester City); 1982 v S, (with Norwich City); 1982 v E, F, S, Y, Hon, Sp, A, F; 1983 v A, WG, Alb, T, Alb, S, E; (with Notts Co); 1984 v A, T, WG, E, W, Fi; 1985 v R, Fi (64)
O'Reilly, H.	(Dublin Freebooters)	1901 v S, W; 1904 v S (3)
Parke, J.	(Linfield)	1964 v S; (with Hibernian); 1964 v Sp, E; (with Sunderland); 1965 v Sw, S, Ho, W, Ho, Alb; 1966 v WG; 1967 v E, S; 1968 v S, E (14)
Patterson, D.J.	(Crystal Palace)	1994 v Col(sub), M(sub) 1995 v Ei (sub) Ei, Lat, Can, Ch (sub)Lat (sub) (8)
Peacock, R.	(Celtic)	1952 v S; 1953 v F; 1954 v W; 1955 v E, S; 1956 v S, E; 1957 v W, I, P; 1958 v S, E, I (2),W,Cz, Arg, WG, Cz; 1959 v E, S, W; 1960 v S, E; 1961 v E, WG, S, WG, I, Gr; (with Coleraine); 1962 v S (31)
Peden, J.	(Linfield)	1887 v S, W; 1888 v W, E; 1889 v E, S; 1890 v W, S; 1891 v W, E; 1892 v W, E; 1893 v E, S, W; 1896 v W, E, S; 1897 v W, S; 1898 v W, E, S; 1899 v W (24)
Penney, S.	(Brighton & HA)	1985 v Is; 1986 v T, R, E, F, D, Mor, Alg, Sp; 1987 v E, T, Is; 1988 v Pol, F, Ma; 1989 v Ei, Sp (17)
Percy, J.C.	(Belfast YMCA)	1889 v W (1)
Platt, J.A.	(Middlesbrough)	1976 v Is(sub); 1978 v S, E, W; 1980 v S, E, W, Aus (3); 1981 v Se, P; 1982 v F, S, W(sub), A; 1983 v A, WG, Alb, T; (with Ballymena Utd); 1984 v E, W(sub); (with Coleraine); 1986 v Mor(sub) (23)
Ponsonby, J.	(Distillery)	1895 v S; W 1896 v W, E, S; 1897 v E, W, S; 1899 v E (9)
Potts, R.M.C.	(Cliftonville)	1883 v E, W (2)
Priestley, T.J.	(Coleraine)	1933 v S; (with Chelsea); 1934 v E (2)
Pyper, James.	(Cliftonville)	1897 v W, S; 1898 v W, E, S; 1899 v S; 1900 v E (7)
Pyper, John.	(Cliftonville)	1897 v E, W, S; 1899 v E, W; 1900 v W, S, E; 1902 v S (9)
Pyper, M.	(Linfield)	1932 v W (1)
Quinn, J.M.	(Blackburn R)	1985 v Is, Fi, E, Sp, T; 1986 v T, R, E, F, D (sub), Mor(sub); 1987 v E(sub), T; (with Swindon T), 1988 v Y(sub),T,Gr, Pol, F(sub), Ma; (with Leicester City); 1989 v Ei, H(sub), Sp (1+1sub) (withBradford City), 1989v Ma, Ch; 1990 v H;(with West Ham Utd); 1990 v N; 1991 vY(sub); (with Bournemouth), 1992 v Lit; (with Reading); 1993 v Sp, D, Alb(sub), Ei(sub), Lat(sub); 1994 v Lat, D(sub), Ei, R, Lic, Col, M 1995 v P, A(sub) Lat (sub) 1996 v Lic, A (sub) (46)
Rafferty, P.	(Linfield)	1980 v E(sub) (1)
Ramsey, P.	(Leicester City)	1984 v A, WG, S; 1985 v Is, E, Sp, T; 1986 v T, Mor; 1987 v E, Is, Y(sub); 1988 v Y; 1989 v Sp (14)
Rankine, J.	(Alexander)	1883 v E, W (2)
Rattray, D.	(Avoneil)	1882 v E; 1883 v E, W (3)
Rea, R.	(Glentoran)	1901 v E (1)
Redmond, R.	(Cliftonville)	1884 v W (1)
Reid, G.H.	(Cardiff City)	1923 v S (1)
Reid, J.	(Ulster)	1883 v E; 1884 v W; 1887 v S; 1889 v W; 1890 v W, S (6)
Reid, S.E.	(Derby Co)	1934 v E, W; 1936 v E (3)
Reid, W.	(Hearts)	1931 v E (1)

Reilly, M.M.	(Portsmouth)	1900 v E; 1902 v E (2)
Renneville, W.T.	(Leyton)	1910 v E, S, W; (with Aston Villa); 1911 v W (4)
Reynolds, J.	(Distillery)	1890 v W, E; (with Ulster); 1891 v W, E, S (5)
Reynolds, R.	(Bohemians)	1905 v W (1)
Rice, P.J.	(Arsenal)	1969 v Is; 1970 v USSR; 1971 v E, S, W; 1972 v USSR, Sp, S, E, W; 1973 v Bul, Cy, E, S, W; 1974 v Bul, P, S, E, W; 1975 v N, Y, E, S, W; 1976 v Se, N, Y, Is, S, E, W; 1977 v Ho, Bel, WG, E, S, Ic; 1978 v Ic, Ho, Bel; 1979 v Ei, D, E (2), S, W, D; 1980 v E (49)
Roberts, F.C.	(Glentoran)	1931 v S (1)
Robinson, P.	(Distillery)	1920 v S; (with Blackburn R); 1921 v W (2)
Rogan, A.	(Celtic)	1988 v Y(sub), Gr, Pol(sub); 1989 v Ei(sub), H, Sp (2), Ma(sub), Ch; 1990 v H, N(sub), U; 1991 v Y, D, A, Y; (with Sunderland); 1992 v Lit(sub) (17)
Rollo, D.	(Linfield)	1912 v W; 1913 v W; 1914 v W, E; (with Blackburn R); 1920 v W, S; 1921 v E, S, W; 1922 v E; 1923 v E; 1924 v S, W; 1925 v W; 1926 v E; 1927 v E (16)
Roper, E.O.	(Dublin University)	1886 v W (1)
Rosbotham, A.	(Cliftonville)	1887 v E, S, W; 1888 v E, S, W; 1889 v E (7)
Ross, W.E.	(Newcastle Utd)	1969 v Is (1)
Rowland, K.	(West Ham Utd)	1994 v Lat (sub) 1995 v Can, Ch, Lat, 1996 v P, (Sub), Lic (Sub), N (Sub) Se, G (Sub) (9)
Rowley, R.W.M.	(Southampton)	1929 v W, S; 1930 v E, W; (with Tottenham Hots); 1931 v W; 1932 v S (6)
Russell, A.	(Linfield)	1947 v E (1)
Russell, S.R.	(Bradford City)	1930 v E, S; (with Derry City); 1932 v E (3)
Ryan, R.A.	(WBA)	1950 v W (1)
Sanchez, L.P.	(Wimbledon)	1987 v T(sub); 1989 v Sp, Ma (3)
Scott, E.	(Liverpool)	1920 v S; 1921 v E, S, W; 1922 v E; 1925 v W; 1926 v E, W, S; 1927 v E, S, W; 1928 v E, W,S; 1929 v E,W, S; 1930 v E; 1931 v E; 1932 v W; 1933 v S, E, W; 1934 v S, E, W; (with Belfast Celtic); 1935 v S; 1936 v E, S, W (31)
Scott, J.	(Grimsby T)	1958 v Cz, F (2)
Scott, J.E.	(Cliftonville)	1901 v S (1)
Scott, L.J.	(Dublin University)	1895 v W, S (2)
Scott, P.W.	(Everton)	1975 v W; 1976 v Y; (with York City); 1976 v Is, S, E(sub), W; 1978 v S, E, W; (with Aldershot); 1979 v S(sub) (10)
Scott, T.	(Cliftonville)	1894 v E, S; 1895 v W, S; 1896 v W, E, S; 1897 v E, W; 1898 v W, E, S; 1900 v W (13)
Scott, W.	(Linfield)	1903 v E, S, W; 1904 v E, W, S; (with Everton); 1905 v E, S; 1907 v E, S; 1908 v E, S, W; 1909 v E, S, W; 1910 v E, S; 1911 v W, E, S; 1912 v E; (with Leeds City); 1913 v W, E, S (25)
Scraggs, M.J.	(Glentoran)	1921 v W; 1922 v E (2)
Seymour, H.C.	(Bohemians)	1914 v W (1)
Seymour, J.	(Cliftonville)	1907 v W; 1909 v W (2)
Shanks, T.	(Woolwich Arsenal)	1903 v S; 1904 v W; (with Brentford); 1905 v E (3)
Sharkey, P.	(Ipswich Town)	1976 v S (1)
Sheehan, Dr.G.	(Bohemians)	1899 v S; 1900 v W, E (3)
Sheridan, J.	(Everton)	1903 v E, S, W; 1904 v E, S; (with Stoke City); 1905 v E (6)
Sherrard, J.	(Limavady)	1885 v S; 1887 v W; 1888 v W (3)
Sherrard, W.C.	(Cliftonville)	1895 v E, W, S (3)
Sherry, J.J.	(Bohemians)	1906 v E; 1907 v E (2)
Shields, R.J.	(Southampton)	1957 v S (1)
Silo, M.	(Belfast YMCA)	1888 v E (1)
Simpson, W.J.	(Rangers)	1951 v W, F; 1954 v S, E; 1955 v E; 1957 v I, P; 1958 v S, E, I, W; 1959 v S (12)
Sinclair, J.	(Knock)	1882 v E, W (2)
Slemin, J.C.	(Bohemians)	1909 v W (1)
Sloan, A.S.	(London Caledonians)	1925 v W (1)
Sloan, D.	(Oxford Utd)	1969 v Is; 1971 v Sp (2)

Sloan, H.A.de B.	(Bohemians)	1903 v E; 1904 v S; 1905 v E; 1906 v W; 1907 v E, W; 1908 v W; 1909 v S (8)
Sloan, J.W.	(Arsenal)	1947 v W (1)
Sloan, T.	(Cardiff City)	1926 v E, W, S; 1927 v S, W; 1928 v E, W; 1929 v E; (with Linfield); 1930 v W, S; 1931 v S (11)
Sloan, T.	(Manchester Utd)	1979 v S, W(sub), D(sub) (3)
Small, J.M.	(Clarence)	1887 v E 1893 v E, S, W (4)
Smith, E.E.	(Cardiff City)	1921 v S; 1923 v E, W; 1924 v E (4)
Smith, J.	(Distillery)	1901 v S, W (2)
Smyth, R.H.	(Dublin University)	1886 v W (1)
Smyth, S.	(Wolverhampton W)	1948 v S, E, W; 1949 v S, E; 1950 v S, E, W; (with Stoke City); 1952 v E (9)
Smyth, W.	(Distillery)	1949 v E, S; 1954 v S, E (4)
Snape, A.	(Airdrie)	1920 v E (1)
Spence, D.W.	(Bury)	1975 v Y, E, S, W; 1976 v Se, Is, S(sub), E, W; (with Blackpool); 1977 v Ho(sub), WG(sub), E(sub),S(sub),W(sub), Ic(sub); 1979 v Ei, D(sub), E(sub), Bul(sub), E(sub), S, W, D; 1980 v Ei, (with Southend Utd); 1980 v Is(sub), Aus(sub); 1981 v S(sub), Se(sub); 1982 v F(sub) (29)
Spencer, S.	(Distillery)	1890 v E, S; 1892 v W, E, S; 1893 v E (6)
Spiller, E.A.	(Cliftonville)	1883 v E, W; 1884 v S, W, E (5)
Stanfield, O.M.	(Distillery)	1887 v E, S, W; 1888 v E, S, W; 1889 v E, S, W; 1890 v E, S; 1891 v W, E, S; 1892 v W, E, S; 1893 v E, W; 1894 v W, E, S; 1895 v E, S; 1896 v W, E, S; 1897 v E, W, S (30)
Steele, A.	(Charlton Ath)	1926 v W, S; (with Fulham); 1929 v W, S (4)
Stevenson, A.E.	(Rangers)	1934 v S, E, W; (with Everton); 1935 v S, E; 1936 v S, W; 1937 v E, W; 1938 v E, W; 1939 v S, E, W; 1947 v S, W; 1948 v S (17)
Stewart, A.	(Glentoran)	1967 v W; 1968 v S, E; (with Derby Co); 1968 v W; 1969 v Is, Tur (1+1sub) (7)
Stewart, D.C.	(Hull City)	1978 v Bel (1)
Stewart, I.	(QPR)	1982 v F(sub); 1983 v A, WG, Alb, T, Alb, S, E, W; 1984 v A, T, WG, S, E, W, Fi; 1985 v R, Is, Fi, E, Sp, T; (with Newcastle Utd); 1986 v R, E, D, Mor, Alg(sub), Sp(sub), Br; 1987 v E, Is(sub) (31)
Stewart, R.K.	(St.Columb's Court)	1890 v W, E, S; (with Cliftonville); 1892 v W, E, S; 1893 v E, W; 1894 v W, E, S (11)
Stewart, T.C.	(Linfield)	1961 v W (1)
Swan, S.	(Linfield)	1899 v S (1)
Taggart, G.P.	(Barnsley)	1990 v N, U; 1991 v Y, D, A, Pol, Fa; 1992 v Fa, A, D, S, Lit, G; 1993 v Alb, Sp, D, Alb, Ei, Sp, Lit, Lat; 1994 v Lat, D, Ei, R, Lic, Col, M 1995 v P (sub), A, Ei (2) Can, Ch, Lat (35)
Taggart, J.	(Walsall)	1899 v W (1)
Thompson, F.W.	(Cliftonville)	1910 v E, S, W; (with Linfield); 1911 v W; (with Bradford City); 1911 v E; 1912 v E, W; 1913 v W, E, S; (with Clyde); 1914 v E, S (12)
Thompson, J.	(Belfast Ath)	1889 v S (1)
Thompson, J.	(Distillery)	1897 v S (1)
Thunder, P.J.	(Bohemians)	1911 v W (1)
Todd, S.J.	(Burnley)	1966 v M(sub); 1967 v E; 1968 v W; 1969 v E, S, W; 1970 v USSR, S; (with Sheffield Wed); 1971 v Sp(sub), Cy (2) (11)
Toner, J.	(Arsenal)	1922 v W; 1923 v W; 1924 v E, W; 1925 v E, S; (with St.Johnstone); 1927 v E, S (8)
Torrans, R.	(Linfield)	1893 v S (1)
Torrans, S.	(Linfield)	1889 v S; 1890 v W, S; 1891 v W, S; 1892 v W, E, S; 1893 v E, S; 1894 v W, E, S; 1895 v E; 1896 v W, E, S; 1897 v E, W, S; 1898 v E, S; 1899 v E, W; 1901 v S, W (26)
Trainor, D.	(Crusaders)	1967 v W (1)
Tully, C.P.	(Celtic)	1949 v E; 1950 v E; 1952 v S; 1953 v E, S, F, W; 1954 v S; 1956 v E; 1959 v Sp (10)
Turner, E.	(Cliftonville)	1896 v W, E (2)
Turner, W.	(Cliftonville)	1886 v E, S; 1888 v S (3)
Twoomey, J.F.	(Leeds Utd)	1938 v W; 1939 v E (2)

Uprichard, W.M.N.C.(Swindon T) 1952 v S, E, W; 1953 v E, S; (with Portsmouth); 1953 v W, F; 1955 v E, S, W; 1956 v S, E, W; 1958 v S, I, Cz; 1959 v Sp, S (18)

Vernon, J. (Belfast Celtic) 1947 v E, S; (with WBA); 1947 v W; 1948 v S, E, W; 1949 v E, S, W; 1950 v S, E; 1951 v E, S, W, F; 1952 v S, E (17)

Waddell, T.M.R. (Cliftonville) 1906 v S (1)
Walker, J. (Doncaster R) 1955 v W (1)
Walker, T. (Bury) 1911 v S (1)
Walsh, D.J. (WBA) 1947 v S, W; 1948 v S, E, W; 1949 v E, S, W; 1950 v W (9)
Walsh, W. (Manchester City) 1948 v S, E, W; 1949 v E, S (5)
Waring, R. (Distillery) 1899 v E (1)
Warren, P. (Shelbourne) 1913 v E, S (2)
Watson, J. (Ulster) 1883 v E, W; 1886 v W, E, S; 1887 v S, W; 1889 v E, W (9)
Watson, P. (Distillery) 1971 v Cy(sub) (1)
Watson, T. (Cardifff City) 1926 v S (1)
Wattle, J. (Distillery) 1899 v E (1)
Webb, C.G. (Brighton) 1909 v S, W; 1911 v S (3)
Weir, E. (Clyde) 1939 v W (1)
Welsh, E. (Carlisle Utd) 1966 v W, WG, M; 1967 v W (4)
Whiteside, N. (Manchester Utd); 1982 v Y, Ho, Sp, A, F; 1983 v WG, Alb, T; 1984 v A, T, WG, S, E, W, Fi; 1985 v R, Is, Fi, E, Sp, T;1986 v R, E, F, D, Mor, Alg, Sp, Br; 1987 v E, Is, E, Y; 1988 v T, Pol, F; (with Everton); 1990 v H, Ei (38)
Whiteside, T. (Distillery) 1891 v E (1)
Whitfield, E.R. (Dublin University) 1886 v W (1)
Williams, J.R. (Ulster) 1886 v E, S (2)
Williams, P.A. (WBA) 1991 v Fa(sub) (1)
Williamson, J. (Cliftonville) 1890 v E; 1892 v S; 1893 v S (3)
Willigham, T. (Burnley) 1933 v W; 1934 v S (2)
Willis, G. (Linfield) 1906 v S, W; 1907 v S; 1912 S (4)
Wilson, D.J. (Brighton & HA) 1987 v T, Is, E(sub); (with Luton Town); 1988 v Y, T, Gr, Pol, F, Ma; 1989 v Ei, H, Sp, Ma, Ch; 1990 v H, Ei, N, U; (with Sheffield Wed); 1991 v Y, D, A, Fa; 1992 v A(sub), S (24)
Wilson, H. (Linfield) 1925 v W (1)
Wilson, K.J. (Ipswich Town) 1987 v Is, E, Y; (with Chelsea); 1988 v Y, T, Gr(sub), Pol(sub), F(sub); 1989 v H(sub), Sp (2), Ma, Ch; 1990 v Ei(sub), N, U; 1991 v Y, A, Pol, Y, Fa; 1992 v Fa, A, D, S; (with Notts Co); 1992 v Lit, G; 1993 v Alb, Sp, D, Sp, Lit, Lat; 1994 v Lat, D, Ei, R, Lic, Col, M (with Walsall) 1995 v Ei(sub), Lat (42)
Wilson, M. (Distillery) 1884 v S, W, E (3)
Wilson, R. (Cliftonville) 1888 v S (1)
Wilson, S.J. (Glenavon) 1962 v S; 1964 v S; (with Falkirk); 1964 v Sp, E, W, U; 1965 v E, Sw; (with Dundee) 1966 v W, WG; 1967 v S; 1968 v E (12)
Wilton, J.M. (St.Columb's Court) 1888 v W, E; 1889 v E, S; (with Cliftonville); 1890 v E; (with St.Columb's Court); 1893 v S (7)
Worthington, N. (Sheffield Wed) 1984 v W, Fi(sub); 1985 v Is, Sp(sub); 1986 v T, R(sub), E(sub), D, Alg, Sp; 1987 v E, T, Is, E, Y; 1988 v Y, T, Gr, Pol, F, Ma; 1989 v Ei, H, Sp, Ma; 1990 v H, Ei, U; 1991 v Y, D, A, Fa; 1992 v A, D, S, Lit, G; 1993 v Alb, Sp, D, Sp, Lit, Lat; 1994 v Lat, D, Ei, Lic, Col, M (with Leeds U) 1995 v P, A, Ei(2) Lat, Can (sub), Ch, Lat 1996 V P, LIC, A, N, SE, G (64)
Wright, J. (Cliftonville) 1906 v E, S, W; 1907 v E, W, S (6)
Wright, T.J. (Newcastle Utd) 1989 v Ma, Ch; 1990 v H, U; 1992 v Fa, A, S, G; 1993 v Alb, Sp, Alb, Ei, Sp, Lit, Lat; 1994 v Lat, D, Ei, R, Lic, Col, M(sub) (22)

Young, S. (Linfield) 1907 v E, S; 1908 v E, S; (with Airdrie); 1909 v E; 1912 v S; (with Linfield); 1914 v W, E, S (9)

23rd October, 1957

Venue: Windsor Park, Belfast.   Att: 10,000
Northern Ireland (3)	**6**	**Rumania (0)**	**0**

S.McCrory, S.Chapman (pen),
D.Dougan (3), J.Scott

N.Ireland: R.Rea, R.Keith, W.Marshall, P.Corr, T.Hamill, W.Wilson, J.Hill, S.McCrory, D.Dougan, S.Chapman, J.Scott.
Rumania: Utu, Pahontu, Szakacs, Alexandru, Hulea, Nunweiler, Copil, Seredai, Bukosy, Georgescu, Semenescu.
Referee: A.Ellis (England)

11th November, 1959

Venue: Windsor Park, Belfast.   Att: 20,000
Northern Ireland (0)	**1**	**France (0)**	**1**

H.Barr   *Stopyra*

N.Ireland: J.Milligan, A.Elder, W.McCullough, M.Harvey, D.Dougan, J.Nicholson, D.Shiels, J.Crossan, I.Lawther, H.Barr, J.Fraser. *Sub:* A.Campbell replaced D.Dougan:
France: Remetter, Lelong, Siatka, Hantow, Kowal, Bariaguet, Stopyra, Bruey, Guillias, Skiba, Rahis.
Referee: T.Wharton (Scotland)

16th March, 1960

Venue: Stade Du Coteau, Annecy .   Att: 9,000
France (2)	**5**	**Northern Ireland (0)**	**0**

Sauvage (3), Skiba, Harbin

France: Rozak, Cornu, Legadec, Harbin, Tyslinski, Marcel, Wisnieski, Douis, Skiba, Van Sam, Sauvage.
N.Ireland: V.Hunter, J.Shiels, W.Marshall, J.Nicholson, T.Lowry, M.Harvey, S.Wilson, D.Shiels, I.Lawther, J.Hill, J.Elwood.
Referee: M.Schitker (Switzerland)

10th May, 1994

Venue: Hillsborough, Sheffield.   Att: 8,258
England (3)	**4**	**Northern Ireland (2)**	**2**

Holdsworth, Merson, Bould,   *G.O'Boyle, J.Quinn*
Scales

England: K.Pressman, W.Barton, J.Beresford, C.Bart-Williams, S.Bould, J.Scales, R.Fox, R.Lee, C.Sutton, D.Holdsworth, P.Merson. *Subs:* A.Stubbs replaced C.Bart-Williams; C.Armstrong replaced C.Sutton; R.Edgehill replaced W.Barton; N.Martyn replaced K.Pressman; N.Summerbee replaced R.Fox:
N.Ireland: A.Fettis, S.Lomas, K.Horlock, D.Patterson, P.McGibbon, N.Lennon, R.Dennison, J.Quinn, G.O'Boyle, M.O'Neill, K.Black. *Subs:* B.Hunter replaced P.McGibbon; S.Robinson replaced J.Quinn; G.McMahon replaced N.Lennon; P.Millar replaced M.O'Neill:
Referee: S.Lodge (England)

21st February, 1995.

Venue: Easter Road, Edinburgh.   Att: 5,067
Scotland (1)	**3**	**Northern Ireland**	**(0)**	**0**

Tweed, Jackson, Wright

Scotland: N.Walker, S.Wright, R.McKinnon, S.Tweed, B.Martin, B.O'Neill, P.Lambert, A.Rae, T.Brown, D.Jackson, P.McGinlay. *Subs:* S.Woods replaced N.Walker; C.McCart replaced R.McKinnon; W.Dodds replaced P.Lambert; C.Cameron replaced T.Brown; J.Henry replaced A.Rae:
N.Ireland: A.Fettis, J.Wright, K.Rowland, G.Dunlop, P.McGibbon, N.Matthews, J.Morrow, D.Sonner, G.O'Boyle, D.Lennon, D.Finlay. *Subs:* W.Lamont replaced A.Fettis; G.McMahon replaced J.Morrow; M.Graham replaced D.Finlay; R.Hamill replaced D.Lennon:
Referee: D.Elleray (England)

26th March, 1996

Venue: The Showgrounds, Coleraine.   Att: 1,600

| **Northern Ireland (1)** | **3** | **Norway Olympic XI (0)** | **0** |

Patterson, Quinn,
Mulryne

N.Ireland: A.Davison, J.Wright, K.Horlock, D.Patterson, P.McGibbon, D.Lennon, J.McCarthy, D.Griffin, J.Quinn, G.O'Boyle, K.Black. *Subs:* T.Wood replaced A.Davison; S.Robinson replaced G.O'Boyle; C.Murdock replaced D.Patterson; P.Mulryne replaced J.Quinn; M.Graham replaced J.McCarthy;
Norway: Baardsen, Andersen, Kindevag, Waehler, Tran, Aarsheim, Fjortoft, Hestad, Fermann, Lund, Iversen. *Subs:* Hoiland replaced Andersen; Helstad replaced Fermann; Baake replaced Fjortoft:
Referee: B.Lawlor (Wales)

NORTHERN IRELAND 'B' INTERNATIONAL APPEARANCES 1957 - 1996

Barr, H.H.	(Ballymena United) 1960 v F (1)
Black, K.T	(Nottingham Forest) 1994 v E; 1996 v N (2)
Campbell, A.C.	(Crusaders) 1960 v F (sub) (1)
Chapman, S.E.C.	(Mansfield Town) 1958 v R (1)
Corr, P.	(Glenavon) 1958 v R (1)
Crossan, J.A.	(Sparta Rotterdam) 1960 v F (1)
Davison, A.	(Bolton Wanderers) 1996 v N (1)
Dennison, R.	(Wolverhampton Wanderers) 1994 v E (1)
Dougan, A.D.	(Portsmouth) 1958 v R; (with Blackburn Rovers) 1960 v F (2)
Dunlop, G.	(Crusaders) 1995 v S (1)
Elder, A.R.	(Burnley) 1960 v F (1)
Elwood, J.P.	(Leyton Orient) 1960 v F (1)
Fettis, A.W.	(Hull City) 1994 v E; 1995 v S (2)
Finlay, D.J.	(Doncaster Rovers) 1995 v S (1)
Fraser, J.W.	(Sunderland) 1960 v F (1)
Graham, M.	(Queens Park Rangers) 1995 v S (sub); 1996 v N (sub) (2)
Griffin, D.	(St.Johnstone) 1996 v N (1)
Hamill, R.	(Fulham) 1995 v S (sub) (1)
Hamill, T.	(Linfield) 1958 v R (1)
Harvey, M.	(Sunderland) 1960 v F (2) (2)
Hill, M.J.	(Newcastle United) 1958 v R; (with Norwich City) 1960 v F (2)
Horlock, K.	(Swindon Town) 1994 v E; 1996 v N (2)
Hunter, B.V.	(Wrexham) 1994 v E (sub) (1)
Hunter, V.	(Coleraine) 1960 v F (1)
Keith, R.M.	(Newcastle United) 1958 v R (1)
Lamont, W.	(Linfield) 1995 v S (sub) (1)
Lawther, W.I.	(Sunderland) 1960 v F (2) (2)
Lennon, D.J.	(Raith Rovers) 1995 v S; 1996 v N (2)
Lennon, N.F.	(Crewe Alexandra) 1994 v E (1)
Lomas, S.M.	(Manchester City) 1994 v E (1)
Lowry, T.	(Falkirk) 1960 v F (1)
McCarthy, J.D.	(Port Vale) 1996 v N (1)
McCrory, S.	(Southend United) 1958 v R (1)
McCullough, W.J.	(Arsenal) 1960 v F (1)
McGibbon, P.	(Manchester United) 1994 v E; 1995 v S; 1996 v N (3)

McMahon, G.J.	(Tottenham Hotspur) 1994 v E (sub); 1995 v S (sub) (2)
Marshall, W.	(Burnley) 1958 v R; 1960 v F (2)
Matthews, P.N.	(Rochdale) 1995 v S (1)
Millar, W.P.	(Cardiff City) 1994 v E (sub) (1)
Milligan, J.	(Cliftonville) 1960 v F (1)
Morrow, J.	(Rangers) 1995 v S (1)
Mulryne, P.	(Manchester United) 1996 v N (sub) (1)
Murdock, C.	(Manchester United) 1996 v N (sub) (1)
Nicholson, J.J.	(Manchester United) 1960 v F (2) (2)
O'Boyle, G.	(Dunfermline Athletic) 1994 v E; (with St.Johnstone) 1995 v S 1996 v N (3)
O'Neill, M.A.M.	(Hibernian) 1994 v E (1)
Patterson, D.J.	(Crystal Palace) 1994 v E; (with Luton Town) 1996 v N (2)
Quinn, S.J.	(Blackpool) 1994 v E; 1996 v N (2)
Rea, R.	(Glenavon) 1958 v R (1)
Robinson, S.	(Tottenham Hotspur) 1994 v E (sub); (with Bournemouth) 1996 v N (sub) (2)
Rowland, K.	(West Ham United) 1995 v S (1)
Scott, J.	(Grimsby Town) 1958 v R (1)
Shiels, D.P.	(Sheffield United) 1960 v F (2) (2)
Shiels, J.M.	(Manchester United) 1960 v F (1)
Sonner, D.	(Erzgebirge) 1995 v S (1)
Wilson, S.J.	(Glenavon) 1960 v F (1)
Wilson, W.J.R.	(Burnley) 1958 v R (1)
Wood, T.J.	(Walsall) 1996 v N (sub) (1)
Wright, J.	(Norwich City) 1995 v S; 1996 v N (2)

NORTHERN IRELAND 'B' INTERNATIONAL GOALSCORERS

Name:	Goals:	Apps:
Derek Dougan	3	2
James Quinn	2	2
Hubert Barr	1	1
Paddy Corr	1	1
Sammy McCrory	1	1
Philip Mulryne	1	1
George O'Boyle	1	3
Darren Patterson	1	2
Jackie Scott	1	1

NORTHERN IRELANDS UNDER-23 INTERNATIONALS 1962-1996

7th February, 1962

Venue: Windsor Park, Belfast.   Att: 10,000
Northern Ireland   **0**   **Wales**   **0**

N.Ireland: R.Briggs, J.Magill, F.Clarke, M.Harvey, T.Neill, J.Nicholson, E.Welsh, W.Johnston, J.O'Neill, J.Elwood, N.Clarke.
Wales: T.Millington, M.England, C.Green, T.Hennessy, F.Rankmore, S.Gammon, B.Jones, A.Griffiths, G.Moore, B.Godfrey, R.Roberts.
Referee: G.Bowman (Scotland)

27th February, 1963

Venue: Vetch Field, Swansea   Att: 7,133
Wales (1)   **5**   **Northern Ireland (0)**   **1**
R.Rees (2), B.Jones, A.Durban,   *J.McLaughlin*
G.Moore

Wales: T.Millington, R.Evans, C.Green, T.Hennessy, M.England, A.Burton, B.Jones, A.Durban, K.Todd, G.Moore, R.Rees.
N.Ireland: R.Irvine, R.Burke, F.Clarke, M.Harvey, T.Neill, J.Nicholson, J.McLaughlin, W.McCaffrey, W.Irvine, T.Harkin, N.Clarke.
Referee: J.Finney (England)

5th February, 1964

Venue: Windsor Park, Belfast   Att: 18,000
Northern Ireland (2)   **3**   **Wales (0)**   **3**
W.Irvine (2), J.McLaughlin.   *R.Evans (pen), B.Jones, A.Durban*

N.Ireland: P.Jennings, F.Clarke, A.Elder, M.Harvey, T.Neill, J.Nicholson, W.Campbell, D.Sloan, W.Irvine, S.McMillan, J.McLaughlin.
Wales: G.Sprake, R.Evans, R.Rodrigues, T.Hennessy, M.England, H.Williams, B.Jones, G.Moore, R.Davies, A.Durban, R.Rees.
Referee: W.Smye (Scotland)

10th February, 1965

Venue: Ninian Park, Cardiff.   Att: 5,105
Wales (0)   **2**   **Northern Ireland (1)**   **2**
B.Hole, W.Davies   *D.Clements, W.Irvine*

Wales: G.Sprake, R.Rodrigues, C.Green, M.England, G.James, B.Hole, R.Rees, G.Humphreys, W.Davies, R.Blore, B.Lewis.
N.Ireland: R.Briggs, D.Craig, F.Clarke, S.Todd, T.Neill, J.Nicholson, W.Campbell, W.Craig, W.Irvine, S.Dunlop, D.Clements.
Referee: G.McCabe (Scotland)

22nd February, 1967

Venue: Windsor Park, Belfast.   Att: 8,000
Northern Ireland (2)   **2**   **Wales (0)**   **1**
V.McKinney (2)   *M.Evans*

N.Ireland: R.McKenzie, D.Craig, W.McKeag, S.Todd, J.Napier, D.Clements, W.Campbell, E.Ross, E.McMordie, D.Trainor, V.McKinney. *Sub:* I.Murray replaced E.Ross:
Wales: D.Walker, J.Collins, R.Thomas, D.Powell, J.Roberts, T.Walley, J.Thomas, M.Evans, D.Hawkins, G.Humphreys, J.Mahoney. *Sub:* M.Page replaced J.Roberts:
Referee: R.Henderson (Scotland)

NB: This match was abandoned after 73 minutes as the pitch became waterlogged.

20th March, 1968

Venue: Ninian Park, Cardiff   Att: 2,669
Wales (0)   **0**   **Northern Ireland (1)**   **1**
                                      S.Dunlop

Wales: D.Walker, J.Collins, R.Thomas, D.Powell, R.Mielczarek, M.Page, B.Lewis, W.Screen, D.Hawkins,

P.W.Jones, T.Walley. *Sub:* J.Roberts replaced B.Lewis:
N.Ireland: R.McKenzie, P.Rice, W.McKeag, T.Jackson, J.Napier, D.Clements, S.Dunlop, W.McAvoy, B.Hamilton, S.Todd, T.Morrow. *Sub:* A.McNeill replaced T.Morrow:
Referee: E.T.Jennings (England)

26th March, 1969

Venue: Comunale Stadium, Brescia.   Att: 12,000

Italy (1)	2	Northern Ireland (1)	1
Reif, Vieri		*B.Mullan*	

Italy: Superchi, Roversi, Pasetti, Esposito, Niccolai, Santarina, Reif, Vieri, Gori, Merlo, Chiarugl. *Sub:* Nastasio replaced Reif:
N.Ireland: R.McKenzie, P.Rice, S.Nelson, S.Todd, A.Hunter, A.O'Doherty, B.Hamilton, J.Johnston, R.Gaston, B.Mullan, T.Morrow.
Referee: H.Seeker (Austria)

11th April, 1989

Venue: Dalymount Park, Dublin.   Att: 3,200

Republic of Ireland (2)	3	Northern Ireland (0)	0
M.McCarthy, D.Irwin, J.Sheridan (pen)			

R.O.I: G.Kelly, D.Irwin, C.Fleming, M.McCarthy, D.Brazil, J.Sheridan, M.Milligan, L.O'Brien, O.Coyle, B.Mooney, M.Kelly. *Subs:* K.De Mange replaced L.O'Brien; D.Swan replaced M.McCarthy; P.McGee replaced M.Kelly:
N.Ireland: T.Wright, G.Fleming, S.Morrow, G.Taggart, N.Matthews, M.Hughes, J.Magilton, M.O'Neill, I.Dowie, N.Whiteside, K.Black. *Subs:* R.Johnston replaced K.Black; A.Diamond replaced M.Hughes:
Referee: P.Kelly (Republic of Ireland)

15th May, 1990

Venue: Shamrock Park, Portadown   Att: 1,500

Northern Ireland (2)	2	Republic Of Ireland (0)	3
S.McBride, J.Devine.		*N.Quinn, D.Kelly (2)*	

N.Ireland: A.McKnight, N.Lennon, S.Morrow, J.Devine, G.Taggart, J.Magilton, M.Todd, N.Bailie, S.McBride, Philip Gray, M.Hughes. *Subs:* P.Agnew replaced N.Bailie; P.Millar replaced S.McBride:
R.O.I: A.Kelly, C.Fleming, T.Phelan, P.Scully, D.Brazil, G.Waddock, B.Mooney, J.Sheridan, N.Quinn, D.Kelly, M.Kelly. *Sub:* M.Russell replaced M.Kelly:
Referee: A.Snoddy (N.Ireland)

NORTHERN IRELAND UNDER-23 APPEARANCES 1962 - 1996

Agnew, P.	(Grimsby Town) 1990 v ROI (sub) (1)
Bailie, N.	(Linfield) 1990 v ROI (1)
Black, K.	(Luton Town) 1989 v ROI (1)
Briggs, W.R.	(Manchester United) 1962 v W; (with Swansea Town) 1965 v W (2)
Burke, R.	(Portadown) 1963 v W (1)
Campbell, W.G.	(Distillery) 1964 v W; (with Sunderland)1965 v W; (with Dundee) 1967 v W (3)
Clarke, F. J.	(Arsenal) 1962 v W; 1963 v W; 1964 v W; 1965 v W (4)
Clarke, N.S.	(Ballymena United) 1962 v W; (with Sunderland) 1963 v W (2)
Clements, D.	(Coventry City) 1965 v W; 1967 v W; 1968 v W (3)
Craig, D.J.	(Newcastle United) 1965 v W; 1967 v W (2)
Craig, W.	(Linfield) 1965 v W (1)
Devine, J.	(Glentoran) 1990 v ROI (1)
Diamond, A.J.	(Blackburn Rovers) 1989 v ROI (sub) (1)
Dowie, I.	(Luton Town) 1989 v ROI (1)
Dunlop, S.	(Coleraine) 1965 v W; 1968 v W (2)
Elder, A.R.	(Burnley) 1964 v W (1)
Elwood, J.P.	(Leyton Orient) 1962 v W (1)
Flemimg, J.G.	(Nottingham Forest) 1989 v ROI (1)
Gaston, R.	(Oxford United) 1969 v It (1)
Gray, P.	(Tottenham Hotspur) 1990 v ROI (1)
Hamilton, B.	(Linfield) 1968 v W; 1969 v It (2)
Harkin, J.T.	(Port Vale) 1963 v W (1)
Harvey, M.	(Sunderland) 1962 v W; 1963 v W; 1964 v W (3)

Hughes, M.E.	(Manchester City) 1989 v ROI; 1990 v ROI (2)
Hunter, A.	(Oldham Athletic) 1969 v It (1)
Irvine, R.J.	(Linfield) 1963 v W (1)
Irvine, W.J.	(Burnley) 1963 v W; 1964 v W; 1965 v W (3)
Jackson, T.	(Everton) 1968 v W (1)
Jennings, P.A.	(Watford) 1964 v W (1)
Johnston, J.	(Blackpool) 1969 v It (1)
Johnston, R.	(Tottenham Hotspur) 1989 v ROI (sub) (1)
Johnston, W.C.	(Glenavon) 1962 v W (1)
Lennon, N.	(Manchester City) 1990 v ROI (1)
McAvoy, W.	(Ards) 1968 v W (1)
McBride, S.D.	(Glenavon) 1990 v ROI (1)
McCaffrey, W.	(Leicester City) 1963 v W (1)
McKeag, W.	(Glentoran) 1967 v W; 1968 v W (2)
McKenzie, R.	(Airdrie) 1967 v W; 1968 v W; 1969 v It (3)
McKinney, V.J.	(Falkirk) 1967 v W (1)
McKnight, A.	(West Ham United) 1990 v ROI (1)
McLaughlin, J.C.	(Shrewsbury Town) 1963 v W; 1964 v W (2)
McMillan, S.	(Wrexham) 1964 v W (1)
McMordie, W.S.	(Middlesbrough) 1967 v W (1)
McNeill, A.A.	(Middlesbrough) 1968 v W (sub) (1)
Magill E.J.	(Arsenal) 1962 v W (1)
Magilton, J.	(Liverpool) 1989 v ROI; 1990 v ROI (2)
Matthews N.P.	(Blackpool) 1989 v ROI (1)
Millar, W.P.	(Port Vale) 1990 v ROI (sub) (1)
Morrow, S.J.	(Arsenal) 1989 v ROI; 1990 v ROI (2)
Morrow, T.	(Glentoran) 1968 v W; 1969 v It (2)
Mullan, B.G.J.	(Fulham) 1969 v It (1)
Murray, I.	(Coleraine) 1967 v W (sub) (1)
Napier, R.J.	(Bolton Wanderers) 1967 v W; (with Brighton & H.A.) 1968 v W (2)
Neill, W.J.T.	(Arsenal) 1962 v W; 1963 v W; 1964 v W; 1965 v W (4)
Nelson, S.	(Arsenal) 1969 v It (1)
Nicholson, J.J.	(Manchester United) 1962 v W; 1963 v W; 1964 v W; (with Huddersfield Town) 1965 v W (4)
O'Doherty, A.	(Coleraine) 1969 v It (1)
O'Neill, J.	(Sunderland) 1962 v W (1)
O'Neill, M.A.M.	(Newcastle United) 1989 v ROI (1)
Rice, P.J.	(Arsenal) 1968 v W; 1969 v It (2)
Ross, W.E.	(Glentoran) 1967 v W (1)
Sloan, D.	(Scunthorpe United) 1964 v W (1)
Taggart, G.P.	(Manchester City) 1989 v ROI; (with Barnsley) 1990 v ROI (2)
Todd, M.K.	(Sheffield United) 1990 v ROI (1)
Todd, S.J.	(Burnley) 1965 v W; 1967 v W; 1968 v W; 1969 v It (4)
Trainor, D.	(Crusaders) 1967 v W (1)
Welsh, E.	(Distillery) 1962 v W (1)
Whiteside, N.	(Manchester United) 1989 v ROI (1)
Wright T.J.	(Newcastle United) 1989 v ROI (1)

NORTHERN IRELAND UNDER-23 INTERNATIONAL GOALSCORERS:

Name:	Goals:	Apps:
William Irvine	3	3
Victor McKinney	2	1
Jim McLaughlin	2	2
Dave Clements	1	3
John Devine	1	1
Shaun Dunlop	1	2
Stephen McBride	1	1
Brendan Mullan	1	1

NORTHERN IRELAND UNDER-21 INTERNATIONALS 1978-1996

8th March, 1978

Venue: Dalymount Park, Dublin.   Att: 6,000

Republic of Ireland (1)	1	Northern Ireland (1)	1
M.Murray		*G.Blackledge*	

ROI: A.O'Neill, P.Nolan, M.Daly, J.Anderson, J.Devine, S.Braddish, M.Madigan, A.Grimes, P.McGee, M.Murray, R.Lane
N.Ireland: B.Johnston, J.Nicholl, M.Donaghy, T.Hayes, V.Moreland, J.O'Neill, T.Sloan, J.Harvey, G.Blackledge, W.Hamilton, D.McCreery. *Subs:* T.Connell replaced T.Hayes; N.Brotherston replaced J.Harvey; W.Murray replaced N.Brotherston:
Referee: D.Byrne (Dublin)

3rd April, 1990

Venue: The Showgrounds, Coleraine.   Att: 1,000

Northern Ireland (1)	2	Israel (0)	1
I.Dowie, Paul Gray		*Moharer*	

N.Ireland: P.Kee, N.Lennon, S.Beatty, J.Devine, N.Matthews, N.Bailie, R.McCoy, J.Magilton, I.Dowie, P.Millar, K.Black. *Subs:* N.Kelly replaced N.Bailie; M.Hughes replaced P.Millar; Paul Gray replaced K.Black:
Israel: Cohen, A.Harazi, Elinellech, Hadad, Ben Dov, Udea, Banin, Melika, Nir-On, Ben Simon, Zohar. *Sub:* Moharer replaced ?
Referee: F.McKnight (Newtownards)

NB: Match abandoned on 88 mins due to floodlight failure.

22nd March, 1994

Venue: The Oval, Belfast.   Att: 700

Northern Ireland	0	Romania	0

N.Ireland: D.Devine, G.O'Hara, M.Glendinning, D.Patterson, P.McGibbon, K.Gillespie, J.Quinn, S.Beatty, S.Robinson, M.O'Neill, N.Lennon. *Subs:* N.Bailie replaced P.McGibbon; S.McBride replaced S.Robinson; T.McIlroy replaced M.O'Neill; J.Magee replaced J.Quinn; G.McMahon replaced K.Gillespie:
Romania: Munteanu, Stanciu, Petre, Mutica, Parashiu, Potocianu, Petrescu, Curt, Filipescu, Calin, Ilie. *Subs:* Lita replaced Ilie; Bujor replaced Curt:
Referee: A.Howells (Wales)

NORTHERN IRELAND UNDER-21 APPEARANCES 1978 - 1996

Bailie, N.	(Linfield) 1990 v Is, 1994 v R (sub) (2)
Beatty, S.	(Chelsea) 1990 v Is, (with Linfield) 1994 v R (2)
Black, K.T.	(Luton Town) 1990 v Is (1)
Blackledge, G.	(Portadown) 1978 v ROI (1)
Brotherston, N	(Blackburn Rovers) 1978 v ROI (sub) (1)
Connell, T.E.	(Coleraine) 1978 v ROI (sub) (1)
Devine, D.	(Omagh Town) 1994 v R (1)

NORTHERN IRELAND UNDER-21 INTERNATIONALS 1978-1996

Devine, J.	(Glentoran) 1990 v Is (1)
Donaghy, M.M.	(Larne) 1978 v ROI (1)
Dowie, I.	(Luton Town) 1990 v Is (1)
Gillespie, K.R.	(Manchester United) 1994 v R (1)
Glendinning, M.	(Bangor) 1994 v R (1)
Gray, Paul	(Luton Town) 1990 v Is (sub) (1)
Hamilton, W.	(Linfield) 1978 v ROI (1)
Harvey, J.	(Arsenal) 1978 v ROI (1)
Hayes, T.	(Luton Town) 1978 v ROI (1)
Hughes, M.E.	(Manchester City) 1990 v Is (sub) (1)
Johnston, B.	(Cliftonville) 1978 v ROI (1)
Kee, P.V.	(Oxford United) 1990 v Is (1)
Kelly, N.	(Oldham Athletic) 1990 v Is (sub) (1)
Lennon, N.F.	(Manchester City) 1990 v Is; (with Crewe Alex) 1994 v R (2)
McBride, S.D.	(Glenavon) 1994 v R (sub) (1)
McCoy, R.	(Coleraine) 1990 v Is (1)
McCreery, D.	(Manchester United) 1978 v ROI (1)
McGibbon, P.	(Manchester United) 1994 v R (1)
McIlroy, T.	(Linfield) 1994 v R (sub) (1)
McMahon, G.J.	(Tottenham Hotspur) 1994 v R (sub) (1)
Magee, J.	(Bangor) 1994 v R (sub) (1)
Magilton, J.	(Liverpool) 1990 v Is (1)
Matthews, N.P.	(Blackpool) 1990 v Is (1)
Millar, W.P.	(Port Vale) 1990 v Is (1)
Moreland, V.	(Glentoran) 1978 v ROI (1)
Murray, W.	(Linfield) 1978 v ROI (sub) (1)
Nicholl, J.M.	(Manchester United) 1978 v ROI (1)
O'Hara, G.	(Leeds United) 1994 v R (1)
O'Neill, M.A.M.	(Hibernian) 1994 v R (1)
O'Neill, J.P.	(Leicester City) 1978 v ROI (1)
Patterson, D.J.	(Crystal Palace) 1994 v R (1)
Quinn, S.J.	(Blackpool) 1994 v R (1)
Robinson, S.	(Tottenham Hotspur) 1994 v R (1)
Sloan, T.	(Ballymena United) 1978 v ROI (1)

NORTHERN IRELAND UNDER-21 INTERNATIONALS GOALSCORERS

Name:	Goals:	Apps:
Black, K.T.	1	1
Dowie, I.	1	1
Gray, Paul	1	1

INTERNATIONAL PLAYERS DIRECTORY 1996

AGNEW, Paul (Defender)
Born: 15.08.1965 Lisburn
Ht: 5.9   Wt: 10.07
Career: Cliftonville; Grimsby Town (15.02.84 £4,000)
219+23 - 3; West Bromwich Albion (23.02.95 £65,000)
17- 1:
Int.Hon: U.23 (1-0); U.18 (11-0); U.15 (4-0):

BLACK, Kingsley (Winger)
Born: 22.06.1968 Luton
Ht: 5.8   Wt: 11.12
Career: Luton Town (07.07.86) 123+4 - 26;
Nottingham Forest (02.09.91) (£1,500,000)
80+18 - 14; Sheffield United (02.03.95 Loan) 8+3 - 2;
Millwall (29.09.95 Loan) 1+2 - 1:
Int.Hon: Full (30-1); 'B' (1-0); U.23 (1-0); U.21 (1-1);
England U.15:

CARROLL, Roy (Goalkeeper)
Born: 30.09.1977 Belfast
Ht: 6.2   Wt: 11.09
Career: Ballinamallard United; Hull City (07.09.95) 23
- 0:
Int.Hon: None.

DAVISON, Aidan (Goalkeeper)
Born: 11.05.1968 Sedgefield
Ht: 6.1   Wt: 13.12
Career: Spennymoor United; Billingham Synthonia;
Notts County (25.03.88) 1 - 0; Leyton Orient (07.09.89
Loan) 0 - 0; Bury (07.10.89 £6,000) 0 - 0; Chester City
(21.03.90 Loan) 0 - 0; Blackpool (28.03.91 Loan) 0 - 0;
Millwall (14.08.91 Free) 34 - 0; Bolton Wanderers
(26.07.93 £25,000) 35+2 - 0:
Int.Hon: Full (1-0); 'B' (1-0):

DENNISON, Robert (Midfielder)
Born: 30.04.1963 Banbridge
Ht: 5.7   Wt: 11.00
Career: Glenavon; West Bromwich Albion (13.09.85
£40,000); 9+7 - 1; Wolverhampton Wanderers
(13.03.87 £20,000) 255+24 - 40; Swansea City
(05.10.95 Loan) 9 - 0:
In.Hon: Full (17-0); 'B' (1-0); U.18 (3-0):

DOWIE, Iain (Forward)
Born: 09.01.1965 Hatfield
Ht: 6.1   Wt: 13.07
Career: Hendon Town; Luton Town (14.12.88 £30,000)
53+13 - 16; Fulham (13.09.89 Loan) 5 - 1; West Ham

United (22.03.91 £480,000) 12 - 4; Southampton
(03.09.91 £500,000) 115+7 - 30; Crystal Palace
(13.01.95 £400,000) 19 - 4: West Ham United (08.09.95
£500,000) 33 - 8:
Int.Hon: Full (36-8); U.23 (1-0); U.21 (1-1):

FETTIS, Alan (Goalkeeper)
Born: 01.02.1971 Belfast
Ht: 6.1   Wt: 11.08
Career: Ards 42 - 0; Hull City (14.08.91 £50,000)
131+4 - 2; West Bromwich Albion (20.11.95 Loan) 3 -
0; Nottingham Forest (13.01.96 £250,000) 0 - 0:
Int.Hon: Full (15-0); 'B' (2-0); U.18 (1-0); U.17 (1-0):

FLEMING, Gary (Defender)
Born: 17.02.1967 Londonderry
Ht: 5.9 Wt: 11.09
Career: Nottingham Forest (19.11.84) 71+3 - 0;
Manchester City (17.08.89 £150,000) 13+1 - 0; Notts
County (08.03.90 Loan) 3 - 0; Barnsley (23.03.90
£85,000) 236+3 - 0:
Int.Hon: Full (31-0); U.23 (1-0); U.18 (7-0):

GILLESPIE, Keith (Winger)
Born: 18.02.75 Bangor
Ht: 5.10 Wt: 11.05
Career: Linfield 0-0; Manchester United (03.02.93)
3+6 - 1; Wigan Athletic (03.09.93 Loan) 8 - 4;
Newcastle United (12.01.95 £1,000,000) 41+4 - 6:
Int.Hon: Full (12-1); U.21 (1-0); U.18 (4-2); U.16 (2-1);
U.15 (6-2):

GRAY, Philip (Forward)
Born: 01.04.1969 Belfast
Ht: 5.10 Wt: 12.09
Career: Ballyclare Comrades; Tottenham Hotspur
(21.08.86) 4+5 - 0; Barnsley (17.01.90 Loan) 3 - 0;
Fulham (08.11.90 Loan) 3 - 0; Luton Town (16.08.91
£275,000) 54+5 - 22; Sunderland (19.07.93 £800,000)
108+7 - 34:
Int.Hon: Full (17-5); U.23 (1-0); U.18 (2-1); U.16 (1-
0); U.15 (5-4):

GRIFFIN, Daniel (Midfielder)
Born: 10.08.77 Belfast
Ht: 5.10 Wt: 10.05
Career: St.Andrews; St.Johnstone (18.02.94) 3 - 0:
Int.Hon: Full (1-0); 'B' (1-0); U.18 (7-2); U.16 (1-0);
U.15 (6-0):

HAMILL, Rory (Forward)
Born: 04.05.76 Coleraine
Ht: 5.10 Wt: 12.02
*Career: **Southampton; Fulham** (18.11.94 Free) 24+24 - 7:*
Int.Hon: 'B' (1-0); U.18 (2-0); U.16 (6-0); U.15 (3-0):

HILL, Colin (Defender)
Born: 12.11.1963 Uxbridge
Ht: 6.0 Wt: 12.07
*Career: **Glebe Athletic; Park Lane; Hillingdon; Arsenal** (07.08.81) 46 - 1; **Maritimo** (Por) (c/s '86 Free); **Colchester United** (30.10.87 Free) 64+5 - 0; **Sheffield United** (01.08.89 £85,000) 77+5 - 1; **Leicester City** (26.03.92 Loan) 10 - 0; **Leicester City** (31.07.92 £200,000) 134+4 - 0:*
*Int.Hon: **Full (14-1):***

HORLOCK, Kevin (Midfielder)
Born: 01.11.72 Plumstead
Ht: 6.0 Wt: 12.00
*Career: **West Ham United** (01.07.91); **Swindon Town** (27.08.92 Free) 123+12 - 14:*
Int.Hon: Full (2-0); 'B' (2-0):

HUGHES, Michael (Winger)
Born: 02.08.71 Larne
Ht: 5.7 Wt: 10.13
*Career: **Carrick Rangers** 17+1 - 1; **Manchester City** (17.08.88) 25+1 - 1; **Strasbourg** (c/s '92 £450,000) 83 - 9; **West Ham United** (29.11.94 Loan) 15+2 - 2; **West Ham United** (02.10.95 Loan) 28 - 0:*
*Int.Hon: **Full (31-2); U.23 (2-0); U.21 (1-0); U.19 (1-0); U.18 (1-0); U.17 (2-0); U.16 (4-0); U.15 (5-1):***

HUNTER, Barry (Defender)
Born: 18.11.1968 Coleraine
Ht: 6.3 Wt: 12.09
*Career: **Newcastle United** 0-0; **Coleraine:** (12.88) 0 - 0; **Crusaders** (02.89) 74+1 - 3; **Wrexham** (20.08.93 £50,000) 88+3 - 4:*
Int: Hon: Full (6-1); 'B' (1-0):

LENNON, Neil (Midfielder)
Born: 25.06.71 Lurgan
Ht: 5.10 Wt: 12.12
*Career: **Glenavon** 0 - 0; **Manchester City** (26.08.89) 1 - 0; **Crewe Alex.** (09.08.90 Free) 142+5 - 15; **Leicester City** (23.02.96 £750,000) 14+1 - 1:*
Int.Hon: Full (6-0); 'B' (1-0); U.23 (1-0); U.21 (2-0):

LOMAS, Steve (Midfielder)
Born: 18.01.74 Hanover, Germany
Ht: 6.0 Wt: 11.09
*Career: **Coleraine** 5-1; **Manchester City** (22.01.91) 67+9 - 5:*
*Int.Hon: **Full (12-1); 'B' (1-0); U.18 (4-0); U.16 (5-0); U.15 (10-1):***

McAREE, Rodney (Midfielder)
Born: 19.08.74 Dungannon
Ht: 5.7 Wt: 10.02
*Career: **Dungannon Swifts; Liverpool** (21.09.91) 0 - 0; **Bristol City** (26.07.94 Free) 4+2 - 0; **Dungannon Swifts** (11.95); **Fulham** (29.12.95 Free) 16+1 - 2:*
In.Hon: U.18 (3-1); U.16 (1-0); U.15 (7-2):

McCARTHY, Jonathan (Winger)
Born: 18.08.70 Middlesbrough
Ht: 5.9 Wt: 11.05
*Career: **Hartlepool United** (07.11.87) 0+1 - 0; **Shepshed Charterhouse** (03.89 Free); **York City** (22.03.90 Free) 198+1 - 31; **Port Vale** (08.95 £450,000) 44+1 - 8:*
*Int.Hon: **Full (1-0); 'B' (1-0):***

McDONALD, Alan (Defender)
Born: 12.10.63 Belfast
Ht: 6.2 Wt: 13.11
*Career: **Queens Park Rangers** (12.08.81) 357+6 - 11; **Charlton Athletic** (24.03.83 Loan) 9 - 0;*
*Int.Hon: **Full (52-3); U.15 (7+1):***

McGIBBON, Patrick (Defender)
Born: 06.09.1973 Lurgan
Ht: 6.2 Wt: 13.02
*Career: **Portadown** 0+1 - 0; **Manchester United** (01.08.92 £100,000) 0 - 0:*
*Int.Hon: **Full (4-0); 'B' (3-1); U.18 Schools (2-0):***

McMAHON, Gerard (Winger)
Born: 29.12.73 Belfast
Ht: 5.11 Wt: 11.00
*Career: **Glenavon** 6+1 - 3; **Tottenham Hotspur** (31.07.92 £100,000) 9+7 - 0; **Barnet** (20.01.94 Loan) 10 - 2:*
*Int.Hon: **Full (7-2); 'B' (2-0); U.21 (1-0); U.18 Schools (2-0):***

MAGILTON, Jim (Midfielder)
Born: 06.05.1969 Belfast
Ht: 6.0 Wt: 14.02
Career: Distillery 1-0; Liverpool (14.05.86) 0 - 0;
Oxford United (03.10.90 £100,000) 150 - 34;
Southampton (11.02.94 £600,000) 88 - 9:
Int.Hon: Full (32-4); U.23 (2-0); U.21 (1-0); U.18 (3-0);
U.16 (1-0); U.15 (5-1):

MASTERS, Neil (Defender)
Born: 25.05.72 Ballymena
Ht: 6.1 Wt: 13.00
Career: Glenavon; Bournemouth (31.08.90) 37+1 - 2;
Wolverhampton (22.12.93 £600,000) 10+2 - 0:
Int.Hon: U.17 (1-0):

MORROW, Stephen (Defender)
Born: 02.07.70 Belfast
Ht: 5.11 Wt: 12.02
Career: Bangor 20+1 - 0; Arsenal (05.05.88) 34+14 -
1; Reading (16.01.91 Loan) 10 - 0; Watford (14.08.91
Loan) 7+1 - 0; Reading (30.10.90 Loan) 3 - 0; Barnet
(04.03.92 Loan) 1 - 0:
Int.Hon: Full (19-1) U.23 (2-0); U.19 (2-0); U.18 (4-0);
U.17 (2-0); U.16 (4-0); U.15 (6-1):

O'BOYLE, George (Forward)
Born: 14.12.67 Belfast
Ht: 5.8 Wt: 11.09
Career: Manchester City (22.10.84) 0 - 0; Distillery
(12.85) 23+1 - 4; Linfield (c/s'86) 20+2 - 12;
Bordeaux (c/s'87) 0+3 - 0; Linfield (09.06.88 loan)
23+1 - 9; Dunfermline Athletic (02.08.89); 86+9-29;
St.Johnstone (24.07.94) 32 - 19:
Int.Hon: Full (8-1); 'B' (3-1); U.18 (6-3); U.17 (1-0);

O'NEILL, Michael (Midfielder)
Born: 05.07.69 Portadown
Ht: 5.11   Wt: 10.10
Career: Chimney Corner; Coleraine 13+5 - 4;
Newcastle United (23.10.87 £50,000) 36+12 - 15;
Dundee United (15.08.89 £300,000) 50+14 - 12;
Hibernian (20.08.93 £250,000) 98 - 19:
Int.Hon: Full (29-4); U.16 (1-0); U.15 (3-0):

PATTERSON, Darren (Defender)
Born: 15.10.69 Belfast
Ht: 6.1 Wt: 12.10
Career: West Bromwich Albion (05.07.88) 0 - 0; Wigan

Athletic (17.04.89) 69+28 - 6; Crystal Palace (01.07.92
£225,000) 22 - 1; Luton Town (21.08.95 £100,000)
21+2 - 0:
Int.Hon: Full (10-0); 'B' (2-1); U.21 (1-0):

QUINN, Jimmy (Forward)
Born: 18.11.59 Belfast
Ht: 6.0 Wt: 11.06
Career: Whitchurch Alport; Oswestry Town; Swindon
Town (31.12.81 £10,000) 34+15 - 10; Blackburn
Rovers (15.08.84 £32,000) 58+13 - 17; Swindon Town
(19.12.86 £50,000) 61+3 - 30; Leicester City (19.12.86
£210,000) 13+18 - 6; Bradford City (17.03.89) 35 - 14;
West Ham United (30.12.89 £320,000) 34+13 - 18;
Bournemouth (05.08.91 £40,000) 43 - 19; Reading
(27.07.92 £55,000) 139+19 - 68:
Int.Hon: Full (46-12):

QUINN, James (Forward)
Born: 15.04.1974 Coventry
Ht: 6.1 Wt: 12.10
Career: Birmingham City 1+3 - 0; Blackpool (05.07.93
£25,000) 80+19 - 20; Stockport County (04.03.94 Loan)
0+1 - 0:
Int.Hon: Full (1-0); 'B' (2-2); U.21 (1-0); U.18 (3-1);
U.16 (1-0):

ROBINSON, Stephen (Forward)
Born: 10.12.74 Lisburn
Ht: 5.9 Wt: 11.03
Career: Tottenham Hotspur (27.01.93) 1+1 - 0;
Bournemouth (20.10.94 Free) 66+7 - 12:
Int.Hon: 'B' (2-0); U.21 (1-0); U.18 (2-1)

ROGAN, Anton (Defender)
Born: 25.03.66 Belfast
Ht: 6.1 Wt: 13.00
Career: Distillery; Celtic (09.05.86) 115+12 - 4;
Sunderland (04.10.91 £350,000) 45+1 - 1; Oxford
United (09.08.93) 56+2 - 3; Millwall (11.08.95 Free)
4+4 - 0:
Int.Hon: Full (17-0); U.18 (2-0):

ROWLAND, Keith (Defender)
Born: 01.09.71 Portadown
Ht: 5.10 Wt: 10.00
Career: Linfield 0-0; Bournemouth (02.10.89) 65+7 -
2; Coventry City (08.01.93 Loan) 0+2 - 0; West Ham
United (06.08.93 £110,000) 46+12 - 0:
Int.Hon: Full (9-0); 'B' (1-0); U.19 (1-0); U.18 (1-1);
U.17 (2-0):

TAGGART, Gerald (Defender)
Born: 18.10.70 Belfast
Ht: 6.1 Wt: 12.03
*Career: **Glenavon; Manchester City** (01.07.89) 10+2 -*
*1; **Barnsley** (10.01.90 £75,000) 209+3 - 16; **Bolton***
***Wanderers** (01.08.95 £1,500.000) 11 - 1:*
*Int.Hon: **Full (28-5); U.23 (2-0); U.18 (2-0); U.17 (1-0);***
U.16 (6-1); U.15 (4-0):

WILSON, Kevin (Forward)
Born: 18.04.61 Banbury
Ht: 5.7 Wt: 11.03
*Career: **Banbury United; Derby County** (21.12.79*
*£20,000) 106+16 - 30; **Ipswich Town***
*(05.01.85 £100,000) 94+4 - 34; **Chelsea** (25.06.87*
*£335,000) 124+28 - 42; **Notts County** (27.03.92*
*£225,000) 58+11 - 3; **Bradford City** (13.01.94 Loan) 5 -*
*0; **Walsall** (04.08.94 Free) 88 - 31:*
*Int.Hon: **Full (42-6)***

WOOD, Trevor (Goalkeeper)
Born: 03.11.68 Jersey
Ht: 6.0 Wt: 13.04
*Career: **Brighton & Hove Albion** (07.11.86) 0 - 0; **Port***
***Vale** (08.07.88 Free) 42 - 0; **Walsall** (18.07.94 Free) 59 -*
0:
*Int.Hon: **Full (1-0); 'B' (1-0):***

WORTHINGTON, Nigel (Defender)
Born: 04.11.61 Ballymena
Ht: 5.10 Wt: 12.08
*Career: **Ballymena United; Notts County** (01.07.81*
*£100,000) 62+5 - 4; **Sheffield Wednesday** (06.02.84*
*£125,000) 334+4 -12; **Leeds United** (04.07.94*
£325,000) 33+10 - 1:
*Int.Hon: **Full (64-0); U.18 (14-0):***

WRIGHT, Jonathan (Defender)
Born: 24.11.75 Belfast
Ht: 5.9 Wt: 11.05
*Career: **Linfield; Norwich City** (01.07.94) 2+1 - 0:*
*Int.Hon: **'B' (2-0); U.18 (2-0); U.16 (5-2):***

WRIGHT, Tommy (Goalkeeper)
Born: 29.08.63 Belfast
Ht: 6.1 Wt: 14.05
*Career: **Brantwood; Linfield; Newcastle United***
*(27.01.88 £30,000) 72+1 - 0; **Hull City** (14.02.91 Loan)*
*6 - 0; **Nottingham Forest** (24.09.93 £450,000) 10 - 0:*
*Int.Hon: **Full (22-0); U.23 (1-0):***

There are other Northern Ireland born players (or players who are eligible to play for N.Ireland) with League clubs in England and Scotland who are no longer on the International scene or who have yet to make the breakthrough into their respective first team.

*Wesley Boyle (M) (Leeds United); **Darren Clyde** (G) (Barnsley); **Stephen Craigan** (D) (Motherwell); **Paul Emerson** (D) (Leicester City); **Roy Essandoh** (M) (Motherwell); **Tom Evans** (G) (Sheffield United); **Darren Fitzgerald** (F) (Rangers); **Sean Friars** (M) (Liverpool); **Mark Graham** (F) (Q.P.R.); **David Henry** (G) (Nottingham Forest); **John Hooks** (D) (Blackpool); **Damien Johnston** (M) (Blackburn Rovers); **Stephen Jones** (M) (Blackpool); **Peter Kennedy** (M) (Notts County); **Danny Lennon** (M) (Raith Rovers); **Tim McCann** (M) (Leicester City); **Brian McGlinchey** (M) (Manchester City); **Jamie Marks** (D) (Hull City); **Colin Murdock** (D) (Manchester United); **Philip Mulryne** (F) (Manchester United); **Paul McKnight** (F) (Rangers); **Paul McVeigh** (M) (Tottenham Hotspur); **Shane O'Neill** (M) (Nottingham Forest); **David Parry** (M); **Graeme Philson** (D) (West Ham United); **Tony Thirlby** (M) (Southampton); **Mark Todd** (M) (Mansfield); **Brian Vaugh** (M) (Celtic); **Lee Waterman** (M) (Portsmouth); **David Waterman** (D) (Portsmouth); **David Wells** (G) (Bournemouth);*

WILKINSON SWORD IRISH LEAGUE 'B' DIVISION
REVIEW OF THE 1995/96 SEASON

The highlight of the 'B' Division season was the achievement of Loughgall in becoming the first Champions for more than twenty years to take the title out of Belfast in successive seasons. Their success was a triumph for manager Alfie Wylie and if he had more money to spend on paying players than any other manager he seemed to have the knack of spending it wisely to build a team which held off the challenge of neighbours Dungannon Swifts who again flattered to deceive. However Dungannon did have the consolation of finishing second and winning the Bob Radcliffe Cup, now the most significant of the three Divisional cup competitions.

At the other end of the table Queen's University had a disastrous season. For some years now the majority of 'B' Division clubs have not regarded the university teams as valued members of the League, an away fixture on an exposed playing field with no cover or even hard standing does not present a very appealing prospect to either players or spectators. Stranmillis withdrew from the League in the 1980's, both University of Ulster teams failed to gain re-election and this year Queen's, who had only won two matches all season, suffered the same fate. They will be replaced by the Londonderry club Institute, so for the first time all 'B'Division games will be played on enclosed pitches.

The other struggling clubs, Cookstown United and Ballymoney United, had a difficult year too, though the Ballymoney club is now well established at the Showgrounds in the town and seem to have put any off-field problems behind them. Millbank Park, Cookstown on the other hand continues to be a millstone around the necks of the other applicant for re-election. Situated more than two miles from the town and a long way from the nearest main road, the club house has continued to be a frequent target for burglars while the combination of a struggling team and a remote location has failed to capture the imagination of the local population.

A club which has been along the same route, apart from the break-ins, is Armagh City which moved the three miles from its roots to the city of Armagh eight years ago and has just completed its second season at Holm Park. The transition from perennial struggle to mid-table security seems complete even if success is still some way away with manager Stephen Uprichard finding it difficult to sustain the improvement of his promising first season in charge. Chimney Corner, whose move a few years earlier took them in the opposite direction from the centre of Antrim to a new ground a couple of miles out, had another solid season without looking like serious challengers for honours. The lack of support from the Antrim public remains a cause for some concern.

In south Londonderry Tobermore United, whose very survival seemed very doubtful a few years ago, have learned to live within their means and chairman Raymond Beatty had the satisfaction of presiding over a measure of improvement sufficient to lift them above local rivals Moyola Park. Moyola, one of the two oldest clubs in the League, have made great strides in recent years but their improvement, for now at least, seems to have come to an end.

Another village club competing successfully at this level is Ballinamallard United whose League progress in 1995 was hampered by their Intermediate Cup campaign. This time around they concentrated more on the League with their largely Omagh-based team progressing to the top half of the table. Whether or not the relative success, achieved as it is with few local players, leads to long term progress remains to be seen though it was interesting to note the level of local interest in Ballinamallard's highly successful second team which consists almost exclusively of Fermanagh players.

Turning to the Belfast area, Brantwood's welcome ground improvements were unfortunately not accompanied by improved playing standards with the departure of long serving manager Ivor McGuckin leaving a gap which proved difficult to fill in the short term. Harland & Wolff Welders, the only one of the League's fifteen survivors not to have a ground which met last season's Irish Cup requirements, had a reasonably successful season finishing 6th in the 'B' Division and more notably finishing runners-up to Limavady United in the Intermediate Cup. The R.U.C. again flattered to deceive, reserving their best performances for the cups, particularly the British Police Championship in which they again represented their Province with distinction.

As usual the best Intermediate team in Belfast were Dundela, though they lacked some of the sparkle of earlier years. The club suffered a grievous loss when their popular and long-serving defender Michael Goddard collapsed and died during the early season game with Dungannon Swifts, leaving a void which in several ways proved difficult to overcome.

In the end Loughgall's nearest challengers, for the second year running, were Dungannon where manager Colin Malone led his side into a position where they lost out only in the closing weeks of the season. This very ambitious club has now cover on all four sides of the ground and some rudimentary terracing on much of it, in line for meeting the IFA's latest changes to the rules governing the staging of games in the later rounds of the Irish Cup. Perhaps the biggest surprise of the season was the consistent improvement in performances of Banbridge Town, who were also in the running until very near the end of the season. The balance of power seems to have shifted firmly to Mid-Ulster at present.

Brian Weir.

SECTION I FINAL LEAGUE TABLE 1995/96

	P	Home: W	D	L	F	A	Away: W	D	L	F	A	Total: W	D	L	F	A	Pts	Gd
1 Loughgall	30	12	3	0	29	10	12	1	2	29	13	24	4	2	58	23	76	+35
2 Dungannon Swifts	30	8	4	3	33	14	13	1	1	58	18	21	5	4	91	32	68	+59
3 Banbridge Town	30	9	2	4	42	16	12	2	1	37	12	21	4	5	79	28	67	+50
4 Dundela	30	10	3	2	52	17	8	2	5	27	18	18	5	7	79	35	59	+45
5 Limavady United	30	11	1	3	35	14	6	6	3	36	24	17	7	6	71	38	58	+33
6 Harland & Wolff W.	30	12	0	3	39	16	5	6	4	32	23	17	6	7	71	39	57	+32
7 Chimney Corner	30	8	3	4	35	18	8	4	3	35	18	16	7	7	70	36	55	+34
8 R.U.C.	30	8	0	7	27	20	5	4	6	27	21	13	4	13	54	41	43	+13
9 Ballinamallard United	30	4	4	7	27	26	6	3	6	23	24	10	7	13	50	51	37	-1
10 Armagh City	30	6	3	6	30	34	4	2	9	16	30	10	5	15	46	64	35	-18
11 Tobermore United	30	6	2	7	19	30	2	2	11	17	49	8	4	18	36	79	28	-43
12 Moyola Park	30	4	4	7	26	34	2	2	11	19	38	6	6	18	45	72	24	-27
13 Brantwood	30	3	5	7	19	32	2	2	11	13	38	5	7	18	32	70	22	-38
14 Ballymoney United	30	4	2	9	24	36	1	3	11	9	38	5	5	20	33	74	20	-41
15 Cookstown United	30	3	4	8	13	34	2	1	12	11	45	5	5	20	24	79	20	-54
16 Queens University	30	1	3	11	10	47	0	2	13	10	51	1	5	24	20	98	8	-78

NB: Queens University were not re-elected to the 'B' Division Section One for 1996/97 season. Their place will be taken by Institute F.C. from Co.Londonderry.

SECTION II FINAL LEAGUE TABLE 1995/96

	P	Home: W	D	L	F	A	Away: W	D	L	F	A	Total: W	D	L	F	A	Pts	Gd.
1 Glentoran II	28	9	3	2	29	17	11	1	2	30	15	20	4	4	59	32	64	+27
2 Bangor Reserves	28	9	3	2	42	15	10	3	1	39	13	19	6	3	81	28	63	+53
3 Glenavon Reserves	28	8	2	4	31	18	10	2	2	36	22	18	4	6	77	40	58	+37
4 Crusaders Reserves	28	8	3	3	39	19	7	7	0	32	14	15	10	3	71	33	55	+38
5 Linfield Swifts	28	7	3	4	34	22	6	2	6	22	22	13	5	10	56	44	44	+12
6 Portadown Reserves	28	4	5	5	28	22	8	2	4	35	25	12	7	9	63	47	43	+16
7 Distillery II	28	2	5	7	18	27	9	2	3	37	26	11	7	10	55	53	40	+2
8 Coleraine Reserves	28	7	1	6	22	26	5	2	7	20	34	12	3	13	42	60	39	-18
9 Ards II	28	5	2	7	26	27	3	5	6	22	29	8	7	13	48	56	31	-8
10 Ballymena United Res	28	4	4	6	28	28	4	2	8	24	33	8	6	14	52	61	30	-9
11 Ballyclare Com. Res.	28	5	0	9	22	33	3	4	7	15	27	8	4	16	37	60	28	-23
12 Larne Olympic	28	3	3	8	22	29	5	1	8	14	31	8	4	16	36	60	28	-24
13 Newry Town Res.	28	3	4	7	14	22	3	2	9	19	34	6	6	16	33	56	24	-23
14 Cliftonville Olympic	28	4	1	9	22	30	3	2	9	11	34	7	3	18	33	64	24	-31
15 Carrick Rangers Res.	28	4	1	9	16	36	1	3	10	15	34	5	4	19	31	70	19	-39

NB: Omagh Town Reserves withdrew from Section Two during the season.

WILKINSON SWORD IRISH LEAGUE 'B' DIVISION

SECTION I RESULTS 1995/96

	Armagh City	Ballinamallard United	Ballymoney United	Banbridge Town	Brantwood	Chimney Corner	Cookstown United	Dundela	Dungannon Swifts	Harland & Wolff Welders	Limavady United	Loughgall	Moyola Park	Queens University	RUC	Tobermore United
Armagh City	–	0-3	1-0	0-3	3-0	2-2	4-1	4-8	1-5	1-1	2-3	0-1	2-1	2-2	1-0	7-4
Ballinamallard United	4-2	–	2-2	1-4	0-1	0-1	2-3	1-2	2-2	2-3	2-2	1-2	3-2	5-0	2-1	0-0
Ballymoney United	0-1	2-3	–	2-4	1-1	0-6	4-0	0-3	2-3	1-1	4-2	1-3	1-5	1-0	1-3	4-1
Banbridge Town	5-0	2-1	3-1	–	3-0	2-0	4-0	1-1	3-5	1-1	0-2	1-2	3-0	4-0	1-2	9-1
Brantwood	1-3	0-1	1-1	1-3	–	0-4	2-1	1-1	0-5	3-1	3-3	1-2	0-0	3-1	3-6	0-0
Chimney Corner	2-0	2-1	7-2	1-2	6-0	–	2-1	0-1	1-3	2-2	2-2	0-1	2-2	5-0	1-0	2-1
Cookstown United	1-2	0-4	1-1	0-1	1-0	2-2	–	0-1	0-4	0-5	0-6	1-4	3-1	2-2	0-0	2-1
Dundela	2-1	5-0	4-0	1-1	1-0	1-1	7-0	–	4-5	1-1	4-1	1-2	7-2	8-0	4-2	2-1
Dungannon Swifts	1-1	1-1	5-0	1-3	4-2	1-2	7-0	1-2	–	1-0	0-0	1-0	4-0	3-1	1-1	2-1
Harland & Wolff Welders	2-1	4-1	2-0	2-0	3-0	1-4	1-0	2-0	1-3	–	6-3	3-1	4-0	4-0	2-0	2-3
Limavady United	3-0	1-1	4-0	1-4	4-1	1-0	3-0	4-1	0-1	2-1	–	0-3	3-0	3-1	2-1	4-0
Loughgall	1-0	4-1	2-0	1-1	2-0	4-3	1-0	2-1	1-0	2-1	0-0	–	2-1	3-0	1-1	3-1
Moyola Park	3-4	1-1	1-0	0-4	1-1	1-4	3-0	0-1	1-5	2-6	1-1	2-3	–	3-2	2-2	5-0
Queens University	1-1	0-2	3-1	0-4	0-3	1-1	2-2	0-5	0-6	1-4	0-5	0-3	1-4	–	0-4	1-2
RUC	2-0	0-2	2-0	1-2	4-2	1-2	2-0	1-0	2-5	2-3	0-1	0-1	1-0	3-1	–	6-1
Tobermore United	2-0	2-1	0-1	0-1	5-2	1-3	1-3	1-0	0-6	2-2	0-5	1-1	2-1	2-0	0-4	–

SECTION II RESULTS 1995/96

	Ards Seconds	Ballyclare Comrades Reserves	Ballymena United Reserves	Bangor Reserves	Carrick Rangers Reserves	Cliftonville Olympic	Coleraine Reserves	Crusaders Reserves	Distillery Seconds	Glenavon Reserves	Glentoran Seconds	Larne Olympic	Linfield Swifts	Newry Town Reserves	Portadown Reserves
Ards Seconds	–	1-0	4-1	0-1	1-1	5-1	2-5	1-1	1-3	2-4	0-2	2-3	1-3	3-0	3-2
Ballyclare Comrades Reserves	0-1	–	0-4	1-5	2-3	3-2	3-1	2-5	0-2	2-1	0-1	4-2	1-2	3-0	1-4
Ballymena United Reserves	2-2	1-1	–	0-3	1-1	3-1	6-0	0-3	3-3	4-5	0-1	4-2	0-1	3-2	1-3
Bangor Reserves	3-1	3-0	6-0	–	4-1	4-1	0-1	1-1	1-3	1-1	3-3	4-0	2-1	6-1	4-1
Carrick Rangers Reserves	0-3	0-2	2-1	0-6	–	0-2	0-3	0-4	1-4	4-2	0-2	4-1	3-2	1-3	1-1
Cliftonville Olympic	3-1	2-1	4-2	1-6	4-1	–	1-1	1-2	1-2	2-4	1-2	L3pt	1-2	0-3	1-3
Coleraine Reserves	2-1	3-3	0-2	2-1	3-0	2-0	–	0-2	0-6	1-3	0-2	2-1	3-2	3-1	1-2
Crusaders Reserves	5-0	3-0	2-5	2-2	4-2	4-1	3-2	–	5-0	0-2	1-2	3-0	0-0	1-1	6-2
Distillery Seconds	2-5	1-1	2-1	2-2	2-1	0-1	1-2	1-2	–	1-3	1-2	1-1	2-2	1-3	1-1
Glenavon Reserves	1-1	3-0	6-1	1-2	3-0	2-0	4-0	1-1	5-2	–	0-4	0-1	3-2	2-1	0-3
Glentoran Seconds	2-2	6-2	1-0	1-1	4-2	1-0	1-1	0-4	1-0	1-2	–	5-1	1-0	2-0	3-2
Larne Olympic	2-2	0-1	2-2	1-3	1-0	0-1	5-1	2-2	4-5	1-2	1-4	–	0-1	3-2	0-3
Linfield Swifts	5-2	2-1	0-2	1-2	2-1	1-1	5-0	2-2	2-4	2-2	4-1	2-1	–	4-0	2-3
Newry Town Reserves	2-1	0-1	2-2	0-2	1-1	0-0	2-1	1-1	1-2	1-2	3-1	0-1	0-2	–	1-5
Portadown Reserves	0-0	2-2	2-1	1-3	2-1	9-0	1-2	2-2	1-1	0-3	1-3	L3pt	5-2	2-2	–

'B' DIVISION CHAMPIONS 1951/52 -1995/96

Season	Section One	Section Two
1951/52	Linfield Swifts	
1952/53	Linfield Swifts	
1953/54	Cliftonville Olympic	
1954/55	Larne	
1955/56	Banbridge Town	
1956/57	Larne	
1957/58	Ards II	
1958/59	Glentoran II	
1959/60	Newry Town	
1960/61	Ballyclare Comrades	
1961/62	Carrick Rangers	
1962/63	Ballyclare Comrades	
1963/64	Larne	
1964/65	Larne	
1965/66	Larne	
1966/67	Larne	
1967/68	Dundela	
1968/69	Larne	
1969/70	Larne	
1970/71	Larne	
1971/72	Larne	
1972/73	Carrick Rangers	
1973/74	Ballyclare Comrades	
1974/75	Carrick Rangers	
1975/76	Linfield Swifts	
1976/77	Carrick Rangers	Dundela
1977/78	Ballyclare Comrades	Linfield Swifts
1978/79	Carrick Rangers	Linfield Swifts
1979/80	Ballyclare Comrades	Linfield Swifts
1980/81	Newry Town	Cliftonville Olympic
1981/82	Dundela	Larne Olympic
1982/83	Carrick Rangers	Linfield Swifts
1983/84	Limavady United	Linfield Swifts
1984/85	Chimney Corner	Linfield Swifts
1985/86	Dundela	Glentoran II
1986/87	R.U.C.	Glentoran II
1987/88	Dundela	Linfield Swifts
1988/89	Ballyclare Comrades	Linfield Swifts
1989/90	Dundela	Glentoran II
1990/91	Dundela	Linfield Swifts
1991/92	Dundela	Linfield Swifts
1992/93	Limavady United	Glentoran II
1993/94	Dundela	Bangor Reserves
1994/95	Loughgall	Bangor Reserves
1995/96	Loughgall	Glentoran II

NB: From 1951/52 to 1973/74 there was only one Section to the 'B' Division. This was made up of Irish League clubs Reserve teams and Intermediate clubs. From 1974/75 to 1975/76 the 'B' Division was split into North and South Sections with the winners of each being involved in a 'Play-off' to decide the overall winners. In 1975/76 the North and South Sections were retained though a 'Play-off' was not held, therefore Carrick Rangers and Dundela shared the Championship. In 1977/78 the 'B' Division was again restructured to its present day format, which is; Section One being made up of Intermediate clubs and Section Two containing Irish League clubs Reserve teams.

ARMAGH CITY

Ground: Holm Park, Armagh. Founded: 1964

Armagh City 1995/96

Back Row L to R: Stephen Uprichard (Player/Manager), Jonathan Pollock, Conor Lavery, Gary Haire, Mark Neill, Sean Casey, Noel Nelson, John Tumilty, Noel Richardson, Stephen Montgomery.
Front Row L to R: Oliver McGeown, Shay Campbell (Mascot), Philip Murphy (Mascot), Paul Murphy (Mascot), Alan Murphy, Harry Fay, Alan Willis, Tony Cochrane, Hugh McAleavey.
(Photo by Ulster Gazette, courtesy of Aidan Murphy)

Playing Staff for 1995/95
Stephen Boyce, Bobby Buchanan, Sean Casey, Tony Cochrane, Harry Fay, Gary Haire, Stephen Hynds*, Conor Lavery, Hugh McAleavey, Andy McCann*, Joe McCourt, Oliver McGeown, Charlie McLoughlin, Paul Matchett, Stephen Montgomery, Darren Mullen, Alan Murphy, Jonathan Neill, Kyle Neill, Mark Neill, Noel Nelson, Brian O'Kane, George Pollock, Jonathan Pollock, Noel Richardson, George Steenson, John Tumilty, Gary Turkington, Stephen Uprichard, Alan Willis.
* Denotes Player has now left the club.

Secretary:
Aidan Murphy
Player/Manager:
Stephen Uprichard
Coach:
Harry Fay
Colours: Azure/Black striped shirts, Black shorts and socks.
Programme Editor:
Brian Weir
Entered 'B': 1975/76

HONOURS:

Irish League 'B' Division	Best Position: 4th 1975/76	
Bob Radcliffe Cup	(1)	1991/92
Mid-Ulster League	(1)	1973/74
Mid-Ulster Shield	(1)	1969/70
Alexander Cup	(1)	1973/74
Alan Wilson Memorial Trophy	(1)	1973/74

TRANSFERS C/S '95 TO APRIL '96

Players Signed:
Sean Casey (Carnbane League c/s'95), Conor Lavery (Dungannon Swifts c/s'95), Joe McCourt (Unattached c/s'95), Stephen Montgomery (Loughgall c/s'95), Darren Mullen (Bessbrook United c/s'95), John Tumilty (Newry Town c/s'95), Andy McCann (Limavady United Sep.'95), Hugh McAleavey (Carnbane League Nov.'95), Paul Matchett (Hanover Dec.'95), Noel Richardson (Distillery Jan.'96):

Players Transferred:
Stephen Hyndes (Arniston Rangers Oct.'95), Andy McCann (Limavady United Feb.'96):

THE NORTHERN IRELAND **football** Y E A R B O O K

ARMAGH CITY COMPLETE PLAYING RECORD FOR 1995/96

Date:	Comp:	Ven:	Opponents:	Result:	Goalscorers:
Aug 12	ILC 1	H	Crusaders	2-3 L	Mullen, Fay
Aug 16	BD	H	Tobermore United	7-4 W	Haire, Willis (4), Casey, Mullen
Aug 19	BD	A	Cookstown United	2-1 W	Mullen, Willis
Aug 22	BD	H	R.U.C.	1-0 W	Casey
Aug 25	BD	A	Loughgall	0-1 L	-
Sep 2	BRC 1	H	Dromore Amateurs	1-0 W	Casey
Sep 9	IC 1	A	Ballymoney United	1-0 W	Willis
Sep 16	BRC 2	A	Seapatrick	5-2 W	Willis (3), Cochrane, Hyndes
Sep 23	BD	A	Ballymoney United	1-0 W	Casey
Sep 30	BD	H	Dungannon Swifts	1-5 L	Willis
Oct 7	BD	A	Moyola Park	4-3 W	Willis (2), Casey, McCann
Oct 14	BD	H	Dundela	4-8 L	Mullen, (M) Neill, Casey, Willis
Oct 21	BD	A	Harland & Wolff Welders	1-2 L	McCann
Oct 28	BRC QF	A	Lurgan Celtic Bhoys	0-2 L	-
Nov 4	BD	H	Banbridge Town	0-3 L	-
Nov 11	IC 3	A	Ards Rangers	1-2 L	Willis
Nov 18	BD	H	Limavady United	2-3 L	Willis, (M) Neill
Nov 25	BD	A	R.U.C.	0-2 L	-
Dec 2	BD	A	Chimney Corner	0-2 L	-
Dec 9	BIC 4	A	Dunmurry Recreation	1-0 W	Casey
Dec 16	BD	H	Cookstown United	4-1 W	Casey (2), Willis, Lavery
Jan 6	BD	H	Chimney Corner	2-2 D	Nelson (2)
Jan 13	BD	H	Loughgall	0-1 L	-
Jan 20	BIC 5	H	Dundela	2-1 W	McAleavey, Casey
Jan 27	BD	A	Limavady United	0-3 L	-
Feb 3	BD	H	Queens University	2-2 D	Montgomery, Willis
Feb 10	BD	H	Ballinamallard United	0-3 L	-
Feb 17	BD	A	Dungannon Swifts	1-1 D	Cochrane
Feb 24	BIC 6	A	Ballymena United	0-4 L	-
Mar 2	BD	H	Moyola Park	2-1 W	(M) Neill, Casey
Mar 9	MUC 4	H	Coagh United	1-3 L	McGeown
Mar 16	SKC 1	A	Loughgall	0-1 L	-
Mar 23	BD	A	Queens University	1-1 D	McGeown
Mar 30	BD	A	Brantwood	3-1 W	Murphy, (M) Neill, Haire
Apr 6	BD	H	Harland & Wolff Welders	1-1 D	McGeown
Apr 20	BD	H	Ballymoney United	1-0 W	McGeown
Apr 25	BD	A	Banbridge Town	0-5 L	-
Apr 27	BD	A	Tobermore United	0-2 L	-
May 1	BD	A	Ballinamallard United	2-4 L	Willis, (M) Neill
May 4	BD	H	Brantwood	3-0 W	(M) Neill, (K) Neill, Cochrane
May 7	BD	A	Dundela	1-2 L	Haire

ARMAGH CITY GOALSCORERS FOR 1995/96

'B' Division: (46): 13 Alan Willis; 8 Sean Casey; 6 Mark Neill; 3 Gary Haire, Oliver McGeown, Darren Mullen; 2 Tony Cochrane, Andy McCann, Noel Nelson; 1 Conor Lavery, Stephen Montgomery, Alan Murphy, Kyle Neill:
Bob Radcliffe Cup: (6): 3 Alan Willis; 1 Sean Casey, Tony Cochrane, Stephen Hyndes:
McEwans Intermediate Cup: (2): 2 Alan Willis:
Bass Irish Cup: (3): 2 Sean Casey; 1 Hugh McAleavey:
Wilkinson Sword Irish League Cup: (2): 1 Harry Fay, Darren Mullen:
McEwans Mid-Ulster Cup: (1): Oliver McGeown:
Smirnoff 'B' Division Knockout Cup: (0): -

Top Goalscorer for 1995/96: Alan Willis with 18:

BALLINAMALLARD UNITED

Ground: Ferney Park, Ballinamallard. Founded 1975

Chairman:
Clive Murray
Secretary:
Alister Cooke
Player/Manager:
Greg Turley
Team Coach:
Ray Sanderson
Club Colours:
Sky Blue shirts, White shorts,
Sky Blue socks
Entered 'B':
1990/91

Playing Staff for 1995/96

Gary Armstrong, Derek Ballard, Mervyn Bell, Anthony Benson*, Paul Bogle, Seamus Bonner, Bob Carroll, Michael Conlon, Martin Doherty, Paul Doherty, John Dougan, Eamon Gallagher, Brian Hampson, Sean Hargan, Dermot Hillen, Roger Howe, Gregory Kearney, Martin Kelly, Nigel Keys, Gordon Lee, Sean McCallion, Michael McConomy, Alan McCutcheon, Gary McGettigan, Kieran McGlinchey, Damien Ming, Shane O'Brien, John Sheridan, Martin Turner, Greg Turley, Martin Woodhead.

Denotes player has now left the club.

HONOURS:

Irish League 'B' Division:	Best Position: 6th 1993/94	
IFA Intermediate Cup:	(1)	1994/95
Fermanagh & Western League:		
Mulhern Cup:	(1)	1988/89
Top Four Trophy:	(1)	1988/89

TRANSFERS C/S'95 TO APRIL '96

Players Signed:
Gregory Kearney (Finn Harps Sep.'95), Derek Elliott (Enniskillen Rangers Jan.'96), Dermot Hillen (Omagh Town Jan.'96), Peter Townsend (NFC Kesh Jan.'96), Liam Williamson (Lisnarick Jan.'96).

Players Transferred:
Anthony Benson (Lisnaskea Rovers Jan.'96).

BALLINAMALLARD UNITED

BALLINAMALLARD UNITEDS COMPLETE PLAYING RECORD FOR 1995/96

Date:	Comp:	Ven:	Opponents:	Result:	Goalscorers:
Aug 12	ILC 1	A	Coleraine	1-3 L	Ming
Aug 15	BD	A	Loughgall	1-4 L	Ming (pen)
Aug 19	BD	H	Queens University	5-0 W	McCallion, Turner, Ming (2), Bonner (pen)
Aug 22	BD	A	Dungannon Swifts	1-1 D	Bonner
Aug 26	BD	H	Brantwood	0-1 L	-
Sep 2	NWIC 1	A	Dungiven Celtic	1-2 L	Bogle
Sep 9	IC 1	H	East Belfast	2-0 W	McCutcheon, Benson
Sep 16	BD	A	Ballymoney United	3-2 W	Benson, Keys, Bonner (pen)
Sep 23	BD	H	Limavady United	2-2 D	Bonner (pen), Keys
Sep 30	BD	A	Cookstown United	4-0 W	Keys, Doherty (2 pens), Carroll
Oct 7	IC 2	H	Brantwood	0-2 L	-
Oct 14	BD	H	Ballymoney United	2-2 D	Bonner, Kearney
Oct 21	BD	A	Banbridge Town	1-2 L	Kearney
Nov 4	BD	A	Moyola Park	1-1 D	Bonner
Nov 11	BD	H	Tobermore United	0-0 D	-
Nov 18	BD	A	Dundela	0-5 L	-
Nov 25	BD	H	Cookstown United	2-3 L	Ming, Bonner
Dec 2	BD	A	Limavady United	1-1 D	Keys
Dec 9	BIC 4	H	Crumlin United	1-1 D	Ming
Dec 12	BIC 4R	A	Crumlin United	0-4 L	-
Dec 16	BD	H	Moyola Park	3-2 W	Bonner, Keys, Carroll
Jan 6	BD	H	Harland & Wolff W	2-3 L	Bonner, McCallion
Jan 13	BD	A	Queens University	2-0 W	McCallion, Hargan
Jan 27	BD	A	R.U.C.	2-0 W	Kelly, Doherty
Feb 10	BD	A	Armagh City	3-0 W	Doherty (2,1pen), Keys
Feb 17	BD	H	Loughgall	1-2 L	Ballard
Feb 24	BD	A	Brantwood	1-0 W	Kelly
Mar 2	BD	H	Dundela	1-2 L	Sheridan
Mar 9	BD	H	Chimney Corner	0-1 L	-
Mar 16	SKC 1	H	Banbridge Town	0-4 L	-
Mar 23	BD	A	Chimney Corner	1-2 L	Ming
Mar 30	BD	A	Tobermore United	1-2 L	Carroll
Apr 10	BD	A	Harland & Wolff W	1-4 L	Bonner
Apr 20	BD	H	Banbridge Town	1-4 L	Dougan
Apr 27	BD	H	R.U.C	2-1 W	Bonner, Ming
May 1	BD	H	Armagh City	4-2 W	Turner, Ming, McCallion, Keys
May 11	BD	H	Dungannon Swifts	2-2 D	Bonner, McCallion

BALLINAMALLARD UNITED GOALSCORERS FOR 1995/96

''B' Division: (50): 12 Seamus Bonner (3p); 7 Nigel Keys, Damien Ming (1p); 5 Sean McCallion; 4 Paul Doherty (3p); 3 Bob Carroll; 2 Gregory Kearney, Martin Kelly, Martin Turner; 1 Derek Ballard, Anthony Benson, Martin Doherty, John Dougan, Sean Hargan, John Sheridan:
North West Intermediate Cup: (1): Paul Bogle:
McEwans Intermediate Cup: (2): 1 Anthony Benson, Alan McCutcheon:
Bass Irish Cup: (1): Damien Ming:
Wilkinson Sword Irish League Cup: (1): Damien Ming:
Smirnoff 'B' Division Knockout Cup: (0): -

Top Goalscorer for 1995/96: Seamus Bonner with 12 (3 pens):

BALLYMONEY UNITED
Ground: The Showgrounds, Ballymoney. Founded 1944.

Playing Staff for 1995/96

Zane Adams, Roger Anderson, Liam Black, Nevin Clyde, Danny Graham, Joe Irwin, Gareth Kearney, Brendan Kirgan, Gary Little, Jackie McAfee, Michael McCaul, Billy McCurdy, John McFall, Gareth Mitchell, Gareth Moody, Gavin Nash, Michael Nash, Tony O'Carroll, Michael O'Donovan, Dominic O'Loughlin, Michael O'Loughlin, Roan O'Neill, Simon Smyth, Richard Wade, Milo Walker, Mark Wilkinson, Jason Wilmot.

Denotes player has now left the club.

No photograph available for 1995/96.

Chairman:
Oliver Muldoon
Secretary:
Robert Morrow
Manager:
Jackie McAfee
Club Colours:
Blue shirts, White shorts, Blue socks
Entered 'B':
1983/84

HONOURS:

Irish League 'B' Division:	Best Position: 4th 1993/94	
N.I. Intermediate League:	(2)	1980/81 and 1982/83
N.I. Intermediate Challenge Cup:	(3)	1980/81, 1981/82, 1982/83
N.I. Intermediate League Cup:	(2)	1980/81 and 1981/82
Irish Junior Cup:	(1)	1960/61

TRANSFERS C/S'95 TO APRIL '96

Players Signed:
Tony O'Carroll (Limavady United c/s'95), Richard Wade (Coleraine Sep.'95), Joe Irwin (Roe Valley Oct.'95), Billy McCurdy (Coleraine Oct.'95), Michael O'Donovan (Limavady United Oct.'95).

Players Transferred:
Billy Pyper (Moyola Park c/s'95), Paul Trainor (Chimney Corner c/s'95), Michael Tully (Chimney Corner c/s'95).

THE NORTHERN IRELAND
football
Y E A R B O O K

Ballymoney United

Date:	Comp:	Ven:	Opponents:	Result:	Goalscorers:
Aug 12	ILC 1	A	Larne	0-3 L	-
Aug 15	BD	A	Limavady United	0-4 L	-
Aug 19	BD	H	Moyola Park	1-5 L	McCaul
Aug 22	BD	A	Chimney Corner	2-7 L	?
Aug 25	BD	H	R.U.C.	1-3 L	Wilmot
Sep 2	SS 1	H	Comber Recreation	3-6 L	O'Carroll (2), McFaul
Sep 9	IC 1	H	Armagh City	0-1 L	-
Sep 16	BD	H	Ballinamallard United	2-3 L	Moody, Nash
Sep 23	BD	H	Armagh City	0-1 L	-
Sep 30	BD	A	Banbridge Town	1-3 L	Kirgan
Oct 7	BD	H	Loughgall	1-3 L	O'Carroll
Oct 14	BD	A	Ballinamallard United	2-2 D	Wade, Kearney
Oct 21	BD	H	Cookstown United	4-0 W	O'Carroll, Irwin, (M) O'Donovan (2)
Oct 28	BD	A	Cookstown United	1-1 D	Irwin
Nov 4	BD	H	Dundela	0-3 L	-
Nov 11	BD	A	Dungannon Swifts	0-5 L	-
Nov 18	BD	H	Queens University	1-0 W	Kirgan
Dec 2	BD	A	Moyola Park	0-1 L	-
Dec 9	BIC 4	H	Larne Tech Old Boys	1-3 L	O'Carroll
Dec 16	BD	A	Dundela	0-4 L	-
Jan 6	BD	A	Loughgall	0-2 L	-
Jan 13	BD	H	Chimney Corner	0-6 L	-
Jan 20	BD	A	Queens University	1-3 L	Moody
Jan 27	BD	H	Brantwood	1-1 D	Moody
Feb 3	BD	A	Tobermore United	1-0 W	O'Carroll
Feb 10	BD	H	Harland & Wolff W	1-1 D	?
Feb 17	BD	A	R.U.C	0-2 L	-
Feb 24	BD	H	Dungannon Swifts	2-3 L	Wilkinson, Black
Mar 2	BD	A	Harland & Wolff W	0-2 L	-
Mar 16	SKC 1	H	Queens University	3-0 W	Wade, O'Carroll, Little
Mar 23	BD	H	Banbridge Town	2-4 L	O'Carroll, Wade
Mar 30	SKC QFA		Dundela	3-1 W	Wade (2), O'Carroll
Apr 6	BD	H	Tobermore United	4-1 W	Wade (2), Kirgan, (M) O'Donovan
Apr 13	BD	A	Brantwood	1-1 D	(M) O'Donovan
Apr 16	SKC SF1.L.	A	Banbridge Town	0-4 L	-
Apr 20	BD	A	Armagh City	0-1 L	-
Apr 23	SKC SF 2.L.	H	Banbridge Town	1-2 L	?
Apr 29	BD	H	Limavady United	4-2 W	?

Ballymoney United Goalscorers for 1995/96

'B' Division: (33): 4 Tony O'Carroll, Richard Wade, Michael O'Donovan; 3
Brendan Kirgan, Gareth Moody; 2 Joe Irwin; 1 Liam Black, Gareth Kearney, Michael McCaul, Gavin Nash, Mark
Wilkinson, Jason Wilmot (7 goalscorers missing):
Calor Steel & Sons Cup: (3): 2 Tony O'Carroll; 1 John McFaul:
McEwans Intermediate Cup: (0) -
Bass Irish Cup: (1): Tony O'Carroll:
Wilkinson Sword Irish League Cup: (0): -
Smirnoff 'B' Division Knockout Cup: (7): 3 Richard Wade; 2 Tony O'Carroll; 1 Gary Little (1 goalscorer missing):

Top Goalscorer for 1995/96: Tony O'Carroll with 9:

BANBRIDGE TOWN
Ground: Crystal Park, Castlewellan Road, Banbridge. Founded: 1947

Banbridge Town 1995/96
Back Row L to R: Ronnie Clarke (Manager), Barry White, Noel McQuaid, Ian Clarke,
Michael Napier, Mario Scappatticci, Paul McStravick, Mark Gracey, Stephen Thompson,
George Falloon (Coach).
Front Row L to R: Francis Shannon (Physio), Frankie Maguire, Kevin Buchanan, Michael
Wilson, Gary Smith, John Johnston, Pat Brannigan.
(Photo courtesy of Damien Wilson)

Playing Staff for 1995/96
Ian Adams, Martin Andrews, Patrick Brannigan, Neil Brown, Kevin Buchanan,
Paul Buchanan, Patrick Burns, IanClarke, Keith Douglas, George Falloon, Mark
Gracey, Tom Gray, Larry Griffen*, John Jonston, Mervyn Kerr, Noel McQuaid,
Paul McStravick, Frank Maguire, Damien Mullan, Michael Napier, Mario
Scappaticci, Gary Smyth, Paul Sneddon, Steven Thompson, Barry White, Michael
Wison. *Denotes players has now left the club.*

Chairman:
Jim Cassells
Secretary:
Norman Livingstone
Manager:
Peter Watson
Club Colours:
Red & Black striped shirts, Black shorts,
Black socks with Red tops
Entered 'B'
1954/55

HONOURS

Irish League 'B' Division:	Champions	(1)	1955/56
IFA Intermediate Cup:		(1)	1985/86
Louis Moore Cup:		(2)	1954/55, 1967/68
Mid-Ulster Cup:		(4)	1948/49, 1958/59, 1973/74, 1979/80
Bob Radcliffe Cup:		(1)	1980/81
Alan Wilson Memorial Cup:		(1)	1986/87

TRANSFERS C/S'95 TO APRIL '96

Players Signed:
Patrick Brannigan (Donegal Celtic c/s'95), Damian Mullan (Moira Albion
c/s'95), Tom Gray (Newry Town Jul.'95), Larry Griffen (Newry Town Aug.'95),
Mark Gracey (Newry Town Feb.'96), Gary Smyth (Donegal Celtic Mar.'96),
Steven Thompson (Newry Town Mar.'96).

Players Transferred:
Fred Scappaticci (Newry Town c/s'95), Larry Griffen (Newry Town Mar.'96).

BANBRIDGE TOWN COMPLETE PLAYING RECORD FOR 1995/96

Date:	Comp:	Ven:	Opponents:	Result:	Goalscorers:
Aug 12	ILC 1	A	Ballyclare Comrades	1-0 W aet	Brannigan
Aug 15	ILC 2	A	Carrick Rangers	0-3 L	-
Aug 19	BD	H	Brantwood	3-0 W	Brannigan, Maguire, McStravick
Aug 22	BD	H	Loughgall	1-2 L	Brannigan
Aug 25	BD	H	Harland & Wolff Welders	1-1 D	Brannigan
Sep 2	BRC 1	H	Hanover	3-2 W	White (2), Burns
Sep 9	BD	A	Harland & Wolff Welders	0-2 L	-
Sep 16	BRC 2	A	Rathfriland Rangers	2-1 W	Maguire, Clarke
Sep 23	BD	A	Tobermore United	1-0 W	White
Sep 30	BD	H	Ballymoney United	3-1 W	Maguire, Clarke, White
Oct 7	BD	A	Dungannon Swifts	3-1 W	Maguire, Wilson, Brannigan
Oct 14	BD	A	Limavady United	4-1 W	Johnston (2), Maguire, Mullan
Oct 21	BD	H	Ballinamallard United	2-1 W	Mullan, Brannigan
Oct 28	BRC QF	H	Bourneview Y.M.	8-1 W	Clarke (3), Brannigan, Johnston, White, McStravick, Mullan
Nov 4	BD	A	Armagh City	3-0 W	Brannigan, McStravick (pen), White
Nov 11	BD	H	Moyola Park	3-0 W	Mullan, Brannigan, Clarke
Nov 18	BD	A	Cookstown United	1-0 W	Johnston
Nov 25	BD	H	Dundela	1-1 D	White
Dec 9	BIC 4	H	Loughgall	3-3 D	Clarke, Mullan, Brannigan
Dec 14	BIC 4R	A	Loughgall	4-1 W	Johnston (3), Brannigan
Dec 16	BRC SF	N	Dungannon Swifts	2-5 L	Griffen, Brannigan
Jan 13	BD	A	Brantwood	3-1 W	Sloan (og), White, Johnston
Jan 20	BIC 5	A	Larne	0-3 L	-
Feb 10	BD	H	Limavady United	0-2 L	-
Feb 17	BD	A	Chimney Corner	2-1 W	White, McQuaid
Feb 24	BD	H	R.U.C.	1-2 L	White
Mar 2	BD	A	Queens University	4-0 W	Clarke, Johnston, Brannigan, Scappaticci
Mar 9	MUC 4	H	Loughgall	2-4 L	Brannigan, McQuaid
Mar 16	SKC 1	A	Ballinamallard United	4-0 W	White, Smyth, McQuaid (pen), (P) Buchanan
Mar 23	BD	A	Ballymoney United	4-2 W	Mullan (3), Smyth
Mar 30	SKC QF	H	Dungannon Swifts	5-1 W	Brannigan (2), Mullan, Clarke, McStravick
Apr 6	BD	A	Moyola Park	4-0 W	Clarke (2), Brannigan, Smyth
Apr 13	BD	A	Dundela	1-1 D	Mullan
Apr 16	SKC SF 1L	H	Ballymoney United	4-0 W	Clarke (3), Brannigan
Apr 20	BD	A	Ballinamallard United	4-1 W	Clarke, Smyth, Brannigan, Mullan
Apr 23	SKC SF 2L	A	Ballymoney United	2-1 W	Clarke, Smyth
			(Banbridge Town won 6-1 on aggregate)		
Apr 25	BD	H	Armagh City	5-0 W	Clarke (3), Smyth, McQuaid
Apr 27	BD	H	Queens University	4-0 W	Clarke (2), Maguire, Smyth
Apr 30	BD	H	Cookstown United	4-0 W	Smyth (3), Clarke
May 4	BD	H	Tobermore United	9-1 W	Johnston (2), Smyth (4), Brannigan (2,1pen), Napier (pen)
May 7	BD	A	R.U.C.	2-1 W	Brannigan, Clarke
May 14	BD	A	Loughgall	1-1 D	Brannigan
May 16	BD	H	Dungannon Swifts	3-5 L	Smyth, McQuaid (pen), Clarke
May 18	BD	H	Chimney Corner	2-0 W	Brannigan, Clarke
May 25	SKC F	N	Limavady United	2-3 L	Brannigan (2)

BANBRIDGE TOWN GOALSCORERS FOR 1995/96

'B' Division: (79): 15 Pat Brannigan (1p), Ian Clarke; 13 Gary Smyth; 8 Damian Mullan; 7 John Johnston, Barry White; 5 Frank Maguire; 3 Noel McQuaid (1p); 2 Paul McStravick (1p); 1 Michael Napier (pen), Mario Scappaticci, Michael Wilson; 1 own goal:

Bob Radcliffe Cup: (15): 4 Ian Clarke; 3 Barry White; 2 Patrick Brannigan; 1 Patrick Burns, Larry Griffen, John Johnston, Paul McStravick, Frank Maguire, Damian Mullan:

Bass Irish Cup: (7): 3 John Johnston; 2 Patrick Brannigan; 1 Ian Clarke, Damian Mullan:

Wilkinson Sword Irish League Cup: (1): Patrick Brannigan:

McEwans Mid-Ulster Cup: (2): 1 Patrick Brannigan, Noel McQuaid:

Smirnoff 'B' Division Knockout Cup: (17): 5 Patrick Brannigan, Ian Clarke; 2 Gary Smyth; 1 Paul Buchanan, Noel McQuaid (pen), Paul McStravick, Damian Mullan, Barry White:

Top Goalscorer for 1995/96: Patrick Brannigan with 26 (1 pen)

BRANTWOOD

Ground:- Skegoneill Avenue, Belfast BT15 Founded: 1903

Playing Staff for 1995/96
David Allen, Paddy Barr, George Beattie, Bill Cardwell, Frankie Caulfield, Mark Cobain, John Coey, Neil Coey, Paul Garrett, Wesley Hanna, Paul Hardy, Robert Ingram, Gordon McBride, Martin McBride, Ronnie McCullough, Robert McDonald, Joseph McGeehan, Anthony McGreevy, Colin McIlwrath, Stephen Maxwell, Brian Mellon, Neil Murphy, Thomas Pearson, Jeff Russell, Ricky Simpson, Stephen Sloan, Mark Taylor.

No Photograph available for 1995/96.

Chairman:
Stephen Forsythe
Secretary:
Tommy Holmes
Manager:
Billy Beggs
Club Colours:
Royal Blue shirts, White shorts.
Blue socks
Entered 'B':
1954/55

Honours:

Irish League 'B' Division:	Best Position: 2nd	1961/62
Intermediate League:	(5)	1920/21, 1924/25, 1947/48, 1951/52, 1953/54
IFA Intermediate Cup:	(4)	1951/52, 1952/53, 1972/73, 1990/91
Steel & Sons Cup:	(8)	1920/21, 1931/32, 1950/51, 1951/52, 1952/53, 1955/56, 1976/77, 1985/86
George Wilson Cup:	(1)	1972/73
Clements Lyttle Cup:	(1)	1947/48
Irish Junior Cup:	(1)	1913/14

Transfers c/s'95 to April '96

Players Signed:
Wesley Hanna (Carrick Rangers c/s'95), Stephen Sloan (Harland & Wolff Welders c/s'95), Frankie Caulfield (Chimney Corner Mar.'96).

Players Transferred:
—

THE NORTHERN IRELAND **football**
Y E A R B O O K

BRANTWOOD

BRANTWOODS COMPLETE PLAYING RECORD FOR 1995/96

Date:	Comp:	Ven:	Opponents:	Result:	Goalscorers:
Aug 12	ILC 1	A	Glentoran	0-3 L	-
Aug 15	BD	H	Queens University	3-1 W	?
Aug 19	BD	A	Banbridge Town	0-3 L	-
Aug 22	BD	H	Harland & Wolff W	3-1 W	?
Aug 26	BD	A	Ballinamallard United	1-0 W	Hardy
Sep 2	SS1		Cliftonville Olympic	4-2 W aet	McIlwrath, Simpson, McCullough (2)
Sep 9	IC 1	H	Wellington Recreation	4-0 W	?
Sep 16	SS 2	H	Bangor Reserves	2-4 L	McIlwrath, Hanna
Sep 23	BD	H	Dundela	1-1 D	Hardy
Sep 30	BD	A	Loughgall	0-2 L	-
Oct 7	IC 2	A	Ballinamallard United	2-0 W	Hanna, Barr
Oct 14	BD	A	Cookstown United	0-1 L	-
Oct 21	BD	H	Tobermore United	0-0 D	-
Oct 28	BD	A	Limavady United	1-4 L	Hardy
Nov4	BD	H	Dungannon Swifts	0-5 L	-
Nov 11	IC 3	A	Dunmurry Recreation	4-3 W	Maxwell (2), McIlwrath, Pearson
Nov 18	BD		Moyola Park	1-1 D	Maxwell
Nov 25	BD	H	Loughgall	1-2 L	Barr
Dec 2	BD	A	Tobermore United	2-5 L	McDonald, Barr
Dec 9	BIC 4	A	Tobermore United	0-1 L	-
Dec 16	IC 4	A	Crumlin United	2-1 W	Barr, McIlwrath
Jan 6	BD	A	Dungannon Swifts	2-4 L	McIlwrath, McDonald
Jan 13	BD	H	Banbridge Town	1-3 L	Russell
Jan 20	BD	H	Moyola Park	0-0 D	-
Jan 27	BD	A	Ballymoney United	1-1 D	Hardy
Feb 3	IC QF	A	R.U.C.	1-2 L	Barr
Feb 10	BD	H	Chimney Corner	0-4 L	-
Feb 17	BD	A	Queens University	3-0 W	Russell, Barr, Ingram
Feb 24	BD	H	Ballinamallard United	0-1 L	-
Mar2	BD	A	Chimney Corner	0-6 L	-
Mar 9	BD	H	Limivady United	3-3 D	Murphy (2), McDonald
Mar 16	SKC 1	H	Dundela	1-3 L	(N) Coey
Mar 23	BD	A	Dundela	0-1 L	-
Mar 30	BD	H	Armagh City	1-3 L	McDonald
Apr 6	BD	H	Cookstown United	2-1 W	McIlwrath, Caulfield
Apr 13	BD	H	Ballymoney United	1-1 D	Ingram
Apr 16	BD	A	Harland & Wolff W	0-3 L	-
Apr 20	BD	A	R.U.C.	2-4 L	(N) Coey, Hanna
Apr 30	BD	H	R.U.C	3-6 L	?
May 4	BD	A	Armagh City	0-3 L	-

BRANTWOOD GOALSCORERS FOR 1995/96

'B' Division:(32): 4 Paul Hardy, Robert McDonald; 3 Paddy Barr; 2 Robert Ingram, Colin McIlwrath, Neil Murphy, Jeff Russell; 1 Frankie Caulfield, Neil Coey, Wesley Hanna, Stephen Maxwell; (9 goalscorers missing):
Calor Steel & Sons Cup: (6): 2 Ronnie McCullough, Colin McIlwrath; 1 Wesley Hanna, Ricky Simpson:
McEwans Intermediate: (13): 3 Paddy Barr; 2 Colin McIlwrath, Stephen Maxwell; 1 Wesley Hanna, Thomas Pearson; (4 goalscorers missing):
Bass Irish Cup: (0): -
Wilkinson Sword Irish League Cup: (0): -
Smirnoff 'B'Divisiion Knockout Cup: (1): Neil Coey:

Top Goalscorers for 1995/96: Paddy Barr and Colin McIlwrath both with 6:
NB: Goalscorers for certain matches have not been located, so above goalscoring records are not complete.

CHIMNEY CORNER
Ground: Allen Park, Antrim. Founded: 1952

Chimney Corner 1995/96

Back Row L to R: Patsy Hennessey (Ass. Manager), Gary Clifford, Mark McCloskey, Paul Trainor, Paul McAteer, Laurence Stitt (Player/Manager),Willie Owens, Aaron Clements.
Front Row L to R: Sean O'Kane, Frank O'Kane, Paddy Mallon, Paul McGurnaguan, Eddie Patterson, Harry Kernohan, Michael Tully.
(Photo courtesy of Norman Wallace)

Playing Staff for 1995/96

Tommy Breslin, Frankie Caulfield*, Aaron Clements, Gary Clifford, Kevin Currier, Liam Hartley, Harry Kernoghan, Eddie McAlea, Kevin McAllister, Paul McAteer, Gary McCaig, Mark McCloskey, Gavin McCrystal, Germanus McGrinder, Paul McGurnaghan, Trevor McNicholl, Patrick Mallon, Frank O'Kane, Sean O'Kane, William Owens, Eddie Patterson, Michael Press, Laurence Stitt, Danny Trainor, Paul Trainor, Michael Tully, Paul Tumilty.
* Denotes player has now left the club.

Chairman:
John Stewart
Secretary:
Raymond Murray
Player /Manager:
Laurence Stitt
Asst.Manager:
Patsy Hennessey
Club Colours:
Red shirts, shorts and socks
Entered 'B':
1973/74

HONOURS:

Irish League 'B' Division:	(1)	1984/85
Steel & Sons Cup:	(3)	1962/63, 1973/74, 1975/76
IFA Intermediate Cup:	(3)	1967/68, 1981/82, 1982/83
'B' Division Knockout Cup:	(1)	1985/86
Amateur League Div.1A	(5)	1961/62, 1968/69, 1969/70, 1973/74, 1974/75
Amateur League Div.2C	(1)	1953/54
Clarence Cup:	(2)	1955/56 and 1969/70
Border Regiment Cup:	(6)	1958/59, 1967/68, 1969/70, 1971/72, 1973/74, 1974/75
Walter Moore Cup:	(1)	1969/70

TRANSFERS C/S'95 TO APRIL '96

Players Signed:
Gary Clifford (Cliftonville c/s'95), Paul Trainor (Ballymoney United c/s'95), Michael Tully (Ballymoney United c/s'95), Harry Kernoghan (Larne Aug.'95), Michael Press (Carrick Rangers Nov.'95), Gavin McCrystal (Ballyclare Comrades Mar.'96).

Players Transferred:
Jonathan Field (Carrick Rangers c/s'95), Frankie Caulfield (Brantwood Mar.'96).

CHIMNEY CORNERS COMPLETE PLAYING RECORD FOR 1995/96

Date:	Comp:	Ven:	Opponents:	Result:	Goalscorers:
Aug 12	ILC 1	H	Ballymena United	0-1 L	-
Aug 19	BD	H	Dundela	0-1 L	-
Aug 22	BD	H	Ballymoney United	7-2 W	Tumilty, McGurnaghan, Kernoghan, Patterson (2), Tully, McAlea
Aug 25	BD	A	Queens University	1-1 D	McAlea
Sep 2	SS 1	H	Shorts Brothers	3-2 W	Kernoghan, Tully, McGurnaghan
Sep 9	IC 1	H	Barn United	5-1 W	McAlea (2), Tumilty, Patterson, Tully
Sep 16	SS 2	H	Queens University	6-1 W	McAlea (2), Clements, Tully, Kernoghan, Mallon
Sep 23	BD	H	Cookstown United	2-1 W	Kernoghan, McAlea
Sep 30	SS 3	A	Ballymena United Res.	2-3 L	Kernoghan, Hartley
Oct 7	IC 2	A	Ballynahinch United	2-3 L	Clifford, (S) O'Kane
Oct 14	BD	H	Dungannon Swifts	1-3 L	(P) Trainor
Oct 21	BD	A	Moyola Park	4-1 W	Tumilty, Tully, (S) O'Kane, Ballentine (og)
Nov 4	BD	H	Harland & Wolff Welders	2-2 D	Kernoghan, Tully
Nov 25	BD	H	Limavady United	2-2 D	Patterson, Tumilty
Dec 2	BD	H	Armagh City	2-0 W	Stitt, Tully
Dec 9	BIC 4	A	Park	2-2 D	(P) Trainor, Kernoghan
Dec 14	BIC 4R	H	Park	2-0 W	Kernoghan, Tully
Jan 6	BD	A	Armagh City	2-2 D	(P) Trainor, Tumilty
Jan 13	BD	A	Ballymoney United	6-0 W	Clifford, Kernoghan, Patterson (2), McCloskey (2)
Jan 20	BIC 5	H	Ballymena United	0-1 L	-
Feb 3	BD	H	Moyola Park	2-2 D	Mallon, McCloskey
Feb 10	BD	A	Brantwood	4-0 W	(P) Trainor (pen), McCloskey, McAlea, Kernoghan
Feb 17	BD	H	Banbridge Town	1-2 L	McAlea
Feb 24	BD	A	Dundela	1-1 D	McCloskey
Mar 2	BD	H	Brantwood	6-0 W	McAlea (2), McCloskey (2), Patterson, Clifford
Mar 9	BD	A	Ballinamallard United	1-0 W	McAlea
Mar 16	SKC 1	A	Moyola Park	2-1 W	Rankin (og), McCloskey
Mar 23	BD	H	Ballinamallard United	2-1 W	Mallon, (P) Trainor
Mar 30	SKC QF	A	Loughgall	0-2 L	-
Apr 6	BD	A	Dungannon Swifts	2-1 W	Tumilty, Patterson
Apr 13	BD	H	R.U.C.	1-0 W	Patterson
Apr 20	BD	A	Cookstown United	2-2 D	Patterson, McCrystal
Apr 23	BD	H	Queens University	5-0 W	McAlea, McGurnaghan, Kernoghan, Clifford, (P) Trainor (pen)
Apr 25	BD	A	Tobermore United	3-1 W	(P) Trainor (2), McAlea
Apr 27	BD	A	Loughgall	3-4 L	(P) Trainor (2,1pen), Kernoghan
Apr 30	BD	H	Tobermore United	2-1 W	Kernoghan (2)
May 2	BD	A	R.U.C.	2-1 W	Kernoghan, (P) Trainor
May 4	BD	H	Loughgall	0-1 L	-
May 7	BD	A	Limavady United	0-1 L	-
May 9	BD	A	Harland & Wolff Welders	4-1 W	Clifford, McCrystal, (P) Trainor, Breslin
May 18	BD	A	Banbridge Town	0-2 L	-

CHIMNEY CORNER GOALSCORERS 1995/96

'B' Division: (70): 11 Paul Trainor (3p); 10 Harry Kernoghan, Eddie McAlea; 9 Eddie Patterson; 7 Mark McCloskey; 5 Paul Tumilty; 4 Gary Clifford, Michael Tully; 2 Gavin McCrystal, Paul McGurnaghan, Patrick Mallon; 1 Tommy Breslin, Sean O'Kane, Laurence Stitt; 1 own goal:

Calor Steel & Sons Cup: (11): 3 Harry Kernoghan; 2 Eddie McAlea, Michael Tully; 1 Aaron Clements, Liam Hartley, Paul McGurnaghan, Patrick Mallon:

McEwans Intermediate Cup: (7): 2 Eddie McAlea; 1 Gary Clifford, Sean O'Kane, Eddie Patterson, Paul Tumilty, Michael Tully:

Bass Irish Cup: (4): 2 Harry Kernoghan; 1 Paul Trainor, Michael Tully:

Wilkinson Sword Irish League Cup: (0): -

Smirnoff 'B' Division Knockout Cup: (0): -

Top Goalscorer for 1995/96: Harry Kernoghan with 15:

COOKSTOWN UNITED

Ground: Millbank Park, Drapersfield, Cookstown. Founded: 1976

Playing Staff for 1995/96
Jackie Canavan, Justin Corr, Conor Devine, Tommy Devlin, Stephen Donnelly, Eamon Eastwood, Jim Eastwood, Gary Fitzpatrick, Derek Hudson, Niall Hunter, Stephen Hunter, Jody Kelly, Danny Lawn, Liam McAllister, Stephen McCombe*, Denis McElhatton, Joe McGuckin, Barry Monaghan, William Montgomery, Darren Mullan, Eugene Mullan, Barton Shannon, Colin Stannex, James Taggart, Jason Talbot.

Denotes player has now left the club.

HONOURS:

Irish League 'B' Division:	Best Position: 6th 1991/92	
NI Intermediate League Cup:	(1)	1978/79
NI Intermediate Challenge Cup:	(1)	1978/79
Mid-Ulster League Div. 4	(1)	1977/78
Div.5	(1)	1976/77
Magee Memorial Trophy	(1)	1977/78
Tyrone Cup:	(1)	1981/82

TRANSFERS C/S '95 TO APRIL '96

Players Signed:
Stephen McCombe (Coleraine Aug.'95):

Players Transferred:
Colin Bell (Ballyclare Comrades c/s'95), Alan Campbell (Ballyclare Comrades Jul.'95), James Irwin (Ballyclare Comrades Jul.'95), Liam McCann (Ballyclare Comrades Aug.'95), Stephen McCombe (Coleraine Oct.'95).

Chairman:
Raymond Shannon
Secretary:
William Jordan
Joint Managers:
Tommy Devlin
Club Colours:
Royal Blue shirts, White shorts, White socks
Entered 'B':
1991/92

THE NORTHERN IRELAND football YEARBOOK

COOKSTOWN UNITEDS COMPLETE PLAYING RECORD FOR 1994/95

Date:	Comp:	Ven:	Opponents:	Result:		Goalscorers:
Aug 12	ILC 1	A	Carrick Rangers	9-1	L	-
Aug 15	BD	A	Dungannon Swifts	0-7	L	-
Aug 19	BD	H	Armagh City	1-2	L	McElhatton
Aug 22	BD	A	Moyola Park	0-3	L	-
Aug 26	BD	H	Limavady United	0-6	L	-
Sep 2	BRC 1	A	Richhill	6-4	W	?
Sep 9	IC 1	A	Bridgend United	7-2	W	McElhatton (2), Shannon, Hudson, Kelly (2), (D) Mullan
Sep 16	BRC 2	H	Lurgan Celtic Bhoys	5-5	L	Kelly, Monaghan, (S) Hunter, ?
			(aet Cookstown United lost 1-3 on pens)			
Sep 23	BD	A	Chimney Corner	1-2	L	McElhatton
Sep 30	BD	H	Ballinamallard United	0-4	L	-
Oct 14	BD	H	Brantwood	1-0	W	Kelly
Oct 21	BD	A	Ballymoney United	0-4	L	-
Oct 28	BD	H	Ballymoney United	1-1	D	Devine
Nov 4	BD	A	R.U.C.	0-2	L	-
Nov 11	IC 3	A	Limavady United	1-8	L	Shannon
Nov 18	BD	H	Banbridge Town	0-1	L	-
Nov 25	BD	A	Ballinamallard United	3-2	W	McElhatton, Montgomery (2)
Dec 2	BD	H	Harland & Wolff Welders	0-5	L	-
Dec 9	BIC 4	A	Crewe United	4-2	W	Devine (3,1pen), Montgomery
Jan 6	BD	A	Dundela	0-7	L	-
Jan 13	BD	H	Dungannon Swifts	0-4	L	-
Jan 20	BIC 5	A	Ards	0-10	L	-
Jan 27	BD	A	Loughgall	0-1	L	-
Feb 3	BD	H	Dundela	0-1	L	-
Feb 10	BD	A	Queens University	2-2	D	McElhatton, ?
Feb 17	BD	H	Moyola Park	3-1	W	McElhatton, Canavan, ?
Feb 24	BD	A	Tobermore United	3-1	W	Lawn, McElhatton, Canavan
Mar 2	BD	H	Loughgall	1-4	L	Montgomery
Mar 9	MUC 4	H	Laurelvale	2-3	L	Lawn, Canavan
Mar 16	SKC 1	A	R.U.C.	0-2	L	-
Mar 23	BD	H	Tobermore United	2-1	W	(A) Moore (og), Montgomery
Mar 30	BD	H	Queens University	2-2	D	?
Apr 6	BD	A	Brantwood	1-2	L	?
Apr 13	BD	A	Limavady United	0-3	L	-
Apr 16	BD	H	R.U.C	0-0	D	-
Apr 20	BD	H	Chimney Corner	2-2	D	Canavan, ?
Apr 27	BD	A	Harland & Wolff Welders	0-1	L	-
Apr 30	BD	A	Banbridge Town	0-3	L	-

COOKSTOWN UNITED GOALSCORERS FOR 1995/96

'B' Division: (24): 6 Denis McElhatton; 5 William Montgomery; 3 Jackie Canavan; 1 Conor Devine, Jody Kelly, Danny Lawn; 1 own goal (6 goalscorers missing):

Bob Radcliffe Cup: (11): 1 Stephen Hunter, Jody Kelly, Barry Monaghan (8 goalscorers missing):

McEwans Intermediate Cup: (8): 2 Jody Kelly, Denis McElhatton, Barton Shannon; 1 Derek Hudson, Darren Mullan:

Bass Irish Cup: (4): 3 Conor Devine (1 pen); 1 William Montgomery:

Wilkinson Sword Irish League Cup: (0): -

McEwans Mid Ulster Cup: (2): 1 Jackie Canavan, Danny Lawn:

Smirnoff 'B' Division Knockout Cup: (0) -

Top Goalscorer for 1995/96: Denis McElhatton with 8:

NB: Goalscorers in certain matches have not been located, therefore the above goalscoring records are not complete.

DUNDELA

Ground: Wilgar Park, Strandtown, Belfast Founded: 1895

Playing Staff for 1995/96

Billy Caskey, Ian Coulter, Stephen Doey, Stephen Fettis, Laurence Fyfe, Stephen Hanvey, Alan Harrison, Allen Huxley, Tony Jones, Brian Kennedy, Mark Lennox, Brian McCarroll, Gary McCormick, Noel McKee, Tony Miskelly, Thomas Parker, Criag Robson, Stephen Shanks, Johnny Simpson, Mark Snodden, Simon Spence, Ronnie Stirling, Sammy Whiteside.

NB: No photograph available for 1995/96.

Chairman:
George McMaster
Secretary:
George Sterling
Manager:
Mervyn Bell
Club Colours:
Green shirts, White shorts, Green socks
Entered 'B'
1956/57

HONOURS:

Irish League 'B' Division: Champions:	(8)	1967/68, 1981/82, 1985/86, 1987/88, 1989/90, 1990/91, 1991/92, 1993/94.
Irish Cup:	(1)	1954/55
IFA Intermediate Cup:	(7)	1946/47, 1954/55, 1965/66, 1974/75, 1983/84, 1988/89, 1992/93
Steel & Sons Cup:	(7)	1945/46, 1963/64, 1980/81, 1982/83, 1987/88, 1988/89, 1990/91
'B' Division Knockout Cup:	(4)	1987/88, 1990/91, 1991/92, 1994/95
George Wilson Cup:	(4)	1964/65, 1967/68, 1971/72, 1974/75
Louis Moore Cup:	(3)	1960/61, 1964/65, 1966/67

TRANSFERS C/S'95 TO APRIL '96

Players Signed:

Alan Harrison (Unattached c/s'95), Stephen Doey (Ballymena United Jul.'95), Gary McCormick (Ballyclare Comrades Nov.'95), Tony Jones (East Belfast Jan.'96), Brian Kennedy (Dungannon Swifts Jan.'96), Allen Huxley (Bangor Mar.'96).

Players Transferred:

Gary Crowe (Harland & Wolff Welders Jun.'95), David Moore (Ballymena United Jul.'95).

DUNDELA

DUNDELAS COMPLETE PLAYING RECORD FOR 1995/96

Date:	Comp:	Ven:	Opponents:	Result:	Goalscorers:
Aug 12	ILC 1	H	Portadown	0-1 L	-
Aug 15	BD	H	R.U.C.	4-2	W Hanvey, Coulter, Goddard, Doey
Aug 19	BD	A	Chimney Corner	1-0 W	Hanvey
Aug 22	BD	H	Queens University	8-0 W	Hanvey (4), Coulter (2), Snodden, Caskey
Sep 2	SS1	H	Connor	3-1 W	Coulter, Brown (og), Hanvey
Sep 9	IC 1	H	Dromore Amateurs	6-0 W	Coulter (2), McCarroll, Snodden (2), Fettis
Sep 16	SS 2	H	U.U.J.	6-0 W	Fyfe, Fettis (2), Harrison (pen), 1 og
Sep 23	BD	A	Brantwood	1-1 D	Hanna (og)
Sep 30	SS 3	H	Comber Recreation	2-1 W	aet McKee, Hanvey
Oct 7	IC 2	A	F.C. Enkalon	3-2 W	Fettis, Coulter, Spence
Oct 14	BD	A	Armagh City	8-4 W	Hanvey (5,1pen), Lennox, Doey, Coulter
Oct 21	BD	H	Limavady United	4-1 W	Caskey, Coulter (2), Hanvey
Oct 28	SS QF	A	R.U.C.	3-1 W	McCarroll, Hanvey, Coulter
Nov 4	BD	A	Ballymoney United	3-0 W	Harrison, Hanvey (2)
Nov 7	SS SF	N	Dromara Village	0-1 L	aet -
Nov 11	IC 3	A	R.U.C.	2-3 L	aet Doey (2)
Nov 18	BD	H	Ballinamallard United	5-0 W	Caskey, Coulter, Hanvey (2), Doey
Nov 21	CAS 1	A	Glenavon	0-5 L	-
Nov 25	BD	A	Banbridge Town	1-1 D	McCormick
Dec 2	BD	H	Loughgall	1-2 L	Hanvey
Dec 9	BIC 4	H	Harland & Wolff W	0-0 D	-
Dec 13	BIC 4 Rep.	H	Harland & Wolff W	3-0 W	Hanvey (3)
Dec 16	BD	H	Ballymoney United	4-0 W	Hanvey (2,1pen), Fettis, Doey
Jan 6	BD	H	Cookstown United	7-0 W	Snodden, Hanvey, Caskey (2), Doey (2), Coulter
Jan 13	BD	A	Moyola Park	1-0 W	Snodden
Jan 20	BIC 5	A	Armagh City	1-2 L	Coulter
Jan 27	BD	H	Tobermore United	2-1 W	Whiteside, Snodden
Feb 3	BD	A	Cookstown United	1-0 W	Doey
Feb 10	BD	H	Dungannon Swifts	4-5 L	McNamee (og), Hanvey, Doey (2)
Feb 17	BD	A	Limavady United	1-4 L	Hanvey
Feb 24	BD	H	Chimney Corner	1-1 D	Mallon (og)
Mar 2	BD	A	Ballinamallard United	2-1 W	Hanvey, Coulter
Mar 9	BD	A	Tobermore United	0-1 L	-
Mar 16	SKC 1	A	Brantwood	3-1 W	Hanvey (2), Doey
Mar 23	BD	H	Brantwood	1-0 W	Doey
Mar 30	SKC QF	H	Ballymoney United	1-3 L	Hanvey
Apr 6	BD	A	R.U.C.	0-1 L	-
Apr 13	BD	H	Banbridge Town	1-1 D	Coulter
Apr 20	BD	A	Queens University	5-0 W	Coulter, Doey (2), Hanvey, Jones
Apr 23	BD	H	Harland & Wolff W	1-1 D	Hanvey
Apr 27	BD	H	Moyola Park	7-2 W	Coulter, Snodden (3), Hanvey (2), Doey
May 4	BD	A	Dungannon Swifts	2-1 W	Coulter, Hanvey
May 7	BD	H	Armagh City	2-1 W	Snodden, Coulter
May 11	BD	A	Loughgall	1-2 L	Snodden
May 14	BD	A	Harland & Wolff W	0-2 L	-

DUNDELA GOALSCORERS FOR 1995/96

'B' Division: (79): 28 Stephen Hanvey (1p); 14 Ian Coulter; 13 Stephen Doey; 9 Mark Snodden; 5 Billy Caskey; 1 Stephen Fettis, Michael Goddard, Alan Harrison, Tony Jones, Mark Lennox, Gary McCormick, Sammy Whiteside:
3 own goals:

Calor Steel & Sons Cup: (14): 3 Stephen Fettis, Stephen Hanvey; 2 Ian Coulter; 1 Laurence Fyfe, Alan Harrison (pen), Brian McCarroll, Noel McKee; 2 own goals:

McEwans Intermediate Cup: (11): 3 Ian Coulter; 2 Stephen Doey, Stephen Fettis, Mark Snodden; 1 Brian McCarroll, Simon Spence:

Bass Irish Cup: (4): 3 Stephen Hanvey; 1 Ian Coulter:

Wilkinson Sword Irish League Cup: (0) -

Calor Co.Antrim Shield: (0) -

Smirnoff 'B' Division Knockout Cup: (4): 3 Stephen Hanvey; 1 Stephen Doey:

Top Goalscorer for 1995/96: Stephen Hanvey with 37 (2 pen)

DUNGANNON SWIFTS

Ground: Stangmore Park, Dungannon   Founded: 1949

Playing Staff for 1995/96
Derek Anderson, Richard Averill, Tony Clarke, Damien Coll, Michael Crowe, Alex Denver, John Gregg, Alan Hammond, Mark Jennings, Brian Kennedy*, Rodney McAree*, Dermot McCaul, Terry McCrory, Chris McKerr, Gary McKinstry, Damien McNamee, Gary Mackey, Jonathaon Magee, Johnny Montgomery, Michael O'Hagen, Damien Robinson, Jeremy Robinson, Jim Robinson, Alan Shaw, James Slater, Sammy Smyth, Stephen Vance.
* Denotes player has now left the club.

HONOURS:

Irish League 'B' Division: Best Position:		Runners-Up 1980/81 1994/95, 1995/96
IFA Intermediate Cup:	(2)	1977/78 and 1991/92
Mid-Ulster Cup:	(3)	1970/71, 1975/76, 1987/88
'B' Division Knockout Cup:	(1)	1993/94
George Wilson Cup:	(1)	1973/74
Louis Moore Cup:	(1)	1975/76
Bob Radcliffe Cup:	(8)	1981/82, 1985/86, 1986/87, 1989/90, 1992/93, 1993/94, 1994/95, 1995/96
Mid-Ulster League:	(2)	1970/71 and 1971/72
Mid-Ulster Shield:	(1)	1970/71
Alexander Cup:	(4)	1967/68, 1969/70, 1970/71, 1971/72

Chairman:
Gordon Lee
Secretary:
David Gallagher
Manager:
Colin Malone
Asst. Manager
Damien Robinson
Club Colours:
Royal Blue shirts, White shorts, Royal Blue Socks
Entered 'B':
1971/72

TRANSFERS C/S'95 TO APRIL '96

Players Signed:
Paul Kee (Institute c/s'95), Chris McKerr (Glenavon c/s'95), Michael O'Hagen (Moyola Park c/s'95), Tony Clarke (Bangor Sep.'95), Rodney McAree (Bristol City Nov.'95), Damien McNamee (Larne Nov.'95), Gary McKinstry (Bangor Dec.'95), Jonathon Magee (Distillery Dec.'95), Dermot McCaul (Omagh Town Jan.'96).

Players Transferred:
Conor Lavery (Armagh City c/s'95), Sammy McFadden (R.U.C. c/s'95), Paul Kee (Institute Aug.'95), Gary McKinstry (Bangor Sep.'95), David Mallon (Harland & Wolff Welders Sep.'95), Brian Kennedy (Dundela Jan.'96), Rodney McAree (Fulham (Eng) Jan.'96), Jonathon Magee (Released Mar.'96).

Date:	Comp:	Ven:	Opponents:	Result:	Goalscorers:
Aug 12	ILC 1	H	Bangor	1-2 L	O'Hagen
Aug 15	BD	H	Cookstown United	7-0 W	McKinstry (2), O'Hagen (3), Mullan (og), Averill
Aug 19	BD	A	Tobermore United	6-0 W	McKinstry (4,1pen), Jim.Robinson, O'Hagen
Aug 22	BD	H	Ballinamallard United	1-1 D	McKinstry
Sep 2	BRC 1	A	Portadown Res.	3-1 W	McKinstry, O'Hagen, Mackey
Sep 9	BD	H	Moyola Park	4-0 W	McKinstry (3,1pen), McCrory
Sep 16	BRC	2	Loughgall	1-1 D(aet)	Smyth won 4-3 on pens
Sep 30	BD	A	Armagh City	5-1 W	(S) Montgomery (og), Denver, Jennings (2), Mackey
Oct 7	BD	H	Banbridge Town	1-3 L	O'Hagen
Oct 14	BD	A	Chimney Corner	3-1 W	Smyth, Jennings, Mackey
Oct 21	BD	H	R.U.C.	1-1 D	O'Hagen
Oct 28	BRC QF	A	Laurelvale	3-0 W	Averill, Gregg (2)
Nov 4	BD	A	Brantwood	5-0 W	Jennings (3), Averill, Gregg
Nov 11	BD	H	Ballymoney United	5-0 W	McCrory (2), Jennings, Denver, (D) Robinson
Nov 18	BD	A	Harland & Wolff Welders	3-1 W	Jennings, Crowe, O'Hagen
Nov 25	BD	H	Tobermore United	2-1 W	McAree, Smyth
Dec 9	BIC 4	H	Moyola Park	2-0 W	O'Hagen (2)
Dec 16	BRC SF	N	Banbridge Town	5-2 W	Magee, McAree, McKinstry, O'Hagen, Crowe
Jan 6	BD	H	Brantwood	4-2 W	McKinstry, Magee (2), Hanna (og)
Jan 13	BD	A	Cookstown United	4-0 W	O'Hagen, Magee, McKinstry, Jer.Robinson
Jan 20	BIC 5	H	Omagh Town	2-4 L	McNamee, O'Hagen
Feb 3	BD	H	Loughgall	1-0 W	Smyth (pen)
Feb 10	BD	A	Dundela	5-4 W	Smyth, Magee (2), McNamee, McKinstry
Feb 17	BD	H	Armagh City	1-1 D	McNamee
Feb 24	BD	A	Ballymoney United	3-2 W	Smyth (pen), Gregg, O'Hagen
Mar 2	BD	A	Limavady United	1-0 W	Magee
Mar 9	MUC 4	H	Lurgan Celtic Bhoys	3-3 W	McKinstry (2), Magee
			(aet Dungannon Swifts won 5-3 on pens)		
Mar 16	SKC 1	H	Harland & Wolff Welders	2-0 W	Jer.Robinson, McKinstry
Mar 19	BD	H	Queens University	3-1 W	McKerr, McKinstry (2)
Mar 23	BD	A	Harland & Wolff Welers	1-0 W	Smyth
Mar 30	SKC QF	A	Banbridge Town	1-5 L	Smyth (pen)
Apr 1	MUC QF	H	Laurelvale	5-0 W	Jer.Robinson, McKinstry (2), McNamee, O'Hagen
Apr 6	BD	H	Chimney Corner	1-2 L	Jer.Robinson
Apr 9	BRC F	N	Lurgan Celtic Bhoys	3-1 W	Smyth (2), McKinstry
Apr 13	BD	A	Queens University	6-0 W	Montgomery, (D) Robinson (2), Smyth (2,1pen), Jer.Robinson
Apr 25	MUC SF	H	Distillery	2-1 W	Jer.Robinson, Smyth (pen)
Apr 27	BD	H	Limavady United	0-0 D	-
Apr 30	MUC F	N	Bangor	1-3 L	Smyth
May 4	BD	H	Dundela	1-2 L	McKinstry
May 7	BD	A	Loughgall	0-1 L	-
May 9	BD	A	Moyola Park	5-1 W	O'Hagen, Averill, McKinstry, Morrow (og), Vance (pen)
May 11	BD	A	Ballinamallard United	2-2 D	Smyth (pen), Averill
May 14	BD	A	R.U.C.	5-2 W	Smyth, Jer.Robinson, O'Hagen, Jennings, McKinstry
May 16	BD	A	Banbridge Town	5-3 W	McKinstry, Shaw, O'Hagen, Smyth (2)

DUNGANNON SWIFTS GOALSCORERS FOR 1995/96

'B' Division: (91): 19 Gary McKinstry (2p); 12 Michael O'Hagen, Sammy Smyth (4p); 9 Mark Jennings; 6 Jonathon Magee; 4 Richard Averill, Jeremy Robinson; 3 Terry McCrory, Damien Robinson; 2 Alex Denver, John Gregg, Damien McNamee, Gary Mackey; 1 Michael Crowe, Rodney McAree, Chris McKerr, Johnny Montgomery, Jim Robinson, Alan Shaw, Stephen Vance (pen); 4 own goals: **Bob Radcliffe Cup:** (15): 3 Gary McKinstry, Sammy Smyth; 2 John Gregg, Michael O'Hagen; 1 Richard Averill, Michael Crowe, Rodney McAree, Gary Mackey, Johnathon Magee: **Bass Irish Cup:** (4): 3 Michael O'Hagen; 1 Damien McNamee: **Wilkinson Sword Irish League Cup:** (1) Michael O'Hagen: **McEwans Mid-Ulster Cup:** (11): 4 Gary McKinstry, 2 Jeremy Robinson, Sammy Smyth (1p): **Smirnoff 'B' Division Knockout Cup:** (3): 1 Gary McKinstry, Jeremy Robinson, Sammy Smyth (pen): **Top Goalscorer for 1995/96:** Gary McKinstry with 27 (2 pen):

H A R L A N D & W O L F F W E L D E R S

Ground: Tillysburn Park, Holywood Road, Belfast BT4. Founded: 1965

Playing Staff for 1994/95
Darren Black, Gary Blackledge, Alan Blackwood, Robert Blair, Andy Clarke, Gary Crowe, Ian Cummings, Gary Cunningham, Edward Dinsmore, Ian Doey, Stuart Doyle, Mark Dunwoody, Paul English, Colin Gallagher, Colin Johnston, Bobby Kincaid, Darren Lockhart, Ryan McCartney, David McCrea, Ian McDonald, David Mallon, Dennis Moore, Billy Neill, David Thompson, Gary Trueick, Paul Wilson, Colin Woods.

Chairman:
Brian Lilley (Sen)
Secretary:
Fred Magee
Manager:
Jim Wilson
Club Colours:
Amber shirts, Black shorts, Amber socks
Entered 'B':
1983/84

HONOURS:

Irish League 'B' Division:	Best Position:	3rd 1983/84 and 1986/87
Amateur League Division 1:	(1)	1978/79
Clarence Cup:	(1)	1968/69

TRANSFERS C/S'95 TO APRIL '96

Players Signed:
Robert Blair (Ards Rangers c/s'95), David McCrea (Moyola Park c/s'95) Gary Crowe (Dundela Jun.'95), Mark Dunwoody (East Belfast Jul.'95), Colin Gallagher (East Belfast Aug.'95), Gary Cunningham (GEC Larne Sep.'95), David Mallon (Dungannon Swifts Sep.'95), Colin Woods (Carrick Rangers Feb.'95).

Players Transferred:
Stephen Sloan (Brantwood c/s'95), Gary Stevenson (Abbey Villa Jul.'95)

THE NORTHERN IRELAND
football
Y E A R B O O K

HARLAND & WOLFF WELDERS COMPLETE PLAYING RECORD FOR 1995/96

Date:	Comp:	Ven:	Opponents:	Result:	Goalscorers:
Aug 12	ILC 1	A	Distillery	1-0 W	Gallagher (pen)
Aug 15	ILC 2	A	Crusaders	0-1 L	-
Aug 19	BD	H	Loughgall	3-1 W	Gallagher (pen), Wilson, Johnston
Aug 22	BD	A	Brantwood	1-3 L	Wilson
Aug 25	BD	A	Banbridge Town	1-1 D	Doyle
Sep 2	SS 1	H	Wellington Recreation	8-2 W	Wilson (3), Lockhart, Dunwoody, Doyle (2), Johnston
Sep 9	BD	H	Banbridge Town	2-0 W	Wilson, Lockhart
Sep 16	SS 2	H	Malachians	1-0 W	Lewsley (og)
Sep 23	BIC 1	H	Civil Service	5-2 W	Blackledge (3), Gallagher (pen), McCrea
Sep 30	SS 3	H	First Bangor Old Boys	1-0 W	McCrea
Oct 7	IC 2	H	Killyleagh Youth Club	4-3 Waet	Crowe, Wilson (2), Kincaid
Oct 14	BIC 2	H	Hanover	5-2 W	Wilson (3), Dunwoody, McCrea
Oct 21	BD	H	Armagh City	2-1 W	Wilson, Lockhart
Oct 28	SS QF	A	Dromara Village	1-2 L	Dunwoody
Nov 4	BD	A	Chimney Corner	2-2 D	Wilson (2)
Nov 11	IC 3	H	Glentoran II	1-1 W	McCrea
			(aet Harland & Wolff Welders won 5-4 on pens)		
Nov 18	BD	H	Dungannon Swifts	1-3 L	Blackledge
Nov 25	BIC 3	A	Annagh United	4-1 W	Lockhart (2), Blackledge, og
Dec 2	BD	A	Cookstown United	5-0 W	Dunwoody, McCrea, Lockhart, Crowe, Wilson
Dec 9	BIC 4	A	Dundela	0-0 D	-
Dec 13	BIC 4R	A	Dundela	0-3 L	-
Dec 16	IC 4	H	Portstewart	2-1 W	Black (2)
Jan 6	BD	A	Ballinamallard United	3-2 W	Lockhart, Kincaid (pen), Black
Jan 13	BD	A	Limavady United	1-2 L	Wilson
Jan 20	BD	A	Loughgall	1-2 L	Wilson
Jan 27	BD	H	Queens University	4-0 W	Black (3,1pen), Moore (pen)
Feb 3	IC QF	H	Glenavon Reserves	5-1 W	Blackledge (2), Black, Dunwoody
Feb 10	BD	A	Ballymoney United	1-1 D	Black
Feb 17	BD	H	Tobermore United	2-3 L	Black, Moore
Feb 24	BD	A	Moyola Park	6-2 W	Wilson (4,1pen), Blackledge, Woods
Mar 2	BD	H	Ballymoney United	2-0 W	Crowe, Lockhart
Mar 9	BD	H	R.U.C	2-0 W	Lockhart, Dunwoody
Mar 16	SKC 1	A	Dungannon Swifts	0-2 L	-
Mar 21	IC SF	N	R.U.C	5-2 W	Lockhart (2), Crowe, Dunwoody, Blackledge
Mar 23	BD	A	Dungannon Swifts	0-1 L	-
Mar 30	BD	H	Moyola Park	4-0 W	Black, Wilson, Lockhart (pen), Blackledge
Apr 6	BD	A	Armagh City	1-1 D	Neill
Apr 10	BD	A	Queens University	4-1 W	Blackledge (2), Lockhart, Dunwoody
Apr 13	BD	H	Ballinamallard United	4-1 W	Lockhart (2,1pen), Blackledge, Black
Apr 16	BD	H	Brantwood	3-0 W	Lockhart, Wilson, Blackledge
Apr 20	BD	A	Tobermore United	2-2 D	Lockhart, Dunwoody
Apr 23	BD	A	Dundela	1-1 D	Dunwoody
Apr 27	BD	H	Cookstown United	1-0 W	Cummings
May 2	IC F	N	Limavady United	2-4 L	Lockhart (2,1pen)
May 9	BD	H	Chimney Corner	1-4 L	Lockhart
May 14	BD	H	Dundela	2-0 W	Lockhart, Blackledge
May 18	BD	H	Limavady United	6-3 W	Dinsmore (3), Black, Wilson, Dunwoody
May 21	BD	A	R.U.C	3-2 W	Crowe (2), Dunwoody

HARLAND & WOLFF WELDERS GOALSCORERS FOR 1995/96

'B' Division: (71): 16 Paul Wilson (1p); 14 Darren Lockhart (2p); 9 Darren Black (1p); 8 Gary Blackledge; 7 Mark Dunwoody; 4 Gary Crowe; 3 Edward Dinsmore; 2 Dennis Moore (1p); 1 Neill Cummings, Stuart Doyle, Colin Gallagher (p), Colin Johnston, Bobby Kincaid, David McCrea, Billy Neill, Colin Woods:
Calor Steel & Sons Cup: (11): 3 Paul Wilson; 2 Stuart Doyle, Mark Dunwoody; 1 Colin Johnston, Darren Lockhart, David McCrea; 1 own goal:McEwans Intermediate Cup: (19): 4 Darren Lockhart (1p); 3 Darren Black, Gary Blackledge, Gary Crowe; 2 Mark Dunwoody, Paul Wilson; 1 Bobby Kincaid, David McCrea:
Bass Irish Cup: (14): 4 Gary Blackledge; 3 Paul Wilson; 2 Darren Lockhart, David McCrea; 1 Mark Dunwoody, Colin Gallagher (p); 1 own goal:Wilkinson Sword Irish League Cup: (1): Colin Gallagher (p)
Smirnoff 'B' Division Knockout Cup: (0) -Top Goalscorer for 1995/96: Paul Wilson with 24 (1 pen):

LIMAVADY UNITED

Ground: The Showgrounds, Rathmore Road, Limavady. Founded: 1876

Limavady United 1995/96

Back Row L to R: Brian Anderson, Robert Crown, Stephen Morrow, John Shiels, Martin Mullan, Stewart McCallum, Ronnie McDowell, Johnny Law, Thomas White, Jackie Humphreys, Michael Foley .*Front Row L to R*: Colin Nutt, Francis Harrison, David King, Damian Mullan, Peter Moran, Neil Painter, Bobby Davies.

(Photo courtesy of Liam Kelly)

Playing Staff for 1995/96
Brian Anderson, Michael Burns, Gabriel Caldwell, Richard Crown, Robert Crown, Robert Davies, Cahal Deery*, Francis Harrison, David King, John Law, Gary Love, Stewart McCallum, Andy McCann*, Brian McConway, Chris McCreadie, Ronnie McDowell, Adrain McLaughlin, Chris Moore, Peter Moran, Kevin Morrow*, Stephen Morrow, Damien Mullan, Martin Mullan, Neil Mullan, Michael Neill, Colin Nutt, Michael O'Donovan*, Neil Painter, John Shiels, Trevor Thompson, Thomas White.
*Denotes player has now left the club.

HONOURS

Irish League 'B' Division: Champions:	(2)	1983/84 and 1992/93
Irish Cup:	(2)	1885/86 and 1886/87
IFA Intermediate Cup:	(2)	1973/74 and 1995/96
'B'Division Knockout Cup:	(2)	1992/93 and 1995/96
North West Senior Challenge Cup:	(2)	1992/93 and 1993/94
North West Intermediate Cup:	(10)	1886/87, 1887/88, 1888/89, 1889/90, 1892/93, 1897/98, 1898/99, 1899/00, 1993/94, 1994/95
North West City Cup:	(1)	1963/64
North West Junior Cup:	(1)	1963/64
Irish Junior Cup:	(1)	1963/64
George Wilson Cup:	(1)	1975/76

TRANSFERS C/S'95 TO APRIL '96

Players Signed:
Cahal Deery (Omagh Town c/s'95), Chris McCreadie (Cliftonville c/s'95), Peter Moran (Omagh Town Oct.'95).

Players Transferred:
Tony O'Carroll (Ballymoney United c/s'95), Andy McCann (Armagh City Sep.'95), Cahal Deery (Institute Oct.'95), Michael O'Donovan (Ballymoney United (Oct.'95), Kevin Morrow (Moyola Park Feb.'96).

Chairman:
William Dunn
Secretary:
Robert Jenkins
Manager:
Jimmy Calvin
Club Colours:
Royal Blue shorts, White shorts, Blue/White socks
Entered 'B':
1972/73

THE NORTHERN IRELAND **football** Y E A R B O O K

LIMAVADY UNITED

LIMAVADY UNITEDS COMPLETE PLAYING RECORD FOR 1995/96

Date:	Comp:	Ven:	Opponents:	Result:		Goalscorers:
Aug 12	ILC 1	A	Cliftonville	0-5	L	-
Aug 15	BD	H	Ballymoney United	4-0	W	McCallum (2), Harrison, (M) Mullan
Aug 19	BD	H	R.U.C.	1-0	W	Painter
Aug 22	BD	H	Tobermore United	4-0	W	Harrison (2), (M) Mullan, McLaughlin
Aug 26	BD	A	Cookstown United	6-0	W	Neill (4), Harrison (2,1pen)
Sep 2	NWC 1	H	Magilligan	4-1	W	(M) Mullan, Harrison, McCallum, og
Sep 9	IC 1	H	Laurelvale	4-2	W	Harrison, Painter, King, McCallum (pen)
Sep 16	BD	A	Tobermore United	5-0	W	(M) Mullan (2), Harrison, King, McCallum
Sep 23	BD	A	Ballinamallard United	2-2	D	Harrison (pen), Painter
Sep 30	NWC 2	H	Moyola Park	2-3	L	Harrison, Law
Oct 7	IC 2	A	Ballymena United Res.	2-1	W	Painter, King
Oct 14	BD	H	Banbridge Town	1-4	L	Neill
Oct 21	BD	A	Dundela	1-4	L	Harrison (pen)
Oct 28	BD	H	Brantwood	4-1	W	Neill (3), White
Nov 4	BD	A	Queens University	5-0	W	Moran (3), Harrison, Neill
Nov 11	IC 3	H	Cookstown United	8-1	W	Harrison, Moran (2), Neill (3), McCallum, (M) Mullan
Nov 18	BD	A	Armagh City	3-2	W	White, McCreadie, Moran
Nov 25	BD	A	Chimney Corner	2-2	D	Harrison (2,1pen)
Dec 2	BD	H	Ballinamallard United	1-1	D	Neill
Dec 9	BIC 4	H	Ards Rangers	1-1	D	Moran
Dec 13	BIC 4R	H	Ards Rangers	2-1	W	Neill, Law
Dec 16	IC 4	H	Loughgall	1-0	W	Neill
Jan 6	BD	H	Queens University	3-1	W	Moran, King, Law
Jan 13	BD	H	Harland & Wolff Welders	2-1	W	Neill, Law
Jan 20	BIC 5	A	Glentoran	1-4	L	Moran
Jan 27	BD	H	Armagh City	3-0	W	Neill, Moran (2)
Feb 3	IC QF	A	Islandmagee	4-0	W	Neill, Law, Nutt, Davies
Feb 10	BD	A	Banbridge Town	2-0	W	Moran, White
Feb 17	BD	H	Dundela	4-1	W	Moran (3), White
Feb 24	BD	H	Loughgall	0-3	L	-
Mar 2	BD	H	Dungannon Swifts	0-1	L	-
Mar 9	BD	A	Brantwood	3-3	D	Moran (2), Neill
Mar 14	IC SF	N	Crusaders Reserves	2-0	Waet	Painter, Moran
Mar 16	SKC 1	H	Tobermore United	5-2	W	Painter (3), Moran (2)
Mar 23	BD	H	Moyola Park	3-0	W	Moran, Kelly (og), Law
Mar 30	SKC QF	H	R.U.C.	1-1	Waet	Harrison (pen) (won 6-5 on pens)
Apr 6	BD	A	Loughgall	0-0	D	-
Apr 13	BD	H	Cookstown United	3-0	W	(M) Mullan, Neill (2)
Apr 16	SKC SF,1L	A	Loughgall	1-1	D	Harrison (pen)
Apr 20	BD	A	Moyola Park	1-1	D	Neill
Apr 23	SKC SF,2L	H	Loughgall	2-2	D	Painter, og
			(aet aggregate 3-3; Limavady United won 7-6 on pens)			
Apr 27	BD	A	Dungannon Swifts	0-0	D	-
Apr 29	BD	A	Ballymoney United	2-4	L	Richard Crown, Moore
May 2	IC F	N	Harland & Wolff Welders	4-2	W	Harrison (2), Painter, White
May 7	BD	H	Chimney Corner	1-0	W	Moran
May 10	BD	H	R.U.C.	2-1	W	Moran, Harrison
May 18	BD	A	Harland & Wolff Welders	3-6	L	Moran (2), King
May 25	SKC F	N	Banbridge Town	3-2	W	Painter, Harrison (pen), White

LIMAVADY UNITED GOALSCORERS FOR 1995/96

'B' Division: (71): 18 Peter Moran; 16 Michael Neill; 12 Francis Harrison (4p); 5 Martin Mullan; 4 Thomas White; 3 David King, John Law, Stewart McCallum; 2 Neill Painter; 1 Richard Crown, Chris McCreadie, Adrian McLaughlin, Chris Moore; 1 own goal:**North West Intermediate Cup:** (6): 2 Francis Harrison; 1 John Law, Stewart McCallum, Martin Mullan; 1 own goal:**McEwans Intermediate Cup:** (25): 5 Michael Neill; 4 Francis Harrison, Neill Painter; 3 Peter Moran; 2 David King, Stewart McCallum (1p); 1 Robert Davies, John Law, Martin Mullan, Colin Nutt, Thomas White:**Bass Irish Cup:** (4): 2 Peter Moran; 1 John Law, Michael Neill:
Wilkinson Sword Irish League Cup: (0): -**Smirnoff 'B' Division Knockout Cup:** (12): 5 Neill Painter; 3 Francis Harrison (3p); 2 Peter Moran; 1 Thomas White; 1 own goal:
Top Goalscorer for 1995/96: Peter Moran with 25:

LOUGHGALL

Ground: Lakeview Park, Loughgall. Founded: 1967.

Playing Staff for 1995/96
Jason Adams, Steven Barnes, Alan Blake, Darren Bruce, Geoff Calvin, Andrew Coulter, Robert Craig, Gary Duke, Des Edgar, James Gardiner, Peter Greer, David Gregge, Nicky Griffin, Keith Halliday, Ian Hamilton, Brian Hanley, Gary Henderson, Trevor Huddleston, John Johnston, Thomas Leeman, Dean McCullough, Gary McCullough, John Montgomery, Randal Morwood, Gary Murray, Jason Murtagh, Stephen Williamsons.

Chairman:
Raymond Nesbitt
Secretary:
Noel McClure
Manager:
Alfie Wylie
Club Colours:
Royal Blue shirts, shorts and socks
Entered 'B':
1991/92

HONOURS:

Irish League 'B' Division Champions:	(2)	1994/95
Bob Radcliffe Cup:	(1)	1979/80
Mid-Ulster League Div. 1	(5)	1973/74, 1976/77, 1977/78, 1978/79, 1979/80
Premier League:	(1)	1988/89
Premier Cup:	(2)	1988/89 and 1989/90
Bass Bowl:	(1)	1990/91
Alan Wilson Memorial Trophy:	(1)	1982/83
Foster Cup:	(1)	1973/74

TRANSFERS C/S'95 TO MAY '96

Players Signed:
Robert Craig (Crusaders c/s'95), Dean McCullough (Glenavon c/s'95),Des Edgar (Newry Town Jul.'95), James Gardiner (Crusaders Oct.'95), Jason Murtagh (Bangor Jan.'96), John Johnston (Bangor (loan) Feb.'96), Gary Murray (Larne Apr.'96), John Johnston (Bangor May'96).

Players Transferred:
Paul Matchett (Hanover c/s'95), Stephen Montgomery (Armagh City c/s'95), Darren Murphy (Glenavon c/s'95), John Johnston (Bangor (loan rtn) May '96).

LOUGHGALLS COMPLETE PLAYING RECORD FOR 1995/96

Date:	Comp:	Ven:	Opponents:	Result:	Goalscorers:
Aug 12	ILC 1	H	Omagh Town	3-4 L aet	Henderson, Craig (2)
Aug 15	BD	H	Ballinamallard United	4-1 W	Edgar, Griffin (2), Blake
Aug 19	BD	A	Harland & Wolff Welders	1-3 L	Duke
Aug 22	BD	A	Banbridge Town	2-1 W	Halliday, Griffin
Aug 25	BD	H	Armagh City	1-0 W	Edgar
Sep 2	BRC 1	H	Warrenpoint Town	8-0 W	Hamilton, Barnes, Halliday, (D) McCullough, Morwood, Henderson (2), 1og
Sep 9	IC 1	H	Roe Valley	4-1 W	Edgar (2,1pen), Duke, Leeman
Sep 16	BRC 2	H	Dungannon Swifts	1-1 L	Barnes
			(aet Loughgall lost 4-5 on pens)		
Sep 30	BD	H	Brantwood	2-0 W	Halliday, Henderson
Oct 7	BD	A	Ballymoney United	3-1 W	Halliday, Barnes (pen), Henderson
Oct 14	BD	H	Moyola Park	2-1 W	Bradley (og), Hamilton
Oct 21	BD	A	Queens University	3-0 W	Henderson (2), Halliday
Oct 28	BD	H	Queens University	3-0 W	Barnes (2), Hamilton
Nov 4	BD	A	Tobermore United	1-1 D	Henderson
Nov 11	IC 3	A	Northern Telecom	4-1 W	Barnes (2,1pen), Blake, Hamilton
Nov 18	BD	H	R.U.C.	1-1 D	Blake
Nov 25	BD	A	Brantwood	2-1 W	(D)McCullough, Hamilton
Dec 2	BD	A	Dundela	2-1 W	Henderson, Barnes
Dec 9	BIC 4	A	Banbridge Town	3-3 D	Barnes (3)
Dec 13	BIC 4R	H	Banbridge Town	1-4 L	Barnes
Dec 16	IC 4	A	Limavady United	0-1 L	-
Jan 6	BD	H	Ballymoney United	2-0 W	Barnes (pen), Hamilton
Jan 13	BD	A	Armagh City	1-0 W	Barnes
Jan 20	BD	H	Harland & Wolff Welders	2-1 W	Henderson, Barnes (pen)
Jan 27	BD	H	Cookstown United	1-0 W	Murtagh
Feb 3	BD	A	Dungannon Swifts	0-1 L	-
Feb 10	BD	H	Tobermore United	3-1 W	Duke, Johnston, Barnes
Feb 17	BD	A	Ballinamallard United	2-1 W	Henderson, Hamilton
Feb 24	BD	A	Limavady United	3-0 W	Henderson, Duke, Barnes
Mar 2	BD	A	Cookstown United	4-1 W	Henderson, Morwood, Duke (2)
Mar 9	MUC 4	A	Banbridge Town	4-2 W	Barnes (pen), Edgar (2), Henderson
Mar 16	SKC	H	Armagh City	1-0 W	Duke
Mar 23	BD	A	R.U.C	1-0 W	Halliday
Mar 30	SKC QF	H	Chimney Corner	2-0 W	Gardiner, Henderson
Apr 1	MUC QF	A	Newry Town	1-3 L	Griffin
Apr 6	BD	H	Limavady United	0-0 D	-
Apr 13	BD	A	Moyola Park	3-2 W	Barnes, Hamilton, Henderson
Apr 16	SKC SF 1L	H	Limavady United	1-1 D	Hamilton
Apr 23	SKC SF 2L	A	Limavady United	2-2 D	Henderson, Edgar
			(aet aggregate 3-3 Loughgall lost 6-7 on pens)		
Apr 27	BD	H	Chimney Corner	4-3 W	Barnes (2), Henderson (2)
May 4	BD	A	Chimney Corner	1-0 W	Henderson
May 7	BD	H	Dungannon Swifts	1-0 W	Henderson
May 11	BD	H	Dundela	2-1 W	Henderson (2)
May 14	BD	H	Banbridge Town	1-1 D	Halliday

LOUGHGALL GOALSCORERS FOR 1994/95

'B' Division: (58): 17 Gary Henderson; 12 Steven Barnes (3p); 6 Keith Halliday, Ian Hamilton; 5 Gary Duke; 3 Nicky Griffin; 2 Alan Blake, Des Edgar; 1 John Johnston, Dean McCullough, Randal Morwood, Jason Murtagh; 1 own goal:**Bob Radcliffe Cup:** (9); 2 Steven Barnes, Gary Henderson; 1 Keith Halliday, Ian Hamilton, Dean McCullough, Randal Morwood, 1 own goal:

McEwans Intermadiate Cup: (8): 2 Steven Barnes (1p), Des Edgar (1p); 1 Alan Blake, Gary Duke, Ian Hamilton, Thomas Leeman:**Bass Irish Cup:** (4): 4 Steven Barnes

Wilkinson Sword Irish League Cup: (3): 2 Robert Craig; 1 Gary Henderson:

McEwans Mid-Ulster Cup: (5): 2 Des Edgar; 1 Steven Barnes (1p), Nicky Griffin, Gary Henderson:

Smirnoff 'B' Division Knockout Cup: (6): 2 Gary Henderson; 1 Gary Duke, Des Edgar, James Gardiner, Ian Hamilton:**Top Goalscorer for 1995/96:** Gary Henderson with 23.

MOYOLA PARK

Ground: Moyola Park, Castledawson. Founded: 1880

Playing Staff fo 1994/95

John Andrews, Nigel Ballantine*, Colin Bell, Neville Bradley, David Braniff, Maurice Devine, Benny Devlin, Dermot Doherty*, Steven Ewing, Issac Glendinning, Rodney Hassan, Brian Holmes, Brian Hutchinson*, Gerry Kelly, John Kelly, Raymond Kennedy, Paul Lavery, Chris Leacock, Bertie McMinn, Stephen McComb, Michael McCormick, Brian Martin, Darren Mawhinney, Graham Mellon*, Kevin Morrow, Adrian Pattison, Mervyn Pattison*, Billy Pyper, Seamus Quinn, Jack Rankin, Richard Ruddock, Jim Scott, Mark Spiers, Thomas Young*.

Denotes player has now left the club.

HONOURS:

Irish League 'B' Division: Best Position: 7th 1993/94

Irish Cup:	(1)	1880/81
Irish Junior Cup:	(2)	1972/73 and 1973/74
North West Intermediate Cup:	(1)	1981/82
NI Intermediate League Cup:	(1)	1987/88
Most capped player:		Arthur Gaussen 6 caps for Ireland

Chairman:
Maurice Lennon
Secretary:
Raymond Loughrey
Player/Manager:
Raymond Kennedy and Gerry Kelly
Club Colours:
Royal Blue shirts, White shorts, Royal Blue socks
Entered 'B':
1991/92

TRANSFERS C/S'95 TO APRIL '96

Players Signed:
Colin Bell (Larne c/s'95), Billy Pyper (Ballymoney United (c/s'95), Nigel Ballentine (Loughgall Sep.'95), Kevin Morrow (Limavady United Feb.'96).

Players Transferred:
David McCrea (Harland & Wolff Welders c/s'95), Michael O'Hagen (Dungannon Swifts c/s'95), Tom Young (Tobermore United Sep.'95), Brian Hutchinson (Glentoran Jan.'96), Mervyn Pattison (Ballyclare Comrades Jan.'96), Dermot Doherty (Larne Feb.'96), Graham Mellon (Ballyclare Comrades Feb.'96), Nigel Ballentine (Carrick Rangers Mar.'96)

THE NORTHERN IRELAND
football
Y E A R B O O K

MOYOLA PARK

MOYOLA PARKS COMPLETE PLAYING RECORD FOR 1995/96

Date:	Comp:	Ven:	Opponents:	Result:	Goalscorers:
Aug 12	ILC 1	A	Glenavon	0-5 L	-
Aug 19	BD	A	Ballymoney United	5-1 W	(A) Pattison, Clyde (og), Pyper, McMinn (2)
Aug 22	BD	H	Cookstown United	3-0 W	?
Aug 25	BD	H	Tobermore United	5-0 W	(A) Pattison (3), (M) Pattison (2)
Sep 9	BD	A	Dungannon Swifts	0-4 L	-
Sep 23	BD	A	R.U.C	0-1 L	-
Sep 30	NWIC 2	A	Limavady United	3-2 W	?
Oct 7	BD	H	Armagh City	3-4 L	Pyper, Andrews, (M) Pattison
Oct 14	BD	A	Loughgall	1-2 L	Scott
Oct 21	BD	H	Chimney Corner	1-4 L	(A) Pattison
Oct 28	NWIC QF	A	Tobermore United	1-2 L aet	(A) Pattison
Nov4	BD	H	Ballinamallard United	1-1 D	Hassan
Nov 11	BD	A	Banbridge Town	0-3 L	-
Nov 18	BD	H	Brantwood	1-1 D	Hassan
Nov 25	BD	A	Queens University	4-1 W	Scott, Quinn, (A) Pattison (2,1pen)
Dec 2	BD	H	Ballymoney United	1-0 W	(M) Pattison
Dec 9	BIC 4	A	Dungannon Swifts	0-2 L	-
Dec 16	BD	A	Ballinamallard United	2-3 L	(A) Pattison, (M) Pattison
Jan 6	BD	A	Tobermore United	1-2 L	(M) Pattison
Jan 13	BD	H	Dundela	0-1 L	-
Jan 20	BD	A	Brantwood	0-0 D	-
Feb 3	BD	A	Chimney Corner	2-2 D	(A) Pattison
Feb 10	BD	H	R.U.C	2-2 D	Holmes (2)
Feb 17	BD	A	Cookstown United	1-3 L	Quinn
Feb 24	BD	H	Harland & Wolff W	2-6 L	(A) Pattison, Quinn
Mar 2	BD	A	Armagh City	1-2 L	Spiers
Mar 9	BD	H	Queens University	3-2 W	Holmes, Hassan (2)
Mar 16	SKC 1	H	Chimney Corner	1-2 L	Spiers
Mar 23	BD	A	Limavady United	0-3 L	-
Mar 30	BD	A	Harland & Wolff W	0-4 L	-
Apr 6	BD	H	Banbridge Town	0-4 L	-
Apr 13	BD	H	Loughgall	2-3 L	Pyper, (A) Pattison
Apr 20	BD	H	Limavady United	1-1 D	(A) Pattison
Apr 27	BD	A	Dundela	2-7 L	Quinn (2)
May9	BD	H	Dungannon Swifts	1-5 L	Holmes

MOYOLA PARK GOALSCORERS FOR 1995/96

B' Division: (45): 13 Adrian Pattison (1pen); 6 Mervyn Pattison; 5 Seamus Quinn; 4 Rodney Hassan, Brian Holmes; 3 Billy Pyper; 2 Bertie McMinn, Jim Scott; 1 John Andrews, Mark Spiers; 1 own goal: (3 goalscorers missing):

North West Intermediate Cup: (4): 1 Adrian Pattison; (3 goalscorers missing):

Bass Irish Cup: (0): -

Wilkinson Sword Irish League Cup: (0): -

Smirnoff 'B' Division Knockout Cup: (1): Mark Spiers:

Top Goalscorer for 1995/96: Adrian Pattison with 13 (1 pen):

QUEENS UNIVERSITY
Ground: Dub Lane, Belfast. Founded: 1900 circa

Playing Staff for 1995/96
Jonathan Anderson, Colin Atkinson, Brian Beattie, Glen Bell, Thorsten Brenker, Mark Browne, Paul Carlisle, Neil Carson, Bonar Clarke, Patrick Connolly, Declan Cooley*, John Crawford, Kieran Crilly, Brendan Crossan, Martin Downey, Neil Evans, Martin Graham, Paul Harding, Stephen Harding, James Harty, Ciaran Harvey, Nigel Haworth, Damian Hillen, Richard Hume, James Hutton, Gareth Johnston, Andrew McClean, Eamon McCourt, Sean McKeown, Paul McNeill, Stephen Morris, Fergal O'Carroll, Rory O'Mahoney, Conor O'Neill, Paul Reid, Stephen Smart, Richard Spratt, Jonathan Steen, Paul Taylor, Mark Todd, Conor Willis.

No Photograph available for 1995/96.

Chairman:
Denis Clarke
Secretary:
Stephen Harding
Manager:
Patrick Connolly
Club Colours:
White shirts, Black shorts, Black socks
Entered 'B':
1951/52

HONOURS:

Irish League 'B' Division: Best Position:8th		1979/80
NI College League:	(6)	1973/74, 1974/75, 1976/77, 1980/81, 1983/84, 1989/90
All Ireland University League:	(2)	1976/77 and 1980/81
Collingwood Cup:	(4)	1974/75, 1976/77, 1981/82, 1984/85
Farquhar Cup:	(6)	1978/79*, 1979/80, 1980/81, 1981/82*, 1983/84, 1984/85

*NB: * Denotes trophy was shared.*

TRANSFERS C/S'95 TO APRIL '96

Players Signed:
Gareth Johnston (Portadown Oct.'95):

Players Transferred:
Mark Looney (Larne Aug.'95); Declan Cooley (Crusaders Feb.'96):

QUEENS UNIVERSITY

QUEENS UNIVERSITYS COMPLETE PLAYING RECORD FOR 1995/96

Date:	Comp:	Ven:	Opponents:	Result:	Goalscorers:
Aug 12	ILC 1	A	Ards	0-2 L	-
Aug 15	BD	A	Brantwood	1-3 L	O'Neill
Aug 19	BD	A	Ballinamallard United	0-5 L	-
Aug 22	BD	A	Dundela	0-8 L	-
Aug 25	BD	H	Chimney Corner	1-1 D	Clarke
Sep 2	SS 1	A	Killyleagh Youth Club	3-2 W	O'Neill (2), Clarke
Sep 9	IC 1	A	Comber Recreation	3-2 W	aet Downey, Taylor, Clarke
Sep 16	SS 2	A	Chimney Corner	1-6 L	Downey
Sep 23	BIC 1	H	Hanover	2-2 D	Morris, McCourt
Sep 27	BIC 1R	A	Hanover	1-3 L	Taylor
Oct 7	BD	A	Tobermore United	0-2 L	-
Oct 14	BD	A	R.U.C.	1-3 L	Downey
Oct 21	BD	H	Loughgall	0-3 L	-
Oct 28	BD	A	Loughgall	0-3 L	-
Nov 4	BD	H	Limavady United	0-5 L	-
Nov 11	IC 3	H	Crumlin United	2-6 L	O'Neill, Reid
Nov 18	BD	A	Ballymoney United	0-1 L	-
Nov 25	BD	H	Moyola Park	1-4 L	O'Neill
Dec 2	BD	H	R.U.C.	0-4 L	-
Dec 16	BD	H	Tobermore United	1-2 L	Harty
Jan 6	BD	A	Limavady United	1-3 L	Reid
Jan 13	BD	H	Ballinamallard United	0-2 L	-
Jan 20	BD	H	Ballymoney United	3-1 W	Crawford (2), Hutton
Jan 27	BD	A	Harland & Wolff Welders	0-4 L	-
Feb 3	BD	A	Armagh City	2-2 D	Harty, Reid
Feb 10	BD	H	Cookstown United	2-2 D	O'Neill, McCourt
Feb 17	BD	H	Brantwood	0-3 L	-
Mar 2	BD	H	Banbridge Town	0-4 L	-
Mar 9	BD	A	Moyola Park	2-3 L	O'Neill, McCourt
Mar 16	SKC 1	A	Ballymoney United	0-3 L	-
Mar 19	BD	A	Dungannon Swifts	1-3 L	Crawford
Mar 23	BD	H	Armagh City	1-1 D	McCourt
Mar 30	BD	A	Cookstown United	2-2 D	Connolly, Reid
Apr 10	BD	H	Harland & Wolff Welders	1-4 L	O'Neill
Apr 13	BD	H	Dungannon Swifts	0-6 L	-
Apr 20	BD	H	Dundela	0-5 L	-
Apr 23	BD	A	Chimney Corner	0-5 L	-
Apr 27	BD	A	Banbridge Town	0-4 L	-

QUEENS UNIVERSITY GOALSCORERS FOR 1995/96

'B' Division: (20): 5 Conor O'Neill; 3 John Crawford, Eamon McCourt, Paul Reid; 2 James Harty; 1 Bonor Clarke, Patrick Connolly, Martin Downey, James Hutton:

Calor Steel & Sons Cup: (4): 2 Conor O'Neill, 1 Bonor Clarke, Martin Downey:

McEwans Intermediate Cup: (5): 1 Bonor Clarke, Martin Downey, Conor O'Neill, Paul Reid, Paul Taylor:

Bass Irish Cup: (3): 1 Eamon McCourt, Stephen Morris, Paul Taylor:

Wilkinson Sword Irish League Cup: (0): -

Smirnoff 'B' Division Knockout Cup: (0): -

Top Goalscorer for 1995/96: Conor O'Neill with 8:

ROYAL ULSTER CONSTABULARY
Ground: Newforge Lane, Belfast BT9 5NN. Founded: 1956

Playing Staff for 1994/95
Darren Crawford, Joe Crawford, Ian Doherty, Stuart Ferguson, Alan Ferris, Stephen Ferris, Tony Frazer, Gary Hunter, Tony Kerr, David Leckey, Harry Love, Gary Macartney, Willie McClean, Stephen McCormick, Sammy McFadden, Philip Matthews, David Mayne, Richard Mercer, Billy Millen, Neil Morrow, David Mulligan, Clayton Pike, Trevior Senior, Gary Spratt, Brian Thompson, Ken Whiteside, Colin Young.

No Photograph available for 1995/96.

Chairman:
Brian Dunlop
Secretary:
Ernest Downey
Manager:
Billy Moore
Club Colours:
Green/Black striped shirts, Black shorts, Red socks
Entered 'B':
1975/76

HONOURS:
Irish League 'B' Division:	(1)	1986/87
IFA Intermediate Cup:	(4)	1978/79, 1979/80, 1984/85, 1986/87
Steel & Sons Cup:	(1)	1993/94
'B'Division Knockout Cup:	(3)	1982/83, 1984/85, 1985/86
UK Police Athletic Assn Cup:	(4)	1981/82, 1982/83, 1986/87, 1994/95
Amateur League Div. 1A	(2)	1970/71 and 1972/73
Border Regiment Cup:	(1)	1965/66
Clarence Cup:	(1)	1960/61
Walter Moore Cup:	(1)	1970/71
Irish Junior Shield:	(1)	1964/65
Templeton Cup:	(1)	1972/73

TRANSFERS C/S'95 TO APRIL '96

Players Signed:
Sammy McFadden (Dungannon Swifts c/s'95), Harry Love (Coleraine Aug.'95), Darren Crawford (Carrick Rangers Sep.'95), Dean May (Ballymena United Feb.'96):

Players Transferred:
Dean May (Carrick Rangers Mar.'96):

THE NORTHERN IRELAND
football
Y E A R B O O K

ROYAL ULSTER CONSTABULARY

R.U.C. COMPLETE PLAYING RECORD FOR 1995/96

Date:	Comp:	Ven:	Opponents:	Result:	Goalscorers:
Aug 12	ILC 1	A	Linfield	0-6 L	-
Aug 15	BD	A	Dundela	2-4 L	Young, Macartney
Aug 19	BD	H	Limavady United	0-1 L	-
Aug 22	BD	A	Armagh City	0-1 L	-
Aug 25	BD	A	Ballymoney United	3-1 W	Macartney, McFadden, Young
Sep 2	SS 1	H	Carrick Rangers Res.	2-0 W	Hunter (2)
Sep 9	IC 1	H	Ballycastle United	4-0 W	Macartney, Millen, Hunter (2)
Sep 16	SS 2	A	First Shankill N.I.S.C.	4-1 W	Hunter, Frazer, McFadden (pen), Macartney
Sep 23	BD	H	Moyola Park	1-0 W	(D) Crawford
Sep 30	SS 3	A	Bangor Reserves	3-2 W	aet Macartney, McFadden, Young
Oct 7	IC 2	A	Seapatrick	5-0 W	Hunter (2), Macartney, Young, og
Oct 14	BD	H	Queens University	3-1 W	Macartney (2), Hunter
Oct 21	BD	A	Dungannon Swifts	1-1 D	Macartney
Oct 28	SS QF	H	Dundela	1-3 L	Hunter
Nov 4	BD	H	Cookstown United	2-0 W	Leckey, Millen
Nov 11	IC 3	H	Dundela	3-2 W	aet Macartney, Leckey, Lennox (og)
Nov 18	BD	A	Loughgall	1-1 D	Young
Nov 25	BD	A	Armagh City	2-0 W	McFadden, Young
Dec 2	BD	A	Queens University	4-0 W	Leckey, Macartney (2), Hunter
Dec 16	IC 4	A	AFC Craigavon	4-1 W	Young (2), Mercer, Hunter
Jan 13	BD	A	Tobermore United	4-0 W	Macartney, McFadden (3)
Jan 20	BIC 5	H	Carrick Rangers	2-3 L	Young, Millen
Jan 27	BD	H	Ballinamallard United	0-2 L	-
Feb 3	IC QF	H	Brantwood	2-1 W	Macartney, Millen
Feb 10	BD	A	Moyola Park	2-2 D	(D) Crawford, Macartney
Feb 17	BD	H	Ballymoney United	2-0 W	Hunter (2)
Feb 24	BD	A	Banbridge Town	2-1 W	Young, Macartney
Mar 2	BD	H	Tobermore United	6-1 W	Macartney (3), Love (3)
Mar 9	BD	A	Harland & Wolff Welders	0-2 L	-
Mar 16	SKC 1	H	Cookstown United	2-0 W	Macartney, Millen
Mar 21	IC SF	N	Harland & Wolff Welders	2-5 L	Macartney (2)
Mar 23	BD	H	Loughgall	0-1 L	-
Mar 30	SKC QF	A	Limavady United	1-1 L	Morrow
			(aet R.U.C. lost 5-6 on pens)		
Apr 6	BD	H	Dundela	1-0 W	Mulligan
Apr 13	BD	A	Chimney Corner	0-1 L	-
Apr 16	BD	A	Cookstown United	0-0 D	-
Apr 20	BD	H	Brantwood	4-2 W	McClean (4)
Apr 27	BD	A	Ballinamallard United	1-2 L	Frazer
Apr 30	BD	A	Brantwood	6-3 W	Hunter (2), Mercer, Millen, Frazer, McClean
May 2	BD	H	Chimney Corner	1-2 L	Hunter
May 7	BD	H	Banbridge Town	1-2 L	Macartney
May 10	BD	A	Limavady United	1-2 L	Young
May 14	BD	H	Dungannon Swifts	2-5 L	Macartney, Millen
May 21	BD	H	Harland & Wolff Welders	2-3 L	Thompson, Hunter

R.U.C. GOALSCORERS FOR 1995/96

'B' Division: (54): 15 Gary Macartney; 8 Gary Hunter; 6 Colin Young; 5 Willie McClean, Sammy McFadden; 3 Harry Love, Billy Millen; 2 Darren Crawford, Tony Frazer, David Leckey; 1 Richard Mercer, David Mulligan, Brian Thompson:**Calor Steel & Sons Cup: (10):** 4 Gary Hunter; 2 Gary Macartney, Sammy McFadden (1p); 1 Tony Frazer, Colin Young:**McEwans Intermediate Cup:** (20): 6 Gary Macartney; 5 Gary Hunter; 3 Colin Young; 2 Billy Millen; 1 David Leckey, Richard Mercer; 2 own goals:**Bass Irish Cup:** (2): 1 Billy Millen, Colin Young: **Wilkinson Sword Irish League Cup: (0):** -**Smirnoff 'B'Division Knockout Cup: (3):** 1 Gary Macartney, Billy Millen, Neill Morrow:

Top Goalscorer 1995/96: Gary Macartney with 24:

TOBERMORE UNITED

Ground: Fortwilliam Park, Maghera Road, Tobermore. Founded: 1965

Playing Staff for 1995/96
..... Campbell, David Crooks, Gerry Kelly, Bert Lamont, Hayden Leacock, Derek Livingstone, Andy McCann, Jason McFadden, Alistair, Rodney McKay, David McLaughlin, Alan Moore, Brian Moore, Gavin Moran, Wesley Nelson, Gerry O'Doherty, Mark Patterson, Stuart Reid, ...Ritchie, Sammy Shiels*, Darren Taylor, Kenny Thompson, Thomas Todd, Paul White, Lawrence Wray, Thomas Young.
*Denotes player has now left the club.

Chairman:
Raymond Beatty
Secretary:
Brian Montgomery
Manager:
Tom Todd
Colours:
Red shirts, Black shorts,
White socks
Entered 'B':
1983/84

HONOURS:

Irish League 'B' Division:	Best Position 5th 1988/89	
NI Intermediate League: (2)		1978/79 and 1981/82
NI Intermediate League Cup: (2)		1978/79 and 1981/82
North West Senior Challenge Cup(1)		1989/90
North West Intermediate Cup: (3)		1981/82, 1988/89,
		1989/90

TRANSFERS C/S'95 TO APRIL '96

Players Signed:
Lawrence Wray (c/s'95 Amateur League), Sammy Shiels (Carrick Rangers Aug.'95), Thomas Young (Moyola Park Sep.'95), Andy McCann (Armagh City Feb.'96).

Players Transferred:
Thomas McLeister (Carrick Rangers Aug.'95); Sammy Shiels (Coleraine Sep.'95)

THE NORTHERN IRELAND
football
Y E A R B O O K

TOBERMORE UNITEDS COMPLETE PLAYING RECORD 1995/96

Date:	Comp:	Ven:	Opponents:	Result:	Goalscorers:
Aug 12	ILC 1	A	Newry Town	0-2 L	-
Aug 16	BD	A	Armagh City	4-7 L	?
Aug 19	BD	H	Dungannon Swifts	0-6 L	-
Aug 22	BD	H	Limavady United	0-4 L	-
Aug 25	BD	A	Moyola Park	0-5 L	-
Sep 2	NWIC 1	H	U.U.C.	4-2 W	Shiels (2), McKay, ?
Sep 16	BD	H	Limavady United	0-5 L	-
Sep 23	BD	H	Banbridge Town	0-1 L	-
Oct 7	BD	H	Queens University	2-0 W	Thompson, Young
Oct 21	BD	A	Brantwood	0-0 D	-
Oct 28	NWIC Q.F.	H	Moyola Park	2-1 Waet	McFadden, Scott (og)
Nov 4	BD	H	Loughgall	1-1 D	Thompson (pen)
Nov 11	BD	A	Ballinamallard United	0-0 D	-
Nov 18	NWIC SF	H	C.K.U.	1-1 L	Taylor
			(aet Tobermore United lost 2-3 on pens)		
Nov 25	BD	A	Dungannon Swifts	1-2 L	McFadden
Dec 2	BD	H	Brantwood	5-2 W	Taylor, Reid (2), O'Doherty, Leacock
Dec 9	BIC 4	H	Brantwood	1-0 W	McFadden
Dec 16	BD	A	Queens University	2-1 W	Crooks (2)
Jan 6	BD	H	Moyola Park	2-1 W	O'Doherty, Leacock
Jan 13	BD	H	R.U.C.	0-4 L	-
Jan 20	BIC 5	H	Ballyclare Comrades	2-3 L	Crooks (2)
Jan 27	BD	A	Dundela	1-2 L	Taylor
Feb 3	BD	H	Ballymoney United	0-1 L	-
Feb 10	BD	A	Loughgall	1-3 L	O'Doherty
Feb 17	BD	A	Harland & Wolff Welders	3-2 W	Reid, Crooks (2,1pen)
Feb 24	BD	H	Cookstown United	1-3 L	Young
Mar 2	BD	A	R.U.C	1-6 L	McFadden
Mar 9	BD	H	Dundela	1-0 W	McFadden
Mar 16	SKC 1	A	Limavady United	2-5 Laet	McCann, Crown (og)
Mar 23	BD	A	Cookstown United	1-2 L	Ritchie
Mar 30	BD	H	Ballinamallard United	2-1 W	Taylor (2)
Apr 6	BD	A	Ballymoney United	1-4 L	Taylor
Apr 20	BD	H	Harland & Wolff Welders	2-2 D	Leacock, McCann
Apr 25	BD	H	Chimney Corner	1-3 L	?
Apr 27	BD	H	Armagh City	2-0 W	Campbell, McFadden
Apr 30	BD	A	Chimney Corner	1-2 L	?
May 4	BD	A	Banbridge Town	1-9 L	McFadden

TOBERMORE UNITED GOALSCORERS FOR 1995/96

'B' Division: (36): 5 Jason McFadden, Darren Taylor; 4 David Crooks (1p); 3 Hayden Leacock, Gerry O'Doherty, Stuart Reid; 2 Kenny Thompson (1p), Thomas Young; 1 .... Campbell, Andy McCann, ...Ritchie: (6 goalscorers missing).

North West Intermediate Cup: (7): 2 Sammy Shiels; 1 Jason McFadden, Rodney McKay, Darren Taylor; 1 own goal: (1 goalscorer missing).

Bass Irish Cup: (3): 2 David Crooks; 1 Jason McFadden:

Wilkinson Sword Irish League Cup: (0): -

Smirnoff 'B' Division Knockout Cup: (2): 1 Andy McCann; 1 own goal:

Top Goalscorer for 1995/96: Jason McFadden with 7:

NB: Goalscorers in certain matches have not been located, so above goalscoring records are not complete.

First Round

9th September, 1995.

AFC Craigavon	?	Drummond United	?	Dumurry Recreation	3	Armoy United	1
Abbey Villa	1	Northern Telecom	2	First Bangor Old Boys	2	Larne Olympic	7
Ards II	0	Glenavon Reserves	1	First Liverpool R.R.	1	British Telecom	1
Ards Rangers	2	First Shankill N.I.S.C.	1	(aet British Telecom won 5-4 on pens)			
Ballinamallard United	2	East Belfast	0	Glebe Rangers	0	Crumlin United	5
Ballymoney United	0	Armagh City	1	Islandmagee	2	Cookstown Royals	1
Brantwood	4	Wellington Recreation	0	Killyleagh Youth Club	6	Civil Service	1
Bridgend United	2	Cookstown United	7	Killymoon Rangers	1	Bangor Amateurs	6
Carrick Rangers Res.	2	Ballymena United Res.	2	Larne Tech. Old Boys	1	Kilmore Recreation	2
(aet Ballymena United Res. won 10-9 on pens)				Limavady United	4	Laurelvale	2
Chimney Corner	5	Barn United	1	Loughgall	4	Roe Valley	1
Coagh United	2	Crusaders Reserves	3	Omagh Town Reserves	1	Connor	4
Comber Recreation	2	Queens University	3	Park	2	Orangefield Old Boys	1
Crewe United	4	Portglenone	1	R.U.C.	4	Ballycastle United	0
Cullybackey	0	FC Enkalon	1	Rathfriland Rangers	1	Coleraine Reserves	0
Distillery II	0	Glentoran II	4	Richhill	1	Ballynahinch United	2
Donard Hospital	2	Portadown Reserves	4	Seapatrick	?	Annagh United	?
Downshire Young Men	2	Malachians	0	Short Brothers	3	Portstewart	7
Dromara Village	3	Southend United	1	Sirocco Works	0	Saintfield United	3
Drumaness Mills	5	Ballymacash Rangers	1	U.U.C.	1	Tandragee Rovers	2
Dundela	6	Dromore Amateurs	0	U.U.J.	2	Hanover	0
Dungiven Celtic	5	Magherafelt Sky Blues	1				

First Round Bye: Harland & Wolff Welders

Second Round

7th October, 1995

Ballinamallard United	0	Brantwood	2	FC Enkalon	2	Dundela	3
Ballymena United Res.	1	Limavady United	2	Harland & Wolff Welders	4	Killyleagh Youth Club	3
Ballynahinch United	3	Chimney Corner	2	Park	1	Drumaness Mills	0
Crumlin United	6	Bangor Amateurs	3	Saintfield United	2	Crusaders Reserves	8
Dungiven Celtic	3	Kilmore Recreation	1	Seapatrick	0	R.U.C.	5

Second Round Byes: AFC Craigavon, Ards Rangers, Armagh City, British Telecom, Connor, Cookstown United, Crewe United, Downshire Young Men, Dromara Village, Dunmurry Recreation, Glenavon Reserves, Glentoran II, Islandmagee, Larne Olympic, Loughgall, Northern Telecom, Portadown Reserves, Portstewart, Queens University, Rathfriland Rangers, Tandragee Rovers, U.U.J.

Third Round

11th November, 1995

Ards Rangers	2	Armagh City	1	Larne Olympic	3	Tandragee Rovers	2
British Telecom	1	U.U.J.	0	Limavady United	8	Cookstown United	1
Connor	4	Ballynahinch United	2	Northern Telecom	1	Loughgall	4
Crewe United	6	Rathfriland Rangers	2	Park	1	Islandmagee	3
Crusaders Reserves	3	Dungiven Celtic	1	Portstewart	6	Downshire Young Men	0
Dromara Village	1	AFC Craigvon	2	Queens University	2	Crumlin United	6
Dunmurry Recreation	3	Brantwood	4	R.U.C.	3	Dundela	2
Glenavon Reserves	4	Portadown Reserves	3				
Harland & Wolff Welders	1	Glentoran II	1				
(aet Harland & Wolff Welders won 5-4 on pens)							

FOURTH ROUND

16th December, 1995

AFC Craigavon	1	R.U.C.	4	Harland & Wolff Welders	2	Portstewart	1
British Telecom	2	Crewe United	0	Islandmagee	2	Ards Rangers	2
Connor	2	Glenavon Reserves	3	(aet Islandmagee won 5-4 on pens)			
Crumlin United	1	Brantwood	2	Limavady United	1	Loughgall	0
Crusaders Reserves	1	Larne Olympic	0				

QUARTER-FINALS

3rd February, 1996

British Telecom	0	Crusaders Reserves	1	Islandmagee	0	Limavady United	4
Harland & Wolff Welders	5	Glenavon Reserves	1	R.U.C.	2	Brantwood	1

SEMI-FINALS

14th March, 1996

Venue: Stangmore Park, Dungannon.

Limavady United (0) **2** **Crusaders Reserves** (0) **0 (aet)**
Painter (98), Moran (100)

21st March, 1996

Venue: The Oval, Belfast

Harland & Wolff Welders (1) **5** **R.U.C.** (1) **2**
Lockhart (5,86), Crowe (58), *Macartney (38,73)*
Dunwoody (75), Blackledge (83)

HWW: Johnston, Mallon, Doey, Cummings, Trueick, Gallagher, Lockhart, Blackledge, Crowe, Wilson, Dunwoody. **Subs:** Thompson replaced Doey; Neill replaced ? Sub not used: Blackwood (gk):
RUC: Matthews, Ferguson, (D) Crawford, Spratt, (J) Crawford, Millen, Love, McFadden, Macartney, McClean, Leckey. **Subs:** Morrow replaced (D) Crawford; Hunter replaced McClean; Sub not used: Young:
Referee: D.Chambers (Belfast)

FINAL

2nd May, 1996

Venue: Stangmore Park, Dungannon Att: 400

Limavady United (2) **4** **Harland & Wolff Welders** (1) **2**
Harrison (5,46), Painter (45) *Lockhart (pen 37,85)*
White (88)

Limavady U: Crown, Nutt, Law, (D) Mullan, King, Neill, (M) Mullan, Davies, Harrison, Moran, Painter. **Subs:** Shiels replaced Neill (45 min); White replaced Harrison (79 min) **Sub not used:** McCallum:
H.W.W: Johnston, Mallon, Doey, Cummings, Trueick, Gallagher, Lockhart, Crowe, Blackledge, Wilson, Dunwoody: **Subs:** Thompson replaced Doey (53 min); Black replaced Blackledge (56 min); Blackwood (gk) replaced Thompson (71 min):
Referee: G.McCabe (Strabane)
Sent Off: Davy King (Limavady United)

IFA Intermediate Cup
Winners 1892/93-1995/96

1892/93	Distillery Rovers	1945/46	Linfield Swifts
1893/94	Glentoran II	1946/47	Dundela
1894/95	Milltown	1947/48	Distillery II
1895/96	Cliftonville Olympic	1948/49	Linfield Swifts
1896/97	Linfield Swifts	1949/50	Ballyclare Comrades
1897/98	Glentoran II	1950/51	Ballyclare Comrades
1898/99	Linfield Swifts	1951/52	Brantwood
1899/00	Cliftonville Olympic	1952/53	Brantwood
1900/01	Linfield Swifts	1953/54	Ballyclare Comrades
1901/02	Cliftonville Olympic	1954/55	Dundela
1902/03	Distillery II	1955/56	Linfield Swifts
1903/04	YMCA	1956/57	Linfield Swifts
1904/05	Woodvale	1957/58	Newry Town
1905/06	Forth River	1958/59	Larne
1906/07	Forth River	1959/60	Ballyclare Comrades
1907/08	Glenavon	1960/61	Ballyclare Comrades
1908/09	Glentoran II	1961/62	Glentoran II
1909/10	St.James Gate	1962/63	Ballyclare Comrades
1910/11	Glenavon	1963/64	Ballyclare Comrades
1911/12	Derry Guilds	1964/65	Coleraine Reserves
1912/13	Glentoran II	1965/66	Dundela
1913/14	Belfast Celtic II	1966/67	Newry Town
1914/15	U.M. Co. Dublin	1967/68	Chimney Corner
1915/16	Glentoran II	1968/69	Coleraine Reserves
1916/17	Strandville	1969/70	Larne
1917/18	Glentoran II	1970/71	Ards II
1918/19	Withheld	1971/72	Linfield Swifts
1919/20	St.James Gate	1972/73	Brantwood
1920/21	Queen's Island	1973/74	Limavady United
1921/22	Linfield Rangers	1974/75	Dundela
1922/23	Dunmurry	1975/76	Carrick Rangers
1923/24	Willowfield	1976/77	Carrick Rangers
1924/25	Linfield Rangers	1977/78	Dungannon Swifts
1925/26	Ballyclare Comrades	1978/79	R.U.C.
1926/27	Crusaders	1979/80	R.U.C.
1927/28	Willowfield	1980/81	Newry Town
1928/29	Linfield Swifts	1981/82	Chimney Corner
1929/30	Dunmurry	1982/83	Chimney Corner
1930/31	Glentoran II	1983/84	Dundela
1931/32	Broadway	1984/85	R.U.C.
1932/33	Dunvilles	1985/86	Banbridge Town
1933/34	Sunnyside	1986/87	R.U.C.
1934/35	Belfast Celtic II	1987/88	Short Brothers
1935/36	Belfast Celtic II	1988/89	Dundela
1936/37	Belfast Celtic II	1989/90	Ballyclare Comrades
1937/38	Crusaders	1990/91	Brantwood
1938/39	Crusaders	1991/92	Dungannon Swifts
1939/40	Belfast Celtic II	1992/93	Dundela
1940/41	Glentoran II	1993/94	Portstewart
1941/42	Bangor Reserves	1994/95	Ballinamallard United
1942/43	Larne	1995/96	Limavady United
1943/44	Bangor Reserves		

SUMMARY OF WINNERS:

9 Ballyclare Comrades, Glentoran II, Linfield Swifts; **7** Dundela, **5** Belfast Celtic II; **4** Brantwood, R.U.C.; **3** Bangor Reserves, Chimney Corner, Cliftonville Olympic, Crusaders, Newry Town; **2** Carrick Rangers, Coleraine Reserves, Distillery II, Dungannon Swifts, Dunmurry, Forth River, Glenavon Reserves, Limavady United, Linfield Rangers, St.James Gate, Willowfield; **1** Ards II, Ballinamallard, Banbridge Town, Broadway, Derry Guilds, Distillery Rovers, Dunvilles, Milltown, Portstewart, Queen's Island, Short Brothers, Strandville, Sunnyside, U.M. Co.Dublin, YMCA:

PRELIMINARY ROUND

26th August, 1995

| Primose F.C. | 3 | Ballycastle United | 2 |

FIRST ROUND

1st September, 1995

| Linfield Swifts | 2 | Dunmurry Young Men | 0 |

2nd September, 1995

Ards II	2	Ballynahinch United	1	Dundela	3	Connor	1
Ballyclare Comrades Res.	0	First Liverpool R.R.	1	First Bangor Old Boys	3	Dundonald	0
Ballymacash Rangers	6	Crusaders Reserves	2	F.C. Enkalon	7	Glentoran II	3
Ballymena United Res.	3	East Belfast	2	Glebe Rangers	1	Downshire Young Men	5
Ballymoney United	3	Comber Recreation	6	Harland & Wolff Welders	8	Wellington Rec.	2
Bangor Amateurs	0	Abbey Villa	1	Killyleagh Youth Club	2	Queens University	3
Bangor Reserves	3	Seacourt	1	Larne Olympic	0	Armoy United	1
Barn United	4	Dunmurry Recreation	1	Malachians	2	Holywood Rangers	1
Brantwood	4	Cliftonville Olympic	2	Northern Telecom	2	Ards Rangers	1
British Telecom	2	Civil Service	1	Orangefield Old Boys	2	Craigyhill Olympic	1
Chimney Corner	3	Short Brothers	2	Portglenone	1	Distillery II	3
Crumlin United	3	Crewe United	2	R.U.C.	2	Carrick Rangers Res.	0
Cullybackey	3	Kilmore Recreation	2	Saintfield United	6	Primrose F.C.	2
Donard Hospital	1	Larne Tech. Old Boys	2	Sirocco Works	2	Islandmagee	2
Donegal Celtic	0	First Shankill NISC		(aet Sirocco Works won on pens)			
Drumaness Mills	1	Dromara Village	2	U.U.J. 1		Harland & Wolff Sports Club	?

SECOND ROUND

16th September, 1995

Abbey Villa	1	British Telecom	1	First Liverpool R.R.	2	Distillery II	0
(aet British Telecom won 3-2 on pens)				First Shankill N.I.S.C.	1	R.U.C.	4
Ballymena United Res.	2	Ballymacash Rangers	0	Harland & Wolff Welders	1	Malachians	0
Brantwood	2	Bangor Reserves	4	Larne Tech Old Boys	0	Barn United	1
Chimney Corner	6	Queens University	1	Linfield Swifts	9	Cullybackey	0
Downshire Young Men	4	Armoy United	0	Orangfield Old Boys	5	F.C.Enkalon	3
Dromara Village	3	Northern Telecom	2	Saintfield United	2	Crumlin United	3
Dundela	6	U.U.J.	0	Sirocco Works	3	Comber Recreation 5	
First Bangor Old Boys	2	Ards II	0				

THIRD ROUND

30th September, 1995.

Ballymena United Res.	3	Chimney Corner	2	Crumlin United	1	First Liverpool	2
Bangor Reserves	2	R.U.C.	3 (aet)	Dundela	2	Comber Recreation	1 (aet)
Barn United	1	Dromara Village	2	Harland & Wolff Welders	1	First Bangor Old Boys	0
British Telecom	1	Linfield Swifts	3	Orangefield Old Boys	2	Downshire Young Men	0

CALOR STEEL & SONS CUP 1995/96
QUARTER-FINALS

28th October, 1995

Ballymena United Res.	1 First Liverpool R.R.	0	Orangefield Old Boys	1 Linfield Swifts	3
Dromara Village	2 Harland & Wolff Welders	1	R.U.C.	1 Dundela	3

SEMI-FINALS

6th November, 1995

Venue: Dixon Park, Ballyclare.

Ballymena United Res.	**(1)**	**3**	**Linfield Swifts**	**(2)**	**2**

McConville (38, 90), Steele (80)   *Johnston (10,27)*

Ballymena Utd. Res: May, Quinn, Wylie, Sloan, (D) Moore, (C) Moore, McConville, Gilmore, Steele, Muir, Lynch.
Subs: Booth replaced Sloan:
Linfield Sw: Caldwell, Crothers, Rainey, McLaughlin, Hill, Knell, Hosick, Ross, Johnston, Feeney, Campbell.
Referee: D.Ross (Killyleagh)

7th November, 1995

Venue: The Oval, Belfast

Dromara Village	**(0)**	**1**	**Dundela**	**(0)**	**0 (aet)**

Woods (91)

Dromara V: Gregg, Graham, (I) Bingham, Johnston, Adams, (K) Bingham, Burns, Treanor, Kirk, Beckett, Cosgrove.
Subs: Dornan replaced Cosgrove; Woods replaced (I) Bingham:
Dundela: Robson, Fyfe, McKee, Harrison, Lennox, Whiteside, Spence, Doey, Hanvey, Coulter, Parker. *Subs:* Fettis replaced Spence:
Referee: R.Penney (Carrickfergus)

FINAL

25th December, 1995

Venue: Seaview, Belfast   *Att:- 1,900*

Dromara Village	**(1)**	**1**	**Ballymena United Reserves**	**(0)**	**1 (aet)**

Kirk (28)   *Sloan (64)*

Dromara V: Gregge, Graham, Kingham, Johnstone, Bustard, (K) Bingham, Woods, Beckett, Kirk, Treanor, Adams.
Subs: Burns replaced Woods (78 min); Hamilton replaced Kirk (116 min):
Ballymena Utd.Res: Smyth, Craig, Wylie, Sloan, (D) Moore, Fullerton, Carlisle, Gilmore, Steele, Lynch, (C) Moore.
Subs: Martin replaced Gilmore (111 min); Quinn replaced Fullerton (115 min):
Referee: R.Penney (Carrickfergus)
Booked: Beckett, Kinghan (Dromara Village); Lynch (Ballymena United Reserves):

FINAL REPLAY

11th January, 1996

Venue: Seaview, Belfast   *Att:- 600*

Dromara Village	**(1)**	**1**	**Ballymena United Reserves**	**(1)**	**2**

Treanor (44)   *Steele (40), Lynch (82)*

Dromara V: Gregge, Graham, Kingham, Johnstone, Bustard, (K) Bingham, Adams, Beckett, Kirk, Treanor. *Subs:* Dornan replaced Kirk (66 min); Woods replaced Graham (86 min); *Sub not used:* Cosgrove:
Ballymena Utd.Res: Smyth, Craig, Wylie, Sloan, (D) Moore, Fullerton, Steele, Gilmore, (C) Moore, Lynch, Carlisle.
Subs: Martin replaced Gilmore (48 min); Booth replaced (C) Moore (71 min); Quinn replaced Fullerton (78 min):
Referee: R.Penney (Carrickfergus)
Booked: Graham (Dromara Village); Fullerton (Ballymena United Reserved):

1896/97 Wesley	1968/69 Larne
1897/98 Dunmurry	1921/22 Cliftonville Olympic
1898/99 Linfield Swifts	1922/23 Crusaders
1899/00 Cliftonville Olympic	1923/24 Bangor
1900/01 Distillery West End	1924/25 Ormiston
1901/02 Cliftonville Olympic	1925/26 St.Marys
1902/03 Highfield	1926/27 Crusaders
1903/04 Mountpottinger YMCA	1927/28 Willowfield
1904/05 Glentoran II	1928/29 Crusaders
1905/06 Mountpottinger YMCA	1929/30 Broadway United
1906/07 Cliftonville Olympic	1930/31 Crusaders
1907/08 Gliftonville Olympic	1931/32 Brantwood
1908/09 Glentoran II	1932/33 Glentoran II
1909/10 Larne	1933/34 Crusaders
1910/11 Glentoran II	1934/35 Belfast Celtic II
1911/12 Black Diamonds	1935/36 Belfast Celtic II
1912/13 Belfast Celtic II	1936/37 Crusaders
1913/14 Cliftonville Olympic	1937/38 Glentoran II
1914/15 Glentorarn II	1938/39 Sirocco Works
1915/16 Linfield Swifts	1939/40 Linfield Swifts
1916/17 Belfast Celtic	1940/41 Bangor Reserves
1918/19 Glentoran II	1941/42 Larne Olympic
1919/20 Dunmurry	1969/70 Larne
1920/21 Brantwood	1970/71 Larne
1942/43 Larne Olympic	1971/72 Larne
1943/44 Ballyclare Comrades	1972/73 Linfield Swifts
1944/45 Bangor Reserves	1973/74 Chimney Corner
1945/46 Dundela	1974/75 Ballyclare Comrades
1946/47 Linfield Swifts	1975/76 Chimney Corner
1947/48 Crusaders	1976/77 Brantwood
1948/49 Linfield Swifts	1977/78 Downpatrick Rec.
1949/50 Albert Foundry	1978/79 Cromac Albion
1950/51 Brantwood	1979/80 Short Brothers
1951/52 Brantwood	1980/81 Dundela
1952/53 Brantwood	1981/82 Ballyclare Comrades
1953/54 Crusaders Reserves	1982/83 Dundela
1954/55 East Belfast	1983/84 Linfield Swifts
1955/56 Brantwood	1984/85 Ballyclare Comrades
1956/57 Larne	1985/86 Brantwood
1957/58 Glentoran II	1986/87 Ballyclare Comrades
1958/59 Larne	1987/88 Dundela
1959/60 Larne	1988/89 Dundela
1960/61 Ballyclare Comrades	1989/90 Glentoran II
1961/62 Carrick Rangers	1990/91 Dundela
1962/63 Chimney Corner	1991/92 Comber Recreation
1963/64 Dundela	1992/93 East Belfast
1964/65 Larne	1993/94 R.U.C.
1965/66 Glentoran II	1994/95 Bangor Reserves
1966/67 Glentoran II	1995/96 Ballymena United Reserves
1967/68 Carrick Rangers	

SUMMARY OF WINNERS

11 Glentoran II, **9** Larne, **8** Brantwood, Linfield Swifts, **7** Crusaders, Dundela, **6** Ballyclare Comrades, Cliftonville Olympic, **5** Belfast Celtic II, **3** Bangor Reserves, **3** Chimney Corner, Carrick Rangers, Dunmurry, East Belfast, Larne Olympic, Mountpottinger YMCA, **1** Albert Foundry, Ballymena United Reserves, Bangor, Black Diamonds, Broadway United, Cromac Albion, Crusaders Reserves, Distillery West End, Downpatrick Rec. Highfield, Ormiston, R.U.C, Short Brothers, Sirocco Works, St.Marys, Wesley, Willowfield.

BOB RADCLIFFE CUP 1995/96

FIRST ROUND

2nd September, 1995.

AFC Craigavon	3	Laurelvale	5	Annagh United	1	Rathfriland Rangers	3
Armagh City	1	Dromore Amateurs	0	Banbridge Town	3	Hanover	2
Bourneview Young Men	2	Mountnorris	1	Coagh United	?	Cookstown Royals	?
Glenavon Reserves	5	Queens Park Swifts	0	Loughgall	8	Warrenpoint Town	0
Newry Town Reserves	3	Coalisland Celtic	3				
(aet Coalisland Celtic won 4-3 on pens)							
Portadown Reserves	1	Dungannon Swifts	3	Richhill	4	Cookstown United	6
Seapatrick	9	Killymoon Rangers	1	Southend United	2	Scarva Rangers	3
Tandragee Rovers	0	Bessbrook United	3				

FIRST ROUND BYE: Lurgan Celtic Bhoys:

SECOND ROUND

16th September, 1995.

Bessbrook United	2	Glenavon Reserves	3	Coalisland Celtic	1	Coagh United	3
Cookstown United	5	Lurgan Celtic Bhoys	5				
(aet Lurgan C.B. won 3-1 on pens)							
Loughgall	1	Dungannon Swifts	1				
(aet Dungannon Swifts won 5-4 on pens)							
Rathfriland Rangers	1	Banbridge Town	2	Scarva Rangers	0	Laurelvale	3
Seapatrick	2	Armagh City	5				

SECOND ROUND BYE: Bourneview Young Men:

QUARTER-FINALS

28th October, 1995.

Banbrige Town	8	Bourneview Young Men	1	Laurelvale	0	Dungannon Swifts	3
Glenavon Reserves	2	Coagh United	2	Lurgan Celtic Bhoys	2	Armagh City	0
(aet Glenavon Reserves won 5-4 on pens)							

SEMI-FINALS

11th December, 1995.
Venue: Mourneview Park, Lurgan

Glenavon Reserves	1	Lurgan Celtic Bhoys	3

16th December, 1995.
Venue: Lakeview Park, Loughgall.

Dungannon Swifts	5	Banbridge Town	2

FINAL

9th April, 1996.
Venue: Lakeview Park, Loughgall   Att:

Dungannon Swifts (1)	3	Lurgan Celtic Bhoys (0)	1

Smyth (4,89), McKinstry (88)   *Maginness (53)*

Dungannon Sw: Vance, Gregg, Clarke, Coll, McKerr, Jennings, Jer.Robinson, McNamee, Crowe, Smyth, McKinstry. ***Subs:*** Montgomery replaced Jer.Robinson; O'Hagen replaced Crowe; Shaw for Montgomery:
Lurgan C.B: Hurle, (N) McCann, (S) King, (D) McCann, Heaney, Maginness, Campbell, (B) King, Woods, Creaney, Donnelly. ***Subs:*** McAreavy replaced Creaney; Maguire replaced (B) King; Reynolds replaced Heaney:
Referee: M.Adamson (Portadown)
Booked: Clarke and McNamee (Dungannon Swifts); Campbell (Lurgan Celtic Bhoys):

BOB RADCLIFFE CUP WINNERS 1978/79 - 1995/96

1978/79 Newry Town	1987/88 Oxford United
1979/80 Loughgall	1988/89 Coagh United
1980/81 Banbridge Town	1989/90 Dungannon Swifts
1981/82 Dungannon Swifts	1990/91 Glenavon Reserves
1982/83 Portadown Reserves	1991/92 Armagh City
1983/84 Portadown Reserves	1992/93 Dungannon Swifts
1984/85 Newry Town Reserves	1993/94 Dungannon Swifts
1985/86 Dungannon Swifts	1994/95 Dungannon Swifts
1986/87 Dungannon Swifts	1995/96 Dungannon Swifts

Summary of Winners 1978/79 - 1995/96

8 Dungannon Swifts,
2 Portadown Reserves,
1 Armagh City, Banbridge Town, Coagh United.

NORTH WEST INTERMEDIATE CUP 1995/96

FIRST ROUND

2nd September, 1995.

Churchill/Kilfennan United	3	Tamnaherin Celtic	2	Coleraine Reserves	6	Magherfelt Sky Blues	1
Drummond United	3	Garvagh	1	Dungiven Celtic	2	Ballinamallard United	1
Limavady United	4	Magilligan	1	Macosquin	1	Draperstown Celtic	2
Park	0	Coleraine Crusaders	1	Roe Valley	3	Ardmore	1
Tobermore United	4	U.U.C.	2				

FIRST ROUND BYES: Bridgend United; Institute; Moyola Park; Omagh Town Reserves; Oxford United Stars; Portstewart; Strabane:

SECOND ROUND

30th September, 1995.

Bridgend United	1	Draperstown Celtic	5	Coleraine Reserves	1	Dungiven Celtic	0
Limavady United	2	Moyola Park	3	Oxford United Stars	5	Coleraine Crusaders	0
Portstewart	0	Institute	1	Roe Valley	3	Omagh Town Reserves	0
Strabane	1	Churchill/Kilfennan Utd	4	Tobermore United v	Drummond United*		

*Tobermore United walkover into Quarter-Finals.

QUARTER-FINALS

28th October, 1995.

Churchill/Kilfennan United	3	Roe Valley	2	Coleraine Reserves	2	Draperstown Celtic	1
Institute	v	Oxford United Stars*		Tobermore United	2	Moyola Park	1 aet

* Oxford United Stars progressed into Semi-Finals after Institute were dismissed from competition for fielding Cathal Deery who was cup-tied after previously playing for Limavady United in an earlier round.

SEMI-FINALS

18th November, 1995.
Venue: The Showgrounds, Coleraine

Coleraine Reserves	**0**	**Oxford United Stars**	**2**

Venue: Fortwilliam Park, Tobermore

Tobermore United	**1**	**Churchill/Kilfennan United**	**1**
Taylor		*Doherty*	

(aet C.K.U. won 3-2 on pens)

FINAL

23rd March, 1996.

Oxford United Stars	**2**	**Churchill/Kilfennan United**	**1**

Smirnoff 'B' Division Knockout Cup 1995/96

First Round

16th March, 1996.

Ballinamallard United	0	Banbridge Town	4	Ballymoney United	3	Queens University	0
Brantwood	1	Dundela	3	Dungannon Swifts	2	Harland & Wolff Welders	0
Limavady United	5	Tobermore United	2	Loughgall	1	Armagh City	0
Moyola Park	1	Chimney Corner	2	R.U.C.	2	Cookstown United	0

Quarter-Finals

30th March, 1996.

Banbridge Town	5	Dungannon Swifts	1	Dundela	1	Ballymoney United	3
Limavady United	1	R.U.C	1	Loughgall	2	Chimney Corner	0

(aet Limavady United won 6-5 on pens)

Semi-Finals, First Leg

16th April, 1996.

Banbridge Town	4	Ballymoney Utd.	0	Loughgall	1	Limavady United	1

Semi-Finals, Second Leg

23rd April, 1996.

Ballymoney United	1	Banbridge Town	2

(Banbridge Town won 6-1 on aggregate)

Limavady United	2	Loughgall	2

(aet aggregate 3-3; Limavady United won 7-6 on pens)

Final

25th May, 1996
Venue: Allen Park, Antrim.

Limavady United (0)	**3**	**Banbridge Town** (2)	**2**
Painter (55), Harrison (pen 60),		*Brannigan (15,22)*	
White (80)			

Limavady Utd: Crown, Nutt, Law, (D) Mullan, King, McCallum, (M) Mullan, Davies, Harrison, Moran, Painter. *Subs:* White replaced Painter; *Subs not used:* Shiels; Morrow

Banbridge T: Napier, Mullan, McQuaid, Scappaticci, Gracey, Johnston, Smyth, McStravick, Clarke, Brannigan, Thompson. *Subs:* White replaced Clarke; Maguire replaced McQuaid; Kerr replaced Thompson:
Referee: K.Ginnett (Belfast)
Booked: Napier (Banbridge Town)
Sent Off: Robert Crown (Limavady United)

Knockout Cup Winners 1982/83 - 1995/96

Season:	Winners:
1982/83	R.U.C.
1983/84	Ballyclare Comrades
1984/85	R.U.C.
1985/86	R.U.C.
1986/87	Chimney Corner
1987/88	Dundela
1988/89	Ballyclare Comrades
1989/90	Omagh Town
1990/91	Dundela
1991/92	Dundela
1992/93	Limavady United
1993/94	Dungannon Swifts
1994/95	Dundela
1995/96	Limavady United

Summary of Winners 1982/83 - 1995/96

4 Dundela, **3** R.U.C; **2** Ballyclare Comrades; Limavady United, **1** Chimney Corner, Dungannon Swifts, Omagh Town.

GEORGE WILSON CUP 1995/96

18th August, 1995
Section A
| Glentoran II | 2 | Crusaders Res. | 0 |
Section C
| Coleraine Res. | 3 | Portadown Res. | 1 |

19th August, 1995
Section A
| Omagh Town Res. | 0 | Carrick Rangers Res. | 1 |
Section B
| Cliftonville Olympic | 0 | Glenavon Res. | 1 |
Section C
| Bangor Res. | 2 | Newry Town Res. | 0 |
Section D
| Ballymena United Res. | 4 | Larne Olympic | 1 |
| Linfield Swifts | 3 | Ards II | 0 |

23rd August, 1995
Section A
| Carrick Rangers Res. | 0 | Crusaders Res. | 5 |
| Omagh Town Res. | 2 | Glentoran II | 1 |
Section B
| Distillery II | 3 | Cliftonville Olympic | 3 |
Section C
| Bangor Res. | 2 | Coleraine Res. | 0 |
| Newry Town Res. | 1 | Portadown Res. | 5 |
Section D
| Ballymena United Res. | 1 | Linfield Swifts | 0 |
| Larne Olympic | 0 | Ards II | 3 |

25th August, 1995
Section A
| Carrick Rangers Res. | 0 | Glentoran II | 1 |
Section B
| Ballyclare Comrades Res. | 1 | Cliftonville Olympic | 8 |
Section D
| Larne Olympic | 1 | Linfield Swifts | 4 |

26th August, 1995
Section A
| Omagh Town Res. | 1 | Crusaders Res. | 0 |
Section B
| Distillery II | 0 | Glenavon Res. | 0 |
Section C
| Bangor Res. | 6 | Portadown Res. | 0 |
| Newry Town Res. | 2 | Coleraine Res. | 2 |
Section D
| Ballymena United Res. | 2 | Ards II | 3 |

28th August, 1995
Section B
| Ballyclare Comrades Res. | 1 | Glenavon Res. | 3 |

29th August, 1995
Section B
| Distillery II | 4 | Ballyclare Comrades Res. | 1 |

FINAL TABLES

Section A
	P	W	D	L	F	A	Pts
1 Glentoran II	3	2	0	1	4	2	6
2 Omagh Town Res.	3	2	0	1	3	3	6
3 Crusaders Res.	3	1	0	2	5	3	3
4 Carrick Rangers Res.	3	1	0	2	1	6	3

Section B
	P	W	D	L	F	A	Pts
1 Glenavon Res.	3	2	1	0	4	1	7
2 Distillery II	3	1	2	0	7	4	5
3 Cliftonville Olympic	3	1	1	1	11	5	4
4 Ballyclare Comrades Res.	3	0	0	3	3	15	0

Section C
	P	W	D	L	F	A	Pts
1 Bangor Res.	3	3	0	0	10	0	9
2 Coleraine Res.	3	1	1	1	5	5	4
3 Portadown Res.	3	1	0	2	6	10	3
4 Newry Town Res.	3	0	1	2	3	9	1

Section D
	P	W	D	L	F	A	Pts
1 Linfield Swifts	3	2	0	1	7	2	6
2 Ballymena United Res.	3	2	0	1	7	4	6
3 Ards II	3	2	0	1	6	5	6
4 Larne Olympic	3	0	0	3	2	11	0

NB: Top two from each Section went through to the Semi-Finals of Competition.

QUARTER-FINALS
30th August, 1995
Bangor Res.	4	Ballymena United Res.	1 (aet)
Glenavon Res.	2	Omagh Town Res.	2
	(aet Omagh Town Res. won 4-3 on pens)		
Linfield Swifts	1	Coleraine Res.	1
	(aet Coleraine Res. won 7-6 on pens)		

31st August, 1995
| Glentoran II | 2 | Distillery II | 2 |
| | (aet Distillery II won 5-4 on pens) | | |

SEMI-FINALS
6th September, 1995
| Distillery II | 1 | Bangor Res. | 4 |

7th September, 1995
| Omagh Town Res. | 0 | Coleraine Res. | 1 |

FINAL
Venue: Seaview, Belfast   *Att:* 150

| **Coleraine Res. (1)** | **3** | **Bangor Res. (1)** | **2** |

Sweeney (28,68)   *McCartan (39), McPherson (88)*
McIvor (84)

Coleraine Res: Platt, Harkin, Mullan, Hagan, Clanachan, Young, McIvor, Sweeney, Larkin, McCallion, McDowell. **Sub:** Logan replaced McCallion (87 min); **Subs not used:** Calvin; Starrett:

Bangor Res: Huxley, Dornan, Clarke, Eddis, Cash, Ferguson, Wilkinson, McPherson, Morrow, McNamara, McCartan. **Subs:** Murtagh replaced McNamara (79 min); McCloskey replaced Ferguson (88 min); **Sub not used:** Massey:

Referee: R.Hawthorn (Belfast)

Ballymena United Reserves

Who successfully beat Dromara Village 2-1 after replay in the Steel & Sons Cup

Coca-Cola Irish Youth Cup 1995/96

First Round

23rd September, 1995

Ards Colts	3	Ballymena United III	5	Bangor Colts	5	Lurgan Town Boys	0
Coleraine Colts	3	Linfield Rangers	2	Dergview Youth	3	Newry Town III	0
Derryhirk United	1	Ballinamallard United III	2	Enniskillen Town Utd. Yth.	4	Chimney Corner Colts	0
Glenavon III	3	Killymoon Rangers Boys	1	Lisnaskea Rovers Youth	8	Rathfriland Youth Club	0
Loughgall Colts	0	Glentoran Colts	2	N.F.C. Kesh III	1	Portadown Boys	1

(aet Portadown Boys won 3-2 on pens)

Oxford Utd Youth	3	Limavady United Youth	0	Townsend United	1	Kilmore Recreation	6

NB: In the following First Round matches the with an asterisk(*) beside their name were dismissed from the competition and their opponents automatically progressed to the next round.

Banbridge Town Youth* v Cliftonville Strollers; Carrick Rangers Colts* v Lisburn United; Enniskillen Rangers Youth* v Crumlin United U.18; Gilford Crusaders* v Rosario Youth Club:

Second Round

14th October, 1995

Dergview Youth	2	Portadown Boys	8	Enniskillen Town Utd. Yth.	3	Oxford United Youth	1
Glentoran Colts	4	Cliftonville Strollers	2	Kilmore Recreation	7	Crumlin United U.18	3
Lisburn United	0	Ballinamallard United III	3	Lisnaskea Rovers Youth	0	Glenavon III	2
Rosario Yth. Club	0	Bangor Colts	2				

Second Round Bye: Coleraine Colts:

Quarter-Finals

4th November, 1995

Glenavon III	0	Bangor Colts	1	Kilmore Recreation	4	Coleraine	2
Portadown Boys	1	Glentoran Colts	0				

NB: Enniskillen Town Utd. Youth received a bye into the Semi-Finals after Ballinamallard United III were dismissed from the competition for fielding an ineligible player in their Second Round match v Lisburn United.

Semi-Finals

26th March, 1996
Venue: Castlereagh Park, Newtownards

Kilmore Recreation	**2**	**Bangor Colts**	**1**

28th March, 1996
Venue: Stangmore Park, Dungannon

Portadown Boys	**1**	**Enniskillen Town Utd. Youth**	**0**

Final

22nd April, 1996
Venue: Dixon Park, Ballyclare

Kilmore Recreation	**(0)**	**2**	**Portadown Boys (0)**	**0**

Kennedy (81,82)

Kilmore Rec: Travers, Mullan, Ferguson, Holland, O'Donnell, Oakes, Burns, Gelston, Kennedy, Smyth, Perry. *Sub:* Keaveney replaced Burns (89 min); *Subs not used:* Murray; Madine:
Portadown Boys: Skelton, McConnell, Kingston, Gallagher, Ward, McCullough, Turkington, Clarke, Bradley, Hill, McArdle. *Subs:* Campbell replaced McCullough (87 min); Fitzpatrick replaced Hill (87 min); *Sub not used:* Pollock (gk):
Referee: K.Glasgow (Belfast)
Booked: Smyth (Kilmore Recreation); Kingston (Portadown Boys): *Sent Off:* Simon Kingston (Portadown Boys):

Cup Fixtures 1996/97

Wilkinson Sword Irish League Cup
First Round: Saturday, 10th August, 1996
Second Round: Tuesday, 13th August, 1996
Quarter-Finals: Tuesday, 1st October, 1996
Semi-Finals: Tuesday 8th/Wednesday 9th October, 1996
Final: Tuesday, 15th October, 1996

Ulster Cup

Saturday, 17th August, 1996
First Round - First Leg

Distillery	v	Linfield
Newry Town	v	Coleraine
Carrick Rangers	v	Ards
Bangor	v	Glentoran
Omagh Town	v	Glenavon
Larne	v	Cliftonville
Ballymena United	v	Crusaders
Ballyclare Comrades	v	Portadown

Saturday, 24th August, 1996
First Round - Second Leg

Linfield	v	Distillery (A)
Coleraine	v	Newry Town (B)
Ards	v	Carrick Rangers (C)
Glentoran	v	Bangor (D)
Glenavon	v	Omagh Town (E)
Cliftonville	v	Larne (F)
Crusaders	v	Ballymena United (G)
Portadown	v	Ballyclare Comrades (H)

Quarter-Finals
Tuesday, 27th August, 1996

(1) Winner of (E)	v	Winner of (B)
(2) Winner of (C)	v	Winner of (D)
(3) Winner of (A)	v	Winner of (G)
(4) Winner of (F)	v	Winner of (H)

Semi-Finals
Tuesday 3rd/Wednesday 4th September, 1996

Winner of (4)	v	Winner of (3)
Winner of (1)	v	Winner of (2)

Final
Tuesday, 17th September, 1996

Sun Life Gold Cup

Saturday, 7th September, 1996
Section A

Bangor	v	Portadown
Newry Town	v	Coleraine

Section B

Ards	v	Crusaders
Larne	v	Ballymena United

Section C

Carrick Rangers	v	Omagh Town
Cliftonville	v	Glentoran

Section D

Ballyclare Comrades	v	Distillery
Linfield	v	Glenavon

Saturday, 14th September, 1996
Section A

Coleraine	v	Bangor
Portadown	v	Newry Town

Section B

Ballymena United	v	Ards
Crusaders	v	Larne

Section C

Glentoran	v	Carrick Rangers
Omagh Town	v	Cliftonville

Section D

Distillery	v	Linfield
Glenavon	v	Ballyclare Comrades

Saturday, 21st September, 1996
Section A

Coleraine	v	Portadown
Newry Town	v	Bangor

CUP FIXTURES 1996/97

Section B

Crusaders	v	Ballymena United
Larne	v	Ards

Section C

Carrick Rangers	v	Cliftonville
Omagh Town	v	Glentoran

Section D

Ballyclare Comrades	v	Linfield
Glenavon	v	Distillery

QUARTER-FINALS: TUESDAY, 22ND OCTOBER, 1996
SEMI-FINALS: TUESDAY 29TH/WEDNESDAY 30TH OCTOBER, 1996
FINAL: TUESDAY, 12TH NOVEMBER, 1996

COCA-COLA FLOODLIT CUP

First Round - First Leg: Saturday, 28th December, 1996
First Round - Second Leg: Tuesday, 7th January, 1997
Quarter-Finals: Tuesday, 11th February, 1997
Semi-Finals: Tuesday 4th/Wednesday 5th March, 1997
Final: Tuesday, 8th April, 1997

CALOR GAS COUNTY ANTRIM SHIELD

First Round: Tuesday, 3rd December, 1996
Quarter-Finals: Tuesday, 17th December, 1997
Semi-Finals: Tuesday 14th/Wednesday 15th January, 1997
Final: Tuesday, 4th February, 1997

BASS IRISH CUP

Fifth Round: Saturday, 25th January, 1997
Sixth Round: Saturday, 22nd February, 1997
Quarter-Finals: Saturday, 15th march, 1997
Semi-Finals: Friday 11th/Saturday 12th April, 1997
Final: Saturday, 3rd May 1997

EUROPEAN COMPETITIONS
UEFA CUP

Preliminary Round
17th July, 1996 - First Leg

Portadown	v	Vojvodina (Yugoslavia)
Zalgiris Vilnius (Lithuania)	v	Crusaders

24th July, 1996 - Second Leg

Crusaders	v	Zalgiris Vilnius
Vojvodina	v	Portadown

CUP WINNERS' CUP

Preliminary Round
8th August, 1996 - First Leg

Glentoran	v	Sparta Prague (Czech Republic)

22nd August, 1996 - Second Leg

Sparta Prague	v	Glentoran

316

SMIRNOFF LEAGUE FIXTURES 1996/97 SEASON

FIXTURES © IRISH FOOTBALL LEAGUE

SATURDAY, 28TH SEPTEMBER, 1996
Premier League

Coleraine	v	Ards
Crusaders	v	Glenavon
Glentoran	v	Cliftonville
Portadown	v	Linfield

First Division

Ballyclare Comrades	v	Omagh Town
Bangor	v	Ballymena United
Distillery	v	Carrick Rangers
Newry Town	v	Larne

SATURDAY, 12TH OCTOBER, 1996
Premier League

Ards	v	Portadown
Cliftonville	v	Coleraine
Glenavon	v	Glentoran
Linfield	v	Crusaders

First Division

Ballymena United	v	Distillery
Carrick Rangers	v	Newry Town
Larne	v	Ballyclare Comrades
Omagh Town	v	Bangor

SATURDAY, 19TH OCTOBER, 1996
Premier League

Coleraine	v	Glentoran
Crusaders	v	Ards
Linfield	v	Glenavon
Portadown	v	Cliftonville

First Division

Bangor	v	Ballyclare Comrades
Carrick Rangers	v	Larne
Distillery	v	Omagh Town
Newry Town	v	Ballymena United

SATURDAY, 26TH OCTOBER, 1996
Premier League

Ards	v	Linfield
Cliftonville	v	Crusaders
Glenavon	v	Coleraine
Glentoran	v	Portadown

First Division

Ballyclare Comrades	v	Distillery
Ballymena United	v	Carrick Rangers
Larne	v	Bangor
Omagh Town	v	Newry Town

SATURDAY, 2ND NOVEMBER, 1996
Premier League

Ards	v	Glenavon
Crusaders	v	Glentoran
Linfield	v	Cliftonville
Portadown	v	Coleraine

First Division

Ballymena United	v	Larne
Carrick Rangers	v	Omagh Town
Distillery	v	Bangor
Newry Town	v	Ballyclare Comrades

FRIDAY 8TH/SATURDAY 9TH NOVEMBER, 1996
Premier League

Cliftonville	v	Ards
Coleraine	v	Crusaders
Glentoran	v	Linfield
Portadown	v	Glenavon

First Division

Ballyclare Comrades	v	Carrick Rangers
Bangor	v	Newry Town
Distillery	v	Larne
Omagh Town	v	Ballymena United

SATURDAY, 16TH NOVEMBER, 1996
Premier League

Ards	v	Glentoran
Crusaders	v	Portadown
Glenavon	v	Cliftonville
Linfield	v	Coleraine

First Division

Ballymena United	v	Ballyclare Comrades
Carrick Rangers	v	Bangor
Larne	v	Omagh Town
Newry Town	v	Distillery

SATURDAY, 23RD NOVEMBER, 1996
Premier League

Ards	v	Coleraine
Cliftonville	v	Glentoran
Glenavon	v	Crusaders
Linfield	v	Portadown

First Division

Ballymena United	v	Bangor
Carrick Rangers	v	Distillery
Larne	v	Newry Town
Omagh Town	v	Ballyclare Comrades

SATURDAY, 30TH NOVEMBER, 1996
Premier League

Coleraine	v	Cliftonville
Crusaders	v	Linfield
Glentoran	v	Glenavon
Portadown	v	Ards

First Division

Ballyclare Comrades	v	Larne
Bangor	v	Omagh Town
Distillery	v	Ballymena United
Newry Town	v	Carrick Rangers

SATURDAY, 7TH DECEMBER, 1996
Premier League

Ards	v	Crusaders
Cliftonville	v	Portadown
Glenavon	v	Linfield
Glentoran	v	Coleraine

First Division

Ballyclare Comrades	v	Bangor
Ballymena United	v	Newry Town
Larne	v	Carrick Rangers
Omagh Town	v	Distillery

TUESDAY 10TH/WEDNESDAY 11TH DECEMBER, 1996
Premier League

Coleraine	v	Glenavon
Crusaders	v	Cliftonville
Linfield	v	Ards
Portadown	v	Glentoran

First Division

Bangor	v	Larne
Carrick Rangers	v	Ballymena United
Distillery	v	Ballyclare Comrades
Newry Town	v	Omagh Town

SATURDAY, 21ST DECEMBER, 1996
Premier League

Cliftonville	v	Linfield
Coleraine	v	Portadown
Glenavon	v	Ards
Glentoran	v	Crusaders

First Division

Ballyclare Comrades	v	Newry Town
Bangor	v	Distillery
Larne	v	Ballymena United
Omagh Town	v	Carrick Rangers

THURSDAY, 26TH DECEMBER, 1996
Premier League

Ards	v	Cliftonville
Crusaders	v	Coleraine
Glenavon	v	Portadown
Linfield	v	Glentoran

First Division

Ballymena United	v	Omagh Town
Carrick Rangers	v	Ballyclare Comrades
Larne	v	Ballymena United
Newry Town	v	Bangor

WEDNESDAY, 1ST JANUARY, 1997
Premier League

Cliftonville	v	Glenavon
Coleraine	v	Linfield
Glentoran	v	Ards
Portadown	v	Crusaders

First Division

Ballyclare Comrades	v	Ballymena United
Bangor	v	Carrick Rangers
Distillery	v	Newry Town
Omagh Town	v	Larne

SATURDAY, 4TH JANUARY, 1997
Premier League

Coleraine	v	Ards
Crusaders	v	Glenavon
Glentoran	v	Cliftonville
Portadown	v	Linfield

First Division

Ballyclare Comrades	v	Omagh Town
Bangor	v	Ballymena United
Distillery	v	Carrick Rangers
Newry Town	v	Larne

SATURDAY, 11TH JANUARY, 1997
Premier League

Ards	v	Portadown
Cliftonville	v	Coleraine
Glenavon	v	Glentoran
Linfield	v	Crusaders

First Division

Ballymena United	v	Distillery
Carrick Rangers	v	Newry Town
Larne	v	Ballyclare Comrades
Omagh Town	v	Bangor

SATURDAY, 18TH JANUARY, 1997
Premier League

Coleraine	v	Glentoran
Crusaders	v	Ards
Linfield	v	Glenavon
Portadown	v	Cliftonville

First Division

Bangor	v	Ballyclare Comrades
Carrick Rangers	v	Larne
Distillery	v	Omagh Town
Newry Town	v	Ballymena United

SATURDAY, 1ST FEBRUARY, 1997
Premier League

Ards	v	Linfield
Cliftonville	v	Crusaders
Glenavon	v	Coleraine
Glentoran	v	Portadown

First Division

Ballyclare Comrades	v	Distillery
Ballymena United	v	Carrick Rangers
Larne	v	Bangor
Omagh Town	v	Newry Town

SATURDAY, 8TH FEBRUARY, 1997
Premier League

Ards	v	Glenavon
Crusaders	v	Glentoran
Linfield	v	Cliftonville
Portadown	v	Coleraine

First Division

Ballymena United	v	Larne
Carrick Rangers	v	Omagh Town
Distillery	v	Bangor
Newry Town	v	Ballyclare Comrades

SATURDAY, 15TH FEBRUARY, 1997
Premier League

Cliftonville	v	Ards
Coleraine	v	Crusaders
Glentoran	v	Linfield
Portadown	v	Glenavon

First Division

Ballyclare Comrades	v	Carrick Rangers
Bangor	v	Newry Town
Distillery	v	Larne
Omagh Town	v	Ballymena United

SATURDAY, 1ST MARCH, 1997
Premier League

Ards	v	Glentoran
Crusaders	v	Portadown
Glenavon	v	Cliftonville
Linfield	v	Coleraine

First Division

Ballymena United	v	Ballyclare Comrades
Carrick Rangers	v	Bangor
Larne	v	Omagh Town
Newry Town	v	Distillery

Saturday, 8th March, 1997
Premier League

Ards	v	Coleraine
Cliftonville	v	Glentoran
Glenavon	v	Crusaders
Linfield	v	Portadown

First Division

Ballymena United	v	Bangor
Carrick Rangers	v	Distillery
Larne	v	Newry Town
Omagh Town	v	Ballyclare Comrades

Saturday, 22nd March, 1997
Premier League

Coleraine	v	Cliftonville
Crusaders	v	Linfield
Glentoran	v	Glenavon
Portadown	v	Ards

First Division

Ballyclare Comrades	v	Larne
Bangor	v	Omagh Town
Distillery	v	Ballymena United
Newry Town	v	Carrick Rangers

Tuesday 25th/Wednesday 26th March, 1997
Premier League

Ards	v	Crusaders
Cliftonville	v	Portadown
Glenavon	v	Linfield
Glentoran	v	Coleraine

First Division

Ballyclare Comrades	v	Bangor
Ballymena United	v	Newry Town
Larne	v	Carrick Rangers
Omagh Town	v	Distillery

Monday 31st March/Tuesday 1st April, 1997
Premier League

Coleraine	v	Glenavon
Crusaders	v	Cliftonville
Linfield	v	Ards
Portadown	v	Glentoran

First Division

Bangor	v	Larne
Carrick Rangers	v	Ballymena United
Distillery	v	Ballyclare Comrades
Newry Town	v	Omagh Town

Saturday, 5th April, 1997
Premier League

Cliftonville	v	Linfield
Coleraine	v	Portadown
Glenavon	v	Ards
Glentoran	v	Crusaders

First Division

Ballyclare Comrades	v	Newry Town
Bangor	v	Distillery
Larne	v	Ballymena United
Omagh Town	v	Carrick Rangers

Saturday, 19th April, 1997
Premier League

Ards	v	Cliftonville
Crusaders	v	Coleraine
Glenavon	v	Portadown
Linfield	v	Glentoran

First Division

Ballymena United	v	Omagh Town
Carrick Rangers	v	Ballyclare Comrades
Larne	v	Distillery
Newry Town	v	Bangor

Saturday, 26th April, 1997
Premier League

Cliftonville	v	Glenavon
Coleraine	v	Linfield
Glentoran	v	Ards
Portadown	v	Crusaders

First Division

Ballyclare Comrades	v	Ballymena United
Bangor	v	Carrick Rangers
Distillery	v	Newry Town
Omagh Town	v	Larne